# FOLK MUSIC:
## MORE THAN A SONG

# FOLK MUSIC:
## MORE THAN A SONG

Kristin Baggelaar

AND

Donald Milton

THOMAS Y. CROWELL COMPANY

NEW YORK/Established 1834

Illustration credits and copyright acknowledgments are in the back of the book.

Manufactured in the United States of America

**Library of Congress Cataloging in Publication Data**

Baggelaar, Kristin.
  Folk music: more than a song.
  1. Folk music, American—History and criticism.
I. Milton, Donald, joint author. II. Title.
ML3551.B17     781.7'73     76-3547
ISBN 0-690-01159-8

10  9  8  7  6  5  4  3  2  1

*This book is dedicated to the makers*
*of the legend and of the songs*
*who have so deeply touched our lives*

# PREFACE

What is a folk song?

"I guess all songs is folk songs," Big Bill Broonzy once said. "I never heard no horse sing 'em."

Regardless of the definition accepted by each of us, the lifeblood of folk music remains unchanged—people. This book is concerned with many of the men and women whose approach to the folk song as an expression of life makes folk music more than a song.

Whether amateur or professional, unknown or star, singers and musicians are responsible for bringing songs to life. "I have always felt that it was the performers' unique ways of performing the songs which caused the songs to be noticed or kept alive," Erik Darling wrote to us recently. "It is my guess that the way these songs rest in a lot of people's minds is not as the song so much, though everyone is certainly going to have favorites, but rather the experience the song or songs gave them when performed by Burl Ives, Richard Dyer-Bennet, the Weavers, the Kingston Trio, etc."

Behind the singers and musicians are others—club owners, composers, concert promoters, festival organizers, magazine staff members, producers, and so on—who play a vital role in folk music.

In an attempt to make folk music most readily available to the reader, we have selected those individuals (along with festivals, music publications, and organizations) who have made or are still making the most conspicuous impact on the folk song and its development. For this reason, there are countless names which are not to be found in the coming pages, and, to those individuals whose song is herein unsung, we deeply apologize.

Although our approach is more personal than scholarly, every possible effort has been made to achieve accuracy and authoritative treatment of subject matter. Whenever possible, an appropriate individual was contacted for verification of material, and we are thankful to the many who responded.

We hope that many discrepancies which exist in this fast-changing field have been further resolved and greater insight gained through interviews conducted within the past three years. Many personal comments by those in the field have been included in the book for these purposes. We are particularly grateful to Dewey Balfa, June Carter, Johnny Cash, Judy Collins, Sis Cunningham, Erik Darling, Dave Guard, Joe Hickerson, Ian and Sylvia Tyson, Charlie McCoy, Don McLean, the Nitty Gritty Dirt Band, Tom Paxton, Jean Redpath, Jean Ritchie, Earl Scruggs, Pete Seeger, Lena Spencer, Mary Travers, and Frank Warner. Others whose cooperation deserves special mention are Moe Asch, Tony Barrand, David Bromberg,

John Cohen, Michael Cooney, Sady (S. D.) Courville, Jim Dawson, Edith Fowke, Steve Goodman, Josh Graves, Arlo Guthrie, Margaret MacArthur, Owen McBride, Dennis McGee, Tommy Makem, Glenn Ohrlin, Bruce (U. Utah) Phillips, John Prine, Malvina Reynolds, John Roberts, Rosalie Sorrels, Artie Traum, Jeff Warner, Doc Watson, and Peter Yarrow. We also appreciated interviews with Doris Abrahams, Eddie Adcock, Dewey Addington, Mike Auldridge, Joan Baez, Roy Bookbinder, Oscar Brand, Maybelle Carter, Len Chandler, Harry Chapin, Liam Clancy, John Cohen, Jimmy Driftwood, Mimi Fariña, Paul Geremia, Dr. Kenneth S. Goldstein, John Herald, Sam Hinton, Janis Ian, Doug Kershaw, Lou Killen, Tom Lehrer, Ed McCurdy, Walt Michael for Bottle Hill, Phil Ochs, Ralph Rinzler, Mike Seeger, Patrick Sky, Arthur Smith, John Stewart, Noel Paul Stookey, Dave Van Ronk, Frank Wakefield, and Hedy West.

An unerring source of inspiration and a selfless contributor to every aspect of this book was Lena Spencer, whose files and friendship were so generously offered to us. Through her, we had the good fortune to meet Jackie Alper, who unhesitatingly gave us virtually complete access to her husband's photographs. Many of Joe Alper's photographs are reproduced herein in his memory.

We are also indebted to Frank and Anne Warner, who, in addition to making us welcome in their home on several occasions and to sharing their vast experience with us, permitted us to photograph their priceless and fascinating collection of instruments for the jacket cover. And our thanks to the photographer, Rick Baggelaar, for capturing on film the essence of the subject.

Among the record companies which rendered valuable aid in our research were ABC Records, A&M Records, Arista Records, Atlantic Recording Corporation, Capitol Records, Columbia Records (especially Mary Ann McCready in the Nashville office), County Records (especially David Freeman), DisCreet Records, Elektra Records, Epic Records, Island Records, MCA Records, MGM Records (especially Pat Drosins), Monument Records (especially Jan Walner), Poppy Records, RCA Records, Reprise Records, United Artists Records, and Vanguard Records. Our special thanks to Sandy and Caroline Paton of Folk-Legacy Records for their assistance.

We also acknowledge the cooperation given to us by Roy Acuff, Alistair Anderson, Arthur Argo, George and Gerry Armstrong, Francine Brown for the Pennywhistlers, Guy Carawan, Elizabeth Cotten, Kyle Creed, Barbara Dane, Doug Dorschug for the Highwoods String Band, Livia Drapkin, Stefan Grossman, Bess Lomax Hawes, Tommy Jarrell, Reverend Frederick Douglass Kirkpatrick, Harold Leventhal for Alan Arkin, Ewan MacColl, John Jacob Niles, Bernice Reagon, Earl Robinson, Jean and Lee Schilling, Peggy Seeger, Irwin Silber, Dan Smith, Tom Smothers, Bill and Andy Spence, Victoria Spivey, Win Stracke, Roger Tracy for Apple Country, and Bill Vanaver.

Also: the Archive of Folk Song (especially Joe Hickerson and Dick Spottswood); Virginia Correll of the Brandywine Valley Friends of Old Time Music; Lou Curtiss, Chairman of the San Diego University Folk Festival; the Great Folk Revival, Incorporated; the Guitar Workshop, Roslyn, New York; the John Edwards Memorial Foundation (especially Norman Cohen); David Kent, president of the Louisiana Hayride; the Lendel Agency for the Country Gentlemen; Bill McNeill of the Smithsonian Institution; the National Folk Festival Association (especially Leo Bernache and Andy Wallace); Marsha Necheles, editor of *Folkscene* publication; Judy Peiser of the Center for Southern Folklore; Winslow Pinney; Anne Romaine of the Southern Folk Cultural Revival Project; Bob Sarlin; *Sing Out!* (especially Bob Norman and Alan Senauke); and Les Weinstein, manager of the Irish Rovers.

Our appreciation to the publications and publishing firms which granted us permission to reproduce printed material. Detailed acknowledgments will be found at the back of the book, along with grateful acknowledgments for the use of photos and other illustrations.

Lastly, our heartfelt thanks to Jillian Propper for putting up with us and our typing without losing her great sense of humor.

Kristin Baggelaar and Donald Milton
Oyster Bay, New York
April 1976

## O. J. Abbott

*Traditional singer of Irish, British, and Canadian lumbering songs, performer, and recording artist*

Toward the end of the nineteenth century, when thousands of square miles of Canadian north country were green with tall pines ready for lumber and paper mills, a lumberman by the name of O. J. Abbott was learning songs from other Ontario shantyboys.

Born in England in 1872, he came to Canada with his brother, and during his youth this Canadian singer from Ontario worked on Ottawa Valley farms and in lumber camps, gathering traditional Irish, British, and Canadian folk songs. In 1957, while living in Hull, Quebec, a prominent Canadian folklorist, Edith Fowke, first met and recorded the eighty-five-year-old Abbott: "He was a very fine traditional singer. One of the best from whom I have collected." She recorded over 120 songs and featured Abbott in her book *Traditional Singers and Songs from Ontario*, published in 1965 by Folklore Associates. She also prepared an album of his songs for Moe Asch of Folkways Records, and this appeared in 1961 as *Irish and British Songs from the Ottawa Valley* (FM 4051). Many of Abbott's songs were printed five years later in Edith Fowke's *Lumbering Songs from the Northern Woods* (University of Texas Press, 1970); and he was among the singers included in Fowke's field recordings, which comprise *Far Canadian Fields* (Leader LEE 4057), to complement her work, *The*

*Penguin Book of Canadian Folk Songs*, published in 1973.

Not a professional singer, "old Mr. Abbott" learned his songs orally and sang them for his own amusement. He sang at the Canadian National Museum, Ontario, in 1958, and he appeared on CBC-TV in 1960. He performed at one Newport Folk Festival, and he was among the performers at the 1961 Mariposa Folk Festival; at each, he was heard to reminisce about the early songs: "I haven't sung that song for sixty years!" On March 3, 1962, he died at the age of ninety.

## Will Abernathy. *See* The Blue
Ridge Mountain Entertainers.

## Doris Abrahams

*Singer, songwriter, and performer*

Turned on to folk music "in the eighth grade by a bunch of beatniks," Abrahams started playing guitar and listening to Bob Dylan and Pete Seeger. Frequent visits to Greenwich Village clubs such as the Cafe Au Go Go and the Gaslight familiarized her with the music of Richie Havens, Dave Van Ronk, the Youngbloods, and Jim Kweskin's Jug Band: "I used to love the Jug Band, I used to go to see them all the time—and I used to go *bananas* over Maria [Muldaur], she was wonderful and *so* strange, and it was wonderful when we ended up playing together years later." Maria Muldaur had come to Kweskin's Jug Band from the Even Dozen Jug Band, and in the early 1970s she sang with Ellie Greenberg as Doris Abrahams's vocal backup, called the Sleazettes. They performed at the Eleventh Annual Philadelphia Folk Festival in 1972 with the four-piece acoustic band, the Sleeve Job, which included Peter Eklund on trumpet and Larry Packer on fiddle.

Abrahams's first gigs were in 1969, and she performed in her hometown of New York City at the Focus and the Gaslight hoots: "It was pretty 'folky' at the beginning—I was doing some country tunes and folk tunes—but it soon started to wander from the folk thing." Although her act is basically acoustic, Abrahams's repertoire has evolved to incorporate a variety of styles—blues, ragtime, country, Cole Porter tunes, original and contemporary songs. Often accompanied by Allen Friedman on electric rhythm guitar, Fred Holman on bass guitar, Larry Packer on fiddle, and Ellie Greenberg on vocals, Abrahams performs at colleges, clubs, and festivals throughout the Northeast.

# Nathan Abshire

*Old-time Cajun accordionist, songwriter, performer, and recording artist*

This old-style Cajun accordionist, sometimes referred to as "Mr. Accordion," is probably best known for the many years he played with the famous band, the Balfa Freres. A native of Louisiana's bayou country, Abshire was born in Gueydan, Louisiana, on June 27, 1913. The accordion was always an integral part of his life; his parents and two brothers played the instrument, and when Abshire was six years old, he started his career on an accordion purchased for $3.50. Abshire is a traditionalist who plays with accordion techniques that reflect the earliest forms of Cajun musical accompaniment; even his instrument, the Cajun accordion, is unique to that culture. This brilliant musician has never had musical instruction, is unable to read music or even write his own

name, but he makes and fixes music in his head, picks up the accordion, and just plays.

Abshire began performing at the age of eight, and his first recording, made in the early 1930s, was a 78-RPM record done in New Orleans with Happy Fats and the Rainbow Ramblers. After serving in World War II, Abshire appeared regularly at the Avalon Club in Basile, Louisiana, where he now lives and works as a watchman for the city. Until recently, he worked occasionally with two old-time fiddlers Dennis McGee and S. D. (Sady) Courville; and, as a trio, they performed in their unique Cajun vocal and instrumental style at several festivals, including the 1974 National Folk Festival. Prior to the event, the traditional Cajun band entertained congressional supporters of folk activities at a July prefestival party. Senator Russell Long and Representative Gillis Long proudly introduced Abshire, Courville, and McGee as representatives of Louisiana's musical tradition.

Abshire has been recorded on albums including various other artists, such as *Nathan Abshire and Other Cajun Gems* (Arhoolie 5013); *Cajun Fais Do-Do* (Arhoolie F5004), on which Abshire plays one of his most famous tunes, "Cajun Two Step," with his Pinegrove Boys; *Cajun Music: The Early 50's* (Arhoolie 5008); *The Roots of America's Music* (Arhoolie R2001/2002); *The String Bands—Vol. 2* (Old Timey X-101); *Louisiana Cajun Music—Vol. 4 "From the 30s to the Early 50s"* (Old Timey X-111); *A Cajun Tradition* (La Louisianne 139); and others. His best-known song is probably "Pine Grove Blues" (also known as "Au Negresse"), and it is the title of his solo album, *Pine Grove Blues* (Swallow LP [T] 6014), with accompaniment by the Balfa Freres. Abshire has performed in recent years on radio station KEUN, and together with McGee and Courville as the Mamou Hour Band. Their fine, old-style Cajun tunes are broadcast for fans and traditional music enthusiasts in the Mamou, Louisiana, area.

"I've had Nathan with me on *The Mamou Hour* off and on for the last two years," says the seventy-year-old Courville, "and to me he's one of the top accordion players of the old style still left. I've played a lot of music in my life, and to me he's one of the easiest men to blend with, as a team, to make music. Teamwork is what makes Cajun music, blending with one another, because we play everything by ear, it's all memorized." (*See also* The Balfa Freres; S. D. [Sady] Courville; Dennis McGee.)

## Ray Abshire. *See* The Balfa Freres.

## Roy Acuff

*Singer, songwriter, fiddler, performer, recording artist, and record company executive*

The opinion held by most country music fans is that Roy Acuff's major contribution to folk and country music—and his major influence on the post–World War II American public—has been his development of a popular traditional style as an alternative to modern and country & western styles.

Roy Acuff's minister-lawyer father played the fiddle and collected fiddle tunes, and he influenced his son to pick up and play the instrument. When he was twenty-five, Roy Acuff joined Dr. Hower's Medicine Show, then went to radio station WNOX, and later to WROL. He had auditioned for a job on the *Grand Ole Opry*, and then, one Saturday night when he and his band successfully filled in for Arthur Smith and Sam and Kirk McGee, Acuff was asked to take a regular job on the show. After two years he became as well-known and popular as its foremost performer, Uncle Dave Macon. Acuff was the first singing star of the *Opry*, and as Bashful Brother Oswald of Roy Acuff's Smoky Mountain Boys says: "There was some comedy, but not much, on the *Opry* before Roy come down here. Roy's show always had comedy." The tradition of center-staging string bands at the *Opry* was changed by Acuff's innovative format. During this era, Acuff and the Smoky Mountain Boys recorded such hits as "Will the Circle

Be Unbroken," "Precious Jewel," "Wreck on the Highway," "I Saw the Light," "The Great Speckled Bird," "Wabash Cannonball," and "Carry Me Back to the Mountains." (The first four of these were rerecorded by Acuff and the Nitty Gritty Dirt Band on the United Artists LP *Will the Circle Be Unbroken* [UA-9801].)

Roy Acuff has influenced many artists, including Ian Tyson, whose relatively new group, the Great Speckled Bird, derives its name from Acuff's famous song of the same name. Acuff is now a record company executive and part-owner of Hickory Records (Donovan's first United States recording company). His popularity is expressed by his friend of thirty-eight years, Brother Oswald: "He's been the best boss in the world, I think. You could never ask for a better guy to work for. He's not lookin' for mistakes. You know he's got to be good by how long his band members stay with him. Jimmy Riddle has been with him nearly thirty years. And Howdy Forrester has been with him over twenty-five years, Gene Martin for fifteen years, and Charlie Collins for ten years now."

Roy Acuff's recordings appear on several different labels, including Capitol, Columbia, Hickory, and Old Timey.

## Derroll Adams

*Country and traditional balladeer, songwriter, banjoist, performer, and recording artist*

Acclaimed by his European fans as a cult figure of folk music and a legendary country and British traditional balladeer, this expatriate American has lived in Europe since the late 1950s.

Adams was born in Oregon in 1925, and his early musical influences were the *Grand Ole Opry*, which he heard on the radio, and the fruit pickers singing in the groves. His first instrument was a harmonica; when he was in his late teens, his mother bought him a banjo, which he learned to play by studying records and by attending college performances by Josh White and others. In his

3

twenties and living near Los Angeles, he met Butch and Bess Lomax Hawes, Woody Guthrie, and Jack Elliott. As close friends, Adams and Elliott traveled together doing numerous gigs in West Coast bars and nightspots. After Elliott married and moved to Europe, Adams followed in 1957 and recorded several tunes for Topic Records in England; and together they recorded *Roll On Buddy* (Topic 105). Between bouts of alcoholism, Adams performed throughout Europe and was—and still is—recognized as a major influence on folk music.

After several years of musical inactivity, Adams made a comeback in the summer of 1972 when he performed at the Cambridge Folk Festival in England. Happy Traum described the event in *Sing Out!* magazine:

> The fact that Derroll Adams was there at all was something of a miracle. Not many months before he was suffering DT's in a hospital in Germany. He fell into a coma, and the doctors thought that he would die or suffer incurable brain damage. As it turned out, Derroll was stronger than they knew; and with the help of his wife, Danny, and the realization of how close to the end he had come, he gave up drinking completely and started his recovery. At Cambridge, people who had known him before told me he looked ten years younger than the last time they'd seen him, and Derroll spoke of his harrowing experience and new life with great pride. The festival at Cambridge was his first English appearance in years, and he saw it as a challenge to himself and his music.

Adams's recent British Village Thing album, *Feelin' Fine* (VGT-17), exemplifies his fine banjo picking and the bass voice often described as reminiscent of Johnny Cash or Bascom Lamar Lunsford. He is famous for his bawdy ballads and traditional songs. Probably his best-known original composition is "Portland Town."

# Eddie Adcock

*Bluegrass baritone singer and five-string banjoist, performer, and recording artist.*

Since the mid-1950s, Eddie Adcock's name has been known throughout the world of bluegrass as a member of the Blue Star Boys, Mac Wiseman's Country Boys, the Bluegrass Boys, and the Country Gentlemen. In the early seventies, he formed his own group, called the II Generation, whose progressive bluegrass sound he describes as on "the cuttin' edge."

Adcock was born in 1938 in Scottsville, Virginia, and as a young boy in the late 1940s he played tenor banjo with the *Church of God* gospel programs on Charlottesville, Virginia, radio stations WINA and WCHV. His first professional job was with Smokey Graves and the Blue Star Boys on WSVS Radio in Crewe, Virginia, in the early fifties. During this period he met Don Reno, who strongly influenced Adcock's banjo-picking style, and Reno was largely responsible for Adcock's getting a job with Mac Wiseman. He played with Wiseman for about a year, traveled widely, and was brought to the attention of the general public. In 1957 he played rhythm guitar with Buzz Busby and bassist Vance Truell; and in late 1958 Adcock joined the Country Gentlemen.

At the time, the Country Gentlemen were considered revolutionary, but their new bluegrass sound is now thought of as the old-style bluegrass. On his first album with the Country Gentlemen, Eddie Adcock contributed his influential baritone singing, his celebrated banjo style, and what is commonly referred to as "hammering on." Eddie Adcock, John Duffey, Charlie Waller, and the group's bassists (the best known of whom was Tom Gray) became one of the most popular bluegrass groups in the country, and their sound has been widely imitated by other bluegrass bands.

Eddie Adcock played with the Country Gentlemen for about thirteen years, and when John Duffey left the group in 1969, Adcock soon followed. In 1970 Adcock went to California and formed a country rock band (under the pseudonym Clinton Kodak), and he played a loud electric lead guitar. Adcock had grown tired of the Country Gentlemen's music and he wanted to play something different; before returning to bluegrass, he played rock and country rock for about a year. In 1971, he put together the II Generation, with Jimmy Gaudreau, Wendy Thatcher, and Bob White (Quail), and their first recording was "Virginia," written by Wendy Thatcher. With both the Country Gentlemen and the II Generation, Adcock has broadened the scope of bluegrass and has created an innovative sound with each group.

To date, the most recent additions to II Generation are Akira Otsuka (formerly with Cliff Waldron) on mandolin and Dan Cade on fiddle, along with Eddie Adcock, Johnny Castle, and Martha Hearon. In addition to several recordings with the II Generation, Eddie Adcock has recorded as a solo artist with other noted performers such as Don Reno. (*See also* The Country Boys; The Country Gentlemen.)

## The Addington Family

*Traditional singers, instrumentalists, and performers*

Like most recorded Virginia musicians, "Doc" and Dewey Addington (Mother Maybelle Carter's brothers) and Carl McConnell hail from the southwestern part of the state. Dewey Addington was born, raised, and still lives in Gate City, with "Doc" Addington and Carl McConnell living in nearby Nickelsville in the shadow of Clinch Mountain.

Still active at age seventy-six, Dewey Addington has never recorded or written any songs, but he still picks the five-string banjo every week or two at the old Carter Family place in Maces Spring, Virginia. There, on A. P. Carter's front porch, he and some friends have a little show, making music and having a good time playing for some folks: "I just do those old-time songs that date way back, like 'Pretty Polly,' 'John Henry,' 'Joe Clark,' and others. Maybelle and I started when we were young, and we used to play around home a lot." When Dewey temporarily stopped playing, Maybelle Carter went on to establish a reputation with the Carter Family in the recording business. Thirty or forty years later, Dewey started playing again, and he made his first public appearance at the 1973 National Folk Festival with his sister Maybelle Carter, two of her daughters, Anita and Helen, "Doc," Carl McConnell, two grandchildren, David and Lorry, and A. P. and Sara Carter's youngest daughter, Janette Carter (Kelly).

Carl McConnell, the unrelated member of the family, has performed and recorded with "Doc" since 1938, and they call themselves the Virginia Boys. McConnell plays banjo, but, according to Dewey Addington: "He plays different than me, I play the old-time way."

The Virginia Boys' career is intertwined with the early years of the Carter Family, as described by June Carter: "Uncle 'Doc' and Carl McConnell worked with us in Richmond, Virginia, when we started there in 1943, and stayed until 1946. They sang and performed with us in our concert work in high schools and in the old auditoriums, and they were part of the group at certain times. Uncle 'Doc' played a very fine, old style of guitar, and Carl played banjo. Uncle 'Doc' was the only one from the Addingtons who played professionally, but they were all talented.

"Dewey played all his life at home, but he never worked commercially and he was never a part of our work. He has gone to a few festivals with mother and Uncle 'Doc' and Carl, but it's probably the only thing he's done outside of just picking on his front porch. Mother had a few nephews who could play anything, and I think that much of the strength of the Carter Family came from the Copper Creek side of the mountain, where the Addingtons lived.

"The Addingtons came from England in the 1700s. We have one ancestor, Henry Addington, who was England's prime minister before William Pitt, and we had another relative who lived to be 104 years old. The Addington Family has done a lot to preserve what they brought from England so many years ago, and I hope that I'm a little bit of both of the families because I'm very proud of the Carters and the Addingtons."

Within the past five years, the Addington Family, with Dewey, "Doc," and Carl, has made several appearances at festivals sponsored by the National Folk Festival Association and the Smithsonian Institution. The Addington Family has provided an important link in the folk process of the United States, and they have shared, and spread, their regional old-time style by the processes of basic, or person-to-person, oral tradition and recorded, or aural, transmission of songs. (*See also* The Carter Family; Maybelle Carter.)

## Dewey Addington. *See* The Addington Family.

## "Doc" Addington. *See* The Addington Family.

## The Albion Country Band.
*See* Ashley Hutchings.

## Lee Allen

*Bluegrass guitarist, singer, songwriter, performer, and recording artist*

Born on June 19, 1946, to a fourteen-member Appalachian mountain family of Kentucky, Leamon "Lee" Allen was influenced by both church music and his favorite group, the Stanley Brothers, whom he heard on the radio.

The nine-year-old Allen accompanied his early singing by learning to play an old four-dollar guitar given to him by his mother. At eighteen he migrated with his bride to southwestern Ohio and began singing in his brother's church and in the bluegrass band, Jim Howard and the Kentucky Ramblers. He started swapping tunes with his neighbor Larry Sparks, who was then lead singer for Ralph Stanley, and, on occasion, Allen played with the band on weekends. He recorded a single entitled "Tragedy of Frozen Creek," followed by his first album, *Songs of Love and Tragedy* (Jalyn JLP 127), with the instrumental backup of Ralph Stanley and the Clinch Mountain Boys. He formed his own group, called the Dew Mountain Boys, which, over the years, with personnel changes, has included Neal Brackett, formerly of the Lonesome Ramblers, Dave Cox, Bob Dooley, Lloyd Hensley, Dolin Jackson, Jack Lynch of Jalyn Records, Harold Staggs, Ron Thomason, who came from the Clinch Mountain Boys, and Sherry Tuttle.

With vocal styling in the Stanley tradition, Lee Allen and the Dew Mountain Boys play traditional tunes and many original Allen compositions based on actual life experiences. In recent years they have recorded for both Jalyn (*Lee Allen and the Dew Mountain Boys* [Jalyn 153]) and John Morris's Old Homestead (*Way Out Yonder* [Old Homestead 90025]). At several of the music festivals that they have attended, Ralph Stanley has sung some of Lee Allen's songs, which he has also recorded.

## The Almanac Singers

*Vocal and instrumental group, performers, and recording artists*

Late in 1940, Pete Seeger, who was traveling around the country singing in bars and union halls, met former college instructor Lee Hays and, together with Millard Lampell, a University of West Virginia graduate and roommate of Hays's, formed a group called the Almanac Singers. Their name came from *The Farmer's Almanac.* (Lee Hays claimed that country folks had only two books, a Bible and an Almanac—one to help you get to the next world, and the other to get you by in this one.) They recorded an album of peace songs and an album of union songs called *Talking Union* (now Folkways FH 5285). In June 1941 the Almanacs were joined by Woody Guthrie, who had traveled from the Pacific Northwest to New York City after composing a group of songs commissioned by the Bonneville Power Administration. The foursome recorded two more albums, *Sod Buster Ballads* and *Deep Sea Shanties*, which were later combined as *The Soil and the Sea* (Mainstream 56005). The few extra dollars made from these recordings were combined with the spare change in their pockets to buy a $125 nine-year-old Buick, and they headed West. They sang their way cross-country through Detroit, Chicago, and Denver, and their songs were often met with unexpected enthusiasm by street-corner audiences, auto workers, and CIO union members. As Pete Seeger tells it in his book, *The Incompleat Folksinger:*

> When we walked down the aisle of a room where one thousand local members of the longshoremen's union were meeting, we could see some of them turning around in surprise and even disapproval. "What the hell is a bunch of hillbilly singers coming in here for? We got work to do."
>
> But when we finished singing for them "Union Maid," "Talking Union," "Which Side Are You On?," and especially "The Ballad of Harry Bridges," their applause was deafening. We walked down that same aisle on our way out and they slapped Woody on the back so hard they nearly knocked him over.

When the Almanacs reached Los Angeles, Hays and Lampell dropped out of the group for a while. Seeger and Guthrie continued their odyssey throughout the Pacific Northwest—singing anywhere people would listen—and then worked their way back to New York. In the fall of 1941, they settled in the first of the Almanac Houses, which was a Greenwich Village cooperative apartment on West Tenth Street. The following year, the Almanac Singers recorded an album which urged full participation in the war effort, *Dear Mr. President,* which included "Reuben James," written by Woody Guthrie and played to the tune of "Wildwood Flower," and "Round and Round Hitler's Grave," which they performed to the tune of "Old Joe Clark." (When Russia was attacked by Nazi Germany in June 1941, an album of antiwar songs, which had been recorded prior to *Dear Mr. President,* had been withdrawn.) The Almanac Singers disbanded in the summer of 1942 when Lampell left, and Guthrie formed the short-lived Headline Singers, with Leadbelly, Brownie McGhee, and Sonny Terry. With the United States entering the war, the members went their separate ways by joining different branches of the armed forces.

Although the Almanac Singers originally comprised Woody Guthrie, Lee Hays, Millard Lampell, and Pete Seeger (who used the name Pete Bowers at the time), at various times the group included Sis Cunningham, Butch Hawes, Cisco Houston, Bess Lomax (Hawes), and Arthur Stern.

The Almanac Singers never regrouped after the war, but each of its members remained active as a folksinger—perpetuating the folk process of sharing music with others. Lee Hays and Pete Seeger joined Ronnie Gilbert and Fred Hellerman to form the influential group the Weavers. Millard Lampell authored such works as *The Wall,* *The Long Way Home,* and *The Hero,* which was made into the film *Saturday's Hero;* and he collaborated with Earl Robinson to compose the cantata "The Lonesome Train."

It is significant that the term "hootenanny," which was so often used during the 1960s, was first popularized nationally by

*Eric Andersen*

Woody Guthrie and Pete Seeger and the Almanac Singers.

## American Folk Festival. *See* Mountain Dance and Folk Festival.

## Jean Amos. *See* The Womenfolk.

## Eric Andersen

*Contemporary singer-songwriter, guitarist, pianist, harmonica player, performer, and recording artist*

During the 1960s Eric Andersen became one of the first folksingers to compose instead of simply interpret material. His highly original, lyrical, and romantic songs are characterized by philosophical and poetic stylings which arise from his deep compassion and sensitivity toward other people.

Eric Andersen was born on February 14, 1943, in Pittsburgh, Pennsylvania. After attending Hobart College near his hometown of Buffalo, New York, he hopped a freight car to the West Coast. Then, hoping to get his material published, he came to New York and arrived on the Greenwich Village folk scene early in the winter of 1964. He made his first nightclub appearance at Gerde's Folk City, followed by an engagement at the Gaslight Cafe and the frequent printing of his songs in *Broadside* magazine. He was acclaimed by Robert Shelton in *The New York Times*, February 21, 1964, as follows: "Here is one antidote to the Beatles: a sensitive, very musical 20-year-old with long hair and a lean and esthetic face who is quietly making his New York nightclub debut. . . . Mentioning Mr. Andersen in the same breath as the Beatles may seem invidious. But it is consoling that the folk revival is continuing to develop first-rate performers and songwriters with something to say."

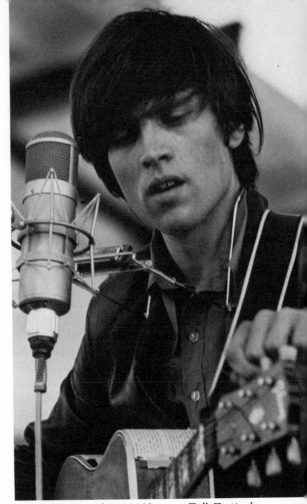

Eric Andersen at the 1966 Newport Folk Festival

Within a few days of his arrival in New York, Eric Andersen secured a music publisher and a recording contract with Vanguard Records, and in 1965 his debut album was released, entitled *Today Is the Highway* (Vanguard VSD-79157). Two songs—"Thirsty Boots" and "Violets of Dawn"—included on his second LP, *'Bout Changes 'n' Things* (Vanguard VSD-79206), established his reputation as a songwriter. His popularity was further spread by Judy Collins's recording of "Thirsty Boots" and by numerous recordings by other artists of "Violets of Dawn."

Two more Vanguard albums followed, and, after the 1968 release of his fifth album, entitled *Avalanche* (Warner Brothers 1748), he entered a period of inactivity. In 1972 he signed with Columbia

Records, and sales of his next album, *Blue River* (Columbia KC 31062), surpassed those of any of his previous efforts. Products of vocal and poetic maturity, all of the selections (with one exception) were written by Eric Andersen.

Three years after the release of *Blue River*, he completed master tapes for a subsequent Columbia LP, but they were lost somewhere between Nashville and Los Angeles—turning up only after production was almost completed on the second set of masters. After the Columbia master tape mishap, he went to contract with Clive Davis's new Arista (formerly Bell) label, and *Be True to You* (Arista AL 4033) was released in 1975. Like his previous album, this disc represents his philosophical statement in his quest for truths relating to love, time, and identity. Some of the songs may be interpreted as reflections of his self-contradictory nature (for example, "Liza, Light the Candle") and one of his best-known compositions, "Time Run Like a Freight Train," evokes images of a journey made weary by the recurrence of names, lovers, and wars.

Eric Andersen still maintains an active touring schedule, and the list of artists who record his songs, including Judy Collins, Peter, Paul and Mary, Pete Seeger, Johnny Cash, and Joan Baez, continues to grow.

## Alistair Anderson

*Performer and recording artist of British traditional music on the English concertina*

"Possibly the most celebrated performer on the English concertina that Britain has ever produced. Anderson and the High Level Ranters have had a profound effect upon the course and aesthetics of British folk music for well over a decade," commented Dr. Kenneth Goldstein in the 1974 Philadelphia Folk Festival program, when Alistair Anderson was among the festival's guest artists during his tour of the United States that year.

Anderson first visited the United States in 1971 with the High Level Ranters, when the band was invited to perform at the Penn State University festival, the Chicago festival, and at coffeehouses in the Midwest and along the East Coast. Like the other three members of the Ranters, Anderson performs both as a solo musician and as a member of the band. His main contribution to the folk revival is as an interpreter of the traditional dance tunes of England, Ireland, and Scotland on the English concertina. He also plays the Northumbrian smallpipes, a bagpipe peculiar to northeast England.

In 1972 Anderson recorded a solo concertina album, *Alistair Anderson Plays English Concertina*, on the Leader-Trailer label (LER 2074). His second solo record is *Concertina Workshop* (Topic 12TFRS501), which is a workshop-tutor LP with instruction booklet. Front Hall Records is planning to release his next album (FHR-08) in 1976.

Alistair Anderson made a successful tour of the United States in 1974, when he was a guest at the Fox Hollow and Philadelphia folk festivals, coffeehouses, and folk music societies. He returned in 1975 and hopes to return annually to play at folk music gatherings of all kinds. (*See also* The High Level Ranters.)

## Kurt Anderson

*Country singer, guitarist, and performer*

In his mid-twenties Kurt Anderson started playing guitar and performing in bars and coffeehouses throughout his native state of Florida. Along with Tony Barrand, Andy Cohen, Paul Combs, Margaret MacArthur, Al McKenney, Bruce (U. Utah) Phillips, John Roberts, Rosalie Sorrels, Bill Vanaver, and others, he became a member of the now-defunct Wildflowers Musicians Cooperative, which was formed around 1970 and located in Saratoga Springs, New York.

Anderson moved to Boston after leaving the struggling musician's co-op, and he became employed in a series of jobs unrelated to music. While living in Boston, he developed a skeptical outlook on life and during this period played mostly for friends. After traveling in Europe for a while, Anderson returned to live in Saratoga. Taking up the electric bass, he played for a few country bands, then went on his own.

His direct, open, honest style is a natural complement to his gentle, nasal vocal presentation, and, says Lena Spencer, owner of Caffé Lena where Anderson has performed, he sings "mostly country songs of the 1930s, '40s, and '50s—songs made popular by people like Hank Williams, Jimmie Rodgers, and the Carter Family." Anderson offers individualistic interpretations of early country music, nostalgic songs of the 1930s and 1940s, and songs written by contemporary musicians. He has appeared throughout the Northeast in colleges and coffeehouses.

# Pink Anderson

*Carolina blues singer, guitarist, old-time medicine-show performer, and recording artist*

With his robust voice and loud, often dissonant, guitar style—frequently using bass runs, brushing the open strings between chords, and snapping the strings during treble runs—this old-time medicine-show performer and legendary blues musician made people hoot 'n' holler 'n' foot-stomp for many years.

Retired since around 1955, Anderson lived in Spartanburg, South Carolina, about thirty miles from the poor farming community of Laurens, where Rev. Gary Davis spent his boyhood. Anderson began his career in 1918 when he signed up with W. R. Kerr's Medicine Show, and before he finally retired he had toured and performed with the traveling shows of Frank

Curry, Emmet Smith, W. A. Blair, and Chief Thundercloud. His older friend, Blind Simmie Dooley, raised him during his youth and taught him guitar accompaniment; in 1928 they recorded two "good-time" blues 78s, "Papa's 'Bout to Get Mad" and "Every Day of the Week," for Columbia Records in Atlanta, reissued on Origin of Jazz and Yazoo Records (*Mama Let Me Lay It on You 1926–1936* [Yazoo L 1040]). Anderson's next record was not made until 1951, when he cut one side of an album for Riverside, and Rev. Gary Davis was recorded on the other side. Ten years later, with the help of Sam Charters of Prestige Records, he recorded three more albums. It is from these four LPs that his songs, such as "Travelin' Man," "Every Day of the Week," "I Got Mine," and "He's in the Jailhouse Now," were passed on and recorded by other artists, such as Tom Rush, Jim Kweskin, Billy Faier, and Paul Geremia.

Anderson suffered a stroke in 1969 and was musically inactive until 1972. During this period, Paul Geremia traveled down to Spartanburg, sat on Pink Anderson's front porch, and taped a lot of old songs and some recently written by the Carolina bluesman. When summer arrived, music club owner Dan Prentice's interest in Anderson had been aroused by Geremia's tape, and with Prentice's cooperation, after almost twenty years, Pink Anderson picked up his guitar and played, sang, and cracked jokes for a nightclub audience in Newport, Rhode Island. The following day, when Anderson was looking at his picture in the *Providence Journal*, he was asked by Roy Bookbinder, the New York blues and ragtime musician: "What'll folks back home say about that?"

"They'll bite their heads off," he [Anderson] answered, "they surely will."

After his last trip North, Pink Anderson died in his hometown on October 12, 1974.

**Pete Apo.** *See* The Travelers 3.

# Appalachian (Mountain) Dulcimer

This traditional Appalachian instrument is a stringed, zither-like descendant of the German *scheitholt*—a folk zither with one to four melody strings and a few drone strings suspended over a thin, rectangular box. The *scheitholt* was the prototype for three Old World instruments: the Norwegian *langeleik*, the French *epinette des Vosges*, and the Dutch *humle*. All three of these instruments share common characteristics with the dulcimer developed in the Southern Appalachian Mountains of the United States.

The Appalachian dulcimer has an elongated hollow sound box (reminiscent of a thin violin) over which a neck board, or a fret board, runs the entire length, terminating at one end with a bridge and tailpiece and at the other end with the tuning pegs and scroll. Traditionally, there are three strings, with one melody string and two drone strings (Richard Fariña used a double melody string), and the melody string is positioned over fixed frets. All of the strings are strummed with a feather (usually a goose or turkey quill) or a small stick while the player's other hand stops the strings by pressing them down on the neck board. When played, the dulcimer is placed across the knees of the player, or on a table.

Although the three-stringed Appalachian dulcimer is most common, other versions are made with four to eight strings. Most dulcimers are handcrafted, and modifications and variations exist from one instrument to the next. In her "Dulcimer Corner," which appeared in the August 1974 *Folkscene*, Holly Tannen describes the dulcimer as follows:

> On some early dulcimers, the frets were nothing more than a nail or a piece of wire bent under the first string alone, so that fretting the other strings would not even have been possible. The scale of the dulcimer fretboard is not chromatic, like that of a guitar or banjo, but rather diatonic—like Schroeder's toy piano, with the black keys just painted on. This makes it difficult to play Beethoven (or any complicated classical piece, with sharps and flats and changes of key) and easy to pick out the modal folk music of the mountains.

The dulcimer is traditionally tuned in any of the ancient diatonic modes, discarded by formal musicians around 1600 but still utilized by English folk singers and their descendants in the Appalachians. The most common modes are the Ionian (C to C on the white notes of the piano: "Go Tell Aunt Rhodie," "What'll I Do with the Baby-O"), mixolydian (G to G: "Old Joe Clark" and "Goin' to Boston"), and the aeolian or "mountain minor" (A to A: "Shady Grove," "East Virginia").

Other modes into which the dulcimer can be tuned are the Dorian (D to D), Phrygian (E to E) and Lydian (F to F). The music that arises from these tunings is purely melodic, free from the modern inventions of harmonies and chords.

In recent years the Appalachian dulcimer has enjoyed a resurgence in popularity with its widespread appeal prompted by such folk artists as Richard Fariña, Howie Mitchell, Jean Ritchie, and Holly Tannen. The dulcimer has expanded from its role as a primitive folk instrument of the Southern mountain region to a prominent and sophisticated musical instrument of the seventies that is used by contemporary artists Joni Mitchell and Steeleye Span, among others.

The hammered dulcimer is a larger instrument, which varies greatly in design and size and is composed of a flat, rectangular or trapezoid-shaped sound box with eight or more groups of strings. The strings in each grouping are tuned in unison, and there are generally three bridges and two soundholes. Howie Mitchell is one of the foremost proponents of the hammered dulcimer in this country today, and he has put together *The Hammered Dulcimer* (Folk-Legacy FSI-43) on how to make it and play it, with an illustrated book of instructions on the instrument.

## Apple Country

*New England six-man bluegrass band, performers, and recording artists*

Active in the greater New Haven area since about 1970, the highly charged bluegrass style of Apple Country has been presented every Thursday night at the Enormous Room and then at the Pickin' Parlor, both in New Haven, and more recently at the Holiday Inn, Meriden, Connecticut, where their music is broadcast live on WIO-FM.

The six members of the group include Dave Kiphuth on rhythm guitar; Gene LaBrie on bass fiddle; Bud Morrisroe on fiddle; Mark Rickart on mandolin; Phil Rosenthal, the group's chief songwriter, on lead guitar; and Bruce Stockwell, from Vermont's Green Mountain Boys, on banjo. One of New England's few bluegrass bands, they have performed at My Father's Place in Roslyn, Long Island, on college campuses, radio and television broadcasts, and at several major festivals, such as the Bill Monroe–Ralph Stanley Festival in Glasgow, Delaware, and the Berryville, Virginia, Festival.

Their first album, *Apple Country Bluegrass* (Orchard XPL-1047) contains four original tunes by Phil Rosenthal, "Wild Country Bound," "Because of Love," "When a Girl I Know Gets Back to Town," and the instrumental, "Apple Country Breakdown." Rosenthal has written songs for the Seldom Scene, and in 1975 one of his tunes was recorded by the Osborne Brothers.

## Jon Arbenz. *See* The Serendipity Singers.

## Archive of Folk Song

*Library of Congress, Washington, D.C.*

In 1928 the Archive of Folk Song was organized within the Music Division of the Library of Congress, operating on a donation basis until staff appropriations were begun by Congress in 1937. Over the years the Archive of Folk Song has been staffed by such noted folklorists as Robert W. Gordon, who gathered early records and documents, including over 500 cylinder recordings; John A. and Alan Lomax, who contributed more than 3,000 disc recordings in the 1930s; Benjamin A. Botkin; Duncan Emrich; Mrs. Rae Korson; Alan Jabbour; and Joseph C. Hickerson.

At present the Archive of Folk Song houses over 26,000 cylinder, disc, wire-spool, and tape recordings, which include folk songs, folk music, folk tales, oral history, and other items of folklore. In addition, there are thousands of 78- and 33-RPM commercial recordings. In the reading room there are thousands of books, periodicals, newsletters, unpublished theses and dissertations. The material encompasses various ethnic groups from every region and state in the United States, and traditional and field collections from the Americas, Africa, Asia, Australia, and the Pacific Islands. A series of sixty-six LP recordings are offered for sale as a sampling of the Archive's collection, and fifteen more are in preparation for the Bicentennial.

To facilitate reference services to the public, the Archive of Folk Song publishes listings such as *American Folklore, a Bibliography of Major Works, An Inventory of the Bibliographies and Other Reference Aids, North American Folklore and Folk Music Serial Publications, A List of Some American Record Companies Specializing in Folk Music, Commercially Issued Recordings of Material in the Archive of Folk Song, Principal Contributors of Field Recordings to The Archive of Folk Song,* and *A Bibliography of Publications Relating to the Archive of Folk Song.*

## Alphonse "Boisec" Ardoin. *See*

Amadie Ardoin.

## Amadie Ardoin

*Cajun accordionist, performer, and recording artist*

Amadie Ardoin was a black musician reputed to be, along with Amadie Breaux, Joe Falcon, and Angelas LeJeune, the best accordionist of his time. He was considered a legend in his own time, and as an active performer from about 1929 to 1935, he was a recording artist for Decca, Bluebird, Columbia, and Brunswick. His last recordings were made in 1935, after which the accordion fell out of favor in Cajun bands. Ardoin played and recorded with Cajun fiddler Dennis McGee during the 1930s, and he was very well known in the Louisiana bayou country around Eunice, Crowley, and Mamou, where he worked dances with another Cajun fiddler, S. D. (Sady) Courville. He died in the mid-1940s in a state mental institution in Pineville, Louisiana.

His cousin Alphonse "Boisec" Ardoin lives in Mamou and is active in the area as an old-time accordionist of the zydeco style. With the Ardoin Brothers and fiddler Conray Fontenot, he recorded *Creole Cajun Blues* (Arhoolie 1070). "Boisec" Ardoin possesses what is believed to be the only existing photograph of Amadie Ardoin—a confirmation picture taken by an unknown photographer when he was about thirteen— and it is included in the book *Tears, Love and Laughter*, by Cajun historian Pierre Daigle.

The work of Amadie Ardoin is included on such contemporary recordings as *Louisiana Cajun Music—Vol. 1: "First Recordings— The 1920s"* (Old Timey X-108) and *Louisiana Cajun Music—Vol. 5: "The Early Years—1928–1938"* (Old Timey X-114).

## Arthur Argo

*Scottish musicologist, recording artist, and BBC producer*

A descendant of one of Scotland's greatest collectors, Gavin Greig, Arthur Argo has established a reputation as a singer and collector of his native country's folk music. A former Scottish newspaperman, now a BBC producer, Argo has done several series of radio programs on the traditional music of Scotland.

In the early 1960s Argo performed a weekend at Caffé Lena in Saratoga Springs, New York, and although he has performed at coffeehouses and music festivals in the United States, he is more renowned as a musicologist. He has recorded several albums of Scottish folk songs on the old Prestige label, Prestige/International. The album *Lyrica Erotica* is composed of his erotic songs, for which he is well known. At one time Argo was founder and editor of the Scottish folk-life magazine, *Chapbook*. As originator and president of the Aberdeen Folk Song Club, he ran the first five Aberdeen folk festivals, which included such artists as Hamish Henderson, Jeannie Robertson, Pete Seeger, and others.

## Arkansas Folk Festival

In April, dogwood blossom time, this annual music and craft festival is held in Mountain View, Arkansas. To commemorate the unique folk culture of Stone County, Arkansas, a state-operated $3.4-million Ozark Folk Center was built one mile north of the county seat, Mountain View. Since its completion in 1973, the Folk Center has been the site of the Arkansas Folk Festival and Crafts Show.

Organizer of the Rackensack Folklore Society and composer of the famous "Battle of New Orleans" and "Tennessee Stud," Jimmy Driftwood ("Daddy of the Cultural Center") is largely responsible for the festival's revival after its World War II abandonment. The tradition of gathering folks together to make music in Stone County is an old one, even older than the first festival held in 1941. Throughout the 1960s, at many of his nationwide appearances at colleges and other folklore gatherings, Driftwood offered blanket invitations to come make music at the Arkansas Folk Festival, promising, "You can sleep in my barn."

Many amateur artists, groups, and traditional singers have performed at the event, along with such well-known performers as Glenn Ohrlin and Almeda Riddle. And, says Driftwood, "The performers are farmers, timber cutters, housewives, ranchers, fox hunters, and maybe a moonshiner now and then." Besides the music and the crafts, there is a handicraft exhibit by the Ozark Foothills Handicraft Guild, parades, jam sessions, country & western music of the Mountain View Folklore Society, which performs year-round at the court square, and "spontaneous jig dancing," Driftwood smiles, "like you never saw before."

In past years the Rackensackers, led by Jimmy Driftwood, Grandpa and Ramona Jones, among others, have performed to festival crowds upwards of 100,000 celebrating springtime and a traditional way of life. Rackensackers derive their society's name from the old Indian term for the region and the Arkansas River. No electric instruments are used in their performances; instead, their authentic old-time music is played on many traditional handmade instruments, such as the dulcimer, guitar, autoharp, pickin' bow, and fiddle. (*See also* Jimmy Driftwood.)

# Alan Arkin

*Singer, songwriter, arranger, performer, recording artist, author, actor, and director*

In recent years, Alan Arkin has been best known for his accomplishments in the motion picture industry and in the theater.

Earlier in his career, this son of *Broadside* songwriter David Arkin contributed to the field of folk music as an arranger, performer, and recording artist.

Born Alan Wolf Arkin on March 26, 1934, in New York City, he was a student at Los Angeles City College from 1951 to 1953 and at Bennington College from 1954 to 1955. He learned to play the guitar and spent many hours listening to records and reading about folk music while attending college. He began working as a musical arranger and, after establishing a reputation as a folksinger, made his first album on the Elektra label. In 1956 he became one of the original members of the Tarriers, with Bob Carey and Erik Darling. For the next two years, he sang with the Tarriers, arranged some of their music, toured extensively throughout the eastern United States, Europe, and Canada, and recorded with the group their top-selling "The Banana Boat Song."

In 1958 he recorded his first album with a group called the Babysitters, which, during the next decade, made several subsequent LPs. Before turning his attention to acting, Alan Arkin taught several music courses, including basic theory and folk guitar.

He appeared on Broadway in *From the Second City* in 1961. Two years later, he was in the short motion picture *That's Me* and in the Broadway production of *Enter Laughing*, followed in 1964 by *Luv*. In 1965 he appeared in *The Last Mohican* and, in the years that followed, starred in *The Russians Are Coming, The Russians Are Coming* (1966), which earned him the Golden Globe Award as best actor in a musical or a comedy in 1967, *Woman Times Seven* (1967), *Wait Until Dark* (1967), *Inspector Clouseau* (1968), *The Heart Is a Lonely Hunter* (1968), *Popi* (1969), *Catch-22* (1970), *Last of the Red Hot Lovers* (1972), *Freebie and the Bean* (1974), *Rafferty and the Gold Dust Twins* (1974), *Hearts of the West* (1975), and *Seven Percent Solution* (1976).

In 1971 he directed the motion picture *Little Murders*, and, in the following year, he directed the Broadway play *The Sunshine*

*Boys.* He is the author of the children's book *Tony's Hard Work Day* (1972). (*See also* The Tarriers.)

## Don Armstrong

*Singer, songwriter, and performer*

Although his musical development has progressed through many different periods of growth, Don Armstrong has achieved recognition during the past few years primarily with the Santa Fe swing sound of Don Armstrong's Silver Lining. The members of his acoustic band include Don Armstrong on vocals, rhythm guitar, and banjo; his wife, Victoria Garvey (a songwriter whose tunes have been recorded by such other artists as Judy Collins, John Denver, Steve Goodman, and the Irish Rovers), on vocals, piano, and maracas; Arlen J. Johnson on lead guitar, pedal steel guitar, and mandolin; and Emil Potel on bass.

At the age of twelve, Armstrong began to hang out at a local coffeehouse, Caffé Lena in Saratoga Springs, New York, and he was influenced by its folk music performers. The beginnings of his career were patterned after his early exposure to the Caffé, and he performed "pretty much folkie stuff," according to Lena Spencer, while playing the coffeehouse circuit.

He considers Santa Fe swing to be a conglomeration of all his musical styles and influences, consisting of original recreations of old and new styles, Bob Wills's western swing, the city swing made popular by Glenn Miller, the Dorseys, Benny Goodman, and Charley Barnett, Will Bradley's boogie-woogie, and the show tunes of Johnny Mercer and Cole Porter. Armstrong's premise for combining nostalgic tunes of the forties and Santa Fe swing is based on his interpretation of western swing as "another idiom of the forties swing," explains Lena Spencer. His own arrangements of oldies and his original compositions capture the spirit of an era within the context of the con-

temporary regional styling of the Southwest.

Don Armstrong's Silver Lining performs in colleges and clubs of New Mexico and upstate New York.

## Frankie Armstrong

*British traditional and contemporary balladeer, performer, recording artist, and social worker*

". . . whether it's a love song, whether it's a ballad, whether it's an erotic song, whether it's an overtly social-industrial song . . . it still says something about the human condition," and about Frankie Armstrong herself, a social worker in drug-treatment programs, and one of Britain's most prominent folksingers. Her personal and universal social concern is reflected in her job and in her performances of traditional and contemporary songs, such as "Doors to My Mind," which she wrote out of her occupational "drug-scene" experience. Her growing involvement in both social work and music evidences her intense commitment, despite a gradual loss of vision over recent years.

At age sixteen, Armstrong sang with a skiffle group, and in the early 1960s she was a member of the Ceilidh Singers, who, influenced by the Weavers, sang blues and traditional American songs. When she began her professional training in social work in 1962, Armstrong became a solo performer and turned to British ballads and blues. She traveled and sang with Lou Killen and around 1964 was associated with the influential singers and songwriters of the Critics Group, with Ewan MacColl and Peggy Seeger. While touring the United States to study American drug problems, Armstrong has made public appearances, playing a few songs on the dulcimer or accompanied by Holly Tannen on dulcimer or piano. Most often, she likes to emphasize the communication of words, and, with her unaccompanied singing, the result is vibrant and spellbinding.

"I think you have to have a certain kind of

enjoyment of the process of being a vehicle," she told Ethel Raim of the Pennywhistlers in an interview that appeared in *Sing Out!* magazine. "And you must know that unaccompanied singing is the ultimate challenge, you just have the air, the sun, and your vocal cords, and the people who are listening . . . and when it works, it works like nothing else."

It worked at the 1973 Philadelphia Folk Festival during her Friday evening performance and during the woman's workshop held the following afternoon with Raun MacKinnon, Diana Marcovitz, Victoria Spivey, Holly Tannen, and Sippie Wallace. Crowds listened enthusiastically as Frankie Armstrong illustrated her talk on male-female roles and conflicts by singing "Barbara Allen" and two erotic British songs.

Frankie Armstrong's first recording for Topic was an album of traditional erotic songs entitled *The Bird in the Bush* (Topic 12T135), with Anne Briggs and A. L. Lloyd. Her first solo appearance on the Topic label was *Lovely on the Water* (Topic 12T216), with accompaniment by Jeff Lowe and Jack Warshaw. She is included on *The Valiant Sailor* (Topic 12T232), and she is among the numerous artists on *Room for Company* (Topic IMP-S 104). Her most recent solo effort is *Songs and Ballads* (Topic 12T5273).

The song that is most often associated with her name is "Gonna Be an Engineer," by Peggy Seeger.

## George and Gerry Armstrong

*Traditional singers, performers, and recording artists*

By profession George Armstrong is a book illustrator and his wife Gerry is a free-lance author (he illustrated three of her children's books—*The Magic Bagpipe*, *The Boat on the Hill*, and *The Fairy Thorn*—all three based on folklore, with a song on the frontispiece, and published by Albert Whitman in Chicago), but they have been influential in the folk song revival for the last twenty years.

The Armstrongs live in Wilmette, outside of Chicago, and they are urban performers of traditional songs collected in the Southern Appalachian Mountains, the Ozarks, New England, and the British Isles. They have recorded a solo album on Folkways called *Simple Gifts* (FA 2335), and they have made several group recordings with the Golden Ring, including *A Gathering of Friends for Making Music* (Folk-Legacy FSI-16) and *Five Days Singing, Volumes 1 and 2* (FSI-41 and FSI-42).

George and Gerry Armstrong have performed at numerous festivals, including the English Folk Song and Dance Society at Stratford-on-Avon in 1954, the University of Chicago Folk Festival, the Ozark Folk Festival, the National Folk Festival, and the Mountain Dance and Folk Festival in Asheville, North Carolina. They have appeared on radio programs for WFMT in Chicago, and on television programs for children, in which they specialize. George Armstrong has his own weekly radio program, called *The Wandering Folksong*, broadcast on WFMT. The Armstrongs are loosely affiliated with the Old Town School of Folk Music (founded by Win Stracke of the Golden Ring) as friends, occasionally as teachers, and as organizers of traditional music concerts. (*See also* The Golden Ring.)

## Howard Armstrong. *See* Martin, Bogan and the Armstrongs.

## Tom Armstrong. *See* Martin, Bogan and the Armstrongs.

## Bob Artis. *See* Mac Martin and the Dixie Travelers.

## Moe Asch

*Cofounder of Oak Publications, editor, and record company executive*

Moses Asch has been recording music for over thirty-five years, beginning in 1939 when he made his first commercial recordings, which he describes as "talking books"—albums with the written text included. In 1941 Burl Ives became his first major recording artist when he made an album of American folk songs directed by Alan Lomax. Asch went bankrupt with his firm Asch Records and again later on with Disc Records in 1948. In the same year, he and Marion Distler founded Folkways Records, and their initial recordings included music of Cuba and the American Indian, square dance tunes, and jazz. The new company was primarily devoted to folk music, and the early Leadbelly recordings made for Folkways Records gave Moe Asch national prominence in the recording industry.

Asch proudly explains the philosophy of Folkways Records: "I've always kept folk music as a manifestation of American culture. What happens with Folkways Records is that it listens, and if it finds that the person has something legitimate to say, it is published. Once it is published, people are cognizant of the fact that there must be a reason why Folkways has issued that person, and so they look at it seriously."

Moe Asch has recorded over 200 songs by Woody Guthrie; over 900 songs by Leadbelly; 63 albums of Pete Seeger; and over 1,500 LPs (including issues in the Asch, RBF, and Broadside series) covering every subject from folk music to language instruction to science. Folkways has remained a small firm in order to promote qualitative and rare recordings, and Moe Asch has maintained a principle of experimentation based on a philosophy of low production and relatively high cost. In the fall of 1965, Moe Asch instigated the formation of another record label, Verve/Folkways, which, under his supervision, was designed to issue recordings for broader distribution.

"Mo Asch, who runs Folkways, has a big burden," remarked John Cohen of the New Lost City Ramblers in an interview for *Pickin'*, March 1975. "He keeps between 1,500 and 2,000 records in circulation all the time. The whole idea of Folkways is that

country music isn't a flash-in-the-pan kind of thing. It's a reflection of people's voices, and the statement that they make. It's a terrific thing and I think that is why we like to work with Mo Asch. We don't make much money from it, but it gives us a voice. He allows us to record what's important to us and makes it accessible to so many people when they need it—not when some big flash fad needs it."

Moe Asch is also the cofounder (with Irwin Silber) of Oak Publications (which was sold in 1967 to Music Sales Limited, London), and he has edited over a dozen works for the company.

## John Ashby

*Traditional old-time fiddler, performer, and recording artist*

With an emphasis on treatment rather than on the tune itself, John Ashby's bowing technique and delicately expressive styling make his traditional fiddle music well-rounded, robust, and snappy.

Ashby hails from the plateau between the coastal plain and the Appalachian Mountains in Virginia, and his homespun lifestyle is reflected in his fiddle playing. He has recorded two inspired albums of old favorite standards and original tunes for County Records of Floyd, Virginia. The Free State Ramblers, with Richard Ashby, Jack Frazier, Ashby Kyhl, and Ronnie Poe, accompany John Ashby on his all-instrumental *Down on Ashby's Farm* (Country 745), released in 1974. Most of Ashby's fiddle band music is played at a medium-fast tempo, highlighted with tunes like the fast-moving "Fox Chase Reel."

## Richard Ashby. *See* The Free State Ramblers.

## Clarence "Tom" Ashley

*Old-time mountain banjoist, singer, performer, and recording artist*

One of the most distinguished and signifi-

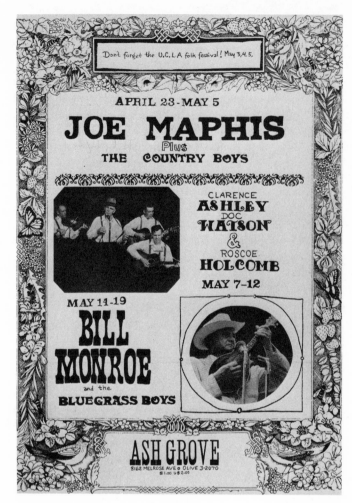

Poster advertising appearance by Clarence "Tom" Ashley, and others, at the now-defunct West Coast "capital of folk music," the Ash Grove in Los Angeles

cant personalities in the early history of country music, Clarence "Tom" Ashley is probably most renowned for his banjo renditions of "The Coo Coo Bird" and "The House Carpenter." Playing his five-string banjo, he first recorded his most famous song, "The Coo Coo Bird," as a solo disc for Columbia in 1929. His second recording of this song was made with Doc Watson accompanying Ashley on guitar. Ashley recorded two versions of "The House Carpenter"—for Columbia in 1930; and two years prior for Victor, as "Can't You Remember When Your Heart Was Mine?," with the Carolina Tar Heels.

Born Clarence Earl McCurry in Bristol, Tennessee, in 1895, he was raised by his grandfather, Enoch Ashley, whose name he adopted later on. An accomplished guitar and banjo player by his teens, Ashley had a comprehensive repertoire of old-time mountain songs, which he utilized to make some money by street singing, or "busting," as he called it. He was often accompanied by blind fiddler George Banman Grayson, who later recorded with Henry Whitter for Victor Records. Traveling shows—the circus and minstrel or medicine troupes—provided the only source of rural entertainment in those days, and they offered one of the few opportunities for musicians such as Uncle Dave Macon or Fiddlin' John Carson to perform. At age sixteen, Ashley joined Dr. Hower's Medicine Show, and he made folks laugh with his songs, banjo playing, and jokes. It was during this period that the young Roy Acuff started to tour with the troupe, and with Jack Tindele as the headliner of the show, Acuff and Ashley both worked as entertainers. In the early 1940s Ashley left the medicine show to play banjo for Charlie Monroe's Kentucky Pardners, and he also played occasionally with the Stanley Brothers, who lived in the same area.

Ashley's first recordings were made in the 1920s with the Blue Ridge Mountain Entertainers, with Will Abernathy on autoharp, Clarence Ashley on banjo, Walter Davis on lead guitar, Gwen Foster on harmonica, and Clarence Greene on fiddle. During the twenties and thirties, Ashley recorded over thirty-five 78s with the Blue Ridge Mountain Entertainers, the Carolina Tar Heels, and Byrd Moore and His Hotshots, on such labels as Columbia (ARC), Victor, Melotone, Perfect, Banner, Romeo, Oriole, Conqueror, Gennett, Okeh, Vocalion, and others. Many years later, Ashley was recorded by Moe Asch of Folkways Records, and two albums were devoted to the old-time musician: *Old-time Music at Clarence Ashley's, Volumes I and II* (Folkways FA 2355 and FA 2359). He is also among the artists included on collections by the Classics Record Library (Book-of-the-Month Club) and Vanguard.

During the sixties Clarence Ashley performed numerous coffeehouse and concert dates. Before his death in the early summer of 1967, he was featured at major folk music events, from Newport to New York, Chicago, Los Angeles, and Europe. (*See also* The Carolina Tar Heels.)

## Leni Ashmore. *See* The Women-folk.

## Mike Auldridge

*Bluegrass dobroist, singer, performer, and recording artist*

A bluegrass music fan from the age of fourteen, Mike Auldridge is considered by many bluegrass musicians to be the best dobro picker in the United States today. Many

dobroists model their techniques and styles after the smooth, split-second rolls and picking patterns of Mike Auldridge's work.

When he was twelve years old, Auldridge started playing the guitar, and within a few years he was playing another instrument, the banjo. He began picking the dobro when he was about twenty, and eight years later he was playing professionally. In 1969 he joined a band called Emerson and Waldron, and when Bill Emerson left a year thereafter to play with the Country Gentlemen, Auldridge stayed on to play with Cliff Waldron. In the meantime, Auldridge's brother Dave, Ben Eldridge, Ed Ferris, and Bill Poffinberger joined Waldron and Auldridge to form the six-piece band called the New Shades of Grass. Waldron's plans for extensive traveling prompted Auldridge and Eldridge to quit and get together with John Duffey, who had left the Country Gentlemen a few years before for the same reason, and, says Auldridge: "We just got together one night just to mess around, and it turned out." Their group, the Seldom Scene, includes Auldridge on dobro and baritone vocals, John Duffey on mandolin and tenor vocals, Ben Eldridge on banjo, Tom Gray on bass, and John Starling on guitar and lead vocals. Like Auldridge, who is a full-time artist for the *Washington Star-News*, the other members also work regular jobs. The Seldom Scene is probably the most popular bluegrass band in the Washington, D.C., area, and the quintet, known for its fast picking and close harmonies, is considered by many to be one of the top bluegrass groups in the country. Mike Auldridge says of their working schedule: "We play once a week regularly at the Red Fox, but we book quite extensively now."

Since the early seventies, Auldridge has been recorded on twenty albums, including several with the Country Gentlemen; two of his own on the Takoma label, *Mike Auldridge: Dobro* (D-1033) and *Blues and Bluegrass* (D-1041), with accompaniment by David Bromberg, Vassar Clements, Linda Ronstadt, and others; and four with the

Seldom Scene on Rebel: *Act One* (SLP 1511), *Act Two* (SLP 1520), *Act III* (SLP 1528), and *Old Train* (SLP 1536), which features Linda Ronstadt on two cuts.

When asked about the future, Auldridge replies: "It was always very frustrating to me to pick and not be able to record because I didn't want the life of a musician who starved to death. As much as I wanted to play, I didn't want to starve for it. So the Seldom Scene was the answer because everybody in the band felt the same way. I'm really just hanging in to see what happens because unless it's possible to make pretty good money making music, I'm just going to do it like I'm doing it now. Part-time." (*See also* Cliff Waldron and the New Shades of Grass.)

## Lonnie Austin. *See* Charlie Poole and the North Carolina Ramblers.

## Autoharp

A stringed instrument with chord bars, which resembles the zither, the autoharp is a derivation of the oldest string instrument, the harp. In the early 1870s music writer and salesman Charles A. Zimmerman (who later composed the music for the United States Navy song "Anchors Aweigh") invented a new musical notation system, but, realizing the difficulty of its implementation, he designed the autoharp—an instrument that could be played only by using his system of musical notation. Zimmerman's original design, with only slight modifications, is still used by instrument makers today.

For several decades its use was limited primarily to Appalachian region musicians, but prior to World War II its popularity spread with the music of the Carter Family, and, after the war, with that of the Seegers. During the recent urban folk revival, the autoharp was used in many recording ses-

sions, including those of Mike Seeger, who was also responsible for taping rural artists performing on the autoharp for the Folkways LP *Mountain Music Played on the Autoharp* (Folkways 2365).

The autoharp comprises forty to fifty metal strings stretched from one end of its frame, across a sound box, to tuning pegs at the opposite end of the instrument's frame. A series of buttons (chord bars, which control the strings) appears in the lower portion of the instrument's frame. Each button produces the sound of a specific chord when the strings are strummed with a fingerpick.

It has been said that the autoharp is one of the easiest instruments to play but one of the hardest to tune. When asked about stringing an autoharp, Maybelle Carter once replied, "I tried that one time and I blistered my hand. I said, 'Never again! I'll throw the thing away before I'll put a whole set of strings on it.'"

## Hoyt Axton

*Singer-songwriter, guitarist, performer, and recording artist*

"My name is Hoyt Axton. I'm a guitar pickin' songwriter & sometimes singer," the Oklahoma-born performer wrote in the liner notes from his third A&M album, *Southbound* (A&M SP-4510), released in 1975. Although he has made a dozen albums for almost as many labels since his career began in the 1950s, it is only in recent years that he has evolved as a prominent artist in the recording industry.

In the late fifties and early sixties, Axton traveled the California coffeehouse circuit and enjoyed national exposure with the Kingston Trio's hit "Greenback Dollar," which he wrote in 1962 with Ken Ramsey. As a popular West Coast folksinger, in 1964 he was heard at the Troubadour in Los Angeles by John Kay, who, later on, as lead singer of the group Steppenwolf, recorded his songs "The Pusher" and "Snowblind Friend." When Axton toured with Three

Hoyt Axton

Dog Night, appearing as their opening act in 1969–70, he wrote "Joy to the World," which became a hit single for the group. Three Dog Night's subsequent recording of his "Never Been to Spain" was another bestselling record for the rock group. During this period, his own versions of both traditional and contemporary songs that appeared on various record labels were picked up and recorded by other top artists, such as Joan Baez and John Denver, among others. He appeared on the *Grand Ole Opry* after his songs "When the Mornin' Comes" and "Boney Fingers" became major country & western hits.

He was joined on his own NBC television special by friends Rita Coolidge, Doug Dillard, Arlo Guthrie, Kris Kristofferson, Linda Ronstadt (with whom he recorded the classic version of his "Lion in the Winter" in 1975), and Buffy Sainte-Marie, among others. His other A&M records include *Less Than the Song* (A&M SP-4376) and *Life Machine* (A&M SP-3604).

"I've always loved music—listening to it, making it—live or recorded—in any language—at almost any time of the day or night.

"I also love women and children, rainbows, pick-up trucks, wild animals, snow, clean rivers, lightnin' bugs, mountains, almost all musical instruments and the people who play them and take care of them, peanut butter & jelly, sex, television, radio, laughing, working, hangin' out, adventure, popcorn, good ideas, singing, motorcycles, antiques, most anything made by human hands, the Christ Spirit, cloudy skies on Lake Tahoe, my dog 'fearless,' my family & friends and you."

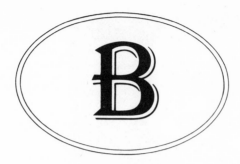

**The Babysitters.** *See* Alan Arkin.

**Elias Badeaux.** *See* The Louisiana Aces.

## Joan Baez

*Singer, songwriter, performer, recording artist, author, and nonviolent activist*

As in all fields of human endeavor, there is a handful of names which comprise an elite roster of innovators in American folk music. Our culture has been both enriched and consequently molded in recent decades by such artists as Bob Dylan, Woody Guthrie, Leadbelly, Odetta, Pete Seeger, and the Weavers. Among the one or two others who have made an outstanding contribution and impact on the contemporary music scene is Joan Baez. Sometimes referred to as the "Queen of Folk Music," and the counterpart of her contemporary and close friend Bob Dylan, she has transcended her role as a vocalist by bridging the gap between her art and her political life. Joan Baez is the personal embodiment of social sensibility and action, and her appeal is woven into the fabric of her personality and her talent for vocal communication.

Joan Baez was born on January 9, 1941, on Staten Island, New York, to physicist Dr. Albert V. Baez and Joan Bridge Baez. Her mother was English, born in Scotland, and her father came to the United States from Mexico; both of her grandfathers were ministers. One of three daughters, Joan Baez grew up in New York and in Southern California and lived abroad for nine months in Baghdad, Iraq, and Switzerland. While she was attending high school on the West Coast, she sang in the choir and learned to play the guitar. At this point in her life, she found herself attracted to folk music, as she explains: "Boredom with school was one reason—I had to fight something. And it was a situation where I was not very social and I had many hours to myself, so I began to listen to Harry Belafonte and Odetta records. I learned to play the guitar, and I would spend hours and hours just picking out tunes and learning chords from friends.

"I think the thing that sold me is that I was looking for something real, and those old songs seemed very pure and very real as opposed to the rock 'n' roll, then R/B, which I was also listening to—and, actually, I did a little of that, but I did it as a parody. The music that filled up my teenage soul was folk music."

When her father was offered a teaching position at the Massachusetts Institute of Technology, the family moved to Boston early in 1958. Although she was enrolled as a drama student at Boston University, Joan Baez was quickly absorbed by the folk music revival in the Cambridge–Boston area. She became an active participant in the urban folk movement, and "the more I got into folk music, the more it became traditional, and I

became a real stodgy purist!" She made her first public appearance at a Boston coffeehouse, and before long she was being billed regularly at the Golden Vanity, Ballad Room, and Club 47. During this period, she was invited to sing at the Gate of Horn in Chicago, and in July 1959 she made her professional debut at the first Newport Folk Festival. Although her appearance was unpublicized, she was received enthusiastically by both the audience and other performers, including Odetta, the Seegers, and the Weavers. She turned down her initial recording contract offers, but after her return engagement at the 1960 Newport Folk Festival she signed with Vanguard Records.

She appeared on CBS-TV's *Folk Sound, U.S.A.*, and in October 1960 her first album was released, entitled *Joan Baez* (Vanguard VRS 9078). In reflecting on her musical development from a traditional to a popular orientation, she says: "I think part of it was a political development, part of it was a musical development, and a lot of it was losing my fear. I had a purist upbringing, in a sense, with the Spanish bloodlines on my father's side, and I literally thought, when I was eighteen, that if you added a bass and drums that you became wicked and vile. They would fight with me to even add an extra guitar! Gradually that fear began to diminish, and then I started to go into music a little bit."

In 1961 she made an extensive tour of colleges and concert halls, and in 1962 she appeared at New York's Carnegie Hall. Her audience was growing in number and scope, and she was attracting many new followers to the field of folk music. By late 1962, three of her albums were on the charts, and she was featured as the subject of the cover story in the November 23, 1962, issue of *Time* magazine.

Joan Baez met Bob Dylan for the first time in Gerde's Folk City, in Greenwich Village, New York City where he "was singing his song to Woody." Along with others, including Peter, Paul and Mary, she played an important role in opening doors for the young singer-songwriter by inviting Bob Dylan onstage as a guest during a number of her concerts. Some of her versions of his songs created tremendous enthusiasm for Dylan material, and, in turn, he gave Joan Baez the words and the music to communicate her spirit of protest.

Political involvement has always been one of the main ingredients in her life and one of the dominant aspects of her public image: "I really don't know what that image is right now, but at the beginning it was Mother Earth–Virgin Mary Teenager, and it was kind of confusing. It was somebody with a social conscience—which is interesting because I had actually done political action before I sang in public—but the songs weren't message songs at the beginning. Although it was straight traditional, I was already mixing the two things one way or another, so there was a message. The political feelings are still exactly the same— and that is, I'm not a violence addict.

"The political drive was stronger than the musical drive, and that may always be the case. In a sense, I have to discipline myself and say, 'Look, you don't have to put messages all over the record, you can just do music.' "

Throughout her career, Joan Baez has reinforced her political convictions through her art. In lieu of concerts, she has often made free appearances for the benefit of charities, UNESCO, civil rights and anti–Vietnam War rallies, and in 1964 she began refusing to pay war taxes to the United States government. By the following year, she had founded the Institute for the Study of Nonviolence at her second California home, in Carmel Valley. October and December of 1967 found her in jail, when she was arrested for civil disobedience in a demonstration opposing the draft and the Vietnam War. In the following year, she continued to make television appearances and speaking tours in the United States and Canada opposing militarism.

In March 1968 she married David Harris,

formerly a Stanford University student leader, who was confronting a three-year prison term for draft resistance. In the same year, her autobiography, *Daybreak*, was published by the Dial Press in New York, and her son Gabriel was born in December.

During the sixties, Vanguard issued nearly two dozen discs by Joan Baez. At a time when other artists were putting 45-RPM folk recordings on the charts, Joan Baez had the distinction of producing bestselling albums in the folk genre. To date, she has recorded an additional five albums (the latest of which is a two-LP set) for A&M Records. Over the years, her music has evolved from its traditional basis to a broader format, encompassing contemporary and original material.

Her concert tours have taken Joan Baez around the world. Late in 1975, she joined Bob Dylan and the Rolling Thunder Revue, with Jack Elliott, Roger McGuinn, Bob Neuwirth, and others, for one of her most memorable tours in recent years.

## Aly Bain. *See* The Boys of the Lough.

## Kenny Baker

*Country fiddler, performer, and recording artist*

One of the most gifted and creative fiddlers performing today, Kenny Baker established his footing in bluegrass by playing and recording with Bill Monroe's Blue Grass Boys from 1956 to 1958, and again from 1961 to 1963. His distinctive style is a combination of different fiddle traditions; influences of his father's old-time music and of Bob Wills and other western swing bands are evident in his country-bluegrass-jazz fiddling.

Born in 1926 in the eastern Kentucky town of Jenkins, Baker learned to play the fiddle at the age of eight. His father taught Baker his early technique and many old-time

fiddling tunes. After World War II, Baker performed regularly at local dances, most often with another hometown fiddler, Bobby Sumner. He also played with the Baily Brothers at WNOX Radio in Knoxville, Tennessee, and with Don Gibson, from about 1953 to 1956. At that time, he joined Bill Monroe's Blue Grass Boys at the *Grand Ole Opry*, where he stayed until 1958; several years later, Baker played again with Monroe and recorded several of Monroe's best instrumental cuts, such as "Scotland" and "Panhandle Country."

Kenny Baker was musically inactive for several years after he left Monroe's Blue Grass Boys to return to his home in Jenkins. In the fall of 1966 he met another fiddler, Joe Greene, at Carlton Haney's Second Annual Bluegrass Festival in Fincastle, Virginia. Baker had been asked by Haney to help put together some of the early Monroe bands, and during the course of the festival he played fiddle with Joe Greene. The following year, *High Country* (County 714) was recorded with the twin fiddles of Kenny Baker and Joe Greene.

Kenny Baker has recorded five solo LPs on the County label: *Portrait of a Bluegrass Fiddler* (County 719); *A Baker's Dozen* (County 730), a collection of country fiddle tunes; *Kenny Baker Country* (County 736); *Dry & Dusty* (County 744); and, most recently, *Grassy Fiddle Blues* (County 750).

## The Balfa Freres

*Cajun band, performers, and recording artists*

With an appreciation for both their cultural heritage and the wishes of their contemporary audience, the Balfa Freres (Brothers) present traditional and modern Cajun music. The modern Cajun sound is generally more popular than its traditional counterpart, and, like other bands which play clubs or dances in large halls, the Balfa Freres find the need to amplify their music. They play the instruments handed down by their Acadian forefathers—violin, accordion, harmonica, *petit fer* (triangle), and spoons—as well as the electric violin, bass and guitar, pedal steel guitar, and drums.

Tenant farmer Charles Balfa settled on Bayou Grand Louie, near Mamou, in southwestern Louisiana, and he sang and played traditional Cajun music for his family (within the Balfa "repertoire," there are songs that have been played over the generations exclusively by family members; in addition, the Balfas play many old traditional songs that have been played by many families in the area). In the oral tradition by which Cajun music is transmitted from father to son, five of Charles Balfa's nine children learned to sing and play in the same manner as he had been taught by his own father. The Balfa Freres's leader, fiddler, and vocalist, Dewey Balfa, recalls their upbringing in the Balfa family: "My father and eldest brother Will played fiddle, and I was about twelve years old when I started to play. Being that we had to learn by ear, it took me several years to play the fiddle fairly well.

"Home entertainment was the only entertainment that we had, there was no radio and very few people could afford to buy a phonograph and records. This is the reason that songs were preserved so well for so long because there were no communications with the outside world. We were isolated and we learned the songs from our parents which they had learned from their parents, and so on. My grandfather and great-grandfather both played fiddle, so it has become a tradition in our family to pick up instruments and start playing, and we all played accordion, harmonica, fiddle, triangle, spoons, and washboard."

In the latter part of 1946, the Balfa Freres started playing for gatherings and dances. They called themselves the Musical Brothers, and, at this point, Harry Balfa played guitar for the band; during the early fifties, Rodney Balfa replaced his brother Harry, who had married and had decided to quit performing for the public. By 1948 they had their own radio program on KSLO in Opelousas, and their music was broadcast for fifteen minutes once a week. They played with other bands which were making recordings of traditional Cajun music, but it was not until the mid-sixties that the Balfa Freres started performing for broader audiences, as Dewey Balfa explains: "I got married and I quit playing for dances and gatherings, but we still played for family reunions and personal occasions. My friend Ralph Rinzler got me interested again, and I began to realize that we had something worth preserving. I was like many people who don't think of their culture, or music, but it was very exciting to reorganize and start traveling and performing at concerts and festivals, and we've been doing it ever since."

Dewey Balfa was among the first Cajun performers at the 1964 Newport Folk Festival, and, three years later, Dewey and his Musical Brothers performed at the University of Chicago Folk Festival. In July 1967, Dewey, Will, Rodney, and Nelda (Dewey's eldest daughter) appeared at the Newport Folk Festival, along with accordionist Hadley Fontenot of Oberlin, Louisiana, who often plays and records with the Balfas.

Dewey Balfa was unsuccessful in his initial attempt to interest Floyd Soileau of the Swallow Recording Company in Ville Platte, Louisiana, in producing a record of traditional Cajun music. He decided to persist with his idea, and, when he approached Soileau on another occasion, an agreement was reached. Dewey and his Musical Brothers made a 45-RPM trial cut for Swallow, and following its release and overwhelming response, they recorded a second disc. Since then, the Balfa Freres have recorded a couple of albums on that label: *The Balfa Brothers Play Traditional Cajun Music* (Swallow LP-6011) and *The Balfa Brothers Play More Traditional Cajun Music* (Swallow LP-6019). They have also made European recordings for Sonet Productions, Ltd., and Cezame, in Paris.

Although the makeup of the Balfa Freres

sometimes varies, the core of its members includes Dewey Balfa on fiddle and vocals, Rodney on guitar and vocals, Harry on guitar, Burke on triangle, and Will on second fiddle (playing baritone or below the melody line). Accordion accompaniment has been provided on different occasions by Nathan and Ray Abshire, Hadley Fontenot, Marc Savoy, and Allie Young; on pedal steel guitar by J. W. Pelsia; and on fiddle by Bessyl Duhon, Walter Lee, Lee Manuel (who also plays guitar), and Ervin "Dick" Richard. Tony Balfa (Rodney's son), who plays many instruments, has also accompanied the band on several tours and in their recording.

All of the Balfas have full-time regular jobs, but they maintain their music and performing in an effort to perpetuate their Cajun heritage; in the words of Dewey Balfa: "We do not wish to become full-time musicians or to promote the Balfa Brothers. We would like to keep it on the basis of playing when we feel that we want to play and putting our hearts fully into the music. However, I am very interested in teaching our America of tomorrow because unless the children pick up and preserve what we have, it will be gone forever."

Since 1967 Dewey Balfa has been the producer and host of his own live radio show on KEUN, called *The Basile Cajun Hour*, which is broadcast every Saturday evening; and for the past six years he has been the announcer for another radio program, *The French Hour*.

For the past two years the Balfa Freres have sponsored *fais-dodos*, or family outings, which bring all aspects of Cajun culture to people in cities such as Chicago—making them the first group to establish an activity outside of Louisiana that includes more than just music.

## Burke Balfa. *See* The Balfa Freres.

## Dewey Balfa. *See* The Balfa
Freres; The Louisiana Aces.

## Harry Balfa. *See* The Balfa Freres.

## Rodney Balfa. *See* The Balfa
Freres.

## Tony Balfa. *See* The Balfa Freres.

## Will Balfa. *See* The Balfa Freres.

## Ballad

By definition, a ballad is a song that tells a story, or a story told in song. The word *ballad* is derived from such medieval terms as *chanson ballade* and *ballata*, but while both of these terms denote dancing songs, this particular connotation has long been absent from its present-day meaning.

As a part of the folk music tradition, the ballad shares with spirituals, blues, work songs, and other folk songs certain features that establish these forms within the context of the folk genre. The ballad, like all folk songs, is traditionally perpetuated by an oral tradition, a process by which a nonwritten song is passed from one person to the next. Changes, such as the alteration of the musical and lyrical content, made by transmission are (like the original) free of authorship, as the writer of any folk song or ballad is anonymous by tradition. Changes in the ballad may range from a subtle alteration of a melody line to the complete revision of the lyrical content; and there are numerous examples of different stories told to the same musical accompaniment. As continuity by means of the folk process is one of the distinguishing characteristics of the ballad, its existence, like that of the traditional folk song, is a source of limitless debate, as many experts feel that the folk tradition has become obsolete in contemporary society. In his book *The Incompleat Folksinger* (Simon and Schuster, 1972), Pete Seeger writes of present-day ballad makers:

Some folklore authorities feel that the day of the true folk ballad maker is irretrievably over. Universal literacy, changing music tastes, canned entertainment, have all combined to make him obsolete, they say.

Yet the interest in folklore and folk music, though a revival, not a survival, has produced not only collectors and listeners. Performers, though they may not fit neatly into any of the old categories of folk singers, nevertheless have more often than not learned their songs by ear, and produced their own variants. In many places one finds singers composing whole new ballads, often without bothering to write them down. And their songwriting method is the same as that of the ballad makers of old: First, they borrow an old melody, using it either note for note, or making slight changes. Second, their verses often start with the words of the older song, changing them to localize the story and make it more meaningful for friends and neighbors who may be listening.

In addition to these common characteristics shared by all musical forms within the folk idiom, the ballad possesses distinguishing traits that set it apart from other types of music in the general folk classification. Most importantly, the ballad is always a narrative; it always tells a story. The ballad is generally straightforward and simple, and as the singer is considered to be only an agent in its transmission, its presentation should be objective and impersonal. Fairly uniform in meter and rhythm, the ballad has a refrain and stanzas that are four lines of verse and rhymed A B C B. Thematically, the ballad dramatizes a memorable event, often marked by fantastic deeds, or a romantic theme, such as requited or unrequited love.

The American ballad has its origins in earlier English and Scottish ballads. The "cowboy's lament," which dates from the era of Western expansion in the United States, is derived from eighteenth-century British ballads. The American ballad is geographically divided into four principal regions: South, North, Midwest, and Far West.

# Banjo

The banjo is a stringed instrument consisting of a long, fretted or fretless neck, and a round, resonating body, or head, which is composed of parchment skin stretched over a wooden or metal hoop. The strings extend from the bottom of the body to tuning pegs, which control the body (head) tension, at the opposite end of the neck.

The oldest traceable ancestor of the modern banjo is an Arabian instrument called the *rebec*. A West African stringed instrument called the *bania* is probably derived from the *rebec*, and it is theorized that the *bania* was brought to America by West Africans who were sold into slavery. However, some experts conjecture the banjo is related to the *bandore*, a European instrument similar to the lute.

Since the days of Thomas Jefferson, who stated in his *Notes on the State of Virginia* (1785) that the "banjar" was a popular instrument among the American Negroes, the banjo has become one of the primary instruments of the folk music genre. Almost 150 years ago a Virginian named Joel Walker Sweeney modified the traditional four-string banjo by adding a fifth string, which was held by a peg mounted only halfway up the neck and tuned higher in pitch than the other four strings. This final development is the basis for the contention that the banjo is America's only native instrument. This pioneer American instrument was used by the early minstrels, who imitated the three-string or four-string banjo playing of the Negro slaves; and, when its popularity waned around the turn of the century, a four-string tenor banjo was devised to play popular ragtime and jazz band music. Despite a general disinterest in the banjo which prevailed throughout the early decades of the twentieth century, the instrument continued to circulate in the Southern Appalachian region of this country; and, during the 1930s, one of the foremost proponents of the five-string banjo was Uncle Dave Macon, whose recordings and freewheeling performances made him a beloved musician and comedian. Around 1940 a young folksinger named Pete Seeger began traveling around the country, playing the banjo and developing a three-finger style of picking; as a member of the Weavers, Seeger was largely responsible for bringing national prominence to the banjo after World War II. About the same time, Earl Scruggs was perfecting and popularizing a three-finger, Scruggs Picking Style, which involves the use of metal fingerpicks, syncopated rhythm, and a solo approach to string band accompaniment.

From 1880 to 1940, three basic banjo-picking styles were developed, which are still used today. Frailing, or down-picking, is the most common style and involves striking the melody string with the middle or index finger while the thumb plucks the fifth string in a constant drone. The clawhammer style is a more refined method of frailing, with the index or middle finger playing the melody while the thumb strikes the second string to fill out the rhythm. The third style, or Scruggs Picking Style, involves the use of the thumb, index, and middle fingers to pick individual strings, and is a popular style among bluegrass and other string band musicians.

**Tony Barrand.** *See* John Roberts and Tony Barrand.

**Skip Battin.** *See* The Byrds.

## The Beers Family

*Traditional singers, instrumentalists, performers, recording artists, and founders of the Fox Hollow Family Festival of Traditional Music and Arts*

The Beers Family is highly respected in the field for their perpetuation of songs which comprise the musical fiber of their American heritage. Traditional Irish and Scottish ballads brought to the United States during its Colonial period are the foundation of the Beers Family repertoire. Their instrumental accompaniment is another aspect of their adherence to the folk tradition, and they play old folk instruments such as the psaltery, fiddlesticks, limberjacks, banjo, fiddle, and guitar, among others.

The family's patriarch, Bob Beers, was born in 1920, and as a youth learned many of his songs and traditional American fiddle music from his grandfather, George Sullivan, a Wisconsin fiddle champion. Before his teens, Bob Beers was one of the contestants who placed at a fiddle contest in North Freedom, Wisconsin, and at fifteen he was playing professionally as a violinist with the St. Louis Philharmonic. He and Evelyne Andresen were married in 1943, and four years later he received a Bachelor of Music Education degree from Northwestern University. After teaching for four years in a Montana secondary school, Bob Beers joined the music staff of Rocky Mountain College in Billings, Montana, where he taught from 1956 to 1959. At this point, he opted for the life of a professional musician and gave up his work in the field of education.

In 1958 Bob and Evelyne Beers (and their daughter Martha, who was not officially added to their performances until 1964) made their first national appearance on the *Today* television show. Since then, they have performed at the White House, Carnegie, Constitution, and Philharmonic halls, and Lincoln Center; on NBC-TV's *Tonight Show*, the CBS Radio Network's *Arthur Godfrey Show*, and NBC's *Monitor*; and at major festivals (Newport, Philadelphia,

University of Chicago, National Folk Festival, and Mariposa), including their own Fox Hollow Family Festival of Traditional Music and Arts. They have also traveled abroad, performing in concert halls on other continents and touring South America and India. The Beers Family has received many honors, including the TV-Radio Gold Medal Award and the Burl Ives Award, given to them in 1964 at the National Folk Festival for "outstanding contribution in preserving traditional music." They have recorded for Columbia, Folkways, Philo, Prestige, and Biograph, and a multirecord set of Fox Hollow Festival performances has been issued on their own label, Fox Hollow.

Bob Beers's sister Janet Boyer and her family have made national appearances as folksingers, and, in the Beers Family tradition, his daughter Martha (who married Eric Nagler in 1968) sings and plays traditional music. In April 1971 the Beers, Boyer, and Nagler families met in Toronto, Canada, where Martha and her conscientious objector husband had moved, to record *The Seasons of Peace* (Biograph BLP-12033). With the concept of a celebration of life, Bob Beers planned the first Fox Hollow Festival, which was held in 1966 on the Beers farm in the Adirondacks (acquired two years prior). Over the years, the festival has become a mainstay of traditional American folk music, and it is considered one of the top musical events in this country today.

A tragic automobile accident claimed the life of Bob Beers on May 26, 1972, and Martha and Eric Nagler left Canada to help Evelyne Beers with the organization of that summer's Fox Hollow Festival. Evelyne Beers (now married to Donald Burnstine) and Martha and Eric Nagler have continued to present faithful renditions of traditional folk songs, and one of their most recent recordings is *The Gentleness in Living* (Philo PH 1010). In 1975 Evelyne Beers Burnstine was involved in the coordination of several festivals, including Fox Hollow. In addition to two previous albums of Fox Hollow performances, *A Place to Be* (Biograph BLP-

12051) and *You Got Magic* (Biograph BLP-12052), Biograph Records is planning the release of a two-record set entitled *Ten Years at Fox Hollow: The Best in Folk Music from the Best in Folk Festivals!* for the tenth anniversary of the annual summer event.

Bob Beers is remembered for his use of the psaltery, an ancient instrument related to the harpsichord and spinet; it has no keyboard, and the strings are plucked by the fingers. The psaltery is still used in performances by the Beers Family.

## Bob Beers. *See* The Beers Family.

## Evelyne Beers. *See* The Beers Family.

## Harry Belafonte
*Singer, performer, recording artist, actor, and producer*

Born on March 1, 1927, Harry George Belafonte became an example of the American success story. A handsome man with a talent for showmanship, Belafonte combined his acting ability with his singing to create a formula for success.

Although born in New York City, Belafonte lived in the Caribbean for five years (his mother was originally from Jamaica, and his father had come from Martinique), returning to New York with his mother and attending George Washington High School. At the outbreak of World War II, Belafonte left school to join the navy. Returning to New York after his discharge from the service, he worked at a number of jobs before finally deciding to use the GI Bill to become an acting student.

Belafonte joined the American Negro Theater and enrolled in Erwin Piscator's Dramatic Workshop in Manhattan, but, much to his disappointment, he found something missing in his work. Although he liked acting, he realized that he needed an outlet for his singing. He left the stage and became a pop singer, signing with Capitol Records; although he was getting closer to what he wanted to do, he was not yet completely satisfied. In 1950 he and a couple of friends decided to open up a small restaurant in Greenwich Village; it featured entertainment by folksingers, and on many occasions Belafonte himself would sing. It was here that he discovered his niche in the field of music, and from here it was back to the stage—this time to sing ballads and folk songs.

In the same year, Belafonte put together a repertoire of folk songs, both American and West Indian, and joined with an old friend, Millard Thomas, to put together an act. Through another friend they were able to get a two-week gig at the Village Vanguard in October 1951. Belafonte was on his way. The two-week engagement was extended twelve more weeks. After leaving the Village Vanguard, Belafonte played every state in the union and was the first black to be booked into the Empire Room at the Palmer House in Chicago.

In 1954, following his acting roles in *Bright Road* and *John Murray Anderson's Almanac*, Belafonte was offered the lead role in the motion picture version of Oscar Hammerstein's *Carmen Jones*. Later that same year he received standing ovations for his role in *Three for the Night*, which toured around the country prior to its New York opening. In the midst of all this, he formed his own motion picture production company, called Harbel, which was set up to introduce creative black artists. In the next few years Belafonte was a frequent guest on network TV shows, including *The Ed Sullivan Show*, *The Colgate Variety Hour*, and several dramatic programs. He later produced his own TV specials.

In the late fifties, Belafonte signed with RCA Victor and recorded a number of hits, including "Jamaica Farewell," "Day-O," "The Banana Boat Song," and "Brown Skin Girl," which started the "calypso boom."

"Matilda" and "Come Back Liza" were two of his later well-known recordings.

Belafonte had a tremendous impact on the folk music revival of the late fifties, influencing such artists as Dave Guard and the Kingston Trio, the Tarriers, Joan Baez, and many, many others. In addition to recording a vast number of songs, he was also responsible for introducing to the world such artists as the Chad Mitchell Trio and Miriam Makeba.

**Derek Bell.** *See* The Chieftains.

**Rafel Bentham.** *See* The Freedom Singers.

**Leo Bernache.** *See* The National Folk Festival Association.

## Leon Bibb
*Singer, guitarist, performer, recording artist, and actor*

Like many singers born and raised in Kentucky, Leon Bibb was surrounded by music, both traditional and gospel. Born in 1935 in Louisville, Bibb grew up amid the songs of the Carter and Ritchie families and the rich gospel music of Tennessee and Kentucky. As a youngster he sang in both the church choir and the school chorus.

Bibb left Kentucky, with his wealth of songs, to do a hitch in the army. While serving his country, he learned songs from various parts of the United States as well as from other countries. Along with learning new songs he perfected his guitar technique.

When he and the army parted company, Bibb came to New York to study acting and voice. Although he had intended to become an actor and Broadway singer, he found himself performing in small clubs around Greenwich Village.

In the late 1950s he played roles in *Fi-*

nian's *Rainbow* and *Annie Get Your Gun*, but instead of progressing in his Broadway ambitions, he started doing more club dates and concerts. He traveled across the country playing popular clubs, from the Hungry i in San Francisco to the Village Gate in Greenwich Village. He also started performing in various festivals such as the 1959 Newport Folk Festival.

Leon Bibb recorded three albums for Vanguard. He later recorded for Washington Records and Liberty Records, and in early 1961 he signed with Columbia Records.

# Theodore Bikel

*Singer, guitarist, performer, recording artist,*
*author, and actor*

In the fashion of a true Renaissance man, this highly acclaimed stage, motion picture, and television actor is well-known for his accomplishments in other areas of the arts. His role as a folksinger has been as brilliant as his theatrical career, and his many recordings and performances of folk music from around the globe have won him an international audience.

Born on May 2, 1924, in Vienna, Austria, to Josef and Miriam (Riegler) Bikel, he emigrated at fourteen with his family to Palestine (now Israel). While living in the Middle East, he worked as a member of a kibbutz, but his acting and linguistic abilities led him to participation in the Habimah Theater in 1943 and the cofounding of the Tel Aviv Chamber Theater in 1945. In 1946 he began studies at the Royal Academy of Dramatic Art in London, from which he graduated in 1948, embarking on a successful career as an actor. His first role was in a London production of *A Streetcar Named Desire*, which brought attention to his work and offers by filmmakers. His initial motion picture role was in *The African Queen* (1951), and from 1950 to 1952 he performed in the London staging of *The Love of Four Colonels*. In 1954 Theodore

Bikel came to the United States; he became a naturalized American citizen in 1961.

Among his many film credits are *The Little Kidnappers*, *The Blue Angel*, *Moulin Rouge*, *The Defiant Ones* (which won Bikel an Academy Award nomination in 1959), *My Fair Lady*, *Sands of the Kalahari*, *The Russians Are Coming, The Russians Are Coming*, *Sweet November*, *My Side of the Mountain*, *Darker Than Amber*, *The Little Ark*, and so on. On the stage, he has made memorable appearances in *Rope Dancers*, *The Lark*, *The Sound of Music*, *Fiddler on the Roof*, and *The Rothschilds*. He has made numerous television appearances, and from 1958 to 1963 he had a weekly radio program called *At Home with Theodore Bikel*.

Theodore Bikel has been a concert folksinger since 1955, and his knowledge of seventeen languages has enabled him to relate with authenticity to audiences everywhere. His appreciation of folklore—particularly Eastern European, Israeli, and Russian folklore—and his broad repertoire of folk songs have won him international repute as one of America's most well-rounded and popular folksingers. In 1958 he signed a recording contract with Elektra Records and in the same year made his debut concert appearance at Town Hall in New York City. Some of his many Elektra LPs include *Folk Songs from Just About Everywhere* ([7]161), with Geula Gill; *From Bondage to Freedom* ([7]200); *A Harvest of Israeli Songs* ([7]210); *Best of Theodore Bikel* ([7]225); *On Tour* ([7]230); and *A Folksinger's Choice* ([7]250). The new Legacy series of Everest Records includes two Elektra reissues of Theodore Bikel, *Song of Songs and Other Bible Prophecies* (LEG-118) and *Theodore Bikel Sings Yiddish Theatre and Folk Songs* (LEG-121), and he is included on *Folk Festival* (LEG-110).

In July 1960 Theodore Bikel was among the new faces (with Joan Baez, the Clancy Brothers, Alan Mills, the Tarriers, the Weavers, and many more) at the Newport Folk Festival. In 1963, along with Bill Clifton, Clarence Cooper, Erik Darling, Jean

Ritchie, Pete Seeger, Peter Yarrow, and producer George Wein, Bikel was instrumental in reorganizing the Newport Folk Festival; as a result of the efforts of this committee of performers, a balance was created between traditional and contemporary forces, and the 1963 event attracted nearly forty thousand paid visitors. In 1963–64 Theodore Bikel was one of the principal participants on the ABC-TV weekly *Hootenanny.*

Theodore Bikel is the author of *Folksongs and Footnotes* (Meridian Books, 1960), which includes eighty-four songs from all over the world, with an introduction and commentaries by this versatile baritone singer.

## The Blue Grass Boys. *See* Bill Monroe.

## The Blue Ridge Mountain Entertainers. *See* Clarence "Tom" Ashley.

## Bluegrass

A term which has attracted widespread interest among urban dwellers in the past quarter of a century, "bluegrass" is an offshoot of hillbilly music distinguishable by special vocal and instrumental stylings and played by bands most commonly comprising guitar, banjo, fiddle, mandolin, and bass fiddle. Although the origins of bluegrass are traceable to "the old corn-shucking party banjo and fiddle music as well as to the ballad songs and religious music of the southern mountains," as Mike Seeger wrote in an article for *Sing Out!* (Vol. 11, No. 1, 1961), it evolved as a distinctive musical entity with the organization by Bill Monroe of the 1945–48 ("original") Blue Grass Boys— Lester Flatt on guitar, Bill Monroe on mandolin, Earl Scruggs on banjo, Howard (Cedric Rainwater) Watts on bass, and

Chubby Wise on fiddle. The name of Monroe's band was derived from an allegiance to his home state of Kentucky, the Bluegrass State; and, with all of the band members well-versed in Southern musical traditions (particularly string band stylings), they introduced bluegrass music to the world in 1945.

One of the key figures of the bluegrass style is Earl Scruggs, who brought new prominence to the banjo by emphasizing its melodic characteristics and using it as a major solo, or lead, instrument. At various times, each instrument in a bluegrass ensemble functions as a lead, a backup to the lead, and a rhythmic accompaniment instrument, with certain instruments such as the banjo, guitar, and dobro used primarily for supplying the central melody throughout a song. In other string band styles, the banjo is used only for rhythmic accompaniment, and today, a bluegrass band is not considered complete without a banjo played in the unique three-finger picking style (or a closely related technique) developed by Earl Scruggs.

Another essential trait of bluegrass music is the restricted employment of nonelectrified stringed instruments. Both vocal and instrumental integration is more sophisticated than that found in preceding mountain music styles; the vocals are typically high-pitched, with harmonization rendered by the musicians singing in multiple parts.

In 1955 Flatt and Scruggs introduced the dobro to their Foggy Mountain Boys band, and, since then, it has appeared more frequently in bluegrass groups. Although the guitar and banjo are the mainstays in the composition of the bluegrass band, other instruments may be added without interfering with the interaction of the basic instruments, and may include drums, autoharp, mouth harp, jew's harp, piano, and accordion. An adherent to the Monroe format would disallow the incorporation of nontraditional stringed instruments; and the electric guitar, organ, and so on, which are used not infrequently in the recording studio, are rarely heard in live performances.

# Blues

While musicologists define the blues in terms of microtones and twelve-measure patterns (in contrast to the eight, sixteen, or thirty-two bars in early jazz and ragtime), the average listener recognizes this musical form by such features as its triple-line stanzas, with repetition of the first line, bottleneck-guitar technique, and characteristic melodic effects, such as flattened (or diminished) "blue notes," which produce the sad and mournful sound that complements the subject matter of the song. The personal, melancholic themes typically deal with the trials and tribulations of daily living, and, says Moe Asch of Folkways Records, "the blues goes back as far as people have known trouble."

Most scholars trace its roots to Africa; when blacks were transported to America as slaves, rudimentary blues-related "hollers" were vocalized by Southern field hands as they labored on another man's land or announced their homecoming. The blues was primarily a vocal form of expression sung "by people to work to or by to make the work easier," states Erik Darling. "There was no real authorship of importance—the most important thing was: 'God, how are we going to get through the day,' or 'Let's make the work easier.'"

Around the turn of this century, widespread attention was brought to the blues by the "Father of the Blues" or the "St. Louis Bluesman" W. C. Handy, whose "Mamie's Blues" (published in 1909) marked the beginning of the recorded history of the blues. The pure blues enjoyed its heyday in the 1920s and was a major influence on the American jazz movement.

Various parts of the United States became centers for the three basic types of blues: classic, country, and city. Classic blues singers were generally accompanied by jazz musicians, and some of the most prominent names which fall into this category are Bessie Smith, Gertrude "Ma" Rainey, Memphis Minnie, and Victoria Spivey. The Mississippi Delta has long been the heartland of the country or black secular blues, which is generally considered the forerunner of modern "race" (a term once used to distinguish black from white country music) and rhythm-and-blues styles—which, in turn, became underlying influences on rock 'n' roll and pop music. Country blues musicians emphasized the role of the guitar by using the instrument as a "second voice" to accentuate the subtle vocal nuances expressed by the singer. Among the numerous country bluesmen who have played an important part in the development of American music are Sleepy John Estes, Mississippi John Hurt, Blind Lemon Jefferson, and Big Joe Williams. (Leadbelly and Sonny Terry are sometimes distinguished as representatives of the "folk" blues sound—country blues influenced by white country and folk music.) Big Bill Broonzy, John Lee Hooker and Sam "Lightnin'" Hopkins typify city bluesmen who play both old-style blues and its more recent (mid-forties) cousin, rhythm-and-blues. Among the white urban interpreters of the blues who began to emerge on the music scene in the sixties are John Hammond, Jr., Dave Van Ronk, Mark Spoelstra, Eric Von Schmidt, and Bonnie Raitt.

# Ted Bogan. *See* Martin, Bogan and the Armstrongs.

# Dock Boggs

*Traditional singer, banjoist, performer, and recording artist*

Over the years, the annual University of Chicago Festival has maintained its reputation as a rendezvous for traditional American folk musicians and scholars of this musical form. Among the many fine old-time country musicians who have enraptured audiences at this major folk event is Kentucky banjoist Dock Boggs, who has also been a guest performer at various other festivals, including Newport. A Brunswick recording artist of the late 1920s, Boggs worked as a coal miner and shared his music with his neighbors until his rediscovery by Mike Seeger, who opened the door for introducing his crystal-clear banjo-picking style to the world.

Moran L. Boggs was born on February 7, 1898, in Norton, Virginia, and he was raised by "hardworking, God-fearing" parents. The youngest of ten children, he began working in the coal mines when he was twelve, and for the next forty-one years he earned his living as a miner. Many years later, his first opportunity to record presented itself, as he once described in a letter to *Broadside* magazine:

I was working on a coal cutting machine at Pardee, Virginia, with a fellow named Emmitt Fletcher for Blackwood Coal & Coke Co. when I got my first chance to record music. There was two men from New York, one I remember named James O'Keefe, and a man from Ashland, Kentucky by the name of Carter. He ran a music store there at that time. That was in 1927, and a friend of mine, Hughie Rollen, then living at Dorchester, Va., asked me why I didn't try out. I told him there was plenty of musicians who didn't do anything but make music, and I figured they would take them if they signed anyone to go make records. But my friend insisted I try out and got me to borrow a banjo from a music store. So I went up to the ballroom of the Norton Hotel. There was a gang on hand. I about lost my nerve, but they had listened to all the others before I got there. I started to play a piece, "Country Blues"—it really was "Hustling Gambler." I seen all three men mark "good" at the end of the title I gave them. They would just let me start and then stop me because they were in a hurry. So I started to play "Down South

Blues" which I learnt from a coloured girl who had an Ace piano.

Dock Boggs started playing the banjo when he was in his early teens, and he based his fingerpicking style on a three-finger blues styling which he learned from two local black musicians. After his Brunswick recording sessions, he continued to sing and play the banjo for his own enjoyment and adhered to his own unique style despite the immense popularity of the three-finger bluegrass or "Scruggs Picking Style" in more recent years. Nine years after he retired from almost half a century of working as a miner, his musical career was set in motion by Mike Seeger.

In addition to numerous recordings made for Folkways Records, other commercial companies, including Disc and Verve/Folkways, have issued material by Dock Boggs.

# David Boise. *See* The Chad Mitchell Trio.

# Gordon Bok

*Singer, guitarist, songwriter, performer, and recording artist*

An established figure in folk music circles, professional singer and sailor Gordon Bok achieved more widespread recognition while working and performing as a member of the *Clearwater* crew. A native of Maine, where the Hudson River sloop was designed and constructed, Gordon Bok communicates universal concerns and ideas through his singing and writing about the sea and the people whose lives are connected with it.

As a teenager, Gordon Bok began working aboard the sailing vessels of yesteryear, and he once wrote: "They've all been sailing boats, mostly traditional in type (like taking a Brixham trawler from England to Portugal—and like the sloop *Clearwater*). Mostly America, but some Virgin Islands,

Bahamas, Nova Scotia and Cape Breton Island, and a few short bits of fishing, now and then."

His vocals are richly imbued with a depth and resonance that mirror his involvement with the sea and the rugged coastline of his home state, and his guitar playing incorporates various styles from classical to traditional folk. He has made a number of recordings, particularly on the Folk-Legacy label, and the song most often requested by his concert audiences—"Bay of Fundy"—is the title song of his most recent solo album (Folk-Legacy FSI-54). (*See also* The Golden Ring.)

# Roy Bookbinder

*Ragtime and blues guitarist, singer, performer, and recording artist*

Well-known on the folk club circuit, Roy Bookbinder draws his "raggy East Coast guitar style" from the work of his two South Carolina mentors, Pink Anderson and Rev. Gary Davis. Both his voice and style have been accorded an acclaim uncommon among white blues artists, and his lively, up-tempo brand of music is a testimony to the men who created the legacy of American blues.

Roy Bookbinder was born in October 5, 1943, in New York City. Influenced by "the rock 'n' roll craze, Buddy Holly and the Crickets, and other fifties groups," Roy Bookbinder started playing guitar in 1963 while he was in the navy. After his stint in the service, where he "met people from Texas and the South," he was introduced to the music of Dave Van Ronk. "One of the first things I heard him play was by Rev. Gary Davis, and, it was shortly after that, I met him [Rev. Gary Davis]." Bookbinder developed a genuine interest in Rev. Gary Davis's blues, and he soon became one of his students and traveling companion, and "that was really the beginning."

In 1968 he went to England, where he caught the "tail end of the blues boom," and he stayed there for six months. While he was abroad, Bookbinder had the opportunity to tour with British blues star Jo Ann Kelly, and on many of the National Blues Federation promotions with Arthur "Big Boy" Crudup, "Homesick" James, and Larry Johnson. His performances in the British Isles brought Bookbinder rave reviews, and he proved himself adept as an interpreter and performer of various American regional blues styles, from the Nashville style of Sam McGee to Bo Carter of Mississippi to the Chicago style of Big Bill Broonzy to New Orleans and Jelly Roll Morton.

When he returned from England to the United States, he had amassed enough press material to arouse the interest of club owners throughout this country. He recorded an album on the Adelphi label entitled *Travelin' Man* (Adelphi AD 1017). Before his second trip to England in 1972, "people like Paul Geremia helped me out and I started doing colleges and club dates. I then went down South and rediscovered Pink Anderson, and, together with Paul Geremia, I helped to put him [Pink Anderson] on tour."

In 1973 he met fiddler and tenor banjoist "Fats" Kaplin, and they have been touring together since then. Although the combination of guitar and fiddle is uncommon in blues today, it is a traditional teaming of instruments which was used by earlier bluesmen such as fiddlers Walter Vincent and Henry Sims and guitarists Charley Patton and Bo Carter. The duo recorded their first effort for Blue Goose Records: *Git-Fiddle Shuffle* (Blue Goose BG-2018), which was released in 1975.

Roy Bookbinder is also included on *These Blues Is Meant to Be Barrelhoused* (Blue Goose BG-2003) and *Some People Who Play Guitar Like a Lot of People Don't* (Kicking Mule KM 104).

# Benjamin A. Botkin

*American folklorist, collector, writer, editor, teacher, head of the Archive of Folk Song (1942–45), and director of the National Folk Festival Association*

One of America's most prominent folklorists, Dr. Benjamin Albert Botkin followed a career spanning thirty-five years of dedication and productivity. He is probably best known for his editing of *A Treasury of American Folklore* (Crown Publishers, 1944) with a foreword by Carl Sandburg. The 932-page volume was considered to be the first definitive endeavor related to American folklore.

Born on February 7, 1901, in Boston, Massachusetts, he usually signed his work B. A. Botkin. He received his BA degree in English at Harvard in 1920, his MA at Columbia in 1921, and his PhD at the University of Nebraska in 1931. Until 1937 he taught English on the college level, but as the recipient of the Julius Rosenwald fellowship, Dr. Botkin went to Washington, D.C., where he served as the folklore editor of the Federal Writers Project from 1938 to 1939. His subsequent involvement with the Library of Congress led to his appointment as head of the Archive of Folk Song during the forties.

Some of his other professional affiliations included the Bureau of Educational and Cultural Affairs of the State Department, the National Committee of Folk Arts, the National Folk Festival Association, and the Workshop for Cultural Democracy. In 1951 he was a Guggenheim fellow, and sixteen years later he was a senior fellow of the National Endowment for the Humanities.

Dr. Botkin authored numerous works which reflected his deep immersion in American folklore, and one of his pioneering efforts in the field was a book called *Lay My Burden Down: A Folk History of Slavery* (University of Chicago Press, 1945). A collection of stories by over two thousand former black slaves, it recounted an aspect of America's past through the lives of those who were held in bondage.

His interests encompassed different regions and periods of American history and folklore, and he edited a broad range of volumes, including *A Treasury of Western Folklore*, *A Treasury of Railroad Folklore* (with Alvin F. Harlow), *Sidewalks of America*, *A Treasury of Mississippi Folklore*, *A Treasury of New England Folklore*, *The Southwest Scene*, *New York City Folklore*, *A Treasury of American Anecdotes*, *A Civil War Treasury of Tales, Legends and Folklore*, and *The Illustrated Book of American Folklore* (with Carl Withers).

Dr. Botkin was a dedicated supporter of the ideals of the National Folk Festival, and, as special folklore consultant of the thirty-third annual event, he said of the program divisions: "From these several vantage points the folk music body and process is conceived as a tree with the workshops and panel discussions as the trunk and the branches and the concerts as the blossoms and fruit, while the land and the folk are the soil and the roots."

He died on July 30, 1975, at his home in Croton-on-Hudson, New York; he was seventy-four years old. (*See also* Archive of Folk Song.)

# Michael Gene Botta. *See* The Travelers 3.

# Bottle Hill

*Contemporary and traditional bluegrass band, performers, and recording artists*

The original group was formed by Jim Albertson in the fall of 1970, and, in addition to Albertson, who ran a New Jersey coffeehouse called Hayes House, Bottle Hill consisted of Davey Burkitt on harmonica, Lew London on guitar and banjo, and Walt

Michael on hammered dulcimer. At the time, Bottle Hill was basically a folk group, and they played at school programs and small concerts. By the following summer, in 1971, they had turned to bluegrass.

Jim Albertson had quit, and Barry Mitterhoff joined the group as the mandolinist, Rex Hunt became the dobro player, and Frazier Shaw was recruited as the bass player. They performed at the Philadelphia Folk Festival, got a manager, and, during the winter, Bottle Hill toured colleges in the Northeast. In the spring of 1972 they recorded their first album, *Bottle Hill: A Rumor in Their Own Time* (Biograph BLP 6006), and the band moved from New Jersey to the Catskills.

The following winter, another personnel change was made when London left, and fiddler David Jaffe and banjoist Lester Bunin, both from New Jersey, joined Bottle Hill. With the arrival of August, another band was put together with Sam and Kirk McGee's nephew, Harry Guffee, who was from Nashville, Rex Hunt, Walt Michael, Barry Mitterhoff, and banjo player and singer Harry Orlove. By this time, Bottle Hill was without a manager, so they did their own bookings in colleges and clubs. Walt Michael describes the final rearrangement of the group's members: "Harry Guffee left two Christmases ago, and we replaced him with Dave Schwartz, who had gone to college and studied music with Barry [Mitterhoff], but unlike Barry, who quit after his first year at Rutgers, Dave went on for the full course. After he had been with the band for six months, David Jaffe quit as fiddler, and we finally replaced him recently with Joe Selly, who was Stevie Snow's backup guitarist for a long time. He roomed with all these people from Rutgers that were our musical core for a while, and he's influenced the group with his special talent for jazz.

"Like many working-traveling groups, Bottle Hill has seen many changes. People get tired and burned out. Last year we came close to 100,000 miles on the road. It seems to me that often musicians will last a year and a half or so, and then they just can't handle it anymore."

Originally called the Bottle Hill Boys, the group has been known for the past five years simply as Bottle Hill, and the membership seems to have stabilized with Hunt, Michael, Mitterhoff, Orlove, Schwartz, and Selly. They live "communally, renting two houses, and they book their own tours."

Bottle Hill has contracted with Biograph Records to record another album, and Walt Michael is involved in a hammered dulcimer recording with about fifteen different musicians, including Bottle Hill.

## The Boyer Family. *See* The Beers Family.

## The Boys of the Lough

*Vocal and instrumental group, performers, and recording artists*

One of the most popular groups from the British Isles, the Boys of the Lough have created a significant impact on the American folk scene as revival musicians. Their repertoire comprises mostly Irish and Scottish music played in what is described by Michael Cooney as "a less arranged, more folky (as 'twere) fashion than the Chieftains."

Top billing is often given to virtuoso fiddler Aly Bain from the Shetland Islands (north of Scotland). He was born in Lerwick, Shetland, and started playing fiddle seriously in his early teens, receiving instruction from Shetland Fiddlers Society organizer Tom Anderson. By 1967 Aly Bain was performing as a professional musician, and several years later he came to the United States with Mike Whellans (from Scotland), who accompanied the fiddler on guitar and bodhran (traditional Irish drum). In 1971 they joined up with two Irishmen, Robin Morton and Cathal McConnell, to form the original Boys of the Lough. Since then, Mike Whellans has been replaced by Dick Gaughan, who, in turn, has been replaced by Dave Richardson, an Englishman.

The Boys of the Lough perform their lively jigs and reels in concert, clubs, and festivals, with Aly Bain on fiddle, Cathal McConnell on flute and whistle, Robin Morton on bodhran and concertina, and Dave Richardson on mandolin, tenor banjo, and concertina. Their first album, entitled *Boys of the Lough* (Leader-Trailer LER 7086), was followed by an American release of their debut LP by Rounder Records, *The Boys of the Lough: Second Album* (Rounder 3006). Their most recent efforts are on the Philo label, *Boys of the Lough Live* (Philo PH 1026) and *Boys of the Lough* (Philo PH 1031).

## Jim Brady. *See* The Kentucky Pardners.

## Oscar Brand

*Singer, guitarist, author, composer, lyricist, performer, recording artist, and host of WNYC's* Folksong Festival

Oscar Brand performing at the Great Folk Revival held at the Nassau Coliseum, Uniondale, New York, on February 2, 1974

With boundless energy and love for music, Oscar Brand has achieved distinction as one of the most productive and ubiquitous figures on the contemporary American folk music scene. Although his accomplishments range far afield, he is best known for his work in folk music, and for many years he has been considered one of its most significant forces in the New York metropolitan area.

Born on February 7, 1920, in Winnipeg, Canada, Brand acquired his love for folk music and a compulsion for singing at a very young age. While he was growing up, his main ambition was to become a writer, as he recalls: "I loved the sound of words. I loved fooling with them, playing with them, moving them around. So along with singing for fun, I became a writer for business—I started writing professionally, for radio and newspapers, while I was in high school." His family had moved to New York during the Depression, and he attended Erasmus Hall High School in Brooklyn. After graduation, he worked at a number of jobs, and he brought his music everywhere he went: "I worked all around and I spent a lot of time singing. It got me along, it got me through work, made friends for me, and, in some cases, helped me pick up some extra money or sandwiches." He attended Brooklyn College to "learn writing and journalism," but earned a BA degree in psychology when it turned out that "these were the only courses in which I got A's."

During the late thirties, Oscar Brand started "traveling around New York and meeting people like Leadbelly, Burl Ives, and Josh White." He gravitated toward the singers who sang the same songs he did— songs with lyrics which could easily be changed and rearranged—and his repertoire included folk, country, pop, and old-fashioned hokey tunes: "I met Woody [Guthrie] around 1939, and he was making up new versions of the songs I sang. We used to fight about that, but since I didn't have an instrument, I needed him to play for me when I sang.

"The important thing to understand is, for me, the folk music also gave me a chance to write. I started rewriting old songs and writing new songs. I went into the army as a psychologist, and at that time, not having Woody to accompany me, I decided to try to do something myself. My cousin lent me his banjo, and I bought a little book, *Learn to Play the Banjo in 10 Minutes*, and I learned to play the banjo in ten minutes—at least a few songs. I took it into the army with me, carried it over my back, and I used it.

"When I got back from the war, Margot Mayo gave a big party with, let's see, Pete [Seeger], Woody Guthrie, Burl Ives, Lee Hays, Josh White, Dyer-Bennet—it was quite a party. We all sang and then Pete came over to me and said that he'd like to start some kind of a newsletter in which we would print songs that weren't printed in most of the collections, like picket line songs and the union songs we were writing then. In the army I had been an editor of a newspaper for psychiatric patients, and so I had all the newspaper equipment to start with. It started as a mimeograph and then went into printing, we called it *People's Songs*.

"When I got out of the army, I didn't want to be a psychologist—that was fine to get through college and even to get through the army—but I wanted to get back to writing. On December 11, 1945, WNYC offered me a

program, and I called it the *Folksong Festival*. We celebrated its thirtieth anniversary this year [1975]."

Oscar Brand is also currently host of the National Public Radio program *Voices in the Wind* and NBC-TV's *Spirit of '76*. He was for four years host and coproducer of the CBC-TV weekly show, *Let's Sing Out*; the host of another top-rated Canadian show called *Brand New Scene*; the host and coproducer for NET's *American Odyssey*; and was among the creators of *Sesame Street*. He worked as music director of the NBC-TV shows *Exploring*, *American Treasure Chest*, *Sunday*, and *The First Look*. Among the many honors which he has received since 1945 are the Peabody, Ohio State, Edison, Freedoms Foundation, and Emmy awards for radio and television. His scripts have been used for ballets, TV commercials (among the hundreds of commercials which he has written, composed, and acted on are those for Cheerios, Rival, Log Cabin, Maxwell House, Oldsmobile, and Ipana), TV musicals for the Methodist Church, a collection of feast day songs for the New York Presbytery, works for the National Lutheran Council, and numerous NBC and NET documentary specials.

"I started writing motion picture documentaries, using folk music as my entering wedge," he says in reflecting on his work involving more than seventy-five films, including Gulf's *Invisible Journey*, Ford's *Highway by the Sea*, Allied Chemical's *The Farmer Comes to Town*, and so on, for which he has accumulated Venice, Edinburgh, Golden Reel, Valley Forge, Cannes, and Scholastic awards. Both his Department of Health, Education and Welfare program, *The World of Music*, and his CBS Radio series of the same name were aired on close to two thousand stations.

He has written for Broadway shows (*A Joyful Noise* and *H\*Y\*M\*A\*N K\*A\*P\*L\*A\*N*); he was music director of *In White America*; he was composer of the songs for the film *The Fox*, and composer and lyricist of *How to Steal an Election* and the Kennedy Center Bicentennial musical *Sing, America, Sing.*

Oscar Brand is vice-president of the Songwriters Hall of Fame; president of Harlequin Productions, Inc., and Gypsy Hill Music, Inc.; a member of the Newport Festival Corporation; on the faculty of Hofstra University, New College, and the New School; and a member of the New York Folklore Society. He has authored ten books and music manuals, including *Singing Holidays* (1957); *Bawdy Songs* (1960); *Folksongs for Fun* (1961); *The Ballad Mongers* (1963); *Songs of '76* (1972); and *When I First Came to This Land* (1975).

He gives concerts for both adults and children, and he adds: "I do a lot of writing now, I've finally become a writer. But I still sing."

## Marie Brate. *See* Fennig's All-Star String Band.

## Broadside

In the cold winter months of 1962 the first several hundred mimeographed copies of *Broadside* magazine were put out as a combined effort by Agnes "Sis" Cunningham, Gordon Friesen, Pete Seeger, and Gil Turner. Conceived within the fabric of the folk song revival, the publication was designed to make available songs composed by contemporary writers such as Eric Andersen, Len Chandler, Rev. Gary Davis, Richard Fariña, Fred Hellerman, Janis Ian, Peter LaFarge, Phil Ochs, Tom Paxton, Malvina Reynolds, Buffy Sainte-Marie, Pete Seeger, Patrick Sky, Mark Spoelstra—and the list continues on to include more than one hundred names.

Throughout the next decade *Broadside* was published semimonthly, then monthly, and by 1972 it was reaching the stands only once every two months. In addition to over a

thousand songs and many poems published over the years, *Broadside* has printed at least one hundred articles pertinent to the folk-topical movement of the 1960s and 1970s— Bob Dylan, the Freedom Singers, Woody Guthrie, folk songs and their popularity, folk music magazines, the Newport Folk Festival, the Philadelphia Folk Festival, and hundreds of clippings from newspapers, magazines, and trade journals—contributed by Josh Dunson (now on the editorial advisory board of *Sing Out!*), Gordon Friesen, Julius Lester, and Pete Seeger, among others. *Broadside* has also put together eight LPs of songs from the publication, issued by Folkways-Broadside Records. *Broadside* has been mentioned extensively in several books published in the United States and in two foreign books, one in French (*Une Histoire de la Musique Populaire aux Etats-Unis*, by Jacques Vassal) and the other in Spanish (*PROTESTA: Ediciones de Cultura Popular*, by Ramon Padilla), which base their texts extensively on material from *Broadside*.

*Broadside's* printing of "Talking John Birch" in the first issue marked the initial publication of material by Bob Dylan; throughout its existence, Dylan has continued to grant *Broadside's* permission to print his songs. Sis Cunningham mentions an interesting fact in connection with *Broadside's* interaction with Bob Dylan: "We printed on the cover of *Broadside #6* his song 'Blowin' in the Wind'—a full year before it was popularized by Peter, Paul and Mary. Bob sang it for us at our place, we taped it. I transcribed words and music, and, within a week, we had it out in *Broadside*. It was first recorded on Volume One of the *Broadside* LPs, sung by Gil Turner's group, the New World Singers. Bob was singing on that record, but he sang a couple of his other songs—or, to be more exact, two and a half, since he stopped during one of the songs, and said, 'That's just two verses to it.' His pronouncement was included on the LP."

In his article *"Broadside: Ten Years—One Thousand Songs,"* printed in *Sing Out!*

BROADSIDE # 49

AUGUST 20, 1964
Price 50¢

THE NATIONAL TOPICAL SONG MAGAZINE

IN THIS ISSUE
SONGS BY:
Mark Spoelstra, Buffy Sainte-Marie,
Mattye Peters Iversen, Tom Paxton,
Dick Fariña, Neruda-Brecht-Bentley,
Amy Lowenstein, Linda Lu DeLorenzo.
* * * * * * *
ARTICLES BY:
Josh Dunson (and others) writing on
the 1964 NEWPORT FOLK FESTIVAL, Pete
Seeger on what are folksongs and why
their popularity, and Gordon Friesen
looks at some recent folk music mag-
azines. * * * * * *

MARK SPOELSTRA
Photo By
Joe Alper

Sample cover page of a well-known topical song publication of the sixties, *Broadside*, published in New York City

(Volume 21, Number 5, 1972), Josh Dunson formulates the significance of *Broadside*'s publication of the most meaningful songs of the day, from 1962 to the present: "Many of the to-be-famous found solace in the coffee and the warmth offered by the Friesens in their tiny apartment on 104th St. in New York City, and many more never-to-be-spotlighted kept writing and working in the movements because they were encouraged by a song in print, a real and smiling greeting, and hours of talk."

Two other *Broadside* magazines commenced publication at the same time that the New York *Broadside* came into existence, each independent of the other. The Boston *Broadside* concentrated on happenings in the New England area and the Los Angeles *Broadside* emphasized editorial and theoretical printed material. (*See also* Agnes "Sis" Cunningham.)

# David Bromberg

*Singer, songwriter, guitarist, performer, and recording artist*

David Bromberg's early reputation was established by his talent as a session man, but since 1970 he has become an increasingly popular solo performer. Since he quit his job as Jerry Jeff Walker's backup guitarist, he has recorded four albums of his own on the Columbia label.

"I started playing guitar because I got turned on by the Weavers and from reading their albums. They talked about people like Big Bill Broonzy, so I started getting some of his records, and one day I bought an album with Muddy Waters singing Big Bill Broonzy and I found another kind of music entirely. I was listening to a lot of rock 'n' roll at the same time, and then in New York I got turned on to country music, especially Doc Watson."

Born in Philadelphia in September 1945, David Bromberg graduated from Tarrytown High and entered Columbia University as a music major. He was immediately drawn to Greenwich Village, playing his guitar in places around MacDougal and Bleecker streets; and after three semesters of studying musicology, Bromberg dropped out of Columbia to become a full-time guitarist.

"The first professional work that I did was behind a gospel singer named Brother John Sours. Then I did a whole bunch of rock 'n' roll gigs, playing guitar for Chubby Checker for a little while, and then recording with Jay and the Americans. I played guitar for Jerry Jeff Walker for a couple of years, and he was a big influence on me. At that time, I was doing a lot of recording work—I think I've been on about eighty albums to date—as a sideman. At one point, I stopped playing electric guitar and I started playing acoustic guitar almost exclusively, but I'm playing both again, now."

Bromberg has backed up other folk artists, including Bob Dylan, Doug Kershaw, Tom Paxton, Paul Siebel, and Patrick Sky. When Jerry Jeff Walker had a hit with "Mr. Bojangles," Bromberg was behind him, playing the guitar licks that made his rendition so memorable. As they started touring around the country, people started to take notice of this talented young backup guitarist, and one night at the Bitter End, Bob Dylan heard him play and asked

Bromberg to be a session man for both his *Self Portrait* and *New Morning* albums. For a brief period of time, Bromberg served an apprenticeship with Rev. Gary Davis, who broadened his musical interests and ability to play a fingerpicking blues style of guitar.

His first job after leaving Jerry Jeff Walker was at the Gaslight. Soon thereafter, he was booked as an accompanist to folksinger Rosalie Sorrels, who was scheduled to play the 1970 Isle of Wight Festival. On opening night, Sorrels was scheduled to perform, and during her set she asked Bromberg to do "Bullfrog Blues." The crowd went wild. The

David Bromberg at the 1975 Mariposa Folk Festival held on the Toronto Islands, Ontario, Canada

promoters asked him to do a solo performance, and after an hour-long set, Bromberg received four encores.

The news of his success at the Isle of Wight Festival traveled quickly, and within a matter of months he was signed to Columbia Records. His first album, *David Bromberg* (C 31104), was released in January 1972, and it demonstrated his gift for working in a diversity of musical styles. *Demon in Disguise* (KC 31753) and *Wanted/Dead or Alive* (KC 32717) was followed by *Midnight on the Water* (PC 33397), which Bromberg considers his best.

"I have a weird band which consists of bass and drums; two fiddlers who double on other instruments like mandolin and banjo; and two horn players—one of whom doubles on trumpet, coronet, and mellophone—and the other on clarinet, saxophone, lute, and pennywhistle. At first I thought that I'd just sing by myself, but the band grew on me 'cause I picked them one by one from different places. We have a repertoire of over two hundred tunes covering all kinds of music—traditional, rock, country, country & western, dixieland, old and modern blues, and folk—so it's pretty hard to put us into one category or another. I'm looking to create satisfying music, and as long as I can do that and still eat, I'm going to keep right on."

## Guy Brooks. *See* The Red Fox Chasers.

## Big Bill Broonzy

*Country blues singer, guitarist, fiddler, songwriter, performer, and recording artist*

When he died of cancer on August 14, 1958, William Lee Conley Broonzy was regarded internationally as one of America's greatest country and folk blues musicians. The career of Big Bill Broonzy was not unlike that of other early folk and blues artists whose rise from obscurity to fame was linked to the popularization of traditional material during the midcentury folk revival.

Broonzy gave his year of birth as 1893, but a certificate found after his death corrected this to June 26, 1898. One of many children, he lived on a farm in Scott, Mississippi, and started working in the fields when he was eight years old. His uncle, Jerry Belcher, had played fiddle with an old buddy, Stonewall Jackson, and the young boy had learned many songs from his father. When he was about ten, Broonzy was impressed by the fiddling of a traveling blues singer who answered to the name C. C. Rider, and, stimulated by this musician, who played with the banjo accompaniment of "Fast Black," Broonzy fashioned a fiddle out of a cigar box. After he found someone to play with him, they made a guitar using a larger box, and together they performed at picnics and suppers.

He played for local events from the time he was in his early teens, and when his family moved to Arkansas, Broonzy entertained at barbecues and "two-way picnics," where blacks and whites performed on separate stages. At the time, Broonzy was playing fiddle, and he didn't start playing guitar until he went to Chicago in 1920 after his discharge from the army.

His uncle had given him a wealth of songs, like "John Henry," "Midnight Special," and "Oh, Susanna," and from the beginning, Big Bill Broonzy developed a musical style that was derived from his background of blues, spirituals, and folk tunes. Broonzy felt that blues were sung differently when he was a boy, and what his uncle called "reels" later became blues to the general public.

Throughout his life, Broonzy was employed in a multitude of occupations—cook, porter, janitor, dishwasher, floor mopper—and when he arrived in Chicago, he got a job with the railroads. He perfected the guitar, and he accompanied such musicians as Big Napoleon Strickland, Papa Charlie Jackson, Theo Edwards, and "Kid Music"; and he composed one of his first guitar solos, "Saturday Night Rub." Within three years, he had played with Sleepy John Estes, Blind Lemon Jefferson, Blind Blake, Jim Jackson, and other well-known bluesmen, and Broonzy made his first recordings of original works, "Big Bill Blues" and "House Rent Stomp." By the end of the decade, he had made numerous recordings, including "Big Bill Blues No. 2," "House Rent Stomp No. 2," "Bull Cow Blues," and "Mama Let's Cuddle Some More," and following the Depression, Big Bill Broonzy became a popular entertainer in Chicago's South Side clubs.

He recorded with other artists on the Champion label, and he came to New York in 1932 with one of his own bands. A few recording sessions were done in the studios of Vocalion, Oriole, and Melotone, and when Broonzy returned to Chicago, he continued to supplement his regular job with club dates. He returned to New York City in 1939 when John Hammond brought him to Carnegie Hall for the Spirituals to Swing Concert.

Throughout the forties, the pattern remained the same, except that Broonzy traveled farther afield to perform in the South and on college campuses while he continued to work at a variety of daytime jobs. The folk movement of the 1950s put an end to the discouragingly slow progress of his career, and fortunately, like so many others who had earned well-deserved recognition, Broonzy began to enjoy the benefits of a recognized country blues musician. He was part of folksinger Win Stracke's group called I Come for to Sing, and they were a respected and well-liked act at folk concerts.

In 1951 he gave his first European concert, in Paris, and during the course of his successful tour he recorded "Black, Brown and White." His European following was stronger than his acceptance in the United States, and his national reputation remained a step behind, even when, in 1953, he was able to support himself for the first time solely by his music. Between African and South American tours, Broonzy appeared with such famed folk personalities as Pete Seeger,

Sonny Terry, and Brownie McGhee, and sales of his early Folkways recordings steadily increased. He had recorded *Big Bill Broonzy Sings Folk Songs* (FS 2328); *Music Down Home* (FS 2691), with Leadbelly, Sonny Terry, and Brownie McGhee; *Big Bill Broonzy Blues* (FS 3586); *Blues* (FS 3817), with Sonny Terry and Brownie McGhee; and *Folksongs and Blues* (FS 3864), with Pete Seeger.

Unfortunately, most Broonzy LPs were issued after his death in 1958, including albums on such labels as Verve/Folkways, Folkways, and Mercury. It was only during the last three years of his life that Big Bill Broonzy was able to focus his attention full-time on his musical talents. In 1954 his biography was written by the Belgian author Yannick Bruynoghe, and in the following year *Big Bill Blues: Big Bill Broonzy's Story as Told to Yannick Bruynoghe* was published by Cassell, London; it was issued in the United States by Grove Press in 1956.

Broonzy claimed to have recorded about 260 blues, of which he wrote about 100, and in his lifetime he composed over 350 songs. By the time of his death, Broonzy was one of the best-known folk blues singers, and in addition to other recordings by Columbia, Fontana, RCA Victor, and the above-mentioned labels, his music is a part of collections by Biograph Records, *Big Bill Broonzy 1932-1942* (BLPC 15), and Yazoo, *The Young Big Bill Broonzy 1928-1935* (L-1011), *Do That Guitar Rag 1928-1935* (L-1035), and *Uptown Blues* (L-1042), with others.

# The Brothers Four

*Vocal and instrumental group, performers, and recording artists*

A West Coast quartet of college fraternity brothers—a medical student, a would-be television director, a hopeful electrical engineer, and a prospective diplomat—banded together as folksingers to ride the crest of the folk boom wave and became one of the most commercially successful folk groups of the sixties.

Bob Flick, Dick Foley, Mike Kirkland, and John Paine projected a youthful, collegiate image which, combined with their showmanship and talent, appealed to audiences everywhere. The foursome started performing in 1959 at the University of Washington, where they were enrolled as students, and before long their singing "just for fun and free beer" was turned into a commercial venture. Columbia Records was interested in this group of all-American college students, and the Brothers Four signed a recording contract and cut an album called *The Brothers Four* (Columbia CL 1402/CS 8197). One of the selections on their debut LP received considerable airplay on a San Francisco radio station, and "Greenfields" was subsequently issued as a single. The song climbed to the top of the national charts to become No. 21 cash box top single of 1960, and one of the most popular folk songs in Europe, Japan, and Australia. Their first time out, the Brothers Four had recorded a million-seller.

The group continued to grow and develop musically, and their stage presence, musicianship, good humor, and personalities kept them in constant demand for college, club, and concert dates. Their repertoire included traditional folk songs, ballads, pop hits, and show tunes, and some of their most enthusiastic audiences were those in Japan, with consistent support readily supplied by their American fans.

The Brothers Four recorded more than twelve albums for Columbia Records during their short but fruitful career, and some of their best-known songs are versions of "Frogg No. 1 and Frogg No. 2," "Nine Pound Hammer," "The Green Leaves of Summer," "Blue Water Line," "Boa Constrictor," and "25 Minutes to Go."

**Mike Brovsky.** *See* The Serendipity Singers.

**Francine Brown.** *See* The Pennywhistlers.

**The Brown's Ferry Four.** *See* The Delmore Brothers; Merle Travis.

**Jim Buchanan.** *See* The Greenbriar Boys.

**Bud and Travis.** *See* Travis Edmondson.

**Grady Bullins.** *See* The Kentucky Pardners.

**Bob Burnett.** *See* The Highwaymen.

**Steve Butts.** *See* The Highwaymen.

## The Byrds
*Vocal and instrumental group, performers, and recording artists*

The recent folk revival in America created a stimulating and challenging framework within which creative musicians functioned as stationary or innovative elements of the overall design. The Byrds were among the innovative forces of the era, and the group is best remembered for their revitalization of folk music by combining this traditionally acoustic and pure musical form with the rock idiom. Folk-rock was ushered in with the Byrds' early 1965 recording of Bob Dylan's "Mr. Tambourine Man," and the group's electric version of the classic folk song set a precedent for the overlapping and integration of musical forms in the music of today.

The early history of the Byrds dates back to the fall of 1964, when Roger (then Jim) McGuinn decided to form a rock group. He had been performing as a folksinger and a sideman to the Chad Mitchell Trio and Bobby Darin, and he was influenced by the Beatles to formulate innovative musical stylings. The original Byrds comprised diversified musicians, with McGuinn acting as the group's leader and guitarist. Gene Clark (a songwriter and country-oriented singer formerly with the New Christy Minstrels) played tambourine; Mike Clarke was the Byrds' drummer; David Crosby (later of Crosby, Stills, Nash and Young) was rhythm guitarist; and bluegrass mandolinist Chris Hillman was recruited as the bass player.

The Byrds mastered their characteristic vocal harmonies, which were influenced by the Dillards, and the use of two twelve-string guitars to amplify their unique sound. They recorded "Mr. Tambourine Man," which was a cash box top single of 1965 and the title song of their first album, *Mr. Tambourine Man* (CS 9172/CL 2372). Shortly after its release, Bob Dylan put together an electric band and the marriage of folk and rock was cemented. Tremendous controversy was aroused by the Byrds' version of "Mr. Tambourine Man," with purists up in arms and progressive musicians applauding the phenomenon, but the immediate result was an energetic vivification of folk music. The term *folk-rock* was coined, and the Byrds' career was under way.

Their next single release was "Turn! Turn! Turn!," which was a modern interpretation of a biblical verse with music composed by veteran folksinger Pete Seeger; like "Mr. Tambourine Man," their second 45-RPM single became an instant hit, climbing to the top of the record charts in 1966. The Byrds ventured into new territory with "Eight Miles High," and many consider this recording to be the fountainhead of psychedelic music.

Gene Clark left the Byrds after the group had recorded their second album, *Turn! Turn! Turn!* (CS 9254/CL 2454), and "Eight Miles High." By this time, the Byrds' audience had diminished in scope, and the group was involved in further exploration and incorporation of musical styles and metaphysical themes. Inner turmoil resulted in the departure of David Crosby; then Mike Clarke left, and country singer-songwriter Gram Parsons was added to the ranks along with Kevin Kelley.

The Byrds' third LP, *Fifth Dimension* (CS 9349/CL 2549), was recorded by the original group minus Gene Clark; it was followed by *Younger Than Yesterday* (CS 9442/CL 2642) and *The Byrds' Greatest Hits* (CS 9516/CL 2716), with the same personnel. *The Notorious Byrd Brothers* (CS 9575/CL 2775) was recorded by three of the original members, Mike Clarke, Hillman, and McGuinn. The Byrds' sound redeveloped with the addition of Gram Parsons and Kevin Kelley, and *Sweetheart of the Rodeo* (CS 9670), issued in August 1968, brought the Byrds to the center of country music and initiated the "country-rock" movement.

Again, dissension within the group created another rift, which resulted in Parsons and Hillman forming the Flying Burrito Brothers. Kelley left, and McGuinn remained as the core of the group with replacements Clarence White, Gene Parsons, and John York, who was soon replaced by Skip Battin.

Born in 1944, Clarence White learned to play the guitar as a youngster; by the late fifties he and his brothers had formed the Country Boys, which evolved as the Kentucky Colonels. They played the top clubs, including the Second Fret, Gerde's Folk City, and Club 47, and in 1964 the Kentucky Colonels were invited to perform at the Newport Folk Festival. Best known for his flatpick guitar style, Clarence White was an accompanist on a number of albums as the disinterest in bluegrass in the mid-sixties caused him to direct his musical ambitions to studio work, finally joining the Byrds in 1968.

The Byrds toured throughout the world for the next several years, and a number of albums were recorded before Gene Parsons left the group in 1972. In 1969 *Dr. Byrds and Mr. Hyde* (CS 9755) and *The Ballad of Easy Rider* (CS 9942) were recorded while John York was playing with the Byrds as drummer; in the same year *Preflyte* (Together Records ST-T-1001) was released, with the original Byrds personnel as the recording artists. McGuinn, Parsons, White, and Skip Battin recorded *The Byrds* (Untitled) (G 30127), *Byrdmaniax* (KC 30640), and *Farther Along* (KC 31050); and in October 1972 Columbia issued *The Best of the Byrds* (KC 31795).

Gene Parsons was replaced by John Guerin on drums, and in 1973 Clarence White decided to return to bluegrass music and acoustic guitar. He recorded *Muleskin-ner: A Potpourri of Bluegrass Jam* (Warner Brothers BS 2787), with selections by Richard Greene (formerly with Bill Monroe, Jim Kweskin's Jug Band, and the country-rock group Seatrain), David Grisman, Bill Keith, and Pete Rowan. Clarence White played with the Country Gazette, signed a recording contract with Warner Brothers and recorded various parts of half a dozen tracks on a solo LP, toured with the regrouped Kentucky Colonels, and did some recordings with the Country Gazette, Gene Parsons, Skip Battin, and Gram Parsons. On July 15, 1973, he was killed by a drunken driver as he was putting instruments into his car. In the same year Gram Parsons died, apparently of a heart attack. *Muleskinner: A Potpourri of Bluegrass Jam* was released in the fall of 1974, after Clarence White's death.

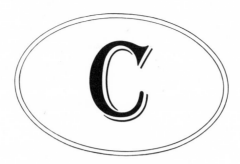

**Dan Cade.** *See* The II Generation.

**The Caffé Lena.** *See* Lena Spencer.

## Cajun

One of America's most distinctive living traditions in folk music is Louisiana Acadian, or Cajun, and the term denotes a native of the state of Louisiana whose first language is French instead of English.

Songs which have grown from this rich and unique heritage of Canadian French ancestry are reflections of its history and the many tastes and styles within the spectrum of Cajun music. The archaic style of Cajun fiddlers S. D. (Sady) Courville and Dennis McGee is reminiscent of the way the music sounded nearly a century ago. According to Cajun music enthusiast Richard Spottswood of the Archive of Folk Song, who wrote the article "Allons A Lafayette, Or: A Brief Glance at the Cajun Tradition of Southwest Louisiana," which appeared in the 1973 National Folk Festival catalogue: "The violin is the oldest in tradition of those instruments found in a standard Cajun band. Throughout the 19th century the violin dominated—to the extent that it was often used singly or in pairs as the only accompaniment for singing and dancing."

Around the turn of the century, the Cajun accordion was introduced, and, today, accordionist Ambrose Thibodeaux and his band present Cajun music as it sounded when first recorded in the 1920s. The Cajun accordion is a simplified version of the standard accordion, and it is described by Spottswood: "There are only two bass keys, played with the left hand, and ten treble keys for the right. It operates something like a harmonica, in that there are no 'black' keys, so that one may play only in two keys, using the tonic and dominant chords of each." The Balfa Freres incorporate both traditional and contemporary Cajun tunes into their repertoire, and they have added the *petit fer*, or *'tit fer* (triangle) and the guitar to the more traditional instrumentation of the fiddle and the Cajun accordion. Influenced by country & western music, the Louisiana Aces are a modern Cajun band which employs electric instrumentation. Contemporary songwriter Doug Kershaw has popularized Cajun fiddle music by such songs as "Louisiana Man," "Diggy Diggy Lo," and his rendition of "Sweet Jole Blon'." "Jolie Blonde" was first recorded in the twenties, and in 1947 its popularity was reborn with the new version recorded by Cajun fiddler Harry Choates. This song typifies the many old Cajun tunes which have been kept alive, revitalized in their southwest Louisiana homeland, and frequently reaching national exposure over the years.

Internationally, an interest in, and an increased cognizance of, Cajun music have been demonstrated in recent years, as exemplified by the French-made movie,

*Dedans le Sud de la Louisiane*, directed by Jean-Pierre Bruneau and partially narrated by Pierre Daigle, Cajun historian and author of *Tears, Love and Laughter*. The film includes the Balfa Freres, Nathan Abshire, Alphonse "Boisec" Ardoin, Dennis McGee, Sady Courville, and others, and it has been distributed in England, France, and the United States.

The term "zydeco" (a phonetic spelling derived from a term used in the title of the first bestselling zydeco record, "Las Haricot Sont Pos Sale") refers to black stylings of Cajun music. One of the best-known zydeco bands is led by Boisec Ardoin, cousin of the legendary Cajun accordionist Amadie Ardoin.

## Thelma Camach. *See* The New Christy Minstrels.

## The Camp Creek Boys. *See* Fred Cockerham; Kyle Creed.

## Guy Carawan

*Singer, instrumentalist, performer, recording artist, collector, author, festival organizer, and music director of the Highlander Research and Education Center in New Market, Tennessee*

"I had my first big dose of the South about twenty years ago," explains California-born Guy Carawan, whose early reputation in the field of folk music was based on his multiple roles as political activist, protest singer and popularizer of such songs as "We Shall Overcome," and participant in the civil rights movement. Since then, his career has continued to encompass many aspects of social involvement, education, and entertainment.

Guy Carawan was born on July 28, 1927, in Los Angeles, California. He was a mathematics major at Occidental College, Los Angeles, where he earned his BA degree; in 1953 he received his MA in sociology from UCLA. His involvement with folk music began with a fundamental interest in his parents' Southern heritage and in the music of Woody Guthrie, Pete Seeger, and Leadbelly. After completing his formal education, he was accompanied by Jack Elliott and Frank Hamilton (later of the Weavers) in his travels throughout the South, stopping "in dozens of cities and farm communities in Appalachia, singing on street corners, in bars and at festivals." While in Tennessee, he visited the Highlander Center, and, after half a dozen years of touring throughout the United States and in Europe, Russia, and Red China, he returned in 1959 to this adult school for social change, where he now works as music director.

Although he was engaged (with his wife, Candie) in field work in Appalachia and among Southern blacks from 1959 to 1967 (and from 1969 to 1972), their activities included a diversity of accomplishments, such as organizing music festivals in the Sea Islands off the coast of South Carolina; doing documentary work for SNCC and SCLC on John's Island and in other parts of Appalachia; performing and speaking on American folk music at colleges, clubs, concerts, and festivals around the United States; and participating in social-musical events outside the South, including *Broadside*'s first "99¢ Hootenanny," held in September 1963 in New York City. Guy and Candie Carawan took part in civil rights marches, sit-ins, and demonstrations, and, in addition to being one of the first whites to fight for this cause, Carawan introduced "We Shall Overcome" to the movement by singing the song at one of the initial SNCC meetings, at Shaw University in Raleigh, North Carolina. For several years (1968 to 1974), he was folklorist-in-residence at Pitzer College in Claremont, California.

Guy and Candie Carawan have co-authored four books based on their personal experiences and work in the southeastern

United States: *We Shall Overcome: The Songs of the Southern Freedom Movement* (Oak Publications, 1963); *Ain't You Got a Right to the Tree of Life?* (Simon & Schuster, 1967), which was chosen by the American Library Association as one of 1967's notable books; *Freedom Is a Constant Struggle: Songs of the Freedom Movement* (Oak Publications, 1968); and, most recently, *Voices from the Mountains* (Alfred A. Knopf, 1975). He has also produced ten documentary records for Folkways, Prestige, Rounder, and SNCC, and has been recorded both here and abroad by such labels as Columbia (of England), CurNon, Folkways, Intercord Xenophone, Plane (Germany), and Prestige. Guy Carawan plays six- and twelve-string guitar, five-string banjo, hammered dulcimer, autoharp, Appalachian dulcimer, and tin whistle; his repertoire consists of both traditional and contemporary (some original) folk material; and he is often accompanied in his performances by Candie.

**Bob Carey.** *See* The Tarriers.

## The Carolina Tar Heels

*Old-time string band, performers, and recording artists*

Early "hillbilly" Columbia and Victor recording artists, the Carolina Tar Heels were among the musicians whose three-finger banjo picking was a fundamental influence on the development of the world-famous "Scruggs Picking Style." As a young boy, Earl Scruggs listened carefully to the work of Carolina Tar Heel banjoist and central figure Doctor Coble "Dock" Walsh, and, many years later, Scruggs emerged as the most significant five-string banjoist to fully develop and to perfect the instrumental techniques employed by such precursors as the Carolina Tar Heels.

The personnel of the Carolina Tar Heels changed and, at different times, included Clarence "Tom" Ashley, Garley Foster, Gwen Foster, and Dock Walsh. Before the formation in 1927 of the original Carolina Tar Heels with Gwen Foster and Dock Walsh, Columbia Records cut in wax four vocals with banjo accompaniment by the "Banjo King of the Carolinas," Dock Walsh, on October 3, 1925. In April of the following year, another solo recording session was arranged with the native North Carolina musician, and he made a subsequent journey to Atlanta to record six additional sides (one of which was not issued) for the Columbia label. A few months later, he teamed up with Gwen Foster as a duet, and then with Dave Fletcher and Floyd Williams as a four-man string band, called the Four Yellowjackets. When they were asked to record for Victor early in 1927, talent scout Ralph S. Peer recorded four duet numbers by Gwen Foster and Dock Walsh as the Carolina Tar Heels. In August of the same year, the duet recorded on a second occasion for Victor at Charlotte.

In October 1928, Dock Walsh returned to Atlanta on another recording excursion—this time accompanied by the "Human Bird," Garley Foster (who was no relation to the previous guitarist and harmonica player associated with Dock Walsh), and by Clarence "Tom" Ashley. As a trio, they cut eight selections for Victor, and, in the following spring, they recorded an additional eight tunes at Victor's Camden (New Jersey) studios. In 1931 Garley Foster and Dock Walsh were recorded by Peer as the Pine Mountain Boys, and in 1932 a final session was scheduled for Gwen Foster and Dock Walsh.

Twenty years later, two original recordings by the Carolina Tar Heels were reissued on *The Anthology of American Folk Music* (Folkways FA 2951-2953), and a new wave of interest in their old-time music led to a subsequent recording session during the sixties. In 1962 Garley Foster, Dock Walsh, and his son Drake Walsh recorded *The Carolina Tar Heels* (Folk-Legacy FSA-24), with three original numbers (written in the

1920s) by Dock Walsh, one 1961 composition by Garley Foster, and the remaining selections comprising traditional material. (*See also* Clarence "Tom" Ashley.)

# Fiddlin' John Carson

*The first commercially recorded hillbilly performer, singer, fiddler, and a principal figure at early old-time fiddlers' conventions in the South*

Credited with being the first hillbilly performer to be recorded and marketed commercially, Fiddlin' John Carson is considered most responsible for the beginning of the country music industry.

Born on March 23, 1868, in the hills of Fannin County, Georgia, Carson worked as a racehorse jockey when a teenager. When he outgrew the size requirements of the job, he went to work at the Exposition Cotton Mill, where he stayed for about twenty years as foreman, and then turned to house painting. Simultaneously, he became well-known as a musical performer in the Atlanta area, where he resided, and by the outbreak of World War I he was a local star, playing fiddle on the instrument brought to this country from Ireland by his grandfather.

The "Champion of Georgia" headlined the annual fall Georgia Old-Time Fiddlers' Association conventions, and between 1913 and 1922 Fiddlin' John Carson won the contest seven times. In the early months of 1922 Atlanta's WSB Radio was established by the *Journal*, and on September 9 of that year Carson became one of the first country performers to be broadcast on radio. During his lifetime, Carson was also active as a political campaigner, composing songs and attracting crowds with his music. He worked for the Populist Tom Watson and for the gubernatorial campaigns of Eugene Talmadge and his son Herman, who later became a United States senator and a member of the Watergate Committee.

In 1923 Atlanta's Okeh Records distributor Polk C. Brockman went to New York City to discuss the promotion of company sales with Ralph S. Peer, who had already broken new ground with his recent recording of "race music," or black folk-blues. In mid-June, Fiddlin' John Carson cut his two best-known songs, "The Little Old Log Cabin in the Lane" and "The Old Hen Cackled and the Rooster's Going to Crow," and the country music industry was born, as described by Bill C. Malone and Judith McCulloh in their essay "Early Pioneers": "Why should Carson be credited with responsibility for the beginnings of recorded country music, when [Eck] Robertson preceded him on record by over a year and Henry Whitter also made earlier test recordings? The answer is that though we must credit Robertson and Whitter for their initiative and imagination in conceiving of themselves as potential phonograph artists when there were no rural southern folk artists on record before them, nevertheless their actions did not lead to any realization by either the industry or the buying public of a significant innovation in the field. . . . it was Carson's discs that first made the industry aware of the vast untapped potential market for southern Anglo-American folk music." When the initially pressed 500 copies sold immediately, Peer recognized the potential for record sales of hillbilly music, and Carson's record was re-pressed for a numbered release.

From 1923 to 1931, Fiddlin' John Carson recorded almost 150 selections for Okeh Records, and, after a couple of recording sessions, he was frequently accompanied by the Virginia Reelers, one of whose members was Rosa Lee Carson ("Moonshine Kate"), the youngest of his ten children. The Depression caused him to cease his recording activities temporarily, but in 1934 he was recorded by RCA Victor, in Camden, New Jersey. Most of the 24 or so records issued at that time were repeats of previously recorded hits.

In his last years he was an elevator

operator in the Georgia State Capitol, and on December 11, 1949, Fiddlin' John Carson died at the age of eighty-one.

Only a relatively small portion of Fiddlin' John Carson's output has been reissued, and the material has been incorporated into collections by different record companies, such as Vetco and County. Rounder Records has put together an entire album of Fiddlin' John Carson, *The Old Hen Cackled and the Rooster's Going to Crow* (Rounder 1003), and the 15 selections are representative of his varied styles and the range of material in his repertoire.

# The Carter Family

*Legendary folk and country group, America's first family of traditional music, with a vocal and instrumental style referred to as the Carter tradition or "Carter Family Style"*

The Carter Family is associated with "Wildwood Flower," "Can the Circle Be Unbroken," "Wabash Cannonball," "Keep on the Sunny Side" (which they used as their radio theme song), and other old-time ballads, traditional songs, and gospel hymns representative of America's Southeastern heritage, folklore, and contemporary musical attitudes toward the selection of songs and their manner of presentation.

Maybelle Addington Carter was born on May 10, 1909, in Nickelsville, Virginia, near the Tennessee border. The Addingtons had come from England in the 1700s, and they settled on the Copper Creek side of Clinch Mountain in southwestern Virginia. Maybelle was one of ten children in a "family that was all musical and used to play around home a lot."

The Carters lived in Poor Valley, on the other side of Clinch Mountain; like the Addingtons, they were very close-knit, religious people who were musically talented. Alvin Pleasant (A. P.) Carter was the eldest of eight children in his family; he had a fine bass

voice, and he became known as a collector of Irish and English folk songs. In 1915 A. P. Carter married Sara Dougherty, who was Maybelle Addington's first cousin.

A decade later, A. P.'s younger brother, Ezra J., journeyed to the Copper Creek side of the mountain to marry Maybelle, who by then could play many instruments, including the banjo, guitar, autoharp, fiddle, and lute. After their marriage on March 23, 1926, Ezra and Maybelle Carter moved to Maces Spring, near A. P. and Sara Carter, and about twenty-five miles from Bristol, Tennessee.

"After I got married we started the Carter Family, with A.P., Sara, and myself," recalls Maybelle Carter, "and we did our first recording on August 2, 1927. A. P. had gone into Bristol, and he happened to run into Ralph S. Peer, who was looking for talent to make some records for Victor. So he came home and told us that he had an appointment for us to make a record the next day, and that's what we did."

Many talented singers and musicians came from the mountains and nearby towns to audition in Bristol, but only the Carter Family and a young singer and guitarist named Jimmie Rodgers became hit recording artists.

"We cut six songs for three records, six sides, and that was the first time that I had done anything like that, ever recorded," Maybelle smiles, "and it was a great surprise to hear yourself singing on a record when you had cut it.

"Then they recorded on wax, a big piece of wax, and if you made a mistake, you had to shave it off and start all over again. We made a lot of mistakes on a lot of 'em, which they didn't take off," she laughs softly, "which they should have, but they didn't. Then it was a lot more trouble than it is now.

"And that's how we got started."

For the next ten years the Carter Family performed in schools, churches, and at socials in Virginia, Tennessee, and North Carolina. Family ties were strong, and only on rare occasions did they travel as far as Pennsylvania, Alabama, or Maryland to perform. It was a difficult decision to leave their homes in Virginia in 1938; but, as musicians, the Carter Family realized that the move to Del Rio, Texas, was important to the growth of their music.

Maybelle Carter describes the early years in Texas: "In 1938 we went to Del Rio to work for the Consolidated Drug Company out of Chicago. I took Anita with me; she was four years old, and she would sing solos and duets with me. In 1938 and 1939 we broadcasted in person over XERA in Del Rio; and in 1940 and 1941 we went to San Antonio to cut the transcriptions, which were broadcast over the border. We took the kids with us to San Antonio, and we cut about four transcriptions in one day because the kids were all in school."

The Carter Family left Texas in 1941; and the following year they went to Charlotte, North Carolina, to work on WBT Radio, as described by June Carter: "There, in the early mornings, we worked with Grady Cole on WBT, which was one of the major 50,000-watt radio stations in the country. We performed our show live every morning for an hour, and sometimes A. P. and Sara's children, Gladys, Janette, and Joe, worked with us." After six months at WBT, A. P. and Sara decided they wanted to retire, and the Carter Family unit broke up.

A. P. and Sara had separated in 1933 and they were divorced several years later. Sara married Coy Bayes in 1938, but she continued to practice, perform, and record with the Carter Family throughout this period. In 1942 the old Original Carter Family did their last radio show together; and on June 1, 1943, Maybelle Carter and her daughters, Anita, Helen, and June, went to work as Mother Maybelle Carter and the Carter Sisters at WRNL in Richmond, Virginia.

Before the original trio split up, they had recorded some three hundred released songs in their seventeen years together, and they had become some of the most influential proponents of traditional, "homemade"

music. Throughout their career, the Carter Family remained faithful to a style based on their heritage, religion, and family unity. After A. P. and Sara retired in the early forties, Maybelle Carter perpetuated the Carter tradition, first by performing and recording with her three daughters, and then by performing as a solo artist, making her recording career the longest continuous one in the history of America's music industry.

Although Maybelle Carter played many instruments, she was the guitarist for most of the Carter Family recordings. Her innovative and distinctive guitar playing included three different styles, including her most famous, and often imitated, "Carter Scratch." In addition to her guitar accompaniment, Maybelle Carter sang harmony; A. P. played violin at the beginning, then just sang bass harmony (as June Carter says, "coming in when the spirit moved him"); and Sara played autoharp and sang alto. Another contribution of the Carter Family was the innovative use of musical instruments—guitar and autoharp—in performing traditional tunes which had always been sung unaccompanied. Their simple, straightforward, melodic style made it possible for their original interpretations of traditional ballads and songs to be enjoyed and perpetuated in the United States. As folklorist Ralph Rinzler claims: "The incidence and continued popularity of numerous old ballads and folksongs in the contemporary country music repertoire, the very persistence of these songs, can surely be attributed to the fact that they were so firmly launched and so solidly established by the recorded performances of the Carter Family."

Woody Guthrie, one of the heroes of the folk movement, used Carter tunes for several of his best-known songs, including "This Land Is Your Land," "The Good Reuben James," and "The Big Grand Coulee Dam"; and as an instrumentalist, Guthrie was unquestionably influenced by Maybelle Carter's guitar techniques. Other urban revivalists, such as the Almanac Singers,

Pete Seeger, Odetta, and Bob Dylan, are indebted to the Carter Family, and their admiration has often been reflected in numerous recordings of Carter tunes. Joan Baez, for example, recorded "Little Moses" and "Wildwood Flower" on *Joan Baez* (Vanguard VRS-9078), "Engine 143" and "Little Darling, Pal of Mine" on *Joan Baez, Vol. 2* (Vanguard VRS-9094), and "Gospel Ship" on *Joan Baez in Concert* (Vanguard VSD-79308). Maybelle Carter humbly acknowledges the widespread admiration for the Carter Family, and she expresses an esteem for other folk and country artists: "I appreciate the interest all of 'em have taken in our music. There are quite a few folksingers that I love to hear, too, like Joan Baez. I have always loved her singing, and I've met others at folk festivals and I appreciate their music very much."

Twenty songs, originally recorded in 1938, have been reissued on the John Edwards Memorial Foundation project LP, *The Carter Family on Border Radio* (JEMF 101), and it includes some tunes that were never recorded commercially by the group. *Carter Family 1936 Radio Transcriptions* (Old Homestead 90045) includes sixteen tunes done during their Decca recording sessions; *The Carter Family, Volumes 1, 2, 3, and 4* (Country Music History CMH 107, CMH 112, CMH 116, and CMH 118) are reissues, with most cuts from 1935 to 1938; and a small label, Pine Mountain, has issued *Last Recordings* (Pine Mountain PMR 206) and *Gospel Album* (Pine Mountain 207). RCA Victor issued one album, *'Mid the Green Fields of Virginia* (LPM-2772); Decca put together *A Collection of Favorites by the Carter Family* (DL4404); and *The Original and Great Carter Family* (CAL586), *The Happiest Days of All* (ACL1-0501), and *My Old Cottage Home* (ACL1-0047) were released on the Camden label.

The bulk of their work has been issued by Columbia Records, including *Country Sounds of the Original Carter Family* (Harmony HL 7422), *The Famous Carter Family* (Harmony HS 11332), *Great Original*

*Recordings by the Carter Family* (Harmony HL 7300), *Give My Love to Rose* (Harmony KH 31256), *Historic Reunion* (CL 2561), which is an album of new recordings made by Sara and Maybelle Carter in 1966, *The Best of the Carter Family* (CS 9119), *I Walk the Line* (HS 11392), *Travelin' Minstrel Band* (KC 31454), *Mother Maybelle Carter* (two records) (KG 32436), and *Three Generations* (KC 33084).

A. P. Carter died on November 7, 1960, in his hometown of Maces Spring, Virginia. (*See also* The Addington Family; Joe and Janette Carter; June Carter; Maybelle Carter.)

## Anita Carter. *See* The Carter Family; June Carter; Maybelle Carter.

## A. P. Carter. *See* The Carter Family; Maybelle Carter.

## Helen Carter. *See* The Carter Family; June Carter; Maybelle Carter.

## Joe and Janette Carter

*Traditional singers, instrumentalists, and recording artists*

The son and youngest daughter of A. P. and Sara Carter, Joe Carter and Janette Carter Kelly sing in the tradition of the Original Carter Family, preserving their style of singing and playing and their authenticity of presentation.

As the second generation of Carters, Joe and Janette made occasional appearances with their parents and their aunt, Maybelle Carter. The Carter Family ideals were instilled in them as children, and although their sound is not an imitation of the Original Carter Family, the overtones can be heard. They play the actual autoharp and guitar that belonged to their parents, and there is a strong similarity between the guitar styles of Joe Carter and his Aunt Maybelle.

Joe Carter is also adept at playing fiddle, piano, and banjo; as a composer, he enjoys writing hymns. A carpentry foreman by trade, he keeps music as a sideline. Janette's vocals are strong, and when she is not accompanied by her brother on vocals and guitar, she accompanies herself on autoharp and guitar. The composition of religious material is not her forte; instead, she writes music of such diverse types as waltzes, blues, humorous and love songs.

Joe and Janette Carter have recorded several LPs: *Storms Are on the Ocean* (Birch Records 1949); *Howdayado!* (Traditional JC-573), a selection of some of the more obscure Carter Family tunes; and *Joe and Janette Carter* (County 706), which includes some Carter Family favorites, some songs from the Original Carter Family repertoire which were never recorded, and two original compositions by Sara, "I'm Going Home" and "Lonesome Blues." Janette Carter was also recorded on *Folk Festival of the Smokies, Volume II* (Traditional FFS-529), singing "I Ain't Gonna Work Tomorrow." (*See also* The Carter Family.)

# June Carter

*Country singer, songwriter, autoharpist, comedienne, performer, and recording artist*

One of Maybelle Carter's three daughters, June Carter was born with the deep-rooted musical heritage that has made her family some of America's foremost pioneers of folk and country music. From her early years with the Carter Family to the pursuit of her own singing career and performances with her husband Johnny Cash, June Carter has followed in the footsteps of a family tradition to establish her own reputation as a television, radio, and recording celebrity.

Born in Maces Spring, Virginia, on June 23, 1929, June Carter and her sisters, Anita and Helen, officially joined the Carter Family in 1939 when they went to San Antonio, Texas, to cut transcriptions for the Original Carter Family broadcasts over the Mexican border radio station XERA. In 1938 Anita went with her mother to Del Rio, Texas, and at the age of four she sang solos and duets with Maybelle Carter. By the following year, June and Helen were also singing and performing with their mother, as June Carter vividly recollects those early years: "When we went down to San Antonio, Texas, Helen, Anita, and I worked with the old Original Carter Family. As bad as we were, we played. That's just the way they were. You stood on your own two feet and you served your apprenticeship. Even if you couldn't play, you hung in there and did the best that you could. Mother always did that for us, she never allowed us to be like anybody else but tried to develop each of us as individuals.

"Helen played guitar, I played autoharp, and we sang as a trio. We did transcriptions three times a week, and they were sent all over the United States to different radio stations, but from the Mexican border stations, they came from XERA. I think that when the Carter Family was performing on those border stations, they were doing the best work that they ever did. My mother was playing better guitar than she ever played in her life. We had about ninety-nine songs. When I was just a tiny little thing, I was piping away on 'Last Railway to Heaven' and a whole bunch of songs."

Next, they went to Charlotte, North Carolina, where the old Carter Family performed a live radio show every morning on WBT. By 1943 Mother Maybelle Carter and the Carter Sisters were on their own; and they worked in Richmond, Virginia, for five years—at WRNL and later at WRVA.

"I had done a comedy character that I used to call Aunt Polly Carter, but I 'buried' her before mother, Anita, Helen, and I went to WNOX, Knoxville, Tennessee, in 1947. I became just June Carter at that point, and I

June Carter in her office at the House of Cash, Hendersonville, Tennessee

Cold Outside,' which was a great big pop hit for us back then. It was frustrating because we had a lot of offers but I wouldn't leave my family, so Homer and Jethro went with Spike Jones, and Chet Atkins came to work with us."

June continued to work with her mother and sisters in Knoxville, Springfield, and at the *Grand Ole Opry* in Nashville. In 1952 she married country singer Carl Smith, and, when her marriage broke up, she studied dramatics for two years in New York City. During this period, she was a guest singer on the television shows of Tennessee Ernie Ford, Jack Paar, Garry Moore, and Jackie Gleason. After getting a start of her own back in the fifties, June Carter remarried.

June Carter started working with Johnny Cash in 1961, and she wrote "The Matador" with him in 1963; in the same year, she and Merle Kilgore authored one of Johnny Cash's biggest hits, "Ring of Fire." Three years later, the three of them collaborated on "Happy to Be with You," which became another smash for Johnny Cash. In 1967 she recorded "Jackson" and "Guitar Pickin' Man" with Cash; and after her marriage of six years to Rip Nix had ended and Johnny Cash's first marriage broke up, they were married in March 1968. They now have a son, John Carter Cash. (*See also* The Carter Family; Maybelle Carter; Johnny Cash.)

did a lot of comedy as June Carter. Lowell Blanchard, who was the announcer for our show, helped me serve the greatest apprenticeship that I had to serve because he gave me a live radio show to play every day to an audience of about twelve hundred to eighteen hundred people who came in from the country; we did not prepare a script but worked on improvisations. So I learned to get laughs with actually no jokes at all, and it really broadened me as a performer.

"Mother, Helen, Anita, and I signed our first recording contract with RCA Victor, and we went to Atlanta to record. Then I did a trio act with Homer and Jethro, and we came to New York with Chet Atkins, the four of us on a train with my father. We did a tune for Victor, a parody on 'Baby, It's

# Maybelle Carter

*Original member of the Carter Family, singer, guitarist, autoharpist, songwriter, performer, and recording artist*

Maybelle Addington Carter is the romantic matriarch of traditional American folk music, and she has been called "The Queen of Country Music." As a pioneer of both folk and country music, Maybelle Carter has always been a proud exponent of her cultural heritage, and she has continued the unique Carter Family style throughout her career. Her work with the Carter Family

Maybelle Carter at the 1965 Newport Folk Festival

and as a solo artist has been revered for almost half a century, and her gentleness and warmth captivate audiences everywhere. "There is such a charm about her, and she is so real," her daughter June Carter says with affection, "she's still Maybelle Carter who came across the mountain to play guitar for the first time with the Carter Family."

Maybelle Addington was born on May 10, 1909, in Nickelsville, Virginia, in the southwestern corner near Tennessee, and June Carter describes her mother's background: "The Addingtons, like the Carters, were close-knit, religious people. I can remember my mother talking about my grandfather cutting the ice out of the river, and dragging it with the oxen, and putting it in the sawdust houses so there would be ice in the summertime.

"All the Addingtons were talented, they could all play."

Maybelle's mother played the five-string banjo, and her brothers played guitar and banjo. Dewey Addington had never played anywhere "outside of just picking on his front porch" until he was in his seventies and he went to a few festivals with his sister Maybelle Carter, his brother "Doc," and Carl McConnell. "Doc" Addington played guitar with banjoist Carl McConnell; they called themselves the Virginia Boys and frequently played with the Carter Family. "Uncle 'Doc' and Carl McConnell worked with us some in Richmond, and they sang and performed with us in our concert work in the high schools and in the old auditoriums," recalls June Carter. "In my early years, I can remember that we had no public-address systems, and just lamps across the front of the stage instead of electricity. I remember playing the commissaries in the old coal-mining towns, the schools, the churches, and the courthouses. These are my early years with the Carter Family and with Uncle 'Doc' and Carl as they were part of that group at certain times."

Maybelle played banjo, fiddle, and lute, but she is best known for her autoharp and guitar playing. There is a style of playing guitar named after her, the "Carter Scratch" or "Carter Family Lick," as described by June Carter: "I think one reason that my mother played the type of guitar that she played, the 'Carter Scratch,' was because many times when they had square dances, they didn't have enough music, and so she made her own. She would play the melody and then the rhythm at the same time. Billy Edd Wheeler noted the three different styles of guitar that my mother plays, and that she's always played. It's not just the 'Carter Scratch,' but a single style with the pick, and a blues style that she actually learned from a black man."

Maybelle Carter began her career with the Carter Family when she, A. P., and Sara recorded for Victor in Bristol, Tennessee, on August 2, 1927. She had married A. P.'s brother, Ezra J. Carter, on March 23, 1926, and their three daughters, Anita, Helen, and June, eventually joined Maybelle in performing and recording with the Carter Family.

In 1938 Maybelle took her four-year-old daughter Anita to Del Rio, Texas, when the Carter Family was working for the Consolidated Drug Company out of Chicago; and in 1939 Anita, Helen, and June went to San Antonio with the Carter Family to cut transcriptions for radio broadcast.

The Carter Family left Texas in 1941, and the following year they went to work at WBT Radio in Charlotte, North Carolina. After only six months, A. P. and Sara decided to retire; so, on June 1, 1943, Maybelle and her daughters went to work at WRNL in Richmond, Virginia, as June Carter explains: "Mother, Anita, Helen, and I started on our own in Richmond at WRNL Radio, and it was almost as if we had to start all over again because it was at this time that we became Mother Maybelle Carter and the Carter Sisters. My mother played guitar, Helen played the accordion. At that point, I still played the autoharp and the tenor guitar, and Anita played the bass fiddle. I remember that Anita had to stand on a chair to play it then. It was during this period at WRNL that my Uncle 'Doc' [Addington] and Carl McConnell performed with us."

Mother Maybelle Carter and the Carter Sisters worked at WRNL Radio from 1943 to 1946, and then they moved to another Richmond station, WRVA, for eighteen months. After a short stay at home, they traveled to Knoxville, Tennessee, where they worked at WNOX for almost a year. June Carter had been doing some comedy and singing on her own, and with Homer and Jethro, and Chet Atkins, but she rejoined her mother and sisters in 1948. At this time, Chet Atkins went to work with Mother Maybelle Carter and the Carter Sisters, and he went to Springfield, Missouri, with them to do a network show and another radio program every day.

In 1950 they went to Nashville, Tenneseee, which was one of the highlights of Maybelle Carter's career, and the last stop in her moves around the country: "We had finally sold our place in Virginia because I didn't figure that we would ever go back there to live, we had been gone so long. I said, 'If I ever get to the *Grand Ole Opry*, I'll never move again,' so I've been stuck here ever since!"

During the fifties the Carter Family toured abroad, and with Johnny Cash, whom Maybelle Carter respected and admired from the beginning, before he and her daughter June were married in 1968: "Johnny needed help when he was at his worst, or, as he would say, 'when he was a Cash.' He's Johnny now, but he was a Cash. We gave him a place to sleep and he lived with us off and on for two to three years, and we did everything that we could to try to get him straightened out. My husband always said, 'There's something good in that boy, and if we turn him away now, I don't know what's going to happen to him.' So we gave him a room and we let him come and go as he pleased, and I'm very proud of Johnny."

Maybelle Carter often tours with the Johnny Cash show, and she and the rest of the family continue to perform in the old Carter tradition, as told by June Carter: "Johnny had four daughters, I had two daughters, and we have a five-year-old son, John Carter Cash, and all our children are very devoted to one another. We're like a bunch of Gypsies, and we travel in a big group, and we encourage my mother to work and to come with us any date that Johnny Cash and I play because she's always welcome. I like to be with my mother and my sisters. Anita is married to Bob Wootton, who is John's guitarist, and that was a lucky break for us because when she married Bob Wootton, we got Anita, too."

Anita Carter has recorded several albums on her own, including *Anita Carter* (Mercury SR 60847) and *So Much Love* (Capitol ST-11085).

Although the Original Carter Family had recorded over three hundred songs for various record companies, an album was not put together until many years later. When Mother Maybelle Carter and the Carter Sisters were in Knoxville in 1947, a recording contract was signed with RCA Victor and an album was cut in Atlanta, Georgia. In addition to the Carter Family LPs, Maybelle Carter has been recorded as a solo artist on the Columbia label, *Mother Maybelle Carter* (KG 32436).

In 1970 the Original Carter Family was selected to become members of the Country Music Hall of Fame, and as one of the original members of the group, Maybelle Carter was honored with one of country music's most esteemed awards. This is only one of many tributes that has been bestowed upon this great, but humble, lady, as summarized by June Carter: "I'm very proud of my heritage. It's a great thing to hear almost any song and to be able to pick out all of the Carter Family someplace in that song. I can find a little bit of the Carter Family in almost any song that I hear. My mother was a pioneer of country music, but I like to call her a 'living antique,' because she's still very active. She's a beautiful lady, and Maybelle Carter is still the gentle Appalachian woman that she's always been."

With her deep concern for the preservation of traditional material, Maybelle Carter is largely responsible for the continuance of the American folk process: "We had a lot of old songs before we even recorded, a lot of old lyrics and pieces of songs. We wrote a lot of them and we put a lot of them together, which, if we hadn't done, many of them would have been lost forever, probably.

"Seems like the folk people like our songs, I guess they must like the type of material that we have. I've had a lot of people tell me that my guitar playing has influenced them to play guitar, and if they hadn't heard the records, they probably would never have played. Chet Atkins, Merle Travis, and several others have told me this, and I have heard that Floyd Cramer was influenced by my playing autoharp. I guess he thought, 'If she can do that on the autoharp, I can do it on the piano.'

"If I had it to do over, I'd do the same thing. I'm proud and happy that they like the style that we started. I think that folk music will never die because there are a lot of people in the world that like it and they will keep it alive. I know I like it because I was brought up on folk and country music and it's all that I've ever known." (*See also* The Addington Family; The Carter Family; June Carter.)

**Sara Carter.** *See* The Carter Family; Maybelle Carter.

# Johnny Cash

*Singer, guitartist, songwriter, performer, recording artist, and author*

"Hello, I'm Johnny Cash."

This one phrase is probably the most famous introduction of any entertainer in any field of music today. Johnny Cash is best known as a country singer, but his repertoire also includes folk and popular music.

Born on February 26, 1932, near Kingsland, Arkansas, John R. Cash was one of six children in a very poor family of sharecroppers. Hard work, religion, and music have always been important parts of his life. His background is rooted in the folk tradition, and the socioeconomic stature of his family is as representative of contemporary Southern life as the singing of old folk and gospel tunes. Both his parents and recordings by the Carter Family, Ernest Tubb, and Hank Williams provided him with a foundation of country music. He began writing songs at the age of twelve, and while he was in high school he sang on KLCN Radio in Blytheville, Arkansas. After his discharge from the air force in the mid-fifties, Cash teamed up with guitarist Luther Perkins and bass player Marshall Grant. Johnny Cash and his Tennessee Two recorded the first side of his first single in one take with his song, "Hey, Porter." That night he wrote, "Cry, Cry, Cry," which became side two of the single and got him a contract with Sun Records. The single became a hit, and it was soon followed by others, such as "Folsom Prison Blues," "So Doggone Lonesome," "There You Go," and "I Walk the Line." Later on, W. S. Holland joined the trio, and they became the Tennessee Three.

Cash signed with Columbia Records in 1958, and his first release, "Don't Take Your Guns to Town," sold over 500,000 copies.

Johnny Cash during a recording session in his own studio at the House of Cash, Hendersonville, Tennessee

Some of his other hits of the sixties include "Seasons of My Heart," "In the Jailhouse Now," "The Matador," "Ring of Fire," "Bad News," "It Ain't Me Babe," "The Ballad of Ira Hayes," "Understand Your Man," "Orange Blossom Special," "The Sons of Katie Elder," "Happy to Be with You," and "The One on the Right Is on the Left." Johnny Cash and June Carter were married on March 1, 1968, and together they recorded two hit records, "Jackson" and "Guitar Pickin' Man."

"I had a lot of rough years of working with Johnny Cash, just being a fellow entertainer and trying to get on the show and trying to be part of his show. I tried to help him to help himself get off drugs, and it would be great if I could say, 'I did it,' but I did not. He did it himself, and it takes a mighty man to turn away from drugs," June Carter explains with pride. "I started working with him in 1961, and after his marriage broke up and he finally began to bring himself together, we began to see that there was a chance that we might find some happiness in life. We were married in 1968 and we've had a very happy marriage."

Johnny Cash has recorded over twenty bestselling LPs on the Columbia label, six of which have become Gold Records: *Ring of Fire* (CS 8853); *I Walk the Line* (CS 8990); *Folsom Prison* (CS 9639); *Greatest Hits, Volume I* (CS 9478); *Johnny Cash at San Quentin* (CS 9827); and *Hello, I'm Johnny Cash* (KCS 9943). His recording career has run simultaneously with appearances on major network television and at folk festivals, clubs, and coffeehouses. From 1969 to 1971 he had his own television variety *Johnny Cash Show*.

On the main street of Hendersonville, just outside Nashville, Tennessee, there is a large plantation-style building that was originally designed as a dinner theater. The stage used to come into the center of what is now the recording studio of the House of Cash. BMI awards decorate the walls of June Carter's study to the right of the main entranceway, and, upstairs, the visitor encounters the conference room, with a long table surrounded by Gold Records from countries around the world. The House of Cash functions as the business extension of the entertainers' home, and June Carter has decorated it with elegant old pieces which have been purchased for each of their children.

Johnny Cash's contribution to the folk process is unique in that he is listened to and enjoyed by a wide audience—consisting of people from all walks of life—and one of his special talents has been to reach prisoners with his music.

Johnny Cash is an advisory committee member of the Peace Corps, the Country Music Association, and the John Edwards Memorial Foundation (JEMF). He composed the movie sound track for *I Walk the Line* and *Little Fauss and Big Halsy*; he is the sub-ject of the documentary films *Trial of Tears* and *Johnny Cash, the Man, His World, His Music*; and he had an acting role in the movie *A Gunfight*.

In 1975 his autobiography, *Man in Black*, was published by Zondervan Publishing House in Michigan. (*See also* June Carter; Maybelle Carter.)

# Johnny Castle. *See* The II Generation.

# The Chad Mitchell Trio

*Vocal group, performers, and recording artists*

At the height of the recent urban folk revival, the Chad Mitchell Trio was one of the most popular performing acts on the college campus circuit. The Chad Mitchell Trio successfully maintained its primary objective of entertaining (similar to the Kingston Trio) while offering satirical songs and material of social significance.

Mike Kobluk, Chad Mitchell, and Mike Pugh formed a singing group while sophomores at Gonzaga University in Spokane, Washington. In 1958, with the encouragement of Father Reinard Beaver (a priest who became their unofficial manager), they turned professional. The vocal trio was accompanied on banjo and guitar by another Gonzaga University student, (Roger) Jim McGuinn, who had toured with the Limeliters as an instrumentalist. The Chad Mitchell Trio traveled by car cross-country to New York, working in clubs along the way, and they made their official debut at the Blue Angel. It was not long before they signed a recording contract with Kapp Records and made personal appearances on radio (*Arthur Godfrey Show*), television (*Bell Telephone Hour*), and at Carnegie Hall, once with Harry Belafonte (on whose *Belafonte Returns to Carnegie Hall* [RCA LOC/LSO 6007] they appeared).

When Mike Pugh left the trio to return to Gonzaga University, he was replaced by Joe Frazier. The Chad Mitchell Trio made a number of major concert tours throughout the United States, and they went to South America on a trip sponsored by the U.S. State Department. Another recording contract was signed, and the Chad Mitchell Trio produced material for the Mercury label.

When Chad Mitchell departed from the trio in 1965 to pursue a solo career, the then-unknown John Denver was recruited as his replacement. The group's original name was changed to the Mitchell Trio, and more personnel changes ensued during the next few years. Joe Frazier left in 1967 and Mike Kobluk departed in the following year, replaced by David Boise and Mike Johnson. With none of the original members remaining, the trio was renamed Denver, Boise, and Johnson. After working with the Mitchell Trio for nearly four years, John Denver decided to strike out on his own, after Mike Johnson had left the group.

After a stint of personal and legal problems which brought his solo career to a halt, Chad Mitchell returned to the stage in late 1975. His initial attempt to follow a cabaret direction had been premature, and his discomfort in this capacity made it difficult for him to relate to his new audience. Although he worked sporadically in the Minneapolis area, it was not until his extended run at the Ballroom (a cabaret-restaurant in the SoHo district of New York City) that Chad Mitchell returned seriously to singing.

The Chad Mitchell Trio's output included *Mighty Day on Campus* (Kapp KL-1262); *The Chad Mitchell Trio at the Bitter End* (Kapp KL-1281), a production of Belafonte Enterprises, recorded live at the Bitter End on March 19, 1962; *The Chad Mitchell Trio* (Colpix Records SCP 411); and *Singin' Our Minds* (Mercury SR 60838/MG 20838). The Mitchell Trio, with David Boise, John Denver, and Mike Kobluk, recorded *The Mitchell Trio "Alive"* (Reprise R-6258). (*See also* John Denver.)

# Dillard Chandler

*Unaccompanied ballad singer, performer, and recording artist*

As one of America's few surviving representatives of the unaccompanied oral tradition, Dillard Chandler has made a significant contribution to traditional music and the folk process. John Cohen is largely responsible for public familiarization with the singer from the mountains of North Carolina; and in the early 1970s Cohen made a documentary film, *The End of an Old Song*, which focused on Chandler's life-style and singing and the perpetuation of ballads.

An old log building was the site of his birth in Marshall, Madison County, North Carolina. His education was short-lived, as he started working at an early age. Since his first logging job, Chandler has been employed in many capacities, including construction and yard work, farming, and odd jobs.

The Smoky Mountain region of North Carolina has always been a source of traditional music, and Dillard Chandler's background is rich in ballads and old-timey tunes. The first songs that he sang were old-timey meeting songs which he learned when folks gathered at molasses-making time or to shuck corn, and whiskey was shared as everyone sang or danced to the sound of banjos. With the advents of radio, television, and tape recorders, the isolation of these traditions was decreased, but Dillard Chandler exemplifies the existence of this living, ongoing process.

Chandler sings with a methodical and relaxed slowness, and his personalized style of rendering a ballad creates a proximity with his music. He delineates arhythmically, emphasizing certain emotional aspects and selected parts of the story within the song. Chandler's distinctive stylization is rooted in versions of the old ballads as sung by his father, mother, and uncle; with only slight variations, each of the ballads has been carried on and on, from one generation to the next. The tunes remain the same, and only the vocal inflection of each singer decorates a song to yield different results.

Chandler has stayed in the mountains for most of his life and worked in and around the Asheville area. In 1967 he traveled to the University of Chicago Folk Festival, which was the farthest away from home he had been since his induction in the army at Fort Jackson, North Carolina, and his earlier logging days in the nearby states of Tennessee, South Carolina, and Georgia.

Dillard Chandler has been recorded by Folkways Records, and he appears on a Rounder Records LP of banjo tunes and ballads collected by John Cohen, entitled *High Atmosphere* (Rounder 0028), which includes Lloyd Chandler and Dell Norton, with whom Chandler sang on occasion, and E. C. Ball, Fred Cockerham, George Lander, Sidna Myers, Frank Proffitt, and Wade Ward.

# Len Chandler

*Singer, guitarist, composer, poet, topical songwriter for radio, founder and codirector of Alternative Chorus–Songwriters Showcase, performer, and recording artist*

A preeminent figure in the recent folk revival of the late 1950s to mid-1960s, Len Chandler shared the limelight with many of this country's best-known folk personalities. He appeared at the major folk festivals, including Newport, Philadelphia, and Mariposa, and in concert at Carnegie and Town halls in New York City.

Len Hunt Chandler, Jr., was born on May 27, 1935, in Akron, Ohio, and he started playing piano at the age of nine, as he describes: "My father was in the army, and my mother bought me a little plastic flute with eight holes in it, and I played songs on it until I ran out of range. I wanted to play this one song, but the instrument didn't have enough notes, so I cut two holes in it to get the two higher notes that I needed; so my mother wrote to my father to tell him that

Len Chandler at the 1965 Newport Folk Festival

she thinks that I ought to start taking music lessons, and he suggested the piano as a foundation. When I was about twelve I started playing classical music, and I played at church and at women's organizations, and so on. When I got to high school, I wanted to join the band, and the only instrument left was the oboe, so I learned to play that, and by my senior year I was playing in the University of Akron orchestra. In high school I had a little singing group, and the first thing that I ever wrote was a commercial for the school's yearbook, and it was a parody based on a popular tune. It was so successful and they played it through the PA system, and all the kids stopped and listened to it, and then I became the school's jingle writer, and every time there was an event, I would write the commercial or song that was broadcast over the school radio. I wrote my senior class song in high school, and I decided to keep writing a lot of tunes from that point on.

"I wasn't interested in folk music at the time—it was the middle of the McCarthy era and my exposure to folk music was very limited. In college, an English professor took me home with him and for the first time I heard Furry Lewis, Bukka White, Josh White, Leadbelly, and chain-gang songs, and Bessie Smith and Bessie Jones of the Georgia Sea Island Singers; and, in essence, Walter Lehrman turned me on to American folk music.

"I got a five-hundred-dollar scholarship by winning a contest in a competition for 'Advanced Orchestral Instrumentalist,' and I played a piece based on two folk songs, and, later on in my life, I did a series of six concerts with the New Jersey Symphony Orchestra that was based on folk music as thematic material for classical works; and the same piece that had originally gotten me to New York, 'The Winter's Past,' was played by the orchestra after I sang the folk songs 'Wayfaring Stranger' and 'Black Is the Color of My True Love's Hair.'

"I went to New York and made arrangements to enroll in the MA summer school program at Columbia, and I got a job as an elevator operator at Columbia. After that, I secured a job as a counselor for neglected children at St. Barnabas House, in Greenwich Village. This is where I met my wife, and we took care of twenty kids between us; she had ten girls and I had ten boys, and we'd go to Washington Square Park with the kids and it was there that I started seeing people like Dave Van Ronk and other folksingers playing their guitars and totally involved in folk music.

"I started borrowing other people's guitars, in the park, and learning more and

more chords and folk songs; and then I would play the folk songs for the children in St. Barnabas House. After I failed to get a teaching certificate because I was a terrible speller, Hugh Romney asked me and two other poets to come to New Haven to play my guitar and to sing some songs for twenty-five dollars, and then he asked me to play with him at the Gaslight. It was mainly a scene for poets, and there wasn't much happening for singers, except for me, at that time. A Detroit television executive saw me there and hired me for a gig in Detroit, so I went there for eighteen weeks, and then I came back to New York.

"At that point, everybody had music, and it was a really high-energy folk music scene. People would play a set and then walk across the street and hear somebody else, and they would trade songs and make different arrangements of songs. I had an arrangement with the Gaslight that I would work when I was in town, and I would give them a month's notice when I was leaving so that they could get somebody else. I was the only singer at the Gaslight for a long time, and then it started going from a poet scene to a music scene around 1960.

"The Gaslight was weird then because there were air shafts up to the apartments and the windows of the Gaslight would open into the air shafts, so when people would applaud, the neighbors would get disturbed and call the police. So then the audience couldn't applaud; they had to snap their fingers instead. So finally they cemented up the air shafts, and they got microphones, and started getting slicker and slicker, and then they expanded; but the club owners still insisted that you couldn't get paid, so they would hire a girl to carry a cornucopia to collect money for us at the door after you played, and she got ten percent of what she collected in the basket.

"The whole Village scene was very heavy, and there were people like Noel Stookey, who was doing sound effects like the sound of a flushing toilet, and singing folk songs, and, eventually, songs that he wrote; then he started rehearsing with Mary Travers and Peter Yarrow. Tom Paxton started coming in from New Jersey, where he was in the army, and he played a nylon string guitar.

"I would be playing at the Bitter End for two weeks and then at the Gaslight for four, and then I would be going out of town for twenty weeks to Toronto, Ottawa, Winnipeg, Saskatchewan, and playing four weeks at each place and then back to New York.

"By 1962, the civil rights movement was under way, and I wrote my first topical song about a bus accident that happened in Greeley, Colorado, and then I started writing many songs about the freedom riders and sit-ins. I was invited to a conference in Atlanta for freedom writers and singers of the North and South, and Tom Paxton and Phil Ochs went, too.

"I started becoming very involved in the freedom movement, and people started asking me to play at demonstrations and rallies, and I began to be known as a topical or protest songwriter."

While he was in the South, Chandler was approached by the director of KRLA Radio in Los Angeles, and he was asked to write some songs related to the Laud's County Alabama Original Black Panther Party, which was the basis for an NBC-TV documentary. Shortly thereafter, Chandler flew to California to write three songs a day for a year for the KRLA show, *Credibility Gap*, and the songs were about each day's news. He then worked for KCET and composed seven songs a week for a thirteen-week summer program called *Newsical Muse Show*.

In 1971 Chandler initiated and acted as codirector with John Braheny of the Alternative Chorus–Songwriters Showcase, which was patterned after *Broadside* hoots in Greenwich Village, where young talent like Janis Ian first performed "Society's Child." The Showcase was held at Ed Pearl's Ash Grove, and then it was moved to Lincoln Center West. Capitol Records donated a studio with technicians for three hours an evening for about a year and a half, and the Showcase then moved to Art Laboe's club for over a year, and then back to the old Ash Grove, now called the Improvisation.

As a result of the Showcase, over three hundred writers have been signed to recording and publishing contracts, and several of the artists have had their records make it to the top-forty chart. Each week, personalities are interviewed, including heads of the major publishing companies, program directors of every major radio station in Los Angeles, talent acquisition directors of major record companies, reviewers of all the trade magazines, such as *Rolling Stone*, *Billboard*, and *Cashbox*, and other writers and performers.

Len Chandler has recorded for Folkways, Broadside, FM, Blue Thumb, King Records, and Columbia. He is associate editor of *Umbra Poetry Anthology*, and his poems have been published in anthologies.

# Harry Chapin

*Contemporary singer-songwriter, guitarist, banjoist, harp player, performer, recording artist, theatrical composer, and filmmaker*

Harry Chapin is revered as a storyteller of modern tales that unfold in a musical medium. Some of his best-known ballads are "Taxi," "W*O*L*D," and "What Made America Famous" (a key number from his New York production of an original musical, *The Night That Made America Famous*). Written by and starring Harry Chapin, *The Night That Made America Famous* was the first show ever to have been allotted a six-figure media budget, and it was described by its creator as "a meeting place of a musical multimedia and a rock concert."

Harry Chapin was born on December 7, 1942, and he and his three brothers were raised in Greenwich Village. He grew up with music as his father, James Chapin, had been a drummer during the Big Band era and he shared with his family his love for

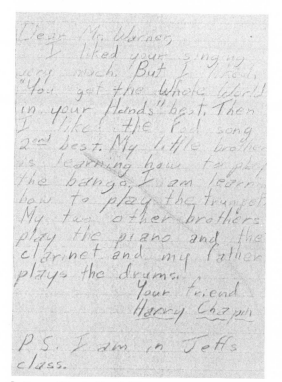

Letter written to Frank Warner by Harry Chapin
when he was in the fifth grade

Brothers recorded an album on the Classic Editions label, in 1966.

Chapin then became involved in the motion picture industry as a film packer (loading reels into crates), a film editor, and, eventually, a filmmaker. He wrote and directed a documentary entitled *Legendary Champions*, which was nominated for an Academy Award and won prizes at the New York and Atlanta film festivals.

After seven years of filmmaking, in the spring of 1971 Harry Chapin decided to return to music, and proceeded to organize another band with Ron Palmer, Tim Scott, and John Wallace. They rented the Village Gate for over three months to polish up their skills as musicians and entertainers, and by the time Harry Chapin signed with Elektra Records, he was working with a well-seasoned band.

His dramatic ballad "Taxi" was included among the selections on his first solo album, *Heads and Tales* (Elektra 75023), and when

Harry Chapin (right) with Pete Seeger at the Huntington, Long Island, PAF Benefit Concert held on January 3, 1976

this art form. When the Chapins moved to Brooklyn Heights, Harry became a member of the Brooklyn Heights Boys Choir, along with Robert Lamm (later with the rock group Chicago) and John Wallace, who was to rejoin his boyhood friend in the sixties as the bassist in his band. As a teenager, Chapin started playing classical trumpet but soon switched to guitar and banjo. When his eldest brother decided to put music aside, Harry Chapin and his brothers Tom and Steve pursued their interest and often played together.

After graduating from high school, Chapin attended the Air Force Academy for a brief time and then studied architecture and philosophy at Cornell. Starting in the summer of 1964, Harry Chapin started performing with his father and two younger brothers. Before the threat of the draft prompted the group to disband, the Chapin it was released as a single, "Taxi" became a smash hit on both AM and FM radio. *Sniper and Other Love Songs* (Elektra 75042) and *Short Stories* (Elektra 75065) were followed by the release of another single, "W*O*L*D" (from his third LP), which became his second major AM radio hit. Before the opening, in February 1975, of his musical *The Night That Made America Famous*, a selection from his next album, *Verities & Balderdash* (Elektra 7E-1012), was issued, and "What Made America Famous" stirred up enthusiasm for his upcoming Broadway production.

Harry Chapin composed the music and lyrics for "The Night That Made America Famous," which ran for seven weeks in New York City. He also played one of the leading roles in the show. Commenting on *The Night That Made America Famous*, he said: "It was an attempt to join the American music theater with more conventional theater. The show was part theater, part concert, and part multimedia experience."

Chapin performs about a hundred concerts each year, mostly with his band, which currently includes Steve Chapin, Howie Fields, Michael Masters, Doug Walker, and John Wallace; he "does benefits alone" or with his brothers; and in 1975 he raised $350,000 for various charity institutions. Harry Chapin is a frequent guest on such network television programs as *Merv Griffin* and *The Midnight Special*. *Portrait Gallery* (Elektra 7E-1041) is his fifth, and most recent, album.

## Milt Chapman. *See* The Gateway Trio.

## Lonnie Chatmon. *See* The Mississippi Sheiks.

## Sam Chatmon

*Blues singer, guitarist, performer, and recording artist*

A celebrated blues veteran "rediscovered" during the recent urban folk revival, Sam Chatmon is known by some as the last survivor of the Chatmon family band and by others for his more recent solo performances and *The Mississippi Sheik* (Blue Goose 2006). The Chatmon name is also associated with one of the top black recording groups of the 1930s, the Mississippi Sheiks, which was a blues duo consisting of Sam Chatmon's brother Lonnie and guitarist Walter Vinson. In recent years, an attempt was made to recreate their sound by bringing together Ted Bogan, Sam Chatmon, Carl Martin, and Walter Vinson, as the New Mississippi Sheiks, and an album by the same name was issued by Rounder Records (Rounder 2004).

Sam Chatmon and his eleven siblings were introduced to music through their fiddler father, who raised his children in South Mississippi. Seven of the ten Chatmon brothers played together as a family band until 1928, when four of its members left for the Delta region. Lonnie Chatmon joined up with Walter Vinson to form the Mississippi Sheiks, and today the duo is probably best known for Vinson's "Sittin' on Top of the World." Two record companies have reissued recordings made between 1930 and 1935 by the Mississippi Sheiks: *Sittin' on Top of the World* (Biograph BLP 12041), with the Beale Street Sheiks of Memphis on the album's flip side, and *Stop and Listen Blues* (Mamlish S-3804).

The vocal and guitar stylings of Sam Chatmon are derived from localized rural techniques typical of his area of the country. Like the Mississippi Sheiks, he plays a broad range of material; his repertoire includes many rare folk songs that predate the blues, and songs popularized by another Chatmon brother, Bo Carter, who was a prominent blues recording artist in the thirties.

Sam Chatmon has toured coast to coast in the past decade, and his music has been heard from the San Diego Folk Festival in California to the National Folk Festival in Virginia.

## The Chieftains

*Irish instrumental group, performers, and recording artists*

Described in *Time* (January 12, 1976) as "Ireland's leading folk band," the Chieftains have sparked a transatlantic interest in their country's traditional music as played on Irish traditional instruments—Uilleann (elbow) pipes, tin whistle (or pennywhistle), tin and concert flutes, bodhran (a large hand-held goatskin drum), concertina, fiddle, Irish harp, and animal bones (used in a castanet-like fashion). The seven-man instrumental ensemble has recently brought to the attention of pop music listening audiences music which has been one of the staples of Irish culture for centuries.

Although the Chieftains have been recording as a group for about fifteen years and have long been regarded with esteem in Irish-folk circles, it was not until the mid-1970s that they achieved significant widespread recognition. The group's leader, Paddy Moloney, is regarded as one of the world's top pipers and a distinguished songwriter, and he has been recorded both with and without the Chieftains. In an interview published in *Folkscene* (February 1976, Vol. 3, No. 11), he gives a brief history of the Chieftains: "During the 50's we sort of knew one another. We played together in twos and threes. In 1960 we joined up with Seán O'Riada and his group called Ceoltoiri Chualanin. As The Chieftains, we wanted to do our own sort of thing. We got our name 'The Chieftains' from the poet John Montague, and his poem 'Death of a Chieftain.' We continued on as The Chieftains and in Ceoltoiri Chualanin on a completely separate basis." When Ceoltoiri Chualanin disbanded a few years ago, the Chieftains continued playing and developing as a group. With the signing of a managing contract in January 1975 with Jo Lustig, the Chieftains embarked on a more encompassing schedule, which, to date, has included several sell-out personal appearances at the Albert Hall in London, a global concert tour, performance of the musical score for Stanley Kubrick's film *Barry Lyndon*, and a recording contract with America's Island Records for their fifth effort, *The Chieftains* (Island ILPS-9334)—thus expanding their market, established when they were recording artists on the Claddagh label.

Four of the original Chieftains—Martin Fay, Paddy Moloney, Seán Potts, and Michael Tubridy—added to their ranks Peadar Mercier in 1967, Seán Keane in 1968, and Derek Bell in 1972, and the seven musicians were joined by Ronnie McShane on bones on their most recent album. With the generation of new interest in Irish traditional music, "it sort of proves the point," says Moloney, "that we have a very strong music that gets across to people." And, adds Moloney, "there are miniature Chieftain groups all over the place now."

## Francis J. Child

*Scholar, folklorist, educator, and author*

Almost a century ago, Francis J. Child, the ambitious offspring of a Boston sailmaker, changed the face of folk song scholarship by classifying and numbering more than three hundred ballads in the five-volume set *The English and Scottish Popular Ballads*, commonly referred to as the Child Ballads. With a specific interest in the poetic content of the verses of the traditional folk ballad, this Harvard professor of English compiled a major and revolutionary songbook which is considered the basic yardstick of reference in the study of folk music in the twentieth century.

Francis James Child was born on February 1, 1825, in Boston, Massachusetts. Through the acquisition of scholarships, he was able to attend Harvard University, where he earned a degree in 1846. He developed an interest in Romantic poetry during his postgraduate studies in Germany, and at the age of twenty-six became a professor at Harvard, remaining there for the rest of his life.

His international reputation was established by his early studies in literature and poetry, and in 1857 he was selected to work on a series involving British poets, resulting in the publication of *English and Scottish Ballads* in 1858. Child became very excited about the relationship between Anglo-Scottish poetry and ballads, but he was displeased with the limited amount of time allotted for the project by the publisher. At this point in his career, he decided to pursue a more comprehensive study of the subject, and embarked on his lifelong work of preserving all existing traditional material before it was lost forever in the progress of the nineteenth century.

He modeled his work after the method used by the Danish ballad editor Svend Grundtwig, and began by acquiring an earlier compilation of traditional ballads, *Reliques of Ancient English Poetry*, by Bishop Percy. When in 1872 he received a letter encouraging him to attempt a thorough and critical edition on the subject, he went to contract with a publishing firm and devoted himself to the realization of his goal.

Francis J. Child collected the bulk of his material from printed sources, and although some ballads were overlooked or ignored (he considered the bawdiness of some unsuitable for publication), his inclusive and qualitative standards provided a model for subsequent collections and scholarly works. He completed the initial part of his work in 1882, and for the next few years concentrated on the compilation of only authentic material. While he managed to finish this monumental task before his death on September 11, 1896, it was not until 1898 that the final volume in the series was published.

The complete collection of 305 traditional ballads was printed first in ten parts and then as a five-quarto volume set entitled *The English and Scottish Popular Ballads.* Today, his name and a catalog number from his collection (for example, "The Half-Hitch," which appears in the Child Ballads as "The Marriage of Sir Gawain" [Child 31]), are commonly mentioned in the discussion of the ballad, and are used repeatedly in record notes and in other printed matter on folk music.

# The Clancy Brothers

*Irish-American vocal and instrumental group, performers, and recording artists*

The Clancy Brothers, either with or without Tommy Makem, have been a part of the American folk music scene since the mid-1950s, and for the past twenty years they have remained active as musicians while simultaneously pursuing individual careers. All of the Clancys, Patrick (Paddy), Tom, and Liam, as well as Tommy Makem, are highly regarded for their achievements in the theater; but like many other performers and groups that got their start during the folk boom, the Clancy Brothers and Tommy Makem became part of the folk circuit from Carnegie Hall to the Royal Albert Hall in London.

Born in Carrick-on-Suir, Ireland, the Clancys got interested in folk music at home, mostly through their parents, as told by Liam Clancy: "It was always there, of course, at home and then through hearing on radio people like Burl Ives. I remember, one day, hearing 'Froggie Went A-Courtin' ' and running down to my mother and telling her that there was someone on the radio singing our song, but it was a different version because she used to sing it as 'There Was a Frog Lived in the Well.'

"There was an interest in traditional Irish music which was fostered to a great extent by the BBC at the time, and every Sunday morning we avidly listened to their program called *As I Roved Out*, and there were many people in Dublin who were involved in the revival, like Colm O'Lochlainn, Seamus Ennis, Donagh McDonagh, Ciaran Mac-Mathuna, and others.

"We started to pick up songs that we didn't have at home, and then I began to play. When a friend of Alan Lomax and Jean Ritchie—Diane Hamilton—came over to Ireland on a collecting trip, I was one of the things that she collected! I traveled throughout Ireland, England, and Scotland with her, and because we had lived in a rather Anglicized part of the country, I had never realized the value of Irish music because I'd never seen much of it in our hometown.

"In the meantime, my brother Paddy had started a record company, Tradition Records, in New York, and he and Tom were living there and running the Cherry Lane Theater, putting on mostly Irish plays. Paddy had formed Tradition Records around 1956, which is the year that I came over to New York with my head full of songs and traditional music.

"I spent some time collecting music down South, in Virginia, North Carolina, and South Carolina, gathering everything from instrumentals to blues and gospel to traditional Irish, English, and Scottish music that had been kept alive in the Southern mountains. So I found a tremendous number of songs that were almost identical to songs that I had heard in Ireland. Paul Clayton was studying at the University of North Carolina, and he was one of the people who led us around down South.

"Ken Goldstein, who was one of the founders of Tradition Records, talked us

into doing an album of rebel songs, so we recorded it in his Bronx apartment with his wife Rochelle keeping her hand over their child's mouth."

As Tommy Makem recalls: "There was accompaniment on only a couple of songs, with Paddy playing harmonica and Jack Keenan on guitar, and *The Rising of the Moon* [TLP 1006] was our first album together. The following year, we did an album of drinking songs called *Come Fill Your Glass with Us* [TLP 1032], with guitar and banjo accompaniment by Jack Keenan, and he was terrific."

Liam Clancy further explains: "Our drinking spot was the White Horse Tavern, which was also frequented by people like Theodore Bikel and Josh White, and we used to have great nights in there. Out of this grew the idea to do an album of drinking songs, which we recorded in a theater on New York's Lower East Side, and from that point on, we kept getting inquiries as to whether or not we would sing in clubs, which we thought, of course, was ridiculous, because Tommy and I were actors, Paddy was running Tradition Records, and Tommy [Makem] had just come down from Dover, New Hampshire, to visit us, and he got into the theater as well, but he and I actually started singing together.

"We played a nightclub out in Chicago, Alan Ribback's Gate of Horn, and even though we had tried to find a name for ourselves, we failed to come up with one. When we arrived, they had up on the billboard, 'The Clancy Brothers and Tommy Makem,' so the name stuck.

"Shortly afterwards, we went into a nightclub in New York, called the Blue Angel, and the Ed Sullivan people picked us up, and that was probably the most important thing that happened as far as our singing career was concerned. We were supposed to do a ten-minute spot on the *Ed Sullivan Show*, and I don't remember who the big star was that night, but whoever it was, he got sick, so we were told live, on air, to improvise another ten minutes. So we ended up with twenty minutes out of the hour on *Ed Sullivan*, in front of fifty million people, and suddenly we were in business. We just took off from there.

"Folk music was in full swing and we were the Irish contingent of it, but the most exciting times were going back to Ireland and discovering the impact that our music had had there. The songs that had been kind of forgotten or had only been known in books were suddenly alive again, so the Irish were really rediscovering their own music through the touch of Americana that we added by bringing guitar, banjo, and pennywhistle to the traditionally unaccompanied music."

Tommy Makem explains his leaving the Clancys: "In April of 1969, I decided that I wanted to do some things on my own. It was a very amicable parting of the ways, we're still very good friends and get together once in a while, and the boys are still going on."

Liam Clancy continues: "After Tommy [Makem] left the group, we continued under different forms for a few years, but we were all a bit tired of the traveling. Our lives had changed. We got married, Paddy had bought a farm and settled down in Ireland to work on it. Tom returned to acting, and he's shooting a movie down in Mexico now, and I have a TV series on folk music called *The Liam Clancy Show*, and it runs a half an hour every week as a semi–talk show with different performers.

"Every now and then we still do a few concerts. We've been doing Philharmonic Hall for the last few years, and we've done either Philharmonic Hall or Carnegie Hall every year for fifteen years."

Each of the Clancys has pursued individual careers while actively engaged in performing and recording as a group. Patrick Clancy has traveled extensively, produced and acted in some plays, and has had many occupations over the years, including editing and arranging songs for Folkways and Elektra and forming Tradition Records. Tom Clancy is a well-known actor; he has worked with a Shakespearean repertory company and appeared in over 150 roles on Broadway, including his highly acclaimed performance in Eugene O'Neill's *Moon for the Misbegotten*. The youngest of the brothers, Liam Clancy, collected folk material for Tradition Records; acted with the Poet's Theater in Cambridge, Massachusetts; and has been seen acting, singing, and playing harmonica on television shows and on theater stages.

The Clancy Brothers and Tommy Makem have made numerous recordings on the Tradition, Columbia, Vanguard, and Audio-Fidelity labels. Their sister has also recorded a solo LP of Irish music, entitled *Peg Clancy Power* (Folk-Legacy FSE-8). (*See also* Tommy Makem.)

## Liam Clancy. *See* The Clancy Brothers.

## Patrick Clancy. *See* The Clancy Brothers.

## Tom Clancy. *See* The Clancy Brothers.

## Gene Clark. *See* The Byrds; The New Christy Minstrels.

## Mike Clarke. *See* The Byrds.

## Paul Clayton

*Singer, composer, guitarist, dulcimer player, collector, author, performer, and recording artist*

Born on March 3, 1933, in the whaling port of New Bedford, Massachusetts, Paul Clayton developed his interest in folk music as a result of his familial sailing heritage.

Paul Clayton performing at Caffé Lena, Saratoga Springs, New York, in autumn 1963

completion of his undergraduate work at the University of Virginia, he became a popular performer at concerts and festivals, and by the mid-fifties had begun a recording career which was to bring him representation on six commercial record labels, in the Archive of Folk Song, the Flanders Ballad Collection at Middlebury College, Vermont, and in the BBC's private recording files.

Clayton collected extensively in the South, and during the fifties he made a collecting tour with Liam Clancy, who spent time in Virginia, North Carolina, and South Carolina gathering instrumentals, ballads, blues, and gospel music. During the fifties and sixties Clayton's reputation as a young professional folksinger spread nationally and internationally, and he became part of the Greenwich Village scene during the folk boom. He was among the first to perform at Gerde's Monday night hoots, a showcase which boasted appearances by such notables as Bob Dylan, Dave Van Ronk, Len Chandler, Judy Collins, Tom Paxton, Jack Elliott, and Arlo Guthrie.

During the early sixties a controversy arose regarding Dylan's use of a tune that had been collected by Clayton on one of his trips to Appalachia. The melody of Dylan's "Don't Think Twice, It's All Right" is based on Clayton's discovery, "Who'll Buy Your Chickens When I'm Gone"; and although the tune is legally in the public domain, many felt that Clayton deserved some measure of credit for its usage. Possibly by way of compensation, Dylan invited Clayton to accompany him on a cross-country, expenses-paid tour in 1964, but whether or not he was paid by Dylan is not known. Although it is denied by Dylan, his friends claim that he composed "It's All Over Now, Baby Blue" as a symbolic termination of his close relationship with Paul Clayton.

Clayton recorded eight discs for Folkways; *Whaling and Sailing Songs from the Days of Moby Dick* (Tradition 1005), reissued by Everest Records; and several LPs on other labels such as Riverside, Elektra, Monument, and Stinson.

From the sea shanties and whaling songs which he learned from his grandfather, Clayton went on to collect and record folk songs of every nature which he found in his travels throughout the United States, in Canada, Cuba, and various European countries.

Both his parents played instruments, and they encouraged their son to take an interest in music. Clayton played the guitar before he was in his teens, and as a high school sophomore wrote, produced, and performed on a fifteen-minute hometown radio program. He attended the University of Virginia, studying with folklorist Professor Arthur Kyle Davis, and started collecting Southern Appalachian ballads. His education was often disrupted by travels to Europe and Great Britain, and he made appearances on a BBC-TV series about folk music. After

After a history of a problem with pills, Paul Clayton took his life on March 30, 1967, and his death brought to light the fine tension between artistic creativity and insanity.

# Clearwater
*Hudson River sloop built for the ecological and educational project of Hudson River Sloop Restoration, Incorporated (HRSR)*

The sloop *Clearwater* was designed and built as a restoration effort to raise funds and to educate the general public to help save the Hudson River from ecological misuse and ruin. The *Clearwater* has sailed along the Hudson, stopping at various ports to solicit donations and to provide entertainment by its crew of folk musicians, who have joined together to share a temporary sailor's life as a means of supporting a worthy cause.

In 1965 Pete Seeger and folksinger Victor Schwartz began researching the project by reading about Hudson River sloops, and their early interest in this field inspired the construction of the *Clearwater* and the formation of its parent organization, Hudson River Sloop Restoration, Incorporated (HRSR). In the summer of 1970, NET-TV filmed a special program about the *Clearwater*, and millions of television viewers learned of this project, thus increasing interest and drawing attention to the goals of HRSR.

In the next five years, the *Clearwater* saw a rise and fall in its continued pursuits; but by 1975 it had reached another peak with the release of an album, *Clearwater* (Sound House PS 1001B/SR0104), with selections by members of the crew: Tony Barrand, Gordon Bok, Jimmy Collier, Jon Eberhart, John Ebert, Mark Gamma, Louis Killen, Bob Killian, Rev. F. D. Kirkpatrick, Tim McGinness, Don McLean, Ed Renehan, John Roberts, Pete Seeger, Keith Sullivan, Andy Wallace, Jeff Warner, Peter Willcox, and Lorre Wyatt. Also included with the album is a descriptive booklet, with sketches

of the *Clearwater* and its crew by Rita Hurault. The songs on the LP range from traditional to sailor's songs, contemporary songs, and satirical tunes; and, due to the lack of sufficient space afforded by one twelve-inch disc, another album is in preparation.

# Vassar Clements
*Country fiddler, performer, and recording artist*

A twenty-five-year veteran of fiddle playing, Vassar Clements was first brought to the attention of the pop world in 1972 through his work on the Nitty Gritty Dirt Band's classic *Will the Circle Be Unbroken*. Since then, he and his new band have been working college and club dates—leaving behind the "corn-pone circuit"—and rousing audiences everywhere with their broad repertoire of country, blues, rock, bluegrass, and western swing.

Born on April 25, 1928, near Kinard, South Carolina, Vassar Clements received his early music education by listening to the *Grand Ole Opry* during his boyhood in Florida. His first instrument was the guitar, but he switched over to the fiddle when he was chosen by the local band, with which he was playing, to change to the instrument for which he is now so famous. In the following year, when he was fourteen years old, Vassar Clements traveled to Nashville to audition for the fiddle vacancy in Bill Monroe's Blue Grass Boys. It was not long before the young fiddler was appearing on Music City's *Opry* stage.

He played with the legendary Bill Monroe intermittently for seven years, followed by a period of relative musical inactivity. Personal problems caused him to stop touring from 1962 to 1967, but he still played, on occasion, with friends (for two years he played tenor banjo, in Tallahassee, Florida). After working as a real estate salesman, mechanic, and operator of a potato chip franchise, Vassar Clements returned to

Nashville in 1967 in a second attempt at a professional music career. In 1968 he started his move toward recognition by touring with John Hartford, Faron Young, and the Earl Scruggs Revue until late 1972. For the past several years, he has been the guest fiddler with musicians representing many fields, appearing in concert with the Grateful Dead, the Nitty Gritty Dirt Band, and, most recently, with Dick Betts of the Allman Brothers Band.

Vassar Clements has recorded with over seventy acts, including Roy Acuff, the Allman Brothers, the Byrds, the Grateful Dead, Tom T. Hall, Kris Kristofferson, Gordon Lightfoot, Paul McCartney, the Nitty Gritty Dirt Band, Linda Ronstadt, Doc Watson, and Bob Wills. Rounder Records has issued a solo LP entitled *Crossing the Catskills* (Rounder 0016), which is the first attempt devoted to his characteristic style, with accompaniment by David Bromberg, Everett Allan Lilly, and Mike Melford. In 1975 Mercury Records issued his debut LP on that label, *Vassar Clements* (Mercury SRM-1-1022), featuring Jeff Hanna and John McEuen of the Nitty Gritty Dirt Band, Charlie Daniels, and John Hartford, among other, followed by *Superbow* (Mercury SRM-1-1058). The Dirt Band's *Circle* LP had made it possible for the virtuoso fiddler to be given a free rein in selecting the material and musical styles for his own albums.

Still playing his 240-year-old fiddle, Vassar Clements is directing his energies to his band and developing a diversity of musical styles, changing instruments, and getting close to rock.

## Sara Cleveland

*Traditional singer, performer, and recording artist*

In many respects, the life and musical career of this Brant Lake, New York, resident are typical of other traditional singers of the Northeast, but what makes Sara Cleveland's contribution to folk music so special is her vast repertoire of over four hundred songs.

Born on January 1, 1905, in Hartford, New York, Sara Jane Creedon learned most of her songs from members of her family. Both her parents were of Irish extraction (her father was born in Ireland and came to the United States in 1873, and her mother was born in the United States of northern Irish parents), and the young girl heard many traditional ballads and songs that could be traced back to her ancestors, in addition to American tunes sung by her neighbors and relatives. She married Everett Cleveland in 1922, and within three years gave birth to two sons, Jim and Billy.

Her Uncle Bobby (Wiggins) provided her with another source of traditional material, particularly lumbering songs. She has compiled a personal "ballad book," which constitutes her repertoire; about half the selections are made up of "old traditional songs" which she acquired prior to 1950, and the other half are "new folk songs" learned in recent years. In the same way that Sara Cleveland's knowledge of folk songs has been expanded by friends who are active on today's folk scene, many singers, folklorists, and collectors have come to her as a source of new material.

Since the death of her husband in 1953, Sara Cleveland has been living in upstate New York with her son Jim, who is a folk music enthusiast and frequent patron of Caffé Lena in Saratoga Springs, New York. On one occasion he mentioned to Bob Beers that his mother was a traditional singer with a wealth of old-time material, and Bob Beers urged him to contact Sandy and Caroline Paton of Folk-Legacy Records. In 1968 *Sara Cleveland* ("Ballads and Songs of the Upper Hudson Valley" [FSA-33]) was issued by the Patons; this album represents only a portion of the thirty-seven tapes they have recorded of her singing.

Sandy Paton recalls their first interaction with Sara Cleveland: "The thrill of finding a truly great traditional singer comes but rarely to the collector, and when it is enhanced by the recovery of a Child ballad which has never before been reported in North America (Child 52—*The King's Dochter Lady Jean*), the excitement is intense. Because it was just such an occasion, I shall never forget the first evening that my wife, Caroline, and I spent in Sara Cleveland's home in Hudson Falls, New York.

"As is the custom in north country homes, we sat at the kitchen table with Sara and her family (parlors are for formal visits only), leafing through the several large notebooks of song texts which Sara had carefully written out over the years, asking if she could remember the melody of first one ballad and then another. Without hesitation, and without reference to the written texts, Sara sang for us all evening, and we barely made a scratch on the surface of her vast repertoire of traditional songs. Indeed, Sara's is the most extensive repertoire of any traditional singer I have ever recorded."

Her most recent album was recorded for Philo Records, *Sara Cleveland* (Philo PH 1020), and released early in 1976.

# Bill Clifton

*Bluegrass bandleader, singer, guitarist, country music director of the Newport Folk Foundation, performer, and recording artist*

Bill Clifton is probably best known for his early efforts at combining the elements of traditional music into the corpus of bluegrass by finding a variety of qualitative material, both old and new, and bringing it to life in his performances. A popular bluegrass bandleader, he sought the accompaniment of the highest caliber of musicians; during his peak recording period of the middle to late 1950s, Bill Clifton made classic recordings on Mercury, Mercury-Starday, and Starday, with such outstanding musicians as John Duffey, Tommy Jackson, Benny Martin, Mike Seeger, Ralph Stanley, and many, many others.

Bill Clifton and Earl Scruggs were among the first to employ techniques reminiscent of

Carter Family and fingerpicking styles, and Clifton drew heavily upon the Carter Family's repertoire for his material. His reintroduction of old-time songs into bluegrass (a direct offshoot of traditional sources) gained Clifton followers among country, folk, and bluegrass fans. An indebtedness to the recorded works of such other bluegrass groups as the Monroe Brothers, the Blue Sky Boys, Mainer's Mountaineers, and Charlie Poole and the North Carolina Ramblers is to be found in Clifton's music; unfortunately, some of his best work, bluegrass music recorded during the late fifties, has become unobtainable since the discontinuation of the recordings in the mid-sixties.

In his mid-forties, Bill Clifton has had many, and diverse, accomplishments and interests since his initial involvement with bluegrass. He earned his master's degree while recording hits for major labels; he collected and edited a songbook of traditional string music; he was a sales broker of radio and television stations; he has been a director in the Peace Corps, a stock broker, and a guitar instructor. In 1961 Clifton produced the first bluegrass festival that brought together Bill Monroe and his former Blue Grass Boys, on July 4 at Luray, Virginia; and in 1963 he coordinated the country music portion of the Newport Folk Festival. *Country Music and Bluegrass at Newport* (Vanguard VRS-9146) was one of the many results of the festival.

A resident of southern England for the past dozen years, Bill Clifton has played an important role in arousing overseas interest in American traditional music and bluegrass; he has also been instrumental in arranging appearances for many bluegrass musicians in Europe, Japan, Australia, New Zealand, and England.

The selections on Bill Clifton and the Dixie Mountain Boys' LP, *Blue Ridge Mountain Blues* (County 740), were originally recorded in 1957 and 1958 for Mercury and Starday. The album includes such cuts as "Corey" (originally "Darling Corey," from the repertoire of the Monroe Brothers), with

Bill Clifton on guitar and lead vocal, John Duffey on mandolin and tenor vocal, Junior Huskey on bass, Benny Martin and Tommy Jackson on fiddles, Curley Lambert on mandolin and baritone vocal, Jimmy Self on guitar, and Ralph Stanley on banjo; the Carter Family tunes "Just Another Broken Heart" and "Dixie Darling," with Mike Seeger on autoharp, introducing this instrument to bluegrass; and several songs from the old-time string band era. In 1972 Bill Clifton and Hedy West recorded *Getting the Folk Out of the Country* for the West German label Folk Variety (FV 12008); it was made in London in the summer of 1972, and the album consists of a collection of mostly old-time country tunes. His most recent recording for County Records is *Come by the Hills* (County 751), made during a return visit to the United States in the summer of 1974 and another album was scheduled for release in mid-1976.

# The Clinch Mountain Boys. *See*
The Stanley Brothers.

# Bruce Cockburn

*Contemporary Canadian singer-songwriter, guitarist, performer, and recording artist*

Unlike Joni Mitchell and Neil Young, who found it necessary to cross the American border to estabish their careers, Bruce Cockburn has made a successful living in his own country, with the help of the Canadian Radio and Television Commission (CRTC) ruling that 30 percent of the music broadcast on Canadian AM radio be works by Canadians. Currently one of Canada's major attractions, Cockburn (pronounced *Coburn*) has made little impact on the American record charts as yet, and only two of his five albums have been picked up by an American company.

Bruce Cockburn, like Murray McLauchlan, has been recorded by True North

Records, a small, custom recording label which was formed after the speculative release of Cockburn's first album early in 1970. The album was distributed by Columbia of Canada, and by the time Cockburn's second LP was issued in Canada, his first album was released in the United States. In 1972 American Epic issued *Sunwheel Dance* (Epic KE-31768), which was Cockburn's third Canadian LP and his second released in the United States. It received minimal publicity (largely as a result of Cockburn's decision not to promote sales by touring the United States), and in 1974 his contract with Epic was terminated.

Cockburn enjoys the status of a superstar in his native country, and his 1975 solo tour of seventeen Canadian theaters and halls was highly successful. Early that year, his fifth album on the True North label, *Salt, Sun and Time*, was released in Canada, and in hopes of expanding his audience, Cockburn has decided to start touring in the United States.

He writes songs with profound imagery, often naturalistic; his best-known work in America is probably "One Day I Walk," which was recorded by Tom Rush and Anne Murray.

# Fred Cockerham

*Old-time fiddler and clawhammer banjoist, performer, and recording artist*

Fred Cockerham has been playing for years with other musicians from his native Beulah section of Surry County in North Carolina; and when Charley Jarrell married Cockerham's aunt, one of his neighbors and musical companions, Tommy Jarrell, became his cousin. Cockerham, like Kyle Creed and Charlie Lowe, is known for his clawhammer style of banjo picking, but he is also a versatile and accomplished fiddler. Unlike Oscar Jenkins, who was raised in Dobson, North Carolina, and plays the fiddle in a manner that reflects his own regional and paternal influences to produce a mellow, easy-listening sound, Cockerham and Jarrell play the instrument with a powerful intensity typical of their region of the state.

As a boy, Fred Cockerham was influenced by a relative, Uncle Troy Cockerham, who used only two fingers to note with on the fiddle. He provided his nephew with versions of "Soldier's Joy" and "Pretty Little Miss" which inspired Fred Cockerham to create his own original interpretations that have become favorites among country musicians and fans. Although other members of his family were talented, Fred Cockerham was the only one to pursue a career in the field of music.

His first professional band was called the Ruby Tonic Entertainers, and they played on WBT Radio in Charlotte, North Carolina, and performed in concerts in the Virginia–North Carolina area. When they broke up, Cockerham played every Saturday night at the Dan River Park Dance Hall and broadcast from High Point, North Carolina, with another group, Fiddling Slim and the North Carolina Ramblers. He began to enter fiddle contests in which he competed against top-notch musicians, including Frank Jenkins and Fiddlin' Arthur Smith, after whose fiddling Cockerham's is patterned. Cockerham also played with the Royal Hawaiians from about 1937 to 1940, and he lived in Galax, Virginia, and played with Fields Ward, his brother Sampson (Simp) Ward, and Herbert Higgins, who had played mandolin for the Ruby Tonic Entertainers.

Fred Cockerham's use of double-noting, or dropping the thumb to the second string of the banjo to increase the number of notes played, creates a complexity which he has developed to perfection on his fretless banjo. His approach is unlike that of Oscar Jenkins, who has eliminated the fifth string and uses his index finger to play the first and second strings while his thumb hits the third and fourth. Tommy Jarrell also employs an individualistic approach to playing the banjo by using unusual tunings and techniques,

such as "hammering-on," which demonstrates his left hand's dexterity and proficiency. Each of their styles is unique, and the instrumental skills of Cockerham, Jenkins, and Jarrell are complemented and enhanced by one another's accompaniment.

Cockerham's driving style of clawhammer banjo yields an intricate combination of down-picking (or frailing) which embodies the melody through use of the thumb on all but the first string, with a distinctive and unsacrificed rhythmic sound. John Cohen collected banjo tunes and ballads for the album *High Atmosphere* (Rounder 0028), which features Fred Cockerham, Dillard Chandler, Wade Ward, Frank Proffitt, and others.

With the encouragement of Kyle Creed to return to his music after an eye operation, Fred Cockerham joined the Camp Creek Boys in 1963. By 1971, as the old-time string band's fiddler, he led the group to victory at the Old Fiddlers' Convention in Galax, Virginia; two years later, the Camp Creek Boys with fiddler Fred Cockerham again took first prize in the contest.

Fred Cockerham has made three albums with Oscar Jenkins and Tommy Jarrell: *Down to the Cider Mill* (County 713), *Back Home in the Blue Ridge* (County 723), and *Stay All Night and Don't Go Home* (County 741). (*See also* Kyle Creed; Tommy Jarrell.)

# Coffeehouse

The concept of the coffeehouse is British in origin. In the seventeenth and eighteenth centuries, the coffeehouse functioned as a club in which clientele of the same occupation or professional interests congregated, with bankers, sailors, and writers enjoying their own exclusive establishments. The coffeehouse was introduced to the United States in the eighteenth century, but it was not until Dominick Parisi opened the Caffé Reggio in Greenwich Village in 1935 that the American venture was firmly established. His imported espresso machine was a novelty which lured customers to gather, play checkers, and chat in a warm and friendly atmosphere; consequently, the Reggio became a prototype for coffeehouses that were to follow. The Café Rienzi opened for business just a few doors down from the Reggio, and its owner offered an extensive list of exotic coffees, checkerboards, and newspapers.

The recent folk revival in the United States generated a need for meeting places where young singers could perform and perfect their art. In his book *The Ballad Mongers*, Oscar Brand describes how the coffeehouse evolved as a folk music enterprise:

At first, the proprietors of the coffee shops prohibited any singing or playing. Many had installed high-fidelity equipment which transmitted Bach and Pergolesi through the coffee-scented air. But a folk singer is usually compelled by nature to sing folk songs, and one did. Others joined in. Coffee drinkers turned to watch and listen. Chess players even smiled a bit over their checkered battlefields. A new audience had been born. The word spread among the folk singing fraternity that a perfect platform for new songs and new singers had been discovered. In Sausalito, Pasadena, San Francisco, and Los Angeles new establishments appeared bearing such names as the Unicorn, the Garret, the Ash Grove, the Troubadour. In Philadelphia the Second Fret; the Exodus, The Tarot and The Spider in Denver; The White Horse and The Door in Seattle; The House of Seven Sorrows in Dallas;—they were springing up like dragon's teeth near colleges and universities everywhere on the American Continent, each complete with appended folk singers and their audiences.

In Greenwich Village, the Rienzi was followed by the Café Wha?, the Lion's Head, the Fat Black Pussy Cat, the Figaro, and tens of others. There were even places where the folk music was featured instead of the coffee—at the Bitter End, or at Gerde's Folk City—one half a bar, one half a hootenanny.

Incessant battles were waged by residents of the Village whose conservative life-styles were threatened by the appearance of bearded and long-haired ascetics, homosexuals, and others who they complained were part of the folk music scene. Pressure was brought to bear on coffeehouse management, and every municipal law in the book was used by the authorities to allay civil disquietude. At one point, monthly park licenses were withheld from folksingers on the premise that their presence and music were undesirable, and Israel Young led a protesting group of folkies in a demonstration in Washington Square Park. The ensuing riot was given wide press coverage; as a result, sympathies with the folksingers led to a recision of permit withholding, and Washington Square was reinstated as the Sunday afternoon folk music domain.

The folk boom was the heyday of coffeehouses, which were scattered throughout this country, but within a matter of a few years the majority of them shut down. With the integration of "folk culture" into the mainstream of mass or "popular culture," the coffeehouse trend over the past fifteen years has been a barometric and significant social phenomenon. With the advent of commercial folk music, many coffeehouses were abandoned for concert halls and larger folk clubs, which are capable of accommodating more people and making more money. Today, the role of the coffeehouse is more modest, tending to the preservation and presentation of traditional folk music, as exemplified by the oldest coffeehouse in America, Caffé Lena. As its proprietress, Lena Spencer, explains the uncommercial function of her operation: "When I think of highlights of the Caffé, I think about the small, day-to-day experiences because the little things have made the Caffé what it is. It's a very modest place, and it hasn't changed. I can't afford to make any changes, and if I could, I wouldn't. A lot of people have said, 'Well, why don't you expand and make the place bigger or move and go to a bigger place?' but I like the way it is." The Caffé Lena—and other coffeehouses like it—is one of the constants in the coffeehouse movement which afford semiprofessionals and new artists an opportunity for expression.

## John Cohen. *See* The New Lost City Ramblers; The Putnam String County Band.

## Leonard Cohen

*Contemporary singer-songwriter, guitarist, performer, recording artist, poet, and novelist*

One of popular music's most well-rounded creative personalities, Leonard Cohen has been lauded for his contributions to the arts as a composer, poet, novelist, and performer. Over the years, his solid reputation has expanded from its original base among the young people of his native Canada to a loyal following on an international scale. While residing on the Greek island of Hydra, he became extremely popular among Europeans, and, with his universal image and artistic appeal, many of his works have been translated into twenty or more languages.

Leonard Norman Cohen was born on September 21, 1934, in Montreal, Canada, and he received his BA at McGill University in 1955, followed by graduate work at Columbia University in New York City. He was the recipient of the McGill Literary Award in 1956 and a Canada Council Grant in 1960–61. The year 1964 brought him the Quebec Literary Award and national recognition through a National Film Board of Canada documentary, *Ladies and Gentlemen . . . Mr. Leonard Cohen*. During the late sixties he was featured on the CBS-TV Sunday morning program *Camera Three*, and, more recently, one of his European tours was filmed and released under

Leonard Cohen

the title *Bird on a Wire*. In 1971 he was awarded an honorary LLB degree at the Dalhousie University commencement.

Leonard Cohen has authored two novels, *The Favorite Game* (1963) and *Beautiful Losers* (1966), published by Viking Press in the United States and by McClelland and Stewart in Canada, with the American editions of both having had several printings as a result of their successful sales. His poetry has been published in six volumes: *Let Us Compare Mythologies* (1956), *The Spice-Box of Earth* (1961), *Flowers for Hitler* (1964), *Parasites of Heaven* (1966), *Selected Poems* (1956–68, 1968), and *The Energy of Slaves* (1973).

The initiation of his recording career turned his artistic acclaim into popular success. Judy Collins presented an alternative for expressive possibilities, and after listening to one of her New York performances during the mid-sixties, Cohen decided to channel his creative, yet uncompromising, energies into songwriting. Judy Collins's classic version of "Suzanne" brought him immediate acclaim as a composer, and both "Suzanne" and "Dress Rehearsal Rag" were recorded by Judy Collins on her album *In My Life*. An exclusive recording contract was arranged by John Hammond of Columbia Records and a new phase of his career was launched as Leonard Cohen began to express his art as a singer, guitarist, and recording artist. His only prior experience with music was in 1954 as a member of a Montreal country group called the Buckskin Boys, and now, over a decade later, he was a solo recording artist premiering with *Songs of Leonard Cohen* (CS 9533/CL 2733), released in December 1967. Since then, he has recorded four more LPs on the Columbia label: *Songs from a Room* (CS 9767), *Songs of Love and Hate* (C 30103), *Live Songs* (KC 31724), and, in 1974, *New Skin for the Old Ceremony* (KC 33167).

Leonard Cohen is enjoyed by a wide cross section of the general public, with his work appealing on its many levels to a universal audience. While literary circles appreciate his poetic craftsmanship, his listening audience is captivated by his ability to relate his beautiful, often mystical, messages through music. Always maintaining an art of the highest caliber, Leonard Cohen fuses with precision poetry and music.

He composed music for the film *McCabe and Mrs. Miller*, directed by Robert Altman, and even in this capacity Cohen proved to be successful in adapting his creativity to another medium. In the fall of 1974, after the completion of his fifth LP, he began an extensive tour of Europe, performing for his many fans in London, Paris, Madrid, Barcelona, Vienna, and other major cities. During the early months of 1975, he returned to North America to commence his first major tour of the United States since 1969.

## Charlie Collins. *See* The Smoky Mountain Boys.

## Judy Collins

*Contemporary singer, guitarist, pianist, songwriter, performer, recording artist, and filmmaker*

One of today's most well-rounded contemporary musicians, Judy Collins has branched out from traditional folk music to explore new areas of creative expression and to offer a diversity of material, innovative arrangements and accompaniments, and a melodic vocal style. She has successfully incorporated her classically based understanding and appreciation of music with the lyrical and communicative attributes of folk music. Her music is testimony to her depth and concern for presenting qualitative works in an art form that ranges from old French songs, Brecht, Debussy, and Ravel to Joni Mitchell, Leonard Cohen, and Jacques Brel.

Born Judith Marjorie Collins on May 1, 1939, in Seattle, Washington, she started studying piano at the age of four: "We lived in Seattle for about four years, then my father, who was in radio, moved down to Los Angeles to work at KFI and KNX. I lived in LA till I was nine, and then my father got a job in Denver, so we moved to Colorado."

Judy Collins's father was aware of his daughter's gift for music, and it was always encouraged. It was not long after they arrived in Colorado that he sought out Antonia Brico, who became one of the most influential musicians in Judy Collins's life and with whom she studied classical piano for about eight years. As a teenager, Judy Collins grew up amid the folk music surge of the fifties. Learning to play guitar to accompany herself when singing, she began her professional music career in Denver area folk clubs: "I was attracted by the music and I was also attracted by the combination of literature and music. The words, the stories,

and the lyric form—folk music is very classically based, the themes are classically based. The way they're structured is not always the same, of course, it's not nearly as complex, but a lot of the basic themes are very similar, and a lot of classical musicians have always recognized that and used the folk patterns of their cultures to work with.

"I think that I was very much a professional musician from the time I could practically walk because I was involved with public performance and I grew up inside a radio station and the concert halls and concert stages, so the difference between not being paid for it and being paid for it wasn't all that great.

"I never had any doubt or question about what I was doing. I always knew that I was doing something that was basically good and satisfactory to me, and it was always very challenging. I don't like to stay in one place very long, and moving in music had always been a challenge—changing direction, changing interest, changing influences—and perhaps that was the strongest point in that period when I was first involved in folk music, because I was not categorizable in a two- or three-year period. Very quickly I was integrating written music and music from the thirties and Brecht and old French songs, and so forth, so it's not easy to categorize my work when you look at the variety of the kind of music that I've always done."

Collins married Peter A. Taylor in April 1958, and at the age of nineteen she gave birth to her son Clark. She recorded her first Elektra albums in the early sixties, and both *Maid of Constant Sorrow* (EKS-7209) and *Golden Apples of the Sun* (EKS-7222) brought her widespread acclaim as a folksinger. By the time *Judy Collins #3* (EKS-7243) was released, Judy Collins's name was connected with the song "Hey Nelly Nelly," but her music was growing as she became more and more attuned to the works of her contemporaries. With her "roots in urban life," Judy Collins was learning about music from other young city singers and songwriters with whom she associated after moving from Colorado to Greenwich Village.

Her range of material expanded with each album that she recorded. *The Judy Collins Concert* (EKS-7280) and *Judy Collins' fifth album* (EKS-7300) included selections by such urban folk musicians as Tom Paxton, Richard Fariña, Bob Dylan, Eric Andersen, Phil Ochs, Gordon Lightfoot, and others, and *In My Life* (EKS-74027) introduced her listening audience to the works of Leonard Cohen and Jacques Brel.

Judy Collins was politically active during the sixties, helping with the registration of black voters in Mississippi in 1964, and becoming involved with Women Strike for Peace, coproducing, with Pennywhistlers' Ethel Raim, *Save the Children*, an album of songs and recitations by various female performers.

In the fall of 1967, *Wildflowers* (EKS-74012) marked Judy Collins's debut as a songwriter, and it made Joni Mitchell a household name with the recording of Mitchell's song, "Both Sides Now." Significantly, the album encompassed her first original compositions, "Sky Fell" and "Albatross," with the works of Mitchell, Cohen, and Brel, and it was her first LP to sell in excess of a million copies.

By the end of the decade, her multifaceted career embraced accomplishments in related areas. She had portrayed Solveig in the New York Shakespeare Festival production of *Peer Gynt*, and she had published *The Judy Collins Songbook*, which contained songs and written reminiscences of her life.

Another milestone in her career was her documentation on film of an interview with her former teacher, Dr. Antonia Brico. *Antonia: A Portrait of the Woman* received wide critical acclaim, and in 1974 opened the American Filmmakers Series at the Whitney Museum of American Art in New York City. The film won the Christopher Award, the Independent Film Critics Award, and others. It was named one of the top ten films of the year by *Time* magazine, and in 1974 was nominated for an Academy Award as the best documentary.

Her fourteenth album, *Judith* (Elektra 7E 1032), was recorded simultaneously with the opening of her film, and, like every LP since *Wildflowers*, it includes original compositions and a variety of musical selections, which, in this case, comprises a Broadway show tune, standard pop classics, works by contemporary songwriters, and a Rolling Stones rock hit.

"There comes a point in your life, if you're really serious about your work, that you have to take a different point of view than the one that you had before. I think all of us tend to feel that we are influenced by our culture, and I think there's a point in your life when you have to seriously consider the fact that you are influencing your culture, rather than vice versa. Or, let's say, it's a mixture, but one of the strengths is that you are giving input to that culture, and, in this sense, I feel that I am making a contribution.

"I feel a responsibility to be individual about my music and not to take the road most easily followed, in pop music, and I feel that's a good, healthy thing to have happening on all levels."

## Concertina

A portable wind instrument patented by Sir Charles Wheatstone on June 19, 1829, the concertina is hexagonally shaped, with an expansible bellows separating two key boxes at either end. The expanding and contracting of the bellows creates air pressure which vibrates free metallic reeds and produces sound, and individual notes are played by pressing finger-operated buttons on the key box. The treble-size concertina covers a four-octave range with complete chromatic scale, and, as a double-action instrument, the same note can be played regardless of whether the bellows is drawn or pressed by the hands.

The tenor, bass, and double-bass (or contrabass) concertinas are single-action instruments which produce sound only by creating pressure. They are constructed in different shapes and sizes, and their range is more limited than that of the treble concertina.

Early proponents of the concertina include Signor Regondi, George Case, and Richard Blagrove. More recently, Alistair Anderson and Lou Killen have played major roles in bringing widespread attention to the instrument.

## Shelley Cook. *See* The Penny-whistlers.

## Rita Coolidge

*Singer, performer, and recording artist*

For many years, in the words of *Rolling Stone* writer Kit Rachlis, "her crystalline voice functioned more effectively in providing ornamentation and flourish than interpretation." Only recently has Rita Coolidge emerged from her role as backup vocalist to that of solo artist in her own right.

Nashville-born, Rita Coolidge was introduced to music through her Baptist minister father, and she began singing in church when she was two years old. Many years later, she put her musical talent to work by earning her art school tuition money, but, after graduating from Florida State, she ended up pursuing singing instead of her master's degree: "Thought I'd work for a year, but at the end of it, I was hooked."

Her professional singing career was launched in Memphis, where she sang on commercials and recorded a locally popular single, "Turn Around and Love Me." From there, she moved on to Los Angeles, where she toured for a while with Delaney and Bonnie and Friends and provided vocal accompaniment on one of their Elektra albums. A tour with Mad Dogs and

Her musical style incorporates a variety of pop, country, and, most recently, jazz interpretations. In commenting on her work with jazz pianist Barbara Carroll, who provided instrumental accompaniment on two cuts from her fifth A&M effort, *It's Only Love* (A&M SP-4531), and on the introduction of jazz material into her repertoire, Rita Coolidge said: "I don't pretend to understand that music. I don't even know where it came from. I just found myself opening my mouth and the sounds flowed out. It was easy, probably the easiest thing I've ever done in a studio." (*See also* Kris Kristofferson.)

## Michael Cooney

*Vocalist, instrumentalist, performer, and recording artist*

One of the most familiar faces in folk music today, Michael Cooney has performed in Mexico, Germany, Great Britain, and at nearly every major music festival in the United States and Canada. Often called a one-man folk festival, Cooney has compiled a wealth of songs ranging from American and British folk songs to ballads, blues, sea shanties, and topical songs, and he delivers them with an inexhaustible supply of anecdotes and information: "The last time I counted, which was about five years ago, I knew about five hundred songs, but I have stopped counting because I realized that for every song I learned, I forgot one. It's not just forgetting, there are songs that I know I'll never sing again that are not my style anymore, and I have a lot of those.

"I always think of myself as being a typical example of what happened in the whole folk music movement, in that we all grew up thinking that you can't play music unless you start when you're six years old and practice for five hours every day, and, for the first time, I heard a kind of music that made me say, 'Gee, maybe I could do that.' "

Rita Coolidge

Englishmen followed, and studio work on recordings by various artists, including Graham Nash and Stephen Stills.

In 1971 she recorded her debut solo LP, entitled *Rita Coolidge* (A&M SP-4291), and began traveling with her future husband, Kris Kristofferson. In addition to recording two albums with Kristofferson, Rita Coolidge has recorded four more solo LPs on the A&M label.

Michael Cooney at the 1975 Mariposa Festival held on the Toronto Islands, Ontario, Canada

Michael Cooney grew up in Arizona, where he had a friend who played the ukelele, and when he was in high school he got a ukelele and learned to play it. It was the heyday of the Kingston Trio, and, like so many of America's youth, Cooney was influenced by their music. He got a four-string banjo that he tuned like a ukelele, and he formed a trio with two friends and they learned Kingston Trio songs. Soon Cooney had another trio that went farther afield for their songs; they played dinners and dances for ten dollars. "Of all the people I met who played music, the ones that were most interesting to me were the ones who played 'real' folk music, a little less commercial. I always drifted around those people who played more traditional styles of music.

"I went to California, but it never occurred to me to be professional. I didn't feel like getting any honest work until I got offered so much money that I thought, 'Gee, a person could make money at this,' and then I started getting serious about it." The talented and dedicated musician, who plays fretted and fretless banjo, six- and twelve-string guitar, and a variety of small instruments, "never cared to get into recording," preferring instead to play live music for people. Cooney sings "Lena, Won't You Open Your Door" on *Welcome to Caffe Lena* (Biograph Records BLP-12046); and he appears on the National Geographic Society album *Songs & Sounds of the Sea* (NGS-705), playing "Sail Away, Ladies," "Can't You Dance the Polka?," and a rendition of a well-known whaling song, "Blow, Ye Winds." In 1968 he made a solo album, *Michael Cooney, Or "The Cheese Stands Alone"* (Folk-Legacy FSI-35), and his next LP is scheduled for release in 1976 on Front Hall Records (FHR-07). For many years, folks have been enjoying his column, "General Delivery," in *Sing Out!*, which is described in the publication as "a column for (a) the exchange of questions and answers, by and for readers, about songs and subjects related to folk music and lore; (b) helpful hints, ideas, and items of interest; (c) opinions, grand pronouncements, and exhortations of the columnist. Questions relating to traditional music, lore, and learning will be given first attention." (*See also* The Golden Ring.)

## Barbara Cooper. *See* The Womenfolk.

## Elizabeth Cotten

*Singer, songwriter, guitarist renowned for the "Cotten Style" of picking, banjoist, performer, and recording artist*

Elizabeth (Libba) Cotten established a dual reputation with her original composition

"Freight Train," as she became as well-known for the song as for her unique instrumental style of guitar accompaniment. Left-handed, she plays with her guitar "upside down," employing two-finger and "banjo" stylings for which her name is most famous. In addition to this "Cotten Style" of guitar picking, she plays a broken rhythm style, using three or four fingers and chording up the neck.

Born in 1893 and raised in Chapel Hill, North Carolina, Libba Cotten wanted a guitar from the time she was a little girl. By the age of twelve, she was working for seventy-five cents a month, doing household chores in a neighboring residence, and when she had saved enough money, she asked her mother to buy a guitar for her. When her mother brought home a $3.75 Stella demonstrator guitar, Libba Cotten spent every spare moment teaching herself to play the instrument. She learned how to strum the guitar from her brother, and, never having had lessons, she figured out the picking styles by herself, with the instrument "wrong side up" from the start.

When her church deacons told her to put down her guitar and serve the Lord, Libba Cotten laid aside her music until the late 1940s. She married at the age of fifteen, and after her divorce, she moved to Washington, D.C., to look for work. After selling dolls in a department store over the Christmas holidays, Libba Cotten started working as a domestic for a Chevy Chase, Maryland, resident. The lady for whom she worked turned out to be Ruth Crawford Seeger, wife of ethnomusicologist Charles Seeger, and Libba Cotten was hired because she had returned the woman's lost daughter, Peggy, when the young girl had wandered away from her mother while shopping in the department store where the middle-aged North Carolina woman was employed.

Sometimes when Mrs. Seeger was playing her guitar, Libba Cotten would pick up Peggy's guitar, which was kept in the kitchen, and start playing in the room with the door closed. One day, Peggy and her brother

Elizabeth Cotten at the Eleventh Annual Philadelphia Folk Festival, 1972

Mike overheard her guitar playing, and, when they asked her to repeat the song that she had been playing, the Seegers heard "Freight Train" for the first time in their own home. It is interesting to note that it wasn't until 1957, after court action in New York and many delays, that Elizabeth Cotten finally secured the copyright to the song that she had composed before the age of twelve.

Libba Cotten's bass runs are used frequently by other guitarists, and her basic picking styles have become standard patterns for folk guitar. Her music is rooted in blues, rag, traditional, and religious tunes that were part of her own unique life experience, and the lyrics and musical accompaniments of her songs reflect this individuality and creative outlook on life.

Her close friend Mike Seeger recorded and edited her 1967 Folkways Records LP, *Elizabeth Cotten Vol. 2: Shake Sugaree* (FTS 31003), which was put together after the success of her first solo album, *Elizabeth Cotten Folk Songs* (Folkways 3526).

In 1972 Elizabeth Cotten received the Burl Ives Award, presented by the National Folk Festival Association on July 29, for her vital role in folk music. The cash prizes are made possible by another folksinger, Burl Ives, and are presented "to those who have made outstanding contributions in the authentic folk music field and have helped spread and preserve folk heritage in everyday life."

Over the years, Libba Cotten has appeared at East Coast folk festivals, such as Newport and Philadelphia, on the West Coast, at the UCLA Folk Festival, and occasionally she plays coffeehouses, concerts, and clubs. In April 1975 she was a guest performer in a program of native American music at Washington's Kennedy Center, and she hopes to complete work on a third album soon.

# Country

One of the basic ingredients of American folk music, "country" is a musical form that evolved during the development of early country or rural Southern folk music, commonly referred to as "hillbilly" music. Along with "mountain" music, which was also derived from rural areas, country music was a predominant force prior to the appearance of "western" styling in the post-Depression years. Solo vocals and nontraditional instrumental accompaniment characterized the country sound, and the country artist most responsible for its commercial emergence was Jimmie Rodgers.

With the merging of cultures, the interaction among servicemen, and the increased mobility of the American populace during the World War II years, country music broke its regional ties to become a nation-wide (and ultimately a worldwide) phenomenon. In devising a highly salable commodity in what had become a major profit-seeking industry, capitalists in the North brought to a close the relative simplicity and ethnic purity of the Golden Age of country music. Some scholars designate 1941, when the Carter Family retired from recording, as the point of commercial corruption of country music.

During the forties, countrywide barn dance shows enjoyed unprecedented financial and popular success, and the *Grand Ole Opry* became firmly established as the principal showcase for country music in the United States. With the resultant prosperity and widespread public recognition of this musical form, a movement was initiated to eliminate its long-standing derogatory connotation by relabeling "hillbilly" music as "country" music in the post–World War II period. The use of more sophisticated instruments and more complex musical arrangements, along with the assemblage of top-notch musicians (session men) in such country music centers as Nashville, created an aura of professionalism in the field.

In the early fifties, Hank Williams overshadowed both the popular honky-tonk sound and western music; and, at this point, country music not only made the final step across the pop border, but it remained there. A temporary lack of public interest in country music during the mid-fifties was reversed by the rise of such country-pop musicians as Roger Miller, whose "King of the Road" created renewed enthusiasm for the musical form.

Reaction against the highly stylized "Nashville sound"—a hybridization of musical styles resulting from the influences of rock amplification and pop arrangements—generated a revival of traditional country music (concurrent with the urban folk revival) in the early sixties. An onslaught of recording artists, including Bob Dylan, Ian and Sylvia, Burl Ives, and Peter, Paul and Mary, among others, traveled to Nashville to record, and it is only recently that a trend away from Music City, along with the increasing prominence of Austin, Texas, threatens to dislodge Nashville's stature as the country music capital of the world.

# The Country Boys. *See* Mac Wiseman.

# The Country Gentlemen

*Bluegrass vocal and instrumental group, performers, and recording artists*

World War II attracted many job-seeking families to the Washington, D.C., area; many musicians started making music together in their leisure time, and a firmly established audience was created as a natural outcome of this centralization of musical activity. The folk boom of the late 1950s generated a new wave of bluegrass enthusiasm, reinforcing the popularity of this musical form and making bluegrass acts highly sought after for club, concert, and college dates. Today the Washington area is the center of operations for many bluegrass string bands, including the Seldom Scene, the Grass Menagerie, the Second Generation, and one of the oldest and best-known groups, the Country Gentlemen.

The Country Gentlemen was founded by Charlie Waller and John Duffey when they played together in a July 4, 1957, Baltimore concert as a substitute act for Buzz Busby, who had been in an automobile accident and was unable to appear. Louisiana-born Charlie Waller had learned to play guitar as a boy, and he moved with his family to the Washington area when he was a teenager. Originally from the Washington–Maryland area, John Duffey was an accomplished musician who was working at radio station WFMD in Frederick, Maryland, when he and Waller played together for the first time. Jim Cox was the group's first bass player, and in late 1958 Eddie Adcock joined the Country Gentlemen as banjoist.

The vocal blending of Waller, Duffey, and Adcock was one of the richest and most unique combinations among bluegrass musicians, and their creative instrumentation was both different and dazzling. Innovators in their field, the Country Gentlemen are considered by many to be the first group to incorporate a bluegrass sound into a contemporary music structure, subsequently termed "progressive bluegrass." Their early recordings on Starday, Folkways, and Mercury encompassed a broad spectrum of music, including jazz numbers ("Heartaches"), folk songs ("Tom Dooley" and "Copper Kettle"), and bluegrass standards, played in an upbeat bluegrass styling. Influenced by the folk music craze, which was running concurrently with their career, the Country Gentlemen selected both traditional and pop-folk songs for their repertoire to keep in step with the contemporary trend and popular demand; as a result, their music reached a wide audience and their commercial success was firmly established.

In the mid-sixties, the Country Gentlemen signed a recording contract with Rebel, a Washington label, and the company's first release was an LP by the Country Gentlemen entitled *Bringin' Mary Home* (Rebel SLP-1478). Since then, the Country Gentlemen have recorded a number of albums on the Rebel label, including *The Traveler* (SLP-1481), *Play It Like It Is* (SLP-1486), *New Look New Sound* (SLP-1490), *Best of the Early Country Gentlemen* (SLP-1494), *One Wide River* (SLP-1497), *The Country Gentlemen Sound Off* (SLP-1489), *The Award Winning Country Gentlemen* (SLP-1506), and *Yesterday and Today*, *Volumes 1, 2, and 3* (SLP-1521, SLP-1527, and SLP-1535). In 1972 the Country Gentlemen signed a contract with Vanguard Records and cut their debut album on that label, *The Country Gentlemen* (VSD-79331), followed in 1975 by *Remembrances & Forecasts* (VSD-79349).

John Duffey left the Country Gentlemen in 1969, and he was replaced by mandolinist

Jimmy Gaudreau, from Rhode Island. Soon after this change in personnel, Eddie Adcock departed from the group, and Bill Emerson was recruited from another bluegrass group called Emerson and Waldron to play banjo for the Country Gentlemen. The group continued to stay abreast of contemporary music, and their repertoire included songs by James Taylor, Gordon Lightfoot, Paul Simon, and other pop-folk singer-songwriters.

The Country Gentlemen now comprises veteran Charlie Waller, emcee, lead singer, and guitarist; Doyle Lawson, tenor, musical arranger, and mandolinist; Bill Yates, bass player and bass singer (formerly of Bill Monroe's Blue Grass Boys); and Bill Holden of Fort Worth, Texas, banjoist.

For three years the Country Gentlemen appeared as regular guests on Ian Tyson's Canadian TV network show, and the group has been seen on Arthur Smith's syndicated television show and other local programs. They work college, club, and concert dates across the United States and in Canada, from the Cellar Door in Washington, D.C., to the Great Southeast Music Hall in Atlanta, Georgia, the Ash Grove in Los Angeles, California, Carnegie Hall in New York City, Constitution Hall in Washington, D.C., and the *Grand Ole Opry* in Nashville, Tennessee. In 1972 they toured Japan, performing in sell-out concerts in eight cities, and in October 1975 they returned from another successful tour of that country. The Country Gentlemen are seen frequently at bluegrass festivals, working approximately twenty events in 1974. (*See also* Eddie Adcock.)

# S. D. (Sady) Courville

*Singer and fiddle player representing the older, traditional instrumental and vocal Cajun music, performer, and recording artist*

S. D. Courville is probably best known for his role as one of the twin fiddlers in a partnership with Dennis McGee, with whom he has played off and on for the last fifty years.

S. D. (Sady) Courville (left), Dennis McGee (center), and Marc Savoy (right) performing in a Cajun Music and Life-style Workshop at the 1975 Mariposa Folk Festival

Together, they have teamed up with many of the most renowned Cajun accordionists, including Nathan Abshire and Angelas LeJeune.

A descendant of French-Canadians who moved to southwestern Louisiana more than two hundred years ago, Courville has spent the seventy years of his life in an area rich in tradition and folklore. As a young boy, he used to listen to his father and uncle play twin-fiddle Cajun tunes, and this older style of instrumentation and singing became the roots of his own music. When Courville was twelve years old, he bought a fiddle from Dennis McGee, which he still owns and plays, and they started working dances together. In 1928 they were invited to make some records for Brunswick-Vocalion, and some of these recordings, such as *Cajun Two Fiddles* (Morningstar MST 16001), are being reissued on the Morningstar label. They appeared at three National folk festivals, 1972 to 1974, and at the Mariposa Folk Festival in 1975.

"In the old days, McGee and I played with Angelas LeJeune, who was a very popular accordion player in his day. He was supposed to come with us to Wolf Trap last year, in 1974, but he died just about three weeks before the festival. We started playing with Marc Savoy about a year ago, and we get together for jam sessions and festivals. And we have just completed a three-week tour in April of the West Coast with Mike Seeger, which was the most enjoyable experience of my life."

A semiretired furniture dealer, Courville and his brother-in-law Dennis McGee have played music together as a hobby, but the goal of their pastime is more far-reaching: "We would like to see Cajun music go further than where it is in South Louisiana because that only covers about one hundred square miles." Courville hosts a radio show called *The Mamou Hour*, which is broadcast from Mamou, Louisiana, and transmitted by KEUN in Eunice: "I've had the three-hour Cajun music show every Saturday morning for the last nine years. One of my most popular guests on the show has been Nathan Abshire, who has been programmed for the last two years. I've known him just about all my life, and he often tells me that when he was a kid and he knew Courville and McGee were going to play for a dance, he'd make that dance. He was with us at the 1974 National Folk Festival, and although he's not on my program at present, anytime he wants to come back, he's welcome, because he's been our most popular guest." (*See also* Nathan Abshire; Dennis McGee.)

**Jim Cox.** *See* The Country Gentlemen.

**Bob Cranford.** *See* The Red Fox Chasers.

# Kyle Creed

*Old-time clawhammer banjoist and fiddler, banjo craftsman, performer, and recording artist*

This old-time clawhammer banjo player, whose roots are deeply entrenched in the musically fertile Beulah section of Surry County, North Carolina, is best known for his crystal-clear, sparse style of playing and for his ability as a country banjo craftsman. His expertise as a clawhammer-style banjoist is marked by a characteristic usage of the instrument's fifth string for simultaneous rhythmic and melodic emphasis, and he has played with nearly every musician in the southwestern Virginia and northwestern North Carolina area.

Music was always interwoven with the daily activities of the Creed family. As a boy, Kyle Creed rode in a wagon to church and listened to various groups sing all day long. His grandfather, Bob Creed, played the fiddle, and his father, Qualey Creed, sang in quartets and played the fiddle with Kyle Creed's Uncle John Lowe. Until he adapted his fiddling to the bluegrass banjo picking of his current Camp Creek Boys' banjoist, Bobby Patterson, Kyle Creed's style of playing strongly resembled his father's old bow licks. He learned to play the fiddle from his father, but Creed's banjo style was acquired from (and is very similar in sound to) John Lowe and Baughy Cockerham. Creed incorporates a distinctive clarity with a strength and drive found in the less sparse clawhammer styles of Fred Cockerham and Charlie Lowe. He uses a metal fingerpick made from Model-T Ford brass headlight reflectors, and generally his hand is situated over the twelfth fret of the fingerboard when he is playing his meticulous clawhammer style.

Kyle Creed constructed his first banjo at the age of sixteen. In the Depression years, he lived with his grandfather, and one day, when he was preparing a fire to cure tobacco with wood that he split from a poplar tree, he discovered a light, soft wood from which to construct a banjo. He made a laminated rim by boiling strips of poplar wood in a tub, and he used the dried skin of a dead cat for the banjo head. Over the years he has continued to experiment in an effort to make an instrument with excellent sound quality; and custom, handcrafted Kyle Creed banjos are sold and distributed by Mountain Records, for whom Creed has recorded. After he returned from doing construction work in Colorado during the early sixties, he made a banjo for Fred Cockerham, who was recovering from a cataract eye operation. He used wood from wild cherry trees that grew along Camp Creek near Cockerham's home. In 1963 Fred Cockerham joined Kyle Creed's band, the Camp Creek Boys. (Prior to the formation of the Camp Creek Boys, Fred Cockerham and Kyle Creed played together as the Galax String Band, with Paul Stuphin and Bobby Patterson.)

Now a resident of Galax, Virginia, Kyle Creed plays old-time music with friends from North Carolina and Virginia. He appeared at the 1974 National Folk Festival with Fred Cockerham and guitarist Bobby Patterson, who has worked with Creed and Cockerham on numerous occasions. His recordings on the Mountain label include *Square Dance Time* (M-301), with Kyle Creed, Bobby Patterson, and the Camp Creek Boys; *June Apple* (M-302), an album of old-time fiddling and clawhammer banjo with Tommy Jarrell, Kyle Creed, Bob Patterson, and A. Lineberry; *Mountain Ballads* (M-303); and *Roustabout* (M-304), with Bobby Patterson. He is featured with other clawhammer banjoists on the album *Clawhammer Banjo* (County 701); and he and his old-time string band have recorded

*The Camp Creek Boys* (County 709) and *Virginia Reel* (L-2053) on Leader, an English, Leader label. (*See also* Fred Cockerham; Tommy Jarrell.)

## The Critics Group. *See* Ewan MacColl.

## David Crosby. *See* The Byrds; Crosby, Stills, Nash and Young.

## Crosby, Stills, Nash and Young
*Vocal and instrumental group, performers, and recording artists*

Some of the top contemporary recordings of this era are the outgrowth of unique combinations of musicians whose temporary fusion has brought about an exciting and significant result. The combination of David Crosby, Stephen Stills, Graham Nash, and Neil Young was a source of musical interest and enthusiasm with their vocal blending, sophisticated lyrics, and original instrumentation. Throughout their career as a group, each member was simultaneously pursuing a solo career, retaining his individuality while functioning as an integral part of a group sound.

Formerly of the Byrds, David Crosby is a Californian who is highly respected as a twelve-string guitarist and a songwriter of such works as "Déjà Vu," "Almost Cut My Hair," "Guinnevere," "Long Time Gone," and "Triad," among others. His vocal harmonies, which contributed to the Byrds' distinctive sound, evolved from background work to lead singing with Crosby, Stills, Nash and Young.

Originally of New Orleans, Stephen Stills established a reputation as lead guitarist, singer, and songwriter of Buffalo Springfield. His work appears on recordings by other top artists, including Joan Baez, Judy Collins, and Richie Havens. Lead guitarist, singer, and keyboard musician for Crosby, Stills, Nash and Young, Stills contributed a number of songs to the group's repertoire, including "Love the One You're With," "49 Bye-Byes," "Carry On," "Find the Cost of Freedom," "Suite: Judy Blue Eyes," and "Helplessly Hoping," among others.

Formerly of Manchester, England, and the Hollies, Graham Nash contributed his talents as guitarist, pianist, vocalist, and songwriter. Well-known for his high harmonies, Nash excelled in composing simple melodies and straightforward lyrics, as exemplified by "Our House," "Teach Your Children," "Marrakesh Express," and "Chicago."

Neil Young, a Canadian who settled in California, came to Crosby, Stills and Nash after the trio had cut its initial LP. Formerly associated with Buffalo Springfield, Young brought to Crosby, Stills, Nash and Young his abilities as a guitarist, singer, and songwriter. His original compositions range in emotional content from bittersweet to fiery rage—"On the Way Home," "Cowgirl in the Sand," "Southern Man," "Don't Let It Bring You Down," "Ohio," "Helpless," and so on.

Crosby, Stills and Nash commenced their combined recording efforts in 1969, and their first album included a broad range of material infused with intelligence and a level of sophistication which set them apart from the mainstream of contemporary styles. Their LP was met with an enthusiastic response, and their subsequent tour was equally successful. Neil Young then joined the group, and they recorded their next album as Crosby, Stills, Nash and Young, followed by another tour. By the summer of 1970 their name was selling out concert halls, and their performances demonstrated their versatility at working alone and with the group. Each member had a solo act which was integrated within the framework of the group act, and, at times, Crosby, Stills, Nash and Young presented an electric set to fill out their sound with bass and drums.

Neil Young was the only member who had recorded on his own—*Neil Young* (Reprise RPS [S]6317) and *Everybody Knows This Is Nowhere* (RPS [S]6349)—prior to working with Crosby, Stills, Nash and Young. Beginning in 1970, each member began recording solo efforts, and Neil Young completed his third album. Since the breakup of the group, David Crosby, Stephen Stills, Graham Nash, and Neil Young have continued to pursue solo careers. In addition to producing numerous solo albums, they have made collaborative efforts, including David Crosby and Graham Nash's *Wind on the Water* (ABC Records ABCD-902).

Crosby, Stills, Nash and Young recorded several albums for Atlantic Records during the course of their career as a group.

## The Cumberland Three. *See* John Stewart.

## Agnes "Sis" Cunningham

*Cofounder and editor of New York's* Broadside *magazine, singer, accordionist, and performer*

Dedicated to organizing and fighting for the right of working people and involved in the American folk music scene since the 1930s, Agnes "Sis" Cunningham is best known for the cofounding (with her writer-journalist husband Gordon Friesen) of *Broadside* in 1962. With the help of Pete Seeger and Gil Turner, the mimeographed topical music publication made possible the printing of songs written in the folk genre, but with contemporary relevance, by young singer-songwriters of the sixties. Since its printing of "Talking John Birch" (which marked the first publication of a song by Bob Dylan) in *Broadside #1*, which came out in February 1962, the magazine has maintained its prominence in the field through the efforts of editor Sis Cunningham, who continues to produce *Broadside* in the Upper West Side

New York apartment where she and her husband now live.

Both Sis Cunningham and Gordon Friesen share a background of protest against injustice—culminating in the concept of combating adverse conditions through music. Sis Cunningham was born in 1909 in Blaine County, Oklahoma; her father was a Socialist and a supporter of labor organizer Eugene V. Debs. After graduating from the high school one and a half miles from her family's small farm, she attended a teachers college and then taught in her home state for four years. When she joined her older brother, who was a teacher at the unaccredited Commonwealth Labor College in Arkansas, she began to compose songs and to sing with a theatrical group. During the summer of 1937 she taught music at a Socialist school near Asheville, North Carolina, and when she returned to Oklahoma at the end of the summer, she became an organizer for the Southern Tenant Farmers Union. In 1939 she participated with the Red Dust Players in presenting topical skits and songs for sharecroppers and for the Oil Workers Union. Two years later, she met Gordon Friesen, who stayed with her family while working on an Oklahoma City committee for the defense of individuals arrested during the backlash of reaction to organizing. They were married in the summer of 1941 and moved to New York, where Sis Cunningham immediately became involved with the Almanac Singers.

The structure of the Almanac Singers allowed various members to become an integral part of the group as some members would not be present and others would fill in. Along with other young radicals, Sis Cunningham sang and often played accordion with the Almanacs at union gatherings and fund raisings. During 1941 and 1942 she and her husband lived in Almanac House in Greenwich Village with Woody Guthrie, Lee Hays, Millard Lampell, and Pete Seeger, and they worked together in composing lyrics for topical songs set to old folk melodies. Sis Cunningham proudly recalls her participation in the Almanac Singers' efforts: "I was duly chosen as a member of the Almanac Singers at a meeting which also included Bess Lomax. After I was designated a member, I lived with my husband at Almanac House as long as it was in existence. The last of the 'Almanac houses'—a third- or fourth-floor walk-up on Hudson Street in the Village—was occupied by myself, my husband, and Woody Guthrie, who was then writing his book *Bound for Glory*." After the summer of 1942, the Almanac Singers ceased to function as a group, and for a while Sis Cunningham performed with Sonny Terry and Brownie McGhee, or with Woody Guthrie and Cisco Houston, as the Almanacs.

The next highlight of her career was the inception of *Broadside* magazine, which came about after a meeting with Pete Seeger and his wife Toshi, Gil Turner, and Cunningham's husband Gordon Friesen. Gil Turner brought the young singer-songwriter Bob Dylan to a subsequent meeting, and Sis Cunningham reflects on the course of events: "He [Bob Dylan] came to *Broadside* editorial meetings for over a year, in 1962–63, and he was on our contributing editors list for quite some time, and he *contributed*—not only songs but a lengthy prose poem in the form of a letter to *Broadside*."

The topical song publication was instrumental in giving exposure to many "undiscovered" songwriters, and *Broadside* reached its peak in this capacity during the mid-sixties. As rock music started to dominate the music scene in the United States, protest songs with simple folk tunes waned in popularity, and it became difficult for *Broadside* to perpetuate its promotion of topical songs in the folk idiom. Sis Cunningham, Gordon Friesen, and their two daughters continue to publish *Broadside* "in the Woody Guthrie tradition," printing topical protest songs by new young writers. (*See also* The Almanac Singers; *Broadside*.)

## DaCosta Woltz's Southern Broadcasters. *See* Tommy Jarrell.

## Barbara Dane

*Singer, guitarist, owner of the club Sugar Hill, Home of the Blues; founder of Paredon Records, performer, and recording artist*

In the past several decades, American folk music has brought forth artists whose ideas have served to revitalize the field by challenging our commercial culture. In some cases, artists have turned their backs on the chance for commercial success, singing, instead, on behalf of personally endorsed causes for audiences which the artist hopes to enlist in those causes. At the peak of the recent folk music revival, Barbara Dane was performing regularly in top folk clubs and had a recording contract; but she turned it all down to sing for causes, not commercialism.

Born on May 12, 1927, in Detroit, Michigan, Barbara Spillman took piano and voice lessons as a young girl. In her late teens, she started working in a Detroit factory, learning her first folk songs during a union strike and singing for a large public "in front of the factory gates to thousands of people at a time" in 1946. She moved to California in 1949 and sang on a radio program called *Light and Mellow*; she worked in a department store and as a door-to-door saleswoman to support her infant son, and

won the Miss U.S. Television talent contest in San Francisco. She started her own (the first commercial) folk music series, *Folksville*, on KGO-TV, for which she was paid sixteen dollars a week. After the birth of two more children, she became active on a program on KPFA-Pacifica Radio, produced small folk music concerts, and sang. Her resumed full-time work in music involved combining folk music and blues, and she often worked with San Francisco jazz bands of the traditional revival, such as Turk Murphy, Bob Mielke's Bearcats, George Lewis, Kid Ory, and others. She toured the Eastern seaboard with Jack Teagarden and Red Nichols, did a television special with Louis Armstrong, worked a nightclub act opposite Lenny Bruce, and recorded with Barbary Coast, Dot, Capitol and Tradition Records.

When she was asked to form a band with which to open in Las Vegas, Barbara Dane refused when she was told that no blacks were allowed. She sang in coffeehouses and performed solo nightclub jobs, and she formed a trio with Kenny Whitson on piano and Wellman Braud on bass. After several television appearances and touring with Bob Newhart, she settled down again in San Francisco to run her own club, Sugar Hill, Home of the Blues, and did a children's television series. In 1964 she dropped out of commercial work to tour Mississippi during Freedom Summer, and she sang on a University of California campus during the Free Speech Movement. She left commercial work completely as a protest against blacklisting and the Vietnam war, and, at this point, devoted her full energies to the antiwar effort.

In 1965 Barbara Dane coordinated the Sing-in for Peace at New York's Carnegie Hall, in which more than sixty top folk music personalities appeared. She edited *The Vietnam Songbook* with Irwin Silber and performed at every major New York and Washington demonstration and many marches elsewhere, devoting her full energies for approximately four years to the GI resistance movement, organizing and singing at bases all over the United States, in England, Japan, and the Philippines. In 1966 she was invited to Cuba as the first people's singer to tour that country, thereby breaking the blockade; when she returned to the United States in 1967, she toured with Vietnamese, Latin American, African, and European political singers. In the winter of 1974–75, Barbara Dane was invited to sing in Vietnam, where she gave a concert in Hanoi's Worker's Hall and sang for workers, farmers, fishermen, and students all the way south to Quang Tri province, which was then the most northerly occupied area of South Vietnam.

Her main goal in founding Paredon Records was to issue and to distribute political songs from United States and liberation struggles everywhere. Her own recordings on the label include *FTA! Songs of the GI Resistance* (P-1003) and *I Hate the Capitalist System* (P-1014), which contains a selection of songs of the American working class and the struggle against oppression.

Barbara Dane has helped many blues artists in making records at a time when blues was not so commercial. She was instrumental in getting Brownie McGhee and Sonny Terry their first records together; helped Jesse Fuller to become known outside the San Francisco area; introduced Memphis Slim and Willie Dixon to white nightclub audiences; and, in the mid-fifties, she was a strong promoter of the blues revival.

Barbara Dane rejected the "folksinger" image as a result of ABC-TV's *Hootenanny's* blacklisting of Pete Seeger because of his confrontation with the House Un-American Activities Committee, and when she was invited to appear on the first show she refused as a matter of principle. After others who originally refused began appearing, she held her position and discovered that the job offers had stopped coming. Barbara Dane decided that the term "folksinger" had become hopelessly compromised, and she began calling herself a "people's singer." Throughout the duration of the folk revival, she was never officially invited to appear at a major folk festival, although several times she appeared spontaneously at the request of fellow performers.

Recently, Barbara Dane has begun performing and working with other musicians, and in 1975 she made appearances in Washington, D.C., at the Orphan in Chicago, at the now-defunct Ash Grove in Los Angeles, and at New York's Folk City. She is also on the editorial advisory board of *Sing Out!* magazine, with which she has been involved for a number of years. (*See also* Irwin Silber.)

## Chan Daniels. *See* The Highwaymen.

## Erik Darling

*Group and solo singer, guitarist, banjoist, songwriter, performer, and recording artist*

Erik Darling has drawn upon multifarious traditions in folk music, and his work encompasses a broad spectrum from blues to ballads, gospel, classical, jazz, folk, and country music. One of the foremost figures of the folk song revival of the mid-1950s to mid-1960s, he is noted for his diversity of roles as solo performer, group singer with the Tarriers, the Weavers, and the Rooftop Singers, and instrumental accompanist on the five-string banjo, six-string guitar, and twelve-string guitar.

Born September 25, 1933, in Baltimore, Maryland, Erik Darling spent a childhood of moving between Canandaigua, New York, and New York City, finally settling in New York City prior to the outset of the popular folk movement. By his late teens, Darling had had exposure to many forms of music, but his main focus of self-expression was in the folk idiom: "As a child, my first musical interests were classical and Negro gospel music. By the age of fifteen or so, I had learned three chords on the guitar and my heroes were Burl Ives and Josh White. About the same time, I became an admirer of the calypso music of Haiti as well as some Jamaican folk songs.

"When I came to settle in New York City, I first heard the sound of the five-string banjo on a recording made by Pete Seeger, and I became an enthusiast of that instrument. In the North, at that time, you could practically count on the fingers of one hand the people who were interested in and played folk songs on the five-string banjo. In New York City there was a small group of people who were banjo and guitar enthusiasts and would gather in Washington Square Park on Sunday afternoons to sing and play songs. It was there that I first heard group singing and became interested in the emotional power of harmony. At about this same time, I found an obscure recording of a black man by the name of Leadbelly, known for singing his way out of prison, his playing of the twelve-string guitar, and his unbending, individualistic way of putting his soul on the line through his music. I responded very strongly to his power and the unique sound that he produced on the twelve-string guitar; apparently he was the only person who was playing that instrument at the time, or, at least, no person I knew spoke of any others, nor was there any mention of other twelve-

string guitar players having been recorded. Also at about this time, I became an admirer of other styles of music that could be found in New York, such as Merle Travis, Lester Flatt and Earl Scruggs with the Foggy Mountain Boys, Brownie McGhee and Sonny Terry, and the Weavers.

"The sound and spirited musical tension created by the Weavers inspired me to want to be in a group that sang in harmony, so at one point I started to form a group, hoping to be able to spend my life expressing the kind of feelings I got from the Weavers' arrangements of such songs as 'Darling Corey' and 'Wimoweh.' What was originally a quartet called the Tunetellers eventually changed and rechanged into the Tarriers, a trio with Alan Arkin, Bob Carey, and myself, and we had a hit record, 'The Banana Boat Song.' A year or two after the hit, Alan Arkin left the group, and he was replaced by Clarence Cooper. A year or so after that, Pete Seeger left the Weavers, and I was asked to help finish a record on which they were working. For a while I worked in both groups, but finally I joined the Weavers on a full-time basis."

Erik Darling worked with the Weavers for four and a half years and then decided to pursue a solo career, performing in the coffeehouse circuit and traveling to many cities in the United States. In the meantime, he came across the song "Walk Right In," and, considering its possibility as a hit, he reworked the lyrics and added the sound of the twelve-string guitar. Almost a year later, he formed a group with Bill Svanoe, who was studying economics at Oberlin College, and Lynne Taylor, a jazz singer. Erik Darling recapitulates their brief career: "With two twelve-string guitars playing the same melodic line, we had a hit, with 'Walk Right In,' as the Rooftop Singers. We never found another song which quite matched us as well as did 'Walk Right In.' Demand for our performances dwindled without strong material, and the personalities and interests of the members became less inclined toward creativity, the result being that we eventually disbanded."

During the last year and a half of the Rooftop Singers, Erik Darling met Patricia Street, who was interested in writing songs, and they began to collaborate as a composing team. Mindy Stuart had replaced Lynne Taylor in the trio, and Patricia Street took the place of Mindy Stuart as the third and last member to make the Rooftop Singers' final recordings and concert appearances. Darling had hoped that he and Street could produce some fresh material for the Rooftop Singers, but the outcome has been more far-reaching, as he says: "Our songwriting style turned out to be best suited to a somewhat different musical ingredient than that which was inherent in the Rooftop Singers, and we very much liked the material that we were creating, so we continued to write songs for the next ten years. We have just finished recording an album for Vanguard Records [released in October 1975] with our best songs, and the album is called *The Possible Dream* [Vanguard VSD 79363], by Darling and Street."

In addition to his recordings with the Tarriers, the Weavers, and the Rooftop Singers, Erik Darling has made three solo LPs, one on Elektra (EKL 154), and two on the Vanguard label, *True Religion* (VRS 9099) and *Train Time* (VRS 9131). He has also recorded many albums with Ed McCurdy, accompanying him on five-string banjo and six-string guitar; and he can be heard as accompanist on over thirty albums of such artists as Oscar Brand, Judy Collins, Jack Elliott, Cynthia Gooding, and others. (*See also* The Rooftop Singers; The Tarriers; The Weavers.)

**Cleo Davis.** *See* The Blue Grass Boys.

**John Davis.** *See* The Georgia Sea Island Singers.

# Reverend Gary Davis

*Gospel-blues singer, guitarist, banjoist, mouth harpist, songwriter, performer, teacher, recording artist, and minister*

Although totally blind, Rev. Gary Davis was a master of the fingerpicking blues guitar style and an animated performer who presented a varied approach to the different types of music in his repertoire—blues, spirituals, ragtime, and dance tunes. He sang and played his perfected guitar styles and techniques throughout the United States and in Canada, and, with his expertise as a singer, instrumentalist, storyteller, teacher, and preacher, became one of the most influential figures in blues history.

Gary Davis was born on April 30, 1896, in the poor farming community of Laurens, South Carolina. He taught himself to play guitar, banjo, and mouth harp, and, when he was about ten, made his first guitar out of a tin can and a stick. By his teens, he had established a reputation as a musician, and he began a career which was to include extensive traveling—even after he was ordained as a minister in 1933. While living in Greenville, South Carolina, he organized a string band which included guitarist Willie Walker, whom Davis considered among the best he ever heard.

Davis was ordained in 1933 in Washington, North Carolina, and by 1935 he was living in Durham, North Carolina. He had become acquainted with Blind Boy Fuller and Sonny Terry, and they often got together to make music. In 1935 Rev. Gary Davis made his first trip to New York City to record for the Perfect Record Company (ARC), along with Blind Boy Fuller. Most of his initial recordings were religious songs (he played only religious material after he was ordained), and, unlike Blind Boy Fuller, whose recordings were commercially popular in the rhythm-and-blues field, Rev. Gary Davis was not invited to make subsequent recordings.

Around 1940, he and his second wife (the former Annie Wright) moved to New York City, where he was seen regularly thereafter,

Reverend Gary Davis at the 1965 Newport Folk Festival

singing and playing in Harlem's streets and churches. Word of his talent spread, and in 1949 he recorded two sides of a 78-RPM disc. In 1951 he recorded one side of an album for Prestige Records, with Pink Anderson recordings being used on the other side. Three years later, he produced recordings for Stinson Records. He appeared regularly in local coffeehouses and started giving guitar lessons while simultaneously maintaining his deep involvement with religion and church activities. Rev. Gary Davis was among the performers at the first Newport Folk Festival in 1959, and throughout the sixties he was featured at other major events, including the Philadelphia Folk Festival.

When Peter, Paul and Mary popularized his composition "Samson and Delilah" with their 1963 version of the song, Rev. Gary Davis used his royalty money to purchase a home in Jamaica, Queens. He continued his guitar instruction and personal appearances at clubs and concerts, and he was recorded on numerous occasions.

In the fall of 1971, Rev. Gary Davis's health began to fail, and although he played his guitar infrequently, he enjoyed listening to visitors who came and played for him. Only rarely did he attend church or give lessons while he was ill, and he performed in only one concert, in April 1972. On May 5, 1972, he suffered a heart attack while en route to New Jersey, and died in a nearby hospital.

Recordings of this finger-style guitar virtuoso appear on a number of different labels, including Adelphi, Advent, Biograph, Fantasy, Kicking Mule, Stinson, and Yazoo.

## Peter Davis. *See* The Georgia Sea Island Singers.

## Walter Davis. *See* The Blue Ridge Mountain Entertainers.

## Jim Dawson

*Contemporary songwriter, singer, performer, and recording artist*

Jim Dawson was born on June 27, 1946, in Miami, Oklahoma. When he was nine years old, he moved with his family to Littleton, Colorado, where he lived until 1964, when he graduated from high school and joined the navy. As a teenager, his involvement in music led to his teaching himself to play guitar and piano, writing his first song at age seventeen, and playing with a group in high school: "Then I joined the navy, which took me away from Colorado to the East Coast, and, when I was there, I started singing again. After the navy, I was faced with a decision to go back to Colorado or to come to New York to try to put something together."

Influenced by the folk music boom and the rock movement of the sixties, Jim Dawson's music "falls someplace between folk music and rock 'n' roll." Dawson plays acoustic guitar and both electric and acoustic piano. His first two albums were recorded on the Kama Sutra label: *Songman* (KSBS-2035), in 1970; and *You'll Never Be Lonely with Me* (KSBS-2049), in late 1971. At this point, Terry Cashman and Tommy West worked intensively with Dawson, and, when he signed with RCA Records in 1974, the outcome of their combined efforts was reflected in *Jim Dawson* (CPL1-0601). Dawson's admiration for Ian Tyson is evidenced by his intimate rendition of "Four Strong Winds," the only nonoriginal cut on the album: "I love his writing, and I have loved the song since 1961, or whenever I first heard it." In 1975 RCA released his next album, entitled *Elephants in the Rain* (RCA APL1-0993).

An active performer, Jim Dawson captivates his audiences with exceptional warmth and sincerity, and his music is a reflection of one of the most genuine personalities in the recording industry today.

## Diane Decker. *See* The Serendipity Singers.

# The Delmore Brothers

*Vocal and instrumental duo, songwriters, performers, and recording artists*

Among the early country music pioneers of the *Grand Ole Opry*, the guitar-playing Delmore Brothers were influential in the development of a unique close-harmony-duet vocal style. Their bluesy brand of country music was derived from an adaptation of Southern black styles, and the Delmores were important for their extensive use of traditional material. Many of their original works are now considered traditional country music standards and are included in the repertoires of various modern country performers.

Alton Delmore was born on December 25, 1908, in Elkmont, Alabama, and his younger brother Rabon was born there almost two years later, on December 3, 1910. They were raised on a farm, and they sang from the time they were young boys. Alton Delmore taught his younger brother to play the guitar, and they were both proficient fiddlers by their teens. For several years they performed at local events and regional contests, and they learned a vast number of traditional songs from their family, friends, and other musicians.

Their professional career, which was to span more than thirty-one years, was initiated by their appearance before an Atlanta, Georgia, radio station microphone in October 1931. In addition to marking their debut performance at a radio station, it became their first recording session, as "Got the Kansas City Blues"/"Alabama Lullaby" was issued by Columbia Records. In the following year, their ambition of joining other entertainers on the *Grand Ole Opry* was realized when they were asked to take the place of the Pickard Family after auditioning with original, traditional, and request songs.

The Delmores played with a relaxed and polished style, and, unlike the majority of contemporary string bands, they used guitars (six-string and four-string tenor guitar) as lead instruments. Another factor which contributed to their individuality and prominence was their perfection at singing in soft, light harmony; they were considered one of the top male duets of this early period. Along with the Monroes and the Bolicks, the Delmores created a vocal-duet craze in country music during the thirties, and they were instrumental in the resurgence of traditional-style music in the post-Depression years. From 1934 to 1939 they recorded on the Bluebird label, and, later, on Decca and King Records of Cincinnati.

When the Delmores left the *Grand Ole Opry* in 1941, they were featured on numerous *Opry*-like shows on such radio stations as WPTF in Raleigh, North Carolina, WFBC in Greenville, South Carolina, WAPI in Birmingham, Alabama, WIBC in Indianapolis, Indiana, and KWHN in Fort Smith, Arkansas. While they were appearing on the *Boone County Jamboree* on WLW in Cincinnati, they became the second artists (following Grandpa Jones and Merle Travis) to record for King Records. Throughout their recording career, the Delmore Brothers cut an assortment of country songs—mostly original numbers by Alton Delmore, who composed in excess of a thousand tunes during his lifetime—and their postwar recordings were among their most successful. Their collaboration with Lonnie Glosson and Wayne Raney, "Blues Stay Away from Me," recorded on May 6, 1949, was a major hit of that year. Their work with harp-playing Wayne Raney produced other successful discs, and the guitar-and-harmonica combination used by the Delmores was employed by other musicians in the years that followed.

Wayne Raney was born on August 17, 1921, near Batesville, Arkansas. As a result of a crippled foot, his boyhood activities were relatively restricted, and he became involved in music at a young age. As a boy of eleven, he was influenced by Lonnie Glosson, whom he met several years later while working on Texas and Mexico border radio stations. When Raney was seventeen years old, he teamed up with Glosson, performing as a dual-harmonica act on KARK in Little Rock, Arkansas, in 1938. They worked together periodically during the forties and fifties, and Glosson later recorded for Raney's Rimrock label in the sixties. The year 1941 found Raney in Cincinnati as host of his own show on WCKY and salesman of what he described as "talking harmonicas," an expression which was used by others in describing Raney's own music. He met the Delmores and began working as a sideman, and in 1946 he made a recording of his "Harmonica Blues" under their names. Their association lasted for several years, and after a year with the *Grand Ole Opry*, Raney returned to Cincinnati. His recording sessions became less frequent, and he finally left the King label in 1955. In 1961, after quitting his job at WCKY, he settled in Concord, near his birthplace of Wolf Bayou, Arkansas, and started his own recording studio called Rimrock.

The Delmore–Raney partnership produced some of the most significant music of the late forties. Another association which yielded memorable results included Alton and Rabon Delmore, with (reputedly) Red Foley, Grandpa Jones, Merle Travis, and others on different occasions, as the Brown's Ferry Four (named after Alton Delmore's well-known novelty song, "Brown's Ferry Blues").

When their career was terminated by the death of Rabon Delmore on December 4, 1952, Alton Delmore continued to engage in professional activities, which included a radio program on a station in southeastern Mississippi in the early sixties.

At the age of fifty-six, Alton Delmore passed away in Nashville, Tennessee, on July 4, 1964.

## Alton Delmore. *See* The Delmore Brothers.

## Rabon Delmore. *See* The Delmore Brothers.

## Sandy Denny. *See* Fairport Convention.

## John Denver

*Contemporary singer-songwriter, guitarist, performer, recording artist, and television personality*

The "Poet Laureate of Colorado," John Denver was the biggest-selling pop music artist in America by the latter months of 1974; and, since then, he has maintained his status as America's top multimedia superstar on records, stage, and television. The naturalistic content of his music, combined with his pure vocals, produces an image of Thoreau-like simplicity and wholesomeness; and, although an enigmatic figure in commercial, popular music, John Denver is a convincing exponent of "clean living" when he sings his dramatic renditions of such songs as "Rocky Mountain High," "Starwood in Aspen," "The Eagle and the Hawk," "Aspen Glow," "Sunshine on My Shoulders," "Take Me Home, Country Roads," and many, many others.

Born Henry John Deutschendorf, Jr., he grew up in an air force family and attended schools throughout the United States. He was first turned on to music by Elvis Presley, and he took guitar lessons on an old 1910 Gibson given to him as a boy (his song, "This Old Guitar," relates to the instrument that his grandmother gave him). In high school he was known as "Mr. Nice Guy, Mr. Average," involved in school, football, church, and a few bands. He played an electric guitar until the Kingston Trio came along with "Tom Dooley," and then, like many other youngsters growing up in the late fifties, John Denver turned his attention to folk music. As a graduation present, he was given a Fender Jazzmaster and Fender Pro Amp, and he played mostly with rock 'n' roll bands as rhythm guitarist.

He majored in architecture at Texas Tech College, pledged a fraternity, played with a band, and sang by himself. His involvement with folk music was growing deeper, and he was listening to Joan Baez, the Chad Mitchell Trio, Peter, Paul and Mary, and the New Christy Minstrels; and the type of music that he had started singing on his own was being labeled by people as "folk music." He left college in the middle of his junior year to pursue music as a living.

He traveled to California, worked for a draftsman, and sang wherever he could; by his second year on the West Coast, he was performing as a solo act at Randy Sparks's Leadbetter's club in Los Angeles. The twenty-year-old Denver worked for a while at the Lumbermill club in Phoenix, and when he returned to Los Angeles, he learned that Chad Mitchell was leaving the Chad Mitchell Trio and a replacement was being sought. His audition tape stirred enthusiasm, and he was sent to New York to audition for the job. He was flown back to Phoenix, where he resumed work at the Lumbermill until he received a phone call a few days later and heard the news that he had been chosen to take Mitchell's place. The Mitchell Trio rehearsed for six days then opened at the Cellar Door, in Washington, D.C.

Overnight, John Denver changed from a West Coast solo folksinger to a member of a well-known folk group which enjoyed a nationwide reputation of commercial prominence. A new element was added to the group when Denver joined up with Joe Frazier and Mike Kobluk: the sound of a six- and twelve-string guitar, which had never been used by the group until then. By 1967 John Denver had composed "Leaving, on a Jet Plane," which was picked up and turned into a smash hit by Peter, Paul and Mary. After working with the Mitchell Trio for nearly four years, with both Frazier and Kobluk being replaced, Denver played for a short while with David Boise and Mike Johnson as Denver, Boise and Johnson. When Johnson pulled out of the trio, John Denver started planning a career as a solo performer.

John Denver decided to make his initial effort as an unknown, solo performer in

John Denver

Winslow Pinney

Aspen, Colorado, a community of ski resorts with less pressure than urban centers. (The expansive beauty of Colorado and a previous glimpse of the Mile High City had moved him to change his name to Denver, which he has used as a stage name since the mid-sixties.) He was successful in Aspen, and after returning to the Cellar Door, he began working the college coffeehouse circuit. He had his first single on the charts with "Take Me Home, Country Roads," which went right to the top as a No. 1 hit in 1969. His first RCA album, *Rhymes & Reasons* (LSP-4207), was released in 1969; and in the following year his second LP, *Take Me to Tomorrow* (LSP-4278), was issued. His third album, *Whose Garden Was This* (LSP-4414), soon followed, and by 1971 *Poems, Prayers & Promises* (LSP-4499) was on the market. This fourth LP contained Denver's first million-selling single, "Take Me Home, Country Roads," and it was his first album

to become a Gold Record. His two suc-
ceeding albums, *Aerie* (LSP-4607) and
*Rocky Mountain High* (LSP-4731) also
turned gold, and the title cut from his sixth
LP, "Rocky Mountain High," was one of the
top hits of 1973. In June of that same year,
*Farewell Andromeda* (APL1-0101) came
out, and, in November, RCA packaged *John
Denver's Greatest Hits* (CPL1-0374).

Originally included among the selections
on *Poems, Prayers & Promises*, "Sunshine on
My Shoulders" was released as a single;
following the television special *Sunshine*,
which used "Sunshine on My Shoulders" as
its theme song, Denver's single soared to the
top of the charts. After his successful ABC-
TV show of 1974, *The John Denver Special*,
another album was released, *Back Home
Again* (CPL1-0548), which included another
smash single, "Annie's Song." The year
1975 brought forth *An Evening with John
Denver* (CPL2-0764), a two-record set of a
live recording at Universal Amphitheater,
Universal City, California on August 26–
September 1, 1974, *Windsong* (CPL1-1183),
and *Rocky Mountain Christmas* (APL1-
1201). To date, John Denver has had nine
consecutive Gold Albums, five of which are
consecutive Platinum Albums.

John Denver and his wife Annie adopted a
son, Zach, and when this superstar of the
seventies is not on the road, touring, he
spends his time with his family at home in
the Aspen community of Starwood.

# The Dew Mountain Boys. *See*
Lee Allen.

# Hazel Dickens. *See* The Strange
Creek Singers.

# The Dillards

*Vocal and instrumental group, performers, and
recording artists*

A number of performers on the contemporary music scene defy classification by the
nature of their versatile and broad-ranging
musical styles. With their foundation in
bluegrass music, the Dillards have
developed to a level of musicianship which is
demonstrative of their consistent high-
quality sound, regardless of its categorization as pop, country, rock, folk-rock, or
bluegrass.

During the early 1960s, the original
Dillards consisted of Doug and Rodney
Dillard, banjo and guitar, Mitch Jayne,
acoustic bass, and Dean Webb, mandolin.
They traveled by car from their Missouri
hometowns to California, where they signed
a recording contract with Elektra Records
and cut their first LP, *Back Porch Bluegrass*
(EKS-7232), consisting of fifteen solid
bluegrass selections. Two of the songs, "Old
Man at the Mill" and "Dooley," were recut
on subsequent albums, and one of the banjo
tunes, "Duelin' Banjo," was popularized
years later by the film *Deliverance*.

Douglas and Rodney Dillard came from a
musical background; their father was an
old-time fiddler who encouraged his sons to
develop their musical talents. The Dillard
family of Salem, Missouri, has boasted a
long line of musicians, many specializing in
bluegrass, and both Doug and Rodney
Dillard are versed in all bluegrass instruments. Another all-instrument man,
Dean Webb of Independence, Missouri,
specialized in bluegrass mandolin; and one
of the Dillards' neighbors, Mitchell Jayne,
acted as the Dillards' spokesman and bassist.

The group began playing various clubs
and making television appearances, most
notably on *The Andy Griffith Show*. Their
act was always a combination of comedy an-
tics and authentic bluegrass music, and the
enthusiasm generated by their live performance led to the recording of their second LP, *The Dillards, Live!!! Almost!!!*
(Elektra EKS-7265). The country-rooted
harmonies of the Dillards were listened to
carefully by other contemporary groups,
especially the Byrds, whose folk-rock vocals
were influenced by these four bluegrass
musicians. In 1965 the Dillards recorded
their third LP, *Pickin' and Fiddlin'* (Elektra

EKS-7285), featuring fiddler Byron Berline. The group continued touring the club and concert circuit, went over to Capitol Records, and recorded singles like Tom Paxton's "The Last Thing on My Mind" and "Nobody Knows." When Doug Dillard left (he later joined up with ex-Byrd Gene Clark to form the Dillard and Clark Expedition), Herb Pederson was recruited as his replacement.

By 1968 the Dillards were again recording for Elektra, and their next album, *Wheatstraw Suite* (EKS-74035), brought their music into the realm of pop instrumentation, with drums, electric bass, and pedal steel used in addition to their standard banjo, mandolin, and acoustic bass. The selections on the album covered a broader range of musical forms; and, in the following year, drummer Paul York was added to the group. *Copperfields* (EKS-74054) reached farther in the Dillards' exploration of new directions while including some traditional Dillard tunes. Pop-folk songs by Eric Andersen, Nilsson, and Kenny O'Dell were among the selections, and Nilsson's "Rainmaker" received substantial airplay. The album was commercially unsuccessful, and the Dillards recorded their next record for the White Whale label (which became Anthem Records). Their single, "One Too Many Mornings," was followed by "It's About Time," and when Anthem became affiliated with United Artists Records, the Dillards were added to the UA roster. Billy Ray Latham had replaced Herb Pederson, who left to form the Country Gazette, and the Dillards recorded a single, "One A.M.," and then an LP, *Roots and Branches* (Anthem ANS 5901), released in 1972. Their most highly acclaimed album to date, it was followed by another single, Paul Parrish's "America," which was also a commercially successful hit for the Dillards. When Anthem parted ways with United Artists, the Dillards moved over to another division of the company, Poppy, recording *Tribute to the American Duck* (Poppy PP-LA175-F), which was released in 1973.

**Doug Dillard.** *See* The Dillards.

**Rodney Dillard.** *See* The Dillards.

**The Dixieliners.** *See* The McGee Brothers; Fiddlin' Arthur Smith.

# Dobro

A stringed instrument similar to the guitar, the dobro produces a sustained, ringing tonal quality reminiscent of the Hawaiian guitar. Four, six, or eight strings are extended between the bridge and the resonator cone, which gives the instrument its unique sound.

The dobro was invented by the Dopera Brothers, who had started constructing guitars with raised strings in the mid-1920s, but, it was not until 1929 that they formed the Dobro Guitar Company and got their instruments patented. The term *dobro* means "good" in the Slavic language (the Doperas were of Czechoslovak extraction), and the name of the instrument was obtained by using the first couple of letters from *Dopera Brothers*. For several years, John, Ed, and Randy Dopera were the sole manufacturers of the instrument; but in 1932 the National Music Company bought the Dopera rights and produced the National Dobro until 1954 when Valco Company took over the business.

There exist today two basic styles of dobro playing: one that is derived from earlier "Hawaiian" stylings; and the other a more modern bluegrass sound that is associated with Brother Oswald of Roy Acuff's Smoky Mountain Boys, Josh Graves (who played for years with Earl Scruggs), and, most recently, Mike Auldridge of the Seldom Scene.

**Jerry Donahue.** *See* Fairport Convention.

# Donovan

*Contemporary singer-songwriter, guitarist, performer, and recording artist*

Among the young singer-songwriters who were catapulted into stardom during the folk boom of the sixties was a soft-spoken, poetic musician from Scotland, named Donovan. His original compositions elicited the attention of music and literary circles, and many of his songs ranked among the favorites of that era's youth culture (his well-known rendition of Buffy Sainte-Marie's "Universal Soldier" was a symbol of the protest and antiwar movements). Although his music, from "Catch the Wind" to "Sunshine Superman," "Hurdy Gurdy Man," "Mellow Yellow" (a Jay Award recipient of 1967), "Josie," and "Colors," may never have exceeded the sales of contemporary sensations, Donovan offered a spirit of warmth and humanity to his audiences throughout the world.

Donovan Leitch was born on February 10, 1946, in Glasgow, Scotland, to a working-class family. Until the age of ten, he lived in the Gorbals section of Glasgow, but in 1956 the Leitches resettled near London. As a young boy, Donovan aroused the interest of his teachers with his creativity, and as a teenager he expressed a desire to study art in college. He attended college for a year, but financial difficulties forced him to abandon his education. A friend named Gypsy Davy accompanied Donovan in his wanderings around the English countryside, pursuing self-education; Donovan took along his guitar, which he had learned to play in his early teens, and he began writing songs and stories.

In 1964 he returned to live in London, and after he had approached several record companies, his talent secured him an appearance on BBC-TV's *Ready, Steady, Go*. Two subsequent appearances on the show were soon followed by a recording contract and the release of his first hit single, "Catch the Wind." He came to the United States and was among the guest performers at the 1965 Newport Folk Festival. In recalling subsequent appearances in concert from New York's Carnegie Hall to the West Coast Hollywood Bowl, Donovan once said: "When people used to come up to me and say, 'Wow, you are really influencing all these people,' I knew it was bullshit. The kids were influencing and producing *me*. I was just their singer. Every night in concert we shared. We were old friends. Whether performing for 5,000 or 20,000, there was always a strong bond between me and the audience. That bond, I suppose, was lost in the later sixties because I did fewer and fewer concerts. My record success has always followed my concert success."

An American recording contract with Epic produced his first single release in the United States, "Sunshine Superman," and, within a two-year span, he had over a dozen hit singles issued in this country. Prior to signing with Epic, Donovan had recorded his debut LP for Hickory Records, *Catch the Wind* (Hickory LPM 123), which was followed by such Epic releases as *Sunshine Superman* (Epic BN-26217), *Mellow Yellow* (Epic BN-26239), *A Gift from a Flower to a Garden* (Epic 8ZN-171), *Hurdy Gurdy Man* (Epic BN-26420), and more recently, *Cosmic Wheels* (Epic KE-32156), *Essence to Essence* (Epic KE-32800), *7-Tease* (Epic PE-33245), and *Slow Down World* (Epic PE-33945).

Neither *Cosmic Wheels* (produced in 1972) nor *Essence to Essence* (produced in 1973) was promoted through any touring, as Donovan explains: "They were still in a period of transition, those albums. Even though I was recording again, I was laying back—and I think the whole generation was laying back, too. I didn't feel the need to bring the music any closer to the people. For once, I let the albums speak for themselves." In late 1974, his complete stage show operetta, entitled *7-Tease* (presented through the album of the same name, which was recorded in Nashville and produced by Norbert Putnam), brought Donovan back to the stage, and he proudly discusses his

Donovan at the 1965 Newport Folk Festival

Donovan and Joan Baez performing at the 1965 Newport Folk Festival

return: "I feel my music is needed. I need it and the people will need it. I get a strong positive vibe from the story I have and the idea I want to bring to the people.

"That's the interesting thing about my reappearing in the seventies. To move the audiences again and to make a new relationship will only make an old one stronger. We're all just friends, really."

Donovan has also composed music for the motion pictures *Brother Sun, Sister Moon* and *The Pied Piper of Hamlin* (in which he makes a cameo appearance). Some of his work also appears in the small publication *Dry Songs and Scribbles.*

## Livia Drapkin. *See* Bill Vanaver and Livia Drapkin.

## Jimmy Driftwood

*Singer, songwriter, instrumentalist, performer, recording artist, folklorist, teacher, and organizer of the Rackensack Folklore Society and the Arkansas Folk Festival*

In 1959 Johnny Horton's hit version of the tradition-based ballad "Battle of New Orleans" brought widespread recognition for the country story-song. Based on an old fiddle tune called "The Eighth of January," its lyrics were written by Jimmy Driftwood, who, in the previous year, had recorded a longer version of the ballad on an album for RCA Victor. As the saga song of Andrew Jackson's victorious battle climbed to the top of both popular and country & western charts, another Jimmy Driftwood composition, "Tennessee Stud," was being popularized by its recording by Eddy Arnold. In addition to setting in motion a country saga-song craze, "Battle of New Orleans" focused renewed attention on material rooted in the American folk tradition, along with "Tennessee Stud," which has become a country music classic.

Born James Morris on June 20, 1907, about seven miles from Mountain View, Arkansas, Jimmy Driftwood was raised on a farm in a "saddlebag" house (a double-log house divided by a hallway). Music had been a part of his family's history for many generations, and his own heritage is deeply rooted in Tennessee. Both his great-grandfather and his maternal grandmother had moved from Tennessee to the Ozarks before the Civil War. Jimmy Driftwood grew up amid a wealth of folk songs, and he learned to play the guitar, fiddle, and banjo as a young boy. He collected numerous folk ballads from relatives and friends in the area, and he proudly accompanied his singing on an old guitar made by his grandfather from a fence rail, thin sides from an ox yoke and top and bottom of a headboard which had been part of a bedstead brought to the Ozark Mountains by his grandmother. While he walked the fourteen miles each day to and from high school, the music which he had memorized and learned to write down in "haystack" notes ran through his head. Later on, when he obtained a tape recorder, he traveled throughout the countryside to track down and collect old tunes. He earned his BS in education at the Arkansas State Teachers College in Conway in the early forties and continued to pursue a career as a schoolteacher while maintaining his avocation of collecting and performing at regional folk festivals. During the fifties, he became a popular performer at events outside his home state, and with the upsurge of interest in folk music during the folk revival of the late fifties and early sixties, Jimmy Driftwood's audience continued to expand. The folk boom aroused new enthusiasm in folk material, and he was requested by RCA Victor to record an album entitled *Newly Discovered Early American Folk Songs* (RCA Victor LPM-1635), which included "Battle of New Orleans."

At the time that "Battle of New Orleans" and "Tennessee Stud" were creating a stir in musical circles, Jimmy Driftwood was employed by the *Grand Ole Opry*. He was receiving many offers to appear at major folk festivals, including Newport, and he was playing an instrumental role in spreading the songs and heritage of the Ozark Mountain peoples. When the idea for building a cultural center at Mountain View was presented to him, Jimmy Driftwood left the *Opry* to work on this project for preserving his Ozark Mountain heritage. After organizing the nucleus of supportive citizens, he joined with others in the newly formed Rackensack Folklore Society in a common effort to raise enough money to construct the cultural center. Jimmy Driftwood traveled extensively to inform university students and other folklore society members around the country of the cultural center project and of the upcoming first annual Arkansas Folk Festival scheduled for April 1963. The initial festival was a success, and Driftwood and other Rackensackers continued to seek support from Washington, D.C. Finally, in 1973, the construction of the Ozark Folk Center was completed. Operated by the Arkansas Commission of Parks, Recreation and Tourism, the $3.4-million Ozark Folk Center is located one mile north of the county seat of Mountain View. Until recently, the "Daddy of the Cultural Center," Jimmy Driftwood, was an active participant in the Ozark Folk Center's activities, which have included performances by the Rackensack Folklore Society, Arkansas College workshops in Ozark folklore, and the Arkansas Folk Festival.

Jimmy Driftwood's first recording in ten years was *A Lesson in Folk Music* (Rimrock RLP-496), which is a teaching aid featuring the sounds of numerous instruments used by traditional musicians. This LP was the first release of the Battle Music Company, which was reorganized by Jimmy and Cleda Drift-wood and Barbara Sanders. (*See also* Arkansas Folk Festival.)

## John Duffey. *See* Bill Clifton; The Country Gentlemen; The Seldom Scene.

## Bessyl Duhon. *See* The Balfa Freres.

## Dulcimer. *See* Appalachian (Mountain) Dulcimer.

## Judith Durham. *See* The Seekers.

## Judy Dyble. *See* Fairport Convention.

## Richard Dyer-Bennet
*Singer, lutist, guitarist, composer, arranger, performer, recording artist, and educator*

Often referred to as a "twentieth-century minstrel," this modern-day counterpart of the medieval troubadour brings to the folk song an artful treatment that revitalizes a long-established custom handed down through the ages. In accordance with this primary intention, he opened this country's first School of Minstrelsy in Aspen, Colorado, in the late 1940s.

Richard Dyer-Bennet was born on October 6, 1913, in Leicester, England. He came to the United States in 1925, and he studied music and English at the University of California from 1932 to 1935. His involvement with folk music was fostered by vocal studies with Gertrude Wheeler Beckman and by his encounter with the seventy-five-year-old European folk music scholar Sven Scholander of Sweden. From Scholander he acquired an appreciation for a masterful and individualistic interpretation of the folk song through harmonious unification of poetry, melody, and instrumental accompaniment, and he learned a vast number of Swedish, French, and German folk songs.

When he returned to the United States, he commenced his minstrel-like performances, and, adopting Scholander's style of singing with lute (and later Spanish guitar) accompaniment, Richard Dyer-Bennet brought to college campuses a unique, yet ancient, presentation of this musical form. In *The Ballad Mongers*, Oscar Brand explains his impact on the folk scene in the postwar years: "A trained countertenor with an artful lute, he attracted many who had considered folk music too 'low down.' Dyer-Bennet sang folk songs as if they were art songs. His 'John Henry' is a delicate ballad with graceful guitar figures. It is a tribute to his taste and artistry that many audiences found Leadbelly's 'John Henry' unacceptable after hearing Dyer-Bennet's paraphrase."

He worked with Gertrude Wheeler Beckman until 1941, and from 1943 to 1946 he received guitar instruction from Jose Rey de la Torre. He began his professional career in 1941 at Le Ruban Bleu in New York City. In 1942–43 Richard Dyer-Bennet performed regularly at the Village Vanguard, and he composed and broadcasted propaganda songs for the Office of War Information (OWI). In 1944 he gave the first of his many recitals at New York's Town Hall, along with an appearance at Carnegie Hall. His initial recordings for Harvard University were followed by recording sessions for such commercial labels as Asch, Concert Hall Society, Decca, Disc, Mercury, Stinson, and Vox; more recently, his music has been presented on his own Dyer-Bennet label and on Everest (reissues). In addition to his numerous recordings, Richard Dyer-Bennet has published his own music as well as arrangements of traditional material.

For the past thirty years, Richard Dyer-Bennet has made annual concert tours of the United States. Since 1955 he has operated Dyer-Bennet Records in Woodside, New York. In 1970 he became associate professor in the Theater Arts Department at the State University of New York at Stony Brook, Long Island.

# Bob Dylan

*Singer-songwriter, guitarist, harp player, pianist, performer, recording artist, prose writer, and poet*

Among the generation considered the progeny of Woody Guthrie is, in the words of *New York Times* folk music critic Robert Shelton, "a deceptively quiet, sparse-boned, tousle-haired singer and instrumentalist whose youthful disarray suggests a cross between a choir boy and a beatnik," who has turned the world of music upside down. Once the emulative disciple of the legendary American folk-poet—now the elusive patriarch of the pop-folk culture—Bob Dylan is destined to ride among America's famous heroes on the same train bound for glory.

In the pages of *Broadside* magazine, Alan Weberman called Dylan "one of the wildest, gonest & freakiest studs that ever stomped through the pages of history." A private man, whose personal life is veiled in mystery and contradiction, Dylan, through his singular preeminence, has become a main attraction in the public eye and a controversial topic for debate. "i accept chaos," he wrote in the liner notes of his fifth Columbia album, *Bringing It All Back Home* (Columbia KCS 9128), "i am not sure whether it accepts me."

His story is that of all mankind—his words are, at once, personal and universal. His work is equally deified and misunderstood; but it remains, as he has remained.

"He was not the only one, of course," reflects Pete Hamill in the liner notes of *Blood on the Tracks* (Columbia X698), citing Dylan's enduring reputation amid the turmoil and decadence in his homeland, "he is not the only one now. But of all our poets, Dylan is the one who has most clearly taken the roiled sea and put it in a glass."

As a poet, Dylan provides a voice for the mute and creates into art that which exists in the world around us. In writing of the human condition, he lays bare his own soul—perhaps it is this potentially destructive vulnerability which makes him retreat into exclusion: "i am called a songwriter. a poem is a naked person . . . some people say that i am a poet."

The Bob Dylan phenomenon started in 1961 when, as described by Jack A. Smith in the *National Guardian* (August 22, 1963), "a roughneck rebel poet and dreamer named Bob Dylan, then 20, packing his guitar and songs," left Minnesota for "New York where he settled unquietly on the Lower East Side and set about to dismember the Establishment, limb by limb."

Dylan claims that his rise to fame was merely an accident: "It was never my intention to become a big star. It happened, and there was nothing I could do about it. I tried to get rid of that burden for a long time. I eat and sleep and, you know, have the same problems anybody else does, and yet people look at me funny."

Born Robert Allen Zimmerman on May 24, 1941, in Duluth, Minnesota, he moved with his family to Hibbing when he was six. A self-taught musician, he began experimenting on the piano, then on a harmonica and a Sears, Roebuck guitar, while still in elementary school. His early influences were Hank Williams and all forms of the blues, but the music that affected him most deeply was that of Elvis Presley, Bill Haley and the Comets, Buddy Holly, and, more than any other, Little Richard. Rock 'n' roll became his *raison d'être*, and he became the leader of a band called the Golden Chords. "I was playing music in the '50s," he said in an interview which appeared in *People* magazine

Bob Dylan in winter 1961–62

Bob Dylan performing at Caffé Lena, Saratoga Springs, New York, in winter 1961–62

(November 10, 1975), "and man, it was all I did. It saved my life." As a boy, he wrote poetry; when he was a teenager, his words were transformed into song lyrics. While he was still in high school, he used to drive to Minneapolis, where he spent his time in the coffeehouse section called Dinkytown, near the University of Minnesota, which he attended for one "fidgety" year before coming to the East Coast early in 1961.

When he arrived on the Greenwich Village scene, he was "Bob Dylan, the folksinger," who had been caught up by the urban folk revival along with millions of college students. From traditional music, his style was directed by the Woody Guthrie tradition, and, following in the footsteps of Jack Elliott, Bob Dylan became a dedicated interpreter of his idol's songs. He shunned his Jewish heritage and Midwestern upbringing, and created a new identity based on the romantic, itinerant image of Woody Guthrie. He came East "to see Woody" and "to make it big."

No one in New York knew for certain who he was, or where he had come from, "or that within a single year [wrote Jack Goddard in the *Village Voice*] he would emerge as one of the most gifted and unusual entertainers in the whole country." Through his visits to Woody Guthrie, he met other prominent folksingers, including Jack Elliott, Cisco Houston, and Pete Seeger, who also spent a considerable amount of time at Bob and Sid Gleason's apartment in East Orange, New Jersey, where Guthrie stayed on weekends while a patient at Greystone Hospital. Clad in a Huck Finn corduroy cap, rough boots, work shirt, and worn trousers, Bob Dylan frequented Izzy Young's Folklore Center on MacDougal Street, the Commons, the Gaslight, the Cafe Wha?, the Mills Tavern, Gerde's Folk City, and parties at Mikki Isaacson's apartment on Sheridan Square.

The breakthrough came in the late fall of 1961 when, following an afternoon of recording for Spivey Records as vocal and harp accompanist for Big Joe Williams, Dylan was billed with the Greenbriar Boys at Gerde's for two weeks, beginning September 26. Robert Shelton came to his opening night performance, and, within a few days, *The New York Times* had printed his rave review, entitled "Bob Dylan: A Distinctive Folk-Song Stylist." On the same day that the four-column headline article hit the newsstands, Dylan provided harmonica accompaniment on three cuts of Carolyn Hester's first Columbia album. John Hammond, who had met Dylan on a previous occasion, was intensely interested in the young singer-songwriter and had a contract drafted after hearing Dylan's first demo, "Talking New York"—a Woody Guthrie-style talking-blues number. Bob Dylan became the first among the young folk performers to be signed by a major record company. A concert produced by Izzy Young and held on November 4 at Carnegie Chapter Hall was attended by only about fifty people, but the "flop" did not impede his progress. He recorded his first LP, *Bob Dylan* (Columbia CL 1779/CS 8579), within four sessions, followed by the signing of a seven-year contract with manager Albert Grossman. By the end of February 1962, his debut LP was released, and he entered a period of writing protest songs.

The year 1962 brought his classic "Blowin' in the Wind," which was written in April and published in *Broadside #6* (late May 1962). The song was immediately adopted as the unofficial anthem of the civil rights movement—and Dylan indirectly became one of its leaders. He was writing prolifically by now, and his songs appeared regularly in New York's foremost topical song publication (in the following year, he was included on *Broadside Ballads, Volume 2* [Folkways-Broadside Series BR 301, now 5301], singing as Blind Boy Grunt—Bob Dylan had signed an exclusive recording contract with Columbia Records, so he used the pseudonym in order to bypass his obligation to CBS). There were concert and television appearances; a tour to Britain; "Don't Think Twice, It's All Right"; "Down the Highway"; "Hard Rain"; and his first single

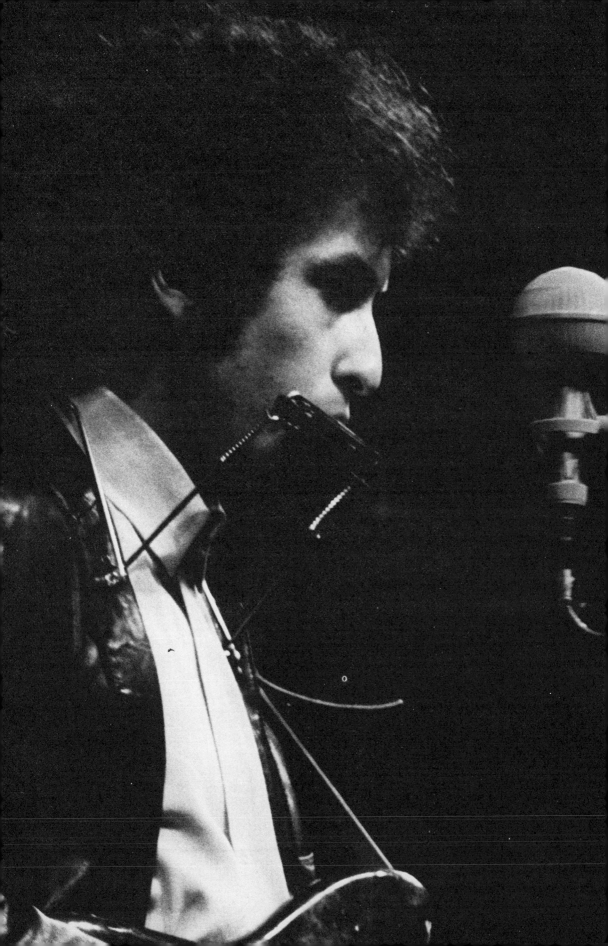

release, "Mixed Up Confusion"/"Corinna, Corinna."

While abroad early in 1963, Dylan composed "Boots of Spanish Leather" and "Girl from the North Country." On April 12, he appeared in his first major solo concert at Town Hall in New York—which was extremely successful and brought enthusiastic reviews in *The New York Times, Billboard*, and other music publications. An offer came from Ed Sullivan to appear on his weekly variety show, but when he was told that he could not sing "Talkin' John Birch Society Blues," Dylan stormed out of the CBS-TV studio (the song was also deleted from his second LP; however, a limited number of copies which included "Birch Society Blues" was issued before the change was finally approved). In mid-May, *The Freewheelin' Bob Dylan* (Columbia CS 8786/CL 1986) was released, and his name began to appear in such publications as *Playboy, The New Yorker*, and *Time*. By midyear, Peter, Paul and Mary had turned his name into a household word with their recording of "Blowin' in the Wind," which sold in excess of 300,000 copies within the first two weeks of its release. Dylan was the box-office attraction at the Newport Folk Festival—and he stole the show as "The Crown Prince of Folk Music," alongside "Folk Queen" Joan Baez. Later that summer Baez invited him to come onstage with her during concerts in the Northeast; then, along with Joan Baez, Harry Belafonte, Mahalia Jackson, Odetta, Peter, Paul and Mary, among others, Bob Dylan participated in the August 28 March on Washington. That fall, he recorded *The Times They Are A-Changin'* (Columbia CS 8905/CL 2105), performed to a full house at New York's Carnegie Hall, and was written up in *Newsweek*.

On February 2, 1964, he set out in a Ford station wagon (along with Paul Clayton and two others) for a cross-country "get-in-touch-with-other-people's-feelings" jaunt à la Woody Guthrie, which yielded another well-known song, "Chimes of Freedom."

While they were in California, Bob Neuwirth (who toured with Bob Dylan's Rolling Thunder Revue late in 1975) became part of the group. By spring, Dylan was on his way to Britain for a concert tour, during which he met and talked with the Beatles, the Rolling Stones, and other rock groups. When he returned home, his music began to show signs of their influences. At Newport and on his next album, *Another Side of Bob Dylan* (Columbia KCS 8993), there was a conspicuous absence of protest material, and the introduction of personal themes. He wrote "Mr. Tambourine Man," which was recorded by scores of artists and was turned into a cash box top single by the Byrds in the following year.

In 1965 Bob Dylan moved "officially" into rock with the recording of his fifth LP, *Bringing It All Back Home*. The change was met with overt hostility at the Newport Folk Festival and again, a month later, at the Forest Hills Stadium in Queens. The pop LP *Highway 61 Revisited* (Columbia KCS 9189) left his listeners divided in their reaction to his music; "Like a Rolling Stone" and "Positively 4th Street" ranked among the year's top-selling singles. After his marriage to fashion model Sarah Lowndes on November 22, 1965, Dylan embarked on a grueling tour of short-term stands, terminating through Canada to the West Coast, where a few tracks were laid for his next album, *Blonde on Blonde* (Columbia C2S 841), which was released early in June 1966, upon his return to New York after a world tour.

On July 29 Bob Dylan suffered serious injuries in a motorcycle accident in Woodstock, New York—echoing Richard Fariña's fatal crash the previous April and the deaths of Paul Clayton and Peter LaFarge. An extended period of recuperation gave him a chance to unwind from the incessant pressures which had been mounting until then; he laid low, and, except for *Bob Dylan's Greatest Hits* (Columbia PC 9463), no new albums appeared for a year and a half. (*The Basement Tapes* [Columbia C2 33682] of 1967 was not released commercially until 1975.)

This period of introspection and tranquillity was reflected in *John Wesley Harding* (Columbia CS 9604/CL 2804), which was put on the market in January 1968. Dylan stayed in Woodstock and sang with a group called the Band; his only major personal appearances included participation in the New York "Tribute to Woody Guthrie," held on January 20, 1968, at Carnegie Hall, and in a Johnny Cash concert. At the end of the year, he recorded *Nashville Skyline* (Columbia KCS 9825) in Nashville (with accompaniment by Johnny Cash on "Girl from the North Country"), and his move into country music, which had been apparent on the *Harding* LP, was further developed with more warmth and intimacy. He hesitantly consented to appear as a special guest on Johnny Cash's weekly TV variety show, and sang "Girl from the North Country" with the host. His appearance at the Isle of Wight Festival in Britain that August marked his first major concert performance in four years.

His next album, entitled *Self Portrait* (Columbia C2X 30050), was highly criticized as a "commercial product," but it was followed only a few months later by his artistically acclaimed *New Morning* (Columbia KC 30290).

Many regard the period from 1966 to 1974 as artistically unproductive in Bob Dylan's career. In addition to a few relatively uninspired albums and a movie soundtrack for the mildly successful film *Pat Garrett and Billy the Kid* (in which he also appeared) his move to Malibu in 1973 was regarded as the ultimate demise of his creative power.

Early in 1974, he undertook his first major tour in eight years, and recorded *Planet Waves* (Elektra-Asylum 7E-1003) with the Band. Toward the end of the year, he cut another album, *Blood on the Tracks*, which completed his reemergence as one of pop music's most vital forces.

One of the highlights in American contemporary culture was Bob Dylan's late 1975 tour—related to his "new" political involvement in the Hurricane Carter case—the Rolling Thunder Revue, which included Joan Baez, Jack Elliott, Roger McGuinn, and Bob Neuwirth (along with others who joined the cast on different occasions).

The potency of Dylan's art has been revealed most recently with the release of his latest LP, *Desire* (Columbia PC 33893), and everyone is left to predict—as always—what Bob Dylan's next move will be.

"There is a voice inside us all that talks only to us," he told interviewer Jim Jerome of *People* magazine. "We have to be able to hear that voice."

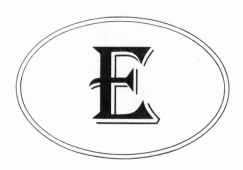

## Ernest East and the Pine Ridge Boys

*Old-time country band, performers, and recording artists*

This North Carolina string band epitomizes the tight, cohesive stylization of old-time country music, and their technical ability as musicians is representative of the Southeastern area of the country. Their sound is distinctively original in that the band complements the notes and tempo of its leader, Ernest East, who plays the fiddle with nuances of inflection that create a broad range of mood and energy. Ernest East, his son Scotty East, Mac Snow, and Gilmer Woodruff play their tunes "straight," unlike many modern regional bands that take the liberty of altering melodies; and their syncopation is less common in the newer styles that adhere to a consistently fast pace. All of the musical elements—inflection, melody, and tempo—of Ernest East and the Pine Ridge Boys tie this string band to its rural past and heritage, and their unpretentious, enthralling sound is the source of their timelessness and piquancy.

At the age of fifty-nine, fiddler Ernest East is the band's oldest member, and he learned about traditional music primarily by listening to early old-time performers. He has instilled a respect for his mountain heritage in the band's members, and his attachment to the musical traditions of the Southeast is professed in the manner in which the old tunes are played in the old way by Ernest East and the Pine Ridge Boys. Each of the band's members lives in the rural area near Mt. Airy, North Carolina, and their lives center around home and church; their music is a reflection of honest and fundamental living.

Banjoist Gilmer Woodruff learned much from clawhammer banjoists Charlie Lowe and Fred Cockerham, and his individualistic style adds animation and an accentuated tempo to the band's timing and expressive vitality. A mellowness is contributed by the bass runs of Mac Snow's and Scotty East's guitars, and Ernest East's son complements his father's fiddling with his high, lilting vocals.

In 1969 Ernest East and the Pine Ridge Boys recorded an album of old-time mountain music on the County label, *Ernest East and the Pine Ridge Boys* (County 718). All of the dozen tunes are traditional and many of the selections, such as "Sally Ann," "Richmond," "Fortune," "Mississippi Sawyer," "Suzanna Gal," and "June Apple," are rooted in the Round Peak, North Carolina, tradition in which Ernest East was born and raised.

## Scotty East. *See* Ernest East and the Pine Ridge Boys.

## Dian Edmondson. *See* The Greenbriar Boys.

## Travis Edmondson. *See* The Gateway Singers.

**Ben Eldridge.** *See* The Seldom Scene; Cliff Waldron and the New Shades of Grass.

**Dave Ellingson.** *See* The New Christy Minstrels.

# Jack Elliott

*Singer, songwriter, guitarist, performer, and recording artist*

Affectionately called the "Singing Cowboy from Brooklyn," this wandering troubadour left behind the "45,000-acre ranch in the middle of Flatbush" where he was born on August 1, 1931, to live out on the open road—claiming everywhere as his home. A protégé of the vagabond minstrel of the 1930s and 1940s Woody Guthrie (long before the young Bob Dylan came on the scene), Ramblin' Jack Elliott has since developed a distinctive style of his own in the course of establishing himself as the foremost interpreter of his folk-poet idol. Through the music of this American balladeer, audiences both in the United States and abroad have gained greater insight into America's folk music traditions—the toughness of Leadbelly, the high-pitched yodeling tenor vocals of Jimmie Rodgers, and the authenticity of the Carter Family—and an understanding of the imaginativeness and excitement of this "folksinger's folksinger."

Born Elliott Charles Adnopoz, the son of a doctor, Jack Elliott became infatuated with the American West and cowboys, particularly Gene Autry (until he discovered that cowboys do not resemble this stereotype), by the age of nine. He changed his name to Buck Elliott to suit his self-image, and, when he was in his early teens, left home to join up with a rodeo. Through Todd Fletcher, he learned to strum a few chords on the guitar; sometime later, he became acquainted with Woody Guthrie, and for half a dozen years he ate, lived, and traveled with his mentor.

His formal education amounted to short-term studies at the University of Connecticut and then at Adelphi College, Garden City, New York; since he had little interest in acquiring knowledge from books, he spent most of his time singing and playing guitar in Washington Square Park. His dream of

Jack Elliott at Mariposa '75

living in the free-spirited Woody Guthrie tradition soon became a reality, and, until his hospitalization in 1954, Guthrie's predominant influence on Elliott allegedly prompted him to say that Elliott "sounds more like me than I do." While in California with the Guthries, Elliott met other folk artists, including Bess and Butch Hawes, Guy Carawan, and Derroll Adams, who became one of his close friends.

Following his first marriage, to June Hammerstein (he has been married several times), Elliott left for Europe, where he quickly established a large and loyal following. Audiences unfamiliar with Woody Guthrie greeted Elliott with unparalleled enthusiasm as he recreated the songs and mannerisms of this famous American folk hero. A recording contract with Topic Records went hand in hand with European tours, radio and television appearances, and numerous major club engagements. For a while he worked with Derroll Adams, who had come to Britain shortly after Elliott's departure from the United States, and they played to eager fans at London's Blue Angel and at the World's Fair in Brussels, Belgium.

When Elliott returned stateside in the late fifties, he lived in California for a year before going back to Britain in 1959. He was billed with the Weavers on one of their European tours, and after a second successful transatlantic stay, he landed back in New York for a billing at Gerde's Folk City. A new generation, caught up in the urban folk boom, was turned onto Jack Elliott and to the life-style which he had assumed long before it became the latest craze. A likable and nostalgic figure of the folk revival era, he was a favorite performer at major festivals (including several Newports) and folk concerts.

In recent years, Ramblin' Jack Elliott has continued to perpetuate his reputation as a major link between the legendary personalities of a bygone age and the contemporary folk scene. In 1971 he appeared at the Mariposa Folk Festival (returning again in 1975) and on the *Johnny Cash Show*. He

plays clubs and beer-parlor joints, but to the average onlooker it seems that he just starts singing and playing the guitar wherever a trucker drops him off.

His recording credits include approximately two dozen albums produced on various labels, including Columbia, Delmark, Everest, Monitor, Prestige, Reprise, and Vanguard, and he has recorded with Johnny Cash and Tom Rush, among others.

## Emerson and Waldron. *See* Mike Auldridge; Cliff Waldron and the New Shades of Grass.

## Bill Emerson. *See* The Country Gentlemen; Emerson and Waldron; Cliff Waldron and the New Shades of Grass.

## Logan English

*Singer, guitarist, performer, recording artist, and actor*

A singer in Greenwich Village bars while Bob Dylan was still a high school student in Hibbing, Minnesota, Logan English was a prominent performer of traditional material in an era when contemporary singer-songwriters seemed to dominate the folk scene.

He was born and raised in Kentucky, and his musical background was steeped in old-time ballads and songs. While he was growing up on a farm in Bourbon County, he acquired from his elders a vast repertoire of traditional tunes, and he learned to yodel by listening to the Girls of the Golden West on radio. Despite his pursuit of an acting career, his classmates at Georgetown College in Kentucky and later at the Yale University School of Drama encouraged him to share his rich treasure of traditional music, and this dual career continued even after he earned his MFA degree from Yale. Following successful coffeehouse engagements during the 1950s, Logan English was billed at various clubs across the country, including Hollywood's Cosmo Alley and Philadelphia's Second Fret. At the height of the folk boom, he was featured at top folk nightspots, including Gerde's Folk City in Greenwich Village, and at Carnegie Hall and Town Hall, in New York. He made recordings for various labels, including Folkways, Monitor, Riverside, and 20th Century-Fox.

When Bob Dylan was frequenting Greenwich Village clubs in the summer of 1975, he ran into Logan English at the Other End. According to Lucian K. Truscott IV in *Rolling Stone*, August 28, 1975, the following transpired between the two veterans of the New York music scene: " 'That you, Logan?' Dylan asked sleepily. 'Yeah Bobby, it's me,' said English. 'Hey man, I thought you were dead,' said Dylan. 'I've heard the same about you a few times,' English replied. They both laughed."

## Séamus Ennis

*Irish piper, singer, storyteller, collector, translater, performer, and recording artist*

For almost two decades now, this Irish piper has maintained his prominent stature as the single most influential figure in his field. A master of the Uilleann or Irish Union pipes, Séamus Ennis approaches the instrument with a "classicist's attitude" and technical proficiency, and his preeminence was once described by Patrick Carroll in the following way: "There are fine chanter players: none better than Séamus, but some comparable. There are interesting users of the regulators: again none better than Séamus, and not including any of those who commit what he regards as a cardinal transgression of traditional discipline, the use of the regulators for constant percussion . . . there is no piper who has Séamus' comprehensive command

of the entire instrument, its music and lore."

Séamus Ennis was born in 1919 in Jamestown, North County Dublin, Ireland. He came from a musical background and, as he was growing up, learned many traditional tunes from his parents. Although he received his first set of pipes as a Christmas present while he was still very young, he did not develop a genuine interest in the instrument until he was in his teens. After graduating from secondary school and commercial college, he worked for four years at the Three Candles Press.

In the early 1940s, Séamus Ennis began collecting British traditional folk material, and for nearly half a dozen years he traveled around Ireland and Scotland gathering songs and stories for the Irish Folklore Commission. Before embarking on a collecting-recording field trip with Alan Lomax, Séamus Ennis worked as a producer, collector, and performer for Radio Eireann. In 1954 his reputation as a collector brought a job offer from the BBC in London, and, along with Wilfred Pickles, he became a primary force behind the British folk revival movement.

Throughout his years of collecting (and translating), Séamus Ennis continued to play, and his music was broadcast on radio and was heard in pubs and at traditional get-togethers throughout Britain. Toward the latter fifties, he began working as an independent performer, translator, and broadcaster in Britain and the United States.

Séamus Ennis has made numerous recordings for various labels, including Caedmon, Claddagh, Ember, Green Linnet, and Leader.

## Sleepy John Estes

*Blues singer, guitarist, songwriter, performer, and recording artist*

Often cited as one of America's pioneer blues singers, Sleepy John Estes was not only among the select number of bluesmen recorded in Memphis prior to the Depression, but his name was one of the few to resurface in the wake of that economic catastrophe. Unlike many other early recording artists who were never heard again, Sleepy John Estes was sought out by commercial record companies—long before the recent urban folk revival brought into vogue the rich tradition of the blues.

One of sixteen children, John Adams Estes was born on January 25, 1900, in Lauderdale County, Tennessee. His father was a tenant farmer who moved his family to Brownsville, Tennessee, when John Estes was eleven years old. Sixty miles from Memphis, Brownsville became his permanent home, and he still lives there today.

As a boy, he was blinded in one eye during a baseball game; over the years, a gradual loss of vision finally resulted in his total blindness. Although his father played the guitar, John Estes learned many of his techniques from singer "Hambone" Willie Newbern, who recorded several songs in Atlanta in 1929. By listening attentively to the highly skilled instrumentalist, John Estes picked up a strong foundation for his guitar playing and was introduced to a wide range of musical stylings. In addition, he acquired the older singer's ability to compose songs based on personal life experiences. John Estes wrote about himself and the world around him, and his music documents his life and the times in which he lived. Some of his best-known compositions include "Brownsville Blues," "Shelby County Workhouse Blues," "Fire Department" (which recounts the burning of a friend's house), and "Floating Bridge" (which depicts his escape from a near-drowning).

The intensity of his highly personalized style was often augmented by the harmonica accompaniment of a young friend, Hammie Nixon, who started playing at country suppers with him in 1927. When he was in his early twenties, Estes met another local musician, James (Yank) Rachell, and in 1929 they traveled to Memphis and played together on Beale Street. A recording session was arranged, and the bluesmen produced their first discs. In 1934 Sleepy John Estes joined Hammie Nixon and another Brownsville musician, Son Bonds, in Chicago, and he made some subsequent recordings.

Until the folk boom brought widespread attention to many blues artists, including Sleepy John Estes, he lived in poverty and played for local social gatherings. Blues enthusiasts helped to bring him international exposure, and his appearance at the 1964 Newport Folk Festival created a sensation. He participated in the American Folk Blues Festival Tour of Europe in 1964 and 1968, and he was among the celebrated guests at the 1969 Ann Arbor Blues Festival, and, more recently, at the 1974 Newport/New York Jazz Festival. In November 1974, Sleepy John Estes became the first country blues artist to tour in Japan, where his LP, *The Legend of Sleepy John Estes* (Delmark 603), was the first blues album to make the top 100 (two weeks at number 92).

Sleepy John Estes is a Delmark recording artist, but his work also appears on such other labels as Adelphi, Folkways, and RBF.

## Skip Evans. *See* Fennig's All-Star String Band.

## The Even Dozen Jug Band

*Vocal and instrumental group, performers, and recording artists*

During the recent urban folk revival, the combined accomplishments of a group of artists have generally been more significant than the later individual efforts of those involved. One of the exceptions to this commonplace phenomenon is the Even Dozen Jug Band. Although many talented musicians were brought together by its formation, its members proved to be less productive as components of this group than might have been expected, and the talent of its members was not fully developed until after they had gone their separate ways.

The Even Dozen Jug Band was formed by Stefan Grossman and old-timey guitarist Peter Siegel. The group was organized for "fun," and it had a nucleus of about seven players and five to seven other friends who frequently joined in to make up a dozen or so participants. They recorded one LP for Elektra (which was released in January 1964); they made a couple of television appearances; and they performed several times in concert, twice at New York's Carnegie Hall.

Some of the Even Dozen Jug Band's members included Dave Grisman, producer and mandolinist who plays with many artists today; Stefan Grossman, virtuoso solo country blues and ragtime guitarist; Steve Katz, later with Blood, Sweat & Tears and the Blues Project; Maria Muldaur, later with the Jim Kweskin Jug Band and now a well-known solo artist; Josh Rifkin, arranger of Scott Joplin fame; John Sebastian, later with the Lovin' Spoonful and now a solo artist; and Peter Siegel, later an A&R head (artist and repertoire producer) for Elektra Records and Polydor Records and now head of ATV Record offices in the United States.

The group finally disbanded after disagreement over its status as primarily a professional or a "fun" band, which left its members divided down the middle over the issue.

## Fairport Convention

*Vocal and instrumental group, performers, and recording artists*

One of the most productive and influential British electric traditional folk music groups, Fairport Convention has assimilated numerous influences and combined balladry and dance tunes with a modern rock sound. Since its formation in 1967, Fairport Convention has undergone a number of personnel changes, giving their sound new directions and spawning solo efforts by Sandy Denny, Ian Matthews, and Richard Thompson, and new groups Steeleye Span and the Albion Country Band. The group's current members include Sandy Denny (its former lead singer who rejoined Fairport Convention in early 1974 after a four-year absence during which she established her career as a solo performer), Jerry Donahue on guitar, Trevor Lucas on rhythm guitar, Dave Pegg on bass guitar, Bruce Rowland on drums, and Dave Swarbrick on fiddle.

The original group evolved from the acquaintanceship of schoolmates Ashley Hutchings, Simon Nicol, and Richard Thompson, who were joined by drummer Martin Lamble, vocalist Judy Dyble, and, later, vocalist Ian Matthews. Sandy Denny replaced Judy Dyble on the group's second album, and in 1969 they had their first hit with "Si Tu Dois Partir." More albums followed, and Fairport Convention's reputation was spread by the introduction of their electric folk music to a wide public.

At this point Ian Matthews left to form his own band (and later to become a successful solo recording artist) and Martin Lamble was killed in an automobile accident, resulting in the recruitment of Dave Swarbrick and Dave Mattacks. When Sandy Denny and Ashley Hutchings left after Fairport Convention's fourth LP, *Liege and Lief* (Island Records ILPS 9115), Dave Pegg was asked to join.

Sandy Denny had left the group to turn her attention to writing and solo performing, becoming one of England's most popular vocalists. On her own she recorded four albums and toured Britain and the United States on several occasions. After her marriage to Australian Trevor Lucas (who by 1973 was a permanent member of Fairport Convention), Sandy Denny started performing with Fairport Convention while maintaining her solo career.

Ashley Hutchings had left the group when it started to place more emphasis on original material rather than on traditional music. He was one of the founding members of the British folk-rock group Steeleye Span, and he played bass guitar on their first three albums. After the recording of their third LP, *Ten Man Mop or Mr. Reservoir Butler Rides Again* (Crest 9), Hutchings left Steeleye Span to become a member of the short-lived Albion Country Band. Sometimes compared with the United States' Golden Ring, the Albion Country Band recorded only one LP, *No Roses* (Pegasus 7), which included such notable musicians as Due Draheim, Robin Dransfield, Nick Jones, Simon Nicol, and Dave Swarbrick, under the direction of Shirley Collins (and her husband Tyger). Ashley Hutchings became increasingly involved in the revival of English folk dancing, and in 1973 he recorded an album of Morris dance tunes, *Morris On* (Island HELP 5), with Barry Dransfield, John Kirkpatrick, Dave Mattacks, and Richard Thompson. He also compiled a music–spoken word history and commentary featuring English country dance music of Playford, *The Compleat Dancing Master* (Island HELP 17), with John Kirkpatrick.

Since his departure from Fairport Convention, in 1971, Richard Thompson has established a strong following as a solo artist. Along the way, he worked with the Albion Country Band, assisted Ashley Hutchings on his *Morris On* project, and played guitar in recording sessions of other artists. During the early seventies, he toured folk music clubs with Linda Peters (now his wife) and recorded a solo folk-rock LP, *Henry the Human Fly* (Island ILPS 9190). The Thompsons' first combined effort, *I Want to See the Bright Lights Tonight* (Island ILPS 9266), features their band, Sour Grapes; and their most recent LP, which was made commercially available in the United States after its initial release in England, is entitled *Hokey Pokey* (Island ILPS 9305), with Aly Bain, John Kirkpatrick, and others; and their most recent effort is *Pour Down Like Silver* (Island ILPS 9348).

Despite the many alterations in Fairport Convention's makeup, the band has evolved and refined its basically traditional repertoire. The group recorded and performed a major conceptual work, *Babbacombe Lee*, and they have toured America half a dozen times. After Sandy Denny rejoined the group, they made a world tour in 1974, which produced their tenth album and their American debut on the Island label, *A Moveable Feast* (Island ILPS 9285). Dave Mattacks left the group in late 1974, and a temporary percussionist was added to Fairport Convention until Bruce Rowland was designated as its permanent drummer.

# Richard and Mimi Fariña

*Singer-songwriters, instrumentalists, performers, and recording artists*

One of the most romantic—and tragic—stories of the folk boom era began in Europe over a decade ago when Joan Baez's younger sister Mimi first met the dashing and talented Richard Fariña. As Mimi tells it: "We started corresponding while he was in London and I was in Paris. Actually, we were writing two love letters a day for about six months, and then Dick moved to Paris. A little while after that, we had a secret wed-

Richard Fariña (left), Joan Baez (center), and Mimi Fariña (right) at the 1965 Newport Folk Festival

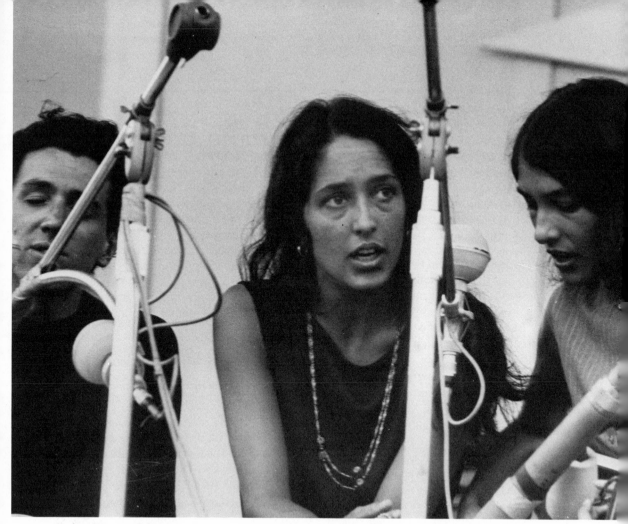

Richard Fariña (left) , Joan Baez (center) , and Mimi Fariña (right) at the 1965 Newport Folk Festival

ding in Paris, and then we had a formal family wedding in California a year later, when I was eighteen."

Richard Fariña was born in Brooklyn in 1937 of Irish and Cuban ancestry. At eighteen he became "associated with the Irish Republican Army" until his presence became known and he was forced to leave the country. He attended Cornell University and made several trips to pre-Castro Cuba. After leaving Cornell, he married folksinger Carolyn Hester, but while on tour with her in Europe, he met Mimi Baez, and they fell in love. When Carolyn Hester returned to the United States, Fariña stayed in Europe to continue working on his novel *Been Down So Long It Looks Like Up to Me*.

"When we were back in the States," Mimi recalls, "Dick was writing his book and we were living in a one-room cabin. We would make music—he on the dulcimer and me on the guitar. Our first public appearance was at Big Sur. We had played at people's houses around Carmel, and then the Big Sur Folk Festival came up with Malvina Reynolds, my sister, Mark Spoelstra, and I can't remember who else—the Chambers Brothers, even—and Dick and I sang for the first time there. Both Vanguard and Elektra and another small company approached us and said: 'Would you like to make an album?' And that was the first time we gave any consideration to becoming professional.

"So we went with Vanguard, and it was at

that time we were going to move back East, hopefully to end up in Europe again. But we got hung up on the East Coast, made our first album, and then started playing and performing on weekends. It worked out okay, because that way Dick could write during the week and we could do clubs on weekends. That was the second year of our marriage but the first year of our singing career." Their first Vanguard LP, *Celebrations for a Gray Day* (Vanguard 79174), which was released in the spring of 1965, included Fariña's classic composition "Pack Up Your Sorrows." About half a year later, *Reflections in a Crystal Wind* (Vanguard 79204) was issued.

"Next we received a letter from my sister saying that she was starting a school in California and that she wanted us to be a part of it. It was to be called the Institute for the Study of Nonviolence. So we were toying around with staying in the States or moving to Europe, and that seemed to fix our minds. So we returned to California and continued with the music. It was a year later, on my twenty-first birthday, that Dick died."

On April 30, 1966, during a party celebrating the publication of *Been Down So Long It Looks Like Up to Me*, Richard Fariña left the premises, got on a motorcycle, and was involved in an accident that took his life—a life of craziness, madness, exuberance, and love.

Late in 1968, two and a half years after his death, Vanguard released the Fariñas' third album, *Memories* (Vanguard 79263). On December 23 of the same year, notes by Mimi Fariña (transcribed from a tape recording of her conversation with Christopher Cerf) were printed in *Long Time Coming and a Long Time Gone*, a collection of short writings, poems, and song lyrics by Richard Fariña. After Fariña's untimely death "people became very protective of me, and a lot of people were asking me to sing." After making numerous unsuccessful attempts to find a new direction in her life,

"which really didn't happen until I was twenty-five," she joined the San Francisco Committee—a political-satirical theater group which was an outgrowth of the Chicago Second City.

"I worked for a year as an improvisational actress, but I did not feel successful at it at all and I kept generally being depressed. At the end of one year I was so thoroughly depressed, and I got a phone call to come back to Newport to sing. So I did, and it was like suddenly seeing the old world of music again. I felt very nostalgic, and I realized how unhappy I had been at the Committee with my private life; I didn't seem to be growing at all. So I decided to quit the Committee and get married. Which, now that I look back, was a cop-out. I was rescuing myself from having to face life alone again. So I was married for three years to a man named Myron Melvin, who was a San Francisco disc jockey." When the marriage broke up, Mimi was twenty-five: "It was just at that time that my life finally began developing on its own. Suddenly, and miraculously, I began writing songs and finally got a driver's license and started to get around."

Still insecure about working as a solo performer, Mimi teamed up with Tom Jans, "who was also writing songs at the time—it was the beginning of his career." They sang together for a year and a half and made an album for A&M before they realized that "we didn't have to rely on each other's company anymore for stage work, and so we separated."

Today, Mimi continues to tour the country as a solo act. She has also founded and is currently running an organization called Bread and Roses: "What we do is to take music into institutions where people normally can't get out—convalescent homes, mental health and psychiatric wards, drug rehabilitation centers—and the program has been so exciting and has developed so quickly and going in the right direction, that it all feels so right that I'm much more confident with life and happier to be singing."

**Cyrus Faryar.** *See* The Whiskeyhill Singers.

**Martin Fay.** *See* The Chieftains.

## Fennig's All-Star String Band

*Vocal and instrumental group, performers, and recording artists*

Fennig's All-Stars' melodic sound and unusual instrumental combination of piano, fiddle, and hammered dulcimer distinguish this string band from upstate New York from other folk groups in the United States. Fennig's All-Star String Band's repertoire is extensive, and although they draw heavily upon traditional American, Canadian, Irish, and Scottish fiddle tunes, they also play country music and old-time and contemporary folk songs. Their specialty is playing for country dancing, which includes such dance forms as the contra, circle, quadrille, and longways, and they have been an important catalyst in the revival of the art of dancing in New York State, as well as performing in concert.

When Bill Spence first became enamored of the hammered dulcimer at the 1969 Fox Hollow Family Festival of Traditional Music and Art, his enthusiasm for the instrument and its creative possibilities interested other musicians in his home region. A number of string band workshops organized in 1971 and 1972 by an east-central New York folk music society known as Pick'n' and Sing'n' Gather'n', Inc., brought together several members, including Bill Spence, who had a special interest in old-time fiddle music (which ultimately led them to Irish and English dance tunes). Seven of the participating members stayed together, and the first Fennig's All-Star String Band was organized with Marie Brate (guitar), Skip Evans (piano), Tom McCreesh (fiddle), John Pedersen (banjo), Joan Pelton (guitar), Bill Spence (hammered dulcimer), and Joe Williams (bass). By the time the band recorded its initial album in May 1973, it had lost three of its original members; *The Hammered Dulcimer* (Front Hall FHR-01) included Tom McCreesh, John Pedersen, Joan Pelton, and Bill Spence. The disc became the first release on Bill and his wife Andy Spence's Front Hall Records label. Explains Andy Spence: "Our business [Andy's Front Hall] grew out of a need in this area for the availability of more traditional records and instruction books. Front Hall Records is our record company, which concentrates on working musicians who perform traditional music."

After further changes in personnel, the Fennig sound stabilized in 1974 with Toby Fink on piano, Tom McCreesh on fiddle, and Bill Spence on hammered dulcimer. With the assistance of Alistair Anderson on concertina and Jack Hume on pedal steel and electric bass, the band recorded, in March 1975, *Saturday Night in the Provinces* (Front Hall FHR-05), before Tom McCreesh left to join up with another band in the Midwest, called the Hotmud Family. George Wilson, fiddle, banjo, and guitar player, is now the third member of Fennig's.

For the past few years Andy Spence has contributed a new dimension to the band by calling dances and by instructing audiences in the arts of country and contra dancing.

In addition to numerous performances in coffeehouses, at high schools and colleges, and for various social functions, in 1974–75 Fennig's All-Stars appeared in concerts and dances at the Buffalo Folk Festival, the Cornell Folk Festival, Mariposa, Passim's in Cambridge, Massachusetts, and the Fox Hollow Festival in Petersburg, New York.

**Jimmy Ferguson.** *See* The Irish Rovers.

## Fiddle

The fiddle is a bowed, stringed musical instrument with a neck and an hourglass-shaped body into which two holes are cut to produce a resonating sound. Four strings, tuned in fifths, are stretched over a fretless fingerboard; tuned by pegs at the head of the neck, the strings pass over a bridge on the soundboard and are secured at the base of the fiddle by a string holder.

In modern use, *fiddle* is a colloquial term for *violin*, generally describing a folk instrument used to play music in a particular manner. Historically, the term *fiddle* predates *violin*, and it is considered the generic name for what is now known as the violin family. Although the origins of the fiddle have not been resolved conclusively, scholarly opinion generally fixes its early history to the Middle East, with its development traceable to both the Far East and Europe. The early instruments varied in size and shape, and there were usually from three to five strings. Evidence of a European fiddle dates back to the early Middle Ages, and these early instruments (now called *rebecs*) were often plucked, not bowed. By the thirteenth century, the fiddle had developed into its final form with a formalization of flat body and neck characteristics. Several centuries later, the violin, as we know it today, was developed from these earlier instruments, and beginning in the seventeenth century, the term *fiddle* referred to the violin in a generic connotation.

The early settlers introduced the fiddle to America, where it was established as one of the chief folk instruments of the people, often used as the lead instrument in old-time string bands of the rural mountain regions of the South. The fiddle was also used as a solo instrument and as the musical accompaniment for regional dances. Fiddle competitions are one of the old traditions that have survived and continue to flourish as a form of entertainment at fairs and festivals in contemporary society. A diversity of styles of fiddle playing has developed over the years; and the various regional styles possess techniques and nuances that are distinctive and indigenous to their area of development, making the eastern Tennessee sound dis-

tinguishable from that of northern Georgia, southwestern Louisiana, and so on.

**Betty Mae Fikes.** *See* The Freedom Voices.

**Judy Fine.** *See* The Womenfolk.

**Toby Fink.** *See* Fennig's All-Star String Band.

**Dave Fisher.** *See* The Highwaymen.

**Flatt and Scruggs.** *See* Lester Flatt; Earl Scruggs.

## Lester Flatt

*Singer, guitarist, songwriter, performer, and recording artist*

For several years a member of Bill Monroe's Blue Grass Boys, Lester Flatt was a part of the combination of musicians who introduced the modern bluegrass sound to country music. As the singing and guitar-picking partner of banjoist Earl Scruggs in the dynamic team of Flatt and Scruggs, this star of the *Grand Ole Opry* helped to popularize bluegrass music for over two decades before embarking on a solo performing and recording career in 1969.

Lester Raymond Flatt was born on June 28, 1914, and was raised in rural Overton County, Tennessee. While receiving his formal education in the state's public school system, he picked up the guitar and learned to play in the popular old-timey country style. During the thirties, playing the guitar remained an avocation, as he was employed as a full-time textile-mill worker. The talented young singer and guitarist performed with other local musicians until 1939, when he followed the advice of family members and friends to pursue a career as a professional musician. He made his debut radio appearance on Roanoke's WDBJ, and in the next several years his name became widely known in the South through both radio and personal performances. By 1944 he was appearing on the stage of the *Grand Ole Opry* as lead singer and guitarist for Bill Monroe, who had asked Flatt to join his band, the Blue Grass Boys. When, in December 1945, Earl Scruggs became the group's banjoist, the final ingredient was added for the evolution of the modern bluegrass sound.

Two weeks after Scruggs left the Blue Grass Boys, in February 1948, Flatt joined up with him, and they organized their own band with Lester Flatt on guitar, Earl Scruggs on banjo, Jim Shumate on fiddle, and Howard (Cedric Rainwater) Watts on bass fiddle. Their music was broadcast live for several weeks on a Danville, Virginia, radio station, and when they shifted their base of operations to Hickory, North Carolina, the foursome was joined by guitarist and tenor vocalist Mac Wiseman. After about a month, the group realized that it was financially disadvantageous to remain in Hickory, so they decided to audition for WCYB in Bristol, Virginia. They were readily accepted by the radio station, and in the wake of commencing their programs in Bristol, the Foggy Mountain Boys were offered a recording contract with Mercury Records. During the next two years, they produced a total of twenty-nine sides, which were issued as selections on three Mercury LPs.

The Foggy Mountain Boys remained with WCYB until the early spring of 1949, at which time they began a four-year stint of traveling and performing on radio stations throughout the South. They switched record labels, and, with their first recording session on November 21, 1950, Flatt and Scruggs became Columbia Records artists and remained with the company for the duration of their partnership. In June 1953 they received the sponsorship of Martha White Mills and settled in Nashville to work seven shows per week on WSM while maintaining an active schedule of nightly live performances. With permission to tape their broadcasts for WSM came the opportunity to work on the *Saturday Night Barndance* program in Richmond, Virginia. Their radio work compounded as they accepted offers to tape shows for WRVA in Richmond and to perform on a couple of daily noon programs in Crewe, Virginia—all while simultaneously booking school, theater, and stadium engagements nearly every night. By January 1955 they had picked up the Martha White television show spots, and each week they traveled about 2,500 miles to appear on the live broadcasts presented by their sponsor in Columbus (Georgia), Atlanta (Georgia), Florence (South Carolina), Huntington (West Virginia), Jackson (Tennessee), and Nashville.

In 1960 Flatt and Scruggs appeared on the nationally televised *Folk Sound, U.S.A.* and at the Newport Folk Festival (Earl Scruggs had made a solo appearance at the 1959 Newport Folk Festival). Throughout the sixties, the duo was featured on numerous radio and television network shows, and the Foggy Mountain Boys played the theme song, "The Ballad of Jed Clampett," for *The Beverly Hillbillies.* Seventeen years after the original recording of "Foggy Mountain Breakdown," Flatt and Scruggs were asked to re-record the selection for the motion picture *Bonnie and Clyde*, and the team of Flatt and Scruggs received international recognition. At about this time, Earl Scruggs's son Randy began accompanying Flatt and Scruggs on guitar, and after the further addition of Gary Scruggs as a sideman, the partnership dissolved. Earl Scruggs went on to form the Earl Scruggs Revue, and Lester Flatt organized another band, called the Nashville Grass.

By the time the duo parted company in March 1969, they had innumerable awards and many bestselling LPs to their credit. In addition to their Mercury and Columbia recordings, the work of Flatt and Scruggs can be found on other labels, including Collectors Classic, Everest, and Kings of Bluegrass.

In recent years, Lester Flatt has continued to tour extensively and to record for RCA. Following open-heart surgery in Nashville in the summer of 1975, the originator of the "Lester Flatt G-run" guitar lick resumed his musical activities on a more restricted basis. (*See also* Earl Scruggs.)

## Bob Flick. *See* The Brothers Four.

## Dan Fogelberg

*Contemporary singer-songwriter, guitarist, performer, and recording artist*

Often cast in the role of the lonely, frustrated artist, Dan Fogelberg produces music reminiscent of Crosby, Stills, Nash and Young, or—as described by its creator and performer—"haunted country music—a synthesis of the feeling of an environment; the antithesis of city living, and the mystique of the hills." Until his rise as a solo musician, Dan Fogelberg's name appeared more and more frequently on albums by other artists such as Eric Andersen, Roger McGuinn, and Buffy Sainte-Marie, but his own recordings of recent years have borne out his widespread acclaim as a solo pop musician.

Dan Fogelberg has been involved with music since the seventh grade, when he started playing with a group of friends. His preference was to perform as a solo musician, and, in the absence of group accompaniment, he became a folksinger. For two or three years prior to studying painting at the University of Illinois, he played coffeehouses in his native area of Illinois. During his junior year of college, he decided to abandon his formal education and began singing and playing his guitar from Illinois to California.

Although his search for a producer ended in failure, while he was in Southern California, he performed at the Troubadour and accompanied Van Morrison on tour. He traveled from Hollywood to Nashville, where he worked with Kenneth Buttrey and Norbert Putnam, who produced his debut Columbia LP, entitled *Home Free* (KC-31751). Fogelberg spent the next couple of years in Nashville, working with other musicians and writing material for his next album, *Souvenirs* (Epic KE-33137), produced by rock musician Joe Walsh and released in the fall of 1974.

After recording his second album, Dan Fogelberg said of his past experiences: "My first album was more a representation of where I come from than where I am now. I wrote the material for this album [*Souvenirs*] with the studio in mind. I was into using the recording studio as an artistic medium, which I think it is. When you're in the studio you should take advantage of all the freedom that's afforded you. You can do whatever you can think of if you can play it and mix it. People can accuse you of overproduction, but it's still your art; besides you've got your soul."

After an extensive and successful tour following the release of *Souvenirs*, *Captured Angel* (Epic PE-33499) was issued in the fall of 1975.

## The Foggy Mountain Boys. *See* Lester Flatt; Earl Scruggs.

## Dick Foley. *See* The Brothers Four.

## Folk Festival of the Smokies. *See* Jean and Lee Schilling.

## Folk Life Center of the Smokies. *See* Jean and Lee Schilling.

## Folk Music

In recent years the increased popularity and interest in folk music has brought forth myriad collections—both printed and recorded—and many literary works related to the various styles within the spectrum of American folk music. The term "folk music" has taken on an ever-increasing number of connotations, and the absence of a universally accepted definition of the term by scholars has contributed to confusion in regard to its meaning.

There are basically two schools of thought in defining folk music. One faction contends that folk music is determined by certain musical, or audible, characteristics which submit to a particular style, or form. Others argue that folk music is a sociological or cultural phenomenon created by peoples of different backgrounds, and consists of the songs derived from the actual life experience (work songs, religious songs, protest and love songs) of the "folk."

Further problems have been caused by the commercial pursuit of folk music, and, in some cases, the label has been applied to material as a means of promoting sales and the marketability of a product for financial gain.

Traditional folk music exists universally, with an abundance and diversity of material, including ballads, religious songs or spirituals, work songs (mining songs, railroad songs, sailors' songs or shanties), cowboy songs, revolutionary songs, dance songs, love songs, and so on, with variations existing within each of the categories. Traditionally, folk songs are transmitted orally from one person to another by the folk process and are, therefore, part of an unwritten custom. A product of evolution, folk songs are altered and varied as they are developed and passed down from generation to generation—subject to adaptation to contemporary situations and to the personal needs of a particular group in society.

The following comments by well-known personalities in folk music are indicative of the differences of opinion regarding the unwritten oral traditions of America's peoples:

There have been people every year who talk about the death of the folk song, of the traditional song, and the same comment is made about the protest song; but they're being written every five minutes, every second, about everything that excites some kind of interest or passion. On election day, you hear only the big pop songs that are written specially for the campaigns, but in every clubhouse all over the country, they're writing a million parodies. Sometimes new songs. Every small contest, every argument, a hundred parodies of "Yankee Doodle," a thousand parodies of "The Battle Hymn of the Republic," they're all being done. In the armed forces, in the Boy Scouts, in the camps, all over the place, in the fraternity houses, in the streets. It's not a dying process, by any means. As far as being a communications blockbuster, that's something else. I don't foresee another big revival like we saw ten years ago, but I think that folk music has had a continuous popularity. It is not like a lightning bolt. It's here, it's sunlight, it stays.—OSCAR BRAND

Well, perhaps it's a really good thing that a lot of people are creating different kinds of music from different ingredients, including folk music. It will probably leave traditional folk music in its more pristine states, at places like the Mariposa Folk Festival and the hills of Kentucky, where it really does live, and it really does have a life of its own, and its offshoots and influences on more popular culture are obvious. I like nothing more than to hear really solid, traditional music, there's nothing like it.—JUDY COLLINS

It's hard to determine what the term "folk music" means because its meaning has changed since the days of the Weavers. Folk music consisted of songs that were written before this era, maybe a hundred years before or even in England; they were undocumented, so the authors, the melodies, the words, the stories were sometimes forgotten or changed, even to the point of being nonsensical. So, when the Weavers came along, they made the old songs intelligible or they wrote songs around them that were based on old melodies, using English ballads or Southern, Jamaican, or Mexican work songs, and so on. But, since then, I think that people have become less interested in the folk process and more interested in writing their own songs.—ERIK DARLING

I think you have to make a distinction between traditional folk songs and contemporary songs in the folk idiom; and there are singers, like Ian and Sylvia, who started out by singing folk songs, but then went to singing their own compositions. I think there are a lot of similarities between Canadian and American folk music; a great deal of American folk music came from Britain, as so much of ours did. The main difference is that American folk music has been influenced to a large extent by Negro music, blues and spirituals, leading to jazz and the influence on rock, whereas our folk songs are primarily French and English.—EDITH FOWKE

Folk music has expanded to mean more than just mountain music, which is a good thing. Folk music should include any kind of music that folks sing or like. If you grew up listening to Beethoven, and whistling his tunes, that should be considered folk music as well. I think the time has come around now when any kind of music that becomes a part of your culture is something that you could classify as folk music. Anything that remains in the cultural mainstream for a long period of time or evokes some kind of memory or emotion and works for the mass of the people, I would consider folk music.—ARLO GUTHRIE

First of all, because it's [folk music] folklore and because it involves oral transmission, aspects of it are always dying out. It's part of the nature of the beast. Orally transmitted music—oral transmission involving music—I think, will always be with us. The folk music revival—that is, the thing that the people in the cities have been doing for thirty years—is what I describe as a cultural transplant of folk materials from the "folk" into a city or urban environment. Folk songs are put into the mainstream of the mass media, so that on the popular charts you'll get one or more aspects of folk music or revival music. There were the Weavers in the early fifties, and the folk music of the early sixties, and interest in calypso at one time, or in the banjo with *Deliverance*; all of these things shoot up from the folk song revival underground to a popular culture, but I also think the folk song revival itself will continue to grow.—JOE HICKERSON

There has never been a lack of interest in folk music, the difference has been in the size of its audience. It was only during the folk boom that I played to fifteen thousand people, at Newport; most of the time, I have played to small audiences, and there is always a bunch of people who like the songs that I feel are unpretentious and uncommercial and speak to basic problems. And this folk music that I am interested in always continues. There have been ups and downs in its popularity, and then other people seized on its popularity to create new things in terms of that popularity that were not particularly long-lasting, but that's an entirely different ball game. I am interested in songs that tell about the people who made them, and I try to keep my own contributions to the **arrangement** of a song to a minimum. —SAM HINTON

At the time that we got hooked on folk music, there wasn't a general interest in folk music. In fact, people said there wasn't any American folk music, except for Negro spirituals and some Appalachian ballads, and people didn't really know about collections that had already been made. Of course, now there isn't a mountain cabin without a TV antenna, I don't care how dilapidated it is, it's got an antenna, and all those folks listen to is the music coming out of Nashville. And how can they compete with that? None of those folks have any training in singing, and they can't compare with the slick. The commercial side of folk music has come on so strongly, but there is one thing that has always interested me. Traditional folksingers may be unlettered, they may be illiterate, but their singing is definitely a discipline of its own; there is a style, and there are rules. Every generation that comes along gets caught by it, and I don't see any reason why folk music won't keep on blooming.—FRANK WARNER

## Folk Process

The folk process is an oral tradition by which folklore (songs, dances, crafts, sayings) is transmitted from one person to another through speech, with modifications and alterations taking place as the culture of the "folk" is handed down from generation to generation. In our modern age of sophisticated and portable recording equipment, and with virtually unrestricted means of travel, the folk process has undergone changes in concept and contemporary meaning and application. The impact of technology and mass communication on the folk process is immeasurable, and the following sampling of opinions regarding its present state of existence is representative of the controversy which has been generated by this issue:

Years ago, in the eighteenth century, there was a man named Percy, and he collected some folk songs and ballads and labeled them *Reliques of Early English Poetry* because he knew that he was collecting the last, nobody would ever write any more, and they would never be sung again, and he was doing the world a favor. In the seventeenth and even the sixteenth centuries, people said the same thing. Walter Scott collected old ballads, thinking he was doing the world a favor because they were never going to persist. In the nineteenth century we had people like George Lyman Kittredge, and we had John Lomax collecting songs because he thought they would die. They're always dying. Folk music is always dying. It died last week; it will die a hundred years from now, in somebody's estimation.—OSCAR BRAND

Multimedia has largely killed traditional folk singing. It's harder and harder to find people who have learned the old traditional songs and who still sing them. There still are some people, however, particularly in Newfoundland and in some rural parts of Ontario, and out in parts of British Columbia. So I think there will be some continuance of the old tradition, but not nearly as much as there used to be.—EDITH FOWKE

To me, the term "folk process" is a good word for plagiarism or something like it, people stealing tunes and ideas from each other. And it's a helluva lot easier to deal with the mass media, so there will be a lot more creativity and the best will rise.—ARLO GUTHRIE

The folk process is one thing, pure and simple, oral transmission, and it will always be with us. The only question is, What will be orally transmitted? And that will always change. And the other question is, How much will there be of oral transmission in our lives? Different forms will come along to be orally transmitted, and I think that we will always be dependent upon oral transmission to a certain extent.—JOE HICKERSON

If you look at all of the definitions of folk music that are used by most of the scholars, they require verbal transmission. I have never agreed with this. To me, it isn't important whether the material is transmitted by word of mouth or by the printed word or by records or radio. As long as people don't treat it as an authoritative thing that cannot be tampered with in any way, they might just as well be passing it on by word of mouth. So, I think the nature of the media doesn't really make much difference. I also feel that to be a fully developed folk culture, you must have this kind of creativity, a non-authoritarian attitude toward the music. At the same time, the creativity that one uses must be within the framework of the folk tradition that is recognized as part of your culture. It is in this respect that I think our culture today is still seeking, it hasn't found itself, and there is no one style or form that you can say is typically American—SAM HINTON

There are some places and little pockets of people who are going about their business involved in folk music. It's an expanding and shrinking universe, but it maintains itself. Out of a sense of oral tradition my daughter came home from school the other day singing two folk songs that I had never taught her. Her music teacher taught them to her, and so the oral tradition is passed unwittingly through the hands of music teachers all over the country. The funny thing is that the concept of the oral tradition in the face of the mass media—the records, the television, the reproduced sound—the one-to-one trans-

mission exists and continues. Slightly modified, slightly distorted in one sense, but not distorted at all in another. —MARY TRAVERS

This question has been kicked around for fifteen years, and I don't think there is a definitive answer to it. Modern electronics have shifted the trend, and Nashville has played an extremely important role. The old-time ballad singers have gotten to be sort of heroes, it's kind of a cult; and the interest in traditional singing, both the songs and the singing styles, is perpetuated by every generation.—FRANK WARNER

My grandmother keeps a little store—it's her life, that store—and she keeps her banjo and her guitar there, and she sings. People come in and she sings for them and they sing for her, and when I was there, practically every day she would make me be the performer. And people would come in, and she would say, "Now Hedy will sing and she sings good and you got to listen to her." You see, folk music keeps on going on in the country, and when local people go out and play, perhaps it has an influence on the folk process itself. I've thought about that with a lot of people who have come from a local situation—like Merle Travis—who have become professionals, and they serve as some sort of catalyst for encouraging local musicians.—HEDY WEST

# Folkscene

*West Coast monthly folk music publication*

The inception of *Folkscene* in March 1973 marked an alternative approach to the coverage of folk music by other media, which, in the words of its editor and one of the original founders of the publication, Marsha Necheles, "utilized writers who either knew nothing or cared very little

75¢

MARCH 1974        Vol. 2 No. 1

**Sam Hinton**

*Folkscene*: A West Coast monthly folk music publication, Los Angeles

about the folk artist who was being covered." With their sights set on offering some alternative, which would cover both traditional and contemporary artists, Marsha Necheles, Howard Larman (promotion advisor), Roz Larman (advertising manager), and V. F. (Vicki) Nadsady (associate editor and art director), pooled their resources as partners dedicated to creating a new dimension in folk music coverage.

*Folkscene* includes a few regular columns, usually consisting of a series of ten or twelve articles on a specific subject, including instruments (the first issue contained the initial column in a series on "Open Guitar Tunings" by folksinger Mary McCaslin). Currently, the regularly printed columns include a diversity of topics: old-timey music ("Everyday Dirt"); country and swing band music ("Hillbilly Jazz"); bluegrass ("Bluegrass Breakdown," written by Bill

Koon, an English professor at a local university); and, the newest addition, on families in the country music tradition ("In the Family Way"). *Folkscene* tries to offer firsthand information and insights by performers and musicians, and the contributing writers have included Mary McCaslin, Jim Ringer, Jon Wilcox, and Bruce Phillips. An annual issue is devoted to the San Diego Folk Festival (a double issue in 1975), and a Women's Issue is designed to focus on important women in all categories of music—blues, folk, country, pop, and bluegrass.

Marsha Necheles elaborates: "Our approach is purely entertainment-oriented—if you learn something from an article, so much the better, but it is not our purpose to educate per se. We have many qualified writers helping us, many are volunteers from the John Edwards Memorial Foundation, and some are well-known free-lance writers in Los Angeles and write for many major magazines besides *Folkscene*.

"Whatever we [Necheles, Nadsady, and the Larmans] make in profit is turned back into the magazine so that we can continue to improve it in some way. We are not out to 'Take Over the World' through folk music or our efforts—all we want to do is share our love of the music with others, so that they can discover it, too."

**Hadley Fontenot.** *See* The Balfa Freres.

**Buffy Ford.** *See* John Stewart.

**Howdy Forrester.** *See* The Smoky Mountain Boys.

**Garley Foster.** *See* The Carolina Tar Heels.

**Gwen Foster.** *See* The Blue Ridge

Mountain Entertainers; The
Carolina Tar Heels.

# Edith Fowke

*Canadian folklorist and collector, author,
magazine editor, fellow of the American
Folklore Society, and college professor*

An early admirer of Burl Ives, Richard
Dyer-Bennet, Josh White, and other folksingers whose recordings were available in
the late 1940s, Edith Fowke developed her
interest in folk music quite casually from a
preference for listening to this particular
genre. From this personal inclination grew
an involvement in the fifties as creator of the
weekly radio program *CBC Folksong Time*.
Since then, she has made Canadian folklore
and folk songs her life's work and has at-
tained an international reputation as one of
her country's foremost authorities in her
field.

Born in Lumsden, Saskatchewan, to Irish
immigrant parents, Edith Fowke (née
Fulton) had a passion for reading which,
later on, led her to the study of literature at
the University of Saskatchewan. After completing undergraduate work in English,
history, and education at the university in
1934, she taught at Readlyn High School in
Saskatchewan. In 1935 she was hired as an
assistant in the University of Saskatchewan's
English Department, and, two years later,
she earned her MA degree at the university.

After her marriage, she and her engineer
husband moved to Toronto in 1938; but it
wasn't until the early fifties that she became
actively involved in folk music, as she explains: "I had become interested in the early
folk song records, but I found that there
were no programs of folk music on the CBC,
so I went to Harry J. Boyle and suggested
that there should be one. He thought it was
worth trying, so I started a program called
*CBC Folksong Time*, which began as a summer show and then it ran all year round.

"From some of the inquiries that I got on
my radio show, I found that there were no
books on folk songs that were suitable to the
general public. All the books that were
available were collectors' works, so that
stimulated me to write my first book, *Folk
Songs of Canada*, published by Waterloo
Music Company in 1954. *Folk Songs of
Canada* was an anthology of Canadian folk
songs that had been collected by other people, such as Helen Creighton, Elisabeth
Greenleaf, and Roy Mackenzie. In 1957 I
wrote another book, *Folk Songs of Quebec*
[Waterloo Music Company], and the idea
behind it was to introduce English-speaking
Canadians to French-Canadian songs; so it
had the original French words and my
English translations of them."

From 1950 on, Edith Fowke was a writer
for the CBC, and she prepared numerous
programs on folklore and folk songs, including these series: *Folk Song Time*
(1950–63); *Folk Sounds* (1963–73); forty-
two programs on "Folklore and Folk
Music" for *The Learning Stage (1965)*; and
seven programs on "The Traveling Folk of
the British Isles" for *Ideas* (1967). In 1967
she authored *More Folk Songs of Canada*
(Waterloo Music Company), and her 1969
publication, *Sally Go Round the Sun* (Mc-
Clelland and Stewart), was chosen Best Book
of the Year by the Canadian Association of
Children's Librarians.

During the sixties, Edith Fowke embarked
on a career of collecting Canadian folk
music, as she recalls: "In *Folk Songs of
Canada* I found that there were no folk songs
west of Quebec, so I started out to see if there
were any in Ontario. I went out there with a
tape recorder and found a whole new group
of old songs and recorded them, and out of
that came a couple of books, *Traditional
Singers and Songs from Ontario* [Folklore
Associates] and *Lumbering Songs from the
Northern Woods* [University of Texas Press,
1970]. It was during this period that I met
and recorded one of our best traditional
singers, O. J. Abbott."

Edith Fowke's books were the first to
make Canadian folk songs known to the
general public; and, unlike previous works
by Canadian collectors who compiled

regional collections of songs, her books offer an overall picture of Canadian music. She has been on the teaching staff at York University in Toronto since 1971, and she teaches three courses in folklore, ballads, and folk songs in the university's English Department. Her most recent publications include *Canadian Vibrations* (Macmillan of Canada, 1972) and *The Penguin Book of Canadian Folk Songs* (Penguin, 1973). She has been an editor for several magazines, and her articles have been printed in both Canadian and American journals. In 1974 Edith Fowke was elected a fellow of the American Folklore Society, and, in the same year, she was presented with an Honorary Doctor of Laws degree at the Brock University convocation.

## Fox Hollow Family Festival of Traditional Music and Arts.

*See* The Beers Family.

## Jack Frazier. *See* The Free State Ramblers.

## Joe Frazier. *See* The Chad Mitchell Trio.

## The Free State Ramblers.

*See* John Ashby.

## The Freedom Singers

*Student Non-Violent Coordinating Committee (SNCC) vocal a capella group, performers, and recording artists*

The Albany (Georgia) civil rights demonstrations of the early 1960s brought together four Student Non-Violent Coordinating Committee field secretaries—Rutha Harris, Bernice Johnson (Reagon), Charles ("Chuck") Neblett, and Cordell Hull Reagon—who, in 1962, organized the original vocal group called the Freedom Singers. Their objectives were twofold: first, to raise funds for SNCC, and, second, to use

music as a vehicle for uniting blacks in the struggle for integration.

The mixed quartet remained intact for about a year, during which time they covered approximately 100,000 miles in a college, university, and church concert tour of the United States. In addition to achieving their goal of raising monies for SNCC, the Freedom Singers were instrumental in spreading their "freedom songs," which, in turn, focused attention on the civil rights movement. One of their most memorable performances was at the 1963 Newport Folk Festival, and they are included on two albums of music recorded live at that event: *Newport Broadside* (Vanguard VRS-9144) and *Evening Concerts at Newport Vol. 1* (Vanguard VRS-9148). After producing a studio recording for Mercury Records, the Freedom Singers disbanded.

The spring of 1964 brought the formation of a new group of Freedom Singers, consisting of six men—Rafel Bentham, Emory Harris (brother of Rutha Harris), Matthew and Marshall Jones, original Freedom Singer Chuck Neblett, and James Peacock—who, unlike the first group, who met and worked together in a single location, were SNCC field secretaries representing different movements across the United States. And although the original group's repertoire was steeped in black traditional material and their style was gospel-oriented, the new Freedom Singers performed many original compositions written by one of its members, ex–jazz musician Matthew Jones, and by other contemporary composers. In April 1964 they recorded live, in Atlanta, Georgia, an album of old and new "freedom songs" on the Mercury label.

By December 1975 a second group, called the Freedom Voices, had been organized, with SNCC field workers Betty Mae Fikes, Walter Harris, James Peacock, and Cordell Reagon; while their coexistence with the Matthew Jones group was designed to broaden the communicative power of the movement, their vocals adhered to the church and gospel styles of the original Freedom Singers. (*See also* Bernice [Johnson] Reagon.)

## The Freedom Voices. *See* The Freedom Singers.

## Kinky Friedman

*Contemporary singer, songwriter, performer, and recording artist*

Kinky Friedman is a musician who strongly portrays the influence of his regional and religious roots, and one of his many talents is the bringing together of elements in his background, as he explains: "Cowboys and Jews, in fact, have a common bond. They are the only two groups of people in the world to wear their hats indoors and attach a certain amount of importance to it."

A Halloween baby, Kinky Friedman was born in Rio Duckworth, Texas, in 1944. He was a classics major at the University of Texas; and in the late sixties, he joined the Peace Corps and went to Borneo. He returned to the United States in 1971, and, laden with a repertoire of original songs, he traveled with his band (then known as the Texas Jewboys) to California. Although he was unsuccessful in his initial attempts to interest record companies in his music, it was not long before a contract was signed with Vanguard Records and his first album, *Sold American* (VSD-79333), was released. A year later, Kinky Friedman was added to the roster of ABC recording artists; and his next album, *Kinky Friedman* (ABC Records ABCD-829), was produced in both Los Angeles (by Steve Barri) and Nashville (by Willie Nelson). The 1974 LP includes a mixed bag of music, with the majority original Friedman compositions (in some cases collaborations with Panama Red or Jeff Shelby) and background vocals by Tompall Glaser, Waylon Jennings, Willie Nelson, Billy Swan, and others.

One of Friedman's strengths is a versatility which allows him to offer both fun-filled and controversial material within the same album. Satirical songs, such as "Get Your Biscuits in the Oven and Your Buns in the Bed," comprise the bulk of his initial LP, but there are also some songs of a serious nature

Kinky Friedman

among the selections. A well-produced country album, *Kinky Friedman* also strikes a balance between the disparate elements of satire and sensitivity, and Kinky Friedman himself represents a well-rounded, new force in popular music.

## The Fruit Jar Drinkers. *See* Uncle Dave Macon.

## Jesse Fuller

*Country and ragtime blues singer, one-man band, songwriter, performer, and recording artist*

In 1954 Jesse Fuller composed the classic "San Francisco Bay Blues," which has been picked up by countless numbers of folk groups and individuals over the past two decades. Jesse Fuller's instrumental-vocal interpretation of "San Francisco Bay Blues" is perhaps the most unusual of its many versions, and he was highly acclaimed as a one-man band and as a stylist of ragtimey, good-time blues which he created with his unique combination of instruments.

139

Jesse Fuller at the 1964
Newport Folk Festival

Jesse Fuller was born in 1896 in Jonesboro, Georgia, and, when his mother gave the six-year-old to another family, he learned the hardship of growing up as a poor black orphan. Despite the struggles of his early years, Fuller developed an optimistic outlook on life, and his hopefulness and love of beauty is expressed through his music. He became interested in music while he was living with the Wilson family of Macedonia, Georgia, and before he was ten he had built a mouth bow and a simple guitar.

He forfeited a formal education when he ran away from Macedonia in 1906, and in his "Drop Out Song" he advises other young people not to follow his example. Appropriately, his nickname was "Lone Cat," and he spent his independent teenage years traveling from one place to another and working at a handful of jobs as a jack-of-all-trades. During these years, he listened to musicians at minstrel shows and dances, and he tried to imitate their songs on his guitar or harmonica.

When he moved to Cincinnati around 1920, he started traveling with a circus, and by the time the Hagenbeck Wallace troupe reached Michigan, Fuller was street singing.

In 1922 he moved to California, and while operating a shoeshine and hot dog stand in Hollywood, he made the acquaintance of Douglas Fairbanks, Charlie Chaplin, and other actors who were instrumental in getting him small parts in such movies as *East of Suez*, *The Thief of Bagdad*, and *Hearts of Dixie*. In the years that followed, he worked as a toymaker, fruit and cotton picker, shipyard welder, and employee of the Southern Pacific Railroad.

During the thirties and forties he worked more regularly as a musician. He became a local favorite in the San Francisco area, where he had settled, and, in addition to playing small clubs and social occasions, he made his first recording for World Song Records in the late forties. By 1954 Fuller was entertaining folk enthusiasts at his shoeshine stand in Berkeley, he was playing the Haight Street Barbeque club often, and he had composed his best-known song, "San Francisco Bay Blues."

As a one-man band, Jesse Fuller accompanied his singing with five instruments: twelve-string guitar, harmonica, kazoo, washboard, and fotdella (a foot-operated bass which he had contrived as part of his instrumental rig). Even his voice was used like an instrument, and his blues intonations created a classic nasal sound appropriate to the idiom.

Fuller appeared at numerous festivals, clubs, and concerts during the late fifties and early sixties, and he successfully toured Europe and the British Isles.

He was in his sixties before he was known outside of his own local following, and the recordings that he made were done late in his career. His initial albums sold well, and, during his career, Jesse Fuller recorded approximately thirty LPs. Among the various record labels which offer his music are Arhoolie (which has reissued an out-of-print Cavalier recording in addition to including Jesse Fuller on the four-record set *The Roots of America's Music* [Arhoolie 2001/2002]), Good Time Jazz Records, Prestige, Stateside (Great Britain), Topic (Great Britain), and World Song Records.

He died on January 30, 1976, in Oakland, California, at the age of seventy-nine.

**The Galax String Band.** *See* Fred Cockerham; Kyle Creed.

**Art Garfunkel.** *See* Simon and Garfunkel.

**Amos Garin.** *See* The Blue Grass Boys.

**Jim Garland.** *See* Sarah Ogan Gunning; Aunt Molly Jackson.

**Victoria Garvey.** *See* Don Armstrong.

## The Gateway Singers

*Vocal and instrumental group, performers, and recording artists*

Typical of many groups that were formed in the late 1950s to profit by the commercialism of the folk boom, the Gateway Singers enjoyed a minor success during their five-year period of existence. As with the Chad Mitchell Trio, the Dauphin Trio, the Wayfarers, the Babysitters, the Travelers, and so on, the Gateway Singers were a product of their time. When the members disbanded in 1961, Gateway Singers spokesman Jerry Walter formed the Gateway Trio with guitarist Betty Mann and bassist Milt Chapman.

Originally from Chicago, banjoist and bass vocalist Jerry Walter worked at a diversity of jobs before settling in Palo Alto, California. Before utilizing his formal training at the American and San Francisco conservatories of music, he was employed as a professional radio actor, a truck driver, an insurance salesman, and a lifeguard. By 1956 Jerry Walter had launched his career as a professional entertainer by teaming up with Oakland-born and -raised Mrs. Elmerlee ("Mama Lee") Thomas, bass player Lou Gottlieb, and guitarist Travis Edmondson (later of Bud and Travis fame) as the Gateway Singers.

Based in San Francisco, the Gateway Singers began performing locally, and after a successful engagement at the city's Hungry i nightclub, their name soon spread around the country. Offers came pouring in for them to appear on television and to perform at major clubs and concerts, and they signed a recording contract with Decca Records which resulted in an output of several albums and singles. In 1958 both *Gateway Singers at the Hungry i* (Decca 8671) and *Gateway Singers in Hi Fi* (Decca 8742) were released. In the following year, Lou Gottlieb left the group to pursue an academic career. He was replaced by Ernie Sheldon, who became the group's lead guitarist.

When the group split up in 1961, the Gateway Trio was organized with Milt Chapman, Betty Mann, and Jerry Walter.

Betty Mann had originally auditioned for the Gateway Singers but was turned down; several years later, she became the guitarist for the Gateway Trio. Milt Chapman amplified the group's sound by playing string bass and by singing bass, which offset the vocals of the other two members. Although it was short-lived, the Gateway Trio recorded a couple of albums for Capitol Records before its demise.

## The Gateway Trio. *See* The Gateway Singers.

## Jimmy Gaudreau: *See* The Country Gentlemen.

## The Georgia Sea Island Singers

*Traditional performers of folk songs related to the Afro-American culture represented by inhabitants of St. Simons Island, Georgia*

In the 1920s, musicologist Mrs. Maxfield Parrish organized the original Georgia Sea Island Singers on St. Simons Island, off the Georgia coast. From the outset, the group comprised singers who were versed in old-time gospel, rowing, longshoremen, work, and play songs, and "shouts," which were the forerunners of spirituals. Each of the members was dedicated to the preservation of their African heritage, and, as younger singers joined the group, this tradition passed from one generation to the next.

Many of the songs in their repertoire typify an ancestral style of black culture that throve among communal workings, religious gatherings, and evening socials in the eighteenth and nineteenth centuries. Over the years, the authenticity of black culture has been diminished by urban forces which have brought about more popular forms of music of Afro-American origin—minstrel shows, blues, jazz, rock 'n' roll, and gospel choirs—but the Sea Island Singers

present the essence of their heritage as enriched by the American experience.

Dancing is an important component of their genuine style of presenting songs, and, instead of instruments, rhythmic complexity is created by harmony, polyrhythmic clapping and tapping the floor with a broomstick or feet. One of the group's many members, John Davis, used the broomstick to tap out the rhythm for such songs as "Knee-Bone Bend" and "Oh, Eve, Where Is Adam? Down in the Garden, Picking Up Leaves."

John Davis, known on the island as Big John Davis, was a native of St. Simons Island, where he was born on March 12, 1903. He learned many of his work songs and shanties from stevedores like Joe Armstrong, and he lived in the settlement of Harrington-and-Fort-Frederica, where his one-room house was surrounded by oaks and pine trees draped with Spanish moss. He died on November 23, 1972, but John Davis's singing of such songs as "Go Down, Brother Moses," "Blow, Gabriel," and "Down in the Mire" will be remembered by all who heard him.

Bessie Jones often led the group, and, with her roots in the hills near Albany, Georgia, she brought an added wealth of songs to her new home on St. Simons Island when she married one of its inhabitants. In the summer of 1964, she and four other members of the black choral group met with Bess Lomax Hawes in California to present a two-week children's activities workshop, which precipitated a collaborative work entitled *Step It Down* (Harper & Row, 1972), by Bessie Jones and Bess Lomax Hawes. With her vast knowledge of children's songs, juba, play, and party songs and games, Bessie Jones provided the valuable content for this volume on Afro-American children's games, songs, dances, and stories. Some of her performances appear on *American Folk Songs for Children*, in the Southern Folk Heritage Series (Atlantic 1350); *Georgia Sea Islands, Volume II*, in the Southern Journey Series (Prestige/International 25002); and *Deep*

South—*Sacred and Sinful*, in the Southern Journey Series (Prestige/International 25005). She has recently recorded a solo album, *So Glad I'm Here* (Rounder Records 2013), with music, work songs, games, stories, and spirituals.

Other members of the Georgia Sea Island Singers include Peter Davis, Henry Morrison, and Emma Ramsay. Another prominent contributor to the group was contralto Mable Hillery, who during the past decade was associated with the "follow-through program" of City College's Interdependent Learning Model, in New York, and with other black cultural projects both in New York and Atlanta. She died on April 27, 1976, at the age of forty-six.

The Georgia Sea Island Singers have appeared at numerous folk festivals (including Newport) during the sixties and seventies. Along with Bessie Jones, they are included in Prestige/International's twelve-volume Southern Journey Series from 1960 field recordings made by Alan Lomax on St. Simons Island.

## The Georgia Wildcats. *See* Clayton "Pappy" McMichen.

## Paul Geremia

*Blues and ragtime guitarist, singer, songwriter, performer, and recording artist*

A creator as well as a performer of blues, Paul Geremia ranges from original ballads to traditional country blues, ragtime, and jazz. He is an accomplished guitarist, pianist, and harmonica player, and his repertoire is a reflection of his personal emotions, experiences, and life-style. He is better known for his work in clubs than for his recorded material, and his sophisticated blues guitar style functions as an accompaniment to his singing. His performances are characteristically lighthearted and easygoing.

"I was born on April 21, 1944, and, as a kid, I used to enjoy folk music. It wasn't until the early sixties that I started hearing finger-style acoustic guitar, which really intrigued me and got me involved in a more serious way. I heard Mississippi John Hurt, and he was the first country blues singer that I ever saw in a performance. When I heard him play, in 1963, my attention turned to country blues, and the early recordings by Robert Johnson, Willie McTell, Pink Anderson, Blind Blake, and others, including some of the white interpreters such as Dave Van Ronk, John Koerner, Tom Rush, John Hammond, Bob Dylan, Pat Sky, and so on, provided the turning point for me.

"The music sort of took over at that point, and it wasn't long before I was performing in coffeehouses and clubs. My first gig was at the Phase 17 coffeehouse in Narragansett, Rhode Island, which is my home state. I started playing coffeehouses in the Boston–Cambridge area, and one of the first clubs of any note that I played was Caffé Lena in Saratoga Springs, New York, where I performed in 1966. In the meantime, I was exposed to a lot of really good music during the folk and blues revival of the sixties, and it affected my own work tremendously.

"I made an album for Folkways in 1968 called *Paul Geremia: Just Enough* [Folkways 31023], which was my first record. Izzy Young had taped a concert that I did at the Folklore Center, and a record deal with Moe Asch of Folkways Records was made through the urging of my friend Patrick Sky. Around 1970 I made another record for Sire, and then, in the spring of 1974, I recorded *Hard Life Rockin' Chair* [Adelphi 1020], and I'm working on a new one for Adelphi Records now."

## Alice Gerrard. *See* The Strange Creek Singers.

# Bob Gibson

*Singer, guitarist, banjoist, songwriter, performer, recording artist, and actor*

Bob Gibson was considered by many to have been an influential and prolific folksinger during the early (mid-1950s) phase of the folk boom, and innumerable urban folk musicians modeled their work after his vocal and instrumental style. His early Riverside and Stinson recordings predated the formation of such commercial folk groups as the Kingston Trio, the Limeliters, and Peter, Paul and Mary (all of whom later recorded Gibson songs), and, through his music, both performers and listening audiences discovered a vast reservoir of folk material. His name gradually faded as rock 'n' roll began to overtake folk on the popular music scene, and he resurfaced only briefly in 1969 as a performer on the club circuit.

Robert Gibson was born on November 16, 1931, in New York City. His father had worked as a singer, and while he was growing up, he developed an interest in folk music by listening to and memorizing songs of Woody Guthrie, Burl Ives, and Leadbelly broadcast on radio. He became a skilled guitarist and five-string banjoist, and following his initial performances for local and educational groups, he soon began to appear before club and concert audiences. During the early fifties, he toured extensively—performing and collecting—and made his debut television appearance in 1954. In the years that followed, Bob Gibson was featured on a number of network TV programs (including *Hootenanny*); was recorded by various labels, including Elektra (beginning in 1959), Riverside, Stinson, and Tradition; and was seen at major clubs (including Chicago's Gate of Horn), festivals (including several Newports), and Carnegie Hall in New York.

Despite his short-lived career, Bob Gibson achieved prominence among contemporary musicians, and although his name is generally unfamiliar to subsequent musical genera-tions, many of his songs have been passed down through performances and recordings by some of today's most prominent artists.

# Gid Tanner and the Skillet Lickers

*Old-time string band, performers, and recording artists*

An old-time group representative of the harsh-sounding, fun-loving north Georgia string bands, Gid Tanner and the Skillet Lickers were among the most prominent and influential performing and recording artists of the golden age of country music.

The band's leader, comedian and fiddler James Gideon (Gid) Tanner, was a poultry farmer who, with his blind guitar-playing partner George Riley Puckett, had enjoyed local recognition as a performer on Atlanta's WSB Radio. On March 7, 1924, the duo became Columbia's first hillbilly artists when they traveled to New York for their initial recording session. In 1926 a subsequent Columbia recording session was arranged, which brought together this duo and two other Georgians and WSB favorites, fiddler Clayton McMichen and five-string banjoist Fate Norris. The name of the newly formed quartet was derived from McMichen's and Norris's previous association with an outfit called the Lick the Skillet Band, and, in the years that followed, theirs became one of the best-known names in early country music history. The original Gid Tanner and the Skillet Lickers disbanded in 1931, but in 1934 the band (with Gid Tanner and his son Gordon, Riley Puckett, and Ted Hawkins) was reformed for a final recording session in Dallas. Other musicians who joined the band on various occasions included fiddlers Bert Layne and Lowe Stokes, and legendary steel guitarist Jimmie Tarleton.

After leaving the band in 1931, Clayton McMichen went on to organize several other groups—the best-known of which was the

Georgia Wildcats, which included, among others, Merle Travis—which were more pop-oriented. Although he retired in 1954, he made a special guest appearance at the Newport Folk Festival a decade later. While Gid Tanner gave up commercial work after the 1934 recording session, Riley Puckett continued to pursue a career in music until his death in 1946.

In recent years, material by Gid Tanner and the Skillet Lickers has been reissued on several labels, including Biograph, County, Rounder, and Voyager (another album put out by the Folk Song Society of Minnesota is now out of print). Selections by the band, or its various members, are also included on a number of group string band LPs.

**Ronnie Gilbert.** *See* The Weavers.

**Tom Gilfellon.** *See* The High Level Ranters.

**Mrs. Texas Gladden.** *See* Hobart Smith.

**Lonnie Glosson.** *See* The Delmore Brothers.

**Joyce Gluck.** *See* The Penny-whistlers.

# The Golden Ring

*Informal collective of traditional folk musicians, or a "Gathering of Friends for Making Music"*

The number of folk musicians involved with this group, informally known as the Golden Ring, is variable, and although they represent a variety of backgrounds, musical abilities, and ages, everyone shares a love of singing together.

The original gathering took place in the Wilmette, Illinois, home of George and Gerry Armstrong, who frequently invite friends over to talk, laugh, sing, and play traditional music. A certain magic was created by the dynamic combination of folk musicians George and Gerry Armstrong, Ruth Meyer, Howie Mitchell, and Ed Trickett (a teacher of psychology at Yale University, who, in his spare time, performs in concert and at colleges and clubs across the country; in 1972, Folk-Legacy Records issued his first solo effort, entitled *"The Telling Takes Me Home"* [Folk-Legacy FSI-46]), and that special quality was maintained as the voices and instruments increased with the arrival of Herb and Betty Nudelman, Shannon Smith, Win Stracke (founder of the Old Town School of Folk Music in Chicago), and Steve White.

Their unique blending of musical talents was recreated at the studios of WFMT, Chicago, and their exuberance and joy in making music together ruled out any self-consciousness or anxiety about the recorded product. The recording session was infused with an air of informality, as songs were done spontaneously and instruments were swapped back and forth. Norm Pellegrini ran his tape recorder for the entire session, and Folk-Legacy Records released an album of this ensemble of folksingers, *Golden Ring* (Folk-Legacy FSI-16), in 1964.

The second recorded gathering took place in Sandy and Caroline Paton's home in Sharon, Connecticut, when the Golden Ring was assembled for five days. The group's number had increased to twenty-six singers and musicians, and enough material was recorded for Folk-Legacy to issue a two-record set by the New Golden Ring, *Five Days Singing, Vol. 1 and Vol. 2* (FSI-41 and FSI-42), which was released in 1971.

The music of the Ring is best described by Michael Cooney's term "living-room music," with stress on the enjoyment of singing together as a group. Each of the twenty-six members is a fine individual performer, and although some, like Gordon Bok, Michael Cooney, and Joe Hickerson, are more well-known in the field, individual predominance is subordinate to the collective effort of the Golden Ring. Their repertoire encompasses a wide range of music, including shanties, spirituals, Child ballads, contemporary songs, and instrumentals.

**The Golden Ring participates annually in the Fox Hollow Festival, and their philosophy of noncommercialism epitomizes the intention of the festival's founders, Bob** and Evelyne Beers, to create a weekend environment of singing spontaneously and into the wee hours of the night, just having a good time.

# Kenneth S. Goldstein

*Educator, author, collector of traditional American and British folk music, record producer, professor of folklore and chairman of the Folklore and Folklife Department at the University of Pennsylvania, and president of the American Folklore Society*

One of America's most distinguished scholars, collectors, and producers of traditional folk music, Dr. Kenneth S. Goldstein has been responsible for the presentation of a vast number of folk musicians on thirteen different record labels. He has produced over five hundred records and has made extensive field recordings in the South, New England, Britain, and Ireland.

Kenneth S. Goldstein was born on March 17, 1927, in Brooklyn, New York, to Irving and Tillie Horowitz Goldstein. He received his BBA degree from the City College of the City of New York in 1949 and his MBA in 1951; in 1963 he earned his PhD at the University of Pennsylvania. Union songs aroused his initial interest in folk music, which "was reinforced during my service in the army in the Second World War, when I first heard a lot of hillbilly and country music." He began to buy records and then books on the subject, and "the more I heard and read, the more I wanted to know."

He worked as a market research analyst for Fairchild Publishers in New York City from 1949 to 1956. During his lunch hours,

he used to visit the nearby Stinson Record Company, "and one of the owners saw my interest and thought that I had sufficient knowledge of folk music. He wanted to reissue material which was originally on 78-RPM discs—Burl Ives, Richard Dyer-Bennet, Josh White—onto LPs." Goldstein agreed to help, and he was paid five dollars a record for selecting the material and producing the albums. In addition to producing the reissue material, he also "got involved in doing original material." He started producing British works and was largely responsible for creating an interest in the United States in such artists as Ewan MacColl and A. L. Lloyd, among others. He also produced other singers of the folk song revival, including Bob Gibson and Robin Roberts, and "was responsible for the recording of the first long-playing record of Rev. Gary Davis." In the meantime, he interested the owner of the newly founded Elektra Records in recording folk music and "occasionally helped him in writing record notes and selecting performers."

In 1957 Goldstein was an assistant to the president of Abelard-Schuman Publishers. He worked for Riverside Records as folk music editor from 1958 to 1959 and produced more than 150 records for that label: "At Riverside, I produced everything from beginning to end. I had quit working as a statistician and had decided to work full-time as a free-lance record producer, and I worked for various other record companies when I could pick up the work.

"I did field work down South, and between 1952 and 1958 I went down there every summer to record traditional singers, and I went up to New England as well. Then I returned to school in 1958 to get my PhD, and I began working for Prestige Records at the same time. After I had been in school for a year, I went off to Britain and did field work in northern Scotland."

In 1961 he formed his own book company, called Folklore Associates, and he soon began to publish various works. He started teaching at the University of Pennsylvania, where he earned his PhD in 1963, and is now chairman of the Folklore Department.

Since 1972 Dr. Kenneth S. Goldstein has been the executive editor of the "Norwood Folklore Series" in Darby, Pennsylvania; he has held various positions in the American Folklore Society since 1965 and is currently president of the organization; he was president of the Pennsylvania Folklore Society in 1964–65; and he is a member of the English Folk Song and Dance Society and an honorary member of the Folklore Society of Great Britain.

He is the author of such works as *A Guide for Field Workers in Folklore* (1964), *Two Penny Ballads and Four Dollar Whiskey* (1965), *Thrice Told Tales* (1971), and *Folklore: Performance and Communication* (1975).

## Steve Goodman

*Contemporary singer-songwriter, guitarist, performer, and recording artist*

Steve Goodman (right) and John Prine at the Eleventh Annual Philadelphia Folk Festival, 1972

With Arlo Guthrie's 1972 hit recording of his classic song, "City of New Orleans," Steve Goodman's reputation was boosted to a new level of recognition. Along with another Chicagoan and friend, John Prine, he is considered by many to be among the top contemporary musicians, composing songs with simple and memorable lyrics.

Born on July 25, 1948, in Chicago, Steve Goodman once described his upbringing in "a Midwestern, middle-class Jewish family" as having been "as normal as you're going to get." His early musical influences were rock 'n' roll and the advent of folk music as a pop force during the urban folk revival. He started playing guitar at the age of thirteen and discovered the music of Bib Gibson, Josh White, and "musicians of those generations," which led him to their influences— artists like Woody Guthrie and Big Bill Broonzy.

Throughout his formal education, he continued to broaden his scope by absorbing related forms of music such as blues and country. With a foundation of listening and playing, he began composing, as he recalls: "I was at the University of Illinois in '65. I listened to a lot of Hank Williams and Jimmie Rodgers, those guys that everyone lists as stock references. Well, guess what—those are the guys that wrote the book on it."

It was not long before Steve Goodman was working almost exclusively on developing his skills as a performer and a songwriter: "I got to the point where it was the only thing I liked to do." The latter part of the sixties found him at both national and international festivals and clubs, and, in his hometown of Chicago, he was a primary force in the revitalization of the local club scene. He subsidized his income as a performer with certain commercial undertakings: "I did a lot of commercial jingles in Chicago. Maybelline Blushing Eye Shadow paid the rent for a while when nothing else was happening."

In 1971 he cut his debut album, entitled *Steve Goodman* (Buddah BDS 5096), which was followed in 1972 by Arlo Guthrie's 45-RPM recording of Goodman's best-known composition, "City of New Orleans." In the same year, his second LP, *Somebody Else's Troubles* (Buddah BDS 5121), was released. He began to concentrate more on performing than recording and, since 1972, has toured extensively. Armed with a new collection of original material, collaborations with other artists, folk, rag, and tunes by John Prine and Mike Smith, he returned to the recording studio and produced his third album, *Jessie's Jig & Other Favorites* (Elektra-Asylum 7E-1037), released in 1975. His most recent album is *Words We Can Dance To* (Asylum 7E-1061).

## Lou Gottlieb. *See* The Gateway Singers; The Limeliters.

## Grand Ole Opry

*Weekly variety program, originating on WSM Radio in Nashville, Tennessee*

Although not the first in its field (WSB and WBAP had presented barn-dance programs as early as 1922, and the WLS *National Barn Dance* in Chicago was a prominent forerunner), the *Grand Ole Opry* has enjoyed a longevity of fifty years, which gives it the honor of being the longest continuous radio show broadcast in the nation. A weekly variety program which attempts to maintain a middle-line position in its music and to avoid controversy, the *Opry* (as it is known locally) presents a range of country music from old-time Appalachian ballads to the electric instrumentation of rock.

The history of the *Grand Ole Opry* dates back to a November 28, 1925, WSM broadcast by announcer George D. Hay, who had originated the *National Barn Dance* on WLS in Chicago in 1924. At eight o'clock on that fall evening, he declared himself "The Solemn Old Judge" and presented as the show's sole attraction an eighty-year-old fiddler named "Uncle" Jimmy Thompson, who played an impromptu sixty-minute session. Originally called the *WSM Barn Dance*, and aired from the small fifth-floor Studio A of WSM in the National Life and Accident Insurance Company Building at Seventh Avenue North and Union Street in downtown Nashville, it marked the inception of what was to become the *Grand Ole Opry* in the following year.

As a result of the show's popularity, several moves were necessitated as the size of the cast (and later of the audience) increased over the years. When Uncle Dave Macon joined the show in 1926, there were about twenty-five members in the cast, and a larger studio was built to accommodate its steady growth. Before long, a live audience of about fifty fans was permitted to attend the show, and during the next several years the show was moved, first, to a newly built auditorium studio (which seated about five hundred people), then to the Hillsboro Theatre (an east Nashville tabernacle), and then to the War Memorial Auditorium. In 1939 the *Opry* gained network status, and a half-hour segment of the show was broadcast on NBC Radio stations across America. When the *Opry* outgrew the War Memorial Auditorium's seating capacity of twelve hundred, it was moved to one of Nashville's historic landmarks, the Ryman Auditorium. This served as the official "home" of the *Opry* from 1941 to 1974; during the sixties the auditorium's facade was converted into a replica of a large red barn with "Grand Ole Opry" spelled out in bold white letters. The show was televised for the first time during the fifties, and within a matter of years the TV version was syndicated on network television across the United States. In March 1974 it moved to its new $15-million home in a $41-million amusement park, Opryland USA, where it celebrated its golden anniversary beginning on October 15, 1975.

In 1926, after the show was moved from Studio A to Studio B of WSM, its name was changed from *WSM Barn Dance* to the *Grand Ole Opry*. After a broadcast of the

*NBC Music Appreciation Hour*, directed by Dr. Walter Damrosch, "Judge" George D. Hay announced that following this presentation of grand opera, WSM listeners would hear music of the "Grand Ole Opry." The name caught on, and the show has been known as the *Grand Ole Opry* ever since that night. On October 21, 1966, "Judge" George Dewey Hay was elected to the Country Music Hall of Fame along with another legendary personality who had contributed extensively to the *Grand Ole Opry*, Uncle Dave Macon. On May 9, 1968, George D. Hay passed away.

Over the years, the cast of the *Grand Ole Opry* has included every major country artist in the music industry, from its early years, which were dominated by Uncle Dave Macon, to the present with Roy Acuff, Dolly Parton, comedienne Minnie Pearl, Jeannie Pruitt, Hank Snow, Ernest Tubb, Tammy Wynette, and countless others.

Josh Graves

## Marshall Grant. *See* The Tennessee Two; The Tennessee Three.

## Josh Graves
*Bluegrass and blues dobroist, songwriter, performer, and recording artist*

Born in Tellico Plains in southeastern Tennessee and raised in a farming family of eight, Josh Graves left home at fourteen with a guitar strapped to his back. Although his roots are in traditional music, he has branched out into bluegrass and blues.

In 1942 he played on radio in Knoxville, Tennessee, and then joined Lulu Belle and Scotty Wiseman. After playing for about a year with Mac Wiseman's Country Boys, he teamed up with Lester Flatt and Earl Scruggs in 1955, and even today he claims the strongest influence on his music has been Scruggs. When the team disbanded, Graves went with Flatt for three years, and then joined the Earl Scruggs Revue. He left the group in 1974 to develop his interest in blues, and he recorded *Alone at Last* (Epic

KE 33168), which evidences his ability as a dobroist and presents his unique brand of blues. Like Scruggs, whose main interest was to find other forms of music for the banjo, Graves has expanded the traditional usage of the dobro as solely a bluegrass instrument.

Graves is probably best known for his song "Just Joshin'," but his greatest contribution to the world of entertainment is his genuine interest in his audience and sharing his love for music. He's known to spend time with young musicians and fans after his performances, playing licks with them and showing them his picking techniques. He tells a story about one concert, which exemplifies his warm personality:

"Now, this happened to me in Steamboat Springs, Colorado, but the story actually began in Utah. I was doing a gig at a high school and this guy named Rob came up to me after the show and he said: 'Mr. Graves, would you have a drink with me?'

"I said: 'Yeah, if you call me Josh, I will, not Mr. Graves.'

"So he said: 'I got lucky today, you see,

I'm from Kentucky and I've been here for 2 years working up in the mountains at a sawmill. I came to Steamboat Springs because I knew you were going to be here, and I've been sleeping in a pup tent with a butane stove for heat and a Colman lantern for light. I've been living on oatmeal for four days, but I got paid today, and that's why I asked you out for a drink.'

"Well, he showed up at about four o'clock in the morning where I was staying, and he knocked at the door and I told him to come on in. The next morning ten people filed right in and said: 'We wanted to see you.'

"When they told me that they had followed me all this time, I said: 'The rent's paid here for two days, why don't you stay here.' "

Josh Graves is also included on *Something Different* (Puritan 5001) and *Bucktime!* (Puritan 5005), both with Kenny Baker. (*See also* The Country Boys; The Earl Scruggs Revue; The Foggy Mountain Boys.)

## Tom Gray. *See* The Seldom Scene.

## The Greenbriar Boys

*Vocal and instrumental group, performers, and recording artists*

Formed in 1958 in the midst of the mid-twentieth-century bluegrass craze, the Greenbriar Boys originally comprised John Herald, Bob Yellin, and Eric Weissberg. The group epitomized the urban bluegrass band, and, as one of the first groups to be organized during the folk boom, the Greenbriar Boys had a strong impact on other performers in the field. Their authenticity was largely attributable to their instrumental prowess and to their field work in the rural South, which they did shortly after the group's formation. As songwriters, the Greenbriar Boys are known by most for "Stewball," popularized by Peter, Paul and Mary in the early sixties.

Born and raised in Greenwich Village,

John Herald attended the Little Red School House. His father was involved in the union movement, and he took his son to Pete Seeger concerts. When he enrolled at the University of Wisconsin, he met Eric Weissberg and Marshall Brickman, who were also freshmen. During his first year of college, he formed the Greenbriar Boys with Eric Weissberg and Bob Yellin, and he acted as the trio's lead vocalist and guitarist.

Bob Yellin came to bluegrass from a classically based musical background—his parents were professional musicians. He attended the City College of New York, and as a member of the Greenbriar Boys, he contributed his skill as a banjoist and songwriter.

A native New Yorker, Eric Weissberg made his first radio appearance on WNYC when he was ten years old. He was a student at the High School of Music and Art (along with Happy Traum) and the Juilliard School of Music. An accomplished and well-versed musician, Eric Weissberg plays bass (he performed as a bassist with the Aspen Festival and Westchester symphony orchestras), guitar, cello, banjo, mandolin, fiddle, kazoo, pedal steel, dobro, and jew's harp.

In 1960 this trio of New Yorkers clinched top honors at the Union Grove Fiddlers' Convention, and in 1960 and 1961 Bob Yellin walked away from Union Grove with a blue ribbon in the banjo contest. When Eric Weissberg left the group in 1959, he was replaced by mandolinist Ralph Rinzler. With John Herald as guitarist and lead vocalist, Ralph Rinzler as mandolinist and baritone vocalist, and Bob Yellin as five-string banjoist and tenor vocalist, the Greenbriar Boys became one of the most popular bluegrass acts in clubs, concerts, and folk festivals around the country. During the early sixties, they recorded several LPs on the Vanguard label.

A few years after their formation, Dian Edmondson became the group's lead singer. She participated in one of their Elektra recordings, and in 1963 and 1964 she sang with them on ABC's *Hootenanny.* When, in 1964, Rinzler left the group to become the

The Greenbriar Boys (left to right): Bob Yellin, Ralph Rinzler, John Herald. In front of an old bottling plant, Saratoga Springs, New York, 1961.

talent and folklore coordinator for the Newport Folk Festival, mandolinist Frank Wakefield was added to the group, along with fiddler Jim Buchanan.

After the breakup of the Greenbriar Boys, John Herald retreated to Woodstock, New York, for six years—avoiding the commercial music scene entirely. By 1972 he had returned to the performing stage as a solo act accompanied by a country-bluegrass band, with David Kapell on electric bass and cello, Alan Stowell on fiddle and guitar, and Bob Tanner on mandolin and fiddle. In the spring of 1972 a recording contract was signed with Paramount Records which resulted in the release of John Herald's first solo album, *John Herald* (Paramount PAS 6043).

In 1972 Vanguard repackaged some of the Greenbriar Boys' recordings as *The Best of John Herald and the Greenbriar Boys* (Vanguard VSD-79317). With only one ex-

ception, all selections feature Herald as lead vocalist, making the album unrepresentative of the full range of work by the Greenbriar Boys.

Since his departure from the Greenbriar Boys, Eric Weissberg has been involved with other groups, beginning with the Tarriers and, more recently, with his own Mt. Airy (with Harry Chapin's brother Tom, Russell George, Bob Hinkle, and Don MacDonald) and Deliverance (with Charlie Brown, Tony Brown, Richard Crooks, and Steve Mandell). His name soared to national prominence with his dazzling performance (with Steve Mandell) of "Dueling Banjo," an Arthur Smith original ("Feuding Banjos") used in the motion picture *Deliverance*. Eric Weissberg is considered a top-notch studio musician as well as an artist in his own right. Among the labels for which he has recorded are Elektra, Olympic, Thimble, and Warner Brothers. (*See also* Ralph Rinzler; Frank Wakefield.)

**Clarence Greene.** *See* The Blue Ridge Mountain Entertainers.

## Joe Greene

*Fiddler, composer, and recording artist*

When Joe Greene met country fiddler Kenny Baker at Carlton Haney's Second Annual Bluegrass Festival at Fincastle, Virginia, in the fall of 1966, he had been musically inactive for five years. As a result of their acquaintanceship, each of these top fiddlers has become a recording artist for County Records and listening audiences have been afforded the opportunity of discovering their music.

Born in 1938 in High Point, North Carolina, Joe Greene played instruments other than the fiddle as a youngster. His father and grandfather were fiddlers, but Greene was not a serious student of the instrument until he was almost twenty. He became interested in the fiddle while he was in the service and befriended an Oklahoma Indian who got him started on the instrument. When his tour of duty with the armed services was completed, Joe Greene went on to become one of the top fiddlers in the Texas–Oklahoma area.

Heavily influenced by his boyhood ties with the "bluegrass belt" of central North Carolina, and growing up in the "golden years of bluegrass" of the forties and fifties, Joe Greene developed a style pervaded by local bluegrass tradition. Traveling and listening to records and radio have enriched his instrumental ability and have enabled him to be fluent in a number of different styles.

In November 1967 he recorded an album with Kenny Baker, *High Country* (County 714), which includes his composition "High Point." He also recorded a solo LP on the County label, entitled *Joe Greene's Fiddle Album* (County 722).

**Richard Greene.** *See* The Jim Kweskin Jug Band.

**Lamar Grier.** *See* The Strange Creek Singers.

## Stefan Grossman

*Country blues and ragtime guitarist, composer, recording artist, teacher, and writer of guitar instruction books*

This virtuoso "revivalist" guitarist is now regarded as one of the leading proponents of basic guitar forms—blues, ballads, marches, jazz, ragtime, waltzes—that were played in the early years of this century. An instrumentalist dedicated to the guitar and to technical expertise in such playing techniques as ragtime, fingerpicking, bottleneck, and slide, Stefan Grossman has been compared in talent to Leo Kottke and John Fahey.

Stefan Grossman was born on April 16, 1945, in Brooklyn, New York. While attending Brooklyn Technical High School, he began to make excursions into New York City to wander around Greenwich Village, where countless numbers of folk musicians gathered to play blues, ragtime, bluegrass, and other forms of folk music. He became a guitar student of the legendary Rev. Gary Davis, and after the death of his teacher, Stefan Grossman became his biographer and documented his lessons in book form. After studying for two years under the exclusive direction of Rev. Gary Davis, Grossman lived with and studied under some of America's foremost country blues and ragtime artists, including Mississippi John Hurt, Skip James, Son House, Mance Lipscomb, and Fred McDowell. These years of invaluable musical education helped to formulate his future; and, like the men with whom he worked, Stefan Grossman chose to devote his life to the performance of music as a living art.

During this period, he also played with other contemporary guitarists, and he formed the Even Dozen Jug Band with old-timey guitarist Peter Siegel. In 1966, after the disbandment of the Even Dozen Jug Band, Grossman put together an instructional record, tab booklet, and notes on *How to Play Blues Guitar*, which, along with his "Country Blues Guitar Series," he feels, "is the work that seems to have influenced the widest assortment in numbers and importance." He joined the Fugs in September 1966, and, during his four months with the group, he mastered some of the techniques of playing electric lead guitar. In January 1967 he became a member of the Chicago Loop and toured with Mitch Ryder, but in May of that year he left to travel, play guitar, and sing in some of Britain's folk clubs.

For the past several years, Stefan Grossman has continued his writing and is nearing completion of his five-volume study, the "Country Blues Guitar Series." To date, the following books in the series have been published (by Oak Publications): *Country Blues Guitar, Delta Blues Guitar, Ragtime Blues Guitar*, and *Rev. Gary Davis—Blues Guitar*. Grossman has also produced other ragtime guitar albums (on the Kicking Mule Records label), and books such as *How to Play Ragtime Guitar* (with Ton Van Bergeyk), *Contemporary Ragtime Guitar, Famous Ragtime Guitar Solos* by Ton Van Bergeyk, *Rags to Riches* by Leo Wijnkamp, Jr., and *The Entertainer—The Classic Rags of Scott Joplin Arranged for the Six-String Guitar*. Grossman is in the process of preparing other books for publication, and has a series of guitar lesson tapes which are distributed by Happy Traum's Homespun Tapes.

Grossman has recorded several albums for Transatlantic Records, and he is now a recording artist, main producer, and copartner (with Ed Denson) of Kicking Mule Records, which specializes in recording acoustic, fingerpicking guitarists "in the tradition of the music developed around the turn of the century in America and brought to great heights by such men as Mississippi John Hurt, Blind Blake, and Rev. Gary Davis." He wrote and performed the soundtrack for the film *Joe Hill*; and he has toured around the world, performing live in concert, appearing on television, and conducting workshops and seminars in the United States and Europe. (*See also* The Even Dozen Jug Band.)

## Dave Guard. *See* The Kingston Trio; The Whiskeyhill Singers.

## John Guerin. *See* The Byrds.

## Guitar

A stringed musical instrument, acoustic (nonelectric) or electric, designed to function as a resonator and played by strumming or plucking. In addition to the flat-top steel-string guitar (folk guitar), there are three other closely related types of acoustic guitar: arched-top, classical, and flamenco.

Different types of wood are used in the construction of the flat-top guitar, which consists of a large, violin-shaped body, with a slight arch in the top (or soundboard) and back, fretted fingerboard, neck, and peghead. Six (four, or twelve) strings are stretched from the tuning pegs in the peghead at the top of the neck over the fretted fingerboard and soundhole in the soundboard to the bridge, where the strings are secured.

The most popular stringed instrument in the world during the twentieth century, the guitar has enjoyed a position of prominence in American folk music. Its steel, copper, or bronze metal strings are played with fingerpicks, flatpicks, and fingers, and the guitar is used for solo work or accompaniment of other instruments.

The origin of the guitar is as obscure as that of most stringed instruments which date back to ancient times. Instruments with a similar body structure and fretted necks, dating from the fourth to eighth centuries, have been excavated in Egypt. Other instruments that are not so readily identifiable as modern guitar prototypes date back to several thousand years B.C. It is believed that the guitar was first introduced into Spain by the Arabs, and the modern guitar is a direct descendant of this thirteenth-century Spanish instrument. The guitar was developed in Europe during the Middle Ages, but its size and shape often varied, with the number of strings ranging from four to twelve. By the eighteenth century, the stringing was simplified from five pairs of strings to six single strings, in a combination of three gut (or, more recently, nylon) and three metalspun silk, or all metal.

The guitar was introduced into America by Spaniards who ventured to the New World. Many years later, European craftsmen came to the United States, as Michael Holmes, editor of the *Mugwumps Instrument Herald*, wrote in his article, "Instrument Makers," which appeared in the 1974 National Folk Festival program:

> In Europe during the second quarter of the 19th century, there was a major disagreement between the Violin Makers' Guild and the Cabinet Makers. This feud first appeared in print in 1826 Guild memoranda demanding an injunction against the "bunglers" and stating that, in effect, only they themselves as artists were suited to build guitars and other instruments, while the cabinetmakers were "nothing more than mechanics" whose product consisted of "all kinds of articles known as furniture." In opposition to this, the cabinetmakers replied that the violin makers had no vested rights to make guitars. In fact, many of the finest instruments, as attested by both players and wholesalers, were those made by the cabinetmakers.
>
> In July of 1832, the authorities granted the cabinetmakers permission to continue making guitars, but this

kind of harassment undoubtedly result[ed] in many craftsmen leaving Europe for the United States. Two of those mentioned by name were Johann Georg Martin and his son, Christian Friedrich Martin. The latter came to this country in 1833 and subsequently founded the C. F. Martin Guitar Company, which has been responsible for many innovations in guitar making and which still does business today as one of the largest makers of quality guitars.

Orville Gibson, born in 1856, was a clerk in a shoe store, taking every opportunity to pursue his hobby—that of building musical instruments. His most important contribution is the application to guitars and mandolins of the violin idea of construction with carved top and back and the Stradivarius arching.

The guitar has experienced rises and falls in popularity as a lead instrument in string bands, at times overshadowed by the fiddle and the banjo, but it has been consistently popular in America as an accompanying instrument. There are many styles and variations of guitar-picking methods. One of the best-known techniques is called the "Travis Style" of picking, introduced by Merle Travis, in which the fingers are used for picking the melody on the higher strings while the thumb picks an alternating base.

# Sarah Ogan Gunning

*Traditional singer, composer of autobiographical and coal-mining songs, performer, and recording artist*

Born Sarah Elizabeth Garland on June 28, 1910, in Knox County, Kentucky, she was raised in an environment that deeply influenced her life and her music. Her personal suffering and struggle for survival in the 1920s and the Depression years, and the hardships in a coal-mining town, are the content of her own original compositions, for example, "I Am a Girl of Constant Sorrow," which is probably her best-known work. Along with her half-sister Aunt Molly Jackson and her brother Jim Garland, she became a spokesman for the plight of coal miners and laborers.

As children, she and her brothers were taught traditional ballads by their mother (after her death Sarah's father married Sarah Elizabeth Lucas, who bore eleven more children), and the entire family was led in their singing by their father, Oliver Perry Garland, who was a miner, Baptist minister, and labor organizer. Sarah acquired a wealth of melodies, and later on she set her labor lyrics to some of the old tunes she had learned as a young girl. Her brother Jim worked as a miner for many years and as a labor organizer during a period when leading workers often met with jail terms or even death. Representative of the 1930s era of topical songwriters, Jim Garland moved from Kentucky to the Pacific Northwest in the late 1940s and ran a broom factory. He was well known as a folksinger and appeared at the 1963 Newport Folk Festival (he is included on *Newport Broadside* [Vanguard VRS-9144/VSD-79144], recorded live at the July event).

When she was fifteen she married Andrew Ogan, and while he worked in the mines each day she was busy raising a family. She sang to her children many of the old songs her mother had taught her as a child, and on occasion she sang at local events and get-togethers. Word of her talent spread, and one of the most prominent collectors of folk songs, Alan Lomax, recorded a number of her songs in 1937; in the following year her duets with her brother Jim were recorded by folklorist Professor Mary Elizabeth Barnicle.

The Ogans had left Kentucky to come to New York City around 1935, and on August 15, 1938, Andrew Ogan died of tuberculosis, brought on by working under poor conditions in the mines for so many years. Sarah married a New York metal polisher, Joseph Gunning, on August 7, 1941. They

lived in New York until the outbreak of World War II, when they moved to the West Coast to work in a defense shipyard. In the late 1940s they returned to Kentucky for a while and then settled permanently in Detroit.

While Sarah Ogan Gunning had been in New York she had made the acquaintance of other artists, such as Earl Robinson, Will Geer, Pete Seeger, Lee Hays, Woody Guthrie, Burl Ives, Leadbelly, and others who were involved in raising funds for Dust Bowl refugees and miners. These were the early years of the folk movement; as its popularity gained momentum in the 1950s, traditional folksingers were in demand and Sarah Ogan Gunning was "rediscovered" out in Detroit. In the fall of 1963 Archie Green and two of his colleagues at Wayne State University, Ellen Stekert and Oscar Paskal, visited the traditionalist, and they recorded her singing on two occasions in early 1964; later in the same year, she was invited to perform at the Newport Folk Festival, and after her appearance at the 1965 University of Chicago Folk Festival Sarah Ogan Gunning was finally on her way to public recognition as a folksinger.

She now lives in Hart, Michigan, and performs at many national folk festivals; in 1975 she appeared at the Mariposa Folk Festival in Canada. She recorded a solo album, *Sarah Ogan Gunning: "Girl of Constant Sorrow"* (Folk-Legacy FSA-26), which includes twenty selections sung in her unique Appalachian style; she is also included on *Come All You Coal Miners* (Rounder 4005), which derives its title from her original song of the same name. (*See also* Aunt Molly Jackson.)

# Arlo Guthrie

*Contemporary singer, songwriter, guitarist, performer, and recording artist*

The contemporary folk scene is an amalgam of old and new elements coexisting within a broad framework amenable to both tradi-

Arlo Guthrie performing at Caffé Lena, Saratoga Springs, New York, in autumn 1974

tional and modern interpretation. Despite the transformation of folk music with the advent of electric instrumentation, some artists have maintained an authentic and personalized style of musical expression. Arlo Guthrie successfully bridges the gap between this era and the days that belonged to his folk-poet father Woody Guthrie; and since his taking by storm of the 1967 Newport Folk Festival with "Alice's Restaurant Massacree," he has maintained his prominent stature in the field.

Born on July 10, 1947, in Coney Island, New York, Arlo Guthrie is the eldest child born to Woodrow Wilson and Marjorie Mazia Guthrie. His father's influence dominated the Guthrie household, and, as a young boy, Arlo Guthrie grew up in the presence of such frequent visitors as Jack Elliott, Cisco Houston, Pete Seeger, and, later, Bob Dylan. He learned to play the guitar and played with a folk-bluegrass group in high school, as he recalls: "Well, I guess when I was finishing up with high school I discovered that I really couldn't do anything else, so I decided to continue playing music for the fun of it, which I did. I went to college and that didn't work out, so I ended up singing anyway, even though it wasn't something that I had really planned to do."

After attending classes for several weeks at a college in Montana, Arlo Guthrie returned to New York City and got his first coffeehouse gig at the Club 47 in Cambridge, Massachusetts, through a phone call by his new manager Harold Leventhal. He started playing "all the clubs around the country," and Oscar Brand (then host of the CTV show *Let's Sing Out*, the WNYC [AM-FM] *Folksong Festival*, and the U.S. government–sponsored radio show *The World of Folk Music*) recalls two of Arlo Guthrie's early engagements:

"I had a radio show for the Health, Education, and Welfare Department, called *The World of Folk Music*, and everybody was on that from the Kingston Trio to Arlo Guthrie. In fact, I took Arlo up to Canada for one of his first engagements on my television show. His second engagement was the WNYC *Folksong Festival* that runs every year—and that year it was at Carnegie Hall—and that was the first time he did 'Alice's Restaurant.'

"He said, 'How long do I have, Oscar?'

"I knew he was a kid, I was just doing him a favor by putting him on because, what the hell, he was Woody's kid, and, in fact, Woody had written a song for him called 'Good Night, Little Arlo,' which not many people knew about.

"So, anyway, I said, 'Twenty-five minutes, everybody's got twenty-five minutes.'

"He said, 'Twenty-five minutes is one song.'

"I said, 'What do you mean that's one song?'

"Anyway, he did his song—it lasted twenty-nine minutes—and it was 'Alice's Restaurant.' "

In the spring of 1967 WBAI Radio in New York broadcast a tape of the ballad which was to become his initial commercial success and his trademark. "Alice's Restaurant Massacree" was played repeatedly on WBAI by request and then in conjunction with a fund-raising effort by WBAI ("Alice's Restaurant" was played continuously until the radio station had reached its monetary goal). Arlo Guthrie's performance at the Newport Folk Festival in the summer of 1967 finalized his emergence as a top performer and recording star of the late sixties.

September brought the release of his first album, *Alice's Restaurant* (Reprise RS-6267), and a single, "Motorcycle Song"/ "Now and Then."

Undaunted by the acclaim precipitated by "Alice's Restaurant," Arlo Guthrie expresses the significance of his popular composition: "I was happy with the record. It turned a lot of commercial wheels for me. I didn't change my style very much, but it sure made it possible to work a lot!

"It also made it possible to entertain a whole new audience, normally middle-of-the-road or country & western, instead of playing to elite college audiences, and, of course, the movie [*Alice's Restaurant*] helped, too. We started to generate interest among a broader range of folks."

In 1968 his second Reprise LP, *Arlo* (RS 6299), and "Motorcycle Song (2 Parts)" were released; and in 1969 a songbook entitled *This Is the Arlo Guthrie Book* (Amsco Music Publishing Company, New York) was published that included lyrics, music, and memorabilia of the entire Guthrie family. Another songbook is planned for the near future, according to Arlo Guthrie: "We're doing another songbook. It has been ten years for me, so we are putting together a lot of different things. It will cover all of the things that I've done, recorded or not, and photographs that we've taken all over the world, and so on."

Arlo Guthrie has recorded an additional six albums on the Reprise label: *Running Down the Road* (RS 6346); *Hobo's Lullaby* (MS 2060); *Washington County* (RS 6411); *Last of the Brooklyn Cowboys* (MS 2142); *Arlo Guthrie* (MS 2183); and, most recently, *Together in Concert* (2R 2214), with Pete Seeger. (*See also* Woody Guthrie.)

# Woody Guthrie

*Singer, guitarist, performer, recording artist, writer, and folk-poet*

In discussing his father, Arlo Guthrie once said: "I don't know if anybody ever knows

Woody Guthrie (left) and Cisco Houston in New York City, autumn 1944. Publicity photo for a traveling revue to promote the election of F.D.R.

what makes somebody do something. I think he felt that he was born to write songs about all of his experiences and involvements with people and projects, and that is all that there is to it."

One of the most glorified and world-famous American folksingers of any period in this country's history, Woody Guthrie evokes a romantic image based on his ramblings through nearly every state in the union, his laboring and singing with coal miners, loggers, migratory workers, farmers, longshoremen, ranch hands, factory workers, and union members, and his chronicling of the 1930s and 1940s in his music and writing. In his travels, Woody Guthrie met and sang with folks from coast to coast, and friendships with Jack Elliott, Cisco Houston, Leadbelly, Pete Seeger, and,

later, Bob Dylan, helped to create vital and memorable occasions which sparked the renewed interest and rise of folk music in the United States during the mid-twentieth century.

Woody Guthrie wrote hundreds of songs about America and its peoples, and, as Cisco Houston once said, "When you hear them, you really hear America singing." Woody Guthrie's deep commitment made him a hero whose life and work have been immortalized and perpetuated with each new generation.

He wrote about the Depression, the Dust Bowl refugees, union organizing, love for his country and its natural beauty, laborers, and World War II. He filled many large notebooks, using whatever writing implement was available, to tell about the social, political, and economic unrest of the times from his own firsthand experiences. His outlook was always positive, as were his actions, and his messages were stated with directness, simplicity, and compassion.

Many of the nearly one thousand songs which he composed from 1936 to 1954, when he became hospitalized, are still sung by people throughout this country and in many parts of the world. For years, his music has been a part of nearly every folksinger's repertoire. His children's songs have remained among those most popular, and some of his classic and most familiar songs include "This Land Is Your Land" (often referred to as the American national folk anthem), "So Long, It's Been Good to Know You," "Pastures of Plenty," "Roll On, Columbia," "This Train Is Bound for Glory," and "Reuben James," among so many others.

Woodrow Wilson Guthrie was born to Charles and Nora Belle Tanner Guthrie on July 14, 1912, in the Oklahoma farming town of Okemah, in Okfuskee County. The Guthrie family had been among the pioneering settlers in the region, and his maternal grandmother was one of the country's first schoolteachers. His father had moved to Oklahoma from Texas; he played banjo and guitar, and, like most members of the Guthrie clan, he knew and sang many folk songs. Woody Guthrie grew up in an environment where music was a part of daily living, and he started singing soon after he learned to talk.

During his school years, life at home was disrupted by his sister's accidental death, his father's failure in the real-estate business, and his mother's commitment to a mental institution. He never finished high school, and, with a harmonica in his pocket, the sixteen-year-old Woody Guthrie started out on the road. To earn some money, he played his harmonica at dances, in pool halls and barbershops, and on street corners, and he worked a variety of other jobs.

He learned to play the guitar later on, while working with his father's half-brother

Jeff Guthrie, as Arlo Guthrie explains: "Jeff, aside from being a peace officer most of his life, was also a magician, and Woody worked magic shows with him in Pampa, Texas, and around that area. He also worked with Cousin Jack Guthrie, who was a well-known country singer back in those days, and they all worked together on Jeff's show. When the show stopped and Jeff settled down, Woody used to travel through there, and, being different—he had long hair in those days—Jeff was one of the only people Woody knew who would put up with him, and so he used to stop by there all the time as he crisscrossed the country."

After his marriage to Mary Esta Jennings, Woody Guthrie headed for the West Coast in 1935 and worked as a painter by day and a singer after working hours. He had already begun his prolific outpouring of songs, writing material conscientiously every day (resulting in a total production of approximately one thousand songs). For a while, he teamed up with "Lefty Lou" Crissman, and they performed regularly in Los Angeles on KFVD. He worked south of the border on XELO on a temporary basis and returned to KFVD as a solo act. His early political involvements took Guthrie and his music to gatherings of migrant workers and union members.

He came to New York before the outbreak of World War II and became involved as a writer for the Communist *Daily Worker*. His performances took him throughout the Northeast, and he recorded a dozen discs in a series entitled "Dust Bowl Ballads" for Alan Lomax, who headed the Archive of Folk Song of the Library of Congress. In New York, Guthrie was featured regularly on such radio shows as *Pursuit of Happiness, Cavalcade of America, Back Where I Come From, Pipe Smoking Time,* and WNYC's *Music Festival.*

Back on the West Coast, Woody Guthrie met Cisco Houston in 1938, when Guthrie was singing for a dollar a day on a Los Angeles radio program. They sang together on the show, and Guthrie, Houston, and actor Will Geer traveled along the coast, entertaining migratory workers. For the next few years, Woody Guthrie and Cisco Houston were constant companions in their traveling and performing on college campuses, street corners, radio programs, and barstools, earning enough money to move on to the next town.

Will Geer had sent the young New York folksinger Pete Seeger a copy of Guthrie's mimeographed songbook, *On a Slow Train Through California*, and on March 13, 1940, Seeger and Guthrie met for the first time at a folk song session for the benefit of California migratory workers, with Will Geer as master of ceremonies. In the same year, Guthrie rejoined his family out West and was commissioned to write songs by the Bonneville Power Administration. In June 1941 Woody Guthrie returned to New York, where Pete Seeger, Lee Hays, and Millard Lampell asked him to join up with the Almanac Singers and head back to the West Coast. The foursome sang their way across the country, returning to New York City in the fall of 1941 and settling in a Greenwich Village cooperative apartment known as Almanac House. After the breakup of his first marriage, Guthrie married Marjorie Mazia Greenblat in 1942 and worked with the short-lived Headline Singers, with Leadbelly, Sonny Terry, and Brownie McGhee. He was asked by Harvard instructor Charles Olson to write an article for *Common Ground* magazine, and, due to the overwhelming response to his "Ear Music," Woody Guthrie began writing his autobiography, *Bound for Glory* (E. P. Dutton & Company), which was published in 1943.

He and Cisco Houston joined the merchant marine in 1943; they collected guitars, mandolins, and fiddles and brought their music to Africa, Sicily, and the United Kingdom. When they survived torpedo attacks, Guthrie and Houston would get the ship's crew to join them in singing "Reuben James."

After the war, Guthrie started recording for Moe Asch, who had just organized his new record company, called Folkways. In the years that followed, Woody Guthrie recorded a couple of hundred songs for Folkways, and the release of a multitude of albums helped to establish a strong foundation for the company. Among the other record companies that issued his work were RCA Victor, Elektra, and Stinson. A collection of prose and poems by Woody Guthrie entitled *Born to Win*, edited by Robert Shelton, was published in 1965.

Woody Guthrie fell victim to Huntington's disease (chorea), and he went into the hospital in 1952. He fought the debilitating illness for fifteen years before it finally claimed his life on October 3, 1967. Many young folksingers came to visit him in his final years, and even before he died, Woody Guthrie had become an eternal source of inspiration and a legend in the field of American folk music.

One of the most memorable tributes to Woody Guthrie in recent years took place at Carnegie Hall on January 20, 1968. Two concerts were planned as a "Tribute to Woody Guthrie," sponsored by the Guthrie Children's Trust Fund, with all proceeds given to the Committee to Combat Huntington's Disease. The program included Judy Collins, Bob Dylan, Jack Elliott, Arlo Guthrie, Richie Havens, Odetta, Tom Paxton, Pete Seeger, and actors Will Geer and Robert Ryan as narrators. The "Tribute" was taped; in 1972 Columbia issued Part I (KC 31171) and Warner Brothers issued Part 2 (BS 2586). The albums include selections from the New York concert and from a second "Tribute" held September 12, 1970, at the Hollywood Bowl in California, with Joan Baez, Jack Elliott, Arlo Guthrie, Odetta, Country Joe McDonald, Richie Havens, Earl Robinson, Pete Seeger, and actors Will Geer and Peter Fonda. The concerts were directed by former Almanac Singer Millard Lampell, who worked out a script using Woody Guthrie's songs and writings.

In 1974 Grosset & Dunlap published *Woody Sez*, which consists of selections from his *People's World* daily column, written in 1939–40 for the West Coast Communist newspaper.

Actor David Carradine was selected to portray Woody Guthrie in the United Artists film *Bound for Glory*, based on the legendary folksinger's life. The screenplay was written by Robert Getchell (who wrote the script for the award-winning *Alice Doesn't Live Here Anymore*) and produced by Harold Leventhal. (*See also* The Almanac Singers; Arlo Guthrie; Cisco Houston.)

**Athol Guy.** *See* The Seekers.

# Kenny Hall

*Old-timey mandolinist, fiddler, guitarist, harmonica player, singer, performer, and recording artist*

A legendary West Coast virtuoso of the mandolin, Kenny Hall has been compared in prowess as an old-timey stylist to the bluegrass mastery of Bill Monroe. He is one of the foremost personalities in traditional music today, and his powerful influence is largely responsible for the development and current popularity of a Northern California regional style of string band music.

At the age of nine, Kenny Hall started playing the "violin" at a school for the blind in Berkeley, California, but his natural inclination to play "fiddle" tunes instead of violin music led him to seek out other fiddlers and old fiddle numbers. When he got his first mandolin, the instrument quickly became his first priority, and, due to his blindness, he formulated a unique method of playing, using his fingernails as flatpicks. He has developed the system so efficiently that if one nail breaks, he can switch to either of the two remaining nails of his first three fingers without skipping a note in the process. His repertoire includes traditional Irish fiddle tunes, 1920s gangster ballads, cowboy music, and old-time American string band music.

He lives in Northern California, about seven miles from Sanger, and he often plays his round-back (old "potato-bug" gourd) mandolin, which is unusual among old-timey musicians. As a hobby he has played

with a "revival" string band called the Sweets Mill String Band, along with Harry Liedstrand on fiddle, Cary Lung complementing Kenny Hall on mandolin and vocals, Jim Ringer on guitar, and Ron Tinkler on banjo (he credits Kenny Hall for his knowledge of the instrument).

Kenny Hall recorded his first album with Sweets Mill for Bay Records of Oakland, California. *Kenny Hall and the Sweets Mill String Band* (TPH 727) features Hall, Liedstrand, Lung, Ringer, and Tinkler doing a selection of old-timey tunes, Irish tunes, and instrumentals. Kenny Hall's second LP, *Kenny Hall* (Philo 1008), was recorded as a solo effort, with guitar accompaniment by Jim Ringer and Holly Tannen on dulcimer; Hall plays fiddle on two cuts, and mandolin for the remainder of the album.

# Frank Hamilton. *See* The Weavers.

# Hammered Dulcimer. *See* Appalachian (Mountain) Dulcimer.

# John Hammond

*Record company executive, author, executive board member of the East Coast Chapter of the National Academy of Recording Arts and Sciences, and jazz musician*

One of the key personalities behind the scenes in the music industry, John Hammond has played an instrumental role in bringing to public attention artists representing all forms of music. Himself the father of a folksinger, John Hammond, Jr., he has been a paternal figure to many musicians, including Count Basie, Big Bill Broonzy, Bob Dylan, Duke Ellington, Billie Holiday, Mitch Miller, Pete Seeger, Bessie Smith, and many, many others.

Born in New York City in 1910, Hammond received his formal education at Hotchkiss and Yale University, and his association with Columbia Records dates to 1932, when he produced Fletcher Henderson. His early recordings included work by Bessie Smith, Duke Ellington, and Mildred Bailey, and he produced most of the classic 1935–38 recordings of Teddy Wilson and Billie Holiday. In the mid-thirties, Hammond worked as American recording representative for English Columbia and Parlophone; and, toward the end of that decade, he initiated the "Spirituals to Swing" concerts at New York's Carnegie Hall, which brought such artists as Count Basie and Big Bill Broonzy to the limelight. By 1939 he had returned to Columbia and was largely responsible for bringing the Budapest String Quartet to the label. Throughout this period, John Hammond wrote many articles and critical works on jazz for several British publications; over the years, his literary pieces have been printed in practically every major magazine and New York newspaper, including *The New York Times* and *The New York Herald Tribune.*

After World War II he became president of Keynote Records, then recording director of Majestic Records. When Keynote was merged with Mercury Records, Hammond's position was raised to vice-president of the parent company, and he gave Mitch Miller a job as head of artists and repertoire. Hammond acted as director of popular music for Vanguard Records from 1953 to 1959, rejoined the Columbia payroll as staff producer, and supervised recordings by Bob Dylan, Carolyn Hester, Pete Seeger, and others during the early sixties. In the spring of 1963 he was appointed director of talent acquisition for Columbia Records and, ten summers later, was promoted to vice-president of talent acquisition, the position he still holds at Columbia. His job includes scouting, auditioning, making recommendations for signing artists to the label, administering and reviewing material submitted to Columbia, and maintaining a liaison with persons in every facet of the music industry.

From 1958 to 1960 he served as president of the East Coast Chapter of the National Academy of Recording Arts and Sciences (NARAS), and he is currently on its executive board. Once described by Leonard Feather as "the most effective catalyst in the development of jazz," John Hammond has also played an important role in the commercial development of such folk and pop artists as Leonard Cohen, Donovan, and, most recently, Bruce Springsteen.

In 1971 Hammond was the recipient of a special Grammy Award, called the Trustees Award, for his major contribution to the reissued works of Bessie Smith. Two years later, he was awarded a Certificate of Merit by the Yale School of Music for his achievements in the field. At present, he is coauthoring (with Michael Brooks) a book entitled *The Golden Age of Jazz*, to be published by Macmillan.

Truly dedicated to his work in the recording industry, John Hammond explains his outlook after nearly half a century in music: "This is the kind of work that I've always loved doing. It is something I can do and truly devote myself to. I consider that the recording industry is the greatest talent developer in the country. The radio and television industries have forfeited their leadership by their heavy reliance on talent developed through recordings. I think the time is right for bringing back to the popular music scene the challenges that can only happen with the discovery and development of new talent."

In 1975 *Soundstage* (a music series on public TV) presented two ninety-minute sessions devoted to "The World of John Hammond." On the national Public Broadcasting Service, the special tribute to John Hammond focused on his talent for discovering musical talent, with appearances and performances by Bob Dylan, Benny Goodman, John Hammond, Jr., Sonny Terry, and others. Bob Dylan's participation in this program dedicated to John Hammond marked his first television appearance in at least half a dozen years. (*See also* John Hammond, Jr.)

# John Hammond, Jr.

*Singer, guitarist, harp player, composer, performer, and recording artist*

Among the beneficial aspects of the recent folk boom was a greater public awareness of the depth of the American folk heritage, and, through the popularization of numerous traditional tunes and styles, many individuals discovered the uncommercial facet of the idiom. Numerous city musicians turned to grass-roots sources for their material and inspiration, and, while some chose to pursue a profit-seeking venture, others delved more deeply into genuine folk music and its interpretation. By the mid-1960s John Hammond, Jr., was regarded as one of the foremost white urban interpreters of the Mississippi Delta blues sound.

Named for his father, the well-known jazz musician and Columbia Records executive, John Hammond, Jr., was born on November 13, 1942, and raised in New York City. Influenced by his father's involvement in music, he taught himself to play guitar when he was eighteen. He began playing jobs in Los Angeles in 1962, and he received wide critical acclaim for his performance at the 1963 Newport Folk Festival. Several months later, his first album was released on the Vanguard label.

The year 1964 brought engagements at New York City's Village Gate and Village Vanguard, another successful appearance at Newport, and his second Vanguard LP. In 1965 John Hammond, Jr., gave his debut performance at New York's Carnegie Hall,

and he completed a highly acclaimed tour of Britain. In the years that followed, several more albums were issued by Vanguard, and his name appeared on the marquees of major clubs and in festival brochures throughout the United States.

He did the soundtrack for the motion picture *Little Big Man*, and he has recorded fourteen albums for various labels, including Atlantic, Capricorn, Columbia, Queen Bee, and Vanguard. (It is interesting to note that prior to his rise to fame as a solo artist, Jimi Hendrix played in Hammond's band, the Screaming Nighthawks.)

# Johnny Handle. *See* The High Level Ranters.

# Tim Hardin

*Contemporary singer-songwriter, guitarist, pianist, performer, and recording artist*

Every generation is represented by the voices of poets who articulate the uniqueness of their age, and during the 1960s, folk music became a popular vehicle for poetic expression. Among the young poet-composers was a singer who had a flair for combining the lyricism of the folk idiom with the rhythmic patterns and chord progressions of other musical forms. Tim Hardin was one of the first musicians to work in the realm of folk-rock, using electric instrumentation and blues-jazz stylings while other folkies were still playing acoustic instruments.

Oregon-born and -raised, Tim Hardin came to New York City after completing an overseas tour of duty with the U.S. Marine Corps. While he was studying acting, he started developing his singing and writing skills. He quit acting school and began hanging around Greenwich Village, and by 1964 he was appearing at the Night Owl Cafe. At this point, Tim Hardin was beginning to move beyond his original folk and country & western stylings to a presentation of jazz-fashioned blues.

He appeared at the 1966 Newport Folk Festival, and his debut album, *Tim Hardin* (Verve/Forecast FT/FTS-3004), was issued in September of the same year. One of the LP's twelve original selections was a song, "Misty Roses," which became a jukebox favorite and a pop music hit with its recording by Johnny Mathis. His second album, *Tim Hardin 2* (Verve/Forecast FT/FTS 3022), was released in the summer of 1967; it included several Hardin songs which were to establish him as a major new star whose material was eagerly sought. "If I Were a Carpenter" became a smash hit for Bobby Darin and led this top entertainer to select other songs by Tim Hardin for recording, including "Lady Came from Baltimore," which was another selection from *Tim Hardin 2*. Within a matter of months, another Hardin LP had reached the record racks of music stores across the United States, and in the winter of 1968 a live recording was released which contained all of his best-known hits to date. After the release of his next album in April 1969, which included romantic compositions inspired by his new role as a father, Tim Hardin seemed temporarily to pull out of the musical limelight. In 1972 he recorded *Painted Head* (Columbia KC 31764), and his most recent album to date is *Archetypes* (MGM 4952), which comprises reissued material.

# Lyndon Hardy. *See* The Putnam String County Band.

# Harmonica

Although there are several types of simple wind instruments which are referred to by this term, the most common harmonica is a popular folk music instrument that consists of a small, flat, metal box with small openings which lead to a pair of reeds of the same pitch. When air is breathed into these openings, pressure is created and operates one set of reeds; when the player exhales, the re-

maining reeds are activated by the suction which is created.

The invention of the harmonica (also called mouth harp, or mouth organ) has not been clearly attributed to one specific individual. In 1821 Friedrich Buschmann of Berlin, Germany, developed an early prototype of today's mouth organ; and, eight years later, Sir Charles Wheatstone of London, England, patented a similar instrument, which he referred to as the aeolina. More primitive ancestors of the harmonica are the mouth organs dating from 1100 B.C. found in China. These Eastern mouth organs consisted of bamboo pipes with either metal or cane reeds arranged in a gourd that acted as a wind chamber.

In the United States, the harmonica is a popular instrument in musical forms such as folk, country, country & western, and blues, and it is used primarily for vocal and/or instrumental accompaniment. Two of the instrument's leading exponents are bluesman Sonny Terry and country musician Charlie McCoy; and, during the recent folk revival, Bob Dylan was instrumental in bringing attention to the harmonica by using it in recording sessions and live performances.

# Emmylou Harris

*Country singer, guitarist, composer, performer, and recording artist*

The mid-1970s has been a period of awakening for a number of veteran performers whose overnight sensation is the end product of a lifetime of working and waiting for a break. Emmylou Harris, who is often compared to Linda Ronstadt, began the initial phase of her musical career in the late sixties, but retired from active performing with the birth of her first child in 1970. In late 1971 she met Gram Parsons, and the rekindling of her career by their acquaintanceship has established her distinction as one of the most celebrated singers of the mid-decade.

Alabama-born and Virginia-raised, she

hanging out in Greenwich Village. She formed friendships with David Bromberg, Paul Siebel, and Jerry Jeff Walker, and played Gerde's Folk City on a regular basis. Influenced by others around her, she was turned on to country music, and her music developed from its ballad-bluegrass roots.

By 1969 she had signed her first recording contract with the now-defunct Jubilee Records; the following year brought the release of her debut album and the birth of her daughter Hallie. After the breakup of her marriage, Emmylou Harris left New York and got back into music with the encouragement of some friends, Billy and Kathy Danoff (composers of "Take Me Home, Country Roads"). One night, while she was performing at Washington, D.C.'s, Red Fox, a bar which has presented other top names, including the Seldom Scene, she was heard by the Flying Burrito Brothers' guitarist, Rick Roberts. The following evening he brought the entire band down to hear her performance, and after the show they asked her to join up with them, but before she could accept the invitation, the Flying Burrito Brothers had disbanded. One of the band's members, Chris Hillman, introduced her to Gram Parsons, and a year later she was in Los Angeles singing as an accompanist on Parsons's Reprise album, *GP*. In the spring of 1973 she toured with the young country-rock singer, and, during the summer, she worked with him on his final LP, *Grievous Angel*. His untimely death turned her world upside down, and instead of flying back to California without him, she decided to remain in the nation's capital to put together her life and her music.

She formed her Angel Band and started working club dates, establishing a solid reputation in the Washington, D.C., area. She was signed to Warner Brothers in mid-1974, and with the release of her new album, *Pieces of the Sky* (MS 2213), her name became known nationally. Her powerful counterharmony was the vocal accompaniment on Linda Ronstadt's 1975 country hit,

Emmylou Harris

sang at parties and idolized Woody Guthrie while attending high school in Woodbridge, Virginia. She went to the University of North Carolina, with a scholarship in drama, and spent her spare time singing in a folk duo. She applied to the Boston University Drama Department after a year and a half of studies in the South, and, in the interim, worked to earn her tuition as a waitress in Virginia Beach. Overwhelmed by the local music scene, Emmylou Harris became serious about singing and came to New York to pursue her career by playing "basket houses" (clubs where the hat is passed in order to pay the entertainer) and

## John Hartford

"I Can't Help It," and Ronstadt's background vocals assisted Emmylou Harris on *Pieces of the Sky.* (Emmylou Harris was also highly praised for her vocal accompaniment on five selections of Bob Dylan's most recent LP, *Desire.*)

By the summer of 1975, she was touring extensively, recording another album (*Elite Hotel* [Reprise MS 2236]), and planning a six-month American and European tour to begin in February 1976.

**Emory Harris.** *See* The Freedom Singers.

**Evelyn Harris.** *See* Sweet Honey in the Rock.

**Rutha Harris.** *See* The Freedom Singers.

**Walter Harris.** *See* The Freedom Voices.

# John Hartford

*Contemporary singer, songwriter, fiddler, banjoist, performer, and recording artist*

A talented banjoist and fiddler from St. Louis, Missouri, John Hartford helped to shape a modern bluegrass sound by developing his straight bluegrass roots into a gentle, personal style which set his brand of music apart from the predominant stylings of the 1960s. Best known for his original composition "Gentle on My Mind" and for his performances on the Glen Campbell TV show, John Hartford has made a significant contribution to the overall acceptance and popularity of bluegrass music.

Born on December 30, 1937, in New York City, he moved with his family to Missouri after his father had completed his medical internship in the North. As a boy, he listened

John Hartford performing at the Friday evening concert at the Eleventh Annual Philadelphia Folk Festival, 1972

to country music radio stations, and he was particularly attracted to bluegrass and country square dance social gatherings. At the age of nine, he started experimenting on an old Washburn mandolin, and within a few years was playing the fiddle and five-string banjo. He started performing at local get-togethers, and, later on, the guitar became a part of his instrumental repertoire.

John Hartford had a number of conventional jobs before he commenced the pursuit of his earliest interest and turned to a career as a professional musician. Music was relegated to his leisure hours as he worked full-time as a sign painter, commercial artist, Mississippi River deckhand, and radio disc jockey, and as he attended St. Louis's Washington University to study art. He became more involved in music as he worked for radio stations in Clinton (Illinois), Balden (Missouri), East St. Louis, St. Louis, and Nashville, but his longing to be at the other end of the business led him to turn from a career as a disc jockey to become a musician. As a Nashville session musician, he attracted the attention of Tom Smothers, who asked Hartford to fly to California to make an appearance on the *Smothers Brothers Comedy Hour*. That summer, he worked with Glen Campbell on the *Summer Smothers Brothers Comedy Hour with Glen Campbell*, which was followed by an offer by Campbell to work as a sideman on the regular *Glen Campbell Goodtime Hour*. His performances with Glen Campbell demonstrated his proficiency both as an instrumental accompanist and as a "songwriter-in-residence," and 1969 proved to be an important year in the formation of his career as a solo artist.

His first recording was a single, "Tall, Tall Grass"/"Jack's in the Sack," which was issued in 1966 after he had signed a recording contract with RCA Victor. That summer, RCA released his first album, followed in 1967 by *Earthwords and Music* (RCA LPM/LSP 3796), which included "Gentle on My Mind." This song became one of the most frequently recorded tunes of the late sixties and is best remembered as a country vocal hit for Glen Campbell and a top-selling instrumental number for Floyd Cramer; "Gentle on My Mind" remained the most performed composition in the BMI catalog for two consecutive years. The year 1968 brought *The Love Album* (RCA LSP 3884).

In recent years, John Hartford has recorded for Warner Brothers and Flying Fish, and he has performed at major festivals and clubs around the country.

# Roy Harvey. *See* Charlie Poole and the North Carolina Ramblers.

# Alex Hassilev. *See* The Limeliters.

# Brooks Hatch. *See* The Serendipity Singers.

# Richie Havens

*Contemporary singer, guitarist, songwriter, performer, and recording artist*

A masterful manipulator of rhythm, Richie Havens adds a magical and individualistic touch to the songs in his repertoire with his distinctive open guitar tuning and his uncanny sense of phrasing and stylistic tension. Whether he is performing material by the Beatles, Bob Dylan, Jesse Fuller, Gordon Lightfoot, or songs penned by his own hand, Richie Havens consistently produces a result which is uniquely his own.

Richard Pierce Havens was born on January 21, 1941, in the Bedford-Stuyvesant section of Brooklyn, New York. He was one of nine children in a family supported by his mother, who was employed in a bindery, and his musician-electroplater father, who played piano for various bands across the country. The neighborhood black church and radio programs (tuned in on sets owned by the less poor inhabitants of the ghetto) provided additional stimuli beyond his father's influence.

As a youngster faced with growing up amid poverty and hardship, Richie Havens found his own avenue of recreation by singing and making music with friends. He began singing professionally at the age of fourteen with the McCrea Gospel Singers, and his further experience with group singing continued to cultivate his affinity for harmonizing and experimenting with vocal and instrumental interpretations of music. Torn by the demands of his environment, he was compelled to become a member of a street gang, but sustained faith in his own dignity and musical ability provided him with incentive to escape both physically and psychologically from his boyhood circumstances. He dropped out of school before completing his secondary education, and he is largely a self-educated man—a fact about himself of which he is very proud.

Richie Havens made his first mark on listening audiences when he began playing small Greenwich Village clubs, such as the

Cafe Wha?, Bizarre, Why Not?, and Fat Black Pussycat, in the pre–Lovin' Spoonful sixties. The size of his fingers made it difficult for him to learn regular guitar tunings, so he resorted instead to an E chord structure (using major, minor, and minor-seventh chords), a styling which soon became a special trademark of his guitar playing. As his reputation grew in the mid-sixties, he began to attract attention among music industry executives. A recording contract was signed with MGM, and his debut album, *Mixed Bag* (Verve/Folkways FT/FTS-3006), was released in the fall of 1967.

In the later sixties, his concert appearances took him to stages from the Fillmore East to the Fillmore West, and he managed to retain his popularity among rock and pop audiences at a time when electric instrumentation was rapidly surpassing acoustic sound. Richie Havens adapted to the demands of a changing era by playing (in addition to guitar) sitar, tamboura, and bongos on his next recording, *Somethin' Else Again* (Verve/Forecast FT/FTS-3034), and he was among the first to use an electric sitar in performing and in recording.

Richie Havens continued to perform extensively, and one of the highlights of his career was his participation in the January 20, 1968 (New York), and September 12, 1970 (Los Angeles), "Tributes to Woody Guthrie." He has been all over the world, and his numerous recordings have enjoyed equal acclaim in the United States, Britain, France, and other countries. In 1974 Richie Havens was selected to be the American representative to the International Festival of Song in Rio de Janeiro, and he was chosen for the prestigious Best Interpreter prize in a competition among artists from over forty countries.

A respected portrait painter, poet, and sculptor, he is also currently writing a book (in prose statement form) on his personal philosophy as it relates to, and is influenced by, the world around him. He is still on the roster of MGM recording artists, and his

Richie Havens at the 1966 Newport Folk Festival

most recent albums have continued to cover a breadth of material as far-reaching as his personal life experience.

## Baldwin "Butch" Hawes. *See* The Almanac Singers; Bess Lomax Hawes.

## Bess Lomax Hawes

*Lecturer, folklorist, teacher, author, singer, guitarist, mandolinist, songwriter, and performer*

Along with her brother, Alan Lomax, Bess Lomax Hawes has continued the Lomax family tradition of achieving fame for significant contributions to the field of folk music. She is a self-taught guitarist, and her early years were highlighted by her participatory role in the influential Almanac Singers. Before her recent move to Washington, D.C., she had established a **reputation on the West Coast as one of its** foremost guitar teachers and performers, as a professor of anthropology at California State University at Northridge (formerly San Fernando Valley State College), and as a summer faculty member at the Idyllwild School of Music and the Arts.

Bess Lomax was born on January 21, 1921, in Austin, Texas. As a child, she was influenced by her father's interest in music, and she studied classical piano for a number of years. After some years in the business field, John A. Lomax returned to a full-time involvement with folk music, and he and his son Alan contracted with the Macmillan Company to write *American Ballads and Folk Songs.* After her mother's death, Bess Lomax was sent to a Dallas boarding school—where she excelled in her studies— while her father and brother traveled widely in search of authentic folk material.

She entered the University of Texas when she was fifteen, and her involvement with folk music expanded as she was introduced to traditional singers, including Leadbelly, by her father and brother. She decided to pursue an academic study of the subject, but, at the time, did not consider a career as a performer. When she was sixteen, she helped to transcribe field recordings for the Lomaxes' second book, *Our Singing Country,* and while she was working with them in Washington, D.C., she assisted Ruth **Crawford Seeger in transcribing tunes.**

After learning to play the guitar while in Europe, she soon gravitated toward others involved in folk music and joined up with the newly formed Almanac Singers in New York City. Woody Guthrie taught her to play the mandolin, and she met scores of people in the field, including her future husband, Butch Hawes, and his older brother John ("Pete"), who were also members of the Almanac Singers.

Baldwin (nicknamed "Butch" by his friends) Hawes was born on September 21, 1919, in Boston, Massachusetts. During the thirties, he temporarily abandoned his pursuit of an art career and turned to music in hopes of finding a more straightforward and relevant medium for expressing his social and political views. As a member of the Almanac Singers, Butch Hawes played primarily backup guitar, sang tenor vocal accompaniment, composed songs (his best-known composition is probably "Arthritis Blues"), and met Bess Lomax, whom he married in 1942. In later years, he returned to fine art and commercial illustration, and before his brother Pete took up residence in Puerto Rico, they often sang together.

When the Almanac Singers disbanded at the beginning of World War II, Bess Lomax Hawes went to work in the Music Division of the Office of War Information (OWI). In the latter forties, Butch and Bess Lomax Hawes moved to Boston, where she began teaching a folk instrument class and composed songs for the Progressive mayoral candidate, Walter F. O'Brien. A collaborative work (with Jacqueline Steiner) of this period, "M.T.A. Song," was later popularized by the Kingston Trio.

The fifties found the Hawes family out on the West Coast, where Bess Lomax Hawes continued her teaching and performing. Her vast knowledge of folk music brought her a reputation as one of Southern California's leading authorities in the field. Today, when she is not teaching, she is frequently lecturing or participating in panel discussions on the subject. Bess Lomax Hawes has been a featured performer at such major festivals as Newport, Berkeley, San Diego, and UCLA, and at numerous concerts, clubs, and workshops.

In addition to teaching folklore and folk music at California State University at Northridge during the sixties, she joined the summer teaching staff of the Idyllwild School of Music and the Arts in Idyllwild, California. She is the coauthor (with Bessie Jones) of a book of Afro-American children's games, *Step It Down* (Harper & Row, 1972). Bess Lomax Hawes is currently living in Washington, D.C., and working for the Division of the Performing Arts, Smithsonian Institution.

Butch Hawes died in late 1971 after a long history of spinal arthritis. (*See also* The Almanac Singers.)

## John "Pete" Hawes. *See* The
Almanac Singers.

## "Judge" George D. Hay. *See*
Grand Ole Opry.

## Lee Hays. *See* The Almanac
Singers; The Weavers.

## Hazel and Alice. *See* The Strange
Creek Singers.

## The Headline Singers. *See* Woody
Guthrie.

## Joe Heaney
*Traditional singer of Irish ballads and songs, performer, and recording artist*

A resident of the United States since the mid-1960s, Joe Heaney is considered by many to be one of the greatest singers of traditional Irish music. He is at his best when he sings a Gaelic song; he considers Gaelic to be his first language because it is what he spoke as a boy. Most of the songs in his repertoire today were learned by Heaney before he was ten, when there were very few radios and family life revolved around gatherings of people sitting around, telling stories, and singing or dancing. Heaney grew up in the tradition of unaccompanied singing and learned the importance of the story within a song.

Joe Heaney was born in 1920 in Connemara, on the western seacoast of County Galway, and he lived there for twenty years, until 1940. His birth came amid the Irish rebellions which were repressed by members of the Royal Irish Constabulary, the Black and Tans, and he grew up hearing his mother recall the suffering and killing of those times. In an interview taped April 9, 1972, by Josh Dunson, Heaney talked about some of the things which concerned him as a youth: "I wanted to get out and see, and what I wanted to find out more than anything was: Why do people have to suffer? Why was there two acres of land and twenty-five acres of rock? And why was there such a thing as somebody with a thousand acres to run their hounds and horses through the fields and collect their money after them? What did they do to deserve it? I suddenly hated the people who did it, you know. Oh, the history . . ."

Joe Heaney recorded *Irish Music in London Pubs* (Folkways FG 3575) with Margaret Barry, Séamus Ennis, and others. It was made from a live recording done by Ralph Rinzler, and it captures the informality and warmth of the performers' presentation in a pub atmosphere.

While he was a boy, Heaney used to sing to himself while tending cattle in the fields; in 1940 he went to Dublin to sing his old-style songs at the Feis Ceoil and won first prize at the National Music Festival. Then he went to England, where he met Peggy Seeger and Ewan MacColl, and he stayed there from 1949 to 1957. He came to the United States in the middle of the sixties, and he has appeared at every major festival in this country, including the 1966 Newport and Philadelphia folk festivals.

Heaney narrates on the Paredon album *This Is Free Belfast* (P-1006), and he has made an album of his unaccompanied, highly ornamental, traditional Gaelic songs, *Irish Traditional Songs in Gaelic and English* (Topic 12T91). He sings "Cunnla" on *From Erin's Green Shore*, Topic Sampler No. 4 (TPS 168); and his most recent album, *Come All Ye Gallant Irishmen* (Philo PH

2004), was released in the summer of 1975.

## Martha Hearon. *See* The II Generation.

## Charlie Heath. *See* The Kentucky Pardners.

## Fred Hellerman. *See* The Weavers.

## Hamish Henderson

*Scottish folklorist, collector, and scholar of the School of Scottish Studies, Edinburgh University, songwriter, and poet*

The name most commonly evoked by any discussion of Scotland's folk song revival, Hamish Henderson was responsible, through his tireless efforts, for the "discovery," in 1953, of the famed Scottish ballad singer Jeannie Robertson, and for the procurement of representation of Scottish traditional music on radio and television airwaves throughout the British Isles.

Prior to the outbreak of World War II, Hamish Henderson was enrolled at Cambridge University. From 1940 to 1945 he served as an intelligence officer, and during night watches he jotted down lines and ideas for a group of poems. In 1948 his poetry was published as *Elegies for the Dead in Cyrenaica*, which, in the following year, won the Somerset Maugham Award. Beginning in 1951, Hamish Henderson devoted his energies to gathering and studying folk songs and folk tales of his native Scotland.

His pursuit has brought him in contact with Scotland's many fine singers and storytellers, including wandering minstrel Jimmy MacBeath, tinker Duncan McPhee, border shepherd Willie Scott, and ballad singer Jeannie Robertson. He began collecting as early as 1938, continuing while he was in the army, and many of these tunes were published in *Ballads of World War Two* (Lili Marlene Club of Glasgow), now a collector's item. After the war Hamish Henderson traveled around the Scottish countryside, befriending countless singers, instrumentalists, and storytellers, and writing down material as he went from village to village.

After an encounter with the Irish singer, piper, and collector Séamus Ennis and the Scottish collector and scholar Calum Maclean, the young amateur collector focused his attention on the folk song. He worked closely with Maclean, and together they collected tapes of traditional singers from South Uist, the Hebrides, Badenoch, and Buchan. Their work attracted a growing audience, mostly of young people, and their enthusiasm for the traditional music of Scotland was one of the primary undercurrents of the folk song revival. Henderson's search took him among tinkers, or "travellers," and, armed with a tape recorder, he collected songs and music which have been transferred and issued by an American company. In 1951 Alan Lomax accompanied Hamish Henderson on a grand tour of Scotland, during which they collected an enormous amount of material. In the late fifties, they worked together on a BBC production of a series call *A Ballad Hunter Looks at Britain*.

For many years Hamish Henderson has been affiliated with the School of Scottish Studies, for which he has collected and conducted extensive correspondence with scholars from other countries. To witness the global acknowledgment of Jeannie Robertson (whom he first met in her Aberdeen home in 1953) is one of the highlights of his career, and, due to his many hours of taping her singing and storytelling, Hamish Henderson compiled an invaluable collection of her work before her death in 1975. (*See also* Jeannie Robertson.)

## Judy Henske

*Singer, performer, and recording artist*

The recent urban folk revival promulgated the rise of innumerable performers, many of whom vanished from the popular music scene as quickly as they had appeared. Although her career is characterized by a conspicuous lack of longevity, Judy Henske is remembered by many for her towering physical stature, her dynamic singing voice, and her emotive facial expressions, which promoted one writer to describe her as "an exclamation point."

Originally from Chippewa Falls, Wisconsin, Judy Henske migrated to the West Coast. By the early sixties, she was singing in San Diego on the same bill with Cyrus Faryar, who encouraged ex–Kingston Trio member Dave Guard to see her perform during an engagement in Oklahoma City. He was moved by her singing and asked her to join up with his new quartet, the Whiskeyhill Singers. The group was organized in December 1961, with Cyrus Faryar, Dave Guard, Judy Henske, and David "Buck" Wheat. In addition to their live performances, they recorded one album, *Dave Guard and the Whiskeyhill Singers* (Capitol T 1728).

Judy Henske reached the peak of her career around 1963; in that one year, Elektra Records issued her three (and only) solo albums, including *Judy Henske* (EKL-231) and *High Flying Bird* (EKL-241). Simultaneously with the release of her debut solo LP in February 1963, Elektra issued her sole single, "Day to Day"/"Dolphins in the Sea."

She married former Lovin' Spoonful member Jerry Yester, who had played briefly with the group until its disbandment in 1968. Judy Henske's name has appeared in recent years only in connection with television reruns of the film *Hootenanny*, in which she performed over a decade ago. (*See also* The Whiskeyhill Singers.)

**John Herald.** *See* The Greenbriar Boys.

# Carolyn Hester
*Singer, guitarist, performer, and recording artist.*

One of the many significant personalities of the early-sixties folk scene, Carolyn Hester came to the Northeast in 1956 from her native Lone Star State. With her rich contralto voice, a guitar, and her intuitive feeling for folk music, she naturally gravitated to the musical circles of her contemporaries and soon was performing at festivals and coffeehouses around the United States and recording for Tradition, Dot, and Columbia.

Born in Waco, Texas, Carolyn Hester participated in singing at family get-togethers and listened to records, with Burl Ives discs among her favorites. Even though folk songs were a part of her early life, theatrical ambitions were foremost among her thoughts— and her primary purpose in coming to New York City. Her family had moved several times since her birth, and the young girl had been exposed to a diversity of musical styles while growing up in Dallas, Austin, and Denver. She had made her first television appearance at the age of thirteen, in Texas, and she decided to study acting with the American Theater Wing in New York.

Carolyn Hester

When she arrived in the East in 1956, the urban folk boom was just starting to gain momentum, and during those early years, she began singing at coffeehouses and college concerts. She toured with the New Lost City Ramblers and recorded her first album, on a small label, long before the revival was in full swing. The late fifties found Carolyn Hester at Gerde's Folk City, the Newport Folk Festival, Chicago's Gate of Horn, the Indian Neck Festival, and, in the early sixties, on a regular basis at the Club 47 in Cambridge, Massachusetts. At this point, she had married the talented writer, singer, and composer Richard Fariña; and, after the release in 1961 of her second LP, *Carolyn Hester* (Tradition TLP-1043), she signed a recording contract with Columbia Records.

In recalling her friendship with the young Bob Dylan, Carolyn Hester once said: "I don't remember exactly how Dylan came to work with me on my first Columbia album. It may have been Richard saying to Dylan, 'Gee, if we get into some gigs or something we'll bring you in, too.' And the record was the first thing to come along. Richard and I were talking about what could be acceptable to the folk crowd and still be a little advanced commercially—to reach out, to be a little different from Joan Baez, say. Odetta had put a bass on her record, so we thought a bass with my guitar and also a harmonica—my father had played a harmonica on my first record—so we thought that's what we'd do. And when we got down to New York around the first of September we asked Dylan to play the harmonica for my record."

Carolyn Hester had established a reputation as a performer in Britain, where her husband, Richard Fariña, was very popular. She appeared on a couple of occasions at the Edinburgh Festival and on British television, and she was among the first female American top folksingers in Great Britain.

She and Richard Fariña had separated in 1962, the year of the release of her Columbia LP (CL 1796/CS 8596), which had brought her praise in *Time, Hi-Fi Stereo Review*, and other publications. After her divorce, Carolyn Hester continued to make personal appearances throughout the United States and in Canada. Her debut appearance at New York's Town Hall produced material for two live albums, and she was among the group of folksingers protesting and boycotting ABC-TV's *Hootenanny*, which had banned Pete Seeger from appearing on the weekly show.

With the introduction of electric instrumentation during the mid-sixties, Carolyn Hester tried to keep in step with the times and formed the Carolyn Hester Coalition. She and her folk-rock band toured, performing mostly college concerts, and made some recordings; but eventually, with the competition by hard-rock groups creating obstacles for a group which was more rooted in folk traditions, Carolyn Hester forfeited further compromise of her music and temporarily abandoned the music industry.

During the seventies, she played various club, concert (including the Great Folk Revival at the Nassau Coliseum, Uniondale, New York, in February 1974), college, and festival dates. She signed a contract with RCA and recorded *Carolyn Hester* (RCA APD1-0086); and, along with Peter Yarrow, she was appointed to the board of directors of the Kerrville (Texas) Folk Festival.

# Joe Hickerson

*Head of the Archive of Folk Song, Library of Congress, singer, guitarist, performer, and recording artist*

As head of the Archive of Folk Song, Joseph C. Hickerson has assumed the prestigious office that has been occupied by such esteemed folklorists as Robert W. Gordon, John A. and Alan Lomax, Benjamin A. Botkin, Duncan Emrich, Mrs. Rae Korson, and Alan Jabbour. Like those who preceded him, he is responsible for the principal U.S. collection of folk recordings, documents, and research data.

Born on October 20, 1935, Joe Hickerson

started singing in church choirs about eleven years later, in 1946. Around 1950, he began playing guitar and singing folk songs: "My family generated the interest in folk music, and there were songbooks and recordings in our home, like *The Fireside Book of Folk Songs*, and popular recordings by the Weavers, and some of Burl Ives and Carl Sandburg.

"I got particularly interested in folk music after I entered Oberlin College, where there were a number of people who played guitar and had recordings. By 1955 I had a radio program of folk music on the Oberlin College station, and I also acted as the campus salesman for the few existing New York folk music record companies.

"About the same time, I started singing in public, and in the summer of 1957 I was involved with seven other Oberlin students in a traveling group that toured mostly summer camps in the Northeast, teaching folk songs, and we called ourselves the Folksmiths. That same year, I entered the graduate program in folklore at Indiana University, where I studied folklore, folk music, anthropology, and ethnomusicology. I had decided to make the study and research of folk music my living, and, of course, I've continued to sing and perform.

"For several years, I worked part-time in the two folklore and folk music archives at Indiana University, which was an exciting experience and led to the job that I have now. I have worked for thirteen years at the Library of Congress, and prior to being appointed as head of the Archive of Folk Song, I was the Archive's reference librarian."

Hickerson is an accomplished vocalist and guitarist. His music can be heard at festivals and on several albums, including *Joe Hickerson with a Gathering of Friends* (Folk-Legacy FSI-39); *Five Days Singing, Volumes 1 and 2* (FSI-41 and FSI-42), as one of several people in the New Golden Ring; *We've Got Some Singing to Do* (Folkways 2407), with the Folksmiths; and recordings made by the Fox Hollow Folk Festival and the National Geographic Society.

Due to his busy work schedule, Hickerson is able to perform at only two or three festivals each year, but, more often, he participates in the activities of local folk song societies and organizations. His appointment as head of the Archive of Folk Song was received by his colleagues, scholars, and others in the field of folk music with approval and acclaim. Hickerson explains his dedication to the betterment of the Archive: "In terms of the future and my work at the Archive, I am hoping to expand the Archive of Folk Song and to make it more viable and useful." (*See also* Archive of Folk Song; The Golden Ring.)

# The High Level Ranters

*Performers of traditional British dance tunes and recording artists*

One of the most popular folk bands in England, the High Level Ranters are widely known in their native country and in Europe for their performances of traditional dance tunes and songs of Northumberland. Northumbrian music is rich in tradition and is still played in homes and pubs by traditional musicians. The music hall songs played by the Ranters are derived from the industrial northeast of England, and the remainder of their repertoire comprises traditional music from other parts of England, Ireland, and Scotland.

The group's unique sound is produced by Alistair Anderson on English concertina; Tom Gilfellon on guitar and vocals; Johnny Handle on accordion, piano, and vocals; and Colin Ross on fiddle, Northumbrian smallpipes, and whistle. They have made six albums in England on the Leader and Topic labels: *Northumberland For Ever* (Topic 12T 186), *The Lads of Northumbria* (Leader LER 2007), *Keep Your Feet Still, Geordie Hinnie* (Leader LER 2020), *High Level* (Leader LER 2030), and *A Mile to Ride* (Leader LER 2037). Their most recent recording, *A Miner's Life* (Topic 2/12TS 271/2) is a double LP of mining songs from the region in which they live. They are also included on *English Garland* (Topic TPSS221 Sampler No. 8), with Dave and Toni Arthur, Peter Bellamy, Anne Briggs, Roy Harris, Oak, Peta Webb, and Bernard Wrigley. (*See also* Alistair Anderson.)

# The Highwaymen

*Vocal and instrumental group, performers, and recording artists*

With their hit version of "Michael," which sold over three million copies while the members of the quintet were still in college at Wesleyan University in Connecticut, the Highwaymen became another overnight success story of the folk boom. Although the Highwaymen produced four other bestselling records, their name is generally associated with this song, with another million-seller, "Cottonfields," and with hundreds of college concerts given between 1961 and 1964.

The group was formed by Bob Burnett, Steve Butts, Chan Daniels, Dave Fisher, and Steve Trott, who attempted to present vocal and instrumental interpretations of greater diversity than offered by other contemporary collegiate-type groups. In their performances they often used over a dozen instruments, and, with their international backgrounds, they rendered with authenticity musical selections covering a broad range of languages and dialects.

Originally from Mystic, Connecticut, tenor Bob Burnett became the rhythm expert of the Highwaymen. While in college, he learned to play the guitar and bongos, and, on a trip to West Africa, he acquired a musical enrichment which brought a new dimension to the group's sound.

Born and raised in New York City, Steve Butts was the most widely traveled member of the Highwaymen; he lived for a while in Australia and journeyed to five continents. His background in classical music, harmony, and counterpoint was an asset to the folk group, and in addition to providing bass

The Highwaymen. Standing, from left, are Bob Burnett, Dave Fisher, Steve Trott. In the center is Steve Butts; at bottom, Chan Daniels

vocal accompaniment, he became the featured banjoist of the Highwaymen.

The group's baritone, Chan Daniels, was born and raised in Buenos Aires, Argentina. His father, who sang and collected songs as an avocation, taught him to play the guitar, and during his school years, he sang with various groups. As a member of the Highwaymen, he contributed to their repertoire the folk songs he had learned while growing up in South America, and his instrumental knowledge of the charango and the bombo.

Dave Fisher, who hailed from New Haven, Connecticut, was the principal arranger and lead tenor for the Highwaymen. With a musical background covering rock 'n' roll, classical theory, harmony, and choral conducting, he was an adept guitarist as well as a proficient accompanist on banjo, bongos, and recorder.

With an interest in folk music first cultivated in Mexico, Steve Trott continued to pick up an international repertoire of folk songs as a student in Europe and Latin America. Guitarist and autoharpist for the Highwaymen, he sang tenor vocals.

One of the subsequent members of the group, Gil Robbins, had previously played bass for another folk group of the early sixties, the Cumberland Three. After about a year and a half with John Montgomery, Mike Settle, and John Stewart, he left to join up with the Highwaymen.

After a short-lived but successful career, the Highwaymen disbanded and its members returned to the pursuit of separate careers. Today, Bob Burnett and Steve Trott are attorneys; Steve Butts is involved in the academic world; Chan Daniels is a record company executive; Dave Fisher is a songwriter; and Gil Robbins is an actor. In 1974 the Highwaymen reunited for a memorable concert appearance at the Great Folk Revival, held on February 2 at the Nassau Veterans Memorial Coliseum, Uniondale, Long Island.

During their brief career, the Highwaymen recorded another popular single, "The Gypsy Rover," and several albums on the United Artists label.

# The Highwoods String Band

*Old-timey string band, performers, and recording artists*

Reputed to comprise one of the best contemporary old-timey string bands in the United States, the five young musicians who compose the Highwoods String Band originally hailed from different parts of the country. Now based on the East Coast, Mac Benford, Jenny Cleland, Doug Dorschug, Walt Koken, and Bob Potts learned their repertoire of Southern Appalachian dance tunes, songs, and tales from field recordings, early 78-RPM discs, and other musicians. "We have tried our darnedest to create our own distinct band style," says Mac Benford, "which will be a product of the 1960s and

1970s and yet can stand in the company of the great string bands of the 1920s and 1930s. We feel very strongly that this music is still alive."

Previously with the Fat City String Band in Berkeley, California, banjoist Mac Benford and fiddlers Walt Koken and Bob Potts joined up with Doug Dorschug (guitar) and Jenny Cleland (bass fiddle) to form the Highwoods String Band. They began playing their genuine old-time country sound for street-corner, festival, concert, and club audiences around the country, and in August and September 1974 the quintet performed for the peoples of Central and South America in conjunction with the National Folk Festival Association's State Department–sponsored tour, "Music of the People—USA."

The Highwoods String Band remains a favorite at fiddlers' conventions (they have won prizes in contests at Galax and in the Old-Time Band Category at Marion, Virginia) and at major folk events, including the annual National and Philadelphia folk festivals. They have recorded two albums for Rounder Records, *Fire on the Mountain* (Rounder 0023) and *Dance All Night* (Rounder 0045), and they are among the performers included on *Good Time Music at the National* (Philo PH 1028).

# The Hill Billies

*Early old-time band, radio, and vaudeville act, performers, and recording artists*

One of the earliest and most significant of the string bands from the Blue Ridge of the Southern Appalachians, the Hill Billies gave a name, "hillbilly," to the type of music that they played. The band was organized in Galax, Virginia, in the mid-1920s, and the Hill Billies made the original recordings of many numbers that have become old standards; their extensive touring brought country music to many of America's major cities, and they performed for President Coolidge in the late twenties. As a commercial country music band, the Hill Billies were primarily showmen; and their radio shows, recordings, and vaudeville act made them the first successful country band in show business.

The band's original members were Alonzo Elvis "Tony" Alderman, Joe and Al Hopkins, the nucleus of the group, and John Rector, operator of a general store near Galax, Virginia. Alderman was a Galax barber at the time of the band's formation; he left the **music profession in the early thirties, and** today resides in the Washington, D.C., area, occasionally playing the fiddle and musical saw at nearby fiddlers' conventions. Banjoist Rector arranged the initial recording session of the Hill Billies; until his untimely death, he was an important part of the band's early work. The Hopkins brothers came from a musical background, and by 1910 Al Hopkins had formed a quartet with his brothers, working at a theater in Washington. Al Hopkins is responsible for the introduction of the piano in early country music recordings, but he was usually photographed with a guitar or banjo. Although the term *hillbilly* was in the American vocabulary of the early twentieth century, it was not used in conjunction with any musical form until a name was selected for the Hopkins-Alderman-Rector band. When they recorded six titles on January 15, 1925, for Ralph S. Peer of the Okeh Recording Company, Peer decided to list the band as the Hill Billies; from then on, many groups have adopted the term, and "hillbilly" came to represent the music of the rural white South.

The Hill Billies' initial 1924 recordings for Clifford Cairns were never issued; but their second New York recording session resulted in their first releases in February 1925, and by March WRC in Washington, D.C., was broadcasting their music. In the years that followed, the Hill Billies traveled to many cities, including New York and Washington, D.C., and in 1928 they made the first film featuring country music for Vitaphone (Warner Brothers).

Most of the Hill Billies' recordings were made with the twin fiddlers Alderman and Charlie Bowman, whom the band had met in 1925 at the Mountain City fiddlers' convention; the resonant vocals of Al Hopkins; (at different times) banjo work by Rector, Jack Reedy, and Walter Bowman; various guitarists, including Elbert Bowman, Joe Hopkins, Walter "Sparkplug" Hughes, and slide guitarist Frank Wilson; and a pioneer of country music recording, fiddler Uncle "Am" Stuart, along with other fiddlers, Fred Roe, "Dad" Williams, and Ed Belcher. While he was with the Hill Billies, Henry Rowe introduced the string bass to country music, and the harmonica and ukelele playing of Elmer and John Hopkins contributed to the hilarity of the Hill Billies' act and the band's hallmark.

The Hill Billies recorded for Victor (the session was never issued), Okeh, Vocalion, and Brunswick. After Al Hopkins's death in a 1932 automobile accident, the Hill Billies disbanded.

County Records has issued *The Hill Billies* (County 405) with selections made by them for Brunswick Phonograph Records. While he was performing with the band, Charlie Bowman recorded for Columbia, and his version of "Forky Deer" is a selection on *Old-Time Fiddle Classics, Volume 2* (County 527).

## "Hillbilly" Music

A colloquial term denoting a type of music that is characteristic of inhabitants of the mountains or backwoods, particularly in the South, "hillbilly" music is used in reference to early country or rural Southern folk music. Evolving in the 1920s, it distinguished white country music from black country, or "race," music, which shares a similar folk origin and orientation.

It is generally accepted that talent scout Ralph S. Peer was responsible for the coinage of both "hillbilly" and "race" music, and, although the word "hillbilly" had been in general usage since the turn of this century, it was not until the mid-twenties that the term was adopted to describe rural Southern folk music. Several months prior to the "official" adoption of the term, "hillbilly" made its initial appearance on a record label with Uncle Dave Macon's seventh issued disc, "All I've Got's Gone"/"Hill Billie Blues" (Vocalion 14904). The three major competitors in the hillbilly field were Okeh, Columbia, and Vocalion, which were soon joined by the mogul of the American music industry, Victor.

The specific sociological and musical marriage of the term "hillbilly" was made on January 15, 1925, when the Hopkins-Alderman-Rector string band was recorded by Peer for the Okeh Recording Company. On that date, Al Hopkins coincidentally referred to the band as a group of North Carolina hillbillies, which, in turn, inspired Peer to list them as the Hill Billies. As a consequence, the name of the group came to represent the type of music which they played, and, over the years, it has developed into a form which is now known as modern country music. No longer a localized phenomenon, "hillbilly" music is a tradition which is kept alive by enthusiasts throughout the world.

## Mable Hillery. *See* The Georgia
Sea Island Singers.

## Chris Hillman. *See* The Byrds.

## Sam Hinton

*Singer, instrumentalist, folklorist, concert and recording artist, author, biologist, illustrator, lecturer, and teacher*

Sam Hinton is said to know more than a thousand songs, both traditional and contemporary, and this California scholar-scientist was one of the first professional entertainers to use the term *folk music* in describing his performances. In 1936 he was on the vaudeville stage, billed as "Texas Sam

Hinton, Novelty Instrumentalist and Folk-singer."

"I was born in 1917 in Tulsa, Oklahoma, but spent most of my boyhood years in the East Texas towns of Beaumont and Crockett. I don't remember when I wasn't interested in folk music. My mother was a musician and piano teacher, and she encouraged this interest and says that I started playing the harmonica at five. At eight, I got my first push-pull accordion, and for years I used that to accompany my singing. But it wasn't until I went to college, in 1934, that I started playing the guitar.

"In 1934, I went to Texas A&M, and that's when I discovered that this material that I liked was known as folk music and that there was a literature and scholarly study of it. I think when I first started calling this folk music was a little before that because for my high school graduation my sister sent me a copy of Carl Sandburg's *American Songbag* that had been published in 1927, and that had a tremendous influence on which way I was going. I was majoring in zoology, and took no courses in folklore, but there was time for this pursuit on the side. I entered into a correspondence with Professor J. Frank Dobie of the University of Texas, and, in my sophomore year, he invited me over to Austin to do a lecture-recital of East Texas folk songs. From that moment on, I have thought of myself as a lecturer-recitalist rather than an entertainer.

"After two years at A&M, I went East to join my folks. My father, a civil engineer, had joined the Department of the Interior in Washington, D.C. My younger sisters, Nell and Ann, joined me in singing; and as the Texas Trio we sang quite a bit around Washington. I was also working as a part-time artist in the National Museum and as a full-time window decorator and sign painter at Woodward and Lothrop's department store. Late in 1936 we appeared on the coast-to-coast radio show, *The Major Bowes Amateur Hour*. Each week the winners of the *Hour* were sent out to join one of the Major's vaudeville units, playing in movie theaters in those dying days of vaudeville. Nell and Ann were too young to go on the road, but I joined the Transcontinental Unit then playing in Danville, Illinois. For the next two years I toured with various units, under the names of Major Bowes and Ted Mack, and played in forty-six states and Canada. While I was on the road, Dad was transferred to Los Angeles, and when the troupe finished its two weeks in LA's old Orpheum Theater, I dropped out and went back to school, this time at UCLA."

After graduating from UCLA with a BS in zoology, Hinton worked for three years as the director of the Desert Museum in Palm Springs, California. From there, he went to the University of California, to become director of the aquarium-museum in the university's famed Scripps Institution of Oceanography in La Jolla. In 1948 he began teaching courses in music, folklore, geography, biology, and education for the University of California Extension, and has done so ever since as an extracurricular activity. When Scripps expanded to become a general campus, University of California at San Diego, Hinton was named director of the Office of Relations with Schools, a post he still holds. He is also lecturer in folklore in the UCSD Department of Literature.

"My first recordings were made in 1947 for the Archive of Folk Song of the Library of Congress. The first commercial recording was made in 1950. This was a 78-RPM single on the Columbia label, 'Old Man Atom,' usually known as 'Talking Atomic Blues.' Then I did an album of California historical songs for Bowmar Records, together with Ben Cruz, a singer of old Spanish and Mexican songs. Then, in 1951, I started recording for Decca. At first the Decca records were singles in their 'Children's Series,' but later I did three LPs—which are all out of print now. Sometime in there was a fun record—a two-record album for RCA Victor called *How the West Was Won* [RCA Victor LP-6070]. I helped Alan

Lomax and Si Rady choose the songs and write the notes, and sang nine of the songs. Other singers on this record were Jimmy Driftwood, Bing Crosby, Rosemary Clooney, and the Salt Lake City Tabernacle Choir. One song is a duet with Rosemary Clooney, but I regret to say that I have never met the lady—our relationship has been purely electronic!

"After that, I joined forces with Moe Asch of Folkways Records, and I've done four solo albums for Moe and am planning others. The most recent recording that I have made was for an album of cowboy songs for the National Geographic Society. I'm also working right now on a college credit course which is a series of thirty one-hour lectures on tape, to be issued with an accompanying book, by the Center for Cassette Studies."

Sam Hinton has given thousands of concerts throughout the United States, in Mexico, Canada, and Europe, appearing primarily at colleges and universities or under the auspices of the Community Concert Association. He has written three books on marine biology, two of which he also illustrated; the latest work is titled *Seashore Life of Southern California*, published by the University of California Press. He has appeared in most major folk festivals, and he has been a host-performer in each of the annual Berkeley festivals. In the summer of 1975, with Jonathan Eberhart, he acted as anchorman in National Public Radio's coverage of the Smithsonian Festival of American Folklife in Washington, D.C.

# Roscoe Holcomb

*Traditional singer, banjoist, guitarist, mouth harpist, performer, and recording artist*

Music has always been a part of Roscoe Holcomb's life, from his boyhood in Daisy, Kentucky, to his years of coal-mining, lumber-mill, and construction work in the Hazard, Kentucky, area, when he sang and played instruments for relaxation and entertainment. Holcomb was among the authentic nonprofessional "discoveries" of the folk movement, and, since 1959, folklorists have helped to make possible for him several recordings and invitations to concerts and festivals.

Born in western Kentucky in 1913, Roscoe Holcomb was an early participant in family singing, and at local gatherings the young boy listened with interest to the banjo, guitar, dulcimer, and mouth harp. One of his early influences was an unaccompanied Baptist style, and, together with the styles of old-time ballad singing and Blind Lemon Jefferson, Holcomb created a unique sound that complemented his high, lonesome, almost angelic singing.

He played banjo by the age of ten, and, after his brother-in-law presented him with a homemade instrument, he began to play with a local fiddler. During his teens, Holcomb learned to play several instruments, and with each year that passed, more and more ballads and dance tunes were added to his repertoire. When Holcomb was in his early twenties, he studied the banjo earnestly, learning to play and sing well over three hundred songs within one year.

His banjo and guitar styles are highly personalized, and basically the same. Holcomb plays with his thumb and index finger only, picking the melody while using the two fingers as a drone, and he often tunes the guitar in an open chord like the banjo.

After being employed by various local farmers, Holcomb looked to the mines for work, and although he often worked more than one job at a time, most of his life was spent as a miner. His leisure hours were devoted to music, and he was in constant demand as a square-dance musician.

When the region's mines closed down after World War II, Holcomb went from one job to another to sustain himself. His musical career was given a boost in 1959 when, during the folk movement, folklorist and musician John Cohen was collecting material for Folkways Records, and Holcomb recorded *Mountain Music of Kentucky* (Folkways FA 2317). In 1962 Cohen made a film, called *The High Lonesome Sound*, about the life and music of Roscoe Holcomb, and Folkways issued an album by the same name, *The High Lonesome Sound* (Folkways FA 2368). In 1963 he recorded *The Music of Roscoe Holcomb and Wade Ward* (Folkways FA 2363), followed recently by *Close to Home* (Folkways FA 2374), and he is among the artists included on *Friends of Old-Time Music* (Folkways 2390).

These recordings helped to bring Roscoe Holcomb the attention that his musical talents deserve, and, as a result, many invitations were extended to him to perform at concerts and at major festivals, including Chicago, UCLA, Berkeley, Cornell, Brandeis, and Newport. In the mid-sixties, he traveled to Europe with the Festival of American Folk and Country Music. During the same period, Oak Publications released the book *Old Time Mountain Banjo*, by Art Rosenbaum. Among the thirty notated songs which illustrate different styles of picking, the playing of Roscoe Holcomb, Uncle Dave Macon, Charlie Poole, Dock Boggs, Hobart Smith, and Wade Ward are represented.

## Bill Holden. *See* The Country Gentlemen.

## W. S. Holland. *See* The Tennessee Three.

## The Hollow Rock String Band

*Old-timey string band, performers, and recording artists*

With material drawn from the rich musical heritage of North Carolina, Virginia, and West Virginia, the forte of the Hollow Rock String Band lies in the recreation of rare old field-recorded fiddle tunes. Today's undisputed specialists on the style and repertoire of Glen Lyn, West Virginia, fiddler

Henry Reed, who was recorded extensively by Hollow Rock String Band member Alan Jabbour, this old-timey trio has paid tribute to its primary source musician by including numerous Reed-derived tunes in its performances and recordings.

The key member of the Hollow Rock String Band is a former head of the Archive of Folk Song, Alan Jabbour, whose robust fiddling is accompanied by Tommy Thompson on banjo and guitar and Jim Watson on guitar, mandolin, and autoharp. Jabbour first played fiddle as one of the original members of the band, along with Bert Levy, Bobbie Thompson, and Tommy Thompson. After the recording of their initial album, *The Hollow Rock String Band* (Kanawha 311), the group was reformed with Alan Jabbour, Tommy Thompson, and Jim Watson. In 1974 the reconstituted Hollow Rock String Band recorded another LP on the Rounder label, *The Hollow Rock String Band* (Rounder 0024), with over half the selections attributable to Alan Jabbour's "master on the fiddle," Henry Reed.

With a career boasting impressive academic credentials and distinction as a scholar, teacher, and writer in the field of folklore and folk music, Alan Jabbour is widely known for his talents as a fiddler and a judge of fiddling contests. His fiddle playing reflects an Irish influence as well as American traditional stylings found in the work of Tommy Jarrell and other old-time fiddlers.

In 1974 Alan Jabbour was appointed by the National Endowment for the Arts to serve as director of folk arts; since then, he has been overseeing festivals and working with American folk musicians and artists in a program of documentation and preservation.

# John Lee Hooker

*Blues singer, guitarist, performer, and recording artist*

John Lee Hooker's versatility within the field of blues has made him a notable performer of the idiom's various aspects, including rhythm-and-blues, rock 'n' roll, folk, and country blues. His musical heritage is rooted in the folk process, which is a viable tradition in rural, close-to-the-earth living, when everyone sings what has been sung for years and years.

Born during World War I on a farm outside Clarksdale, Mississippi, John Lee Hooker was raised in a region of the country where folk blues were passed on from one generation to the next. Singing was an established tradition, and many leisure hours were spent making music with friends and relatives.

The area from which he came had produced a previous generation of legendary country bluesmen—Mississippi John Hurt, Sonny Boy Williamson, and Big Bill Broonzy—and John Lee Hooker and Muddy Waters, his contemporary, followed in the footsteps of these itinerant blues singers. At the age of seventeen, Hooker left home and traveled around the United States for nearly a dozen years, going from one job to the next, but always singing and playing in his inherited, blues-oriented style.

After World War II, more jobs were available in the field of music, and Hooker found work in Detroit's cafés and clubs, primarily as a rhythm-and-blues musician. While he was performing at the Monte Carlo club, he attracted the attention of a local record company, which made Hooker's first recording of a countless number on many labels. During the fifties, his name was associated with rhythm-and-blues and rock 'n' roll, and he recorded some hit songs under such pseudonyms as John Lee Cooker, and Texas Slim.

By the mid-sixties, after several years of recording exclusively with Vee-Jay Records, Hooker was recorded by different companies, such as Atco, Galaxy, and Fortune. The following albums offer a sampling of the many aspects of blues, with old traditional, country, folk, rock, and rhythm-and-blues representing John Lee Hooker's wide range of musicianship: *I'm John Lee*

*Hooker* (Vee-Jay Records VJLP 1007); *Big Maceo Merriweather* (Fortune FRT 3002); *I Feel Good* (Jewel 5005); *The Country Blues of John Lee Hooker* (Riverside RLP 12-838); *John Lee Hooker* (Atlantic 7228); *The Blues—John Lee Hooker* (Crown CLP 5157); and *House of the Blues* (Marble Arch [Great Britain] MAL 663); and he is among the artists who were recorded on *Detroit Blues—Early 1950's* (Blues Classics BC-12).

## Hootenanny

A commonplace term in the American vocabulary during the recent folk revival, *hootenanny* may be defined as an informal and festive assemblage of folksingers for swapping, sharing, and performing many kinds of music, with audience participation.

The coining of the term is usually attributed to the Almanac Singers, who heard *hootenanny* used in the context of a social, fund-raising affair, when they were touring in Seattle, Washington, in the summer of 1941. Pete Seeger explains the derivation and subsequent usage of *hootenanny:* "The word *hootenanny* came from the Midwest. It's a term for an informal party, like *wingding* or *shindig*, and I think it's an old French word. Somebody's even told me they think they heard it used in France by people who have never heard the modern use of it. You see, St. Louis was originally a French city—a French settlement. Louisville, Kentucky, was French, so some of the French words probably lasted. Then one of these Midwesterners went to Seattle. In 1941 Woody and I found them using the term in Seattle for a monthly fund-raising party, where they had some singing and dancing, a little bit of everything, food, and we took the word to New York and used it for our weekly rent parties to pay the rent. Leadbelly, Burl Ives, Josh White, and many other people used to drop in to Almanac House and sing with us on a Sunday afternoon. Then after World War II we used the word for the fund-raising songfests of the organization called People's Songs."

In the early sixties, Ed McCurdy inaugurated Tuesday-night "hoots" at the Bitter End in Greenwich Village, and both professional and amateur folksingers had the opportunity to participate in these jam sessions. By 1963 the term *hootenanny* was adopted for commercial purposes when ABC-TV bought the Bitter End's concept and usage of the name for a weekly show. Each week *Hootenanny* was videotaped on a different college campus, with a commercially successful performer as headliner and acting host. The result was a musically unconstructive situation which imposed a prevalent overtone of entertainment, thus equating a hootenanny with a television variety program. As Pete Seeger describes it: "Then what happened was the word got stolen by ABC television in 1963, and it was a sad thing. The word almost got ruined. Two hundred million Americans looked at their televisions and said, 'Is that a hootenanny show?' White college kids all grinning like fools, no matter what it was, half an hour of happiness, but it really was kind of phony. It was a phony program, it wasn't a real hootenanny. I almost stopped using the word after ABC got through using it."

## Sam "Lightnin'" Hopkins
*Country blues singer, guitarist, songwriter, performer, and recording artist*

Sam "Lightnin'" Hopkins's intense and earthy brand of country blues is rooted in the unrefined melodies of work and field songs with which he grew up on a farm in eastern Texas. His voice conveys the lonely experience of his youth with a mournful, "wailing" vocal style that is unlike the distinctive, rhythmic style of northern Louisianans such as Leadbelly, or the intricate style of Mississippi bluesmen.

Born on March 15, 1912, in Leon County, Texas, Sam Hopkins was raised amid poverty, farm work, and singing in a small, rural community between Houston and Dallas.

Poster advertising performances by Sam "Lightnin'" Hopkins and others at a Great Southeast Music Hall presentation in Atlanta

When Hopkins was a young boy, he taught himself to play guitar, and then, one Sunday at a church picnic in Buffalo, Texas, he met Blind Lemon Jefferson. The youth watched attentively as the famous bluesman played licks on his guitar for Hopkins that day, and on subsequent occasions, when Blind Lemon Jefferson was in Waxahatchie.

Sam Hopkins worked on the family farm near Centerville, and he sang and played guitar whenever there was an audience to listen. A cousin who lived on a nearby farm was the renowned blues singer Texas Alexander, who had made recordings for Okeh in the 1920s, and he shared his love and knowledge of the blues with Hopkins. After World War II, his Uncle Lucien Hopkins encouraged Hopkins to go to Houston and to become a singer. With his uncle's support, Hopkins purchased an electric guitar, and he worked with Texas Alexander and then on his own, in Houston.

He made a recording in Hollywood for the Alladin label in 1946, and it was while he was working with piano player "Thunder" Smith that Sam Hopkins adopted the name "Lightnin' " (the duo was called "Thunder" and "Lightnin' "). When he returned to Houston, Hopkins made his first solo blues recordings for a local company, Gold Star Records, and the most popular numbers sold in excess of eighty thousand copies. His contract with Gold Star was terminated in the early fifties when Hopkins went to New York to record his biggest hits for another company.

With the increased popularity of rhythm-and-blues and folk music, Hopkins became much sought after for appearances on folk programs and concerts throughout the country. He made almost 200 blues recordings on various labels, including Imperial, Time Records, Vee, Folklore, and Bluesville (Prestige Records). During the 1960s, most of his recordings appeared on the Bluesville label, but he also recorded for Verve/Folkways, Herald, and World. His Arhoolie albums are numerous and include *Lightnin'*

*Sam Hopkins* (F 1011); *Early Recordings* (R 2007), *The Texas Blues Man* (F 1034), *In Berkeley* (1063), and *Early Recordings Vol. 2* (2101). He is also featured on many Arhoolie and Blues Classics collections, and on other labels such as Fantasy, Jewel, Everest (reissues), and Tradition.

# Son House

*Blues singer, guitarist, composer, performer, and recording artist*

One of the legendary Delta blues musicians, Son House is revered as a topnotch artist and as the forerunner of Muddy Waters and Robert Johnson. Like many other bluesmen, Son House was strongly influenced by Charley Patton, who became his close companion and brought him to the Paramount Records studio in Grafton, Wisconsin, to make his initial recordings in 1930. Over the years, Son House developed a unique bottleneck guitar style that was still considered definitive when he retired in the sixties.

Eddie "Son" House was born on March 21, 1902, in Lyon, just outside Clarksdale, Mississippi. After his parents separated, he moved with his mother to Louisiana when he was about seven years old. Although his father and uncle performed in a small brass band, his mother's religious scruples prevented him from playing the guitar or singing blues at home. During his teens, he brought home some additional money by gathering moss, which was used for stuffing cushions and mattresses. When his mother died, he returned to Mississippi and found employment as a field hand.

The prospect of earning higher wages drew him to East St. Louis in 1922, and he worked for a dollar an hour at the Commonwealth Steel Plant. Less than a year later, he returned to Mississippi and, at the age of twenty-five, started playing the guitar. His early source of inspiration was the bottleneck style of a musician named Willie Wilson, whom he heard play one day in Matson, Mississippi. Wilson lived in Leland, and Son House had the opportunity of hearing him play often. Some of the songs he was to record several years later, including "My Black Mama" and "Preachin' the Blues," were taught to him by another friend, James McCoy.

In the late 1920s, he was involved in a fight and was sentenced to fifteen years at Parchman Farm on a conviction of homicide. He was released after serving only a year, and moved to Lula, where he met musicians Charley Patton and Willie Brown. A Paramount recording artist, Patton took House and Brown to the company's studio in the summer of 1930, and each of the bluesmen was recorded. After receiving forty dollars for recording songs such as "My Black Mama," "Preachin' the Blues," and "Dry Spell Blues," Son House returned to Mississippi to join Willie Brown. They organized a blues band which performed at country suppers and dances.

In 1933 Jackson music store owner Henry C. Speir made test recordings of Charley Patton, Willie Brown, and Son House, which he sent to the New York offices of the American Record Company (ARC). Although the company was interested in Patton (W. R. Callaway of the ARC traveled to Mississippi to collect Patton's last recordings early in 1934), Son House was overlooked. For the next decade, he was joined by other musicians in his performances around Robinsonville, and in 1941 Fiddlin' Joe Martin, Leroy Williams, Willie Brown, and Son House were recorded on location at Lake Cormorant by Alan Lomax for the Library of Congress.

In the mid-forties, Son House moved to upstate New York, and for the next two decades, he worked for the railroads and played music with Willie Brown, who had also moved north. With the regeneration of interest in blues during the sixties, he was sought out by collectors, musicians, and fans, and for several years he was a popular performer at college concerts and at major festivals, including Newport.

In addition to his Library of Congress recordings, some of the commercial record labels which offer his work are Biograph, Blue Goose, CBS (Great Britain), Columbia, Folklyric, Folkways, Verve/Folkways, and Yazoo.

# Cisco Houston

*Singer, guitarist, songwriter, performer, and recording artist*

When cancer claimed the life of forty-two-year-old Cisco Houston, American folk music lost one of its most authentic voices and a legendary figure who came to symbolize one of the most unique economic and social periods in this country's history. His romantic image and life experiences have been immortalized in his music, which, during his lifetime, he often sang and played with his pal Woody Guthrie.

Cisco (Gilbert Vandine) Houston was born on August 18, 1918, in Wilmington, Delaware. He moved with his family to the West Coast, where he spent the majority of his childhood, and later adopted his first name of Cisco from the Sierra Nevada town near the Donner Pass. He had picked up folk tunes from members of his family and he learned to play the guitar before finishing high school in Los Angeles. He began his itinerant life during the Depression years and he worked at various jobs out West, and as a ranch hand in Colorado Houston expanded his repertoire with cowboy songs. Throughout his travels, he carried his guitar slung over his shoulder, and music was always incorporated into his daily life. He performed informally for friends and fellow workers and occasionally he shared his music with audiences at clubs and over Western radio stations. His life-style attracted him to others who shared a similar philosophical outlook, and his friendships with Woody Guthrie, Leadbelly, and Jack Elliott were natural extensions of his life and music.

In his book, *Bound For Glory* (E. P. Dutton & Company, 1943), Woody Guthrie describes how he and Cisco Houston first met:

> The months flew fast and the people faster, and one day the coast wind blew me out of San Francisco, through San Jose's wide streets, and over the hump to Los Angeles. Month of December, down along old Fifth and Main, Skid Row, one of the skiddiest of all Skid Rows. God, what a wet and windy night! And the clouds swung low and split up like herds of wild horses in the canyons of the street.
>
> I run onto a guitar-playing partner standing on a bad corner, and he called his self the Cisco Kid. He was a long-legged guy that walked like he was on a rolling ship, a good singer and yodeler, and had sailed the seas a lot of times, busted labels in a lot of ports, and had really been around in his twenty-six years. He banged on the guitar pretty good, and like me come rain or sun, or cold or heat, he always walked along with his guitar slung over his shoulder from a leather strap.

Houston and Guthrie traveled and sang together in the years before World War II, parting company when Houston joined the merchant marine, and sailed to ports around the globe. After his stint in the service, Cisco Houston stayed in New York for a while before crossing the continent to resettle in Hollywood. He rejoined forces with Guthrie and often teamed up with Leadbelly, John Jacob Niles, Burl Ives, and other prominent performers and recording artists. He was part of Moe Asch's first Folkways recording sessions, and was among the singers who often performed and recorded with the Almanac Singers, along with Butch, Pete, and Bess Lomax Hawes, Sis Cunningham, Gordon Friesen, Arthur Stern, Josh White, Brownie McGhee, Sonny Terry, and Earl Robinson.

During the fifties, Cisco Houston performed college, club, and church concert dates, with memorable appearances at Town Hall and Madison Square Garden in New York City and the 1960 Newport Folk Festival. He toured India with Sonny Terry, Brownie McGhee, and Marilyn Child under the auspices of the State Department and the American National Theater and Academy; and, on his way home, he performed for enthusiastic audiences in England and Scotland. He was also a guest on numerous radio and television programs. His recording career boasted widespread representation on labels including Disc, Stinson, Folkways, Vanguard, and others. In 1965, Oak Publications put out a songbook entitled *900 Miles: The Ballads, Blues and Folksongs of Cisco Houston.*

One of Cisco Houston's ardent admirers was a young singer by the name of Bob Dylan, who used to hitchhike out to Bob and Sid Gleason's apartment in East Orange, New Jersey, where Woody Guthrie spent almost every weekend while a patient at Greystone Hospital in central New Jersey. Cisco Houston, Jack Elliott, Pete Seeger, and other friends of Woody Guthrie often dropped by, and Bob Dylan was particularly attracted to Houston, who, by then, was dying of cancer. Cisco Houston continued performing at Gerde's Folk City and other clubs in New York, never dwelling on his fate or letting the terminal disease prevent him from sharing his music. By the end of February 1961 he had made his final appearance on stage, and after remaining in New York for several more weeks, he returned to his West Coast home. He died in San Bernardino, California, on April 29, 1961. *(See also* The Almanac Singers.)

## Rex Hunt. *See* Bottle Hill.

## Hurdy-Gurdy

A stringed folk instrument resembling the dulcimer in design, tuning, and relative ease of playing, the hurdy-gurdy functions by means of a rotating crank attached to a wheel that rubs the surface of the strings to produce a sound similar to that of the bagpipes. Sometimes confused with the street organ or barrel organ once used by organ grinders, the hurdy-gurdy is of European origin.

Over the centuries, the hurdy-gurdy has been reduced from a length of five feet (operated by two men and used in churches and monasteries until it was replaced by the organ) to a smaller dimension which made it portable and required only one person to play it. Its portability led to its increased usage among street and folk musicians, and the number of melody strings was reduced and drone strings were added.

By the late Middle Ages, its popularity had diminished as many street musicians switched over to playing newer, portable mechanical pipe organs, which operated in a fashion similar to the player piano, thus requiring no musical skill. These street or barrel organs were also referred to as hurdy-gurdies, and they were largely responsible for the drastic decrease in number of the authentic hurdy-gurdy. In modern times, the hurdy-gurdy has survived in the rural regions of Eastern Europe, particularly in Hungary, France, and western Russia. Although uncommon in the United States, the hurdy-gurdy is sometimes rebuilt from a guitar or a lute, and there are several American craftsmen who construct handmade hurdy-gurdies today.

Renewed interest in the hurdy-gurdy was created by Donovan's hit single of 1968, "Hurdy Gurdy Man," which was also used as the title for his album, *Hurdy Gurdy Man* (Epic BN 26420), released in October 1968.

# Mississippi John Hurt

*Blues singer, guitarist, songwriter, performer, and recording artist*

The folk revival of the 1950s and 1960s was a catalyst for the rediscovery of formerly obscure musicians such as Mississippi John Hurt who reserved music for their personal amusement. Mississippi John Hurt had been musically inactive since his first recordings of 1928, and, tragically, he died only three years after blues collector Tom Hoskins sought him out in 1963 to play as a professional blues artist.

John Hurt was born on March 8, 1892, in Carroll County, in the delta region of Mississippi which has spawned other great bluesmen. Unlike the harsh, biting blues typical of this area, Mississippi John Hurt's blues sound is characterized by the self-expression of many emotions and moods.

His mother paid $1.50 for her nine-year-old son's first Black Anne guitar, and he played "Black Annie" for nearly his whole life. He worked at a variety of occupations, and he learned songs from field workers, cotton pickers, and cattle hands. He developed his own style of playing guitar and performed occasionally for meager wages at dances and festivities from the time he was a teenager.

In 1928 Tommy Rockwell of Okeh Records traveled to Mississippi to find new talent in country music. When he heard John Hurt, the recording director sent the bluesman to Memphis to cut eight recordings, including "Frankie" and "Nobody's Dirty Business." Hurt received his first substantial remuneration for his music —$240 and expenses—and when the initial recordings sold better than expected, Mississippi John Hurt recorded more songs on the Okeh label in a New York recording session during the last month of that year.

He returned to his home in Avalon, where he resumed his normal routine of working at a steady job and making music for his own amusement. Three decades later, Mississippi John Hurt picked up his guitar to perform commercially, and, returning to Washington, D.C., with collector Tom Hoskins, he started gigging at the Ontario Place cafe, where a live recording was made for the Piedmont LP *Worried Blues* (PLP 13161).

Several albums were made for Piedmont Records, and, during the same year of his comeback, in 1963, he was a guest at the Newport Folk Festival, where he was presented with a new guitar by the Newport Foundation.

His name spread widely in 1963 and 1964; major articles were written about him and appeared in such magazines as *Time* and *Newsweek*, and in *The New York Times*; and he made appearances on Johnny Carson's *Tonight Show* and at New York's Carnegie Hall and Town Hall. Other recordings were made by Piedmont, such as *Mississippi John Hurt: Folk Songs and Blues* (PLP 13157) in 1963, and, in the following year, *Worried Blues* was released. Vanguard Records issued several LP's, including *Mississippi John Hurt/Today* (VSD 79220), *The Immortal Mississippi John Hurt* (VSD 79248), and *Last Sessions: Mississippi John Hurt* (VSD 79327), recorded the year that he died, 1966, and produced by Pat Sky.

Biograph Records has issued an album by the country blues musician, *Mississippi John Hurt, 1928: Stack O' Lee Blues* (BLP C4), which is a remastering of some of his best known, early recordings, such as "Frankie," "Nobody's Dirty Business," "Louis Collins," "Avalon Blues," "Candy Man Blues," and "Spike Driver Blues." Hurt is included in a number of important collections, such as *The Anthology of American Folk Music* (Folkways FA 2951, and FA 2953), *Friends of Old-Time Music* (Folkways 2390), *They Sang the Blues—1927–1929* (Historical HLP 17), and *Mississippi John Hurt* (Fontana [Great Britain] TFL 6079).

He died on November 2, 1966, in Grenada, Mississippi.

**Ashley Hutchings.** *See* Fairport Convention.

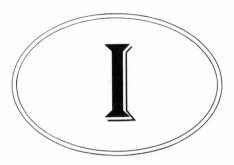

## Ian and Sylvia

*Vocal and instrumental duo, songwriters, performers, and recording artists*

One of the first popular Canadian groups of the recent urban folk revival was Ian and Sylvia, whose meeting in Toronto in 1959 came at a perfect time. The setting in this capital of Ontario was similar to that of New York's Greenwich Village, with folk clubs and folksingers on the rise. Drawing on a wealth of traditional Canadian material as well as contemporary songs, the young folk duo of Ian and Sylvia was a welcome addition to the music scene.

Ian Tyson was born on September 25, 1933, in British Columbia. He was raised on a small farm, worked as a rodeo performer and a lumberjack, and, at the age of twenty-one, entered the Vancouver School of Art to become a commercial artist. Upon graduation, he returned to British Columbia but, unable to find steady employment, left for Toronto. While supporting himself by working full-time as a commercial artist, he found spare hours to play his guitar and to sing with a group of friends. He soon discovered that music was his first love and, at this time, he met "a shy girl from the country," named Sylvia Fricker.

Sylvia Fricker was born on September 19, 1940, in Chatham, Ontario. Her mother was a music teacher and the organist and choir leader in their church; her father was employed in the appliance section of a large department store. After graduating from high school, she worked for a jeweler in her hometown but, unhappy with the direction

her life was taking, began venturing up to Toronto on weekends. She had always enjoyed music, particularly the folk idiom, so she decided to pursue a career as a professional singer. After a year of traveling back and forth to Toronto, she quit her job and moved up there. She first met Ian Tyson while both were performing at a local spot called the Village Corner Club. They formed their music partnership early in 1959, and, in 1964, their personal lives were joined by marriage.

Toronto audiences found the duo's style both refreshing and exciting, but even though they were drawing sellout crowds, their recognition was only local, so they decided to go to New York to enlarge their audience. Shortly after their arrival they met Albert Grossman, who, during the sixties, managed such acts as Dylan, the Band, Peter, Paul and Mary, and another Canadian folksinger, Gordon Lightfoot. Grossman signed them to a contract, says Tyson, "hoping he'd have another big-selling act like Peter, Paul and Mary," and they began playing major clubs around the United States, including Chicago's Gate of Horn, Los Angeles's Ash Grove, and New York's Bitter End.

Their first Vanguard album, *Ian and Sylvia* (Vanguard VRS 9109), was recorded in a Brooklyn Masonic temple, and although it did not sell in large quantities, it precipitated a small but loyal following. But times were changing, and, taking Dylan's lead, they started writing much of their own material—with Ian writing songs about the open plains and the lonesome traveler, and

Ian and Sylvia at the 1965 Newport
Folk Festival

Ian Tyson and his son, Clay, at home in Toronto, Canada

Sylvia penning many blues-style compositions. With the recording of their second and
third LPs in 1964, *Four Strong Winds*
(Vanguard VRS 9133) and *Northern Journey*
(Vanguard VRS 9154), Ian and Sylvia
achieved the international recognition
which they had sought. Written by Ian, the
title song from *Four Strong Winds* has
become a folk classic, and Sylvia's "You
Were on My Mind" (a selection on *Northern
Journey*) became a best-selling single for the
We Five.

Despite their production of five more
albums in the next few years, Ian and Sylvia
were uncertain in which direction to take
their music. After deciding to utilize
Nashville's top-notch musicians by recording in Music City, they realized their commitment to country music—which came as
no great surprise, for their musical roots
were in country. Although some "people
really got uptight," explains Tyson, "when
we made the transition to country music,"
they have never regretted their choice, "and
besides," smiles Tyson, "country music
today seems to be the most valid type of pop
music." Out of the Nashville venture came
another album for Vanguard, a subsequent

193

LP on the MGM label, and the formation of a country band called the Great Speckled Bird.

After recording two albums for Columbia, the duo decided to pursue separate recording careers. Ian Tyson began hosting his own CTV television series (originally called *Nashville North*) in Canada, and his first solo album, entitled *Ol' Eon* (A&M Records of Canada SP-9017), was released in his native country in 1975. He also produced Sylvia's first solo effort, *Woman's World* (Capitol SKAO 6430). Sylvia maintains a busy schedule which includes performing, writing new songs, hosting her own CBC Radio folk music show, *Touch the Earth*, and filming a CBC-TV special with singers Maureen Forrester and Pauline Julien.

## Janis Ian

*Contemporary singer-songwriter, pianist, guitarist, performer, and recording artist*

"Beginning in the ninth grade, my parents moved to New York and I started 'hoots' for *Broadside* magazine and I met Rev. Gary Davis. I was fourteen and a half when he took me down to the Gaslight, where I did an audition, and this guy saw me, and he said that he wanted to manage me, and took me up to a lawyer, and he took me to cut 'Society's Child.' Lucky. And then nobody would play it. And then Leonard Bernstein did a special, and I was featured in it, I guess, and then, all of a sudden, everybody was playing it, and it was a hit. It was 1967, and I worked for about a year and a half, and quit."

A comeback was inevitable for this young artist, who has surmounted the impediments of being a child prodigy and who has demonstrated a maturity and conviction for her music. An aficionado of poetry and music, Janis Ian has developed from a child star of protest songs to a composer whose intensity and emotional magnitude is manifested in a universal expression.

"I was born [Janis Fink] in New York, and

Janis Ian (center) participating in a Songwriter's Workshop at the Eleventh Annual Philadelphia Folk Festival, 1972. Raun MacKinnon and Bruce (U. Utah) Phillips are at her left; Keith Sykes is at the right

I grew up in New Jersey. My father is a music teacher, and I started classical piano when I was about three, and I started playing guitar when I was eleven, and when I was twelve, I started writing and performing."

Janis Ian pulled out of music for about four years, when it "got too insane." She studied and continued writing, and like many artists who are confronted with a premature success, she "laid low," trying to put back together her personal life and her music. She lived in Philadelphia for three years, and then moved to California in 1971, teaching herself to score music, and writing numerous songs within this brief period of time: "I stayed out of it, but it was 'Stars' that brought me out of isolation. I had these songs lying around that I had to get rid of somehow, and 'Stars' was like a catharsis. We started recording 'Stars' in 1973, and it came out in March of 1974."

After the release of "Society's Child," Janis Ian recorded four albums for Verve/Folkways, followed by an LP on the Capitol label. She stopped recording temporarily at the age of nineteen, and "Stars" initiated the second round of making records.

She performs with a backup of Jeff Layton on guitar, Stu Woods on bass, Barry Lazarowitz on drums, and Claire Bay providing vocal harmony. Her latest albums, *Stars* (Columbia KC-32857), *Between the Lines* (Columbia PC-33394), and *Aftertones* (Columbia PC-33919), evidence a vocal maturity that has been developed by Janis Ian over the past few years.

Fame has brought the personal satisfaction of meeting other performers and composers whom she has admired: "One of the highlights of my career has been getting to meet people. I mean, it's great that I get to meet all my heroes like Joan Baez, Odetta, and Bob Dylan, but the real highlights in my life are when I write a good song, really. I also admire Emmylou Harris, she's a great performer. I wish that I were home more because I don't get the chance to see that many performers."

Today, some of Janis Ian's "heroes" are turning their heads in her direction, and the admiration has become mutual, as expressed by Joan Baez: "I think Janis Ian's music is really stunning, and beautiful. She kind of reminds me of myself—I think she's developed from a really hostile ugly duckling during the sixties. She's writing exquisite things, and she even looks lovely on the cover of her new album [*Between the Lines*]."

# The Irish Rovers

*Vocal and instrumental group, performers, and recording artists*

Within the past decade, these five Canadian residents—Jimmy Ferguson, Wilcil McDowell, George Millar, Joe Millar, and Will Millar—have established an international reputation as television, nightclub, and concert performers. Their success as recording artists began in 1968 with their second single release, Shel Silverstein's "The Unicorn" (which sold in excess of three million copies), and, to date, the Irish Rovers have recorded numerous other singles and ten albums on Decca and on their own Potato label.

Born in Ireland, the Millars (brothers George and Will and cousin Joe) and their boyhood friends Jimmy Ferguson and Wilcil McDowell played in variety shows in the town halls of their homeland, as the group's leader, Will Millar, recalls: "There we were, doing our song and dance to a sniffing crowd in damp-smelling clothes and they're yelling 'Ye're quare boys! Give us another'n.' Now only some of the crowd came to hear us—the rest came in to get out of the wet." While in their teens, they emigrated to Canada, and in 1964 the Irish Rovers was officially organized as a professional group. Their reputation quickly spread across the American border, and on New Year's Eve of 1965 they opened a twenty-two-week engagement at the Purple Onion in San Francisco.

Since then, the Irish Rovers have toured throughout the United States, Canada, Ireland, Japan, New Zealand, and Australia, and they have performed to sellout audiences from New York's Carnegie Hall to Boston's Symphony Hall, Nashville's *Grand Ole Opry*, Toronto's Massey Hall, and Montreal's Place des Arts. They have been featured on TV shows with the Smothers Brothers, Mike Douglas, Merv Griffin, and many others, and they have performed both singing and acting roles in several segments of *The Virginian*. The Irish Rovers are currently hosting their own highly successful CBC-TV weekly variety show, and in 1975 they were presented with the Actra Award for Best Variety Performers on Radio or Television. "Last year," smiles Jimmy Ferguson, "we outdrew Hockey Night in Canada!"

After returning to Ireland in 1972 to film a CBC St. Patrick's Day special, the Irish Rovers decided to eliminate patriotic tunes from their repertoire until the fighting has ceased in Northern Ireland. "The good old songs," explains Will Millar, "have become vehicles of hatred instead of happiness.

"We've always loved the old patriotic songs. What is it they say about Ireland? 'The saddest love songs and the happiest wars'? Well, after what we saw over there, the songs just didn't seem as happy to us anymore."

Their success formula remains unchanged, however, and their performances and recordings abound with whimsy, nostalgia, and good music. "We just go out there and enjoy ourselves," says Jimmy Ferguson. "We're very happy people enjoyin' what we're doin'."

In 1974, McClelland and Stewart Limited of Canada published a book about the Irish Rovers, entitled *Children of the Unicorn*, by Will Millar.

# Burl Ives

*Singer, guitarist, banjoist, collector, performer, recording artist, actor, and author*

An artist who has made significant contributions to many fields, Burl Ives played a vital role in attracting millions of people to folk music and, through his early recordings, helped to formulate the public's views on folk material and its presentation in the post-World War II years. A prominent radio and television performer, a Broadway musical, dramatic, and motion picture actor, a prolific recording artist, a masterful storyteller, and an author, this "wayfaring stranger" began his career by traveling as a troubadour throughout nearly every state in the union, collecting, singing, and memorizing about five hundred songs of our land. Since then, he has made both countrywide and international concert tours and has shared his vast knowledge of American folk music with audiences here and abroad.

One of six children in a musical family, which derived its sustenance from farming, Burl Icle Ivanhoe Ives was born on June 14, 1909, in Jasper County, Illinois. Many traditional British and Irish tunes had been passed down through his family, and singing was a part of daily life in the Ives household.

From his grandmother, Katie White, the young boy learned numerous songs and ballads, and when he was four years old, he sang "Barbara Allen" at a local veterans' reunion. While he was in high school, his singing and learning to play the banjo were overshadowed by his star performance as a fullback on the football team, and he decided to pursue his education and to become a football coach. After attending Eastern Illinois State Teachers College for several years, he quit his studies and spent nearly two years roaming throughout the North American continent, working at various jobs, singing, playing the banjo, becoming acquainted with the guitar, and collecting folk material.

After studying briefly at Indiana State Teachers College and singing on a local Terre Haute radio station, he traveled to New York. While studying voice and acting at New York University from 1937 to 1938, he frequently sang with Woody Guthrie, Lee Hays, Millard Lampell, Pete Seeger, and other members of the Almanac Singers. During the summer of 1938 he was cast in several summer stock theater productions at Rockridge Theater in Putnam County, New York, followed by an appearance on Broadway in *The Boys from Syracuse*. His folk-singing career ran concurrently with his acting career, and in addition to appearing regularly on major radio network shows and hosting his own CBS Radio program called *The Wayfaring Stranger* from 1940 to 1942, he was a popular performer at the Village Vanguard in New York's Greenwich Village.

After serving in the army for a year and a half, he returned to the stage as the star of Irving Berlin's *This Is the Army*. In 1944 he was billed at Cafe Society Uptown in Manhattan, and he appeared on Broadway in the folk song presentation *Sing Out, Sweet Land*. Although the cavalcade did not receive high praise from the critics, Burl Ives's contribution to the production earned him the Donaldson Award as Best Supporting Actor in the 1944–45 Broadway season. His first major concert at Town Hall in late 1945 was met with unanimous acclaim; in the following year, his portrayal of a singing cowboy in *Smoky* introduced him to movie screen audiences.

By 1954 Burl Ives had returned to Broadway to play Cap'n Andy in the revival of Jerome Kern's *Showboat*, and in 1955 he made a memorable appearance as Big Daddy in Tennessee Williams's *Cat on a Hot Tin Roof* (he later portrayed the same role in the 1958 film version of the play). Among the numerous motion pictures in which he has appeared are *So Dear to My Heart, Sierra, East of Eden, The Power and the Prize, Cat on a Hot Tin Roof, Let No Man Write My Epitaph, Our Man in Havana, The Big Country* (for which he won an Academy Award), and *Those Fantastic Flying Fools.*

Burl Ives is the author of a number of juveniles, songbooks, an autobiography entitled *The Wayfaring Stranger* (1948), *Tales of America* (1954), and *The Wayfaring Stranger's Notebook* (1962). Throughout his career he produced many albums on various labels, including Columbia, Decca, Stinson, United Artists, and, most recently, MCA; he also recorded six discs in an historical song series for the *Encyclopedia Britannica.* In 1962 he had three single hits on the Decca label: "A Little Bitty Tear," "Call Me Mr. In-Between," and "Funny Way of Laughin'," by which he is probably best known to the general public.

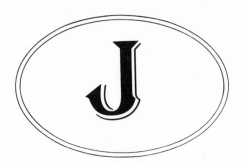

## Alan Jabbour. *See* The Hollow Rock String Band.

## Aunt Molly Jackson

*Singer, songwriter, performer, recording artist, and union organizer*

Along with her half-sister Sarah Ogan Gunning and her half-brother Jim Garland, this fiery organizer and protest and labor songwriter was one of the most significant representatives of the eastern Kentucky coal miners who were striving for unionization and adequate living conditions in the 1930s. The Garland family was a model for the battle against the political, social, and economic injustices which existed at that time in the Southern rural region of Harlan County, Kentucky. Both Aunt Molly Jackson and Sara Ogan Gunning played important roles in developing an awareness of the hostility and misery which prevailed by employing music as a call for action, and they brought their music to New York and other urban centers far away from their home state of Kentucky.

In the tradition of ballad making, lyrics were devised to express contemporary sentiments and grievances, and they were adapted to older melodies by Aunt Molly Jackson. Her method of songwriting was akin to the technique employed by Woody Guthrie, who composed most of his songs by writing lyrics based on his reading of newspapers and his own personal ex-

periences, and setting the words to existing tunes. Her Kentucky hill country heritage was steeped in folk tradition, and her ballads were a natural consequence of her background and existence in the coal-mining region during this turbulent period. Aunt Molly Jackson was an influential spokeswoman for the Appalachian coal miners, and her songs served as a rallying point for the labor movement in the United States.

Mary Magdalene Garland was born in 1880 in Clay County, Kentucky, to a family whose subsistence was derived from the coal mines which had been discovered in the area before the turn of this century. Along with nearly all of his friends and neighbors, her father worked under unhealthy, hazardous conditions and for meager wages as a miner. As a young girl she was influenced by her father's efforts to organize unions, and she often accompanied him on the picket lines. At the age of four, she composed her first song. When she was six years old, her mother died of starvation. Her family's involvement in labor protesting led to her being put in jail when she was ten. She was married at fourteen and worked as a nurse during her teens.

As conditions worsened over the years, Aunt Molly Jackson became a more adamant proponent of union causes, and she wrote numerous songs about the miners' hardships and struggles. Her father and one of her brothers were blinded in a mining accident, and another brother, her husband, and a son were killed while working in the mines. She was a powerful singer in a style rooted in the old-time, unaccompanied church singing of Appalachia, and she used her voice to convey the plight of the coal miners with her songs "Poor Miner's Farewell," "Hard Times in Colman's Mines," and many others.

In the Depression years, violence became more widespread, and Aunt Molly Jackson's work threatened the mine owners, whose position of power was growing less and less tenable. In 1931 the local authorities chased her from Kentucky, and she traveled to New York, where she continued to fight for her cause.

She was recorded by the Lomaxes for the Archive of Folk Song, and many private collectors solicited her material. As her health began to fail during the fifties, she was no longer able to sing, but her songwriting efforts were continued as part of her lifelong fight for justice. Arrangements were made for folklorist John Greenway to sing a selection of her songs, with introductory narration by Aunt Molly Jackson, for Folkways Records, but shortly before the taping was commenced in September 1960, she died. *The Songs and Stories of Aunt Molly Jackson* (Folkways 5457) was recorded by Greenway and released a year after her death. Over a decade later, Rounder issued *Aunt Molly Jackson: Library of Congress Recordings* (Rounder 1002), which offers a sampling of coal-mining songs, union songs, and stories from the several hundred recordings made in 1939 by Alan Lomax for the Library of Congress.

Aunt Molly Jackson died on September 1, 1960, in poverty and relative obscurity in California at the age of eighty, and, like so many others, she was never reimbursed for the use of her songs. In a letter to *Sing Out!* magazine, she wrote:

> I am 3,000 miles away from my old Kentucky home, barely existing on the old age pension. Nobody seems to pay me any attention. Only the folksong collectors, that want me to teach them the songs I learned from my Kentucky ancestors 75 years ago. But if I ask them

where I can get a few pennies for the songs I teach them, they just don't know. . . . I have had the songs I composed translated in five different languages and records made of my songs, but I have never received one cent from anyone out of all the protest songs I have composed. . . . Some of the people that is putting out records and using my songs think I am dead and I am forgotten. But I am not. All said and done, I am still standing by my union, one for all and all for one, even if I am almost eighty-one. . . .

(*See also* Sara Ogan Gunning.)

# Mahalia Jackson

*Gospel singer, performer, and recording artist*

The sacred music of the "Queen of the Gospel Singers" has been a source of inspiration for both her audience and other blues and soul singers throughout the world. From her greatly moving performances which have broken attendance records at Carnegie Hall to her singing on the steps of the Lincoln Memorial during the historic March on Washington in 1963, Mahalia Jackson has left an indelible impression in the minds and hearts of millions of Americans and peoples of all nations.

Born in New Orleans in 1911, she grew up in a neighborhood with blacks, French, Creoles, and Italians. Both her grandparents had been born into slavery, and as a young girl she heard many stories of the struggle and hardships of her ancestors. She came from a religious background; her family attended church every day, and she sang in her Sunday school choir. Two of her relatives were professional entertainers and traveled with blues singer Ma Rainey, who was one of the early influences on her life.

After the death of her mother, the five-year-old Mahalia Jackson went to live with her aunt and uncle, who raised her on religion and hard work. The omnipresence of music in New Orleans was a significant

**199**

memory of her childhood—ragtime, jazz, and blues overflowed from the city's cabarets, cafes, and the Mississippi River showboats. She heard records by Bessie Smith, Ma Rainey, Mamie Smith, and others, and she loved to listen to the live music played by many New Orleans brass bands.

In 1928 the sixteen-year-old Mahalia Jackson left the South to seek her fortune in Chicago, along with thousands of blacks who had made their home on Chicago's South Side. She became a member of the Greater Salem Baptist Church choir and sang with a group called the Johnson Gospel Singers. Ironically, the Depression was largely responsible for her career as a gospel singer, for the Johnson Gospel Singers were asked by many churches to perform for a nominal fee at suppers and socials which were organized to raise money to keep the churches open. The Johnson Gospel Singers started to receive invitations outside the Chicago area, and when Mahalia Jackson was only twenty years old, they sang at the Baptist conventions in St. Louis and Cleveland. More dedicated to gospel singing than the other members of the group, she started singing more and more on her own, and by the middle of the Depression, Mahalia Jackson was singing in churches from coast to coast.

She began making records of her gospel songs, and in the late forties her single release of "I Will Move On Up a Little Higher" was so commercially successful that "Movin' On Up" became known as her song. In 1950 Mahalia Jackson was invited to a symposium at the Music Inn in Massachusetts, and it was not long before she was asked to appear on the Ed Sullivan television show and was made the official soloist of the National Baptist Convention. Finally, an offer came for her to make her first appearance on the stage of New York's Carnegie Hall.

A successful European tour was followed in 1954 by an invitation to host her own radio program on WBBM in Chicago, which, by 1955, had evolved as a television show. During the mid-fifties she became involved with the civil rights movement, and she often worked side by side with her close friend Dr. Martin Luther King, Jr. When John F. Kennedy was elected president, Mahalia Jackson was asked to sing "The Star-Spangled Banner" at an inauguration gala celebration produced by Frank Sinatra in Washington, D.C. In the summer of 1963 she stood on the steps of the Lincoln Memorial and sang during the March on Washington for Jobs and Freedom. Following her unforgettable rendition of "I Been 'Buked and I Been Scorned," Dr. King delivered his famous "I Have a Dream" speech.

Her first marriage, to Isaac Hockenhull, ended in divorce when she was thirty years old, and in the mid-1960s she married Sigmund Galloway. In 1966 her autobiography, *Movin' On Up* (written with Evan McLeod Wylie), was published by Hawthorn Books; portions of the book appeared in both *The Saturday Evening Post* and *Good Housekeeping*.

A Columbia recording artist, Mahalia Jackson has made nearly two dozen LPs for CBS.

# Joyce James. *See* The Womenfolk.

# Skip James
*Blues singer, guitarist, pianist, composer, performer, and recording artist*

As a consequence of the recent urban folk revival, many talented artists enjoyed a resurgence of interest in their lives and their music. Among the Mississippi bluesmen who received recognition as significant folk artists was Skip James, who had developed an intimate and introverted brand of blues. Prior to his rediscovery in the mid-1960s, Skip James was known only to the handful of collectors who were familiar with his 78-RPM recordings made for Paramount in 1931.

Born Nehemiah James on June 9, 1902, in Bentonia, Mississippi, he was nicknamed "Skippy" by his schoolmates. Musical influences were present in his family, as his Baptist minister father played guitar and organ. His interest in music was further aroused by listening to local performers Henry Stuckey and Rich Griffith, who represented an older generation of blues musicians. By the age of eight, Skip James was the proud owner of a $2.50 guitar which he learned to play by listening, practicing, and working earnestly to acquire skill as an instrumentalist. Before starting high school, he traveled to Jackson to hear one of the area's best-known blues artists, Mississippi John Hurt. He was encouraged by his mother to take piano lessons but gave them up after only two lessons because of the expense.

While still in his teens, Skip James worked and traveled throughout Mississippi and Texas. After working by day in a sawmill and by night as an accompanist for piano player Will Crabtree, he headed north to Memphis, where he met other musicians and landed a job in a barrelhouse. When he eventually settled in Jackson, his blues style included both his own individualistic approach and the prevalent musical influences of his environment.

In 1931 he auditioned for Henry C. Speir, whose music company was searching for talent to record for the Paramount label. Impressed by his rendition of "Devil Blues," Speir presented him with a two-year recording contract. Two days later, he was in the Paramount recording studios in Grafton, Wisconsin. In the next two days, he recorded about two dozen songs, including such original compositions as "Hard Times" and ".22-20" (which he prepared in three minutes' time). He returned home and never recorded again until many years later. Only a few of his initial Paramount cuts were issued, and their distribution was limited.

After playing on only an occasional basis for a while, Skip James abandoned music— and the flame was only briefly rekindled in the thirties, when he organized a quartet which sang spirituals. In 1942 he was ordained as a Methodist minister, and in 1943 he was ordained as a Baptist minister. In the years that followed, Skip James worked at a variety of jobs—as a miner, a timber cutter, a tractor driver, and a plantation overseer.

In 1965 John Fahey of Takoma Records went down to Mississippi in hopes of finding Skip James and his original 78s. Along with Bill Barth and Henry Vestine, Fahey followed every conceivable lead to his whereabouts and finally located him in a Mississippi hospital. In an effort to raise enough money for Skip James to pay his extensive medical expenses, "Devil Blues," "All Night Long," and several verses of another tune were recorded and played for other folk music enthusiasts around the country.

Skip James made his first public appearance at the Bitter Lemon in Memphis, followed by performances at the 1965 Newport Folk Festival, Mariposa, Ontario Place in Washington, D.C., a Montgomery Junior College concert, the Unicorn in Boston, and two weeks at the Gaslight in Greenwich Village, New York City. Along with Mississippi John Hurt, Libba Cotten, Sleepy John Estes, and others, Skip James rediscovered his own musical interests as others throughout the world rediscovered his talent.

His later recordings appear on such labels as Adelphi, Biograph, Historical, Melodeon, Storyville, Vanguard, Verve/Folkways, and Yazoo.

Nehemiah "Skip" James, once called "the fastest fingerpicker in the world" and "Mr. Genius," died on October 3, 1969, in Philadelphia, after a prolonged illness.

**Tom Jans.** *See* Richard and Mimi Fariña.

**Ben Jarrell.** *See* Tommy Jarrell.

# Tommy Jarrell

*Old-time fiddler and banjoist, singer, performer, and recording artist*

The Beulah section of Surry County, North Carolina, boasts many great old-time country musicians, including Tommy Jarrell, Fred Cockerham, and Kyle Creed. These three men have been playing together (often with Oscar Jenkins of Dobson, North Carolina), in various combinations, for nearly half a century.

Of Scots-Irish descent, Tommy Jarrell was born in 1901 in a close-knit community of farm families living on the Old Low Gap Road, just to the north of Round Peak. Everyone shared a love for music, and it was integrated into all aspects of their existence. Collective work efforts, or "workings," were followed by dances, and everyone rewarded themselves for raising funds for schools, chopping wood, shucking corn, or helping a neighbor with any number of jobs that were too big for him to manage alone. The Jarrell family, like so many others, often hosted the dances, and when the furniture was moved aside, Tommy's father Ben Jarrell would take out his fiddle and play dance reels with other local musicians. (This isolated existence was terminated in the early 1920s with the popularization of dance halls and the beginning of radio.)

Ben Jarrell, who was a member of DaCosta Woltz's Southern Broadcasters string band, made several records in the 1920s which have been reissued on *DaCosta Woltz's Southern Broadcasters* (County 524). Ben Jarrell was the primary influence on his son's career in music, and, today, Tommy Jarrell still plays the old-style fiddle, called "rocking the bow." His Uncle Charley Jarrell, who married Fred Cockerham's aunt, was another fiddler who influenced the young boy.

Tommy Jarrell's family moved to Mt. Airy in 1921, and, four years later, he started his job with the state highway department, from which he retired in 1966.

Tommy Jarrell has combined his talents with Oscar Jenkins and Fred Cockerham—sometimes he plays with only one of his two old friends—and other times Jarrell plays alone. County Records has recorded three albums under their joint names: *Down to the Cider Mill* (County 713), *Back Home in the Blue Ridge* (County 723), and *Stay All Night and Don't Go Home* (County 741). In his typical, uncompromising style of traditional mountain singing and fiddling, Jarrell presents such songs as "When Sorrows Encompass Me 'Round," one of the best examples of old-time music.

Jarrell is included on *June Apple* (Mountain M-302) with other old-time fiddlers and clawhammer banjoists Kyle Creed, A. Lineberry, and Bob Patterson; and he was recorded on the Union Grove LP, *50th Annual Fiddlers Convention* (SS 9), with Bluegrass Pardners, Buddy Pendleton, Ned Smathers, Smokey Valley Boys, and Swamp Root String Band. County Records has recently issued a Tommy Jarrell banjo album, *Come and Go with Me* (County 748), which is his first solo effort. (*See also* Fred Cockerham; Kyle Creed.)

# Mitchell Jayne. *See* The Dillards.

# Blind Lemon Jefferson

*Blues singer, guitarist, songwriter, performer, and recording artist*

The history of the blues is interspersed with accounts of the lives of many blind singers and instrumentalists who have devoted themselves to the pursuit of a career in the music business. His handicap of blindness prevented Blind Lemon Jefferson from earning a living as a laborer, and, like many others who shared his misfortune, he turned to music. A master of the blues who taught his onetime companion Huddie Ledbetter (Leadbelly) more about the idiom than any other man, Blind Lemon Jefferson was a professional performer and a pioneer recording artist who was instrumental in the molding of a distinctive Texas brand of blues.

Born about 1895 near Wortham, Texas, Blind Lemon Jefferson made certain references in some of his songs which suggest that he may have enjoyed partial vision as a child. He was never permitted to work side by side with his brothers and sisters in the cotton fields, however, and he acquired his compassionate understanding for the tradition of hard labor and music by listening to work songs and hollers as sung by the field hands.

At a young age, Blind Lemon Jefferson began to sing and play guitar for pay on the streets of Wortham. Although various dates for their first meeting have been given, Jefferson and Huddie Ledbetter became acquainted and traveled together in the area around Dallas. They played for nickels and dimes wherever audiences were to be found, and they were known in bars and brothels between Dallas and Silver City. The partnership was particularly beneficial to Ledbetter, who learned new guitar techniques and vocal stylings from the talented blind musician. Blind Lemon Jefferson was a virtuoso guitarist who employed such techniques as "hammering-on" and the complementing of his singing with instrumental responses, and his high vocals approximated the holler in both intensity and sparcity. Along with Texas Alexander, he was considered the most influential blues musician in Dallas during the early decades of the twentieth century, and was recognized as an important force even in his own lifetime.

Blind Lemon Jefferson made his first recordings in 1926, preceding the initial efforts by Texas Alexander, Charley Patton, Willie Brown, and Son House. He was a major recording artist for "the popular race record" company, Paramount Records, and his material sold in large quantities, thus creating an awareness of the potential Southern market.

Whether or not Blind Lemon Jefferson would have continued to maintain his stature as a songwriter, performer, and recording artist will never be known, as he died of a heart attack in Chicago in 1930. As a tribute to this outstanding bluesman, Rev. Emmet Dickenson composed and recorded on Paramount a sermon entitled "Death of Blind Lemon," which was released shortly after the musician's death.

"Black Snake Moan," "Hangman's Blues," "Rabbit Foot Blues," and "Piney Woods Money Mama" are among his best-known compositions. Various commercial record labels offer his work, including Biograph, Everest (reissues), Folkways, Historical, London (Great Britain), Roots (Austria), and Yazoo.

## Oscar Jenkins. *See* Fred Cockerham; Tommy Jarrell.

## Jew's Harp

The jew's harp is a primitive, ancient folk instrument consisting of a small metal (horseshoe-shaped) frame, to which a flexible metal vibrating tongue is attached. Depicted in a Chinese book of the twelfth century, the oldest forms of the jew's harp have been found in Southeast Asia, with other variations of the instrument traced to Japan, Formosa, India, and the Philippines. The European jew's harp is of Asian derivation, and it was first seen in the Western Hemisphere around 1350, ancient instruments having been excavated in Norway and England. In modern times, the jew's harp has enjoyed popularity on the European, Asian, and American continents.

The jew's harp is played by holding the instrument to the mouth, with the lips making contact with the outer edges of the tines, which are pressed against the upper and lower teeth (the teeth should be slightly apart to accommodate the size of the instrument). With the free hand, the player strikes the tongue of the harp, pushing it forward.

The mouth acts as a resonator, and the pitch is changed by altering the shape of the oral cavity. The jew's harp can be played in only one key (which is often approximate), and the key is determined by the length, width, and thickness of the instrument's tongue.

Several theories exist regarding the etymology of the jew's harp, but none are conclusive. Some experts believe that the term is a misnomer for "jaw harp," and others trace its origin to early England and an instrument sold by Jews. Still others conjecture that it is so called because of the instrument's resemblance to the biblical lyre, and many feel that the jew's harp has no relation to either Jews or jaws.

## The Jim Kweskin Jug Band

*Vocal and instrumental group, performers, and recording artists*

One of the results of the folk boom was the revival of jug band music—originally a black folk style, related to English skiffle music, which was popular in the ragtime era South—and the Jim Kweskin Jug Band was probably the most widely recognized, influential, and entertaining group in its field. For its nearly six-year existence, the Jim Kweskin Jug Band played (almost consistently) capacity-crowd club and concert engagements and recorded a number of albums for Reprise and Vanguard. Another notable feature of the Jim Kweskin Jug Band was its impressive lineup of personnel—Maria D'Amato (Muldaur), Richard Greene, Bill Keith, Jim Kweskin, Mel Lyman, Geoff Muldaur, and Fritz Richmond, among others—many of whom went on to achieve fame as solo artists after the disbandment of the group in 1968.

Born on July 18, 1940, and raised in New England, Jim Kweskin was a popular singer and guitarist in the Cambridge (Massachusetts) area prior to assembling the Jug Band. In 1963 the group was formed with Bill Keith (formerly a banjoist for Bill Monroe's Blue Grass Boys), Mel Lyman, Jim Kweskin, Geoff Muldaur, and Fritz Richmond. Over the years the band members changed, and other prominent names, such as Maria Muldaur and Richard Greene (formerly with the Greenbriar Boys and Bill Monroe's Blue Grass Boys), became associated with the Jim Kweskin Jug Band. Along with the Even Dozen Jug Band, Dave Van Ronk's Ragtime Jug Stompers (featuring Sam Charters), and countless other jug bands across the continent, the Jim Kweskin Jug Band played an instrumental role in the revitalization of good-timey, ragtimey, and blues music.

After the breakup of the band, Jim Kweskin temporarily withdrew from the music scene, but he returned three years later as a solo performer (appearing at such major clubs as the Ash Grove in Los Angeles and at such folk events as the 1971 National Folk Festival) and Reprise recording artist. Richard Greene became involved in various musical endeavors—from working with the Blues Project, Seatrain, and the Blue Velvet Band (with Bill Keith, Jim Rooney, and Eric Weissberg), to organizing his own band, performing with other top musicians (David Grisman, Bill Keith, Peter Rowan, and Clarence White) on a KCET-TV special show on bluegrass music, and recording (most notably *Muleskinner* [Warner Brothers BS 2787] with Greene, Grisman, Keith, Rowan, and White, who also performed as the Bluegrass Dropouts). More recently, Richard Greene has played with Maria Muldaur, who has emerged (along with her ex-husband Geoff Muldaur) as a prominent solo performer and recording artist of the mid-seventies, and with David Grisman, David Nichtern, and Taj Mahal in the Great American Music Band.

## The John Edwards Memorial Foundation

*Educational, nonprofit corporation, with its archive of American folk music located at the Folklore and Mythology Center, UCLA*

The John Edwards Memorial Foundation (JEMF) is similar in many respects to the Library of Congress Archive of Folk Song in Washington, D.C. It houses 15,000 78-RPM recordings; 800 33⅓-RPM and 15,000 45-RPM recordings of folk, hillbilly, country, blues, and related types of music; thousands of issues of 500 different music magazines; several hundred song folios; 1,500 vertical files of data related to music; and nearly 100 taped interviews of country musicians. Headquartered on the UCLA campus in the Folklore and Mythology Center, JEMF makes available to researchers in the field one of the most extensive collections of folk-related materials consolidated in one place.

Born in 1932, John Edwards was an Australian who dedicated his life to the study and compilation of American folk music material. Although he never traveled to the United States, he corresponded with many early country music pioneers in this country. He managed to accumulate an invaluable collection of commercial country music recordings, correspondence, photographs, and other biographical and discographical information, and was considered one of the world's most renowned authorities in the field. He specified in his will that his private collection was to be turned over to an American collector and friend, Eugene W. Earle, who, in turn, would provide for its preservation and availability for study. On December 24, 1960, twenty-eight-year-old John Edwards was killed in a car accident near his Cremorne, Australia, home.

Arrangements were made by Earle to have Edwards's collection transported to UCLA, where a Center for the Study of Comparative Folklore and Mythology was located. In the summer of 1962, the John Edwards Memorial Foundation was chartered as an educational, nonprofit corporation in the state of California. Dr. D. K. Wilgus was put in charge of operations. Currently, the directors of the foundation are Eugene W. Earle, president; Archie Green, first vice-president; Fred Hoeptner, second vice-president; Ken Griffis, secretary; and D. K. Wilgus, treasurer. There are a couple dozen advisers, including John Cohen, John Greenway, John Hammond, Bess Lomax Hawes, Joseph C. Hickerson (head of the Library of Congress Archive of Folk Song), Ralph Rinzler, and Charles and Mike Seeger. Norm Cohen is executive secretary and editor of the foundation's publication, the *JEMF Quarterly*.

John Edwards's original collection has been expanded to include country, western, country & western, hillbilly, bluegrass, mountain, cowboy, old-time, sacred, and contemporary American folk music (with files on Joan Baez, John Denver, Malvina Reynolds, and others). Its operations involve cataloguing, indexing, compiling, publishing, distributing, and storing all materials pertaining to such music, and the main goals of the JEMF are to preserve and to perpetuate American folk music.

In addition to regularly issuing the *JEMF Quarterly*, the foundation reprints important scholarly articles dealing with various aspects of commercially recorded and **published American folk music; maintains a special series of biographical and discographical publications; and has initiated an LP record project, devoted primarily to the reissuing of out-of-print, historically important recordings.**

# Arlen J. Johnson. *See* Don Armstrong.

# Larry Johnson

*Country blues guitarist, singer, songwriter in the "good-time" blues tradition, performer, and recording artist*

A former pupil of Rev. Gary Davis, Larry Johnson is a young black musician who recreates East Coast country blues in a style reminiscent of the early bluesmen.

He was born in Atlanta, and, after his

mother's death, was raised in the small town of Riceville, Georgia, where he heard country music. When he visited his father in Atlanta, the young boy listened to blues by Blind Boy Fuller, B. B. King, and Muddy Waters. He started playing a harmonica given to him by his grandmother, and his first songs were traditional folk standards, such as "Rock Island Line" and "John Henry." One day his grandmother played one of her records by bluesman William "Jazz" Gillum, and "12 Keys to the Highway" became the first song in the blues idiom that Johnson played on the harmonica.

When he was twenty-one years old, Larry Johnson traveled with three or four harmonicas to New York City, where he met and finally studied with his mentor, Rev. Gary Davis. Johnson's harmonica accompaniment to Davis's guitar playing can be heard on the 1969 recordings done at John Townley's Apostolic Studios, a session that resulted in *O, Glory* (Adelphi Records AD 1008). Johnson considered Davis the strongest influence on his musical development, his guitar playing, and his life.

Johnson made some records for Prestige; and then, for Blue Goose Records, *Larry Johnson—Fast & Funky* (2001), which was highly praised by *Rolling Stone* magazine. On *Country Blues* (Biograph BLP 12028), he was accompanied by John Hammond, Jr., on harp, steel guitar, and vocals on one cut; and, most recently, he was among the featured artists on Spivey Records' *Spivey's Blues Cavalcade* (LP 1015). He is also included on *These Blues Is Meant to Be Barrelhoused* (Blue Goose 2003).

In 1973 the thirty-four-year-old country blues guitarist played with Doc and Merle Watson at Yale; that same year, he worked Max's Kansas City and Kenny's Castaways, in New York City and other clubs and colleges. When he is not teaching guitar in New York City, he is often seen at major festivals, which, in recent years, have included the Mariposa, Ann Arbor, Philadelphia, and National festivals.

**Mike Johnson.** *See* The Chad Mitchell Trio.

**Pat Johnson.** *See* Sweet Honey in the Rock.

**Bessie Jones.** *See* The Georgia Sea Island Singers.

**Marshall Jones.** *See* The Freedom Singers.

**Matthew Jones.** *See* The Freedom Singers.

# The Journeymen

*Vocal and instrumental group, performers, and recording artists*

The formation of the Journeymen, with Scott McKenzie, John Phillips, and Richard (Dick) Weissman, was a direct outgrowth of the late 1950s and 1960s folk boom. Their rise to commercial success was rapid, but their career was short-lived, as prevailing attitudes changed in the mid-1960s, and the Journeymen, along with many other folk groups, disappeared from the music scene.

The Journeymen were considered one of the most promising of the many groups that were formed during that period, and the trio performed with considerable vocal and instrumental skill. Dick Weissman's background was musical, and his education at the Philadelphia Conservatory of Music, Goddard College in Vermont, and Columbia University provided a strong foundation for his talents as a banjoist and guitarist. Aside from working as a studio musician, Weissman established a reputation as a folklorist and musicologist.

It was during a recording session that

Weissman met John Phillips and his friend from Arlington, Virginia, Scott McKenzie. Phillips and McKenzie were members of a group called the Smoothies, but Phillips's love for bluegrass and McKenzie's talent as a vocalist brought them together with the gifted musician, Weissman.

The man responsible for the Journeymen was Frank Werber, who had discovered and guided the Kingston Trio, and he believed this new group would rise to fame as a result of the new interest in the "modern" folk style. In 1961 the Journeymen made a successful debut at Gerde's Folk City, and, with the help of Werber, a recording contract was signed with Capitol Records. Their first LP was released in the fall of that same year, and with the auspicious sales of *The Journeymen* (Capitol [S]T-1629), a second album was recorded in 1962, *Coming Attraction—Live!* (Capitol [S]T-1770), and a third in 1963, *New Directions* (Capitol [S]T-1951), which included a mixed bag of music peculiar to American culture and traditions.

John Phillips was the acknowledged leader of the group, and he composed material that was recorded by them, including "Ride, Ride, Ride" and "Stackolee." Phillips and Weissman collaborated on such songs as "Ben and Me" and "Chase the Rising Sun," and Scott McKenzie excelled as the Journeymen's lead tenor and soloist.

When the group disbanded, John Phillips achieved a national reputation as Papa John of the Mamas and the Papas, with Denny Doherty, Cass Elliot, and Michelle Phillips. They formed the Mamas and the Papas in the winter of 1965–66 and for the next couple of years were one of the country's most popular and commercially prosperous pop groups.

After his initial success as a solo artist and his hit single "San Francisco (Wear Some Flowers in Your Hair)," Scott McKenzie's career waned after the summer of 1967, when his name became closely associated with the romanticism of California and flower power.

Dick Weissman's first solo effort after the breakup of the Journeymen was an album of topical songs entitled *The Things That Trouble My Mind; Dick Weissman Sings and Plays Folk Songs of Protest!* (Capitol T 2033), with many of the selections penned by the five-string banjo virtuoso and guitarist. His subsequent recordings were released by various commercial companies, including Counterpoint, Judson, Riverside, and Stinson. He taught music in Philadelphia and in New York, and he also wrote several songs for the production *Jesse James*, written by Bump Heeter and James Keach and supported by Judy Collins and Rocky Mountain Productions.

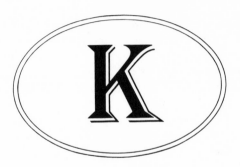

**"Fats" Kaplin.** *See* Roy Bookbinder.

## Buell Kazee

*Kentucky mountain banjoist and balladeer,
retired Baptist minister, collector, pioneer
recording artist of the 1920s, performer, and
author*

Born at the turn of this century in Burton
Fork, Kentucky, Buell Kazee is among the
early country, or "hillbilly," performers
who place heavy emphasis on traditional
music. Along with five-string banjoists
Clarence "Tom" Ashley and Dock Boggs,
and unaccompanied singer Kelly Harrell,
Buell Kazee played a vital role in the early
history of old-time American folk music.

Buell Hilton Kazee was raised in the
mountains of Magoffin County, Kentucky,
where traditional music and religion were
significant elements of daily life. He learned
many tunes from his mother and his
neighbors; and he was taught religious
songs, spirituals, and gospel favorites by his
father, who supervised musical activities at
their local church. His father made a banjo
for the five-year-old Kazee, and by the time
he started his education at the area's log
schoolhouse, the young boy was a popular
entertainer, playing old-time music at
neighborhood events and festivities.

He was ordained as a Missionary Baptist
minister in 1917, and three years later, when
Kazee graduated from the secondary school,

Baptist Magoffin Institute in Salyersville, he
entered Georgetown College in Kentucky as
an English major. In addition to banjo,
Kazee had learned to play piano and guitar,
and his studies in music, voice, and
literature provided a background and appreciation for his musical heritage. During
his college years, Kazee became an enthusiastic collector of American folk music,
and his acclaim as a folksinger led to his first
concert recital in 1925 at the University of
Kentucky.

Throughout his career of more than fifty
years as a Baptist minister, Buell Kazee collected folk material as a hobby, and
although his commitment to the ministry
ruled out commercial pursuit of his own
music, he made fifty-two recordings for
Brunswick and Vocalion from 1926 to
1930. Before the Depression caused the
Brunswick Company to fold, terminating
Kazee's recording career, he had made some
classic recordings of such songs as "The
Waggoner Lad," "Lady Gay," "Rock Island
Line," and "Darling Cora." He was
recorded during the thirties by Library of
Congress field collectors, and his reputation
as a performer spread throughout Appalachia as he continued to sing at colleges
in the Southeast. His literary efforts have included many articles on religion, and a full-
length work entitled *Faith Is the Victory*,
published in 1941.

During the folk music boom of the fifties
and early sixties, many of today's renowned
old-time folksingers and instrumentalists
were rediscovered through the efforts of field

investigators, and such artists as Clarence "Tom" Ashley, Dock Boggs, and Buell Kazee were recorded by Folkways Records. The subsequent release of *Buell Kazee Sings and Plays* (Folkways FS 3810), brought Kazee's old-time country banjo technique and his smooth, melodious vocals to the American public.

Now retired from the Baptist ministry, Buell Kazee devotes more time to his folk music "hobby," and he frequently appears at folk festivals in the United States and Canada.

*The Anthology of American Folk Music* (Folkways FA 2951, FA 2952, FA 2953), Vols. 1, 2, and 3 (six records), includes Buell Kazee, Clarence "Tom" Ashley, the Carter Family, Mississippi John Hurt, Dock Boggs, and Uncle Dave Macon, among others.

## Seán Keane. *See* The Chieftains.

## Bill Keith. *See* The Jim Kweskin Jug Band.

## Kevin Kelley. *See* The Byrds.

## Norman Kennedy

*Traditional Scottish singer, storyteller, performer, and recording artist*

With his roots in the native traditions of Scotland's northeastern Aberdeen area, Norman Kennedy is among the storytellers, balladeers, musicians, and culture bearers who are vital to the continuity of a heritage.

Norman Kennedy was born in 1933 in Aberdeen. His father earned a living in the shipyards, often going to sea as his forefathers had done before him. Kennedy began singing at an early age, and, with a keen memory for tunes, he learned songs and ballads from his family and neighbors— including one of Scotland's most famous

ballad singers, Jeannie Robertson, who lived nearby. When he was seven years old, his family had moved across the road from the home of Jeannie Robertson and her mother, and she was to have a considerable influence on him.

At the age of sixteen, Kennedy left Aberdeen Academy to work as a messenger, and, later, as a tax collector. He was skilled as a craftsman, and he learned a great deal about weaving from the remaining weavers in his native country. He spent his holidays on the island of Barra, west of Scotland, in the Outer Hebrides, and he became very knowledgeable concerning the Gaelic way of life and music.

In 1951 he met Annie Johnston at a folklore convention in Stornoway on the Isle of Lewis. She became his mentor, and, through her, he became acquainted with Highland living, traditional arts, and the west coast style of singing.

Although he returned to Aberdeen, he often traveled to Methlick and other villages in the rural northeast, collecting traditional material. In the early sixties, he joined the Aberdeen Folk Song Club, and his reputation as a singer gradually spread throughout the area. Mike Seeger heard one of Kennedy's performances at the club, and was very impressed by his singing, but "Mike didn't talk about it at the time," says Kennedy. "I got a letter inviting me [to perform at the 1965 Newport Folk Festival] and, although it came as a complete surprise, he [Seeger] certainly was the moving force in getting me to this country." He was a popular entertainer at the festival and, as a consequence, was asked to attend every subsequent Newport Folk Festival until its demise.

Norman Kennedy has been in the United States since 1965, and he has performed at the Philadelphia, Smithsonian, National, and Mariposa folk festivals and other events in the Midwest and California. He has pursued music simultaneously with weaving and crafts. He was employed in a Cambridge, Massachusetts, shop (and later, in Colonial Williamsburg), and he now runs a weaving school in Vermont.

On his Folk-Legacy LP, *Ballads and Songs of Scotland* (FSS-34), he has recorded a version of a song which he learned from Jeannie Robertson, "I'll Lay Ye Doon, Love," and "Johnny, My Man, Dae Ye Nae Think O' Rising?," which was taught to him by Jeannie Robertson's daughter, Lizzie Higgins, who is a fine balladeer in her own right.

## The Kentucky Pardners. *See*
Charlie Monroe.

## Doug Kershaw

*Cajun fiddler, singer, songwriter, performer, and recording artist*

Often referred to by his friends as the "Cajun Conjurer," Doug Kershaw is largely responsible for the current revival of Cajun music. As composer of the popular hits "Louisiana Man," "Diggy Diggy Lo," and "Joli Blon," Kershaw has created an infectious national enthusiasm for his southwestern Louisiana heritage.

One of four sons born to Jack and Rita Kershaw, Doug Kershaw lived for the first seven years of his life in Tiel Ridge, Louisiana, where he was born on January 24, 1936. After his father died, the Kershaw family moved to Lake Arthur, Louisiana, where he started school and learned to speak English, having been raised in a French-speaking environment. The young Kershaw worked as a shoeshine boy, but one day he brought a fiddle to town, and after he had been playing for two or three hours, a crowd gathered around him, listening: "They just wanted me to keep playing. So I said the only way I'd play is if y'all let me shine your shoes, and I wound up making $10.20. Brought it back home and we cried and ate beans and everything."

Kershaw's mother accompanied him on guitar, and occasionally they played the Bucket of Blood club in their hometown. When he was eleven, the family moved to Jennings, Louisiana. Kershaw completed high school, and he formed a band with two of his brothers; they called themselves the Continental Playboys.

At the age of fifteen, Kershaw wrote and recorded a song for J. D. Miller of Feature Records, in Crowley, Louisiana, and the following year he and his brother Rusty recorded another original composition, "No, No It's Not So," which led the Kershaw brothers to Acuff-Rose and Hickory Records in Nashville, Tennessee. Their recording of Kershaw's "So Lovely Baby" established the Cajun musician's career as a songwriter and singer.

By May 1956, "Rusty and Doug" were regular members of the *World's Original Jamboree*, a Saturday-night show in Wheeling, West Virginia; the following year, they joined the *Grand Ole Opry*.

After his discharge from military service, in 1960, Kershaw composed "Louisiana Man," and recorded that song along with "Diggy Diggy Lo" and "Joli Blon."

In 1964 Kershaw and his brother Rusty terminated their career as a team and each went his separate way. Doug Kershaw continued writing songs, and he signed a contract with Warner Brothers. When Johnny Cash asked Kershaw to perform on his premier television variety show, the Cajun musician's musical career was confirmed: "I always wanted to be a professional musician, and I've been playing all my life. My first big break was my appearance on *The Johnny Cash Show*, with Bob Dylan. I had cut an album right before, and it was released after the show was aired. Offers to do club, concert, and television appearances started pouring in."

Doug Kershaw plays twenty-eight other instruments besides the fiddle, and his most recent recording effort is a live album, *Alive & Pickin'* (Warner Brothers BS 2851), which captures his flamboyant style and musicianship. "Louisiana Man" has been recorded over 850 times, and its popularity has been instrumental in the revitalization of the Cajun tradition.

## The Kessinger Brothers

*Old-time instrumentalists, performers, and recording artists*

The "Gentleman of Old-time Music," fiddler Clark Kessinger, and his nephew, guitarist Luches Kessinger, started playing as a duo after World War I. When they recorded for Brunswick in 1928 they acquired their name as the Kessinger Brothers, as the record company's engineer, James O'Keefe, suggested that a sibling relationship was more marketable.

Born on July 27, 1896, in South Hills, West Virginia, Clark Kessinger learned to play the banjo as a young boy and, by the age of five, was playing his brother-in-law's fiddle. When he was seven years old, Clark Kessinger was earning more than his father, who worked in a foundry, by playing fiddle and dancing in the local saloon for ten or fifteen dollars a night. Before he was in his teens, he was performing at country dances. Throughout his career as a musician, Clark Kessinger paid strict attention to all the music that he heard, learning tunes from other musicians, and borrowing and adapting to give his own special brand to each of the tunes that he played.

After serving in the army during World War I, Clark Kessinger started playing with his brother Charles's eldest son, Luches Kessinger, around 1919. Less than ten years later, they were performing on their own radio show on WOBU in Charleston, West Virginia. Their recording career was begun in the temporary setup of Brunswick in Ashland, Kentucky; in addition to gaining their name as the Kessinger Brothers, they used the pseudonyms "Wright Brothers," "Birmingham Entertainers," and "Arnold Brothers" for some of their recordings. Fourteen cuts were made at the initial recording session, and in 1929 to 1930, over seventy sides were recorded in a number of New

York sessions. At the time of the first Kessinger Brothers' releases, Clark Kessinger was employed as a caretaker for Harrison B. Smith of Charleston. During the 1920s, he had the opportunity of listening to recordings of violinists such as Heifetz, Kreisler, and Szigetti, and he saw performances by Kreisler and Szigetti when they appeared in concert in Charleston in the 1930s.

Although their recording career was affected by the Depression, the Kessinger Brothers continued their dance jobs and their radio performances on Charleston's WCHS *Old Farm Hour*. Clark Kessinger also performed with Sam and Kirk McGee, the Delmore Brothers, Clayton McMichen, and Fiddlin' Arthur Smith, among others, and in the late 1930s he was one of the performing artists at the National Folk Festival.

Luches Kessinger died in 1943, and Clark Kessinger played from time to time at local dances, working by day as a house painter. In 1964 he won first place in a Pulaski, Virginia, fiddle contest and, later on, went on to win prizes at Galax, Union Grove, and Weiser. He appeared at various festivals, including Newport, University of Chicago, and Smithsonian Folklife, on network television, and on the *Grand Ole Opry*; from recording sessions of this period, four LPs have been issued.

Shortly after recording an album for Rounder Records, Clark Kessinger suffered a stroke on July 2, 1971, and on June 4, 1975, he died on the way to the hospital after another stroke.

Several rare original 78-RPM recordings have been reissued on *The Kessinger Brothers* (County 536), released in 1975. The album consists of recordings made by Clark and Luches Kessinger from 1928 to 1930. One of the most variously issued old-time recordings, *The Legend of Clark Kessinger*, has been on four labels (Folk Promotions FP828, Kanawha 304, Folkways FA 2336, and County 733). Other recordings by Clark Kessinger include *Sweet Bunch of Daisies* (Kanawha 306, forthcoming on County); *Live at Union Grove* (Kanawha

312); and *Old-Time Music with Fiddle and Guitar* (Rounder 0004), fiddle tunes and waltzes with Gene Meade.

# Clark Kessinger. *See* The Kessinger Brothers.

# Luches Kessinger. *See* The Kessinger Brothers.

# Lou Killen

*Traditional folksinger, concertina and five-pennywhistle player, member of the* Clearwater, *performer, and recording artist*

Active in England's folk song revival during the late 1950s, Lou Killen is largely responsible for the current popularity of the concertina in the United States today. Before leaving his native England, he helped to establish one of the country's better traditional clubs, Folk Song and Ballad—Newcastle, and since he began his professional career as a folksinger in 1962, Lou Killen has been acclaimed for his expertise as both an unaccompanied vocalist and concertina player.

"I was born in January 1934, at Gateshead-on-Tyne, County Durham, in England, and I was the youngest of four sons. We all sang in the family. My father played a little mandolin, my eldest brother took up the guitar when he was about sixteen, another brother played a little piano and then he took up the concertina, but he died when I was about fourteen. He was about three or four years older than I was, but this is where the concertina entered my life because I started picking at it for a while and then left it alone for almost ten years before I picked it up again.

"But the real thing was that we all just sang, not necessarily folk music, but there were always some folk songs in there. We'd sing a lot of dialect songs, which we were taught in school, along with other tunes.

"We just liked to sing, and we used to sing in harmony. Two of us spent some time in choirs. I spent a good ten years, from the age of ten to twenty, in and out of church choir. It helped to develop a sense of harmony for different types of music.

"When I was about seven, my older brothers were interested in cowboy music, which meant, basically, anything that was American folk music. So I was learning songs like 'Get Along Little Dogies,' 'Chisholm Trail,' 'Riding Old Paint,' and a bunch of others that we picked up from radio programs and from some Jimmie Rodgers records. We didn't used to think of the local songs as folk music then, but I went through a whole personal musical education just picking up things that interested me, among which were classical music, grand opera, and church music, which I always loved singing. When I was about fourteen, I discovered 'bee-bop,' which put me on another whole track, and about two years after that, I discovered New Orleans jazz.

"I suppose I have a tendency to approach anything that I get involved in with an historical, antiquarian attitude, so, with jazz, I eventually landed back to country blues and then to white American folk music.

"By the time I was twenty, I had come full circle, and I was really involved with folk music, especially British folk music, and I made a conscious choice to follow English, Scottish, Irish, or American folk music, in 1956 or 1957.

"When I was at Oxford, over a two-year period there, I came across my first folk club, the university's Heritage Society, and that changed my whole attitude. I got very involved in music, and life has never been the same for me ever since. When I returned to Newcastle I started its first folk song club, Folk Song and Ballad—Newcastle, during the summer of 1958.

"I worked at a variety of jobs until 1961, when I found myself out of work, and I started singing in a few folk song clubs. This is when I turned professional, and I turned the club over to one of the other lads because the work started coming in. I suppose I was making one or two pounds more by singing at a couple of clubs a week than I was collecting from unemployment, but eventually the demand became such that if I wanted to sing, which I wanted to do, I could do it professionally.

"I don't know what the influences were, as far as British folk music was concerned, except that Ewan MacColl and Bert Lloyd were very instrumental in creating a folk song revival, and had an inevitable effect upon me. There were others, who were well-known and recorded, but there was so little in the British record catalogues that was available, or that anyone ever knew about.

"I emigrated to America in 1967, and I've been back and forth several times since then, but I make my home in Maine. When I came over, the folk boom had died somewhat, and everybody was into 'folk-rock' and the coffeehouses weren't interested in traditional music, especially British traditional music, so I spent the summer sailing up in Newport. I went to California in 1968, but there was no work, so I ended up in San Francisco with ten cents in my pocket. I picked up odd dollars singing here and there, but nobody knew me in California, and I spent several months earning my living in the shipyards around the Bay Area, and I came back East in 'sixty-nine to join the crew of the *Clearwater* to bring it down from Bristol, Maine. That was the original crew, and we did twenty-odd concerts coming down the coast. During one of the concerts, in Provincetown, I met my wife Sally, because she had come down to the boat looking for Gordon Bok, who had been taught by her father up in Maine, something like ten years beforehand."

Killen left for England to perform at several festivals, and when he returned to the United States, he joined the Clancy Brothers, in February 1971. Since then, he has sung with the Clancys for two or three tours each year; in between, he's been singing around clubs and folklore societies, and lecturing at schools and colleges. Since 1973 Sally Killen has been singing with him, and they sing duets in the classic British traditional style of harmony.

Lou Killen's singing and instrumental accompaniment can be found on about thirty-five albums, and he has recorded solo LPs for Topic, South Street Seaport Museum, ESP, and, most recently, *Bright Shining Morning* (Front Hall Records FHR-06), with Sally Killen.

## Sally Killen. *See* Lou Killen.

## The Kingston Trio

*Vocal and instrumental group, performers, and recording artists*

Considered by many to be the most influential group of the recent urban folk revival, the Kingston Trio—formed in 1957 to play for free beer at a local college-oriented nightspot—went on to become one of the best known and most popular folk acts in the United States. People in all parts of the country started playing the guitar and banjo in imitation of the Kingston Trio, and new groups sprang up everywhere as the country "rediscovered" folk music. The folk boom was precipitated by the Kingston Trio's recording of the Southern murder ballad "Tom Dooley," originally collected by Frank Warner from the singing of Frank Proffitt. Out of the folk boom phenomenon came some of this country's most acclaimed folksingers and composers, including Joan Baez, John Denver, Bob Dylan, Tom Paxton, Peter, Paul and Mary, and many others. The Kingston Trio also influenced many of

The Kingston Trio at the Newport Jazz Festival, July 1959: (left to right) Dave Guard, Bob Shane, Nick Reynolds.

today's traditional singers, such as Michael Cooney and Jeff Warner, who were awakened to the spirit of folk music and then traced the music to its roots. Although the reasons for the success of the Kingston Trio are complex, sociologically, conditions were ripe for them. There was a musical void left when Elvis Presley went into the army, and, besides, people—especially collegians—were becoming generally more aware and more actively involved with others in various activities. With the arrival of the Kingston Trio, the guitar became standard equipment on every college campus, and a timeless musical form of expression was rediscovered as the youth of the late fifties and early sixties armed themselves with the music and the basics of communication learned from the Kingston Trio.

Dave Guard, "the acknowledged leader" of the Kingston Trio, was born on November 19, 1934, in Honolulu, Hawaii. He left Hawaii for the mainland to attend Stanford University, completing his BA in 1956 and then entering the Stanford School of Business Administration. Bob Shane, "the sex symbol" of the group, was born on February 1, 1934, in Hilo, Hawaii, where he met and became friends with Dave Guard during high school. Later on, he left Hawaii to attend Menlo Park School of Business Administration. Nick Reynolds, "the runt of the litter," was born on July 27, 1933, in San Diego, California. After trying different colleges, he enrolled at Menlo Park School, where he met Bob Shane, who then introduced him to his friend Dave Guard. The three started hanging around together, swapping songs and singing at parties and for free beer at local bars.

The group started performing professionally at a small San Francisco club called the Purple Onion. The Purple Onion had a reputation as a "discovery club," and the trio had been trying, initially with little success, to obtain a booking there; when it finally happened, they were given a one-week stand. The trio proceeded to send postcards to everyone they knew, asking them to come.

The postcard idea worked. The place was packed, and the Kingston Trio became its headliner one month later—remaining there for another eight months.

In January 1958, the trio cut its first album, called *The Kingston Trio* (Capitol T996), which was released in June of the same year and included "Tom Dooley," which was issued as a single soon thereafter. By November, "Tom Dooley" was No. 1 on the charts. In 1959 the trio logged close to three hundred days on the road, performing everywhere from the Newport Jazz and Folk Festival to Forest Hills in New York to college field houses to nightclubs across the nation.

In 1961 the famous singing trio lost its leader Dave Guard as a result of irreconcilable internal strife, leaving Reynolds and Shane to look for a replacement. Reynolds then invited John Stewart, who had previously written songs recorded by the trio ("Molly Dee" and "Green Grasses," among others), to Shane's house in San Francisco to audition for the vacancy. They liked Stewart and offered him the job.

Filling Dave Guard's spot with the trio was not an easy job, as John Stewart explains: "At first it was an exciting idea to take the place of Dave Guard, but then, when I got into it, I realized that the reason I had liked the Trio was because Dave Guard was in it! It was a thrill to be part of it, a great thrill, but I felt alien because I hadn't started it, I was the new guy, and I no longer enjoyed the Kingston Trio because I was doing it. The sound was different, and I thought it was much better with Dave. I was a salaried member, hired by the Trio, and I got five hundred dollars a week whether or not we worked."

Finally, in 1968, with over thirty albums released, the Kingston Trio disbanded—leaving behind a generation turned on to a great heritage of folk music.

Today, Dave Guard lives in the San Francisco area and is involved in teaching music and writing; Nick Reynolds lives on his ranch in Oregon; Bob Shane continues to tour with a band called the New Kingston Trio; and John Stewart is a successful solo performing and recording artist. (*See also* John Stewart; The Whiskeyhill Singers.)

## Dave Kiphuth. *See* Apple Country.

## Beecher "Pete" Kirby

*Old-time dobroist and vocalist for Roy Acuff's Smoky Mountain Boys, performer, and recording artist*

Beecher R. "Pete" Kirby, better known as Brother Oswald, has played the dobro for Roy Acuff's Smoky Mountain Boys for nearly forty years. He has contributed to the increasing popularity of the dobro guitar, and his old-time style of playing has been a significant influence on other musicians.

He left his home in Sevierville, Tennessee, when he was thirteen. He had been exposed to the music of his native Smoky Mountains at an early age, and when he was five years old, he played both guitar and banjo. Today, he is best known as a dobroist, although he was not introduced to the instrument until late in his teens. In 1931 he got his first job as a dobro guitar player at a club in Chicago. Around 1936 he met Roy Acuff, and when Acuff moved to radio station WROL in Knoxville, Kirby would play occasionally on the show. He started to fill in for members of Acuff's group on some of their road trips, and soon Acuff asked Kirby to join him on the *Grand Ole Opry* with his Smoky Mountain Boys, replacing Clell Summey ("Cousin Jody") as dobro player.

In addition to playing with Roy Acuff's Smoky Mountain Boys for almost forty years, Kirby also performs with Charlie Collins. Both mainstays of Acuff's band, stars of Opryland and WSM Radio, they recorded *That's Country* (Rounder 0041) with dobro, fiddle, and mandolin instrumentals and accompanied by Sam Bush and Norman Blake on several cuts. Kirby's first solo album was recorded on Rounder Records, *Brother Oswald* (Rounder 0013), and its fifteen cuts show him at his best on this all-dobro album. (*See also* The Smoky Mountain Boys.)

## Monica Kirby. *See* The New Christy Minstrels.

## Mike Kirkland. *See* The Brothers Four.

## Reverend Frederick Douglass Kirkpatrick

*Singer, guitarist, performer, composer, founder and director of Hey Brother coffeehouses, and Baptist minister*

"I've found a lot wrong with the present way this society is being run, and I am going to fight for change until death. We cannot afford to compromise to evil making, generated by greed-filled men and their coworkers."

This statement by the Rev. Frederick Douglass Kirkpatrick reveals his strong commitment to education in regard to justice and change among various ethnic groups in the United States. Over the past twenty years he has been actively working toward this end, and he is highly respected for his role as cultural director of the Poor People's Campaign in the spring of 1968, leader of the Gospel Tent in Resurrection City in Washington, D.C., and founder (and director since 1970) of Hey Brother coffeehouses. From 3:00 P.M. until midnight in June 1968, he led an audience of thousands in a songfest in Resurrection City—armed with music and a message—and he continues to inspire listeners in this fashion at concerts, festivals, colleges, and lectures, and on radio, television, and records.

Born on August 12, 1933, in Haynesville, Louisiana, Kirkpatrick assimilated his rich Southern black heritage through his family and his father's work as a minister. His family suffered many hardships, and music was often its only source of consolation. He worked as a barber while finishing high school and as a scholarship student at Grambling College in Louisiana, where he was an All-American quarterback in 1955. After playing professional football for a while, he quit to teach in the Louisiana public school system, working in black, segregated schools from 1959 to 1965. He was a pro-ball player for the Kansas City Chiefs in 1962, and in 1965 he founded Deacons for Defense and Justice, which is still active throughout the South and Midwest. A professor at his alma mater from 1966 to 1968, he also attended Louisiana Technical University in Ruston, Louisiana, in 1966. The year 1967 found Kirkpatrick serving as chairman of the Student Non-Violent Coordinating Committee and leading demonstrations at Texas Southern University in Houston. He was Texas state director of the Southern Leadership Conference and leader of the campaign to release Martin Luther King, Jr., from jail in Birmingham, Alabama.

In 1968 he acted as leader of the New York area Poor People's Campaign and Resurrection City, and he formed (and has acted as president of) the Many Races Cultural Foundation. The Church of St. Gregory on West Ninetieth Street in New York City permitted Kirkpatrick to use its basement for a Saturday-night Hey Brother coffeehouse, and the opening concert of "Hey Brother I" was held on Feburary 28, 1970. An extension of the oral tradition, Hey Brother is a place for sharing and communicating through music, and participation is the crux of its operation. Organized on a spiritual-educational basis, Hey Brother offers an opportunity for all to perform as well as to listen. Volunteers have opened other Hey Brother coffeehouses in New York City and elsewhere on the East Coast.

A lay minister since 1968, Rev. F. D. Kirkpatrick was one of the founding members of the Hudson River Sloop Restoration (he had sung with Pete Seeger in previous concerts). He was among the performers at the Newport Folk Festival and was elected to the Newport Jazz Festival board in 1969. Since 1970 he has been the chairman of the People's Platform Conference, director of the New York West Side Folk Festival, and director of bookmobile tours in both the north Louisiana and New York areas. In the last several years he has been a member of the White House Conference for Children (for which he won a grant as an outstanding panelist) and teacher of black studies at Fordham University. He has made widespread appearances as a singer and lecturer and has been involved in the making of a number of films, such as *Black Roots, Circle of Lights, Many Faces of America, Music That Moves Mountains, Down Home, Street Preacher*, and *Patchwork of Quilt*.

His music incorporates religious material, country blues, and topical protest songs. He learned the essentials of guitar playing from his brother, Robert Kirkpatrick, with whom he appeared at the 1971 National Folk Festival. Robert Kirkpatrick has performed throughout his life, beginning with high school gatherings and college dances. Now a resident of Dallas, he has been among the performers at the Newport Folk Festival, Tompkins Square Park Festival in New York, and events in Texas, Oklahoma, Louisiana, and Arkansas.

Rev. Frederick Douglass Kirkpatrick has made over half a dozen recordings, including *Everybody's Got a Right to Live* (Folkways [Broadside Series] BR 308), with Jimmy Collier; *Pete Seeger Now* (Columbia CS 9717), with Bernice Reagon; *Square Dance with Soul* (Folkways 7623, originally in the Asch Series AH[S] 823), Rev. F. D. Kirkpatrick with the Hearts; *Ballads of Black America* (MPI/Harlem Black Media Productions); *The Black Struggle in Song and Story* (Kimbo Records, New Jersey), with Fred Starner; *Pete Seeger and "Kirk"*

*Visit Sesame Street* (Columbia Records); and *Clearwater* (Sound House PS 1001B/SR-0104).

## Robert Kirkpatrick. *See* Reverend Frederick Douglass Kirkpatrick.

## Sarah Gertrude Knott. *See* The National Folk Festival Association.

## Mike Kobluk. *See* The Chad Mitchell Trio.

## Alice Kogan. *See* The Pennywhistlers.

## Bernie Krause. *See* The Weavers.

## Kris Kristofferson

*Singer, songwriter, performer, recording artist, actor, television personality, and writer*

For some creative personalities, folk music is merely a stopover in a journey that includes multitudinous forms of self-expression. By the mid-1970s, one of the most prolific poet-songwriters of the late sixties was concentrating his artistic efforts on acting; however, many of the songs written by Kris Kristofferson, such as "Me and Bobby McGee," "Casey's Last Ride," "Help Me Make It Through the Night," "(The) Pilgrim: Chapter 33 (Hang In, Hopper)," "Sunday Mornin' Comin' Down," "To Beat the Devil," "The Silver-Tongued Devil and I," "Loving Her Was Easier (Than Anything I'll Ever Do Again)," and others, have become permanent additions to the American folk music repertoire.

Born Kristoffer Kristofferson on June 22, 1936, in Brownsville, Texas, he moved with his family to California when he was in high school. One of his early interests was country music, and he spent many hours listening to his personal collection of Hank Williams records. After graduating from high school, Kristofferson attended Pomona College, near his home in San Mateo, and he excelled in his studies, played sports, was the sports columnist for the campus paper, and an ROTC commander. It was assumed that he would follow in the footsteps of his air force major general father and pursue a military career, but Kristofferson's real ambition was to become a writer. In the late fifties he submitted a short story to a contest sponsored by the *Atlantic Monthly*, and won hands down. He was the recipient of a Rhodes Scholarship, and upon completion of his studies at Pomona, Kristofferson traveled abroad to attend Oxford University in England. While he was studying literature as part of his formal education, he commenced work on a second novel and composed songs which he sang under the name of Kris Carson. With his manuscripts rejected by publishing firms and his degree work completed at Oxford, he got married and enlisted in the U.S. Army. During the course of his five-year stint in the service, Kristofferson wrote songs and performed in enlisted men's and noncommissioned officers' clubs while stationed in Germany. Encouraged to show his material to someone in the music industry, Kristofferson sent some songs to Nashville; and, with his curiosity aroused, he went to Music City for two weeks between assignments. It was during these two weeks in June 1965 that Kris Kristofferson met Johnny Cash and decided to become a full-time musician instead of an English literature instructor at West Point.

He worked at a number of odd jobs, but songwriting remained his primary concern; financial problems were a part of everyday living in Nashville, and his marriage broke up in the late 1960s. By June 1969, Kristofferson got his first break when Roger Miller recorded three of his original compositions, and, before long, the talented young songwriter signed an exclusive recording contract with Monument Records. The songs started to circulate and his record sales soared; by the fall of 1973, two albums, *The Silver-Tongued Devil and I* (Monument Z-30679) and *Jesus Was a Capricorn* (Monument KZ-31909), and a single, "Why Me," had achieved Gold Record status. More recently, he has recorded *Spooky Lady's Sideshow* (Monument PZ-32914), *Who's to Bless and Who's to Blame* (Monument PZ-33379), and two with his second wife, Rita Coolidge: *Full Moon* (A&M 4403) and *Breakaway* (Monument PZ-33278).

Most recently, Kris Kristofferson has focused his attention on filmmaking, and he has appeared in a number of leading roles in such movies as *The Last Movie, Cisco Pike, Blume in Love, Pat Garrett & Billy the Kid,* with James Coburn and Bob Dylan, *Bring Me the Head of Alfredo Garcia, Alice Doesn't Live Here Anymore*, and *The Sailor Who Fell from Grace with the Sea.*

His other albums include *Me and Bobby McGee*—formerly *Kristofferson* (Monument SLP-18139)—and *Border Lord* (Monument KZ-31302). (*See also* Rita Coolidge.)

## Jim Kweskin. *See* The Jim Kweskin Jug Band.

## Ashby Kyhl. *See* The Free State Ramblers.

**Gene LaBrie.** *See* Apple Country.

## Peter LaFarge

*Singer-songwriter, guitarist, performer, recording artist, and writer*

When he died on October 27, 1965, at the age of thirty-four, Peter LaFarge left behind in his songs and in his writings a vivid remembrance of his posture on social injustice and the oppression of the American Indian. Of Pima Indian heritage, this one-time radio performer, dramatist, poet, painter, rodeo rider, and boxer is best remembered as a singer-songwriter who, in his performances, recordings, and original compositions, such as "Ballad of Ira Hayes" and "As Long as the Grass Shall Grow," sought to reveal the inequitable conditions and hypocrisies in American society.

The son of Pulitzer Prize–winning author and fighter for Indian rights Oliver LaFarge, Peter LaFarge was born in Fountain, Colorado. Although there seems to be no available record of his birth date, he once gave it orally as 1931. He was raised in the American West and, from a very young age, was involved with folk music. As a teenager, he hosted a radio program broadcast over a station in Colorado Springs, and he became acquainted with Cisco Houston, who befriended and guided him in developing his skills as a performer, instrumentalist, and songwriter.

Peter LaFarge continued to pursue his musical ambitions in the post–World War II years, but his career was temporarily interrupted when he served as a soldier in the Korean War. He was decorated five times for wounds received in battle; he later commented that Korea was a "stupid war that should never have been fought in the first place." When he returned to civilian life, he worked as a rodeo hand and a boxer before turning his attention to writing and performing.

His name began to spread as he played to enthusiastic audiences on the local coffeehouse circuit, and he soon became a popular performer at festivals and concerts across the country (including the 1963 Newport Folk Festival) and a Columbia recording artist. His song "Ballad of Ira Hayes" was printed in the August 1962 *Broadside #11-12*, and until his death three years later, the protest song publication presented his material on a regular basis. He became a *Broadside* contributing editor, along with Eric Andersen, Len Chandler, Bob Dylan, Julius Lester, Phil Ochs, Gil Turner, and others, and he was included on the first *Broadside* LP, *Broadside Ballads, Vol. 1* (Folkways 5301, formerly BR 301), and on subsequent recordings in the *Broadside* Series. Peter LaFarge was also a contributing writer for *Sing Out!*; in the fall of 1963 he was among the performers in the annual *Sing Out!* hootenanny at Carnegie Hall (held on September 21) and the singing host of the second program in the monthly *Broadside* folk series at Town Hall called the "99 ¢ Hoot" (held on October 4), with Len Chandler, Danny Kalb, Malvina

Reynolds, and Hedy West. In 1964–65 he participated in *Broadside* "Get Togethers," devoted to new topical songs, and a series of old-style hoots at the Village Gate in New York City. The year 1964 brought the release of his fourth and fifth Folkways LPs, and by the fall of that year, Johnny Cash's recording of "Ira Hayes" was at the top of country & western charts.

In the weeks before he died, Peter LaFarge spoke at length with several friends, including Len Chandler, about his desire to retire as a singer and to direct his energies into writing and painting (one of his paintings had recently been purchased). He died suddenly in New York City, and his passing was officially recorded as a stroke.

## Joseph Ronald "Joe" Lamanno.
*See* The Travelers 3.

## Darrell "Pee Wee" Lambert. *See* The Stanley Brothers.

## Martin Lamble. *See* Fairport Convention.

## Millard Lampell. *See* The Almanac Singers.

## Billy Ray Latham. *See* The Dillards.

## Doyle Lawson. *See* The Country Gentlemen.

## Bert Layne. *See* Gid Tanner and the Skillet Lickers.

# Leadbelly
*Singer, guitarist, songwriter, performer, and recording artist.*

Almost three decades have passed since the death of one of America's most widely acknowledged folksingers, whose influence is still a viable and significant force in American music. Sometimes called the "King of Fannin Street" or "King of the Twelve-String Guitar," Leadbelly created a legacy of original works, and some of his compositions, such as "Good Night, Irene," "Midnight Special," "Boll Weevil," "Rock Island Line," and "Old Cottonfields at Home," among others, have become standards of American folk music. His black skin and scrapes with the law are tied to his forty-nine years of struggle in the Deep South and, along with his music, are vital factors in the understanding of the man and his times.

Leadbelly

## Leadbelly

Born Huddie Ledbetter around 1885 in Mooringsport, Louisiana, he was raised on a farm in the Caddo Lake district of the state. He suffered the hardships of poverty and of growing up in the bitter aftermath of the Civil War, when suppression and mistreatment of blacks remained relatively unchanged in the Deep South. His background of exposure to illiteracy, crime, and death affected the course of his life, but it also provided him with an environment for the development of his unique brand of music. From his elders, he learned work songs, spirituals, lullabies, and hymns, and before he was ten years old, he played an accordion given to him by his uncle. Later on, he was given a guitar by his father, and, when Leadbelly was sixteen, he left home with the instrument strapped to his back.

For the next sixteen years or so, he led a life of roaming, working, making music, and fighting. He worked whatever jobs were available to blacks—field hand, trainer of unbroken horses, mule and oxen driver, ranch hand, and so on—and, in his free time, frequented local nightspots, bars, and pool halls. Throughout his life, Leadbelly accumulated a wealth of music and experience. In 1910 he heard jazz band music for the first time in his life, in Dallas; his acquaintance with brothels from Deep Elm in Dallas to Fannin Street in Shreveport, Louisiana, provided him with another source for the blues; and his daily work gave him the opportunity to learn music ranging from cowboy songs to ballads and work songs. While he was in Dallas, sometime before his arraignment before a judge on May 24, 1918, Leadbelly met a young blind singer named Blind Lemon Jefferson. For a while, they traveled and worked together, and, from his partner, Leadbelly learned new techniques of playing the six-string guitar and new songs. During his years in prison, Leadbelly continued to assimilate material, picking up hollers, work songs, and chain-gang chants from the other prisoners.

His life was filled with passion and blood, and his existence in an atmosphere of violence and disorder led to several separate prison terms during his lifetime. In each case, Leadbelly was convicted of assault (twice with intent to kill) committed against other blacks. His two longest prison terms involved his serving over six years (1918 to 1925) of a thirty-year term at the Shaw State Prison Farm in Texas, when he was convicted of murder, and, five years after his release from the Shaw State Farm, the period from February 28, 1930, to August 1, 1934, when he was imprisoned at the Louisiana State Farm at Angola. In both cases he was given a reprieve of his sentence by the governors of the respective states. His singing and guitar playing moved Texas Governor Pat Neff to set him free from his confinement at Shaw State; and, later on, he was released from the Louisiana State Farm by Governor O. K. Allen, when prison authorities felt that Leadbelly had been "broken" and should be freed.

While he was serving his last term at Angola, he was visited in 1933 by folklorists John A. and Alan Lomax, who were seeking out material on a folk-song collecting trip in the South. In late 1934, after Leadbelly was granted his pardon, he traveled to New York City with the Lomaxes, who arranged a joint concert tour of Northern colleges for the following year. In 1936 the Macmillan Company published forty-eight songs and commentary by Leadbelly in the now-out-of-print *Negro Folk Songs as Sung by Leadbelly*, edited by John A. and Alan Lomax.

New York City was used as a base of operations during this last phase of his life, and he spent most of his last thirteen years there. With the Lomaxes guiding him, he traveled from one college town to another, giving concerts. His performances were a combination of singing, playing, explaining his songs, and storytelling. As a storyteller, he outshone all other performers, and his tales (both fictitious and real) held audiences enthralled. Although Leadbelly was capable of playing a number of instruments, including the six-string guitar, harmonica, mandolin, string bass, and piano, many years before, he had adopted the twelve-string guitar as his primary vehicle for instrumental accompaniment. Leadbelly's vocals have a rough, nasal quality, and **through his singing he is able to convey an intensity and excitement.**

He married Martha Promise on January 21, 1935, and, two days later, he began his recording sessions with the American Record Company (later Columbia Records). Today, these first recordings made during his early days in New York City are considered priceless documents of Leadbelly's songs and stories. He was among the folk-singers who participated in the benefit session for California migratory workers in March 1940, along with Burl Ives, Woody Guthrie, Pete Seeger, and Josh White. In June of the same year, he made recordings for RCA Victor.

In addition to his numerous concert appearances (including Times Hall and Town Hall), Leadbelly played such clubs as the Village Vanguard in Greenwich Village, New York City. He appeared on the Columbia Broadcasting System radio show *Back Where I Come From*, and on WNYC. For a brief period, he performed with Woody Guthrie, Brownie McGhee, and Sonny Terry, as the Headline Singers. Leadbelly was acquainted with many contemporary folksingers, and he played with Big Bill Broonzy, Cisco Houston, and Josh White, among numerous others.

In 1944 he left New York for Hollywood, and in 1949 he embarked on a European concert tour. He returned to New York after several months, when he became seriously ill with amyotrophic lateral sclerosis, a rare, but fatal, disease which causes the muscles to atrophy. On December 6, 1949, Leadbelly died of the same disease that had claimed the life of the legendary baseball player Lou Gehrig. Tragically, Leadbelly never achieved commercial success during his lifetime, and he left his widow nearly penniless. Only six months after his death, his song "Good Night, Irene" became a ma-

jor hit and sold over two million copies.

During the last thirteen years of his life, Leadbelly made numerous recordings. Moe Asch taped over nine hundred songs by Leadbelly, and the Folkways record catalogue boasts one of the most extensive (and still extant) collections of Leadbelly albums available commercially. Among the many labels which have issued Leadbelly recordings are Allegro, Capitol, Columbia, Elektra, Everest, Folkways, Playboy Records, RCA Victor, Stinson, and Verve/Folkways.

Leadbelly's contribution to the folk song revival is inestimable, but he is considered by many to be the key figure in the history of American music to introduce the broadest representation of the world of black music. Less than two months after his death, Alan Lomax arranged a Leadbelly Memorial Concert, which was held on January 28, 1950. A host of folk musicians gathered at New York's Town Hall for the celebration, and, in Leadbelly's honor, performances were given by Count Basie, Rev. Gary Davis, Tom Glazer, Woody Guthrie, Brownie McGhee, Tom Paley, Jean Ritchie, Sonny Terry, Frank Warner, the Weavers, and many others.

In 1976 Paramount Pictures released *Leadbelly*, starring Roger E. Mosley and directed by Gordon Parks.

## Huddie Ledbetter. *See* Leadbelly.

## Walter Lee. *See* The Balfa Freres.

## Tom Lehrer

*Topical and satirical songwriter, singer, pianist, performer, recording artist, writer, and teacher*

Tom Lehrer's career as a songwriter and performer coincided with the folk movement of the 1950s and 1960s; and as a contemporary virtuoso of topical and humorous material, he created an impact with his controversial "Wernher Von Braun," "Vatican Rag," and others, and original compositions such as "Pollution," written for the weekly NBC television show *That Was The Week That Was.*

Born in New York City on April 9, 1928, Lehrer took piano lessons at an early age, and he attended the city's primary and secondary schools. He excelled in mathematics and, upon completion of high school, enrolled at Harvard to pursue a career in that field. With his sights set on teaching, Lehrer received both a bachelor's and a master's degree from Harvard, and he taught math as a graduate student. His musical talents were always a sidelight to his teaching ambitions, but his audiences soon expanded from his circle of friends to nightclub and concert patrons: "At first, I just did it for the fun of it, and then people started offering me money, but I quit when I had gone everywhere that I'd wanted to go."

During his first active period as a nightclub and concert entertainer, from 1953 to 1954, Lehrer was a mathematician at Baird-Atomic, Incorporated, in Cambridge. His initial album was released in 1953, and, the following year, the *Tom Lehrer Song Book* was published. In 1955 he was inducted into the army, and, after his discharge in 1957, he spent most of his time traveling: "I traveled from 1957 to 1960, and I got to England, Australia, New Zealand, Canada, and various cities in the United States. And then, after the last album, *That Was The Week That Was* [Reprise (S) 6179], came out in 1965, I performed in Norway, Denmark, Germany, and England. My main incentive in continuing to perform was to go somewhere I'd never been. Once you've been to Detroit, there's no real reason to go back, so I haven't done any performing in this country since 1959, except for fund raising and benefits and a nightclub job in 1965. Before I did the last record in 1965, I thought I'd better try the songs out in front of a live audience, so I got a job at the Hungry i in San Francisco for a couple of weeks, and ended up staying on for about four weeks."

Two more albums were recorded in 1959 and another in 1960. From 1962 Tom Lehrer was a lecturer at Harvard's Graduate School of Business Administration, and, from 1963 to 1966, at the Harvard Graduate School of Education. He was a lecturer in psychology at Wellesley College in 1966, in political science at the Massachusetts Institite of Technology from 1962 to 1971, and he taught at the University of California at Santa Cruz in 1972.

Nine of the cuts on his last LP were composed, and first sung, on NBC's *That Was The Week That Was.* More recently, he has written songs for the children's television show *Electric Company,* but with the exception of special projects that stimulate his musical interest, Tom Lehrer devotes himself full-time to teaching.

# Angelas LeJeune

*Early traditional Cajun accordionist, performer, and recording artist*

Along with his contemporaries, Amadie Ardoin, Amadie Breaux, and Joe Falcon, Angelas LeJeune is reputed to be one of the best early Cajun accordionists, and is best known for his unique style. Dick Spottswood describes LeJeune in an article entitled "Angelas LeJeune," which appeared in the 1974 National Folk Festival program: "People who knew him when he was at the height of his powers remember the wild, abandoned way he performed, singing in a high, free voice while his fingers leaped over the keys, throwing his head back to punctuate his music with the Cajun cry— aaaaaeeeeeeeee!—with his long hair flying high over his head."

In 1929 LeJeune made a 78-RPM recording for Brunswick, "Valse de la Louisianne"/"Perrodin Two-Step." His strong vocals and accordion playing were backed up by two violins, one of the violinists being none other than Dennis McGee. In 1973, when Spottswood visited LeJeune in Opelousas, Louisiana, the seventy-three-year-old Cajun musician again played to the dual-fiddle accompaniment of Dennis McGee and S. D. Courville. LeJeune was scheduled to perform at the 1974 National Folk Festival, but he died on June 12, just a few weeks before the event. (*See also* S. D. [Sady] Courville).

## Lionel LeLeux. *See* The Louisiana Aces.

## Harry Liedstrand. *See* Sweets Mill String Band.

## Gordon Lightfoot

*Contemporary singer-songwriter, performer, and recording artist*

Gordon Lightfoot has been a folk hero for over a decade in his native country—he was voted top Canadian folksinger in 1966 and top male vocalist in 1967—and in recent years his rugged romanticism and poetic compositions have been heard and acclaimed around the globe. Lightfoot's early successes in the United States, resulting from the popularity of his songs among prominent folk music recording artists, have led to his position as one of today's most widely known and favorite performers.

Born on November 17, 1938, and raised in Orillia, Ontario, he traveled to Los Angeles after completing school. For a brief period of time he studied and earned a professional music degree at the Westlake College of Music in Hollywood, but playing the guitar and writing songs were only part-time activities of his early life. By 1960 Lightfoot was listening closely to the music of Bob Gibson, Pete Seeger, and Ian and Sylvia, who were among the first to use his material. He started performing professionally—singing and playing songs by other artists—and he worked on the CBC show *Country Hoedown*. The year 1963 found him in England as host of the BBC-TV series *Country and Western*, and, upon his return to Canada, he toured the bar and coffeehouse circuit and made a number of solo appearances on television.

Bob Dylan was changing attitudes toward songwriting and performing original material, and Gordon Lightfoot was among the young singer-songwriters who were influenced by contemporary events. He had begun to write more extensively while he was in London, but he explains Dylan's effect on his songwriting: "Dylan changed my whole viewpoint about songwriting.. After getting turned on to Bob Dylan, I started getting some identity into my own songwriting. It's not that Dylan's acceptance as a singer/songwriter made it easier—that wasn't the total thing—it just changed my outlook. I'd already written about 75 songs by the time I first heard him on record but most of them didn't really mean anything."

Lightfoot continued to write, and he incorporated more and more original material into his performances. Ian and Sylvia were largely responsible for his early recognition, and all three of these talented performers were instrumental in giving Canadians a decisive role in the urban folk revival of the sixties.

By the mid-sixties, Lightfoot had signed a recording contract with United Artists, producing nearly half a dozen albums for that label. His first LP, *Lightfoot* (UAL 3487), included all but three of his own compositions, and many of these eleven songs were picked up by other artists for performing and recording purposes. "Ribbon of Darkness" was a No. 1 hit on country & western charts for Marty Robbins, and "For Lovin' Me" and "Early Morning Rain" were substantial hits for Peter, Paul and Mary. Within a relatively short period of time, Lightfoot's works were recorded by artists in a diversity **of fields, including Glen Campbell, the Carter Family, Johnny Cash, Bob Dylan, Waylon Jennings, Jerry Lee Lewis, Anne Murray, Elvis Presley, and Barbra Streisand.**

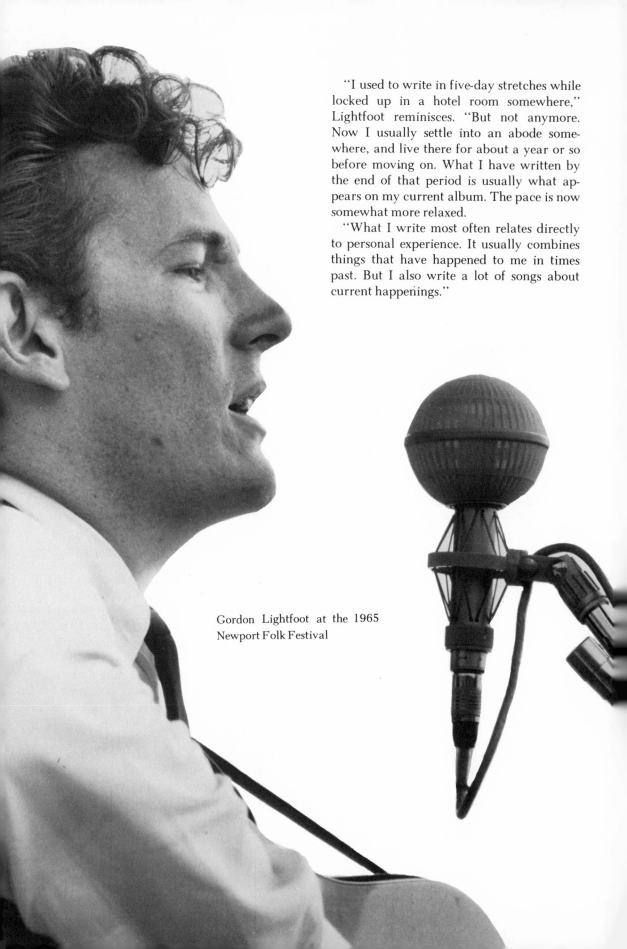

"I used to write in five-day stretches while locked up in a hotel room somewhere," Lightfoot reminisces. "But not anymore. Now I usually settle into an abode somewhere, and live there for about a year or so before moving on. What I have written by the end of that period is usually what appears on my current album. The pace is now somewhat more relaxed.

"What I write most often relates directly to personal experience. It usually combines things that have happened to me in times past. But I also write a lot of songs about current happenings."

Gordon Lightfoot at the 1965
Newport Folk Festival

In 1969 Lightfoot's name was added to the roster of Reprise Records, and, to date, he has recorded seven albums for the company: *If You Could Read My Mind (Sit Down Young Stranger)* (MS 6392), *Summer Side of Life* (MS 2037), *Don Quixote* (MS 2056), *Old Dan's Records* (MS 2116), *Sundown* (MS 2177), *Cold on the Shoulder* (MS 2206), and *Gord's Gold* (2RS 2237).

Lightfoot has appeared at numerous festivals (including Newport), and he remains much in demand as a concert performer in both Canada and the United States. "I'm out there to create a vocal point for the audience," says Lightfoot. "I try to set up a coffeehouse atmosphere at center stage, a small intimate space where everyone's thoughts are focused on the same thing at the same time. I always keep in mind that everyone has to go through the hassle of buying the ticket and getting to the hall and all that, so it's up to me to give out a good feeling in return—musically, emotionally, sound-wise, et cetera. I try never to give my audience less than they expect, nor do I ever take them for granted."

# The Lilly Brothers

*Bluegrass band, performers, and recording artists*

The bluegrass style of the Lilly Brothers is similar to that of Red Allen, Bill Monroe, Earl Taylor, the Lonesome Pine Fiddlers, and others whose music is characteristic of the late 1940s. Their work exemplifies a purity of sound that has survived pressures to compromise and to adapt to changing attitudes and musical styles.

Born in West Virginia in the twenties, Everett and Mitchell (Bea) Lilly were deeply influenced, like so many others, by the Carter Family and the Monroe Brothers. While they were growing up, they learned songs at church or at local gatherings of friends and relatives, and their performances and recordings have always included some of the tunes that they heard during their youth.

The bluegrass duet was part of WWVA Radio's *Jamboree* until the early fifties, when Everett Lilly joined Flatt and Scruggs as mandolinist and vocalist. His old-fashioned hard harmony blended with Lester Flatt's full-bodied singing on some of their best work, including such songs as " 'Tis Sweet to Be Remembered," "I'm Gonna Settle Down," "Get in Line, Brother," "I'm Working on a Road," and "Over the Hill to the Poor House."

For the next eighteen years, the Lillys made nightly appearances at the Hillbilly Ranch, a bar in Boston, Massachusetts. They played with fiddler Tex Logan and banjoist Don Stover, who contributed to the distinctively strong instrumental backup that set off the high, sharp vocals. Despite the adverse conditions created by the atmosphere in any barroom, with its noise, fights, and smoke, the Lilly Brothers and Don Stover initiated a wave of popularity for the bluegrass idiom that stemmed from their musical ability and showmanship.

Today, the Lilly Brothers, often accompanied by veteran banjoist Don Stover, have added Bea Lilly's twelve-year-old son Mark as banjoist for the band, while Bea Lilly plays rhythm guitar and Everett Lilly plays banjo or mandolin.

The Lilly Brothers are included on the Folkways LP *Mountain Music Bluegrass Style* (Folkways FA 2318), and on a solo album, *The Lilly Brothers and Don Stover: Folk Songs from the Southern Mountains* (Folkways FA 2433). They have recorded two albums for County Records, *Early Bluegrass Recordings* (County 729), with Don Stover, and *What Will I Leave Behind* (County 742), which consists of twelve religious tunes. Dick Spottswood selected the Lilly Brothers, among other pure bluegrass musicians, for the first album in a series of at least ten LPs devoted to reissued cuts from the late forties to mid-fifties. The Lillys recorded "They Sleep Together Now at Rest" and "What Are They Doing in Heaven Today?" for *The Early Days of Bluegrass, Volume One* (Rounder 1013). A three-volume set was recorded in Tokyo, Japan, on

September 13, 1973, during live sessions with the Lillys and Don Stover, and probably the best music that they played in their two-and-a-half-hour concert appears on *Holiday in Japan, Part 3* (Towa Records TWA-103-S). (*See also* Earl Scruggs.)

# The Limeliters

*Vocal and instrumental trio, performers, and recording artists*

A distinguished West Coast folk-pop trio of the recent urban folk revival, the Limeliters based their formula for success on a fundamental social approach to the folk song. With their exhilating and entertaining combination of adroit musical arrangements, sophisticated prefacing comments to the traditional and contemporary songs in their far-reaching repertoire, polished style, and clever, witty, and explosive performances, the Limeliters—Lou Gottlieb, Alex Hassilev, and Glenn Yarbrough—enjoyed a prolific and prosperous career.

Louis Gottlieb was born in 1923 in Los Angeles. The comic spokesman and bass player for the Limeliters, he had acquired experience in the entertainment business as a member of another folk group called the Gateway Singers. After several years of performing and recording with Travis Edmondson, Mrs. Elmerlee Thomas, and Jerry Walter, Lou Gottlieb left the Gateway Singers to earn a PhD in musicology at UCLA. In mid-1959, Dr. Lou Gottlieb left behind the academic life to join up with Alex Hassilev and Glenn Yarbrough as the Limeliters.

Alex Hassilev was born on July 11, 1932, in Paris, France. Banjo and baritone vocalist of the Limeliters, Alex Hassilev contributed his musical, acting, and linguistic talents (among the languages in which he is versed are English, French, Portuguese, Russian, and Spanish) to the diverse makeup of the trio.

Glenn Yarbrough was born on January 12, 1930, in Milwaukee, Wisconsin. The warmth and clarity of his lyric tenor vocals, along with his classical guitar-playing ability, were a vital asset to the Limeliters. His professional singing career was launched at the Gate of Horn in Chicago, and after touring on the coffeehouse circuit, he went into partnership with Alex Hassilev and opened the Limelite club in Aspen, Colorado. While performing at the Cosmo Alley Club in Los Angeles in mid-1959, Hassilev and Yarbrough met Lou Gottlieb. They teamed up and named their trio after the Limelite.

Their first engagement, at San Francisco's Hungry i club, established the trio as a top-notch performing act, and for the next several years they were in constant demand for radio, television, and personal appearances. They toured extensively and played concerts and clubs from the Hollywood Bowl to the Village Vanguard in Greenwich Village, New York, and they were billed with such other acts as Shelley Berman, Mort Sahl, and Johnny Mathis.

A recording contract was signed with RCA Victor shortly after the group's inception, and, until their disbandment in 1963, the Limeliters produced about a dozen albums of studio and live recordings for that label.

When the trio broke up in the summer of 1963, Lou Gottlieb returned to academic life, while Alex Hassilev remodeled his Hollywood home and prepared for the intensive study of classical music in his newly designed and furnished recording studio. Several of his original compositions became popular song hits, and he abandoned his interest in classical music to produce albums for Hoyt Axton, Theodore Bikel, and Glenn Yarbrough, among others. (He also played an acting role in the film *The Russians Are Coming, The Russians Are Coming*.) Glenn Yarbrough went on to establish a successful follow-up career as a solo pop and folk performer and recording artist. After producing several albums for RCA Victor, he had a hit single with "Baby the Rain Must Fall," followed by more recordings on such labels as RCA Victor, Elektra, Tradition, Warner

Brothers, and, most recently, Stax.

In 1974 the Limeliters reformed for a ten-week reunion, and they recorded an album entitled *Glenn Yarbrough and the Limeliters* (Stax 5513).

## Mance Lipscomb

*Blues singer, guitarist, performer, and recording artist*

Along with Mississippi John Hurt and Furry Lewis, who were first recorded in 1928, Mance Lipscomb was representative of a generation of songsters whose breadth of music ranges from blues to ballads, reels, jigs, and breakdowns. The rediscovery of both John Hurt and Furry Lewis during the recent folk revival coincided with the initial recordings made by Mance Lipscomb in 1960, when he was sixty-five years old.

Mance Lipscomb was born on April 9, 1895, in Navasota, Texas, to a former Alabama slave. As a boy he worked in the fields to help support his ten siblings. When he was thirteen, he was given his first guitar by an itinerant gambler, and throughout his life as a Navasota sharecropper and tenant farmer, he played ballads, spirituals, blues, waltzes, ragtimey, jazz, and children's songs on the battered instrument for friends and relatives. He mastered the bottleneck blues style and, with his guitar, produced a distinctive "crying" sound for which he is well-known. He is a frequent performer at parties and dances, and his roots in dance music led to his development of a rhythmic bass styling and a distinctive waltz and jig tempo. Ethnic influences pervaded the dances in Texas, and musicians provided accompaniment for a diversity of dances, from the buck-and-wing to the buzzard-loop, the hop-scop, and the heel-and-toe polka.

Fifty years after he started playing the guitar around the Navasota area, Lipscomb was taped by Arhoolie Records founder Chris Strachwitz, who had traveled to East Texas to record the Navasota songster. The tape of about forty of his songs made that evening constituted both his initial record and his first Arhoolie release. Shortly thereafter, Mance Lipscomb was asked by Barry Olivier to perform at the 1961 Berkeley Folk Festival (which marked the first time he set foot outside of the Lone Star State). During the next fifteen years, he recorded several albums for Arhoolie Records; was a guest at major folk festivals around the United States, including Newport, Philadelphia, UCLA, and Monterey; and was featured in Les Blank's film *A Well Spent Life.*

Mance Lipscomb died on January 30, 1976, at the age of eighty.

## Little Wilma. *See* The Kentucky Pardners.

## Alan Lomax

*Folklorist, collector, producer, lecturer, educator, writer, singer, performer, and assistant archivist of the Library of Congress (1937–42)*

Once described by Pete Seeger as "the most important single figure" in the world of folk music, Alan Lomax is considered America's most eminent folk song collector and scholar. As a teenage assistant to his father, folklorist John A. Lomax, he began a lifetime of documenting folk music as sung by the authentic voices of people in Southern prison camps, remote dwellings in the mountains of east Kentucky, lumber camps in the Midwest, farms in New England, sponge docks in the Bahamas, and in countries across the Atlantic.

Alan Lomax was born on January 31, 1915, in Austin, Texas, to John A. and Bess Baumann (Brown) Lomax. After attending public grade school and a college preparatory school in Dallas, he entered the University of Texas, where he graduated in 1936 with a BA degree. In the following year, he was a student at Harvard, and in

Alan Lomax (right) with Woody Guthrie, and Lily Mae Ledford of the Coon Creek Girls. In New York City, about 1946

1938 he engaged in postgraduate work at Columbia University.

His father's first collection of folk songs had been published in 1910; then, two years after Alan Lomax was born, another volume, *Songs of the Cattle Trail and Cow Camp* (1917), was released. While growing up, Alan Lomax was greatly influenced by his father's love for folk music, and in 1933 he accompanied John A. Lomax on a major collecting-recording tour of Southern prisons. In the years that followed, he worked very closely with his father in the scholarly pursuit of the folk song, and they collaborated on several works, including *American Ballads and Folk Songs* (1934), *Negro Folk Songs as Sung by Leadbelly* (1935), *Cowboy Songs and Other Frontier Ballads* (revised edition, 1937), *Our Singing Country* (1939), and *Folk Song, U.S.A.* (1947).

As assistant archivist of the Library of Congress from 1937 to 1942, Alan Lomax worked under his father and traveled extensively, collecting material for the Archive of Folk Song. His efforts yielded three thousand 12-inch records from Southwestern, Southern, Northern, and Midwestern states, Haiti, and the Bahamas, and the Lomaxes made an immeasurable contribution to the expansion of the Archive collection.

In 1939 Alan Lomax initiated a radio program on Columbia's School of the Air, called *Wellsprings of America*, and he wrote, conducted, and sang on the series. For the next several years, he maintained his involvement with radio broadcasting and rendered his talents to such programs as *American Folk Music, Transatlantic Call,* and MBC's *Your Ballad Man Alan Lomax.* During World War II, he worked for the Office of War Information (OWI) and with the Special Services section of the U.S. Army.

Following the war, Alan Lomax received

a Guggenheim grant and continued to do field work, record, and present recitals and lectures on such topics as songs and lore from Haiti, songs of the cowboy, hobo and jailhouse songs, and Bahamian songs and stories. From 1947 to 1949 he was director of folk music for Decca Records, and in 1949 he taught at Columbia University. During this period, he gave a series of concerts at New York's Town Hall in which he presented material expressing "a part of human life"—an approach which he continued to use in subsequent performances at the Newport Folk Festival and at other concerts and festivals. His advice was eagerly sought by festival committees, and during the sixties he served as a member of the board of advisers of the Mountain Dance and Folk Festival (Asheville, North Carolina). He was also among the founders of the Newport Folk Foundation and one of the members of the festival's board of directors.

His constant search for genuine folk songs led to extensive recording trips in England, Scotland, and Ireland; he made complete recording surveys of Spanish and Italian folk music; he produced thirty documentary radio programs on folk music for the BBC in London; and he lectured on folklore at Indiana University, the University of Chicago, the University of Texas, and New York University. During the mid-fifties, he was editor of the Columbia Records World Library of Folk and Primitive Music and was responsible for the production of a nineteen-volume set of records of traditional material. In 1960–61 he was coeditor of a ten-LP set on Folk Music of Great Britain, released by Caedmon Records, and collector and editor of a seven-LP set on the Southern Folk Music Heritage, issued by Atlantic Records. In 1961 he became a research associate in the Department of Anthropology at Columbia University, and was the recipient of a Rockefeller Foundation grant in 1961 and 1962. Since 1963 he has been engaged in the systematic classification of world song styles (cantometrics) and of world dance styles (choreometrics).

Alan Lomax has recorded a number of albums for such labels as Kapp and Tradition; and he is the author of numerous articles and books on folk music, which, in addition to the works which he coauthored with his father, include *Mister Jelly Roll* (1949), *The Rainbow Sign* (1959), *Folk Songs of North America* (1960), *Penguin Book of American Folk Songs* (1961), *Folk Song Style and Culture* (1968), and *3000 Years of Black Poetry*, with R. Abdul (1969). (*See also* The Archive of Folk Song; John A. Lomax.)

# John A. Lomax
*Folklorist, collector, lecturer, honorary consultant and head of the Archive of Folk Song (1937–42), educator, and author*

In the pioneering spirit of the Lomax family, John A. Lomax broke new ground in American folk music scholarship with the same dedication displayed by his ancestors when they ventured to America as early settlers. A Harvard scholar who was motivated by America's vast treasure in music, he journeyed on horseback, by rail, by car, and often on foot in search of folk songs.

John Avery Lomax was born on September 23, 1875, in Goodman, Mississippi, and he was raised in the American Southwest. Early in his life, he listened with interest to the songs heard in that area of the country and copied down lyrics and melodies which were known by local inhabitants and traveling musicians who passed through the region. Near the turn of the twentieth century, he packed up his assortment of collected notations and folk material and traveled to Austin to attend the University of Texas. During his college years, he was informed by an English professor, Dr. Morgan Callaway, Jr., that his material was of inconsequential value, so he temporarily put it aside. In 1897 he earned a BA degree and proceeded to substantiate his qualifications as an English instructor by studying at the University of Chicago in

1903 and 1906, while simultaneously enrolled at the University of Texas, where he **earned his MA degree in 1906. As the recipient of an Austin Teaching Scholarship, he** entered Harvard University, where, in 1907, he earned another master's degree in American literature.

Through one of his Harvard instructors, Barrett Wendell, he met folklorist George Lyman Kittredge, who encouraged Lomax to continue collecting folk material. For the rest of his life, he pursued this interest, which he then passed along to his own children. Lomax returned to the Southwest and, with **the financial assistance of a Shelden Travelling Fellowship, worked for three years doc**umenting folk material with an Ediphone cylinder recording machine. The publishing firm of Sturgis & Walton contracted for his work, and in 1910 *Cowboy Songs and Other Frontier Ballads* was published with the texts of 122 songs—18 with music. The book was highly praised and compared in its importance to the monumental Child Ballads of the nineteenth century.

John A. Lomax kept the study of folklore as an avocation. From 1903 to 1910 he was an associate professor of English at Texas A&M College, and from 1910 to 1917 served as secretary of the University of Texas in Austin. In 1917 another volume of songs (collected on his first recording trip) was published, entitled *Songs of the Cattle Trail and Cow Camp*. Until 1933 he was involved in the banking business, and folk music remained on the sidelines. When the Depression caused his bank to fail, he went to contract with a publisher in hopes of offsetting his monetary loss by producing another volume of songs. Along with his seventeen-year-old son Alan, John A. Lomax headed for the Southern states to collect folk songs of black convicts. In midsummer of 1933 his request for assistance from the Library of Congress came in the form of a 315-pound portable recording machine—complete with Edison batteries, a rotary converter, amplifiers, a double-button carbon microphone, a dynamic speaker, and cutting and reproduc-

ing heads—which he mounted in his Ford sedan. The Lomaxes embarked on their collecting-recording trip through Louisiana, Mississippi, Kentucky, and Tennessee, and in 1934 *American Ballads and Folk Songs* was published by Macmillan. In the same year John A. Lomax was requested by officials at the Library of Congress to serve in Washington, D.C., as honorary consultant and head of the Archive of Folk Song. Along with his son, John A. Lomax helped to further the goals of the Archive by contributing more than three thousand disc recordings during the 1930s. During the next decade, John A. Lomax continued to produce scholarly works (many in collaboration with his son) and to lecture on folk music.

John A. Lomax died on January 26, 1948, in Greenville, Mississippi, leaving behind a legacy of printed and recorded material and **an insight into the importance and utilization of the Archive of Folk Song in the pursuit of folk music. (***See also* **The Archive of Folk Song; Alan Lomax.)**

**Joseph Lopez.** *See* The Louisiana Aces.

**The Lost Gonzo Band.** *See* Jerry Jeff Walker.

## The Louisiana Aces

*Cajun dance band, performers, and recording artists*

A group of modern Cajun musicians from the Lafayette area of Louisiana, the Louisiana Aces have been together for over fifteen years. With the addition of electric steel guitar and drums to the more traditional instruments of this musical style, the Louisiana Aces introduce to Cajun music the influences of country & western stylings and honky-tonk songs.

The band was formed in 1950 by Elias

Badeaux, who, two years later, was joined by the "Cajun Hank Williams," D. L. Menard. They played together until 1967 and recorded eight (still available) sides for Swallow Records. After the band had broken up and its members had joined up with other bands, Dick Spottswood of the Archive of Folk Song in the Library of Congress encouraged D. L. Menard to reassemble the musicians for the 1973 National Folk Festival. That summer, Joseph Lopez, D. L. Menard, John Suire, Arconge Touchet, and Curley Veroney left the Bayou country for the first time, to make an appearance at the annual event at Wolf Trap Farm Park in Vienna, Virginia. They continued to work together on occasion, and, in the following year, the Louisiana Aces—Lionel LeLeux, D. L. Menard, Ervin "Dick" Richard, Marc Savoy, and John Suire—returned to perform at the 1974 National Folk Festival.

The band's personnel changes, and at various times has included Dewey Balfa on fiddle, Lionel LeLeux on fiddle, Joseph Lopez on fiddle, D. L. Menard on vocals and guitar, Dick Richard on steel (slide) guitar, Marc Savoy on accordion, John Suire on drums, Arconge Touchet on steel guitar, and Curley Veroney on accordion. The band members grew up together and still enjoy fishing and hunting with one another. A renowned accordion maker, Marc Savoy often appears with other Cajun musicians, including S. D. (Sady) Courville, Dennis McGee, and the Balfa Freres. Lionel LeLeux has earned a living as a barber since he was ten, and he began fixing and making violins two years later. D. L. Menard is a chair manufacturer; John Suire is employed as a construction worker; Dick Richard is a foreman, and, on different occasions, he provides instrumental accompaniment for the Balfa Freres.

In August and September 1974, the Louisiana Aces participated in the National Folk Festival Association's State Department–sponsored tour of Central and South America—"Music of the People—USA." In the same year, an album recorded by the original band, entitled *The Louisiana Aces* (Rounder 6003), with Elias Badeaux, Joseph Lopez, D. L. Menard, John Suire, and Arconge Touchet, was issued by Rounder Records.

# Louisiana Hayride
*Weekly variety program originating on KWKH Radio in Shreveport, Louisiana*

By the end of World War II, country music was enjoying an unprecedented international popularity. Record company sales soared to new heights, and more and more radio stations were broadcasting country music. By the fall of 1949, *Billboard* magazine estimated that there were no less than 650 radio stations which aired live country music. Changes in scheduling were made, and instead of restricting the broadcasting of country music to the early-morning hours (as had been done in the early commercial years of country music), prime time was now partially devoted to this highly salable commodity. Among the barndance radio shows which were instituted during the postwar period was Shreveport's *Louisiana Hayride*, which proved to be one of the most significant offshoots of this country craze.

*Louisiana Hayride* was first broadcast on April 3, 1948, and within a few months' time, Hank Williams had joined the program; he remained in its cast until the following June (singing his classic rendition of "Lovesick Blues" on his closing night). Over the years, *Louisiana Hayride* grew in prominence and boasted such national personalities in the entertainment field as Johnny Cash, Johnny Horton, David Houston, Johnny and Jack, Webb Pierce, Elvis Presley, Jim Reeves, Red Sovine, Slim Whitman, Hank Williams, Faron Young, and many, many others.

The basic difference between *Louisiana Hayride* and the *Grand Ole Opry* was a substantial one. In principle, only established stars were invited on the *Opry*. The

*Hayride*, on the other hand, welcomed newcomers and accented this policy to such an extent that it took on the subtitle "Cradle of the Stars." As a result of this policy, the *Hayride* attracted budding young talent from across the nation and began turning out stars on a monthly basis. The *Grand Ole Opry* remained the "Palace" of country music, and most of the *Hayride*'s early top talent left Shreveport to join the cast of Nashville's No. 1 country show. Many believe that had the *Hayride* developed the support services of recording studios, publishing houses, and booking agencies, Shreveport would have become what Nashville is today—the country music center of the nation. Another difference between the *Opry* and the *Hayride* is that while the *Opry* was (and still is) essentially an informal stage presentation, the *Hayride* adhered to a produced format that fitted the broadcast requirements of KWKH, and was primarily a radio broadcast show.

The first superstar of *Louisiana Hayride* was either Elvis Presley or Hank Williams. It remains an either/or proposition because Williams had been up and down the ladder of success, alternating between the *Opry* and the *Hayride*, each becoming disenchanted with the drinking habits of the now-immortal star.

Elvis Presley provided the key turning point in the history of the *Hayride*. He "exploded" on the *Hayride* stage with a hip-swiveling style of rock 'n' roll that attracted thousands of teenagers to the Municipal Auditorium. For eighteen months they squealed, they stormed the stage, and they swooned. This un-country-like conduct swept aside the old regulars, and even those who remained tried to adopt Elvis's mannerisms. As a result, the solid foundation of country music began to crumble, and the steady customers who came to hear Red Sovine and the Bailes Brothers drifted away. When Elvis left behind the country & western music world, the old regulars had also disappeared.

*Louisiana Hayride* was aired every Saturday night until the early sixties, when it was scheduled on a monthly basis. During the decade, performances were made by guest artists instead of a regular cast, and until 1974 the *Hayride* was a sporadic production.

In 1974 Shreveport businessman David Kent and veteran *Hayride* master of ceremonies Frank Page put the show back on a full-time operating basis by building a $750,000 auditorium-restaurant complex in Bossier City, Louisiana—across the river from Shreveport, where it all began.

The Saturday-night show is again aired on 50,000-watt KWKH Radio. Although the old format has been retained, *Louisiana Hayride* is involved in publishing, recording, and artist management.

## Trevor Lucas. *See* Fairport Convention.

## Cary Lung. *See* The Sweets Mill String Band.

## Bascom Lamar Lunsford

*Old-time singer, banjoist, fiddler, songwriter, performer, recording artist, collector, and founder of the Mountain Dance and Folk Festival (Asheville, North Carolina)*

A prominent representative of the Southern mountain music tradition, Bascom Lamar Lunsford was once described as the "Minstrel of the Appalachians." Despite his diversity of achievements—as attorney, teacher, politician, newspaper editor, auctioneer, and fruit tree salesman—music always played a central role in his life.

Bascom Lamar Lunsford was born on March 21, 1882, in Mars Hill, North Carolina. Throughout his lifetime, he collected folk material in the Smoky Mountain region, and he played the five-string banjo in a typical North Carolina picking style, which emphasizes the use of the index finger, as opposed to the thumb, as the vital element and lead. In 1924 he made his initial commercial recording on the Okeh label with "I Wish I Was a Mole in the Ground," which he later recorded for Brunswick (1928) and for Folkways (1953). His subsequent recording efforts included several sides on 78-RPM discs, a number of Folkways and Riverside albums, and several hundred songs for such major collections as the Archive of Folk Song in the Library of Congress, the Columbia University Library, and the Frank C. Brown Collection (Duke University).

In 1927 he organized the first Mountain Dance and Folk Festival, in Asheville, North Carolina, which remains one of the major events related to the preservation of traditional American folk music and dance to this day. He also played an instrumental role in organizing other festivals around the country, including the Renfro Valley Festival in Kentucky (with John Lair) and the North Carolina State Fair Folk Festival in Raleigh.

His best-known composition is probably "That Good Old Mountain Dew," written in 1921.

Bascom Lamar Lunsford died on September 4, 1973, at the age of ninety-one. (*See also* Mountain Dance and Folk Festival.)

# Lute

The lute is a stringed instrument which dates back in origin to Mesopotamia of 2000 B.C., when it was constructed with a small egg-shaped body and a long fretted neck. By the time the lute had spread to Egypt, around 1500 B.C., it had assumed an almond or oval shape, and its only players are thought to have been women. The Greek and Roman models were similar in design. A descendant of the Egyptian model is still used today in northwest Africa.

The short-necked lute is the more recently developed of the two types, and evidence of this version is found on Persian clay figurines of the eighth century A.D. Unlike the long-necked type, with a neck much longer than the body, the neck of the short-necked variety is slightly shorter than its body. Traces of its existence have been found in both India and China, developed many centuries after the Persian lute, and its characteristics resemble those of Near and Far Eastern and European lutes. The Arabs are credited with the introduction to Europe of the classical lute, which had reached France by the mid-thirteenth century. The fifteenth century saw the addition of a fifth treble string and fretted neck; and by the mid-seventeenth century a system of tuning had been introduced by lutanist Denis Gaultier which was generally accepted as a standard tuning.

The lute is shaped like a half pear; its body is round, but the soundboard is flat, with a hole in its center. The strings are suspended over the neck, which is situated between the pegbox (or tuning head) and the body. Distinctions are made between bowed (violin-like), plucked, short-necked, and long-necked lutes.

A descendant of the lute, the modern guitar superseded the lute's popularity (it was used extensively in Europe until the end of the eighteenth century) as an instrument for the accompaniment of folk songs.

# Mel Lyman. *See* The Jim Kweskin Jug Band.

## Margaret MacArthur

*Vocalist, instrumentalist, Vermont folklorist, performer, and recording artist*

Born in Chicago, Margaret Crowl MacArthur spent her childhood moving around the country with her family, and singing in the car with her father established the foundation for her interest in music: "I suppose this started me really thinking about the beauty of music with two voices blending to sing melody and harmony." When she was about eight, her family moved to Licking, Missouri, near the Arkansas border, and, like most of the places they moved to in those years, they lived out of town in isolated circumstances: "The only contacts that I had outside of my family were at school, and when I was in the fourth and fifth grades, I used to team up with some boys who sang and played guitar, and this was my first singing with instrumental accompaniment.

"If I had stayed in Missouri, I probably would have become a country & western singer because that music became an important influence in the Ozarks, but when I was sixteen, I went to the University of Chicago. Later, I married John MacArthur, a physicist, and we moved to Vermont, where I became interested in collecting folk music of New England. This changed my idea of the poetry that I wanted to study, and the songs that I've learned have poetry that is important to me because it's either beautiful or tells a story that I like."

Margaret MacArthur's favorite songs are those of her adopted home, Vermont. Many of these songs might have been lost if she had not perpetuated the folk process by collecting them from the traditional singers of the area. MacArthur has also collected songs in western Kentucky, where her parents finally settled.

In 1951 the shy young singer started working professionally when she and Barbara Dretzin provided all the music for a Brattleboro radio station every Friday night. She made her first record in 1960 for Folkways, *Folksongs of Vermont* (Folkways FH5314), with her husband, John, playing banjo on one cut. In 1971 she and her family recorded *On the Mountains High* (LVF 100) for Living Folk Records in Boston, with her sons Gary on fiddle and Dan on guitar, her husband on banjo, and everyone singing on choruses, including her daughter Megan and her son Patrick. She accompanies herself on the Appalachian dulcimer, and on a small hand-held harp found in a local barn.

Her most recent album, *The Old Songs*, was recorded with Dan for Philo Records.

## Leon McAuliffe

*Steel guitar player, performer, and recording artist*

Best known as the first full-time steel guitarist in any country & western band, Leon McAuliffe joined Bob Wills and his Texas Playboys early in 1935.

Born in Houston in 1917, McAuliffe began playing the guitar at fourteen, then, strongly influenced by the duet Jim and Bob, he was drawn to the steel guitar. In 1933 McAuliffe got his first job, with W. Lee O'Daniel, the former sponsor of Bob Wills's original group, the Light Crust Doughboys. Two years later, when he played with the Texas Playboys, the band's recording of "Steel Guitar Rag" became a steel guitar hit and did more to popularize the role of that instrument in country & western music than any other single record. McAuliffe established a reputation by maintaining a stand-up, standard steel style, and since 1950 he has used a Fender electric guitar with four eight-stringed necks. Through his influence, the steel guitar has become a standard lead instrument in country & western music.

His 33-RPM recordings include *Take It Away, Leon* (Stoneway STY 139) and *Mr. Western Swing* (Pine Mountain PMR 271).

# Owen McBride

*Singer of traditional Irish music, guitarist, performer, and recording artist*

Now a commercial artist by profession, Owen McBride first became interested in Irish songs and ballads when he was living in Dublin and frequently spent his evenings at a local coffeehouse. This interest was further developed when he later attended a folk festival: "There were all sorts of singers, dancers, fiddlers, and pipers, and it was there that I really got interested in Irish music." McBride traveled around his native countryside for about six months, collecting songs, about the same time that Liam Clancy was moving about through Ireland for the same reason. While he traveled, McBride used to sing in public houses in return for a few drinks: "One time, I was in a pub in Tipperary. I had met this farmer in a pub ten or fifteen miles down the road, and he came up to this pub because I was singing up there this night. He had to leave early, but he left his donkey and cart with the back loaded with straw. I don't remember actually leaving the pub, but I think I was carried out and thrown in the back of the cart, and a man hit

Owen McBride performing in a workshop at Mariposa '75

the donkey with a stick and the animal brought me back to the farmer's house."

McBride emigrated to Canada, and he sang at the Bohemian Embassy in Toronto. Estelle Klein, the artistic director of the Mariposa Folk Festival, happened to be there, and McBride was invited to sing at the festival. He has appeared at Mariposa many times since then, and, in fact, he has performed at more Mariposa festivals than any other artist; he adds: "It is because of Mariposa, basically, that I've gotten the exposure that I've had.

"I'm a commercial artist, but I would like to sing professionally, full-time. However, traditional music is a specialty music, it hasn't got a very wide appeal, although it's getting wider. So it makes it literally impossible to do it for a living. I'm in the beautiful position of working from nine to five, and being able to sing my music the way I want to sing it without having to be commercial, and that's what I love about it."

Owen McBride's first solo album, *Owen McBride* (Philo 1005), consists of Irish ballads and songs recorded with his own guitar accompaniment. McBride attempted to include those traditional songs which are difficult to find, and traditional Irish music fans welcomed this collection of ancient tunes. He hopes to make another album: "I want to make a live album next because I much prefer to sing to an audience."

# Ewan MacColl

*Singer, songwriter, collector, performer, recording artist, author, and playwright*

A native of Scotland now residing in London, Ewan MacColl has made a significant contribution to folk music on both sides of the Atlantic Ocean. A traditional and revival singer, he has been recorded internationally, has written numerous articles on folk music, and is considered by many to be an expert in the field.

Born on January 25, 1915, in Auchterarder, Perthshire, he spent most of his childhood in Salford, Lancashire. His father was an iron molder, and from his parents, both Lowland Scots, he learned a myriad of songs, melodies, and stories. He left school at the age of fourteen and worked at various jobs, including motor mechanic, factory worker, street singer, and so on. Prior to World War II he became involved in a number of experimental theater projects, and in 1945 MacColl and an associate, Joan Littlewood, formed the Theater Workshop in London. For the next seven years he was the resident dramatist, writing eight plays, and art director of the company. Five of his plays have been translated into German, French, Polish, and Russian, and they have

been produced in those languages and have run in the principal cities of Germany, France, Poland, and the U.S.S.R.

In 1950 MacColl turned his attention to traditional music and played a key role in initiating and promoting the British folk song revival. He was among the first to recognize the importance of the folk club as a basic unit in this revival, and he was instrumental in the founding of the Ballads and Blues Club (later to become the Singers Club), now the leading folk club in England. By the latter fifties, he was acknowledged to be one of the foremost singers and major theorists of the revival.

In 1957 MacColl (in collaboration with his wife, Peggy Seeger, and Charles Parker) was commissioned by BBC Radio to write a documentary program called *The Ballad of John Axon*. This program, comprising recorded speech, sound effects, new songs in the folk idiom, and folk instrumentation, was the first in a series of eight such "radio-ballads," six of which have been issued by Argo Records.

Ewan MacColl's work in television and films is extensive and covers a broad range of entertainment, education, and documentation. He has written scripts and music for BBC films, commercial television, the National Coal Board, and many independent film companies and organizations. Between 1965 and 1971, he devoted a large portion of his time to the training of young singers in both singing and theater techniques to create a foundation from which a folk theater could be developed.

In addition to his other activities, MacColl has been an active collector and has collaborated in the production of several folk song anthologies; he is currently engaged (with Peggy Seeger) in the preparation of three scholarly folk song collections. As leader of the influential group of singers and songwriters known as the Critics Group, Ewan MacColl has worked with Frankie Armstrong, Peggy Seeger, and others in dealing with problems of content, style, and performance of traditional material. Primarily a workshop group, London's Critics Group also focuses attention on theater accompaniment, politics, and composing (the words and music of "Grey October," for example, are by the Critics Group), and they have recorded several LPs.

In England, MacColl has been recorded by English Decca, H.M.V., and Topic; in Australia, Wattle Records has sponsored his appearances. American record companies that have presented his work include Folk-Lyric, Folkways, Riverside, Rounder, Stinson, Tradition, and Vanguard. Many of his recordings have been made with Peggy Seeger, including his recent *At the Present Moment* (Rounder 4003).

Ewan MacColl has composed many songs in the folk idiom, including "The First Time Ever I Saw Your Face," which won the 1973 Grammy Award for Song of the Year (in England it was the recipient of the Ivor Novello Award). (*See also* Peggy Seeger.)

## Carl McConnell. *See* The Addington Family; The Carter Family; Maybelle Carter.

## Cathal McConnell. *See* The Boys of the Lough.

## Charlie McCoy

*Nashville studio musician, performer, and recording artist*

Charlie McCoy established his reputation as a harmonica player in the early sixties, when he played as a sideman on several demo sessions. As Nashville's producers started to hear this new talent, it was not long before the young musician was asked to perform his first recording session, playing the harmonica on Ann-Margret's first, and only, single: "Needless to say, I was scared to death, but I had something to go by because I had played the demo and they wanted it ex-

Charlie McCoy and his daughter, Ginger, at home in Madison, Tennessee

actly the same. Well, the record came out and it was a hit. . . ." The music that he put down that day marked the modest beginning of the fascinating and brilliant career of one of today's best-known studio musicians.

"My interest in music started when I was eight years old. I got a harmonica out of a comic book for fifty cents and a box top. Shortly after that, I got a guitar, and that became my main interest."

Influenced by rock 'n' roll, the popular musical craze of the fifties, McCoy started hearing records with harmonica, and this, in turn, cultivated an interest in blues: "Late one night, I happened to hear a Nashville radio station, WLAC, that played nothing but blues every night. They sold mail-order records, almost all of which had harmonica on them, so I started buying records from Nashville."

While in high school, McCoy had one of the hottest rock 'n' roll bands in Miami, and, with the money he won in a local contest, he bought a bus ticket to Nashville. Unable to establish himself as a musician during his first trip to Music City, he returned after his first year of college: "The one thing I had remembered on my first trip to Nashville was a recording session, with Brenda Lee, that I had been allowed to watch, and I remembered that session. After my disappointment with college, I decided I would go back to Nashville to be a guitar player and try to be a singer, and, if I have to work for somebody else as a musician, that's fine, because that's what I want to do."

Today, Charlie McCoy owns two hundred harmonicas and plays about four hundred recording sessions every year. He has been a top sideman for just about everyone: "I've worked with artists on both ends of the spectrum—Perry Como, Vicki Carr, Ringo Starr, Bob Dylan, Joan Baez, Buffy Sainte-Marie, and Elvis." In addition to guitar and harmonica, McCoy is proficient on piano, organ, bass, trumpet, sax, marimba, and vibraphone.

After a decade of working as a sideman, McCoy is now becoming known as a solo artist: "It took all this time of doing sessions, backing up other people, to develop my own style." He has recorded, and produced, several albums for Monument Records, including *The Real McCoy* (Z-31329), *Charlie McCoy* (KZ-31910), *Good Time Charlie* (KZ-32215), *Fastest Harp in the South* (KZ-32749), and *The Nashville Hit Man* (KZ-32922).

"I'm playing a few concerts, and I'm still working my sessions every week, and I'm making my own records, which, to me, is the most satisfying thing I've ever done."

## Tom McCreesh. *See* Fennig's All-Star String Band.

## Ed McCurdy

*Singer, songwriter, guitarist, writer and performer for radio and television, entertainer, and recording artist*

One of the most recorded and prominent figures of the folk movement of the 1950s and early 1960s, Ed McCurdy became as well known for his rich baritone as for his interpretations of Elizabethan ballads, early English folk songs, and traditional folk music. As a songwriter, he is probably best known for the composition "Last Night I Had the Strangest Dream," but his talents have not been limited to folk music and he has produced songs and stories for children.

A native of Pennsylvania, Ed McCurdy was born on January 11, 1919, in Willow Hill. Although he grew up in a relatively isolated rural area in the Northeast, his exposure to folk music was extensive. After one semester at Panhandle A&M College, McCurdy transferred to Oklahoma Central State College, but as he became more convinced that he wanted to pursue a musical career, he abandoned his formal education and never earned his degree.

He had learned to play guitar, and his first professional employment was as a singer at WKY Radio in Oklahoma City, in 1937. McCurdy studied and listened with enthusiasm to all music, and his repertoire broadened with children's songs, lusty ballads of the American West, his own compositions, and English folk songs and ballads.

He moved to Canada in the mid-forties and started in radio in March 1946, singing folk songs over the Canadian Broadcasting Corporation network. Soon he was performing on television and making personal appearances, and he recorded his first album for a Canadian company, Whitehall. In 1952 he commenced writing and performing for children on Canadian radio and television programs and, in late 1954, moved to New York City.

He became involved in a diversity of activities, including conducting a children's

Ed McCurdy (left) and Erik Darling

television show, contributing music to *The Ballad Book*, by Dr. MacEdward Leach, and the recording of ballads for an album on the Riverside label. In the late fifties and sixties, McCurdy recorded numerous albums for various companies, including Tradition, Elektra, and Prestige/International, and he was one of the most prolific recording artists of that period.

Beginning in 1955 Ed McCurdy was part of the CBS television production *Camera Three*, and in 1959 he was invited to perform at his first Newport Folk Festival, returning in 1960 and 1963. In the early sixties, McCurdy emceed Tuesday-evening jam sessions at the Bitter End, in Greenwich Village, and he was instrumental in bringing together both established and new talent.

Before his career was interrupted in 1966 due to a serious illness, McCurdy had re-recorded for over eight Canadian and American record companies. On many occasions he was accompanied on banjo and guitar by Erik Darling, who organized the Tarriers in 1956.

In April 1976 he made a three-week tour of Germany and Switzerland, and he plans to schedule other concerts and tours in the future.

## Fred McDowell

*Blues singer, guitarist, performer, and recording artist*

The decade of the 1950s witnessed the beginning of a new wave of interest in document-

241

ing American blues, and within a matter of a few years, the rediscovery of blues musicians reached an unprecedented height. While Samuel B. Charters was actively researching and interviewing country bluesmen in the South in 1959, Alan Lomax was engaged in field work that yielded the final recordings of Forest City Joe Pugh and the initial tapes by Fred McDowell.

Born in 1905 in Rossville, Tennessee, Fred McDowell spent over a decade in Memphis before moving on to Como, Mississippi, in 1940. Considered by many to have been among the last great bottleneck guitarists from Mississippi, Fred McDowell enjoyed a brief but substantial period of recognition throughout the sixties. His first recordings, made by Alan Lomax, generated enthusiasm for his music, and he received numerous invitations to appear at major festivals (including Newport), clubs, and concerts both in the United States and abroad. Blues enthusiasts in Europe and Great Britain created an expanded market for the genre, and, in fact, they witnessed more live performances by blues artists than most American aficionados ever experienced. Although his reputation spread widely and his two European tours were met with success, Fred McDowell always came back to his Mississippi home to perform for his personal acquaintances at social gatherings and country suppers.

Fred McDowell recorded for several companies, and his work can be heard on such labels as Arhoolie, Biograph, Everest, and Testament. Like Rev. Gary Davis, Fred McDowell is remembered for talking to his guitar in the midst of an instrumental break. During his live performances, he would rock back in his seat, bring his bottleneck up on the fretboard, and say: "Do it now . . . do it . . . you can play that thing."

He died of cancer on June 3, 1972, in Memphis, at the age of sixty-eight.

# Wilcil McDowell. *See* The Irish Rovers.

# Kate and Anna McGarrigle

*Singer-songwriters, instrumentalists, performers, and recording artists*

A sister team of singer-songwriters from Montreal, Kate and Anna McGarrigle made their first mark on the folk scene as participants in that city's initial "folk boom" in the early 1960s. More recently, they have attracted considerable attention with their original compositions—sometimes written jointly, often separately—recorded by such other artists as Linda Ronstadt (who used Anna's "Heart Like a Wheel" as the title track of one of her recent albums) and Maria Muldaur (who included Anna's "Cool River" and Kate's "Work Song" as selections on two of her albums).

The McGarrigles' background is steeped in a diversity of Canadian material, and while growing up in a French household, they learned many traditional tunes in both French and English. Along with their sister Jane, with whom they performed briefly as the McGarrigle Sisters, they sang in multipart harmony with their parents and played a wide assortment of instruments found around their home—piano, zither, ukelele, guitar, banjo, fiddle, and "squeeze box."

By the time the McGarrigle Sisters made their initial public appearance (as last-minute entrants in a talent contest) in the summer of 1958, the family had moved from the small Laurentian village of St.-Sauveur-des-Monts in Quebec to Montreal. As high school students, Kate and Anna performed as a trio with a friend named Michele Forest in local coffeehouses, at college concerts, and on CBC-TV. When Kate was a senior, she and her sister joined up with Peter Weldon and Jack Nissenson to form the Mountain City Four. At this point, their scope of material broadened to include, among others, the songs of Woody Guthrie, Leadbelly, Bob Dylan, and Rev. Gary Davis, along with French *chansons*, blues, and gospel tunes. They gained considerable acceptance in Montreal, and other folk musicians would often join or replace the four

Kate (left) and Anna McGarrigle at Mariposa '75

core figures during performances by the Mountain City Four.

In 1967 Kate and Anna McGarrigle were commissioned by the National Film Board of Canada to compose a song for the centennial film *Helicopter Canada*, which was nominated for an Academy Award. Within the next few years, their emergence as songwriters was soon followed by an interest in their material among other entertainers. The 1972 recording by McKendree Spring of "Heart Like a Wheel" was subsequently used in the soundtrack of the film *Play It as It Lays*. During the early seventies, Kate became a resident of the United States and

for a year lived in Saratoga Springs, New York, and performed in coffeehouses and at festivals with guitar and cello accompanist Roma Baran. After Kate relocated to New York City and worked intermittently as a solo performer, she was joined regularly in 1974 and 1975 by Anna. Together they played gigs at the Golem in Montreal; the Towne Crier in Beekman, New York; Caffé Lena in Saratoga Springs, New York; the Ark in Ann Arbor, Michigan; the Mainpoint in Bryn Mawr, Pennsylvania; and Mariposa '75 in Toronto. In January 1976 Warner Brothers released their first album, *The McGarrigle Sisters* (Warner Brothers BS

2862), composed almost entirely of their own songs.

Kate lives with her husband, Loudon Wainwright III, in New York City, while Anna resides in an Alexandria, Ontario, farmhouse.

# The McGee Brothers

*Old-time country music pioneers, original stars of the* Grand Ole Opry, *vocalists, instrumentalists and recording artists*

Sam McGee and his younger brother of five years, Kirk McGee, are among the best-known names of the early days of country music. On the same night in 1925, the McGee Brothers and Uncle Dave Macon joined the *Grand Ole Opry*, which was in its first month of existence on WSM Radio in Nashville, Tennessee.

Of English-Irish descent, Sam McGee was born on May 1, 1894, and Kirk McGee was born on November 4, 1899, on the family farm near Franklin, Tennessee. Their father was a talented fiddler, and when he was twelve years old Sam was given a five-dollar banjo, which he used to accompany local fiddlers. Kirk McGee used to listen for hours while his father and older brother played fiddle and banjo, and in a few years he was playing, too. While in their teens, the family moved to Perry, in central Tennessee, and the boys had the opportunity of encountering black street musicians, whose syncopated guitar playing influenced their music. Sam McGee was among the first to incorporate the instrumental breaks and runs of the blues into the basic guitar accompaniment style of country music.

In 1923, they heard their first professional performance by a country musician who traveled to their hometown schoolhouse, Uncle Dave Macon. The McGees invited Macon and his fiddler, Sid Harkreader, to spend the night at their house, where Sam was asked by Uncle Dave Macon to play a few tunes on his guitar. Macon was impressed with his ability, and the following year Sam McGee joined Macon's troupe and traveled to New York to record with one of country music's most prominent entertainers.

Kirk McGee joined his brother and Uncle Dave Macon in 1925, and they began their performances on WSM's brand-new show, the *Grand Ole Opry*. They toured with the WSM road shows, which included country musicians heard on the Saturday night broadcasts, and in 1928 the McGee Brothers made their initial contact with Gennett recording company of Richmond, Indiana. They made several records, including the solo guitar classic by Sam McGee, "The Railroad Blues," which reflects the influence of the Perry street musicians who were responsible for making the guitar Sam McGee's chief instrument.

They formed a trio with Fiddlin' Arthur Smith in 1930, and their new group, the Dixieliners, became a popular road show and *Grand Ole Opry* act. They never recorded together, but the McGees made **recordings with Uncle Dave Macon, and Smith recorded with the Delmore Brothers. Prior to World War II, Smith left the trio,** and Sam and Kirk McGee started doing a comedy act as part of a tent show that toured with Bill Monroe and the Blue Grass Boys. The McGees continued to appear regularly on the *Grand Ole Opry*, and they toured frequently. Each of the brothers was pursuing an occupation aside from music; Kirk was in the real estate business and Sam ran a farm, which was the focal point of his personal life from 1945 to 1955, when he was devoting his energies to its development. The *Grand Ole Opry* had undergone many changes—influenced by Roy Acuff's shift in emphasis to vocals and vocalists, and Bob Wills's introduction of instruments such as the saxophone, trumpet and drums, in the early 1940's—and in 1955 a confrontation developed between the McGees and new *Opry* personnel. After speaking with the owner of National Life and of the *Opry*, Edwin W. Craig, it was decided that the old-time musicians would continue to perform their basic traditional music as members of the *Grand Ole Opry.*

In the late 1950s, as the folk revival became increasingly popular, renewed attention was given to old-time music, and the McGee Brothers were "rediscovered." They were performing as sidemen for Grandpa Jones at the time, and, in 1957, Mike Seeger traveled to Nashville to urge that the brothers record an album. *The McGee Brothers and Arthur Smith* (Folkways FA 2379) reunited them with the third member of their original group, the Dixieliners, and the LP marked their first recording as a trio. The success of the initial album brought about a second recording by the McGees and Fiddlin' Arthur Smith, *Milk 'Em in the Evening Blues* (Folkways FTS 31007). The trio was sponsored by the Newport Folk Foundation in a series of concerts held in several major cities, including New York, Boston, and Philadelphia, and they appeared at the Newport Folk Festival and the Festival of American Folklife in Washington, D.C.

Sam McGee recorded a solo album, *Grand Dad of the Country Guitar Pickers* (Arhoolie 5012), and a now-out-of-print album was made by Sam and Kirk McGee and the Crook Brothers on the Starday label. With the support of friends, the McGees started producing their own records—a practice which has become increasingly popular among folk artists over the years—and two albums were recorded, *Pillars of the Grand Ole Opry* (MBA Records MBA-6078) and *Flat-Top Pickin' Sam McGee* (MBA Records MBA-606-S). Fortunately, many hours of Sam McGee's guitar playing were recorded on tape by his lifelong friend, Fuller Arnold, who was one of the major forces behind the inception of MBA Records and had the foresight to document the older brother's music before McGee's arthritis affected the agility of his fingers.

The original version of "Railroad Blues" by Sam McGee was recorded on *Mountain Blues* (County 511), and his original version of "Knoxville Blues" is included on *Old-Time Mountain Guitar* (County 523). The McGees cut eight selections on *Uncle Dave Macon, Early Recordings* (County 521); and "When the Train Comes Along," with the McGees and Uncle Dave Macon, is featured on *Songs of the Railroad* (Vetco LP 103). An album was recorded on the Guest Star label, *Whoop 'Em Up, Cindy* (1501), and on Starday, *Opry Old Timers* (Starday SLP 182); and two selections by Sam McGee appear on *Mr. Charlie's Blues* (Yazoo L-1024).

Sam McGee died tragically on August 21, 1975, when he suffered multiple injuries in a tractor accident on his 400-acre farm in Williamson County, Tennessee. (*See also* Uncle Dave Macon; Fiddlin' Arthur Smith.)

# Dennis McGee

*Old-style Cajun fiddler and vocalist, performer, and recording artist*

"I learned tunes from my daddy that are one hundred fifty to two hundred years old. There are lots of tunes I can play that nobody knows what they are."

The eighty-two-year-old Dennis McGee has become a legend in his own time. Interest in the traditional Cajun musician was renewed a few years ago by the rediscovery of his first 78 RPM discs recorded with S. D. Courville in 1928 on the old Vocalion label. McGee made other recordings, with fiddler Ernest Fruge in 1929 and with Amadie Ardoin during the thirties. McGee performed at the 1974 National Folk Festival, accompanied by S. D. Courville, who had played the second fiddle on the 1928 recording of "Mon Cherie Bebe Creole," which has been reissued on *Louisiana Cajun Music, Volume 1—First Recordings: The 1920s* (Old Timey X-108). His rendition of "Madame Young Donnez Moi Votre Jole Blonde" can be heard on *Louisiana Cajun Music, Volume 5—The Early Years: 1928–1938* (Old Timey X-114), and collector Richard Nevins is planning a full reissue LP of McGee's early recordings. His first recordings with S. D. Courville are also scheduled to be rereleased on the Morningstar label.

A retired barber who plays fiddle as a pastime, McGee has entertained numerous fans in the Mamou, Louisiana, area when he has appeared as a guest of S. D. Courville and Revon Reed on their radio show, *The Mamou Hour.* He and Courville were invited to perform at the 1972 National Folk Festival, and again in the following year. In 1974 they returned to the National Folk Festival with Nathan Abshire and Revon Reed; and McGee and Courville appeared with accordionist Marc Savoy at the Mariposa Folk Festival in 1975. (*See also* Nathan Abshire; S. D. [Sady] Courville.)

# Kirk McGee. *See* The McGee Brothers.

# Sam McGee. *See* The McGee Brothers.

# Brownie McGhee

*Blues singer, guitarist, pianist, jazz-horn player, songwriter, performer, and recording artist*

Brownie McGhee is one of the best-known personalities on the American folk music scene, and his partnership with singer and harp player Sonny Terry has been one of the most productive and durable in the history of the blues. Highly acclaimed as a guitarist, Brownie McGhee also capably provides instrumental accompaniment on the piano or on the kazoo-trombone bell novelty instrument known as the "jazz-horn."

Born Walter Brown McGhee on November 30, 1915, in Knoxville, Tennessee, he was introduced to the blues by his father,

who was a singer and country guitarist and often accompanied the fiddle playing of an uncle, John Evans, at local social gatherings. The four-year-old Brownie McGhee was stricken with polio, after the birth of his brother Granville "Sticks," and, unable to perform rigorous physical tasks, turned to music. His parents separated when he was six, and his song "Born with the Blues" is based on this personal life experience. When his father moved his children farther south into rural Tennessee, the young Brownie McGhee was raised amid the country music sounds of guitars, banjos, and jew's harps. When bluesman T. T. Carter traveled through the little town of Kingsport, he deeply impressed the teenaged McGhee, and it is to this episode in his life that McGhee attributes his serious love for the guitar. Around 1935 that love was deepened when a successful operation on the polio-stricken McGhee eliminated a cane from his life— making his right leg only an inch and a quarter instead of five inches shorter than the left—and made it possible for him to carry his guitar and to seek his fortune as a musician.

During the thirties, McGhee organized a washboard band which included Robert Young ("Washboard Slim") and Leroy Dallas, who, many years later, played guitar with McGhee during a recording session in New York City. During his early years as an itinerant musician, he was joined by harmonica player Jordan Webb, and, in their wanderings through North Carolina, they met Blind Boy Fuller and Sonny Terry, with whom McGhee started "street playing."

From 1939 to 1942, Brownie McGhee was a recording artist for Okeh Records, and in 1944–45 he recorded for Savoy Records. He had followed Sonny Terry to New York City, where he met Woody Guthrie, Lee Hays, Leadbelly, Pete Seeger, and Josh White, and for two years he lived with Leadbelly and Sonny Terry in a loft at Eighth Street and Sixth Avenue. In 1941 the three musicians joined up with Woody Guthrie to form the

Brownie McGhee performing at the Lenox Music Barn, Connecticut, in July 1961

short-lived Headline Singers, and in 1942 Brownie McGhee made a memorable concert appearance with Paul Robeson. By 1945 he had raised sufficient funds to open a music school, called Home of the Blues, which remained in existence until 1960. When Sonny Terry joined *Finian's Rainbow*, Brownie McGhee formed a trio called the Three B's. His next group, Brownie McGhee and His Mighty House Rockers, included washboard, guitar, and piano (from the Three B's), with the addition of drums, bass, and saxophone. Playing the electric guitar with the Mighty Rockers, Brownie McGhee recorded "I Feel So Good" and "Brownie's Blues." One of his most successful early recordings was an original composition, "My Fault," which was a bestselling rhythm-and-blues hit in 1948.

Brownie McGhee appeared in the 1955 motion pictures *Face in the Crowd* and *Cat on a Hot Tin Roof*, with Sonny Terry. Throughout the fifties, the blues duo was a popular performing act at clubs, concerts, and festivals around the country. In addition to numerous radio and television appearances, Brownie McGhee and Sonny Terry recorded a multitude of albums. In January 1960 they made a State Department–sponsored tour of India and Nepal, and subsequent tours have taken them to Europe and Australia.

Recently added to the A&M roster of recording artists, Brownie McGhee also appears on such labels as Alert, Atlantic, Decca, Fantasy, Flyright, Folkways, Mainstream, Olympic, Prestige, Savoy, and Verve/Folkways. (*See also* Sonny Terry.)

## Michael McGinnis. *See* The New Christy Minstrels.

## Roger (Jim) McGuinn

*Contemporary singer, guitarist, five-string banjoist, songwriter, performer, and recording artist*

After touring as guitarist and five-string ban-joist with the Limeliters and then with the Chad Mitchell Trio, Roger McGuinn established a national reputation as the central figure in the Byrds, the influential folk-rock group of the mid-1960s to early 1970s. With his leadership, the Byrds established new guidelines in the synthesis of the musical genres of folk, rock, country, and country & western, and the Byrds paved the way for many of the groups that constituted the late-sixties musical scene in the United States.

While in his teens, James Roger McGuinn listened to folk music and traditional blues, and he learned to play guitar and five-string banjo. He played at a small club where he was heard by a member of the Limeliters, but he turned down an offer to join the group until after he had finished high school. He then toured with them as banjoist and guitarist and, shortly thereafter, was offered the same position with the Chad Mitchell Trio. His next job was with Bobby Darin, who hired McGuinn to back him up instrumentally during the "folk" segment of his club act.

McGuinn made his way to Greenwich Village, and he played on Judy Collins's third Elektra album, *Judy Collins #3* (EKS-7243). He picked up and traveled to Los Angeles, where he, David Crosby, and Gene Clark decided to form a band that would incorporate the amplified instrumentation of rock, as popularized by the Beatles' 1964 hit, "I Want to Hold Your Hand," with their roots in folk music. With Chris Hillman, Michael Clarke, and producer Jim Dickson, they recorded numerous tracks in the World Pacific Studios, but it wasn't until April 1973 that eleven of the cuts were released on *Preflyte* (Columbia KC 32183).

With the recording of Bob Dylan's "Mr. Tambourine Man," in 1965, the Byrds emerged as one of the most innovative groups of the decade. Their unique version of Dylan's classic song helped to revitalize folk music, and in June of that same year, *Mr. Tambourine Man* (CS 9172) was released, followed in December by *Turn, Turn, Turn* (CS 9254).

Known at the time as Jim McGuinn, the young leader of the Byrds was a forerunner of the adaptation of music to the technology of the space age. The Byrds' rock interpretations of folk music were labeled by the media as "folk-rock"; their other experimental works included "space music" and changing the forms of country and bluegrass by amplified presentation.

In total, the Byrds recorded fifteen albums before the group disbanded early in 1973. McGuinn composed the music for several movies—most notably, *Easy Rider*, for which he wrote the title song. One of the problems that plagued the Byrds throughout their existence was the incessant change of personnel, and even before the group reached its peak in 1970–71, McGuinn was the only remaining original member.

In 1973 McGuinn (now known as Roger McGuinn) embarked on a solo career, and by June of that year he had recorded his first album, *Roger McGuinn* (KC 31946). The following summer, his second LP, *Peace on You* (KC 32956), was released. He put together a new band of working road musicians and in 1975 recorded his third LP, *Roger McGuinn & Band* (Columbia PC 33541). During late 1975 and early 1976, he toured with Bob Dylan as a regular member of the Rolling Thunder Revue. (*See also* The Byrds.)

## Barry McGuire. *See* The New Christy Minstrels.

## Scott McKenzie. *See* The Journeymen.

## Murray McLauchlan

*Contemporary Canadian singer, songwriter, performer, and recording artist*

In Canada, this young singer-songwriter enjoys the status of an established artist with a devoted legion of fans, and although Murray McLauchlan has yet to make a dent in the American record charts, his fairly frequent tours in the United States have led to increased and better publicity for his music. His career is similar in many respects to those of both Bruce Cockburn and Gordon Lightfoot, whose popularity in their own country preceded recognition across the border. While Lightfoot was selling out Massey Hall in Toronto, his name was known in the United States only for having composed "Early Morning Rain"; and even though McLauchlan is a Canadian concert hall sell-out, he is usually known here for his "Child's Song."

Born in 1948 in Paisley, Renfrewshire, Scotland, Murray McLauchlan came to Canada with his family in the early fifties. He lived in Montreal for a while, and later in Toronto; as a young teenager, he started playing the guitar. After graduating from high school, he attended Central Tech in downtown Toronto to study art. Before long, he found himself in the company of young musicians in Yorkville, and Murray McLauchlan discovered an abundance of exciting music in this section of Toronto where about eight folk clubs were flourishing. He learned fingerpicking styles of playing guitar, and, with a nagging sense of adventure urging him to hit the road, he and his friend Nick Ipanovich followed in the footsteps of Woody Guthrie, riding freights, working in logging camps and sawmills, and picking fruit as they traveled across the continent.

McLauchlan began writing songs (his first was "Murray's Mountain"), and two of his works, "Child's Song" and "Old Man's Song," were recorded by an influential American performer, Tom Rush. By this time, he had taken up residence with Bruce Cockburn, whose career was running fairly parallel to McLauchlan's. Encouraged by his manager to take a vacation, McLauchlan headed south to Connecticut to try to put together a band with Tom Rush's guitarist Trevor Veitch. The venture failed, but he managed to get to Albert Grossman's office in New York, where he received an advance of several thousand dollars from this well-known music business manager. McLauchlan stayed in New York for four months to play some concerts and to increase his exposure with American audiences, and, when he returned to Toronto, his career finally took off.

His first album was released in Canada in the fall of 1971, and, by the following year, *Song from the Street* (E-31166) had been issued under the same title in the United States by American Epic. Similar in content to his initial effort, *Murray McLauchlan* (Epic KE-31902) includes "Billy McDaniels," "Big Bad City," and "No Time Together." In 1973 he had a smash single with "Farmer's Song," followed by "Hurricane of Change" and "Linda Wontcha." Toward the end of that same year, Epic released his third LP, *Day to Day Dust* (KE-32859), which became a top-selling Canadian record of 1973–74 and earned McLauchlan three Juno awards. He was recognized by the Canadian Music Industry as Composer of the Year, and "Farmer's Song" was declared Folk and Country Single of the Year.

By the mid-seventies, Murray McLauchlan had performed in a number of prestigious clubs throughout the United States, and a tour with Neil Young helped to pave the way for his fourth album, *Sweeping the Spotlight Away* (KE-33344).

# Don McLean

*Contemporary singer-songwriter, guitarist, banjoist, performer, and recording artist*

"I had done an enormous amount of work from 1968 to 1970. I was playing nightclubs all the time and opening other acts. I was always on tour with some big act and my name was around a lot and I was putting a lot of effort into it, and then 'American Pie' came out and I just went into outer space, it's just that simple.

"And then I began to ask myself, 'What's this all about?' It just seemed like a merry-go-round. I think that a lot of things began to come into focus, but the constant work made

Don McLean at his home

it very difficult to make up my own mind about what I wanted to do. Things had gotten out of control—bookings were so far in advance, and it seemed like my life was planned out of sight of the future that I could see, and that bothered me. All my life I had always just plodded along from job to job, and although that was very insecure, the other thing was more unsettling to me because I didn't like knowing where I was going to be next year."

Born in New Rochelle, New York, on October 2, 1945, Don McLean came from a family with no musical background, but he had a natural affinity for music. He always loved to sing and as a young boy spent hour after hour listening to records and the radio: "I was a singer since I was a little kid of four or five years old, and although I always wanted to sing, I didn't ever realize that I'd be a musician. All my life I had spent a lot of time listening to records, because I'd been sick when I was a kid and my whole life, more than I realized, revolved around listening to these records. I've since met a lot of people who were nuts about Little Richard or Elvis Presley or some other person, and they remember their whole youth spent with their ears just glued to their radio or their record player, and I was one of these people.

"But for about five or six years, from the time I was ten to about fifteen, I lost it. My voice changed, I couldn't sing, I forgot about music, and also, I was healthier by then, so I was living a normal life like any other kid. But then I heard the Weavers sing 'Wimoweh,' and again I was hooked. I couldn't stop listening, and I started collecting singles—I had Bo Diddley, and all those hits—and I had maybe twenty albums, all different kinds, nobody had albums, but I saved up all my money and got them. And Buddy Holly became an enormous influence on me, and every time I listen to him the same old feelings keep coming back.

"So, when I was fifteen I started playing a little bit on the ukelele, and my father convinced me that I should learn to play the guitar because it was a real instrument and the ukelele wasn't. So I bought myself a Harmony Sunburst and got a pickup and was in a couple of rock 'n' roll groups, but when I heard 'Wimoweh,' it pulled me away from that kind of music and I got into folk music—and I really got into it.

"I got into Brownie McGhee, Josh White, Leadbelly, Pete [Seeger] and the Weavers, Wade Ward, Roscoe Holcomb, all the commercial and noncommercial folksingers. At that time, of course, the music was booming, so there were tons of people around, and gradually, as I got older, I started going back to the other music that I had liked in the beginning. I didn't abandon my solo performing because I'd spent ten or twelve years learning how to do that. Instead, I adapted all the influences that I had, and I lost the folk musician's prejudice toward anything that doesn't have five strings, and I began to open my mind up to all the feelings that I had—all the memories that I had, all the music that I have loved—and from then on, I began to develop into what I am now."

McLean graduated from Iona Prep in New Rochelle and attended Villanova for half a year. He abandoned his formal education to work clubs, schools, and coffeehouses as a solo performer. He began gigs at Caffé Lena in Saratoga Springs, New York, in 1966, and, two years later, owner Lena Spencer recommended him to the New York State Council on the Arts to be the "Hudson River

Troubadour" and perform free concerts to arouse public awareness of ecology and community affairs. When Pege Seeger organized the Hudson River Sloop Restoration project to promote pollution control, he invited McLean to come aboard the sloop *Clearwater*.

His first album was turned down by almost thirty record companies. Ironically, one of the songs included on the LP, "And I Love You So," which was one of the main reasons why the album was incessantly rejected, has turned out to be McLean's most recorded song. It was finally issued by Mediarts, and shortly after the release of *Tapestry* (Mediarts 41-4), the company was taken over by United Artists. McLean continued touring throughout the country, working sporadically on "American Pie," which was completed early in 1971 and recorded in June of that same year. With the release of the song, and the album *American Pie* (United Artists UAS-5535), Don McLean was catapulted into superstardom. Another composition on the LP, "Vincent," was a hit in the United States and in England; McLean cites one of the highlights of his career as related to this song: "Aside from being No. 1 around the world, it's also in the Van Gogh Museum in Amsterdam, as part of their time capsule, and it's played in the entranceway."

In the fall of 1972, *Don McLean* (UAS 5651) was released; it contained his hit record "Dreidle," which depicts McLean's internal reaction to the instant fame and fortune brought on by "American Pie." A year later, McLean made an album with Frank Wakefield and other local Saratoga musicians, *Playin' Favorites* (UA-LA161-F); the LP includes bluegrass-rock material by writers other than McLean, and an attempt was made to expose the cross section of traditional, country, country-rock, and bluegrass roots in the music.

In an attempt to put his overnight commercial success into perspective, he "just took a year off and made the *Homeless Brother* [UA-LA315-G] album in 1974, and got reacquainted with friends that I had lost contact with for years that I was out there, and in 1975 I started doing some good hard work again."

One of the songs on the *Homeless Brother* LP, "The Legend of Andrew McCrew," was inspired by a story in *The New York Times* about a black hobo who died in 1913, was mummified, and was displayed as "the petrified man" in a carnival. He was finally buried in 1973, and as a result of McLean's recording, the fourth verse was adopted as the inscription for McCrew's headstone, which was donated by Bob Williams of Chicago's Jensen Corporation.

Don McLean has come full circle in his career, but his outlook is basically unchanged: "All the influences are always present, but to a lesser emphasis, because more influences are coming out. It's the same as in my life. I don't have the time to go to Lena's like I did, but I'll always play there because she was very important to me."

The friendship with Lena Spencer is typical of many of Don McLean's warm and personal relationships, and Lena Spencer expresses the confidence and admiration for him that remained unchanged during the difficult period of learning to cope with commercial success: "After the third or fourth time that he performed at the Caffé [Lena] he started writing songs, and the first time he sang his own songs, he wanted to know what I thought of them. So a highlight for me was to see what happened to Don and to see how it affected him as a person. He's a very beautiful person, and he was not affected at all by the things that have happened to him, in any negative way. He hasn't allowed all of this to really corrupt him, and still never fails to mention my name, and the Caffé Lena."

# Clayton "Pappy" McMichen.
*See* Gid Tanner and the Skillet Lickers.

# Uncle Dave Macon

*Pioneer country recording artist, star performer on WSM's Grand Ole Opry, singer, songwriter, and banjoist*

Today, increased scholarly and personal interest in country music has precipitated a rejuvenation of this musical form, with a significant outgrowth of new information, insights, recordings (including reissues), and critical acclaim for a growing number of artists in this field. Until recently, only one album and inadequate published material were available on one of the legendary figures in country music, Uncle Dave Macon. A beloved and well-known performer in the early years of country music, he suffered a lapse of interest in his art during the late forties, and it was not until fourteen years after his death that Uncle Dave Macon was elected by the Country Music Association to the Country Music Hall of Fame, on October 21, 1966, thus initiating a revived concern for the man and his music.

He was born David Harrison Macon on October 7, 1870, in Warren County, Tennessee, to Martha Ramsey and Captain John Macon, a farmer and ex-soldier in the Confederate army. In 1883 he moved with his family to Nashville, where his father had bought a hotel; from its theatrical clientele, the young boy heard songs, stories, and banjo music. He went to what is presently Hume-Fogg High School, married, and settled down in Kittrell, Tennessee. In 1900 he established a hauling firm, Macon Midway Mule and Wagon Transportation Company, with the central office at his farm.

His neighbors were often entertained by his banjo playing and his comic routines, but Uncle Dave Macon's talents went unremunerated until 1918. A talent scout for Loew's Theaters was impressed with Macon's act and booked him into a Birmingham, Alabama theater. From then on, the offers came pouring forth, and Uncle Dave Macon's career in show business was launched. By 1923 he was playing with fiddler Sid Harkreader, and they made their first recordings in New York in the summer of 1924. During this initial recording session, fourteen sides featuring Macon, assisted by Harkreader, were made; and in April 1925 twenty-eight more tunes were recorded. In the following year, he was asked to join the *WSM Barn Dance* (which was to become the *Grand Ole Opry*), and his combination of music and country yarns brought a new dimension to radio listeners, who were used to larger doses of instrumental renditions of dance tunes. He became one of the show's most popular performers and remained so for fifteen years.

He made his next recordings with guitarist Sam McGee, and in September 1926 he made twenty-eight solo recordings. In the same year, at the age of fifty-six, he became the *Grand Ole Opry*'s first singing star, and for fifteen years, he remained its most beloved single attraction. Some of his best recordings were made in the spring of 1927, with the Fruit Jar Drinkers, which consisted of Sam and Kirk McGee and fiddler Mazy Todd; eighteen cuts were recorded and issued as Uncle Dave Macon and His Fruit Jar Drinkers. They also recorded ten tunes under the name the Dixie Sacred Singers; three songs were recorded by the McGee Brothers and Todd (Macon was featured as banjoist on one cut); nine duets were recorded by the McGee Brothers; and Uncle Dave Macon recorded a handful of songs. Three of the total of fifty songs, "Rock About My Saro Jane," "Sail Away Ladies," and "Jordan Is a Hard Road to Travel," were revived during the recent folk boom.

One of his most unique recording sessions involved duets with Macon on five-string banjo and Sam McGee on six-string banjo (banjo-guitar), done at Chicago's Brunswick Laboratories in the summer heat of 1928. The next year, Macon returned to the Windy City to record some solo discs and duets with Sid Harkreader. On the last two days of March 1930, Macon made his first record-

ings with his son Dorris; and, that winter, Macon and Sam McGee cut ten sides for Okeh in Jackson, Mississippi.

His performance with his son Dorris of "Take Me Back to My Old Carolina Home" is one of the highlights of the Republic Productions film *The Grand Ole Opry*, in which the seventy-year-old Uncle Dave Macon was featured. Several years later, during the forties, he toured with Bill Monroe's tent show as banjoist and comedian.

Uncle Dave Macon gave his last performance on the *Grand Ole Opry* on March 1, 1952, and he died three weeks later, at the age of eighty-two.

His vast repertoire drew upon vaudeville and minstrel show traditions, sacred music, dance tunes, songs of British origin, American ballads, Tin Pan Alley pop songs, and banjo instrumentals. He stands out among his peers for selecting songs with a political and social commentary, many of which were probably written by Uncle Dave Macon, such as "From Earth to Heaven," about the automobile, "Governor Al Smith," "Farm Relief," about the plight of the farmer, "All In Down and Out Blues," and others.

His early recordings were made on the **Aeolian Vocalion record label, and were** followed by those recorded for the Vocalion Division, B.B.C. Company, Brunswick Division, B.B.C. Company, Okeh Phonograph Corporation, Starr Piano Company (Gennett Records), Victor Company, Montgomery Ward, Supertone, and others. Albums and 45-RPM discs appear on such labels as Brunswick, Camden, Coral, County, Decca, Folkways, Record, Book and Film Sales (RBF), Victor, and Yazoo; and two of his most recent reissue LPs have been put on the market by Historical and Biograph Records. (*See also* The McGee Brothers.)

# John Madden. *See* The Serendipity Singers.

## Carol Maillard. *See* Sweet Honey in the Rock.

## Tommy Makem

*Singer, songwriter, instrumentalist, recording artist, actor, storyteller, and Canadian television personality*

Although an artist in his own right, Tommy Makem is closely associated with the Clancy Brothers, with whom he worked for a dozen or so years until April 1969.

Makem was born in Ireland in 1932 to music-loving parents who were responsible for "there always being a bit of music around the house." His mother is a well-known source of folk songs, and the BBC, Jean Ritchie, and Pete Seeger, among others, have collected material from her. Makem's father played the fiddle, his brother played fiddle, whistles, and Uilleann pipes, and they all could sing. Even though his roots were in the folk tradition, he sang with a pop group and, at the age of fifteen, formed his own *ceili*, or country band. He met Liam Clancy in Ireland before they emigrated to the United States: "Both of us came over with the idea of going into the theater, actually, which we did. I was over for only a couple of months when I had an accident with my hand. I was working at a foundry in New Hampshire, and a printing press fell on my hand. I had a lot of operations to save the hand, and while I was recuperating after the first operation, I went to New York for a visit and met up with Paddy, Tom, and Liam Clancy. They asked me to do a concert, and I remember that it was March and there was an awful lot of snow, and we sang at the Circle in the Square in Greenwich Village, and two of the people in the audience turned out to be Alan Lomax and Pete Seeger.

"The Clancys and I recorded an album of rebel songs called *The Rising of the Moon* [TLP 1006] in Kenny Goldstein's kitchen in the Bronx, and Israel Young was there. About a year later we did another album on

Tommy Makem at Mariposa '75

Tradition Records, which is the company that was started by Paddy Clancy, but even after we did *Come Fill Your Glass with Us* [TLP 1032], we still had no intention of becoming singers. We were all still acting, but we used to sing at the White Horse on Hudson Street, and there were lots of people, like Theo Bikel and Odetta, who used to come in. Around 1960 when Liam and I were in an off-Broadway show that was about to close, we got offered a job at

Gerde's Folk City, known then as the Fifth Peg. We started singing there, and Tom and Paddy would come over at night and sing a few songs with us."

When Tommy Makem went to Chicago to act in another play, the Gate of Horn club owners asked him to perform for a couple of weeks at that major Chicago folk nightclub. Shortly after his return to New York City, he and the Clancys decided to devote their energies to singing: "At that time, we were getting offered forty-five dollars a week to act off-Broadway, which was about the same as unemployment, and when someone offered us a hundred twenty-five dollars a week per person, we thought it was a fortune and, being corrupt, we took the money and started to sing. One day, we had a mass meeting with the four of us and we decided to give this singing lark six months, and it lasted for about twelve years."

Since 1969 Makem has been working on his own: "I've been working like mad, harder than I've ever worked in my life, touring all over the place. A new record of mine was released in early June 1975 in England, and I did three weeks over there. I've been to Australia, and all over the States and Canada."

Tommy Makem has a television series called *Tommy Makem and Ryan's Fancy*, which is going into its third year. He collaborates with three Irishmen now living in Newfoundland, and it is a syndicated show taped in Hamilton, Ontario.

Now a resident of Dover, New Hampshire, where he first emigrated from Ireland, and where he had the accident to his hand, he writes "a little bit once in a while, but not very much."

Tommy Makem plays tin whistle, warpipes, banjo, pennywhistle, drums, piccolo, guitar, and bagpipes. During the sixties, he recorded several LPs on his own, including *Songs of Tommy Makem* (TLP 1044) on the Tradition Records label, and he has continued to record up to the present. He has written many songs, including "Bold O'Donahue," "I'll Tell My Ma," "The Cob-

bler," "Freedom's Sons," "Lord Nelson," "Winds of Morning," and "Four Green Fields," which he considers to be his most popular song, especially in Ireland. (*See also* The Clancy Brothers.)

# Mandolin

A stringed instrument, often used in accompaniment with the guitar, the mandolin has a relatively small, pear-shaped sound box which is attached to a fretted neckboard. There are either one circular, or two narrow, elongated soundholes cut into the top of the sound box, four pairs of strings (tuned in fifths), a pegdisc, and rear pegs. The bridge is low, and the metal strings are played with a plectrum to produce either a rapid, rhythmic sound or a melancholic, mournful sound.

As it is known today, this widely used country instrument is actually a Neapolitan mandolin introduced to this country by Southern Europeans. Near Eastern in origin, the mandolin found its way to southeast Europe, and during the eighteenth century, variations of the instrument were made in different Italian towns. Various modifications in structure and stringing resulted in such versions of the *mandolino* as the *mandolino fiorentino* (a smaller version of the Neapolitan mandolin, but with a longer neck and five pairs of strings); *mandolino genovese* (similar to the Neapolitan mandolin, but with a wider neck and five or six pairs of strings); *mandolino milanese* (actually a small lute); and the *mandolino napolitano*, or Neapolitan mandolin, which was used for classical music performances, employed by Mozart in *Don Giovanni* and by Verdi in his 1887 opera *Otello*. Before the mandolin lapsed into disuse, Beethoven had composed five pieces for mandolin and piano; today, it is used as a popular instrument predominantly in Italy and America.

Around the turn of the twentieth century, mandolins and guitars became common items in mail-order catalogues, and many rural Southern families ordered mandolins and learned to play the instruments with the aid of the accompanying instruction books. The *National Barn Dance* boasted two influential mandolin-guitar ensembles, Mac and Bob (blind musicians Lester McFarland and Robert A. Gardner) and Karl and Harty. Mac and Bob employed a country music styling which was to become more widely popularized by the Monroe Brothers in the thirties; and many decades later, the "Father of Bluegrass," Bill Monroe, is still considered one of the foremost proponents of the mandolin as a primary instrument in string band music. Among the other early country music acts which used the mandolin-guitar combination with success were the Callahan Brothers, the Blue Sky Boys, and, more recently, the Bailes Brothers, the Bailey Brothers, and the Louvin Brothers.

## Betty Mann. *See* The Gateway Trio.

## Lee Manuel. *See* The Balfa Freres.

## Jody Maphis. *See* Earl Scruggs.

## Mariposa Folk Festival

*Annual daytime festival of folk music, dance, and crafts, held on the Toronto Islands, Ontario*

In recent years, this fourteen-year-old annual festival, which has been called "a **multinational smorgasbord**," has placed emphasis on the interrelatedness of musical traditions. Links are demonstrated by individuals and groups representing various types of traditional folklore, such as that of the east coast of Canada, French Canada, Louisiana's Cajuns, Appalachia, Scotland, and Ireland—and blues, gospel and work songs. Contemporary singer-songwriters, such as David Bromberg, Steve Goodman, John Hammond, Jr., Murray McLauchlan,

Adam Mitchell, Utah Phillips, John Prine, and Malvina Reynolds, contribute to the primarily traditionally oriented music offered, and there is a conscious effort to avoid "stars" in the lineup of performers.

In 1968 the Toronto Islands were selected as the site for the Mariposa Folk Festival, and the setting has proved to be ideal, with its open spaces, cool breezes off Lake Ontario, groves of shady trees—only a ferry ride from Toronto. The year 1971 marked the tenth festival and the abandonment of big-name entertainers; instead, miniconcerts were interspersed with workshops, the atmosphere became more intimate, and many lesser-known artists participated in the daytime activities. In 1975 there were workshops on six stages, an additional area devoted exclusively to native peoples, games, and play parties for children, and a crafts area. Among the performers were the Boys of the Lough, David Bromberg, Charlie Chin, Michael Cooney, Jack Elliott, Joe Heaney, Larry Johnson, the Lilly Brothers, Margaret MacArthur, Tommy Makem, Martin, Bogan and the Armstrongs, Kate and Anna McGarrigle, Dennis McGee, S. D. Courville, and Marc Savoy, Adam Mitchell, Glenn Ohrlin, Bruce (U. Utah) Phillips, Ola Belle Reed, Malvina Reynolds, John Roberts and Tony Barrand, Rosalie Sorrels, and many, many others.

## Martin, Bogan and the Armstrongs

*Early black old-timey string band, performers, and recording artists*

The backgrounds of each of the band's four members are rich and varied in musical traditions and influences, and although Martin, Bogan and the Armstrongs are basically an old-timey string band, their repertoire includes blues, swing, ragtime, jazz, early pop, rock, country, and a diversity of ethnic songs.

The leader of the Chicago-based band, Howard Armstrong, was born in Lafayette, Macon County, Tennessee. As a young boy, Armstrong learned to play violin, and when he was sixteen years old, he was getting paid to perform his music. His self-education includes the knowledge of Spanish, Mandarin Chinese, and five other languages, and he is a professional artist, besides. Although Howard Armstrong generally plays fiddle for the group, he is also a highly skilled mandolin player.

Virginia-born Carl Martin was influenced by the traditions of the coal-mining region in which he was raised as a boy. He played guitar at an early age and was in his older brother's band for several years. Around 1930 he met the teenage Howard Armstrong, and they started performing together with road shows and on radio broadcasts. They called themselves the Tennessee Chocolate Drops, and their music was broadcast over WORL Radio, Knoxville, Tennessee. Later, they changed the name of their group to the Wandering Troubadours.

Before long, they met up with Bill Ballinger and Ted Bogan, who had been traveling with a medicine show in the Southeast. They traveled, performed, and recorded as the Four Keys. While Armstrong was ill for a short period of time, Martin, Bogan and Ballinger toured through Kingsport and parts of West Virginia. After Armstrong rejoined the group, Ballinger left to get married, and Martin, Bogan and Armstrong have performed together ever since, playing music for a wide audience and for a variety of events.

After 1933, Carl Martin played with various blues artists, including Big Bill Broonzy, Tampa Red, Muddy Waters, and Johnny Young. Martin, Bogan and Armstrong had gone to Chicago, and when Armstrong went home to get married, Martin and Bogan played together until 1937. During that period, while Martin was also interacting with blues musicians, Bogan was playing with Jimmy Dudly, Jimmy Hazely, and Les Paul. Carl Martin is included on the Yazoo Records LPs *East Coast Blues 1924–1935* (L-1013) and *Guitar Wizards 1926–1935* (L-1016), and he has written many songs, including "New Deal Blues," "Joe Louis Blues," and "1937 Flood."

Carl Martin's "Barnyard Dance" is the title track of the group's first album, *Barnyard Dance* (Rounder 2003), which also features their theme song, Ella Fitzgerald's "Lady Be Good," and other old standards. They have recorded a second album, *Let's Give a Party* (Flying Fish Records 003), and their third LP is in its planning stages.

In recent years, Howard Armstrong's son Tom has played bass for the band while his father plays fiddle, Martin plays mandolin, and Bogan plays guitar. They live in Chicago and travel around the country and to Canada, performing at such festivals as the National Folk Festival and Mariposa Folk Festival.

One of the highlights of their career was representing the United States as part of a six week-tour, "Music of the People—USA," which was sponsored by the U.S. State Department. The August–September 1974 tour also included the Highwoods String Band, the dancing Bannerman family, and Andy Wallace, who was then program director of the National Folk Festival Association. They traveled throughout Central and South America, covering nine countries and entertaining audiences in over seventy performances.

## Carl Martin. *See* Martin, Bogan and the Armstrongs.

## Gene Martin. *See* The Smoky Mountain Boys.

## Mac Martin and the Dixie Travelers

*Bluegrass group, performers, and recording artists*

The group's authentic bluegrass music is

allied to the deep-rooted traditions of this genre; and, in a dedicated fashion, Mac Martin and the Dixie Travelers have preserved and contributed to a long-established bluegrass style that has been handed down through the generations. This highly personal approach to a form of music has created a selective, but strong, following, and although the achievements of Mac Martin and the Dixie Travelers have gone largely unnoticed, the band is respected for its unique sound and integrity.

Born on April 26, 1925, in Pittsburgh, Pennsylvania, William D. Colleran (Mac Martin) was an early admirer of country music and its old-time favorites the Monroe Brothers, the Carter Family, the Mainers, and the Blue Sky Boys. He collected some of the recordings that had made their way to the North and in the mid-thirties had his first experience with live country music when he heard a touring Georgia string band perform in his hometown. In his teens, he started singing with his first partner, medicine show entertainer Ed Brozi, who taught him many old-time ballads and hymns.

After World War II, he started listening closely to the music of Bill Monroe's Blue Grass Boys, with Lester Flatt, Earl Scruggs, and Chubby Wise; and, putting aside old-time music, he decided to pursue what was to become known as bluegrass. In 1949 he and his band worked for WHJB in Greensburg, Pennsylvania, and when mandolinist Earl Banner joined the group, their bluegrass sound was firmly established. There were three members in the band named Bill, and to help alleviate the confusion, Bill Colleran changed his name to Mac Martin.

By the early fifties, Mac Martin was devoting his energies to the five-string banjo, and in 1953 he was playing with a group on WHOD in Homestead, Pennsylvania. The Dixie Travelers' sound has been compared to that of the mid-fifties Flatt and Scruggs, and Mac Martin's vocals are reminiscent of the expressive singing of Lester Flatt.

In 1957 the Dixie Travelers started per-forming at Walsh's Lounge in Pittsburgh, and they played there every week for the next fifteen years. It was not until 1963 that the Dixie Travelers made their first recording, but only one of the two albums they made for Gateway Records was issued, and a single from the second LP. Five years later they recorded the first of four albums for Rural Rhythm, with one LP released each year through 1971. In 1965 Frank Basista joined the band as bassist; Bob Artis became mandolinist and tenor vocalist for Mac Martin and the Dixie Travelers in 1968.

Bob Artis was born on July 26, 1946, in Santa Monica, California. When he came East in 1968, he was attracted to the Mac Martin sound and soon became a regular member of the band. His style of mandolin playing is unique in that he uses a thumb pick instead of the traditional flatpick; he has made four albums with the band and has played lead guitar and banjo, as well as mandolin, on some of their recordings. In addition to performing and recording, Bob Artis has been actively involved in teaching and writing, publishing a bluegrass newsletter, contributing articles on a regular basis to *Bluegrass Unlimited* and *Muleskinner News*, and his book, *Bluegrass*, was published in 1975 by Hawthorn Books, Inc., in New York. He became the leader of the Dixie Travelers when Mac Martin left in 1972.

In 1974 Mac Martin and the Dixie Travelers, with Mac Martin, Bob Artis, Frank Basista, Billy Bryant, and Mike Carson, recorded *Dixie Bound* (County 743), with lesser-known bluegrass selections, an original composition by Carson, "Natchez," and several Mac Martin songs, including "Does It Have to End This Way."

**Dave Mattacks.** *See* Fairport Convention.

**Ian Matthews.** *See* Fairport Convention.

# Melanie

*Contemporary singer, songwriter, guitarist, performer, and recording artist*

In her late twenties, Melanie has become an artist of international acclaim whose aura of intimacy has endeared her to audiences in the United States, Europe, Japan, and behind the Iron Curtain. Her songwriting has brought her a couple of ASCAP awards; both *Billboard* and *Cash Box* have selected her as Top Female Vocalist; and she has earned several Gold Records. In addition to her regular tours around the world, in 1971 Melanie was asked by UNICEF to act as its official spokeswoman—a distinction which enabled her to bring her music to ten nations on behalf of this organization.

Melanie Safka was born on February 3, 1947, in Astoria (Queens), New York. One of her primary musical influences was her former jazz singer mother, as Melanie remembers: "I started writing my own little songs, mostly imitations of what I'd hear my mother singing around the house. It wasn't until I was 13 or 14 that I began to write about things I found in myself."

As a teenager, she started singing in Greenwich Village coffeehouses where a hat was passed to secure a meager night's salary for the performer. After graduating from high school, Melanie became an acting student at the American Academy in Manhattan, which led her to the doorstep of a music publishing company. Soon thereafter, one of its employees, Peter Schekeryk (now her husband), directed Melanie in obtaining a recording contract, and her debut album was released in the late sixties.

Her second LP contains one of her best-known songs, "Beautiful People," which Melanie retains in her repertoire and never fails to sing during her live performances. The summer of 1969 found Melanie at the Woodstock Festival, where, despite the preceding performance by Ravi Shankar and the heavy rain, she received a standing ovation for her appearance. During the course of her singing, candles began to flicker in the audience of several thousand as a symbolic sign of solidarity; Melanie's single release of "Lay Down (Candles in the Rain)" in the following spring was a tribute in song to this event. The song became a cash box hit, and the album by the same name became Melanie's first Gold Record.

By the following summer, "Peace Will Come (According to Plan)" had soared to the top of the charts, and Melanie was invited to perform at the 1970 Isle of Wight Festival. Her initial live LP, *Leftover Wine* (Buddah BDS 5066), was released, and, before changing record labels, Melanie recorded *The Good Book* (Buddah BDS 95000), *Four Sides* (2-Buddah 95005), and *Please Love Me* (Buddah 5132).

Melanie and her husband Peter Schekeryk organized their own Neighborhood Record label; the company's first single release, "Brand New Key," became Melanie's first Gold Single, followed by "Ring the Living Bell," another top-twenty hit. The acclaim aroused by *Gather Me* (Neighborhood 47001) was repeated with the 1973 release of *Melanie at Carnegie Hall* (2-Neighborhood 49001), made from a tape of her twenty-sixth-birthday celebration at New York's Carnegie Hall. Some of her subsequent Neighborhood LPs include *Stone Ground Words* (Neighborhood 47005), *Madrugada* (Neighborhood 48001), and *As I See It Now* (Neighborhood NB 3000).

Melanie is now an Arista Records artist. Her most recent album is *Sunsets and Other Beginnings* (Arista NL 3001), issued in 1975.

# D. L. Menard. *See* The Louisiana Aces.

# Peadar Mercier. *See* The Chieftains.

# Ruth Meyer. *See* The Golden Ring.

# Walt Michael. *See* Bottle Hill.

**Paul Miles.** *See* The Red Fox
Chasers.

**George Millar.** *See* The Irish
Rovers.

**Joe Millar.** *See* The Irish Rovers.

**Will Millar.** *See* The Irish Rovers.

**The Mississippi Sheiks.** *See* Sam
Chatmon.

**Chad Mitchell.** *See* The Chad
Mitchell Trio.

## Howard (Howie) Mitchell

*Traditional singer, dulcimer player and maker,*
*performer, and recording artist*

Highly respected among traditionalists, this
Washington, D.C., resident appears frequently at the smaller folk festivals and at
the annual Fox Hollow Festival in Petersburg, New York. His favorite pastime is
making music with friends, and Howie
Mitchell is one of the original members of
the informal collective of friends and folk
musicians known as the Golden Ring.

Born on February 22, 1932, in Lexington,
Kentucky, Mitchell is a graduate of Cornell
University with a degree in electrical
engineering. He started making dulcimers
while he was in the navy during the mid-
fifties, and his main goal was to construct an
inexpensive instrument that would be af-
fordable by practically everybody. This concept led him to produce the "dulciless," a
cardboard box that he used on the concert
stage, and in the course of his experimentation, he "reinvented" the old Kentucky
"courtin' dulcimer," calling it the "twi-

cimer." He still makes dulcimers on occasion but now uses the best materials
available to yield products of the highest
quality and skilled craftsmanship.

A versatile dulcimer player, Howie Mitchell is knowledgeable about many styles.
He and his wife Ann play separately, or
together, and their repertoire includes Appalachian ballads, traditional New England
songs, and classical pieces. Howie Mitchell
has recorded for Folk-Legacy as a solo artist
and as part of the Golden Ring. He made his
first recording in 1962, entitled *Howie Mit-*
*chell* (FSI-5); and Folk-Legacy has put
together two sets of instructional booklets
with companion records: *The Mountain*
*Dulcimer: How to Make It and Play It (After*
*a Fashion)* (FSI-29) and *The Hammered*
*Dulcimer: How to Make It and Play It*
(FSI-43). Howie Mitchell is also a proficient
guitarist, banjoist, and autoharpist. (*See also*
The Golden Ring.)

## Joni Mitchell

*Contemporary singer-songwriter, guitarist,*
*pianist, performer, and recording artist*

A ten-year veteran of the folk scene, this
Canadian poet-composer has demonstrated
unerring artistic growth in the past decade—
from her beginning as an introverted performer and songwriter whose material was
popularized through recordings by such
other artists as Judy Collins ("Both Sides,
Now") and Tom Rush ("Urge for Going"
and "The Circle Game"), to a prestigious
and enviable level of sophistication and confidence as a writer, performer, and interpreter of her own material. An undisputed superstar in the pop music field, she
has often been compared to Bob Dylan (they
have both had their songs recorded incessantly by artists representing various
fields of music). In an interview with Malka
which appeared in *Maclean's* magazine
(June 1974), she said: "I don't feel like my
best work is behind me. I feel as if it's still in
front."

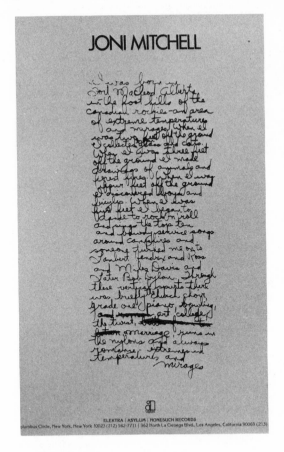

JONI MITCHELL

ELEKTRA | ASYLUM | NONESUCH RECORDS
olumbus Circle, New York, New York 10023 (212) 582-7711 | 962 North La Cienega Blvd., Los Angeles, California 90069 (213)

Born Roberta Joan Anderson on September 27, 1943, in McLeod, Alberta, Canada, Joni Mitchell had a strong inclination toward painting as a young girl, as she recalls: "My childhood longing mostly was to be a painter, yet before I went to art college my mother said to me that my stick-to-itiveness in certain things was never that great, and she said you're going to get to art college and you're going to get distracted, you know." After graduating from high school, Joni Mitchell entered the Alberta College of Art in Calgary. However, she found many of the courses to be meaningless and began to spend more and more time singing folk songs and accompanying herself on the ukelele. Following her first year of college, she performed at the Mariposa Folk Festival in Toronto, where she decided to re-

main to pursue a career as a folksinger. She established a strong local following as she played various coffeehouses in the city, and both her singing and her original compositions attracted considerable attention.

In June 1965 she married Chuck Mitchell, and about six months later they moved to the United States and settled in Detroit. Despite their separation, which occurred shortly thereafter, she continued to use Mitchell as a professional name. Her performances were highly praised by Detroit journalists, and she soon received offers to appear at clubs in New York. Shortly after her arrival on the East Coast, her name was added to the Reprise recording artists' roster, and following her initial recording sessions, she packed her bags and headed for California.

Many artists started to take special notice of her songs, and her material was gradually added to the repertoires of such performers as Johnny Cash, Judy Collins, Gordon Lightfoot, Tom Rush, Buffy Sainte-Marie, and Dave Van Ronk. In 1969 she was invited by Johnny Cash to appear on his network television weekly variety show, and for the next several years appeared as a guest performer on various TV programs.

Her first album, *Joni Mitchell* (Reprise RS 6293), produced by David Crosby and released in 1968, was followed a year later by her chart hit album *Clouds* (Reprise RS 6341), which contains two prominent compositions, "Both Sides, Now" and "Chelsea Morning." In 1970 her third Reprise effort, *Ladies of the Canyon* (Reprise RS 6376), earned her a Gold Record award, and in the following year, *Blue* (Reprise MS 2038) marked a transformation of her vocal technique from timidity to sensuality and maturity. In looking back on her first records, Joni Mitchell feels that "the *Blue* album, for the most part, holds up." Music critics proclaimed it one of the top albums of 1971.

In 1972 she switched to Asylum Records, and in addition to recording a popular single, "You Turn Me On I'm a Radio," produced another bestselling LP, entitled *For the Roses* (Asylum SD 5057). Since then, Joni

Mitchell has recorded three additional albums on the Asylum label: *Court and Spark* (Elektra-Asylum 7E 1001), *Miles of Aisles* (Asylum AB-202), and *The Hissing of Summer Lawns* (Asylum 7E-1051).

In looking to the future, she commented shortly after her thirtieth birthday: "Well, I really don't feel I've scratched the surface of my music. I'm not all that confident about my words. Thematically I think that I'm running out of things which I feel are important enough to describe verbally. I really think that as you get older life's experience becomes more; I begin to see the paradoxes resolved. It's almost like most things that I would once dwell on and explore for an hour, I would shrug my shoulders to now. In your twenties things are still profound and being uncovered. However, I think there's a way to keep that alive if you don't start putting up too many blocks. I feel that my music will continue to grow—I'm almost a pianist now, and the same thing with the guitar. And I also continue to draw, and that also is in a stage of growth, it hasn't stagnated yet. And I hope to bring all these things together. Another thing I'd like to do is to make a film. There's a lot of things I'd like to do, so I still feel young as an artist."

## The Mitchell Trio. *See* The Chad Mitchell Trio.

## Barry Mitterhoff. *See* Bottle Hill.

## Paddy Moloney. *See* The Chieftains.

## The Monroe Brothers. *See* Bill Monroe; Charlie Monroe.

## Bill Monroe

*Singer, instrumentalist, composer, performer, and recording artist*

Among the musicians connected with the evolution of the bluegrass style, none is more prominent in stature and more influential in the contemporary musical field than Bill Monroe. Credited with its founding, Bill Monroe is commonly referred to as the "Father of Bluegrass Music." With his driving mandolin-picking style and his distinctive tenor vocals, he developed traditional Appalachian string band music into a formal and intimately expressive musical style. In naming his band of musicians the Blue Grass Boys, in honor of his home state of Kentucky, Bill Monroe inadvertently coined a phrase for a renewed tradition of American folk music.

Bill Monroe was born on September 13, 1911, on a western Kentucky farm near Rosine. Along with his five brothers and two sisters, he gained an early appreciation of country music from his mother, who played old-time fiddle and was a well-versed singer of mountain songs. Before he was in his teens, Bill Monroe started playing the guitar; he was influenced by the fiddlin' and pickin' of his Uncle Pen Vanderver and a black country dance musician, Arnold Schultz, both of whom Bill Monroe accompanied at local social gatherings. Black musical stylings played a significant role in Monroe's personal approach to his art form, and blues artists—along with Jimmie Rodgers—made a decisive impact on his formative years as a musician. Another pervading influence in his youth was church singing, which provided a musical foundation for innumerable Southern musicians, both black and white.

Although he played several stringed instruments, Bill Monroe adopted the mandolin as his primary vehicle of musical expression, and as a result of his experimentation and virtuosity, he is considered to be the individual most responsible for attracting widespread interest in the instrument.

After his parents died, Bill Monroe traveled North to join his older brothers Birch and Charlie, who were employed as industrial workers in the Chicago area. In their spare time, Birch and Charlie Monroe played music as a guitar-fiddle duet; when

Bill Monroe

their teenage brother Bill teamed up with them, they commenced their career as professional performers in 1927. After several years of working with the WLS *Barn Dance* road show, they received an offer to appear on WWAE in Hammond, Indiana, in 1930. They participated in a number of programs aired on Midwestern radio stations, and, even today, Bill Monroe has strong musical ties with Indiana as owner of the Jamboree Park in Bean Blossom—the site of year-round bluegrass music events (including the annual Bill Monroe Bean Blossom Bluegrass Festival).

Around 1934 the Monroes switched their base of operations to the Carolinas, where they established themselves as one of the top performing acts in the region. Two years

later, with Birch now back at his regular job in the oil refineries, Bill and Charlie Monroe made their initial recordings on February 17, 1936, for RCA Victor, on the Bluebird label, as the Monroe Brothers. Their first release was a sacred song which Bill Monroe had learned in church when he was fourteen, "What Would You Give in Exchange for Your Soul?," backed up with "This World Is Not My Home." In the ensuing three-year period, the Monroe Brothers produced a number of classic recordings, such as "Roll in My Sweet Baby's Arms" and "Nine Pound Hammer," among the sixty songs recorded for Bluebird. Their reputation spread widely as their music reached into both rural and urban homes, where radios or phonographs provided a rich source of entertainment and a learning tool for prospective musicians. Many of the fundamental elements of bluegrass music—vocal and instrumental—are found in the collaborative work of the Monroe Brothers.

By 1938 the Monroe Brothers had separated. Charlie Monroe continued his musical career, first with the Monroe Boys, a trio, and then with his famous band, the Kentucky Pardners. Bill Monroe went on to organize the Blue Grass Boys, which consisted originally of guitarist Cleo Davis, bassist Amos Garin, and fiddler Art Wooten. Over the years, the band's personnel has changed many times, and some of country music's best-known artists have been members of Bill Monroe's Blue Grass Boys at some point in their careers.

For the first time in his career, Bill Monroe sang solo and lead vocals as the twenty-seven-year-old leader of the Blue Grass Boys. He and his band became regulars on WSM's *Grand Ole Opry* in October 1939, and he is still a participant in this world-famous country music institution today. In 1942 he started touring, taking with him a large circus tent that he set up in every small town he played along the way. By 1945 his band had evolved as a distinctive musical entity created by the addition of Earl Scruggs, who developed a position of prominence for the five-string banjo in the traditional string band and provided the final ingredient for the modern bluegrass sound. Three years prior, David "Stringbean" Akeman had been hired by Monroe as the band's first banjoist, but the instrument was used solely to provide rhythmic accompaniment. Earl Scruggs revolutionized the role of the five-string banjo as a string band instrument and became its foremost proponent in the United States. From 1945 to 1948 the Monroe style was perfected as the "original" bluegrass band, with Lester Flatt, Bill Monroe, Earl Scruggs, Howard (Cedric Rainwater) Watts, and Chubby Wise brought national prominence to the modern bluegrass sound. In the postwar years Bill Monroe and the Blue Grass Boys became one of the most important groups in the entire history of country music, and countless numbers of country musicians became their imitators.

In 1948 Lester Flatt and Earl Scruggs left the Monroe organization to form their own band, the Foggy Mountain Boys. Like many of the others who played with Bill Monroe and then struck out on their own—including Carter Stanley, Jimmy Martin, and Mac Wiseman—Flatt and Scruggs played initially in the Monroe style.

After a few years of recording with Columbia, Bill Monroe signed a contract with Decca (now incorporated, with Kapp and Uni, into MCA Records, Inc.) in 1949. To date, he has recorded nineteen albums on the MCA label. Some of his best-known compositions include "Kentucky Waltz," "Blue Moon of Kentucky," "Mule Skinner Blues," and "Uncle Pen."

In 1970 the Country Music Association acknowledged Bill Monroe's influence by electing him to the Country Music Hall of Fame. (*See also* Charlie Monroe.)

## Birch Monroe. *See* The Monroe Brothers.

## Charlie Monroe

*Singer, guitarist, songwriter, performer, and recording artist*

When Charlie Monroe died of cancer on September 27, 1975, country music lost one of its legendary and most influential performers. From his start as a dancer with the WLS road show to his contribution as a member of the most popular Southern recording group of the 1930s—the Monroe Brothers—to his role as a bandleader of the Kentucky Pardners, Charlie (Charger) Monroe remained one of the most revered artists in the music business.

The sixth of eight children, Charlie Monroe was born on July 4, 1903, near Rosine, Kentucky. Old-time music was an important part of his early life, and he learned to play the guitar as a boy. Later, when Charlie Monroe and his brother Birch traveled to the Midwest to seek industrial jobs, they performed informally as a guitar-fiddle duet. In 1927 the Monroe Brothers were joined by their teenage brother Bill, and they started touring the Midwest and upper South with the WLS *Barn Dance* road show. They began their initial radio broadcasts in 1930 on WWAE in Hammond, Indiana, and then on WJKS in Gary, Indiana. Within a few years, they moved their base of operations to the Carolinas, where they were among the most popular performing acts in the region.

With Birch Monroe no longer actively performing with his brothers, the "houn'-dog guitar" and "potato-bug mandolin" duet of Charlie and Bill Monroe made their debut recordings on the Victor Bluebird label in 1936 as the Monroe Brothers. In the initial three-year phase of their recording careers, they produced sixty songs, which, in their musical styling, established the rudiments of the modern bluegrass sound—the high harmony (rendered by Bill Monroe), the driving instrumentation, the bass guitar runs, and the incorporation of traditional material.

When the Monroe Brothers disbanded in 1938, Charlie Monroe maintained his acclaimed stature, first as a member of the Monroe Boys trio, and later with the Kentucky Pardners, which at various times included such notables as Lester Flatt, Ira Louvin, and Curly Sechler. Bill Monroe organized his own band, the Blue Grass Boys, which attracted national attention in the postwar years. Charlie Monroe and the Kentucky Pardners remained Victor recordings artists until 1952, at which time they changed over to Decca Records.

When Charlie Monroe retired as a professional musician in 1957, he continued to appear in public on occasion, and during the early sixties he recorded two albums on the Rem label. His first wife's serious illness forced him to leave his Kentucky farm for employment in Indiana, where he worked for Howard Johnson and Otis Elevator in order to pay a steady stream of medical expenses. After his wife's death, Charlie Monroe remarried in 1969 and moved to his second wife's native state of Tennessee, but remained inactive as a musician until the summer of 1972. That August, he appeared with Jimmy Martin at Carlton Haney's Blue Grass Music Festival in Gettysburg, Pennsylvania, which became the first of a new series of personal appearances on the festival and schoolhouse circuit.

In late 1974, Charlie Monroe learned that he had cancer—the same fatal disease which had claimed the life of his first wife, Betty. He gave his last public performances in the Rosine, Kentucky, area in the early fall of 1975, returning to his home in Reidsville, North Carolina, where he died at the end of September of that year.

The music of Charlie Monroe appears on such record labels as Bluebird, Camden, County, Decca, King, Pine Tree, Rimrock, and Starday. Early in 1976, Grady Bullins took over as leader of the Charlie Monroe and the Kentucky Pardners band, with Jim Brady on fiddle, Grady Bullins on guitar, Charlie Heath on banjo, Donald Smith on mandolin, and Little Wilma on bass. (*See also* Bill Monroe.)

**John Montgomery.** *See* The Cumberland Three.

**McKinley Morganfield.** *See* Muddy Waters.

**James Morris.** *See* Jimmy Driftwood.

**Henry Morrison.** *See* The Georgia Sea Island Singers.

**Bud Morrisroe.** *See* Apple Country.

**Peter Morse.** *See* The New Christy Minstrels.

**Robin Morton.** *See* The Boys of the Lough.

## Mountain Dance and Folk Festival

For nearly half a century, this annual folk festival has been held in the shadow of Beaucatcher Mountain, Asheville, North Carolina, where, in 1927, Bascom Lamar Lunsford set up his dancing platform and invited his neighbors to dance and make music with their fiddles, banjos, dulcimers, guitars, tune bows, and mouth harps.

One of the oldest gatherings aimed at preserving traditional Southern Appalachian mountain music, the Mountain Dance and Folk Festival is an occasion that is met with a whoop and a slap of clogging feet. Dancers of all ages circle and weave on the dancing platform, perpetuating a tradition indigenous to the mountain ballad country that lies between the Great Smokies and the Blue Ridge Mountains. Several hundred folk performers congregate to sing and play music that ranges from old-time mountain to modern bluegrass music, allowing listeners to reach back into their past as they look toward their future.

As it is a mountain dance festival, a variety of English and Irish jigging and clogging is represented. Appalachian Mountain square dancing, a form of dancing that evolved from such social events as barn raising, corn shucking, and bean stringing, is also an important part of the festival. With the presentation of traditional American folk music and dance, the festival's main purpose is to preserve the traditional ballads and tunes brought to this country from England, Ireland, and Scotland which have been passed along unwritten from one generation to the next, undaunted by the popular urban folk movement.

The Mountain Dance and Folk Festival is sponsored by the Asheville Area Chamber of Commerce. The original advisory board members who worked closely with Bascom Lamar Lunsford (who produced this event for forty-six years before his death at the age of ninety-one) included Lunsford's son, Carl Sandburg, Alan Lomax, Harry Golden, and Paul Green. (*See also* Bascom Lamar Lunsford.)

## Mouth Bow

An old type of musical instrument still used today by the bushmen of Africa and some musicians of Appalachia, the mouth bow derives its resonating sound from its player's mouth. It is made from thin, but reasonably stiff, wood (a fallen branch from a tree, a lathing strip, or a wooden yardstick). Grooves are cut at both ends of the wooden stick and are used to hold a piece of string—or wire banjo or guitar string—securely in place. A mouth bow is strung in a manner similar to a bow for shooting arrows: One end of the stick is tied, and while the stick is in a bent position, the other end is tied with the string. The tightness of the string determines the pitch (tuning) of the bow—the looser the string, the weaker the tone.

To play the mouth bow, the player's lips should make the shape of an O while the cheeks are kept taut. When the flat side at the end of the bow is pressed against the cheek near the player's mouth and the string is plucked, a sound is produced. Opening and closing the mouth to change the size of the O yields different pitches, and tunes reproduced.

Three well-known folk performers who have used the mouth bow in personal appearances are Jimmy Driftwood, Buffy Sainte-Marie, and Patrick Sky.

**Mouth Organ.** *See* Harmonica.

## Geoff Muldaur. *See* The Jim Kweskin Jug Band; Maria Muldaur.

## Maria Muldaur

*Contemporary singer, performer, and recording artist*

After a decade of recording and touring, national attention has focused on Maria Muldaur, whose musical development and recognition in the mid-1970s are reminiscent of Linda Ronstadt and Emmylou Harris. Her musical style defies definition, and, with a repertoire ranging from jazz to blues, country, gospel, folk, contemporary, and 1940s swing music, it is impossible to put a label on her music.

Maria Grazia Rosa Domenica D'Amato Muldaur was raised in Greenwich Village, in New York City, where she had the opportunity of interacting with different types of people and art, as she recalls: "Every seven feet or so was another cluster of musicians. There was a non-stop 24-way hootenanny going on. Something like that doesn't exist now. There'd be bluegrass groups and funky folk music groups . . . people would walk around and catch the music, like a little condensed folk festival happening all at once every Sunday afternoon."

Maria Muldaur was an avid fan of Bessie Smith and a loyal listener of the Alan Freed radio show. During high school, she organized a singing group called the Cashmeres, but when a contract with Gone Records and some backup work for Jerry Butler were arranged, her mother stepped in and would not allow her sixteen-year-old daughter to make any commitments at that time. After her graduation from Hunter College High School, Muldaur went to the premier concert sponsored by the Friends of Old-Time Music and was enraptured by the fiddling of Doc Watson's father-in-law, Gaither Carlton. As a result, she traveled to Deep Gap, North Carolina, to visit the Watson family, and she sang with them and

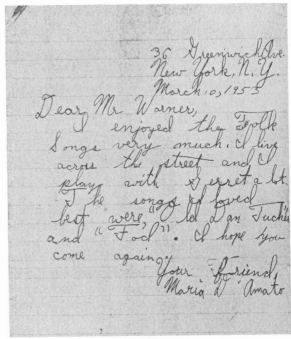

A childhood letter written by Maria Muldaur to Frank Warner

learned to play fiddle from Gaither Carlton. Her days in Greenwich Village consisted of singing and playing at parties and participating in hoots at Gerde's Folk City, and her musical development coincided with the blossoming of the folk scene in her hometown of New York.

Her first break came during the summer of her twenty-first birthday when Victoria Spivey organized the Even Dozen Jug Band, with David Grisman, Stefan Grossman, Steve Katz, Maria Muldaur, Josh Rifkin, and John Sebastian, to record an album of jug band music for her own label, Spivey Records. When Vanguard signed the Kweskin Jug Band, Elektra Records made a bid for the Even Dozen Jug Band in anticipation of a jug band music fad, and they switched labels and cut an album in two days. Before the group disbanded, they had performed two concerts at New York's Carnegie Hall and a *Hootenanny* television show.

While the Kweskin Jug Band was appearing at the Bitter End around this same time, Maria met, and later married, Geoff Muldaur. When Bruno Wolf left the Kweskin band, she was asked to be his replacement. She performed with the group through the seventh month of her first pregnancy and picked up with their touring schedule three weeks after giving birth to her daughter. After six years, the Kweskin Jug Band split up, and the Muldaurs went on to record two albums for Reprise: *Pottery Pie* ([S]6350) and *Sweet Potatoes* (2073). After the breakup of her marriage, she embarked on a solo career and recorded *Maria Muldaur* (Reprise 2148), which was hailed by Jon Landau in the September 27, 1973, *Rolling Stone* as one of the year's top albums. Her single hit, "Midnight at the Oasis," soon followed, and by the following June she had begun a thirty-day road tour, which was extremely successful. Her small, devoted following was expanded as she was catapulted into stardom.

"I'm not a belter," reflects Muldaur. "I'm not a screamer. But my voice is getting heavier as I get older. It's like I've had a flute all these years, a little delicate flute. But I started wanting to express other things. I thought somehow I'm gonna find a corner in my voice to convey more than just a crooning lullabye. Now I find there's a saxophone in there."

Maria Muldaur remains on the Reprise Records roster. One of her most recent LPs is *Waitress in a Donut Shop* (Reprise MS 2194). (*See also* The Jim Kweskin Jug Band.)

**Martha and Eric Nagler.** *See* The Beers Family.

**Graham Nash.** *See* Crosby, Stills, Nash and Young.

## National Barn Dance

*Weekly variety program originating from WLS Radio in Chicago, Illinois*

One of the pioneer, and most important, country radio shows in the United States, the *National Barn Dance* was patterned after the earlier barn-dance programs offered by WSB and WBAP in the early years of the 1920s. Although not the first, Chicago's WLS country music show achieved distinction by its longevity and nationwide acknowledgement. The originator of the show, George D. Hay, was also responsible for the beginnings of what was to become the *Grand Ole Opry*, after he left Chicago.

Sponsored for the first four years of its existence by Sears, Roebuck, WLS (World's Largest Store) commenced its broadcasts in the spring of 1924. When sponsorship was taken over by the *Prairie Farmer* newspaper in September 1928, WLS became known as the "Prairie Farmer Station." One of the station's original goals was to offer a show which would appeal to its basically rural audience. On April 19, 1924, only one week after WLS went on the air, the Chicago radio station presented its first barn-dance show from the city's Sherman Hotel. The overwhelming acceptance of what was then called the *WLS Barn Dance* paved the way for the development of the *National Barn Dance*.

The WLS broadcast included a more encompassing scope of musical forms, and, in addition to country music, the show presented pop and folk tunes. The radio station enjoyed another distinction in being one of the pioneers in the commencement of personal appearances. The station's own booking bureau was operating extensively by the thirties, organizing road show units which played brief stands throughout the Midwest. As a result of its *National Barn Dance* broadcast and its affiliated tours, WLS is considered largely responsible for the integration of the country idiom into the mainstream of music in the Midwest. With the rise in stature of the *Grand Ole Opry*, the *National Barn Dance* gradually lost its position of national prominence and was reduced to merely local significance in the post–World War II years, leading ultimately to its final broadcast in May 1960.

The *National Barn Dance* helped to bring attention to many country performers, including Rex Allen, Gene Autry (who was in its cast from 1930 to 1934), Homer and Jethro, Clayton McMichen (known for his work with Gid Tanner), Joe Maphis, Bill Monroe, and Jimmy Osborne, among many, many others.

# National Folk Festival

The original idea for the National Folk Festival is attributed to Sarah Gertrude Knott, one of the concerned individuals who, in her own words, "saw reasons for using folklore to meet artistic and recreational needs." The National Folk Festival was originated in St. Louis in 1934, and for the next thirty-six years, the festival site was moved around the country. Since 1971 the annual event has been held at Wolf Trap Farm Park in Vienna, Virginia, and, with an emphasis on music and dancing, it continues to bring together people from diverse traditions and various regions of the country.

Although the evening concerts are most publicized, the heart of the weekend festival held every August rests with the daytime activities which are scheduled Friday through Sunday. The Thirty-fourth Annual National Folk Festival instituted a special children's day on Thursday, making it a four-day event. The daytime activities have featured miniconcerts and workshops with evening performers and participants from the National Folk Festival Association's regional and affiliated festivals, traditional woodcarvers from across the United States, musical instrument construction and repair teaching workshops, and square, contra and ethnic dancing, with participation and demonstration.

The spirit of the National Folk Festival is best described by Andy Wallace, who was program director of the National Folk Festival Association for over four years: "What you see at this festival is homegrown. It is to be hoped that you will be inspired by these folk musicians, dancers and craftsmen to explore your own traditional heritage and the others that make up the rich American Patchwork Quilt. Make your own music, dance, work with your hands. We're all a part of the American tradition."

With the cooperation of the National Park Service, the festival is sponsored by the National Folk Festival Association, which for "almost 40 years . . . has encouraged, organized and been consultant to many regional, state and local festivals across the United States," including the National Folk Festival, the Northwest Folk-Life Festival in Seattle, the Ashland Area Kentucky Folk Festival (Lexington, Kentucky), Folklore in America (an accredited seminar in cooperation with George Washington University), and "an on-going effort to realize the most exciting potential of the 1976 Bicentennial celebrations: *reminding Americans of the diverse folk traditions that make this country what it is.*"

In August 1975 Philo Records in Vermont released *Good Time Music at the National* (Philo PH 1028), with fifteen cuts from four National folk festivals. Recorded live, with various artists represented, all cuts and production were contributed by the participants, staff, Philo Records, and friends of the National Folk Festival Association. (*See also* The National Folk Festival Association.)

# The National Folk Festival Association

The history of the National Folk Festival Association (NFFA) evolves from the educational and recreational foresight of Sarah Gertrude Knott, who initiated the concept of a "national" folk festival in 1934. Her first organized folk festival took place from April 29 to May 2, 1934, in the St. Louis Municipal Auditorium, with several hundred participants from over a dozen states. Her work with actors, writers, unemployed blacks, and immigrants in the twenties and early thirties created an awareness of cultural diversity and the common ties that unite all Americans; and her insight into the worth and dignity of both similarities and differences among her countrymen is the seed from which the National Folk Festival Association originated.

Sarah Gertrude Knott was lauded for her

accomplishment, and she received the support of a number of celebrities, such as North Carolina playwright Paul Green (who was an advisory board member of Bascom Lamar Lunsford's Mountain Dance and Folk Festival, Asheville, North Carolina, established in 1928) and critic Constance Rourke, whose association with her festival lent additional prestige and importance to the enterprise. From its inception, the festival has presented workshops (originally called "educational programs"), music, dance, drama, and crafts, with a broad linguistic and ethnic representation. Sarah Gertrude Knott's guideline for the selection of "arrangers" (today, the term *performers* is used) was based on her inherent conviction that the undercurrent of tradition, not commercial success, should predominate.

It was not until thirty-three years after the first annual festival that the event found a permanent site at Wolf Trap Farm Park in Vienna, Virginia; from 1934 to 1969 the National Folk Festival had moved about the country (there were no festivals in 1945, 1956, 1958, 1962, or 1970). In 1959 a permanent headquarters for the festival was established in Washington, D.C., and, at this point, Sarah Gertrude Knott and the festival organizers formed the National Folk Festival Association, Incorporated. In 1971 Sarah Gertrude Knott retired. For the past several years, the NFFA has been funded by Federal grants from the National Endowment for the Arts and the National Park Service. There are over two dozen names on the current list of the NFFA board of directors, and the festival staff consists of Leo Bernache, executive director, and others, who cover program coordination, operations, publicity, audio, and the National Folk Festival program book. (*See also* National Folk Festival.)

# Charles ("Chuck") Neblett. *See* The Freedom Singers.

# The New Christy Minstrels

*Vocal and instrumental group, performers, and recording artists*

Perhaps no other group of the recent urban folk revival saw as many changes in personnel as the well-known folk chorale called the New Christy Minstrels. The origin of the group's name dates back to Edwin P. Christy's original Christy Minstrels, organized in 1842; but the new group took nothing from his vaudeville act (which was designed primarily to promote the work of Stephen Foster) but its title. The New Christy Minstrels epitomized the commercial answer to the demands of the folk boom, and their mellow and carefree approach to the idiom led to a successful career.

With the premise of organizing a group offering modernized and lively arrangements of old folk tunes as well as contemporary material, Randy Sparks gathered together a handful of male and female musicians in 1961 to form the New Christy Minstrels. From the beginning, various members wrote original songs which were performed and recorded by the group and which contributed to a relative longevity not enjoyed by contemporary groups lacking this attribute. Among the early hits of the New Christy Minstrels were "Green, Green" (a Barry McGuire–Randy Sparks collaboration), "Today," "Saturday Night," and "Liza Lee."

By 1963 the New Christy Minstrels were enjoying nationwide prominence, were making numerous television, radio, and concert appearances, and were producing a number of albums and singles on the Columbia label. In 1964 they starred on their own summer television program and were invited by President Lyndon Johnson to perform on the steps of the White House. Shortly after Randy Sparks relinquished his position in the peroming lineup to become the group's full-time manager, he turned over his concern in the New Christy Minstrels to the George Greif and Sid Garris management organization for a quarter of a million dollars. In the following year, the group made their initial tour abroad, which was highlighted by their participation in Italy's San Remo Festival. Until their demise a few years ago, the New Christy Minstrels continued their steady outpouring of recordings, and their album sales reached the multi-million-dollar mark.

In the mid-sixties, Mike Settle joined the New Christy Minstrels as musical director. Originally from Oklahoma, he had met Mason Williams while attending Oklahoma City University; Williams prompted him to play the guitar and was instrumental in lining up a billing for him at a local coffeehouse called the Gourd. A few months later, Mike Settle met the Cumberland Three, who passed through Oklahoma while on tour, and he was asked to join up with them. After a year of performing and recording with the Cumberland Three, followed by a brief stint as a radio disc jockey on a Muskogee, Oklahoma, station, he teamed up with Mason Williams. The duo lasted only two months before Williams went into the navy, and Settle decided to come to New York. He contributed his talent as musical director of the New Christy Minstrels for eighteen months (while simultaneously recording three solo albums); then, taking three other members—Thelma Camach, Kenny Rogers, and Terry (Benson) Williams—with him, he formed another group called the First Edition. After leaving this group, he turned to television script writing before eventually returning to performing and recording for the Uni label.

Another New Christy Minstrel who achieved individual recognition was Barry McGuire, whose "Eve of Destruction" was a major hit of 1965.

# The New Lost City Ramblers

*Vocal and instrumental group, performers, and recording artists*

A trio of musicians whose primary objective is to perform a variety of old-time string band sounds, the New Lost City Ramblers have played a vital role in the revival of this older style of country music. By popularizing traditional string band music, the New Lost City Ramblers have generated renewed enthusiasm for some of its original proponents, such as Gid Tanner and his Skillet Lickers, the Fruit Jar Drinkers, Sam and Kirk McGee, the Kessinger Brothers, the Carolina Tar Heels, and other early country recording artists from whom the urban folk group has derived its material.

John Cohen, Tom Paley, and Mike Seeger formed the New Lost City Ramblers in mid-1958. Their music is based on the prevailing cultural stylings of the 1920s and 1930s, and their employment of the fiddle has enhanced their unique and genuine sound. "I feel that, perhaps more important than the actual music we play," says Mike Seeger, "we have brought attention to the value of the many songs and styles of old-time music—this consciousness did not exist in any way before we started working for it."

"For me," John Cohen explains, "old-time music and the authentic styles and instruments used to perform it gave me a vehicle to participate in music myself. If the New Lost City Ramblers did anything, it was that they made it possible for urban-based musicians to step out of the demands of the music business and away from the insulated middle-class classical sound which permeated most of the so-called folk songs available then—and, instead, to look out into America, to come in touch with the genuine energy, drive, and craziness which existed out there somewhere. I think it was this spirit of departure and this quest which gave us our validity. And it was this spirit—more than our musicianship—which opened doors for many other musicians to follow a similar path, regardless of where it led.

"In a sense, the musical platform of old-time music became an informal launching station for a variety of young musicians who went on to other things, from blues to country, bluegrass, or rock 'n' roll. Apparently

The New Lost City Ramblers (left to right): Tracy Schwarz, Mike Seeger, John Cohen, at the 1965 Newport Folk Festival

we had some influence on the Byrds as well as on Ry Cooder, and a lot of significant musicians played old-time music at some point on their way elsewhere.

"Another important factor was our introduction of so many traditional performers to the urban audience. This pattern became the basic ingredient of the folk festivals, moving away from the Baez, Weavers pattern. Today there is a large and active place for old-time music, and the new urban string bands are touring with some regularity. It seems as if the crusades are over and people are settling into enjoying music for itself and developing new standards of excellence in musicianship."

Born in 1933 in New York City, John Cohen was first introduced to folk music through his older brother Mike, who played with the Shantyboys. John Cohen learned to play a number of stringed instruments, and when he enrolled at Yale University in 1952, he started playing hillbilly music informally with another Yale student, Tom Paley.

Tom Paley was born on March 19, 1928, in New York City, and his background centered primarily around classical music and science. While he was finishing high school in the Bronx, he developed an interest in folk music and learned to play the banjo and guitar. By the time he had completed his degree work in mathematics at the City College of New York in 1950, he was regarded as one of the area's talented young folk performers (he appeared at the Leadbelly Memorial Concert at Town Hall in January 1950). While he was engaged in advanced studies at Yale, he met John Cohen.

Later on, while Paley was teaching in Maryland, he and his visiting friend John Cohen were invited by John Dildine to be on his FM radio folk music program. Mike Seeger heard about the arrangement and got together with Cohen and Paley to play for the first time in 1958. All three musicians were excited about the combination, and John Cohen contacted Moe Asch (of Folkways Records) to set up a recording session and Israel Young to arrange a concert in New York. It was originally planned for the Carnegie Chapter Hall, but when the concert tickets were sold out in advance, two performances were held in September 1959 at Carnegie Recital Hall. Their debut LP, *The New Lost City Ramblers* (Folkways FA 2396), was recorded in one session on the following day.

The original members of the three-piece band were together for about four years. In August 1962 Tracy Schwarz joined the Ramblers as a replacement for Tom Paley, who returned to teaching and moved to England. Tracy Schwarz was born in 1938 in New York City and was raised in New Jersey and New England, where he developed an appreciation for country living. As a member of the New Lost City Ramblers, Tracy Schwarz has played primarily fiddle, but he is also an accomplished guitarist, five-string banjoist, and bassist, and he sings lead and tenor vocals. With the group's change in personnel, their repertoire was broadened to incorporate unaccompanied ballads and more modern bluegrass music, as Mike Seeger explains: "We worked a lot of folk festivals and colleges, and when Tracy joined the group, we started going more deeply into country music. Our repertoire changed, which was very purposeful on our part. Tracy had just gotten out of the army, but while he was still in college he had

been getting heavily into music, and he brought a new orientation to the Ramblers."

The New Lost City Ramblers performed at the first Newport Folk Festival in 1959. Their appearance was significant in that they were virtually the only representative of traditional American folk music during a period when the folk scene was dominated by commercial groups such as the Kingston Trio, Peter, Paul and Mary, and others. They played mostly colleges, some coffeehouses, and clubs such as the Gate of Horn in Chicago and the Ash Grove in Los Angeles. In 1964 John Cohen and Mike Seeger edited the *New Lost City Ramblers Songbook* (Oak Publications), which contains over one hundred selections played by the group and, says John Cohen, "has a greater circulation today than it did ten years ago."

The group is no longer active on a full-time basis, as each of its members performs and records with other musicians. "Perhaps what is interesting for me," notes John Cohen, "is to see how all three Ramblers are living out of the city and participating in the rural life to some degree. Tracy, on occasion, gets real serious about farming. Both Mike and myself are owners of barns—but they are often used as studios for editing records and films." John Cohen has done numerous field recordings and has produced documentary films, including *The End of an Old Song*, *The High Lonesome Sound*, and *Musical Holdouts*. He is currently teaching music at the State University of New York at Purchase and he is a contributing writer to many folk music publications. He has teamed up most recently with Lyn Hardy, Jay Ungar, and Abby Newton as the Putnam String County Band, and they have recorded *The Putnam String County Band* (Rounder 3003).

In the late 1960s, Mike Seeger and Tracy Schwarz formed the Strange Creek Singers with Alice Gerrard, Hazel Dickens, and Lamar Grier. Mike Seeger has been active in making field recordings, and he has recorded five solo albums and another five with his sister Peggy. He works primarily as a solo artist but performs on occasion as a duo with his wife, Alice Gerrard. Tracy Schwarz also plays on his own and has recorded extensively with the New Lost City Ramblers, the Strange Creek Singers, Hazel and Alice, and a number of bluegrass bands. He recorded *Home Among the Hills* (Folk Variety FV 12007) with his wife, Eloise, and he has recorded for Folkways and Rounder Records. In addition to his recordings with the New Lost City Ramblers and an earlier solo recording on Elektra (EKL 12), made in the 1950s, Tom Paley has recorded a couple of albums with Peggy Seeger and he has recently done limited tours in Europe.

To date, the New Lost City Ramblers have recorded fifteen albums for Folkways Records.

## The New Shades of Grass. *See* Cliff Waldron and the New Shades of Grass.

## The New World Singers. *See* Gil Turner.

## Mickey Newbury

*Contemporary singer-songwriter, performer, and recording artist*

Cited by many top artists and composers as a major influence on American music, Mickey Newbury has expanded his career to include public performances only in recent years—rendering his own expressive interpretations of original songs that have been so profusely performed and recorded by other artists. A veteran songwriter of ten years, he has accumulated a string of hits recorded by such varied artists as Lynn Anderson, Ray Charles, Elvis Presley, Kenny Rogers and the First Edition, and Linda Ronstadt.

Born on May 19, 1940, in Houston, Texas,

he spent his boyhood years in the Lone Star State. In 1959 he crossed over into Louisiana, where he signed up for a four-year hitch with the air force, spending three of his four years in England. After his discharge, he returned to Houston and began writing, wandering around, and searching for his future. During this odyssey, Mickey Newbury's talent for writing brought him a contract with the Acuff-Rose publishing firm. By the mid-sixties, he had settled in the Nashville area, composing songs for a variety of artists representing a diversity of musical styles. His early years as a writer in Music City reaped immediate acclaim and distinction, and his songs appeared simultaneously on country, easy-listening, rock, and rhythm-and-blues charts. He was discouraged by fainthearted response to his initial recording efforts on RCA and Mercury, and by the late sixties he had retreated from the mainstream of musical activity. In 1969 he worked on a John Hartford television special with Kris Kristofferson, and while he was in Los Angeles, he met ex-New Christy Minstrel singer Susan Pack, whom he soon married.

Basically, his music has been shaped by the diversification of people and kinds of music with which he grew up in Houston. Country music was most commonly broadcast on radio, but Mickey Newbury also listened to "race" and jazz stations. The wide range of elements found in his style is largely traceable to his background, and his ability to write without restriction in a broad musical spectrum has resulted in his widespread appeal.

In 1970 he moved with his wife and son to Eugene, Oregon; in the same year, Mickey Newbury signed a recording contract with Elektra Records. To date, he has made seven albums, but he has yet to attain a hit record on his own; most of his commercial success is based on recordings of his songs by others. In 1975 he was engaged in his most active concert schedule of recent years, and his latest album, *Lovers* (7E-1030), was released.

# Randy Newman

*Contemporary singer, songwriter, pianist, performer, and recording artist*

Folk music provides a natural medium for the genesis of poetic expression, and, with the interaction of musical forms, the work of many talented individuals in the field spills over into the realms of rock, pop, jazz, and so on. With his roots in the folk tradition, Randy Newman has emerged as a cult idol and composer whose music has been chronicled by various media and by a diversity of musical stylists. Since Bob Dylan, contemporary poet-songwriters have assumed a more active role in the recording of their own material; in some cases, the combination warrants self-expression, but often the best-known renditions of a song are those recorded by artists other than its creator.

Randy Newman was born in New Orleans, and his background is musical, medical, and Western. As a young boy, he moved to California with his father, who was a doctor. Three of his uncles are musicians, and Newman was undoubtedly influenced by their prestigious status as conductors and film score composers.

His music has been a source of inspiration for many, and, through him, other people have found the articulated expression of what they have experienced in their personal lives. Known primarily by recordings of his songs by other musicians, he has gone into the recording studio to employ his own ragged, raspy singing style as self-interpreted versions of his music. The release of his first Reprise LP, *Randy Newman* (RS 6286), in 1968, initiated a strong following. In May of that same year, a single was issued, "I Think It's Going to Rain Today"/"Beehive State," which was picked up by Judy Collins and recorded on her album *In My Life* (Elektra EKS-74027). "I Think It's Going to Rain Today" was also recorded by Dave Van Ronk, among others.

His commercial success has evolved around his compositions, which have been made into hit records by such groups as Three Dog Night, which recorded Newman's "Mama Told Me Not to Come." Throughout the seventies, Randy Newman songs have been among the selections on albums by such artists as ex-Animal Alan Price, who recorded an LP of which half comprises Newman songs; Art Garfunkel, who recorded Newman's "Old Man" on his debut solo album of 1973, *Angel Clare* (Columbia KC 31474); Linda Ronstadt; Bonnie Raitt; Sonny Terry and Brownie McGhee; Harry Nilsson; and many others.

He was acclaimed for his contribution to the soundtrack of Mick Jagger's *Performance*, in which he conducted, sang, and played piano self-accompaniment on "Gone Dead Train." His next two albums, *12 Songs* (Reprise RS 6373) and *Randy Newman "Live"* (Reprise RS 6459), strengthened his following; and, in 1972, his fourth album, *Sail Away* (Reprise MS 2064), was premiered at Philharmonic Hall in New York City, with one of his uncles (Emil) conducting. In 1974 *Good Old Boys* (Reprise MS 2193) was premiered with the Atlanta Philharmonic.

# Newport Folk Festival

When Pete Seeger first proposed his idea for rehabilitating folk festivals by supplanting commercial profiteering with a nonprofit foundation concept, he was met with skepticism by the coproducers of the first (1959) and second (1960) Newport folk festivals, George Wein and Albert Grossman. Seeger was convinced that his idealistic notion (of a festival run by the artists, with profits used to benefit the field of folk music) was viable, and, together with Theodore Bikel, he won the confidence and support of George Wein, who had originally undertaken the Newport venture as a commercial enterprise. With its alteration in orientation (as suggested by Seeger and Bikel), the Newport Folk Festival became not only the largest, most controversial, and most widely publicized folk music event in memory, but it also became an exemplar for the presentation of both contemporary and traditional aspects of the idiom.

In 1963 George Wein organized (after a two-year hiatus) a committee comprising seven performers to act as the first board of directors—Theodore Bikel, Bill Clifton, Clarence Cooper, Erik Darling, Jean Ritchie, Pete Seeger, and Peter Yarrow—responsible for the selection of entertainment and the supervision of operations. The directorship was rotated on a regular basis, and later board members included Oscar Brand, Judy Collins, Ronnie Gilbert, Julius Lester, Alan Lomax, Ralph Rinzler, and Mike Seeger. All foundation and festival activities were controlled by the board of directors (George Wein, along with New York attorney Elliot L. Hoffman and Boston CPA Arnold London, served as a nonvoting member), who met approximately once a month to handle current business affairs and, in the spring, to formalize arrangements for the presentation of the annual Newport Folk Festival, generally held the third week in July.

What was even more significant than its success in terms of sheer numbers of both spectators and performers was the Newport Folk Festival's furtherance of the best in contemporary and traditional folk music. The diversity of musical orientation among the board members was reflected in its selection of performers representing all facets of the genre, from contemporary sensations such as Joan Baez, Bob Dylan, and Peter, Paul and Mary to authentic unknowns such as the Balfa Freres, Almeda Riddle, and Eck Robertson.

The foundation also addressed itself to the study, research, and support of projects related to folk music as specified in its original charter:

> To promote and stimulate interest in the arts associated with folk music; to coordinate research and promotion of these arts in the United States of America and elsewhere and to furnish a central source of assistance or information to groups or individuals interested in folk music and the folk arts; to foster the development everywhere of an understanding and appreciation of the folk arts, with particular emphasis on folk music, by presenting and causing to be produced, musical productions, seminars, and entertainments, and by taking part in activities having this end in view: to encourage and promote study, research and scholarship in the area of folk music and the folk arts through voluntary grants for such purposes by scholarships or otherwise, to individuals, institutions and organizations.

In discussing the inherent problems of such a large-scale operation, Theodore Bikel once said of the Newport Folk Festival: "The **Newport Folk Festival remains a big unwieldy mammoth.** Some problems will be solved, others will of necessity remain unremedied. The size of the festival is both its pitfall and its ultimate saving grace. Its pitfall—for intimacy disappears, parallel presentations create dilemmas both for performer and spectator, personal discomfort often becomes the price of participation. Its saving grace, however—for the very magnitude of the undertaking creates the attraction for some 15,000 to flock to Newport, to listen, to learn, to applaud or to disapprove, to sing along or sing alone; and to provide the revenue which, unlike on other days of the year, the performers do not take for **themselves but make available to those** from whom we learned and who, until now, have mostly gone unrewarded."

From the 1959 attendance figure of approximately 13,000, the size of the audience increased in 1963 to 40,000, in 1964 to 70,000, and in 1965 to a record 80,000. Toward the end of the decade, persistent pressure was imposed on festival officials by the Newport City Council, and in a letter to *Broadside* magazine, one of the directors of the Newport Folk Foundation, Toshi Seeger, clarified the reasons for the cancellation by the board of directors of the 1970 event: "Rock music had absolutely nothing to do with the Newport Folk Foundation's decision to not hold a festival this summer.

There was no rock music at the 1969 Folk Festival, and hence could not have drawn 'record crowds' to 'swamp facilities,' or 'disturb Newport residents.'

"Due to the paying for one-half of a $25,000 hurricane fence at the city's request *after* the jazz festival (where the above might have happened), an enormous bill for required police protection, and smaller attendance than usual, Newport Folk Festival is penniless. . . ."

At the last minute, the Newport Folk Festival was canceled again in 1971 when the city council, in response to youths (without tickets) storming the fences during the July 3 Jazz Festival, rescinded its license. At this point, producer George Wein relocated the annual Newport Jazz Festival to New York City, and in an attempt to recover $30,000 in losses incurred by its folk counterpart, a benefit concert was held on July 7, 1972, at Carnegie Hall.

A number of LPs of live recordings taped at the annual event have been issued by Vanguard Records, covering various years and areas, including country music, blues, bluegrass, old-time music, and evening concerts.

## Abby Newton. *See* The Putnam String County Band.

## Simon Nicol. *See* Fairport Convention.

## John Jacob Niles

*Singer, instrumentalist, songwriter, composer, collector, performer, recording artist, teacher, and author*

Along with Richard Dyer-Bennet, John Jacob Niles was considered one of the foremost "artistic," as opposed to "popular," folksingers in the period preceding the urban folk music "boom." Active in the field since World War I, this eminent folklorist

and collector is a representative of the "old school" of folk music, and his renditions of original and traditional material are graced with elegant high tenor vocals and simple yet sophisticated and gentle instrumental accompaniment on dulcimer (he is largely responsible for the popularization of the eight-string dulcimer). He is an accomplished composer, lauded for his musical arrangements, his cantata "Mary the Rose," his oratorio "Lamentation," and "Rhapsody for the Merry Month of May." The best-known folk compositions of this "Dean of American Balladeers" include "I Wonder as I Wander," "Go 'Way from My Window," "Black Is the Color of My True Love's Hair," and "Venezuela," among others.

John Jacob Niles was born on April 28, 1892, in Louisville, Kentucky. His farmer-carpenter father was one of the most respected folksingers in the area, and many of the traditional tunes which had been passed down from generation to generation in the Niles family became part of John Jacob Niles's early repertoire. His mother was a church organist and an accomplished classical pianist, and his father was adept on a variety of stringed instruments. When Niles was a young boy, he learned to play a three-string dulcimer, which his father had purchased for him. Before he was in his teens, however, by constructing a homemade dulcimer to replace the one which had been bought for him, Niles fulfilled his father's expectation that he make all instruments in his personal collection. Since then, he has made a variety of dulcimers, which he has used in performances and recordings.

When he was fifteen, Niles began his lifelong task of collecting traditional American folk music, and, using his own musical notation system, jotted down tunes found in his locality. After graduating from DuPont Manual High School in 1909, he worked as a surveyor, continuing to gather folk material wherever his job took him. Before long, he was performing at local get-togethers.

During World War I, he was seriously injured in a plane crash while serving in the U.S. Army Air Corps in France. After his discharge he remained in Europe and studied classical music at the University of Lyon and the Schola Cantorum in Paris, in 1919. Upon his return to the United States, he pursued his formal education at the Cincinnati Conservatory of Music from 1920 to 1922, and he recommenced his folk music performances.

He came to New York City, and while continuing his involvement with folk music, he supported himself with various jobs, including horse grooming, working as a nightclub master of ceremonies, and gardening. Most importantly, he worked as assistant and guide to famed photographer Doris Ulmann, who was then working extensively in the Southern mountains—thus affording Niles an invaluable opportunity to enrich his private collection of folk material. His college performances led to his acquaintanceship with contralto Marion Kerby, and they teamed up together for a while to present a folk music program to audiences in the United States and Europe.

By this time, his collection of folk material was quite extensive, and, three years prior to the publication of Carl Sandburg's famous *American Songbag* (1927), John Jacob Niles's first of several important works on folk music was published. *Singing Soldiers* consisted of selections compiled during his war experience, and it was followed in 1927 by *Songs My Mother Never Taught Me*, and in 1929 by *One Man's War* and *Seven Kentucky Mountain Songs*. The next decade brought additional publications, including *Songs of the Hill Folk* (1936) and *Ballads, Carols and Tragic Legends from the Southern Appalachian Mountains* (1937), numerous concert appearances and a recording contract with RCA Victor.

In 1940 he began work on "Lamentation," which was completed and performed for the first time on March 14, 1951, at Indiana State Teachers College. Throughout this period he continued to produce folk music recordings and to maintain an active performing schedule, while also completing another folk music collection, entitled *The Anglo-American Study Book* (1945).

On April 28, 1975, John Jacob Niles celebrated his eighty-third birthday by performing in concert at the Actors Theater in Louisville, Kentucky. At the close of the one-and-a-half-hour program, Mayor Harvey Sloane presented Niles with a "Distinguished Citizen of Louisville" scroll and with a key to the city.

His other publications include *Shape-Note Study Book* (1950); the major collection, *Ballad Book of John Jacob Niles* (1961), consisting of Appalachian ballads arranged by Child groupings with the author's variations; *Folk Ballads for Young Actors* (1962); *Folk Carols for Young Actors* (1962); and the G. Schirmer Bicentennial publication, *The Songs of John Jacob Niles.*

In addition to recordings made for RCA Victor, John Jacob Niles has produced albums for other labels, including his own Boone-Tolliver, Everest, Folkways, and Tradition.

John Jacob Niles is the recipient of five honorary doctoral degrees.

# The Nitty Gritty Dirt Band

*Vocal and instrumental group, performers, and recording artists*

Often loosely defined as a "rock band committed to a country music sound," the Nitty Gritty Dirt Band is probably best known for bringing together on a three-record set some of America's most prominent traditional country musicians, including Roy Acuff, Mother Maybelle Carter, Vassar Clements, Jimmy Martin, Earl Scruggs, Merle Travis, Doc Watson, and others. Masterminded by the group's manager and producer Bill McEuen, *Will the Circle Be Unbroken* (United Artists 9801) fostered an artistic bond which bridged the many likes and dislikes of its participants, and it introduced

The Nitty Gritty Dirt Band (clockwise, from left): Jeff Hanna, John McEuen, Jim Ibbotson, Les Thompson, Jimmie Fadden. Backstage at the now-defunct Max's Kansas City, in New York City, December 1972

both traditional country music and the Nitty Gritty Dirt Band to a broader audience.

Initially, their music was a potpourri of Spike Jones, Jim Kweskin's Jug Band, the New Vaudeville Band, and English skiffle band styles. They were based in Southern California and performed around that area for about a year before recording. Bill McEuen describes the visual emphasis in their performances: "The Dirt Band used to be a really visual act before Alice Cooper and other people got weird onstage. They put powder on their faces and wore costumes—acted out songs and used lighting and strobes—and everything was theatrical. People playing each other's instruments. Everything was visual. And that's why peo-

ple in the Los Angeles area said they'd never make it on record."

Since its beginnings early in 1966, the Nitty Gritty Dirt Band has undergone several personnel changes which have somewhat altered the group's sound. Before the group made its first recording, singer-songwriter Jackson Browne was a member, but when he embarked on a solo career, he was replaced by John McEuen. Early in 1967, Liberty Records released their single recording of "Buy for Me the Rain," which became a hit. Their first three LPs were basically combinations of jug band, vaudevillian, and contemporary pop tunes, and the theatrical orientation of the group was depicted in the jacket photographs and drawings of *The Nit-*

ty Gritty Dirt Band (Liberty LST-7501), *Ricochet* (Liberty LST-7516), and *Rare Junk* (Liberty LST-7540).

The Nitty Gritty Dirt Band made a memorable appearance in the film *Paint Your Wagon* to become the first pop group to secure a starring role in a Hollywood musical extravaganza.

After the recording of their next album, *Alive!* (Liberty LST-7611), the group temporarily disbanded when its members were in conflict over their musical direction. With Chris Darrow returning to Linda Ronstadt's band and Ralph Barr being replaced by Jim Ibbotson, the Nitty Gritty Dirt Band regrouped with Jimmie Fadden, Jeff Hanna, Jim Ibbotson, John McEuen, and Les Thompson. They had a minor hit in late 1969 with Mike Nesmith's "Some of Shelley's Blues," followed by their acclaimed version of Jerry Jeff Walker's "Mr. Bojangles." *Uncle Charlie and His Dog Teddy* (Liberty LST-7642) was designed to increase the size of their audience, as Bill McEuen explains: "*Uncle Charlie* is an AM album, it wasn't meant for FM. It's not perfect, but it sells. It's what we are—with strings and horns—and it got play on the radio."

The band moved to Colorado, and in 1971 *All the Good Times* (UAS 5553) was issued by United Artists. In that same year, Bill McEuen was making arrangements for the uniting of legendary bluegrass and country performers, accompanied by the five members of the Nitty Gritty Dirt Band. The eternal circle of music was a major theme of the *Circle* LP, and its contribution to the world of music was cited in publications from *The Nashville Tennessean* to *Rolling Stone*.

For the past few years, the Nitty Gritty Dirt Band has toured extensively, culminating in the release of a live recording, *Stars and Stripes Forever* (United Artists UA-LA184-J2). With Les Thompson gone from the group, its current personnel consist of Jimmie Fadden on drums, harmonica, and vocals; Jeff Hanna on lead guitar and vocals; Jim Ibbotson on bass, guitar, and vocals; and John McEuen on banjo, fiddle, mandolin, and numerous other instruments. Their most recent recording is *Symphonion Dream* (United Artists UA-LA 469-G).

"Where we want to go," says Bill McEuen, "is to become an act that can handle acoustic music or electric music, handle a Las Vegas audience or a college campus audience. The roots of the Dirt Band are in folk music, but we'll do whatever we feel qualified to do, and do what we like—to entertain people."

**Fate Norris.** *See* Gid Tanner and the Skillet Lickers.

**Herb and Betty Nudelman.** *See* The Golden Ring.

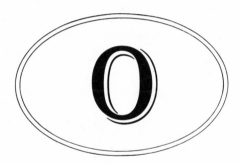

# Phil Ochs

*Singer-songwriter, guitarist, performer, recording artist, and producer*

Phil Ochs was well-known for his role as a political activist, and his social consciousness was a powerful force behind his protest songs and his involvement in civil rights and antiwar movements. He was an integral part of many social protest gatherings, from the stage of New York's Carnegie Hall to Greenwich Village coffeehouses, international folk festivals, and marches in cities throughout the United States.

Philip David Ochs was born on December 19, 1940, in El Paso, Texas, and was raised in New York and Ohio. After two years at Virginia's Staunton Military Academy, he studied at Ohio State for two years before becoming a journalism major: "I quit school and went to Florida, where I was arrested for vagrancy. I spent fifteen days in jail, where I started to become a songwriter—out of boredom, I guess, which still plagues me."

When Ochs returned to Ohio State, he started singing in Columbus and Cleveland with his roommate Jim Glover (later of Jim & Jean), who had taught him how to play the guitar. They sang together, first as the Singing Socialists and then as the Sundowners. When they broke up, Ochs spent the summer at a club called Farraghers, in Cleveland, along with such other performers as Bob Gibson, Judy Henske, and the Smothers Brothers. In the fall, Ochs left for Greenwich Village: "I was very arrogant at

the time, and I thought I'd be the best songwriter in the world. But then I immediately met Dylan, and I decided that I'd be the second-best songwriter in the world. I had walked into what happened to be the hotbed of songwriters of this century. There was Dylan, Tim Hardin, Paxton, Van Ronk, Pat Sky, Mark Spoelstra, Gil Turner, Peter LaFarge. About twenty talented people showed up at the same time—within a two-year span—and it ran for about five years, from 1961 to 1965."

Ochs was active as a songwriter from 1961 to 1970; some of his better-known works include "There but for Fortune," "State of Mississippi," "Draft Dodger Rag," "I Ain't Marchin' Any More," and "Changes." He recorded several albums on the Elektra label, including *All the News That's Fit to Sing* (EKL-269/EKS-7269), *I Ain't Marching Any More* (EKL-287/EKS-7287), and *Phil Ochs in Concert* (EKL-310/EKS-7310). In 1967 he signed with A&M Records and produced five LPs, the best of which he claims are *Gunfight at Carnegie Hall* (A&M SP-9010), a live recording of the 1970 "Gold Suit Show," and an album of his greatest hits. He is also included on several Folkways albums in the Broadside Series.

In 1973 Ochs was strangled while traveling in Africa: "My voice is ruined for life. My high notes are gone forever as a result from the damage." He continued to participate in the antiwar movement, and in January 1974 he performed at a rally for the impeachment of President Nixon, held at the

Phil Ochs at the 1966 Newport Folk Festival

Westbury Music Fair, Westbury, New York. Several months later he appeared at the now-defunct Max's Kansas City in Manhattan.

After living for a while on the West Coast, he moved back to New York, where he organized the War Is Over rally in Central Park on May 11, 1975. In addition to working as a record producer, Ochs became more active in the production of movies, and he made his final public performance on October 23, 1975, at a birthday celebration for the owner of Gerde's Folk City, Mike Porco.

On April 9, 1976, Phil Ochs hung himself in his sister's house in Far Rockaway, Queens, where he had been living since December. "Phil had been very depressed for a long time," a family friend said, according to The New York Times. "Mainly, the words weren't coming to him anymore."

A "Concert Tribute to Phil Ochs by his Many Friends" was held on May 28, 1976, at the Felt Forum in New York City. Among those present were Eric Andersen, David Blue, Oscar Brand, Len Chandler, Jack Elliott, Bob Gibson, Jim Glover, Tim Hardin, Fred Hellerman, Ed McCurdy, Melanie, Odetta, Tom Rush, Pete Seeger, Patrick Sky, Dave Van Ronk, and Peter Yarrow.

# Odetta

*Singer, guitarist, actress, performer, and recording artist*

A prominent contributor to the folk song revival of the 1950s and early 1960s, Odetta became a well-known personality on New York's Greenwich Village scene. Her richly embued performances and her sensitivity as a folksinger made her very popular and highly imitated. Younger aspirants were captivated by her genuine and complex style, which incorporated the dignity and warmth of a spiritual, the ethnic folk blues of Leadbelly, Vera Hall, Dock Reed, and others, and a contemporary identity which expressed an empathy and comprehension of gospel music, blues, and jazz.

Born Odetta Holmes on December 31, 1930, in Birmingham, Alabama, she enjoyed plunking notes on her grandmother's piano as a child. The interest became more tangible while she was growing up in Los Angeles, where the family had moved when she was six years old. She took voice lessons, joined a glee club, studied classical music in Belmont High School, and, employed as a domestic helper by day, Odetta was able to pay for her night courses in music at Los Angeles City College. In 1949 she became a member of the chorus in *Finian's Rainbow*, but, influenced by friends who had become involved in folk music, Odetta decided to make the idiom her form of musical expression.

After returning from her San Francisco tour with *Finian's Rainbow*, Odetta finished her college studies in Los Angeles but quickly went back to San Francisco to begin her **professional folk singing career at the** Hungry i club. Her next engagement was at the Tin Angel, where she worked for a year. Then Herb Jacobi of New York's Blue Angel read a review about her in the *San Francisco*

*Chronicle*, traveled to the West Coast to hear her perform, and she was booked for a two-week engagement at the Blue Angel. When she came to New York City, Odetta started on her fast rise to fame as a folksinger.

Pete Seeger and Harry Belafonte were among her early admirers, and they introduced her to other folksingers who were active in New York. Odetta went back to California to sing "Santy Anno" in the film *Cinerama Holiday*, and she stayed for the next two years, working at the Los Angeles Turnabout Theater. Her performance at Chicago's Gate of Horn was followed by her first album, *Odetta Sings Ballads and Blues* (Tradition TLP-1010), in 1956. Her second LP, *Odetta at the Gate of Horn* (Tradition TLP-1025), was based on her live performance at the club, and was recorded in 1957.

Odetta made guest appearances at concerts in the United States and Canada, including Chicago, Boston, Toronto, Vancouver, and Town Hall in New York City, in 1959. That same year, Odetta headlined the December television special with Harry Belafonte called *TV Tonight*. In 1960 she signed with Vanguard Records and was a featured singer at the Newport Folk Festival, where thousands of people were entranced by her magical style and her strong, hypnotic singing voice. Her second appearance at Carnegie Hall was on May 8, 1960, and, during that year, she was asked to perform one of the roles in the motion picture *Sanctuary*.

Odetta embodies an emotional and vocal range of expression that makes her universally appealing to all ages, colors, and creeds. Within the twenty-year span of her recording career, she has produced thirteen albums, and her continued performances attest to an unwavering popularity and acceptance that afford her the distinction of being one of the few folksingers of the folk boom who have remained active and commercially productive over the years.

Odetta has also performed with symphony

Odetta at the 1965 Newport Folk Festival

orchestras, and her interest in acting remains very strong. One of her most recent endeavors combines her talents as a vocalist and an actress, in the opera *The Medium*, by Gian-Carlo Menotti. Some additional recordings by Odetta appear on labels such as Everest (Archive of Folk & Jazz Music), Tradition, and Vanguard.

## Glenn Ohrlin

*Singer, guitarist, recording artist, and Arkansas ranch owner*

In 1963 folklorist Archie Green went down South to Arkansas, where he attended a small festival and heard the singing and guitar picking of a local rancher, Glenn Ohrlin. Owner of his own ranch since 1954, Ohrlin had spent most of his early life "cowboying and rodeoing" in Arizona, Montana, Wyoming, Nevada, and California. Arche Green encouraged Ohrlin to share his lifetime experiences of rodeo performing, working as a cowboy on ranches, and learning, swapping, and singing of traditional cowboy songs, folk and western music.

Born in Minnesota in the fall of 1926, Ohrlin learned to play guitar at an early age; even before he was in his early teens, he knew about a hundred songs, most of which were cowboy tunes. In 1943 he was a bareback riding contestant in the Caliente, Nevada, annual rodeo: "I started cowboying in Nevada when I was sixteen and I started rodeoing at the same time. I kept rodeoing for twenty-three years, through 1965, and I picked up songs everywhere I went."

Ohrlin's reputation as a talented singer of western music began to spread, and during the sixties he was invited to perform at colleges and coffeehouses. He made an album for the Campus Folksong Club of the University of Illinois, entitled *The Hell-Bound Train* (CFC 301), with most of the cuts taken from a live recording of his first concert on that college campus. The *Hell-Bound Train: A Cowboy Songbook*, by Glenn Ohrlin, with a Biblio-Discography by Harlan Daniel, was published by the University of Illinois Press, Urbana, Chicago, and London, in 1974. It is essentially a folio which includes about a hundred songs, with some cowboy standards and other selections less recognized as belonging to working cowboys or rodeo men exclusively. Dave Samuelson of Puritan Records reissued the album as Puritan 5009, and Philo Records has scheduled for release another LP entitled *Cowboy Songs* (Philo PH

1017). Ohrlin is also included on *Folk Festival of the Smokies, Volume II* (Traditional Records FFS-529), singing "Jake and Roaney and the Bald Faced Steer" and "The Hanging of Eva Dugan" with Kay Ohrlin.

Ohrlin has appeared at most of the major festivals, performing at two or three each year. During the sixties, he was a guest at the Newport Folk Festival and, more recently, was among the popular performers at the Mariposa, National, and Philadelphia folk festivals.

**Harry Orlove.** *See* Bottle Hill.

**Brother Oswald.** *See* Beecher "Pete" Kirby.

**Akira Otsuka.** *See* The II Generation.

**Charles Oyama.** *See* The Travelers 3.

**Ozark Folk Center.** *See* Arkansas Folk Festival.

Glenn Ohrlin (left) and Jack Elliott at Mariposa '75

Ozark Folk Center: Site of the Arkansas Folk Festival

287

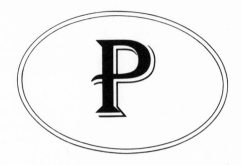

**Sue Pack.** *See* The New Christy Minstrels.


**John Paine.** *See* The Brothers Four.


**Tom Paley.** *See* The New Lost City Ramblers.


**Gene Parsons.** *See* The Byrds.


**Gram Parsons.** *See* The Byrds.


## Sandy and Caroline Paton

*Traditional singers, folklorists, cofounders of Folk-Legacy Records, performers, and recording artists*

Sandy and Caroline Paton have been singing together since they first met in 1957, and they have actively collected traditional folk music in their travels in the United States, Canada, and the British Isles. As scholars, they document the origin and provide interesting accounts for each of the songs in their repertoire, and in the interest of providing qualitative traditional music for the general public, they founded Folk-Legacy Records, Incorporated, with Lee Haggerty, in 1961.

Caroline Paton spent her childhood in Whiting, Indiana, an industrial suburb of Chicago, and she was the oldest of four children in the Swenson family. She first became involved with folk music when she was a summer camp counselor, and her interest in the field was strengthened during her college years. She studied for two years at Oberlin College, then transferred to the University of Chicago, where she completed her work toward a BA degree. After a period of traveling, she took a job at the University of California at Berkeley library, and when she met Sandy Paton in 1957, she incorporated her interests in anthropology, literature, and music in the field of folklore.

Florida-born Sandy Paton spent his childhood moving around the country with his family, finally leaving home to travel on his own. He worked at several unrelated jobs, studied art in Washington, D.C., then headed West to learn about acting at the Seattle Repertory Playhouse. He was introduced to folk music, first, by Burl Ives, then by Carl Sandburg, Richard Dyer-Bennet, and Leadbelly. Like so many others who were affected by the folk music contagion of the late forties and early fifties, Sandy Paton roamed around the country with his guitar in a style that befits the itinerant folksinger. After traveling to New York in 1953, he returned to the West Coast, where he met Caroline in Berkeley in 1957; they were married shortly thereafter. That summer, they started hitchhiking cross-country, singing and collecting songs, then sailed across the Atlantic Ocean to spend a year in the British Isles. Sandy Paton performed in London's pubs and cafés, he made several recordings by himself and one record with his wife, and they both devoted a considerable amount of time listening to field recordings and reading books in the Cecil Sharp House collection. In their 1958 travels in Scotland, they met Jeannie Robertson, who bestowed upon them a wealth of folklore, songs, and ballads and an unforgettable enthusiasm for traditional music.

They returned to the United States, and for several years Sandy Paton continued to perform as a solo act at colleges, schools, and clubs. After living in the Midwest for about a year, where they met Lee Haggerty in Chicago, the Patons settled in New England. Sandy Paton had done some field recording in Appalachia, primarily to collect works by Frank Proffitt and Horton Barker, and when Lee Haggerty came to visit the Patons, their universal enthusiasm for traditional music resulted in the formation of Folk-Legacy Records, Incorporated. They operate the record company out of their remodeled farmhouse in Sharon, Connecticut, where they moved when they outgrew their home in Huntington, Vermont. Sandy Paton acts as the company's vice-president, and Caroline Paton is the promotional director. Their own recording, entitled *Sandy and Caroline Paton* (EGO-30), is among the more than fifty albums issued by Folk-Legacy Records.

Currently, the Patons divide their time between recording artists for Folk-Legacy, working on record production and promotion, and traveling and singing. They participate in many folk festivals, sing in numerous coffeehouses, and present community concerts. Their first children's album, *I've Got a Song!* (Folk-Legacy FSK-52), is a collection of songs designed to encourage family and classroom participation in the Paton approach of singing with, not at, children, and it was issued in August 1975. (*See also* The Golden Ring.)

**Bobby Patterson.** *See* Kyle Creed.

# Ray and Ina Patterson

*Traditional country singers, instrumentalists, performers, and recording artists*

The Pattersons heard, and were influenced by, country radio of the 1930s and their traditional two-part harmony and guitar and mandolin accompaniment is reminiscent of such groups as the Delmore Brothers, the Carter Family, and the Blue Sky Boys. Their performing style is modest, and, like the material presented on local and regional family radio programs of the thirties and forties, their repertoire consists basically of old-time ballads and hymns.

Ray Patterson was born on April 17, 1926, in a rural area near Clayton, New Mexico, and, while he was growing up, he listened to his grandparents' country music recordings of Jimmie Rodgers, Peg Moreland, Vernon Dalhart, and Riley Puckett. When he moved to the farming country of Roswell, New Mexico, in 1934, the teenaged Ray Patterson heard such radio favorites as the Carter Family, Asher Sizemore, and Little Jimmie; and by 1939 he had been exposed to the music of the Blue Sky Boys. Ray Patterson started playing the mandolin at the age of sixteen; today, it is his principal instrument.

Born on March 13, 1929, in Dexter, Texas, Ina Patterson was a fan of country music, particularly the Carter Family, the Delmore Brothers, and the Chuck Wagon Gang. She and Ray Patterson were married in 1946, and by the following year they were regular performers on KGFL Radio's *Western Jamboree*. They worked with the Blue Sky Boys on WNAO in Raleigh, North Carolina, in 1948, and for the next few years played on radio stations in New Mexico, Texas, Missouri, Kentucky, and Alabama. In 1949 they made a recording for Gold Star Records and a series of recordings for the Texas–Mexico border stations.

Ray and Ina Patterson recorded for the Cozy label in the early 1950s, and in 1957 they moved to Colorado and worked for

KPIK in Colorado Springs. In 1962 they
made a permanent move to Woodland Park,
Colorado, where Ray Patterson works as a
local photographer. The Pattersons spend
much of their time making public appearances (they have performed at the San Diego
Folk Festival for the past five years and they
play annually at the Colorado Rocky Mountain Bluegrass Festival), collecting country
recordings, and recording traditional country music.

Ray and Ina Patterson have made several
albums on the County label, including *Old
Time Ballads and Hymns* (County 708); *Old
Time Songs* (County 715); and, most recently, *Songs of Home and Childhood* (County
737), released in 1973. The Pattersons are
currently working on their fourth album.

## Tom Paxton

*Contemporary singer-songwriter, performer,
and recording artist*

"I was born on October 31, 1937, in
Chicago, and I moved to Oklahoma when I
was ten. I grew up there, and then I went to
the University of Oklahoma. At the time, I
thought that I wanted to be an actor, so I
was a drama major, but in the meantime I
discovered folk music. About the same time,
I was starting to write songs, and it was the
first thing I had found that I really felt I
could do."

After graduating in 1959 with a BFA
degree from the University of Oklahoma,
Tom Paxton came to New York City in 1960
and joined the many talented young artists
who were part of the Greenwich Village coffeehouse scene. He began his professional
career by singing in such clubs as the
Gaslight, which issued his first (now-out-of-
print) LP. Along with original compositions
by other young singer-songwriters of that
era, many Paxton songs were printed in New
York's *Broadside* and *Sing Out!* magazines.
Tom Paxton was also among the participants in *Broadside's* first topical song

Tom Paxton at the Gaslight, New York City, in
August 1961

workshop held on November 1, 1964, at the
Village Gate, with Eric Andersen, Len
Chandler, Julius Lester, Phil Ochs, Bernice
Reagon, Buffy Sainte-Marie, Pete Seeger,
and Patrick Sky. Early in 1965 Tom Paxton's first of seven LPs on the Elektra label
was released, entitled *Ramblin' Boy* (Elektra
EKS-7277). The diversity of its content—
love songs, protest songs, and children's

songs—appealed to a wide audience, with "The Last Thing on My Mind," "I Can't Help But Wonder Where I Am Bound," and "What Did You Learn in School Today?" among the selections.

On August 5, 1963, he married Margaret Ann Cummings. Today, he claims this to be the most significant event of his life. He and his wife Midge traveled cross-country, planning his coffeehouse dates, and, soon thereafter, they embarked on their first trip to England: "We went to England as tourists, more or less, and, unknown to me at the time, my first Elektra album had been released over there, and many of the songs on that LP had been grabbed up by many English folk song clubs. So, when I got there, I was flooded with invitations to sing in clubs. This was the start of my English career, which has always run several laps ahead of my American career."

His subsequent recordings for Elektra were *Ain't That News* (EKS-7298); *Outward Bound* (EKS-7317); *Morning Again* (EKS-74019); *The Things I Notice Now* (EKS-74043); *Tom Paxton 6* (EKS-74066); and *The Compleat Paxton* (EKS-7E-2003), made from a live recording at the Bitter End in June 1970 and released in the following year. After Paxton signed a recording contract with Reprise in 1971, he and his family moved to England, where he made three albums: *How Come the Sun* (RS 6443), *Peace Will Come* (MS 2096), and *New Songs for Old Friends* (MS 2144).

Paxton is probably best known for his ability as a songwriter, and many of his songs have become well-known through other artists, such as Peter, Paul and Mary, who recorded "Going to the Zoo," "The Marvelous Toy," and "The Last Thing on My Mind" (which Paxton claims to be his

Tom Paxton (left) and Pete Seeger at the 1966 Newport Folk Festival

favorite composition). John Denver has popularized "Forest Lawn" and "Jimmy Newman"; the Kingston Trio recorded several of Paxton's songs, including "Ramblin' Boy," which was also performed by the Weavers; "The Marvelous Toy" and "Willie Seton" were recorded by the Chad Mitchell Trio; and so on.

"I'm very proud of the songs that I've written. I've worked hard at it, and I've learned a lot about writing songs. I've learned to write for my own voice, which I think is important for the song. I have the feeling of a tune in my head when I write the lyrics, but usually the words come first."

The Paxtons now live in the eastern Long Island rural community of East Hampton. His most recent album, *Something in My Life* (PS 2002), was issued in 1975 by Private Stock Records in New York City.

## James Peacock. *See* The Freedom Singers; The Freedom Voices.

## John Pedersen. *See* Fennig's All-Star String Band.

## Herb Pederson. *See* The Dillards.

## Dave Pegg. *See* Fairport Convention.

## J. W. Pelsia. *See* The Balfa Freres.

## Joan Pelton. *See* Fennig's All-Star String Band.

## The Pennywhistlers

*Female vocal group, performers, and recording artists*

A New York City–based women's ensemble whose members—Francine Brown, Shelley Cook, Joyce Gluck, Alice Kogan, Ethel Raim, and Dina Suler—were born in the United States in the late 1930s and early 1940s of Polish and Russian Jewish immigrants, the Pennywhistlers specialize in the recreation of characteristic stylings of Slavic and Balkan music. Whether singing *a capella* or with minimal instrumental accompaniment, the strength and directness of their vocals express their commitment to, in their words, "the open spaces, the echoing mountains, and the long river valleys of the Balkans and Eastern Europe where women have sung for hundreds of years in full, penetrating voices that carry over the distances."

While growing up, they experienced both American and Yiddish cultures, and music and singing played an important role in their early lives. The Pennywhistlers' inception was based on a need to perpetuate the meaningfulness derived from their ethnic experience, and when they had outgrown the formal activities of their community, the women continued to sing together on an informal basis.

As the group became increasingly absorbed by their ancestral heritage, their allegiance to Slavic and Balkan musical stylings became more firmly established, and, under the direction of Ethel Raim, considerable time was spent acquiring a more total comprehension of the music and its content. Vocal "relearning" became a necessary step in their attainment of the vitality and vigor of the songs in their repertoire—traditional American and topical tunes in addition to unaccompanied Balkan and Eastern European songs—and the reclamation of their own voices for this purpose has been an ongoing process and a major focus of the Pennywhistlers over the years.

The Pennywhistlers have performed at New York's Town Hall and Carnegie Hall, at the Fox Hollow, Mariposa, National, and Newport folk festivals, and at universities, colleges, churches, clubs, and coffeehouses.

They have been heard on numerous radio broadcasts and have appeared on Pete Seeger's *Rainbow Quest* (NET-TV), among other television programs. In addition to providing vocal accompaniment on recordings by other artists, such as Melanie and Rachel Faro, they have produced a number of their own albums (and one with Theodore Bikel) on various labels, including Elektra, Folkways, and Nonesuch.

## People's Artists, Inc. *See* Irwin Silber.

## People's Songs, Inc. *See* Irwin Silber.

## Luther Perkins. *See* The Tennessee Two; The Tennessee Three.

## Peter, Paul and Mary

*Vocal and instrumental trio, performers, and recording artists*

The outstanding commercial success of the Kingston Trio created a precedent for designing in a systematic way folk acts which offered to the public a blending of contemporaneity and the folk tradition. During the recent urban folk revival, the visual and vocal combination of Peter, Paul and Mary stood out among the rest, making their star-studded story one of the most memorable of that era. Their conception was masterminded by manager Albert Grossman, whose formulations, in the years that followed, were the bases of such success stories as Bob Dylan, Odetta, Richie Havens, Ian and Sylvia, and others. After several years of working out of Chicago, where he built and managed the first folk music club—the Gate of Horn—and produced the 1959 and 1960 Newport folk festivals, Albert Grossman moved his offices to New

York City, where he discovered Peter, Paul and Mary during the early sixties. The trio became one of the major forces in attracting a broader audience to the folk idiom by popularizing such standards as "If I Had a Hammer," by Pete Seeger and Lee Hays, and they brought the young Bob Dylan to the attention of the entire world when they recorded his "Blowin' in the Wind."

Mary Allin Travers was born on November 9, 1936, in Louisville, Kentucky, and came to New York City with her newspaper-writer parents when she was two years old. She attended progressive private schools where "folk music came with the education," and she grew up in Greenwich Village which "was full of folksingers." Mary Travers recalls some of her early experiences: "My life was full of people who were involved, seriously involved, in folk music. I had met Pete [Seeger] when I was about ten, and I also met people like Paul Robeson. But it never occurred to me that it would become my profession—it was a hobby, an avocation, something that was wonderful and inclusive and non-snobby and anybody could sing, even if they couldn't sing!" When she was fourteen, she was part of the children's chorus called the Songswappers, which recorded three albums with Pete Seeger, including a Folkways reissue of material by the Almanac Singers, *Folk Songs of Four Continents* (Folkways 6911), and *Bantu Choral Folk Songs* (Folkways 6912). By the age of fifteen, she was frequenting the White Horse Tavern, where "the Clancy Brothers and their friends often sang late into the night," and she began to sing in various places around the Village: "Freddy Hellerman or Theodore Bikel would say, 'Come on, sing a song.' I was very shy about singing in front of people, but I could be made to do it or embarrassed into doing it."

Noel Stookey, who adopted the name "Paul" in devising a title for the trio (based, as he explains, on "a piece of folk music in which one of the verses is 'I saw Peter, Paul and Moses playing around the roses' "), was

Sketches by Peter, Paul and Mary

born on December 30, 1937, in Baltimore, Maryland. He "grew up listening to radio," and his musical background was rooted in rock 'n' roll: "I had my own rock 'n' roll band back in the fifties, wrote some original material, and did some work as an MC and had a chance to sing some original material when I was at Michigan State from 1955 to 1958." When he came to New York, he brought along his guitar "as a hobby," and while he worked by day as a production manager for the Cormac Chemical Corporation, he started performing songs and sound effects as an evening and weekend avocation: "In terms of folk music, it was only because I started singing in the Village and was exposed to people like Paxton, Ramblin' Jack Elliott and especially Dave Van Ronk that I became interested in doing some of those songs." He gave up his daytime job with the photographic chemical company in 1960 and commenced his career as a professional entertainer, appearing at such clubs as the Club 47 and the Golden Vanity, in Boston, and the Gaslight, in New York City.

Born on May 31, 1938, in New York City, Peter Yarrow came to the trio via Cornell University where he earned his BA degree in psychology. He had been raised in a family which "placed a great emphasis on ethics, values, and culture." In addition to taking

both violin and art lessons, he went to "operas and Josh White concerts, along with the classical." He was exposed to folk music in the High School of Music and Art, and he greatly admired Woody Guthrie, Burl Ives, Pete Seeger, and Josh White. While he was at Cornell, Peter Yarrow became actively involved in folk music as an assistant to an English professor who taught a course in folklore and folk music: "In the process of teaching this material, I would sing songs to them, and with them, and I realized that something very fundamental and mean-

Peter, Paul and Mary performing at the 1965 Newport Folk Festival

ingful was happening—I was acting as a catalyst, opening people to themselves and to ideas and to feelings." After graduating from college, he decided to "take a year or two to perform," came to New York's Greenwich Village, and eventually met up with Mary Travers and Noel Stookey. In 1960 Yarrow appeared on the CBS-TV production of *Folk Sound, U.S.A.,* which led to an invitation to perform at the Newport Folk Festival that summer.

Noel Stookey had met Mary Travers at the Gaslight, where he frequently performed, and they decided "to work out some songs together." One night, after one of his performances, Noel Stookey was approached by Albert Grossman and asked if he would like to sing in a group, but Stookey turned him down. "About two weeks later," Stookey smiles, "Mary called and asked if she could bring a friend over to sing. I didn't even know at the time that it was the same Peter Yarrow that Albert had in mind and was handling." The trio put together several tunes for Albert Grossman, who then suggested that Noel Stookey change his name to Paul; and Peter, Paul and Mary was formed, with Grossman as their manager.

They started performing together in the spring of 1961, and after successful engagements in coffeehouses around the country and a television debut, they signed a recording contract with Warner Brothers Records. In 1962 their first album, entitled *Peter, Paul and Mary* (Warner W 1449), was released, along with their first single, "If I Had a Hammer"/"Lemon Tree." The year 1963 brought the release of "Blowin' in the Wind" (which helped to give Bob Dylan a boost in his career and earned Peter, Paul and Mary a Grammy Award) and two more albums, *Moving* (Warner W 1473) and *In the Wind* (Warner W 1507).

By the mid-sixties, the trio was one of the most popular folk acts in the United States and abroad, appearing in concerts, at clubs and festivals, and on television. They were among the main attractions at the Newport folk festivals, and Peter Yarrow became one

of its founding incorporators and a member of the Newport Folk Foundation's initial board of directors. Peter, Paul and Mary were also among the first entertainers to get involved in the civil rights movement and, later, the antiwar movement during the period of the Vietnam War. They took a position on certain issues before it was popular to do so, and, owing to their large following, they indirectly involved many others in current events of the sixties.

During their nine years together, Peter Yarrow and Noel Stookey contributed about half the material that was in the trio's repertoire, with the remainder derived "from outside sources." Finally, in 1970, Peter, Paul and Mary disbanded, leaving a legacy of hit recordings. "Eight out of the ten albums went Gold," says Mary Travers, "and five of them went Platinum."

Since the breakup of the trio, Mary Travers has recorded four solo albums on the Warner label, and her single release of "Follow Me" was a popular hit of the early seventies. In 1975 she hosted a syndicated radio show called the *Mary Travers Show,* and she is currently performing and writing an autobiography to be published by Delacorte Press. Peter Yarrow has continued to record for Warner Brothers; his most recent album is *Hard Times* (Warner BS 2860), released in 1975. He had a substantial hit with "Weave Me the Sunshine," and at present he is actively pursuing his solo recording and performing career. Although he has discontinued touring, Noel Stookey takes "maybe three or four weeks every year to go out and sing." He recorded one album, *Paul and Paul Stookey* (Warner WS 1912), from which his single hit of 1971, "Wedding Song (There Is Love)," was taken.

**Linda Peters.** *See* Richard Thompson.

# Philadelphia Folk Festival

In recent years, Abe Pool and his sister Maud Godshall have hosted this annual August event on the spacious wooded fields of their farm in Montgomery County, Pennsylvania. Undaunted by heat, humidity, sudden cloudbursts, and flashes of lightning across a summer evening sky, capacity crowds flock to Upper Salford Township, near Schwenksville (northwest of Philadelphia), to enjoy an impressive lineup of talent representing folk musicians from many cultures, covering all aspects of the folk idiom.

Today it is considered one of the nation's most important and prestigious folk festivals. It has grown tremendously from its modest beginnings in the late fifties, when it was originated as a cooperative effort to work hard in the interest of folk music and to have fun in the process. The Philadelphia Folk Festival is sponsored by the Philadelphia Folksong Society, a nonprofit, educational Pennsylvania corporation, which was founded in 1957 by a handful of people concerned with the encouragement of young performers and the promotion of folk music in the Philadelphia area. Since 1970, the society has received matching grants-in-aid from the Pennsylvania Council on the Arts, and additional Federal grants from the National Endowment for the Arts, Washington, D.C.

The weekend festival comprises afternoon workshops and concerts beginning on Friday; a children's concert; and three major evening concerts, which, by agreement with the local community, end by midnight. There is folk dancing, both organized and spontaneous; jam sessions; craft displays and demonstrations; instruction by instrument makers; and food, beverage, and camping facilities. In 1972 the daytime program was expanded from seventeen to twenty workshops, and a third stage area was added to accommodate the more than one hundred singers, instrumentalists, and dancers.

Over the years, entertainment has been provided by both amateurs and professionals. In 1975 there was a conspicuous absence of "name" performers in an attempt by the program committee to arrange "a more legitimate" folk festival. The overwhelming response to advance ticket sales indicated the public's enthusiasm for grassroots and uncommercial music and dancing.

# Bruce (U. Utah) Phillips

*Singer, songwriter, guitarist, performer of music, stories, puns, and jokes, recording artist, poet, essayist, and Spokane truck farmer*

"In the army, they call you either by your last name or by your state, so that's where the 'Utah' came from. The 'U. Utah' is a play on T. Texas Tyler. I got that in Yellowstone National Park in 1951 when I was working with a fellow named Norman Ritchie up in the kitchens there. I was always talking about T. Texas Tyler, so he started calling me U. Utah Phillips."

While the "Golden Voice of the Great Southwest" considers himself to be "a rumor in his own time," others regard Bruce (U. Utah) Phillips to be a legend in the field of folk music. Proud of his outrageous puns, which flow unmercifully in conversation or in concert, Phillips has a magic that engages folks whether he is reciting a terrible joke or singing "handmade songs" about "his West," railroads, bums, or small towns.

"I was born in Cleveland in 1935, and my parents were labor organizers. I spent the war years in Cleveland and Dayton, Ohio, and then in 1947 my stepfather moved us all out to Utah, where I became politically involved during the sixties. I think it was the experience of Korea when I was overseas from 1956 to 1959 that I got a chance to see what terms like 'cultural imperialism' meant, how the imposition of a foreign army could completely corrupt a culture which prior to that time had had a lot of integrity, and it infuriated me. So, when I got out of the army, I was willing to fight it anyplace that I saw it. I got involved in a thousand committees, the whole alphabet soup of the New and Old Left, all through the sixties, and it got me involved in migrant organiza-

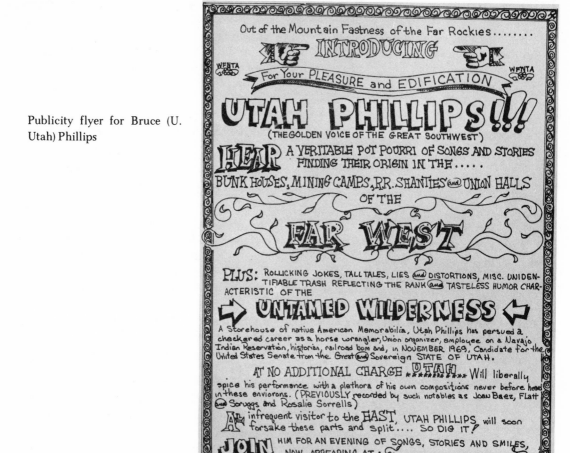

Publicity flyer for Bruce (U. Utah) Phillips

tion, the Peace and Freedom Party, Poor People's Party, just the whole spectrum of activities, some of which were constructive, I suppose, most of which were simply instructive as educational experiences by themselves. They've helped me to change the way that I go about doing things, and it culminated in running for the Senate in 1968 on a Peace and Freedom ticket. After the campaign, I finally decided that the election route and politics was not the way to do it, there were a whole lot of other changes that had to take place first.

"The consequence of that was I was no longer employable in the state, so I had to find a trade. Now, I had been using songs in field organizing and things like that, but it had never occurred to me to try to make a living at it. So, I went to New York to sell some songs that I'd written, flat out, copyrights and all, so I could get the money and go back home and dig in and fight. Then I found out, having left Utah, that things were pretty much the same all over, that no matter where you were, there was more than enough around you to dig in and fight against. The problem was systemic, general, rather than being specific to Utah, and whether it was war, racism, sexism, or what, you might as well fight it where you are.

"I also found that because other people had been singing my songs around the country, that there were audiences that wanted to listen. So in 1969 I started traveling and singing, and my first show was right after Thanksgiving in Norfolk, Virginia. I starved for a couple of years, but it's been getting better and I've been doing more and more writing."

In 1974 Phillips settled down on a farm just outside of Spokane, Washington, where he has been truck farming, writing essays and poetry, and working on a book about bumming and hoboes. Among other things, he has had the experience of riding the rails in boxcars of freight trains that carry hoboes from coast to coast. Phillips also ran Joe Hill House, which is a home for transients and migrants in Salt Lake City, Utah.

Phillips describes his first LP as "discouraging from a standpoint of recording. Occasionally I find a copy of that old Prestige record that was produced by Ken Goldstein in about 1960, and I find it in the ninety-nine-cent bin, and I take it out and jump up and down on it. I stand on my own record—'Phillips breaks his own record.' "

He recorded an album for Philo Records, *Good Though!* (Philo 1004), which contains songs, stories ("Moose Turd Pie"), some narration, and sound effects—entirely about trains and hoboing. All but two of the songs were written by Phillips, and they include "Starlight on the Rails," "Going Away," "Old Buddy, Goodnight," and "Daddy, What's a Train?," which he had recorded on a previous album entitled *Welcome to Caffe Lena* (Biograph Records BLP-12046). His second Philo LP includes songs of the West, with extensive notes, and is called *El Capitan* (Philo PH 1016), released in the fall of 1975. Among the other artists who have recorded his songs is Joan Baez, who sings "Rock Salt and Nails" on her Vanguard LP *David's Album* (VSD-79308).

Many of Phillips' songs, including "Goin' Away," are reproduced in the publication by Wooden Shoe, *Starlight on the Rails & Other Songs.*

**John Phillips.** *See* The Journeymen.

**The Pine Ridge Boys.** *See* Ernest East and the Pine Ridge Boys.

**The Pinegrove Boys.** *See* Nathan Abshire.

**Ronnie Poe.** *See* The Free State Ramblers.

# Charlie Poole and the North Carolina Ramblers

*Vocal and instrumental group, performers, and recording artists*

A pioneer of early country music, Charlie Poole sang with a distinctive nasal twang and used a three-finger style of banjo picking that helped to popularize this method of playing the five-string banjo. Charlie Poole and his North Carolina Ramblers were immensely popular while they were actively performing and recording, and they have greatly influenced modern country, particularly bluegrass, performers. Charlie Poole and the North Carolina Ramblers are representative of 1920s string band music at its peak of humor and instrumental expertise, and they have played an important role in the revival of old-time music.

Charlie Poole and the North Carolina Ramblers began their musical career around 1918, when the original members—Charlie Poole, Posey Rorer, and Norman Woodlieff—performed at dances and fiddlers' conventions in north central North Carolina. During the early years, each of the group's members worked regular jobs, mostly in textile mills; but by the mid-twenties, after their initial New York recording session for Columbia Records, they enjoyed sufficient financial security to devote themselves full-time to music.

While working for a Passaic, New Jersey, car manufacturer, Poole, Rorer, and Woodlieff went into New York City for their first recording session on July 27, 1925. One of the four cuts recorded that day, "Don't Let Your Deal Go Down Blues," better known as "The Deal," became the group's bestselling record; it featured Charlie Poole on the five-string banjo and vocals, Posey Rorer on fiddle, and Norman Woodlieff on guitar. Due to the overwhelming response to this first release, their second disc was issued almost immediately after "The Deal."

Charlie Poole and the North Carolina Ramblers started touring extensively, particularly in the upper South and Ohio. In 1926 West Virginia guitarist Roy Harvey joined the group when Norman Woodlieff left. A former railroad engineer, Harvey had become a professional musician before being added to the ranks of the Ramblers. In spite of the personnel changes, there was no significant change in the group's sound throughout its half decade of recording. In 1928 Posey Rorer left the group to return to Spray, North Carolina, and fiddler Lonnie Austin became his replacement on the Ramblers' recordings.

Lonnie Austin had joined a vaudeville act and was touring as a member of H. M. Barnes's Blue Ridge Ramblers; it was during this period that most of the recordings of the North Carolina Ramblers with Lonnie Austin were made, as he would meet the group in New York for recording sessions. After he had fulfilled his contract with H. M. Barnes's Blue Ridge Ramblers, Lonnie Austin went back to Spray, where he played with Charlie Poole for about a year.

Charlie Poole became sick and died on May 21, 1931; less than four years later, in March 1935, Posey Rorer suffered a heart attack and died. Rorer was buried near the gravesite of his lifelong friend Charlie Poole, in the Spray village cemetery. Roy Harvey continued with his recording career, performing some classic duets with guitarists Leonard Copeland and Jess Johnson. After

World War II he worked with the Florida East Coast Railroad, and he died of cancer in New Smyrna Beach, Florida, in 1958.

After leaving Charlie Poole and the North Carolina Ramblers, Norman Woodlieff recorded with a number of other musicians. In 1929 Posey Rorer, Walter Smith, and Norman Woodlieff made recordings for the Gennett label in Richmond, Indiana. Two years later, Odell Smith, Walter Smith, and Norman Woodlieff recorded as the Virginia Dandies for Crown, and as the Carolina Buddies for Columbia, and, in the same year, this trio was joined by Walter Smith's daughters Dorothy and Thelma to make a single recording for RCA Victor. By 1938 Norman Woodlieff was employed as a painter in his hometown of Spray and was performing with a new group called the Four Pickled Peppers, which engaged in two recording sessions for Bluebird.

Thirty-five of Charlie Poole's recordings have been reissued on three LPs by County Records: *Charlie Poole and the North Carolina Ramblers (1925–1930)* (County 505); *Charlie Poole and the North Carolina Ramblers, Volume 2* (County 509); and *The Legend of Charlie Poole* (County 516). One of the most recent reissues of Charlie Poole and the North Carolina Ramblers is on the Historical label, *Charlie Poole 1926–1930* (Historical HLP 8005); released in 1975, it includes some of his less well-known recordings, and two cuts from the Ramblers' last recording session, with Odell Smith playing fiddle on "Where the Whip-or-will Is Whispering Goodnight" and "Mother's Farewell Kiss."

A half century after the first recording sessions of Charlie Poole and the North Carolina Ramblers (which included Norman Woodlieff), a British label has issued an album entitled *Lonnie Austin & Norman Woodlieff* (Leader LEE 4045), released in the summer of 1975. Although they do not play together on the LP, it includes numerous personal reminiscences of these early old-time recording artists.

**Emil Potel.** *See* Don Armstrong.

**Keith Potger.** *See* The Seekers.

**Seán Potts.** *See* The Chieftains.

**Peg Clancy Power.** *See* The Clancy Brothers.

# John Prine

*Contemporary singer-songwriter, guitarist, performer, and recording artist*

A performer whose stature is based largely on the exceptional quality of his first album (*John Prine*, Atlantic SD 8296), Prine is well-known for his poignant character sketches and his philosophical reporting of current events. Like some of his other Midwestern contemporaries, such as Bob Dylan (to whom he has been likened) and his friend Steve Goodman, John Prine transcends the specificity of his background and grasps a spirit which exceeds the limitations of his immediate reference. His unique insights into a diversity of significant issues have captured the interest of a widespread audience, and, with depth and precise imagery, he presents the universal common denominators in our lives.

Now in his late twenties, John Prine was born and raised in Chicago, spending a portion of his childhood in Muhlenberg County, Kentucky (his song "Paradise" refers to the strip-mining in this region of the United States). His is basically an introspective personality, and many of the ideas for his songs arise from his own personal experiences (his satirical "Your Flag Won't Get You into Heaven Anymore" was generated by his brief employment as a mailman, when the weight of his mailbag was increased by the

John Prine at an afternoon workshop at the Eleventh Annual Philadelphia Folk Festival, 1972

flag decals included within the pages of *Reader's Digest*).

Some of the other short tales on his debut LP, which created such a stir (and a wave of comparisons to the genius of Bob Dylan) in the music industry, are "Donald and Lydia," "Sam Stone," "Hello in There," and "Illegal Smile." Many of these songs have been picked up by other artists. Soon after the album's release in 1971, he recorded his second effort, entitled *Diamonds in the Rough* (Atlantic SD 7240). Although its selections make further personal statements, its country-flavored tunes limited its airplay on pop radio stations, and the album sales were disappointing. Lighter in content than its predecessors, his third LP, *Sweet Revenge* (Atlantic SD 7274), paved the way for a successful third tour, during which he headlined and filled Los Angeles's Troubadour for a solid week. Prine is often seen with Steve Goodman (with whom he frequently works and tours), and his career has paralleled the rise of his friend (of "City of New Orleans" fame) from their beginnings in Chicago bars to national acclaim. Both Prine and Goodman travel extensively, playing festivals, clubs, and concerts from coast to coast.

John Prine's fourth, and most recent, album is called *Common Sense* (Atlantic SD 18127), released in 1975.

## Willis Proctor. *See* The Georgia Sea Island Singers.

## Frank Proffitt

*Traditional singer, collector, guitarist, banjoist, instrument maker, and recording artist*

The Kingston Trio's 45-RPM recording of "Tom Dooley" was a cash box top single of 1958; based on cumulative sales, it won a Gold Record award and became one of the key propellants of the recent folk song revival. Based on an actual incident in Wilkes County, North Carolina, "Tom Dooley" had been passed on to regional descendant Frank Proffitt, who, in turn, taught the ballad to his friends Anne and Frank Warner, in 1938. Without copyrighting his version of "Tom Dooley," Frank Warner recorded the ballad for Elektra Records in 1952. Six years later, the Kingston Trio's leader Dave Guard copyrighted his arrangement of "Tom Dooley," and thus created a stir of con-

troversy regarding the problems of unethical use and copyrighting of folk songs in the public domain.

Born in 1913 in Laurel Bloomery, Tennessee, Frank Noah Proffitt moved with his family to Watauga County, North Carolina, where his father Wiley Proffitt supported his family as a farmer, cooper, and tinker. As a youngster, Frank Proffitt learned a multitude of songs from his father, his Uncle Noah, and an aunt, Nancy Prather, and the skill of handcrafting banjos was handed down from father to son.

Throughout his lifetime, Frank Proffitt collected traditional material from friends and neighbors in Watauga County. His proud mountain heritage was communicated to Anne and Frank Warner, who traveled to North Carolina and collected songs from Proffitt and others, as described by the Warners: "Once we got there, someone in Boone said they were having a big county sing. We inquired about Nathan Hicks of Beech Mountain, who had made a dulcimer and sent it to us, and when we got to his house, which was way back into the mountains, there was a group of people sitting around the front yard, and among those in the photograph that we took was Frank Proffitt, who was Nathan's eldest son-in-law.

"He had walked eight miles from the valley over to meet us from 'the beyont.' We were from 'the beyont.' He became a blood brother of ours. That afternoon, we wrote down the words of two songs, 'Moonshine' and 'Tom Dooley.' At the time, Anne wrote down, 'Hang down your head, Tom Dewey,' because he had made such a name for himself as the district attorney in New York City, and 'Tom Dewey' is what was in her mind, so that is what she heard.

"He had a mountain banjo that he had made himself and played, and I fell in love with it. All of the banjos that Frank Proffitt made were fretless.

"We were there in June of 1975, and we had a big reunion on Beech Mountain. Nathan Hicks's son Ray, who recorded the 'Jack Tales' for Folk-Legacy, lives there, and

Ray Hicks dancing to the music of Frank Proffitt and Buna Hicks on Beech Mountain, North Carolina, while Mrs. Nathan Hicks and local children look on

the house has hardly changed in the more than thirty years that we have known it. We had about forty people gathered 'round for our homecoming, and we had taken a cassette of Frank Proffitt singing, before he died, and there they all sat, listening to Frank sing.''

During the course of the Warners' friendship with Frank Proffitt, they collected over 120 songs from him. Proffitt's name became known in folk circles with the widespread publicity of the Kingston Trio's commercial hit, "Tom Dooley," and he made his initial public appearance at the University of Chicago's First Annual Folk Festival. Frank Proffitt's first album was recorded by Folkways Records, *Frank Proffitt Sings Folk Songs* (FA 2360). In 1962 Folk-Legacy Records issued their company's first recording, *Frank Proffitt* (FSA-1), which was made at Proffitt's home that January, and includes his version of "Tom Dooley."

Frank Proffitt made his living as a tobacco farmer, part-time carpenter, and instrument maker, and traditional music was an authentic part of his Anglo-American heritage. Since his death on Thanksgiving morning, November 24, 1965, his name has been honored in memorial concerts throughout the world, and, in the spring of 1969, Folk-Legacy released *A Memorial Album* (FSA-36) from the last tapes made before he died, and recorded in tribute to Frank Proffitt's memory and friendship.

## George Riley Puckett. *See* Gid Tanner and the Skillet Lickers.

## Mike Pugh. *See* The Chad Mitchell Trio.

## The Putnam String County Band

*Vocal and instrumental group, performers, and recording artists*

Each of this group's members is an accomplished musician who is highly respected for work both with and outside of the Putnam String County Band. "The Putnam String County Band is a reflection of musical and social forces of the early 1970s," explains one of its members, John Cohen, "and brings together a much more varied set of musical backgrounds into a semi-quasi-crazy country sound."

John Cohen is well-known for his role with the New Lost City Ramblers, which is one of a number of influences on the Putnam String County Band. His involvement in traditional music has led to his branching out in a variety of activities, including teaching, writing for folk music publications, making field recordings, and producing documentary films.

Publicity flyer of the Putnam String County Band

Jay Ungar has played with an old rock 'n' roll band named Cat Mother and the All Night Newsboys, and, says John Cohen, "when he joined that group, he gave them more of a fiddle–country music orientation for a while." An outstanding fiddle player, Ungar made an album with John Townley with the intention of mixing rock sounds and more traditional approaches, along with some experimental ideas. John Cohen reflects on Jay Ungar's musical growth: "As the Putnam String got moving, David Bromberg hired Jay to tour and record with him. This served to slow things down for us, although we had several excellent years of concerts and festivals.

"Jay writes songs as does his wife Lyndon Ungar [Hardy]. Her singing is more of the folk revival style, although she 'feels' country as well, and she writes some good sentimental women's songs. She acts more like Moonshine Kate!

"Abby Newton and her cello come from a more classical music background, and the message here seems to be that playing music can be informal and fun—if not traditionally or aesthetically correct."

Formed in 1971, the Putnam String Band recorded an album entitled *The Putnam String County Band* (Rounder 3003), which shows the influence of the New Lost City Ramblers, rock music, and folk sources. The group plays together rarely now, as each of its members is engaged in other pursuits. Abby Newton tours with a classical group; John Cohen is teaching at the State University of New York at Purchase; and the Ungars play as the duo Jay Ungar and Lyndon Hardy— they have recorded their first solo effort, *Songs, Ballads, and Fiddle Tunes* (Philo PH 1023), released on July 25, 1975. Jay Ungar also appears on numerous current records as a backup fiddler.

"We all remain good friends," smiles John Cohen, "and get together when we can."

## The Rackensack Folklore Society.  *See* Arkansas Folk Festival; Jimmy Driftwood.

## Ethel Raim. *See* The Pennywhistlers.

## Bonnie Raitt

*Contemporary singer, guitarist, songwriter, performer, and recording artist*

In a brief half decade or so, this soulful singer of the blues has established a widespread reputation as one of the music industry's most natural and earthy artists. Her basically black-oriented repertoire ranges from traditional blues music to old blues tunes (composed by Robert Johnson, her close friend Fred McDowell, Son House, and others), classic blues of Sippie Wallace, modern blues, Motown oldies, jazz, calypso, and contemporary popular music. A proficient guitarist who is well-known for her own bottleneck accompaniment, Bonnie Raitt is an impressive writer and interpreter of blues and modern material and an entertainer with a sincere and irrepressible nature.

Born Bonnie Lynn Raitt on November 8, 1949, in Burbank, California, to Marjorie and actor John Raitt (star of such Broadway hits as *Carousel*, *Oklahoma!*, and *Pajama Game*), she spent most of her early life in New York, where her father was engaged in

theatrical work. The Raitts returned to Los Angeles in 1957 when John Raitt was asked to star in the movie version of *Pajama Game*. Bonnie Raitt and her brothers Steven and David grew up in musical surroundings, and they all sang. She received her first guitar—a twenty-five dollar Stella—when she was eight years old and within a couple of years was playing on her grandfather's Hawaiian slide guitar. She took piano lessons for several years and by the age of eleven had saved enough money to buy a red Guild gut-string guitar.

As a young girl, she listened to the rhythm-and-blues of the late fifties, which appealed to her more than contemporary rock 'n' roll. She spent seven consecutive summers at a politically oriented camp in the Adirondacks, which was run by friends of her Scottish Quaker parents, and it was there that Bonnie Raitt's love for music and her social consciousness were fostered. She became involved in the peace movement during the early sixties, and her attention turned to the music of Joan Baez and Pete Seeger. When she was fifteen, she and a friend sang at a "hoot" night held at the Troubadour in Los Angeles. She went to University High School in Hollywood (with Randy Newman) and, later, to an activist Quaker secondary school in Poughkeepsie, New York. Although she sang at folk hoots and informal sessions while attending Radcliffe College, her main interest resided with blues. After the first semester of her sophomore year at Radcliffe, she went to Philadelphia and was hired by the Second

Fret to open for the Sweet Stavin' Chain local band—which resulted in her own four-night booking. She returned to Cambridge to complete another year of her college education, and landed a job as opening act for John Hammond, Jr. For two and a half years, she traveled and performed gigs with ex-Edison Electric Band (another local Philadelphia group, which she had met on a return engagement at the Second Fret) bass player Dan "Freebo" Friedberg, who has played as a member of her entourage throughout the seventies.

Bonnie Raitt performing at the Friday evening concert at the Eleventh Annual Philadelphia Folk Festival, 1972

Bonnie Raitt started playing blues in the early sixties after listening to records by Mississippi John Hurt and other blues singers. She was deeply attracted to country blues and delta stylists such as Robert Johnson, Fred McDowell, and Son House, and during her college years she became friends and traveled with Son House, Fred McDowell, Robert Pete Williams, and other bluesmen. She often performed club, concert, and festival dates with Fred McDowell, and since his death, in 1972, she will frequently include a selection of his songs during her performances.

From her first public performance in 1969 to gigs around the Worcester, Massachusetts, area, Philadelphia's Main Point, the Philadelphia Folk Festival, and the Gaslight (with Fred McDowell), in 1970, her career has developed rapidly. She became one of the regular performers at the Philadelphia Folk Festival and has appeared in clubs, concerts, and festivals across the country (in the summer of 1971 she was among the select few white artists to perform at the Ann Arbor Blues and Jazz Festival). She signed with Warner Brothers in the spring of 1971, resulting in the release of her first album, *Bonnie Raitt* (Warner WS 1953). Since then, she has made four more LPs on the Warner label: *Give It Up* (2643), *Takin' My Time* (2729), *Streetlights* (BS 2818), and *Home Plate* (B 2864).

## Emma Ramsay. *See* The Georgia Sea Island Singers.

## Wayne Raney. *See* The Delmore Brothers.

## Bernice (Johnson) Reagon

*Singer, songwriter, performer, recording artist, oral historian, and folklore specialist for the Smithsonian Institution*

One of the original Freedom Singers and

now the central figure in an all-black women's ensemble called Sweet Honey in the Rock, Bernice (Johnson) Reagon has played a significant role in the fight for black sociopolitical change for the past fifteen years.

In her own words: "Bernice Johnson Reagon is first the daughter of a Baptist minister from Albany, Georgia, and a product of Baptist music and cultural traditions. My present-day usage of music began in Albany, as a song leader in the Albany, Georgia, mass movement of 1961 to 1962. From this position I moved to become one of the original Freedom Singers, along with Cordell Reagon (my former husband), Rutha Harris, and Chuck Neblett." With a strong interest in black traditional music, she avidly collected material in this genre in 1962–63 while concurrently fostering social action by singing at Student Non-Violent Coordinating Committee (SNCC) benefit concerts in the North and at freedom rallies in the South.

In the mid-sixties, Bernice Reagon appeared frequently in folk clubs in the North, and, in addition to her appearance with the Freedom Singers at Newport in 1963, she was among the performers at several subsequent Newport folk festivals. She was also instrumental (along with Anne Romaine) in organizing the Southern Folk Festival, the Soul Roots Festival, and the Penny Festival, and other college, church, and community folk music events in every state in the South. In 1968, "responding to political and cultural realities of the black struggle," she withdrew from the more interracial folk music scene and put together the Harambee Singers—an all-black female quartet of political activists who sang "songs reflecting the growing moods of black nationalism and Pan-Africanism."

The early seventies found Bernice Reagon in Atlanta, where she was working on the compilation of a tape library for the Atlanta Center for Black Art. In May 1975 she earned a PhD in oral history at Howard University, and she was awarded Smithso-

nian Foundation grants for research in Africa and the Caribbean. She is currently folklore specialist for the Smithsonian Institution, vocal director of the Black Repertory Theater in Washington, D.C., a songwriter, and a performer with Sweet Honey in the Rock.

Bernice Reagon has recorded for Folkways and KinTel Records (Atlanta, Georgia), and, most recently, for Paredon Records. (*See also* The Freedom Singers; Sweet Honey in the Rock.)

# Cordell Hull Reagon. *See* The Freedom Singers; The Freedom Voices.

# The Red Fox Chasers
*Old-time band, performers, and recording artists*

The core of the Red Fox Chasers' homespun, down-to-earth music was the vocal harmonizing of A. P. Thompson and Bob Cranford, who had grown up together in Surry County, North Carolina. The Red Fox Chasers were organized in 1928, and although the band did not experience the longevity enjoyed by other early old-time groups, A. P. Thompson, Bob Cranford, Paul Miles, and Guy Brooks are historically significant for a stylization that is congruous with the uncomplicated life of mountain people of the twenties.

As young boys, A. P. Thompson and Bob Cranford sang duets together. They were neighbors in Thurmond, North Carolina, and they used to meet every day at the local schoolhouse. They were given singing lessons by a traveling music teacher, and, in combination with much practice, Thompson and Cranford perfected harmony singing. By their teens they had learned to accompany their singing with Thompson on guitar and Cranford on mouth harp, and they began to perform old-time regional songs, such as "Goodbye Little Bonnie," "Devilish Mary," and "Katy Cline," for local audiences.

Paul Miles and Guy Brooks were brought up with roots in fiddle music, and when they teamed up with Thompson and Cranford they modified their fiddle and banjo styles to complement the mountain vocals. Miles and Brooks had also grown up together in Alleghany County, North Carolina. Paul Miles learned to play the banjo as a youngster, and, with his homemade fretless banjo, he played with Guy Brooks, who earned a $3.50 fiddle by gathering chestnuts.

The four musicians met at the 1928 Union Grove Fiddlers' Convention. The Red Fox Chasers was organized by Paul Miles, who suggested that their primary objective should be to make records. As the band's leader, he set up an audition with the Gennett Company of Richmond, Indiana, and on April 15, 1928, the Red Fox Chasers recorded eight sides. Guy Brooks wrote the lyrics to many of the forty-eight sides recorded by the band. Some of the songs for which he wrote the words have been reissued on *The Red Fox Chasers* (County 510), including "Honeysuckle Time" and two others with his lyrics set to music by A. P. Thompson, "Stolen Love" and "The Blind Man and the Child."

The Red Fox Chasers made their last recordings in 1929, and in January 1931 Thompson and Cranford recorded a dozen sides by themselves. Each of the band's members returned to his regular job after their last recording session, and they went back to making music as a pastime and not as a profession.

# Jean Redpath

*Scottish traditional singer, performer, and recording artist*

Since her emigration to the United States in March 1961, Jean Redpath has received widespread critical acclaim for her consis-

tent contributions to the American folk music scene. She was an integral part of the folk movement during the 1960s and, from the beginning, was recognized as a viable force in traditional folk singing.

"I was born on April 28, 1937, in Edinburgh, Scotland, and by the age of ten I was already recognized as 'having a voice,' I believe is the expression at home. It was a gradual process of opting for traditional music versus other types. When I was growing up, it was no longer a case of being raised in a rural community with only one kind of music available. There were record players, radios, and traveling concert groups, and I don't believe I actually heard the expression 'folk music' until I was about nineteen.

"I went to the University of Edinburgh, and I met a girl from California. So, when I decided it was time to travel, the only place where I had a roof over my head was in California with this girl's family. So I headed for California, and Hamish Henderson had written ahead to an agent in Michigan and to Ken Goldstein in Philadelphia to let them know that I was coming. About four or five months after I landed, I got a letter from this chap in Michigan, whom I had yet to meet, telling me that he had booked me into a club in Philadelphia for three weeks and had arranged a recording session with Kenny, and he gave me the specific dates for both, and so on. Well, being very green, and never having done anything so special, I begged, borrowed, and stole my fare across country, and when I landed in Philly I discovered that the club owner had skipped out of town three weeks before and hadn't paid his last performer . . . [Dave] Van Ronk. And when I called Kenny, he said, 'I don't know where this guy got these dates because I'm not even going to be in town then,' so the whole venture was a bust. So I went to visit with Ken and his wife Rochelle for about five days. While I was there, Bob and Evelyne Beers drove through Philly and stopped to see Ken and Rochelle and, discovering that I was thinking of going to New York, said, 'If you're headed for New York, we'll give you a ride.' So they gave me a ride to the city, and they took me to Miki Isaacson's apartment in Greenwich Village. It was a Thursday afternoon and we walked in on a jam session with Dylan, Jack Elliott and the Greenbriar Boys, who were working at Gerde's at the time.

"So essentially what happened is that I walked into the hard-core folk scene in Greenwich Village, and, by going to that apartment, I met everyone who was doing this for a living.

"One of the highlights of my career was playing Gerde's Folk City in 1961, six weeks after I landed in New York City. And getting a review in *The New York Times* gave me a good hard push off the road of starvation because I had been living on peanut butter and jelly up until then.

"The kind of music that I sing tends to be highly personal and dependent on intimate situations, which is almost self-destructive in terms of making a living because you can't ask a big fee from a place that doesn't hold many people. But ideally, a group of fifty people or less is what I like to work with. Even getting letters from somebody in the sticks somewhere who has happened to stumble onto one of my records and who writes just to say thanks for the pleasure I've given him, that's probably more of a highlight than any of the other things that I could mention. There's always something that seems to come up just at the right moment that reminds me of my sense of responsibility to my music. I'm happy with the type of music that I'm doing because this is the language that I speak better than any other, so I stick with it.

"I must know several hundred songs, and they span everything from bluegrass to 'Will You Love Me When I'm Old' to kid's songs to ghastly English translations of Italian opera to fifty-verse ballads in the Scottish tradition. When I use guitar, I use the simplest possible accompaniment because essentially I'm concerned with the song and not how I can dress it up or do variations of

it. I find that if I can vary the piece for an audience that is not accustomed to *a cappella* singing, by using guitar, I do it. But the less I use the instrument, the less I feel that I am compromising.

"My first recording was *Skipping Barefoot Through the Heather* [Prestige/International PR 13020], which was cut before, but released after, *Scottish Ballad Book* [Elektra EKL-214]. I made two more albums for Elektra, *Songs of Love, Lilt and Laughter* [EKL-224] and *Laddie Lie Near Me* [EKL-274], but all of these recordings have been out of print for a considerable time. A Folk-Legacy recording which I made about two years ago, in 1973, *Frae My Ain Countrie* [FFS-49], is still available. A new album, *Jean Redpath* [Philo PH 2015], was released in November of 1975, and, hopefully, I'll have two more records out by the summer of 1976."

Jean Redpath is currently lecturing full-time in Wesleyan University's Music Department: "It's a chance to stay in one place, with the books and all the records, and I can really sink my teeth into the things that I'm singing. I'm also acquiring all sorts of repertoires as well because classic ballads, with which I'm most involved, need a lot of living with before you can sing them."

## Henry Reed. *See* The Hollow Rock String Band.

## Ola Belle Reed
*Country, clawhammer-style banjoist, traditional folksinger, songwriter, performer, and recording artist*

Well-known for her earthy, mountain style of singing and her old-timey, clawhammer style of banjo picking, Ola Belle Reed is a traditionalist who reflects the cultural heritage of the mountain region of western North Carolina where she was born in 1915.

As a child, Ola Belle Reed learned to play banjo on a borrowed instrument. She performed with a group called the North Carolina Ridge Runners, and after World War II she and her brother formed the New River Boys and Girls, which played at local gatherings, such as picnics, festivals, and carnivals. Ola Belle Reed has done radio work for forty years and has performed at numerous festivals, entertaining crowds with Appalachian ballads, bluegrass, gospel, country & western, and banjo tunes. At home with audiences of any size, she is often accompanied by her husband Bud and her son David.

Her song "High on a Mountain" is the title track of a record by Del McCoury & the Dixie Pals, *High on a Mountain* (Rounder 0019), and the song is among those included on her album *Ola Belle Reed* (Rounder 0021).

# Revon Reed. *See* Dennis McGee.

# Malvina Reynolds

*Contemporary songwriter, singer, guitarist, recording artist, publisher, and record producer*

The list of this prolific Berkeley songwriter's accomplishments is long, but Malvina Reynolds's niche in folk music has been established primarily by recordings of her songs by other artists.

The seventy-five-year-old songwriter was born of immigrant parents in San Francisco at the turn of the century. When she was six her aunt took her to the city's repertory theaters: "I used to watch the curtain go up and the lights go out, and I was just fascinated." Woody Guthrie, Pete Seeger, and Earl Robinson were among her early contacts with folk music: "After Woody, I think I was one of the first who was primarily interested in writing songs based on labor and the folk tradition, songs with a social content. I write topical songs because I feel as though they are necessary." In 1934 she and

Bud Reynolds, who was a radical activist and labor organizer, were married. One of her early songs, "Bury Me in My Overalls," was written to cheer him up when he was recovering from a heart attack, in 1956. In July 1971, he suffered a stroke and, the following year, in September, died in his sleep.

The turning point in her career as a songwriter was Harry Belafonte's recording of "Turn Around," which she wrote in the late fifties. Other songs of that decade include "Magic Penny," "Bury Me in My Overalls," "Bring Flowers," "Let Us Come In," "Little Land," "Nobody," "Pied Piper," "We Don't Need the Men," "Don't Talk to Me of Love," "Faucets Are Dripping," "Oh, Doctor," "Patchwork of Dreams," "Somewhere Between," "The Little Mermaid," "The Miracle," "There'll Come a Time," "We Hate to See Them Go," and "Where Is the Little Street"; in 1957 she wrote the lyrics to music composed by Woody Guthrie for "Sally, Don't You Grieve."

During the sixties, Malvina Reynolds and her friend Pete Seeger worked on several songs, including "From Way Up Here," "Andorra," and "Mrs. Clara Sullivan's Letter." Many of her songs have been recorded by Seeger, but "Little Boxes" is probably the most notable: " 'Little Boxes' was actually his first hit single after the long years of boycott, and I was glad to be the one that helped to break him through that situation. A funny thing happened in connection with that song. There were many big-name people, like the Kingston Trio and the Limeliters, and as commercial as they were, they had such respect for Pete that they wanted him to have that song, and they wouldn't cover it." "Little Boxes" is on one of his earlier Columbia LPs, *We Shall Overcome* (Recorded Live at His Historic Carnigie Hall Concert of June 8, 1963 [CS 8901]), and five of her songs appear on one of Seeger's more recent albums, *God Bless the Grass* (ICS-9232). " 'What Have They Done to the Rain' turned out to be a big,

Malvina Reynolds at Mariposa '75

cluding *Malvina* (Cassandra CFS 2807), *Malvina Reynolds* (Century City CCR 5100), and, most recently, *Malvina—Held Over* (Cassandra CFS 3688); and three 45-RPM records. Her albums *Artichokes, Griddle Cakes Etc.* (Pacific Cascade LPS 7028) and *Funnybugs, Giggleworms, Etc.* (Pacific Cascade LPS 7025) were issued by Joan Lowe Productions in Vida, Oregon. She recorded an album for Folkways Records entitled *Another Country Heard From* (FN 2524), and for Columbia Records, *Malvina Reynolds Sings the Truth.* Oak Publications has issued two songbooks: *Little Boxes and Other Handmade Songs* and *The Muse of Parker Street.*

## Nick Reynolds. *See* The Kingston Trio.

## Ervin "Dick" Richard. *See* The Louisiana Aces.

## Dave Richardson. *See* The Boys of the Lough.

## Larry Richardson

*Bluegrass singer, banjoist, songwriter, performer, and recording artist*

An enigmatic personality in the field of bluegrass music, Larry Richardson has been in and out of bands since his early days of Scruggs-style banjo picking and singing in his 1949 duets with Bobby Osborne on WPFB in Middletown, Ohio.

Larry Richardson hails from one of America's most fertile areas of old-time music—Mt. Airy, North Carolina. When he began his professional career in music, bluegrass was a young and viable form of country music. He opted to perform in the old style of bluegrass, and his style was influenced by early recordings of "The Father of Bluegrass," Bill Monroe.

practical hit and lots of fun because it was recorded as a rock song at the time when rock was beginning to bloom." It appears on *Joan Baez in Concert* (Vanguard VRS-9112) and the Seekers' LP *The Seekers* (Capitol T-2319), among others. The Seekers also recorded "Morningtown Ride" on that same album. Reynolds wrote a song about demonstrations, which was rewritten by Barbara Dane after it was issued. "It Isn't Nice" was picked up and recorded by Judy Collins on her album *Judy Collins' fifth album* (Elektra EKL-300).

Malvina Reynolds set up her own publishing firm, Schroder Music, and her own recording company, Cassandra Records. They have produced *The Malvina Reynolds Songbook, Cheerful Tunes for Lutes and Spoons, Tweedles and Foodles for Young Noodles,* and *Not in Our Stars;* albums in-

Bobby Osborne was inspired by the musical drive and musicianship of Larry Richardson, and they performed together, with Osborne's band, for a very brief time in the summer of 1949. After a dispute with the management of WPFB, they decided to head South, hoping to find a radio station that would be more receptive to their music. They started working for WHIS in Bluefield, West Virginia, and, after playing with one band led by Rex and Eleanor Parker, Richardson and Osborne joined up with the Lonesome Pine Fiddlers. The Cline family had been the backbone of the Fiddlers for the previous decade, and in the fall of 1949 the band was led by bassist Ezra Cline. Within a year, they made their first recordings with the Lonesome Pine Fiddlers, with two vocal duets by Larry Richardson and Bobby Osborne—"Lonesome, Sad, and Blue" and "Pain in My Heart," which later became a Flatt and Scruggs standard on Mercury. After playing an instrumental role in establishing a bluegrass identity for the Lonesome Pine Fiddlers, Richardson left the group in the early fifties.

In 1949 Richardson joined Republic, Mercury, and Capitol recording artist Carl Sauceman, and during this period he developed his clear, high tenor singing voice and his distinctive banjo style. After a brief reunion with the Lonesome Pine Fiddlers, Richardson again departed in the late spring of 1951, and commenced performing on WCYB in Bristol.

After several years of traveling, Richardson returned to his North Carolina home, where he continued to sing and play bluegrass music. In 1955 he and banjoist Happy Smith recorded "Let Me Fall" and "I'm Lonesome" on the now-defunct Blue Ridge label. The mid-sixties found Larry Richardson recording with the Blue Ridge Boys for County Records, and *Blue Ridge Bluegrass* (County 702) contains his classic arrangement of "Let Me Fall." The album also offers two original compositions by Richardson, "You Left Me So Blue" and an earlier hit, "Pain in My Heart," written with Bobby Osborne; and it features Red Barker on

guitar and vocals, Curly Blake on bass, Buddy Crisp on guitar and vocals, Buddy Pendleton on fiddle, Ronnie Pervette on mandolin, and Larry Richardson on banjo and vocals.

## Fritz Richmond. *See* The Jim Kweskin Jug Band.

## Mark Rickart. *See* Apple Country.

## Almeda Riddle
*Traditional singer, performer, and recording artist*

This traditional singer from the Ozarks has provided the contemporary music scene with a link to its roots in an oral tradition. Her unaccompanied singing of old-time ballads breathes new life into this country's folk heritage as she revives legends which have been kept alive, generation after generation, by ballad singers. For a number of years, Almeda Riddle has charmed festival audiences with the narrative and vocal qualities of her art, and she has performed at folk music events across the United States, from Newport, to the National Folk Festival, to local gatherings near her home in Heber Springs, Arkansas.

Almeda Riddle was born in 1898, and most of her life has been spent either in White County or in Cleburne County, Arkansas. As her family moved frequently while she was growing up, her education was largely acquired at home. Music was an important part of her upbringing, and through her singing-teacher father, the young Almeda Riddle learned to read music, to accompany her singing on fiddle and parlor organ, and to understand the principles of harmony.

She was recorded for the Library of Congress by Alan Lomax, and she was included on his twelve-volume *Southern Journey* set of field recordings issued by Prestige/International in 1961. In addition to her own now-out-of-print *Almeda Riddle: Songs and Ballads of the Ozarks* (Vanguard VRS-9158), she was included on Vanguard recordings of the Newport folk festivals. More recently, Rounder Records has issued *Ballads and Hymns from the Ozarks: Almeda Riddle* (Rounder 0017), a collection of a dozen songs performed by Almeda Riddle in a traditional style, with her typical high-pitched vocals.

## Jimmy Riddle. *See* The Smoky Mountain Boys.

## Jim Ringer

*Singer, songwriter, guitarist, performer, and recording artist*

Sometimes said to be one of America's true western singers, this ex-construction worker, ex-con, and ex-prizefighter-turned-professional-musician has enjoyed a substantial and loyal following on the West Coast, where he has lived and worked from job to job, for most of his forty years. In the past several years, his name has spread to other areas of the United States and to Canada through his appearances at various clubs and festivals (including Fox Hollow and Mariposa), articles by and about him in such music publications as *Folkscene* and *Sing Out!*, and his recordings for Folk-Legacy and Philo.

Jim Ringer was born on February 29, 1936, in Arkansas, and he moved with his family to California in 1945. In an interview with Bruce Phillips, published in *Sing Out!* (Vol. 22, No. 3, 1973), he explains his early involvement with music: "As far back as I can remember, there's always been singing and people comin' around. We had the only radio in the country back there, and Saturday nights people would get together and listen to the 'Grand Ole Opry,' and then sing afterwards." When he was seventeen, he left high school and did a four-month hitch in the air force, then returned home and

followed his father into construction work. At nineteen, he received a two-year jail term on a burglary conviction; while he was serving his sentence, he organized a country band and was a country & western disc jockey on the prison radio station. After his release in 1961, he went back to construction work and, in his spare time, played with Kenny Hall and other musicians. Occasionally he and the other members of the Sweets Mill String Band would take time off from work to play, but after about half a dozen years of earning a living as a construction worker, a vacuum cleaner and insurance salesman, a logger, and "probably everything else," he turned to music for his primary source of income.

For over a decade, Ringer has been writing many of his own songs, and his repertoire consists of both traditional and contemporary material. In 1972 Folk-Legacy issued his debut solo album, entitled "Waitin' for the Hard Times to Go" (Folk-Legacy FSI-47). More recently, he has recorded *Good to Get Home* (Philo PH 1012), followed by *Any Old Wind That Blows* (Philo PH 1021), with David Bromberg and his band. (*See also* The Sweets Mill String Band.)

## Ralph Rinzler

*Singer, mandolinist, performer, recording artist, collector, director of field research programs for the Newport Folk Foundation (1964–67), director of the Festival of American Folklife, Smithsonian Institution, and author*

One of the most significant personalities connected with the Newport Folk Festival, Ralph Rinzler was largely responsible for the introduction of traditional folk performers into its programming. After serving as the director of field research programs for the Newport Folk Foundation from 1964 to 1967, he became director of the Festival of American Folklife, Smithsonian Institution, and today continues to act as a primary force in American folk music as the current director of this major folk festival.

Ralph Rinzler was born on July 20, 1934, and grew up in the New York–New Jersey area. Although he became acquainted with classical music as a young boy, his interest soon turned to folk music. He read books and listened to recordings of traditionalists, and he adopted the mandolin as his favorite instrument.

He received his BA degree in 1956 from Swarthmore College and had additional training in the Middlebury College graduate program and in Paris in French language and culture from 1957 to 1958. In 1958 he went to London to work under folklorist A. L. Lloyd, and from 1964 to 1966 he did field work under the direction of Alan Lomax.

During the fifties, he was involved with a group known as the Friends of Old-Time Folk Music, which was a New York–based organization dedicated to the preservation of traditional American folk culture. In 1959 he became a member of the Greenbriar Boys and over the next five years performed and recorded with this top bluegrass group. He maintained an active role as a collector of traditional material, doing field work and making recording trips for Folkways Records (in 1956, and from 1960 to 1963) in the Southeastern region of the United States, and with Gaelic and French language, music, and oral history in Nova Scotia.

He was selected by the board of directors of the Newport Folk Festival to seek new talent for the event. When he left the Greenbriar Boys in 1964 to become director of field research programs for the foundation, he was replaced in the group by mandolinist Frank Wakefield. For the next three years, Rinzler was involved in field recording, collecting, and mounting presentations of traditional performers at the annual Newport folk festivals.

In 1967 he became the director of the Festival of American Folklife, a position which he still holds today. His film credits include *Cheever Meaders: Technology of a North Georgia Potter* (1970) and *Southern Korea Kitchen Pottery Making: A Study in Folk Technology* (1971); he has produced, edited, and recorded in the field more than fifty LPs; and he has edited and written articles for the Newport Folk Festival programs (1964–68) and the Smithsonian Folklife Festival programs (1968, 1970, and 1972). His other publications include *Uncle Dave Macon, a Bio-Discography*, John Edwards Memorial Foundation Special Series, No. 3; *Cheever Meaders: North Georgia Potter*; *Forms upon the Frontier*, Utah State University monograph series, Volume 2, April, 1969; Introductory Preface to the Dover Publications reissue, *Handicrafts of the Southern Highlands*, by Allen Eaton, 1972; Introduction to the *Doc Watson Song Book*, Oak Publications, 1971; and "Bill Monroe," in *Stars of Country Music*, edited by Bill Malone and Judith McCulloh, University of Illinois Press, 1975. (*See also* The Greenbriar Boys.)

# The Ritchie Family. *See* Jean Ritchie

# Edna Ritchie. *See* The Ritchie Family.

# Jean Ritchie

*Traditional singer, dulcimer player, guitarist, American traditional folk music collector, songwriter, performer, recording artist, and author*

Jean Ritchie's untrained voice is representative of the authenticity and forthright simplicity of her Cumberland Mountain heritage, and in the United States and abroad she is considered one of the foremost performers, recording artists, and writers of Appalachian music. Although she often sings unaccompanied, or with guitar accompaniment, her name has become synonymous with the dulcimer, and she is probably the individual most responsible for bringing national attention to that instrument.

The youngest of Abigail and Balis Ritchie's fourteen children, Jean Ritchie was born on December 8, 1922, in Viper, Kentucky. The Ritchie Family has long been considered an invaluable source of traditional folk songs and culture, and musicologists have enthusiastically collected material from these descendants of early English settlers who sailed to America in 1768. In 1917 folklorist Cecil Sharp visited the Ritchies and wrote down many of the tunes that were sung by Balis Ritchie and his family. During the thirties, John A. and Alan Lomax collected songs and made field recordings of the Ritchie Family for the Archive of Folk Song of the Library of Congress.

Singing and playing instruments such as the dulcimer, banjo, guitar, and fiddle were a part of Jean Ritchie's childhood, as she recalls: "We always used to sing around the house, but we never thought of it as folk music.

"I remember when we finally got a radio and we started listening to hillbilly and country music. We had never heard it called that before, and even though we were the 'hillbillies,' we never even knew it!"

Balis Ritchie showed his five-year-old daughter Jean how to play the family's old black dulcimer, which she had been playing without his knowing by sneaking behind the sofa and strumming the instrument softly. The instrument had been made by J. Edward Thomas of Bath, Kentucky; to the best of everyone's knowledge, Thomas was the area's first dulcimer maker, and Thomas gave his pattern to her cousin Jethro Amburgy, of Hindman, in Knott County, Kentucky. Slight variations have been made from the original pattern, but the dulcimer has always been played in a very simple style. Traditionally, ballads and songs were sung unaccompanied, so it was felt that the accompaniment of any instrument, including the dulcimer, should be basic and secondary to the song and its content.

As a youngster, Jean Ritchie performed at community programs, 4H Club meetings, and at the county fair in Hazard, but she recalls her mother's reaction to the singing of certain folk songs: "My mother would not allow me to sing 'Pretty Polly' because she felt that it was indelicate for a woman. But after folk music became more recognized and respectable, she changed her mind and said, 'I guess it is all right because it is a part of your heritage.' "

While she attended Cumberland College in Williamsburg, Kentucky, and, later, the University of Kentucky in Lexington, Jean Ritchie participated in the glee club and choir, and took voice and piano lessons. She taught elementary school during World War II, and in 1946 she received her BA in social work from the university. By mid-June of the following year, she was in New York, working at the Henry Street Settlement, where she acquired the nickname "Kentucky." She began to perform for audiences and met other singers, such as Oscar Brand, Mrs. Texas Gladden, Hobart Smith, Brownie McGhee, Vera Hall, Leadbelly, and Pete Seeger, and was recorded for the Library of Congress Archive of Folk Song by Alan Lomax.

She performed at the Spring Fever Hootenanny, along with the Weavers, Woody Guthrie, Betty Sanders, Oscar Brand, and Ernie Leiberman. On February 6, 1949, she was a guest on Oscar Brand's WNYC radio program *Folksong Festival* and by October of that year was a regular on the show. Beginning in the fifties, the dulcimer started to enjoy a boom in popularity, and Jean Ritchie was closely associated with this phenomenon. She began writing a work about her family and music, *Singing Family of the Cumberlands* (Oxford University Press, 1955).

In 1950 Jean Ritchie was married to photographer George Pickow. She signed a contract with Elektra Records which led to the recording of a 10-inch LP, *Jean Ritchie,*

*Singing Traditional Songs of Her Kentucky Mountain Family* (EKS-2), issued in 1952. She was awarded a Fulbright scholarship to study folklore in the British Isles, where she and her husband traced many of the Ritchie Family tunes. When they returned to the United States, Jean Ritchie began appearing on television programs and continued performing, writing, and recording. By 1959, with the help of an uncle, Morris Pickow, she and her husband had started building dulcimers in their basement. In the same year, Jean Ritchie participated in the Newport Folk Festival, along with the Kingston Trio, Sonny Terry and Brownie McGhee, Pete Seeger, Earl Scruggs, Jimmy Driftwood, Frank Warner, Oscar Brand, Leon Bibb, Odetta, John Jacob Niles, and the New Lost City Ramblers. In 1963 she was asked by Pete Seeger and Theodore Bikel to be one of the seven original members of the board of directors of the Newport Folk Festival, along with Bill Clifton, Clarence Cooper, Erik Darling, and Peter Yarrow. By then, she had been recorded by Elektra, His Master's Voice (London), Esoteric Records, Collector Limited Editions, Tradition, Pacific Cascade, Riverside, Argo, Washington and Prestige/International. In 1963 she made an instructional LP entitled *The Appalachian Dulcimer* (Folkways FI 8352) to accompany her new book, *The Dulcimer Book* (Oak Publications). Since then, Jean Ritchie has recorded for Warner Brothers (*A Time for Singing* [WS 1592]), Sire Records (*Clear Waters Remembered* [SES 97014, which has been reissued as Geordie 101]), and Verve/Folkways. Her most recent publication is *Jean Ritchie's Dulcimer People* (Oak Publications, 1975).

Edna Ritchie, Jean's sister, represents a different aspect of the family tradition. Formerly a student at Pine Mountain Settlement and a graduate of Berea College, she has worked as a teacher and a librarian in Perry County. Until about fifteen years ago, her singing was heard only at local festivals and Kentucky Folklore Society gatherings; since then, she has performed at such national events as the University of Chicago Folk Festival, and has recorded *Edna Ritchie* (Folk-Legacy FSA-3).

## Gil Robbins. *See* The Cumberland Three; The Highwaymen.

## John Roberts and Tony Barrand

*English traditional folk musicians, performers, and recording artists*

Well-known for their ability to entertain audiences of folk music enthusiasts and people as yet unfamiliar with their particular brand of music—English traditional ballads, bawdy and drinking songs, and sea shanties—John Roberts and Tony Barrand organize their repertoire thematically to make the material instructional as well as entertaining, as Tony Barrand explains: "We tend to push in new directions when we get a central idea. The songs in our repertoire are entertaining, but there's more to it. They're much more participatory than a lot of forms of music because it's basically social music—songs sung in pubs—but there is a lot more in them, such as the people that they came from and the people who've created them and the people they've gone through. All of that is in the song, and we try to put it together so that is visible as well."

Tony Barrand came from England to Swarthmore College on an exchange program in 1966–67, and he sang with a rhythm-and-blues band called Merry Lion, in Philadelphia. He had gone to folk clubs in England, and his mother had sung many English vaudeville music hall songs, but Barrand had not sung English folk songs in public as unaccompanied singing seemed too difficult. He met John Roberts in 1968 when they both attended graduate school at Cornell University, and Tony Barrand spent many hours listening to his new friend's

John Roberts (right) and Tony Barrand at Mariposa '75

tapes of English folk music. They started working as a duo in 1969, doing mostly unaccompanied two-part harmonies, and over the years have added to their performances instruments such as the banjo, concertina, and button accordion, depending on what was needed for a song in their repertoire. Together with another colleague from Cornell, they began teaching a program called Psychology and the Arts at Marlboro College in Vermont, when they completed their graduate work in 1972.

In the winter of 1973–74, they organized a Morris dance team and a sword-dance team to establish a ceremonial dancing tradition in the village of Marlboro, where they live. Their energies have been devoted to another project which they call "An Evening at the English Music Hall," as Tony Barrand describes: "We try to recreate a London music hall as it would have been in about 1895, with a cast of nine or ten people

that work in costume. We put it on in old vaudeville halls or theaters in this country in an attempt to recreate the form of entertainment that existed in that period at the end of the Victorian era in London. It's really very interesting to take people who sing traditional folk songs—Maggie Pierce, David Jones, Murray Callahan, Susan Warner, Kathleen and Jan Oosting, as well as ourselves—and use music to relate to audiences and get them to be actors and to use their skills with audiences and songs to recreate a style of entertaining that existed eighty years ago."

John Roberts and Tony Barrand have been recorded on many albums, such as the National Geographic Society LP *Songs & Sounds of the Sea*, which also includes the Boys of the Lough, Michael Cooney, Joe Hickerson, David Jones, Lou Killen, Tony Saletan, and Jeff and Gerret Warner. They have made three exclusive albums: *Spencer

318

the Rover Is Alive and Well and Living in Ithaca (Swallowtail Records ST-1), *Across the Western Ocean* (Swallowtail Records ST-4), and *Mellow with Ale from the Horn* (Front Hall Records FHR-04).

# Jeannie Robertson

*Scottish traditional ballad singer, storyteller, and recording artist*

One of the finest of Scotland's traditional ballad singers and storytellers, Jeannie Robertson was once described by Alan Lomax as "a monumental figure of the world's folksong." From her "discovery" in Aberdeen in 1953 until her death on March 13, 1975, she provided a wellspring of her country's deep-rooted traditions. The magnitude of her legendary stature is a tribute to her talents and services to the English-speaking world of folk song.

Born in 1908 of nomadic ancestry, Jeannie Robertson was brought up amid traditional music and folklore. She acquired most of her vast repertoire from her mother and grandmother, and during her early travels "up the Dee and down the Don," she learned many tunes from other traveling folk of Scotland. Music was an inextricable element throughout her entire life, with her famous fiddler husband Donald Higgins, her three singing brothers, her brother-in-law Isaac playing the pipes, her next-door neighbor Albert Stewart (one of Scotland's finest fiddlers), and her daughter Lizzie Higgins, who is highly regarded as an artist in her own right.

Jeannie Robertson is remembered for her powerful and dignified presentation through which she fulfilled her role as a vehicle for the song, transmitting through the folk (oral) tradition numerous ballads listed in Child and an incalculable number of fragments of material. Her sensitive interpretations of traditional ballads were an integral aspect of her music and undoubtedly served as a basis for her own shaping of new songs. Her storytelling repertoire included a selection of international tales, and she was the first of the Lowland storytellers to be recorded by

the School of Scottish Studies at the University of Edinburgh. The comic tale was her specialty, and her authoritative and compelling style befit her inherited traditional artistry, which was perpetuated over the years as a source of entertainment among traveling clans.

In 1968 Jeannie Robertson was honored with the award of the MBE (Member of the Order of the British Empire) in acknowledgement of her lasting gifts to folk song. Over the years, her friendship with folklorist Hamish Henderson produced hours of tape of her singing and storytelling, and her work is considered by many to have been an inspiration for, and an impetus to, the folk song revival and the folk festival in the British Isles.

Jeannie Robertson's first recordings were released as 45-RPM discs by Collector Records, in Scotland. Her albums have been issued by Collector as well as several other companies, including H.M.V. (7EG 8534); Prestige/International (*World's Greatest Folksinger*, 13006, and Prestige/International 13075); Tangent (*The Muckle Sangs*, TNGM 119/D Scottish Tradition Volume 5); Topic (*Jeannie Robertson*, 12T96); and Tradition (*Heather and Glen*, TLP 1047), with three cuts by her in "a collection of folk songs and folk music from Aberdeenshire and the Hebrides collected by Alan Lomax, Calum McLean and Hamish Henderson." (*See also* Hamish Henderson.)

# Paul Robeson

*Singer, performer, recording artist, and actor*

Despite his athletic accolades, scores of recordings, radio appearances, and motion picture and theatrical roles, Paul Robeson has been immortalized as a symbol of strength and of the struggle for freedom of all oppressed peoples—a folksinger in the classic and universal connotation of the term. A humanitarian denounced by his countrymen and a prime target of McCarthyism, Robeson found his name deleted from American history because of his personal conviction that "the artist must elect to fight for freedom or slavery. I have made my choice. I have no alternative."

His father was a former slave who left the South and became a Methodist minister in Princeton, New Jersey, where Paul Robeson was born on April 9, 1898. When he was seventeen, he became the third black to enter Rutgers College; when he graduated in 1919 with a Phi Beta Kappa key, he had amassed over a dozen varsity letters, had been twice chosen All-American football end, was among the four graduates elected to the prestigious Cap and Skull honor society, and gave his class commencement oration. But his scholastic and athletic achievements were overshadowed by racism, and he was barred from the glee club and harassed by his teammates.

A brief stint as a professional ball player paid for his tuition at Columbia Law School, from which he earned his LLB degree in 1923. But his marriage to Eslanda Goode in 1921 changed the course of his life; instead of pursuing a law career, he was encouraged by his wife to turn to theater. In 1920 he accepted an acting role in a YMCA production of *Simon the Cyrenian*, followed by its 1921 run at the Lafayette Theater. The next year brought Paul Robeson to Broadway's Sam H. Harris Theater, where he portrayed Jim in *Taboo* and to Britain, where he played opposite Mrs. Patrick Campbell in the same play (renamed *The Voodoo*). Upon his return to the United States, he became a member of the Greenwich Village Provincetown Players and starred in Eugene O'Neill's *All God's Chillun Got Wings*. After his acclaimed performance in *The Emperor Jones*, the Provincetown Players sponsored his premier concert of black spirituals, in 1925.

For the next several years, he traveled between London and New York to give concerts and to perform theatrical roles. In 1928 he left British audiences stunned when, in his portrayal of Joe in *Showboat*, he delivered his rendition of "Ol' Man River"—the song by which he is most widely

known today. During the thirties, Paul Robeson turned his back on the social and political climate in the United States and remained abroad. In London he appeared in the principal roles in *Othello* and *The Hairy Ape* in 1931, and in *Stevedore* in 1933, and he toured Europe in 1931 and 1938. He traveled to Russia on several occasions and was lauded by that country and its people. Toward the end of the decade, he sang for opponents of the Franco revolt in Spain. It was at this point that he fully comprehended his commitment as an artist to participate in the fight for freedom of the oppressed, and he decided to return stateside.

Back on native soil, in late 1939 he created a sensation with his radio performance of the Earl Robinson–John Latouche collaboration, "Ballad for Americans," which was rebroadcast and recorded by Paul Robeson and the American People's Chorus for Victor Records. (His name is also closely associated with Earl Robinson's "Joe Hill.") The height of his career was marked by his outstanding performance as the first black to play the lead role in *Othello*, supported by an all-white cast, in the Theater Guild production which opened on October 19, 1943, on Broadway. Among the numerous honorary degrees and awards which accompanied his rise to fame as a stage actor and concert artist were a Doctor of Humane Letters degree from Howard University, a Donaldson Award, and the NAACP's Spingarn Medal.

In the late forties, he was sharply criticized for founding and acting as chairman of the Progressive Party, which backed 1948 presidential candidate Henry A. Wallace, and for his ardent support of the civil rights movement. A 1949 Peekskill, New York, concert resulted in an embittered battle between Robeson supporters and rock- and bottle-throwing dissidents. In 1950 his passport was revoked when he refused to put his signature on a House Un-American Activities Committee non-Communist affidavit. Eight years later, his passport was restored, and he left for Britain. Throughout his career, he enjoyed widespread popularity abroad, and until illness caused him to return to New York in 1963, he entertained audiences in Europe and Australia as a singer and, in 1959, made a memorable appearance as the Moor in *Othello* at Stratford-on-Avon.

He lived retired from public notice in Harlem and, after his wife's death in 1965, moved to his sister's home in Philadelphia. On Sunday, April 15, 1973, a celebration of his seventy-fifth birthday was held at New York's Carnegie Hall, with many theatrical figures, artists, and speakers taking part. Although illness prevented him from attending this salute in his honor, he sent a taped message to this large gathering of admirers.

After suffering for many years with circulatory ailments, Paul Robeson had a severe stroke and entered Presbyterian University Hospital on December 28, 1975. On January 23, 1976, he died in the Philadelphia hospital at the age of seventy-seven.

During his career, Paul Robeson starred or played a feature part in the motion pictures *Emporer Jones*, *Showboat*, *Saunders of the River*, *King Solomon's Mines*, and *Jericho*.

# Earl Robinson

*Composer, singer, conductor, lecturer, folklorist, author, musical editor, and recording artist*

Earl Robinson has been called "the folk composer and poet-singer of America," and since his graduation from the University of Washington in 1933, his interest and love for native American music has begotten a career filled with memorable achievements. Along with important contributions to folk music, he is renowned for his film scores, cantatas, conducting of choruses and orchestras, teaching, and singing.

Born on July 2, 1910, in Seattle, Washington, Earl Hawley Robinson was part of a musically gifted family. His mother was a talented classical musician, and she and her three children were, among them, proficient on cello, harp, violin, viola, flute, clarinet, various saxophones, guitar, and piano. She started her sons Earl and Duane and her daughter Claire on piano very early in their lives. By the age of six, Earl Robinson was improvising a "Ghosts Dance" and other compositions. His father, Morris John Robinson, was considered the "black sheep" of the family because, while possessing a penetrating harmonizing tenor voice, he could not read music and played only one instrument, the mandolin.

Young Earl Robinson's attraction to music grew over the years, and he decided to major in that field when he entered college in 1928. After receiving his bachelor of music degree from the University of Washington in 1933, he postponed advanced studies to travel to China, working his way back home—playing piano on a passenger liner—and acquiring on the boat a guitar for two dollars. On his subsequent journeys across the American continent, he became friends and traded songs with Woody Guthrie, Lee Hays, Burl Ives, Leadbelly, Pete Seeger, and others who began to sing Robinson compositions such as "Joe Hill." His association with Woody Guthrie, Lee Hays, and Pete Seeger led to his frequent singing with the Almanac Singers, and he collaborated with another of the group's members, Millard Lampell, to write "The Lonesome Train." "I am especially proud," reflects Earl Robinson, "that Huddie Ledbetter took my 'The Same Boat Brother' and song sections from 'The Lonesome Train' and made them his own."

During the thirties, he was recorded by the Lomaxes for the Archive of American Folk Song, and he joined a Workers Theater in New York City "as musical director, actor, sweeper, cook, and other shared communal jobs." During 1936 and 1939, he wrote the music for Federal Theater shows, including *Processional*, *Life and Death of an American*, and *Sing for Your Supper*. And, says Robinson: " 'Ballad for Americans' had been the finale of *Sing for Your Supper*. When the run of that play was interrupted by the closing of the WPA projects, 'Ballad' was chosen for the CBS *Pursuit of Happiness* program in late 1939, and Paul Robeson's rendition of it produced a sensation." Robeson recorded it (with the American People's Chorus, which Robinson had formed and conducted from 1937 to 1943) for Victor Records. It was purchased by MGM for a movie and was instrumental in Robinson's being awarded a Guggenheim fellowship to create the musical setting for Carl Sandburg's *The People, Yes.*

While still in New York, Earl Robinson and Will Geer produced the *Cavalcade of American Song.* Robinson also worked as master of ceremonies on the CBS sustaining program *Back Where I Come From,* and "in addition to Leadbelly, Woody Guthrie, Pete Seeger, and Josh White, other folksingers such as Richard Dyer-Bennet and the Golden Gate Quartet would join us on the program from time to time."

Robinson moved to Hollywood in 1943, and for nearly a decade he wrote for radio-theater, films, and television. He composed songs for the films *A Walk in the Sun, California,* and *Romance of Rosie Ridge;* a song and the background score for the documentary film *The Roosevelt Story;* and songs and the background score for *Texas Story.*

In the early fifties, Robinson wrote (with Waldo Salt) the folk opera *Sandhog,* which was presented at the Phoenix Theater in New York from late 1954 to early 1955. He composed the songs and background score for the General Motors industrial film *Giants in the Land,* and he produced and appeared with the children's chorus in the film *When We Grow Up.*

He returned to the New York City area, and after a period of lecturing, composing, and conducting, acted as music director of Elisabeth Irwin High School from 1957 to 1966. The year 1967 found him back in California, conducting the Extension Chorus of the University of California at Los Angeles. From 1969 to the present, he has composed for films and the theater. His

television scores include *The Great Man's Whiskers* (Universal-NBC), *Maybe I'll Come Home in the Spring* (ABC Movie of the Week), and *Adventures of Huckleberry Finn* (ABC special, 1975).

His numerous cantatas include "Ballad for Americans," "The Lonesome Train," "Tower of Babel," "In the Folded and Quiet Yesterdays," "Illinois People" (which was commissioned by the state of Illinois for the Sesquicentennial Year in 1968), "The People, Yes" (with Carl Sandburg and Norman Corwin), "Battle Hymn," "The Town Crier," "When We Grow Up," "Strange Unusual Evening" (A Santa Barbara Story), and "Ride the Wind." He has composed songs for the children's musical *Gingerbread John,* scores for ballet and opera, a piano concerto entitled "Concerto for Five String Banjo and Orchestra," and a symphonic tone poem, "A Country They Call Puget Sound," for voice and orchestra. His best-known songs are probably "Hurry Sundown" (which was nominated for a Grammy Award), "Joe Hill," "The House I Live In," "My Fisherman—My Laddio," and, most recently, "Black and White," which was a million-seller Gold Record for the rock group Three Dog Night. Robinson's publications include *Young Folk Song Book, Songs of the Great West, Folk Guitar in Ten Sessions, Songs of Brecht and Eisler,* and *German Folk Songs.*

Earl Robinson has recorded on various domestic labels, including Decca, Disc, Folkways, and Mercury. In his live performances, he brings songs to life with his insights and explanations as a folklorist and humanist. Most recently, he has been composing and singing for Bicentennial celebrations in his home state of Washington. An orchestral work, "To the Northwest Indian," was commissioned by the Spokane EXPO World's Fair and the National Foundation for the Arts, and was performed by the Spokane Symphony on September 4, 1974, with Robinson narrating. A cantata inspired by another Washingtonian, former Associate Justice of the Supreme Court William

O. Douglas, is the finale of a musical pageant, *Washington Love Story*. This full evening work includes another major cantata, "Grand Coulee Dam." Robinson confesses: "I began where Woody left off, using several of the twenty-six songs he wrote in the weeks he spent in the great Northwest."

# Louise Robinson. *See* Sweet Honey in the Rock.

# Jimmie Rodgers

*Singer-songwriter, guitarist, performer, and recording artist*

The romantic "Singing Brakeman" and reputed "Father of the Country Field," whose recording career was launched simultaneously with that of the famous Carter Family, Jimmie Rodgers was the undisputed hero of hillbilly music in the late 1920s and early 1930s. He singlehandedly converted a nation to country music—singing and guitar picking—and his profound influence on the development of American folk music is immeasurable.

His impact on other musicians was evidenced by the increasing number of amateurs and professionals alike who turned to this musical form. Other performers (as well as audiences) were captivated by his easygoing stage presence, his versatile guitar techniques, and his vocal stylings, particularly his "blue yodeling." His music was meant for everyone, and his audiences comprised farmers, coal miners, ranch hands, schoolteachers, and clergymen. A vast and loyal national following was soon accompanied by worldwide acclaim, and his music and winning personality made a significant impact on a global scale.

During his brief career, which was tragically brought to a close by his death on May 26, 1933, from tuberculosis, he composed and recorded over a hundred songs—which retained their immense popularity for years after he passed away. As a tribute to

his invaluable contribution to early country music, he was elected on November 3, 1961—nearly three decades after his death—as one of the first members, along with Fred Rose and Hank Williams, of the prestigious Country Music Hall of Fame.

James Charles Rodgers was born on September 8, 1897, in Meridian, Mississippi. When he was four years old, his mother passed away, and he was raised by his father, whose job with the railroad forced him to be constantly on the move, taking his small son with him. A formal education was virtually replaced with knowledge gained by traveling from one city to the next, and during his itinerant existence as a child, Jimmie Rodgers encountered various musical influences prevailing in the South. As a teenager, he and a friend used to carry buckets of water for black railroad hands; from them, he learned to play guitar and banjo and became familiar with black musical stylings, which played an important role in his own musical development many years later.

Jimmie Rodgers worked for the railroad for fourteen years, mostly as a brakeman or flagman, and his job took him through the towns and countryside of the Deep South and the Southwest. He contracted tuberculosis and, with the draining of his physical energy, retired from his job in 1925 when he was twenty-eight years old.

Aside from playing guitar and banjo and singing for his fellow workers, his only other musical experience was performing with a small dance band for various social occasions. In 1925 he joined up with a medicine troupe, acquiring basic skills as a professional entertainer which helped to cultivate an informality that became the trademark of his performing style. After leaving the show, he settled with his wife Carrie in Asheville, North Carolina, and formed the Jimmie Rodgers Entertainers with Jack and Claude Grant (the Grant Brothers) and Jack Pierce. For several weeks in early 1927 he was featured on local WWNC Radio, but when his contract was terminated by station officials, he became discouraged and took a job as an Asheville detective.

The breakthrough in his career came in 1927 when he phoned Ralph S. Peer to arrange an audition with the Victor hillbilly talent scout. Like the Carter Family, who journeyed from their home in Maces Spring, Virginia, Jimmie Rodgers went off to Bristol in hopes of fulfilling his dream of fame and fortune as a musician. When he reached Bristol, Jack and Claude Grant and Jack Pierce decided to strike out on their own—without him—as the Tenneva Ramblers. Jimmie Rodgers ended up singing alone, accompanied only by his own guitar playing. His two selections, "Sleep, Baby, Sleep" and "The Soldier's Sweetheart," brought immediate attention to his roots in Southern country music and to his unique vocal technique of yodeling.

Toward the end of 1927, there was a noticeable increase in his popularity. With Victor executives eager to turn his potential into the reality of stardom, another recording session was lined up in their Camden, New Jersey, studios. As a result of this historic event, Jimmie Rodgers became a country music legend.

In addition to his numerous recordings, he toured in the Southern and Southwestern states and performed on radio; although a tour in the North was planned by Peer, Rodgers's deteriorating physical condition led to its cancellation. In 1931 he recorded his song "The TB Blues," which related to his own personal life experience. As his affliction steadily progressed, he made fewer and fewer solo appearances, but he remained the major attraction of every tent show with which he traveled, from the Paul English Players to W. I. Swain's Hollywood Follies (except in regions of the country, such as the Dust Bowl, where he was as yet unknown).

He moved to the warm, dry climate of Texas for health reasons and, toward the end of his career, performed almost exclusively in the Lone Star State. Two years before his death, he built his $50,000 "Blue Yodeler's Paradise" mansion in Kerrville, where he lived until medical expenses and the financial draining of a high-fashioned life-style made it necessary to put the dwelling up for sale. For the remainder of his life, he lived with his wife and daughter in a modest home in San Antonio.

For the eighteen months prior to his death, he continued to record, to make personal and radio appearances, and to undergo expensive TB treatments. Finally, in May 1933, he came to New York to record—realizing that this session would be his final one. By this time he was so weak that he was forced to lie down on a cot between each recording. Two days after his final recording session, he died in his room at the Taft Hotel.

When the train carrying his body home approached the mourning town of Meridian, the engineer pulled the whistle cord slowly two times—producing a sad, wailing sound—as the final ride of the "Singing Brakeman" drew to an end.

Two decades later, in June 1953, approximately thirty thousand people gathered in Meridian to witness the unveiling of a statue of Jimmie Rodgers. Almost a decade later, the newly founded Country Music Hall of Fame chose Jimmie Rodgers, Fred Rose, and Hank Williams as its first enshrined members.

Along with reissues marketed by RCA Victor since 1949, other companies which have compiled and released albums of his work include A&M, Dot, and Roulette.

## Kenny Rogers. *See* The New Christy Minstrels.

## Linda Ronstadt

*Contemporary singer, performer, and recording artist*

Linda Ronstadt's evocative natural soprano voice first caught the attention of millions of radio listeners with her late 1967 hit single

Linda Ronstadt

with the Stone Poneys, "Different Drum," written by Mike Nesmith. Now one of pop music's latest stars, her rise to fame was made in spite of haphazard recordings and nearly a decade of management upheaval and shoddy tours. Although her public self-image as a "high priestess of heartache" has changed, she is often still at her best when adapting her sweet, but sad, voice to a ballad or love song such as Gary White's "Long Long Time" or Hank Williams's "I Can't Help It If I'm Still in Love with You."

Linda Maria Ronstadt was born on July 15, 1946, in Tucson, Arizona. Her family was musical, and as a child she used to listen to music on the radio. Her mother played the ukelele and her father played guitar, sang,

and introduced her to the music of Peggy Lee and Billie Holiday. From her sister, who played Hank Williams records all day long, Linda Ronstadt acquired a love for country music.

She attended the University of Arizona but left at the end of her freshman year and headed for Los Angeles, where she formed the Stone Poneys with two friends, Bob Kimmel and Ken Edwards. Three Capitol albums and one successful single ("Different Drum") later, Linda Ronstadt went out on her own.

Her debut album as a solo artist, *Hand Sown, Home Grown* (ST-208), was released in the spring of 1969. She started touring with her own backup band and performed at colleges, the Troubadour in Los Angeles, the Bitter End in New York, and the Cellar Door in Washington, D.C., and made a number of television appearances. In 1970 her second LP, *Silk Purse* (Capitol ST-407), was issued, containing her first solo hit, "Long Long Time." After traveling to Europe, she returned to the United States to put together another band, called the Eagles, and recorded her third album, *Linda Ronstadt* (Capitol SMAS-35).

In September 1973 after a period of management difficulties and prolonged recording sessions, her first album on the Asylum label was released. The mood throughout is created by her typical predilection for country-style ballads, and, with her natural affinity for performing in the country-rock genre, she received a favorable response to *Don't Cry Now* (Asylum SD 5064).

Anna McGarrigle's original composition, "Heart Like a Wheel," is the title track of Ronstadt's next album, produced by Peter Asher. *Heart Like a Wheel* (Capitol ST-11358) completed her recording career with Capitol Records. The LP is probably most significant for its diversification of musical form—expanding beyond Ronstadt's repertoire of country- and folk-rock. Two singles from the album, "You're No Good" and Phil Everly's "When Will I Be Loved," were both hits for Linda Ronstadt in 1975.

Classic country laments comprise the more successful half of the selections on her most recent album, *Prisoner in Disguise* (Asylum 7E1045), released in the fall of 1975. Similar in many respects to her previous LP, which established Ronstadt as a pop music star of the mid-seventies, *Prisoner in Disguise* holds promise for more experimentation and an ever-broadening repertoire. "Love Is a Rose"/"Heat Wave" was the first single release to be extracted from *Prisoner in Disguise*, and in late 1975 the 45-RPM recording turned into one of her fastest-selling records to date.

# The Rooftop Singers

*Vocal and instrumental group, performers, and recording artists*

With their national success of 1963, "Walk Right In," the Rooftop Singers achieved instantaneous notoriety among city musicians of the urban folk music revival. Rooted in the tradition of group singing as masterfully set forth by the Weavers, the young trio attempted to link traditional folk, blues, and gospel music with a modern element. Their recording of "Walk Right In" was unique in that it introduced the twelve-string guitar as the predominant musical motif, and it was the first time that the instrument had been used in the commercial 45-RPM singles market.

Before forming the Rooftop Singers in 1962, Erik Darling had been a member of the Weavers, as the replacement for Pete Seeger. In 1956 he had put together the Tarriers with Bob Carey and Alan Arkin, and with them he recorded the hit song "The Banana Boat Song." After working both the Tarriers and the Weavers simultaneously, Darling decided to stay on with Hays, Gilbert, and Hellerman until he organized his own group, the Rooftop Singers, as he recalls: "After I left the Weavers, I went on to pursue a solo career singing in coffeehouses and clubs across the country and in Canada. Meanwhile, I had found this song, 'Walk Right In,' on an old recording of a jug band, Gus Cannon and His Jug Stompers, and I thought that it had to be a hit if done in a certain way with a new group. So I brought together two friends, Bill Svanoe and Lynne Taylor, along with myself, to record 'Walk Right In.'

"Bill Svanoe was the only person I knew who could play the guitar with the kind of rhythmical feel I had grown to experience. His background, as far as musical interests were concerned, was similar to mine. He was also a fan of Josh White and he had an

The Rooftop Singers (left to right): Bill Svanoe, Erik Darling, and Lynne Taylor

appreciation for the rhythmical nuances found in Negro gospel music.

"Lynne Taylor started her professional singing career at age fourteen and was the featured vocalist with the Benny Goodman band and appeared at the Empire Room at the Waldorf-Astoria and Birdland. In 1958 she was featured with the Buddy Rich band. She had the ability to harmonize anything and to follow the subtlest rhythmical nuances.

"It had been my experience with making recordings that the engineers or producers tended to hide the sound of acoustic guitars, so I figured that if I got two twelve-strings playing the same thing, there would be no way the sound could be hidden, and that's the way the record was made. And once it was a hit, the sound of the twelve-string guitar became 'in' for a while, and the instrument became more readily available in stores.

"Before 'Walk Right In' was a hit, however, you couldn't buy a twelve-string guitar. The only ones that you could find then were in pawnshops and quite old. Eventually, I ordered one from the Gibson Company, but in order to record 'Walk Right In' with two twelve-strings, we had to wait for the company to build a second one for Bill!

327

"We never found another song which we could get our teeth into quite like 'Walk Right In' or which fit the format of two driving twelve-strings. So after doing college concerts and TV shows for four and a half years and an Australian–New Zealand tour, we concluded that the group, which had been put together mainly for 'Walk Right In,' had fulfilled its usefulness, and so we disbanded."

Before the group disbanded in 1967, Lynne Taylor had been replaced by Mindy Stuart, who was then replaced by Patricia Street. She assisted in their last recordings on Atlantic Records, performed in their later concerts and TV appearances, and began to write new songs for the group with Erik Darling. When the Rooftop Singers broke up, Patricia Street and Erik Darling continued to write songs together, and, in October 1975, their first LP was released. The Rooftop Singers recorded three albums for Vanguard Records: *"Walk Right In!"* (VRS-9123), *Good Time* (VRS-9134), and *Rainy River* (VRS-9190). (*See also* Erik Darling.)

## Posey Rorer. *See* Charlie Poole and the North Carolina Ramblers.

## Phil Rosenthal. *See* Apple Country.

## Colin Ross. *See* The High Level Ranters.

## Bruce Rowland. *See* Fairport Convention.

## Tom Rush

*Contemporary singer, songwriter, guitarist, performer, and recording artist*

During the recent folk revival, there were several major areas of the United States which became spawning grounds for a number of young performers. The flourishing Boston–Cambridge scene yielded such names as Joan Baez, Jim Kweskin, Eric Von Schmidt, and a folkie who was closely tied with the Club 47, Tom Rush. From the beginning, Tom Rush has presented material from a broad range of styles—country blues, jazz, English ballads, traditional, and contemporary—and he has always remained in step with current trends by developing and reshaping his own skills as a singer and songwriter.

Born on February 8, 1941, in Portsmouth, New Hampshire, Tom Rush was raised in Concord, where his father was a teacher at a boarding school. He was educated in the public school system until the eighth grade, when he was sent to Groton School in Massachusetts, as he recalls: "It was straight out of Dickens. They had a black-mark system and depending on the nature of the offense, you could be given up to six black marks. Each black mark was worth an hour's time doing something. Sometimes it was copying out of the Bible, sometimes it was walking in circles. Every now and then they would have you do something constructive, like sweep up the woodworking shop or model for an art class."

One of his most significant experiences as a teenager was receiving his first guitar, which led to his involvement with folk music during his years as a student at Harvard. He explains: "I never did take lessons on the guitar, which is probably why I enjoyed it so much. I got a little band together and we played before the Saturday night movies and for parties and things. We were doing Gene Vincent imitations and Carl Perkins imitations, you know, old rock 'n' roll.

"Subsequently, I became interested in a folkier type of music. When I went to Harvard, I found that Cambridge was the hotbed of folk."

Tom Rush started performing at local coffeehouses one or two nights a week and, before long, he had attracted a loyal following. His first experience with recording was something less than professional, in his words: "I made a record on a little fly-by-night label. It wasn't quite a vanity record. Somebody was paying me to make it.

"It was really a small-scale operation. The guy was distributing it to stores out of the trunk of his car. Then, a friend of mine, Paul Rothchild, got a job as A&R man for Prestige Records and signed up most of the Cambridge folk scene, except for a few artists who went with Vanguard Records."

Tom Rush's *Got a Mind to Ramble* (Prestige/Folklore FL 14003) was released in December 1963, followed in May 1965 by *Blues/Songs/Ballads* (Prestige 7374). He had left Harvard in the middle of his junior year to find out if he could make a living as a folksinger, but he later returned to earn his degree in English literature in 1964.

He signed a recording contract with Elektra Records early in 1965, and *Tom Rush* (Elektra EKS[7]288) was released in March of the same year. Boston *Broadside* selected Tom Rush as the favorite male performer of 1964, 1965, and 1966, and he was chosen by *Billboard* as the most promising new male folksinger of 1965. He began to travel farther and farther away from his Boston home base, and his bookings took him to such clubs as the Brickskeller (Washington, D.C.), the Riverboat (Toronto), Le Hibou (Ottawa), and the Troubadour (Los Angeles). He also appeared in major theaters in New York and Chicago and at major folk festivals, including Newport and Philadelphia. His initial electric recording was precipitated by the advent of amplified instrumentation during the mid-sixties, and *Take a Little Walk with Me* (Elektra [7]308) was issued in the summer of 1966. The following year brought his single release of an early Joni Mitchell composition, "Urge for Going," and in March 1968 this mildly successful hit was reissued on his final Elektra LP entitled *Circle Game* (EKS-74018).

Toward the end of 1969 Tom Rush was added to the roster of Columbia Records; since then, he has recorded four albums for the label: *Tom Rush* (2-Fantasy 24709), *Merrimack County* (KC-31306), *Wrong End of the Rainbow* (C-30402), and, most recently, *Ladies Love Outlaws* (KC-33054).

Tom Rush maintains an active performing schedule which includes college and club dates across the nation. When he is not touring, he lives a relaxing life on a four-hundred-acre farm in New Hampshire.

## Buffy Sainte-Marie

*Contemporary singer, instrumentalist, songwriter, performer, and recording artist*

One of the best-known personalities of the contemporary folk circuit, Buffy Sainte-Marie has contributed a special dimension in musical expression with her Indian heritage and humanitarian concerns as set forth in original compositions such as "My Country 'Tis of Thy People You're Dying," "Now That the Buffalo's Gone," "Cod'ine," "Universal Soldier," and others. Along with such other performers of Indian descent as Patrick Sky and Peter LaFarge, she has generated an interest in, and awareness of, a minority culture that represents a significant, and often neglected, aspect of the total American folk culture. Together with her knowledge and understanding of white American traditional music, Buffy Sainte-Marie is revered as one of this country's most gifted, poetic, and well-rounded artists.

Born in Canada on February 20, 1941, Buffy Sainte-Marie was raised by foster parents in New England. Music was one of her childhood hobbies, and she had learned to play guitar by the time she was in high school. She attended the University of Massachusetts, where she was an honors graduate in Oriental philosophy and education, but before entering the teaching profession she decided to go to New York City for a weekend—which subsequently altered the course of her life. While she was in college, she had played some of her songs, as yet untitled, for her fellow students and teachers,

and she had sung in an off-campus coffeehouse for five dollars a night. Upon graduation, she left for New York, stayed at the YWCA, sang at a coffeehouse in Greenwich Village, and ended up staying for a while. She played the Gaslight, the Bitter End, and Gerde's Folk City, and her performances brought her acclaim and offers from agents, managers, and record companies. Herb Gart became her manager, and she signed a recording contract with Vanguard Records.

Within a short span of time, Buffy Sainte-Marie was invited to sing at coffeehouses, clubs, and major concert halls along the Eastern seaboard. She performed her own material but kept its authorship unannounced. Her first hit was "Universal Soldier," which was recorded by many other artists, including the Highwaymen, Glen Campbell, and Donovan, whose smash hit recording of her song led listening audiences to believe that it was his composition. Buffy Sainte-Marie underwent several transformations; her singing style changed, and her appearance onstage altered with her shift in wardrobe from tight dresses and high heels to blue jeans and boots. Underneath it all, Buffy Sainte-Marie was searching for a way to best express her own experiences, insights, and music.

Patrick Sky had taught her to play the Indian mouth bow, and she started using this unusual instrument at such festivals as Newport. In 1963 her poor state of health caused her to cease singing for six months. She became addicted to the codeine which

Buffy Sainte-Marie playing the mouth bow at the 1966 Newport Folk Festival

she was taking, and, after her recuperation, she composed a song about the experience, "Cod'ine." At this point, she also took her first formal voice lessons.

The following year, she started touring around the United States and Canada, playing clubs and colleges. One of the highlights of her early career was performing at New York's Carnegie Hall with Johnny Cash and Chuck Berry. Her songs were being popularized by such other artists as Bobby Darin, who recorded her classic song "Until It's Time for You to Go," and Bobby Bare, who had a country hit with her "Piney Wood Hills." During this period she continued to compose works that related to her personal experiences, including "Native North American Child," "My Country 'Tis of Thy People You're Dying," and "Now That the Buffalo's Gone."

Buffy Sainte-Marie has endured all the changes that have occurred in her musical field, but her music has remained. She has traveled to Europe, Asia, and Australia, and she has been recorded in New York and Nashville. Some of her Vanguard LPs include *It's My Way!* (VSD-79142), *Many a Mile* (VSD-79171), *Little Wheel/Spin and Spin* (VSD-79211), *Fire, Fleet, Candlelight* (VSD-79250), *Quiet Places* (VSD-79330), and *Native North American Child: An Odyssey* (VSD-79340). More recently, she has recorded for MCA Records.

## Tony and Irene Saletan

*Singers, songwriters, instrumentalists, performers, and recording artists*

Now very familiar and highly respected names within folk music circles, Tony Saletan began his career in the early 1960s as a Boston area folksinger who, even then, impressed contemporaries with his vast knowledge of obscure folk material and his unusual renditions of songs, and Irene

Saletan first established a reputation as a singer through her recordings on the Tradition label, by her participation in the Washington Square folk scene, and by her appearance at the Newport Folk Festival with her sister Ellen as the Kossoy Sisters. The Saletans are skillful performers who possess a special talent for generating audience participation. In commenting on their respected position in the field of folk music, Bob Beers once said: "In the midst of a very frenetic and changing folk scene, Tony and Irene have maintained a welcome consistency. Not only do they occupy a special area of their own, one they have built themselves, but their stature has grown in it, until they must be counted among our major artists."

Among the highlights of Tony Saletan's diverse background are a Master of Music Education degree from Harvard University, private study with conductor-composer Leonard Bernstein, and employment as music consultant to the Harvard Preschool and the Newton (Massachusetts) public school system. An established singer and guitarist, he was chosen by the International Recreation Association for a two-year global tour, which enabled him to expand his international repertoire with songs from scores of countries. His national reputation is largely based on his creation and performance as host of four public TV series (of which *Let's All Sing* and *The Song Bag* are broadcast both in the United States and in Canada). He has also been featured on *Sesame Street, Circle of Lights*, and NBC's *Take a Giant Step*.

A Harvard alumna and formerly on the music faculty of Salem State College in Massachusetts, Irene Saletan has, in recent years, become a frequent performer in schools, colleges, and coffeehouses, and on such television shows as *Take a Giant Step*.

Tony and Irene Saletan have made several recordings on such labels as Folk-Legacy, Folkways, ITV, Old North Bridge, Prestige/International, Tradition, and Western. Tony Saletan is credited with finding "Michael, Row the Boat Ashore" in an 1867 song col-

lection and bringing international prominence to this folk standard. One of his recent accomplishments was serving as music director of *Songs & Sounds of the Sea* (National Geographic Society 705), for which he also wrote (with James A. Cox) the text and annotation.

# San Diego Folk Festival

An annual event which has been billed as the "largest festival west of the Mississippi," the San Diego State University Folk Festival is held in the spring of each year at the SDSU's Student Union. Now in its tenth year, it has grown from its original $350 budget ($200 of which covered the cost of featuring Bill Monroe and the Blue Grass Boys at the First Annual San Diego State College [SDSC] Folk Festival in 1967) to a six-day event with 75 to 100 performers.

Sponsored by the Folk Arts Rare Record Shop and the Associated Students Cultural Arts Board of SDSU, the San Diego Folk Festival comprises workshops, evening concerts, all-day folk dancing, and special unrehearsed, spontaneous moments which arise when musicians pick up their instruments and blend their voices in the patio and corridors and out on the campus lawn—swapping tunes, jamming, teaching a special lick to an inquisitive fan, and enjoying the opportunity of being a part of this special springtime celebration.

A notable feature of the San Diego Folk Festival has been the first-time appearances by such old-time and traditional performers as Sam Chatmon, Kenny Hall, Wade Mainer, Ray and Ina Patterson, and Jim Ringer, among others. In the words of festival director Louis F. Curtiss: "Others who have appeared at the festival comprise a *Who's Who* of old-time and traditional music and blues, including the Balfa Freres, the Boys of the Lough, S. D. Courville and Dennis McGee, Roscoe Holcomb, Skip James, Bessie Jones and the Georgia Sea Island Singers, Martin, Bogan and the Armstrongs, Sam and Kirk McGee, Jean Ritchie, Mike Seeger, the Strange Creek Singers, Merle Travis, 'n' lots more. We also feature some contemporary artists, such as Mary McCaslin, U. Utah Phillips, Jim Ringer, Bodie Wagner, Tom Waits, and others.

"As a result of our work, involving collecting and researching connected with the festival over the last couple of years, my wife Virginia and I have received a separate grant to develop traditional artists in the western United States.

"We feel strongly that local old-timers mingling with better-known traditional artists and young pickers both well-known and not-so-well-known is what keeps this music alive."

# Carl Sandburg

*Poet, author, journalist, singer, guitarist, recording artist, and collector of American folk music*

Well-known as one of America's most accomplished and immortal poets, and author of the Pulitzer prize-winning *Abraham Lincoln: The War Years*, Carl Sandburg made enduring and significant contributions to the field of American folk music with his collection of 280 songs and ballads in *American Songbag*, his *New American Songbook*, his performances of folk music, and his recordings on such labels as Disc, Caedmon, Decca, and Lyrichord.

He was born on January 6, 1878, in Galesburg, Illinois, to Swedish immigrant parents. His father, August Sandburg, was a stern and reserved man who tried to support his large family on his less-than-ten-dollars-a-week salary as a blacksmith's helper for the Chicago, Burlington & Quincy Railroad. After completing the eighth grade, young Carl ("Curly" as he was called by his family and friends) left school to seek employment in order to supplement the family income. As a young man, he worked at a succession of jobs, which included delivering milk, selling fruit, cutting ice, changing scenery at an opera house, and laboring on nearby farms. In later years, he would remark that the most significant job he held during this early period was that of shining shoes and sweeping the floor of a town barbershop, for it was there that he developed a feeling for Midwest-flavored attitudes toward religion, politics, and work. He would listen to the men in the shop as they spoke in a familiar language that impressed Sandburg with its strength and honesty. Later in his life he was to draw upon these experiences to formulate a direct, hard-hitting literary style.

Sandburg grew restless with life in his hometown and set out for Chicago; although he returned, he had begun an existence that would always include a sense of adventure and wandering throughout the United States. In 1897, at the age of nineteen, he headed West, hopping a freight train and riding in a boxcar to Keokuk, Iowa, where he worked for a day as a waiter, then traveled to Missouri. His wandering took him to various cities and rural areas as far west as Denver; he returned to Galesburg to work as an apprentice to a house painter until February 1898. He joined Company C of the Sixth Illinois Regiment of the state militia but did not get to see much of the Spanish-American War as his regiment was stationed in Puerto Rico. Upon his return to Galesburg, he enrolled in Lombard College (the episodes leading up to the enrollment at Lombard are included in Sandburg's autobiography *Always the Young Strangers*, published in 1952); before he left in 1902, he had served as the business manager and, later, the editor in chief of the *Lombard Review*.

During his college years, Sandburg's literary aspirations and social conscience were developed. He was greatly influenced by Professor Philip Green Wright, who met on Sunday afternoons with Sandburg and a small group of students called "The Poor Writers Club" to recite poetry and to discuss politics. Wright was also responsible for the publication of two of Sandburg's books of poetry, *In Reckless Ecstasy* (1904), and *The*

*Plaint of a Rose* (1905), and a volume of essays entitled *Incidentals* (1905), which he financed and published privately after Carl Sandburg had left without graduating from Lombard College.

Sandburg worked in New York as a reporter for the *Daily News*, but by 1907 he was back in the Midwest working as a district organizer for the Social Democratic party in Milwaukee. He continued to work as a journalist, and 1912 found him in Chicago as a reporter for the *Daily Socialist*. From 1917 to 1927 Sandburg was on the staff of the *Chicago Daily News*.

One of his literary breakthroughs occurred in 1914 when his poem "Chicago" was printed in *Poetry* magazine and awarded the Helen Haire Levinson prize of two hundred dollars. Sandburg's second book of verse, *Cornhuskers*, was published in 1918 and included two poems which clearly expressed his love for American folk music. "Singing Nigger" and "Potato Blossom Soup and Jigs" not only dealt with the subject of music, but they imitated the rhythmic patterns of the songs. In 1919 a book of essays entitled *The Chicago Race Riots* was published; and in 1920 Sandburg's third book of verse, *Smoke and Steel*, came out with another poem dealing with music, "Jazz Fantasia."

In 1926, on the 125th anniversary of Abraham Lincoln's birth, Sandburg had published the first two volumes of his Lincoln series (four more were to follow), *Abraham Lincoln: The Prairie Years*. The Lincoln works were completed by 1939, and he was the recipient of the Pulitzer prize for *Abraham Lincoln: The War Years*.

A portion of Sandberg's lectures was devoted to American folk songs, and, although he knew only a few rudimentary chords, he accompanied himself on guitar as he sang many traditional songs and ballads. Over the years, he had collected a vast amount of material and, with the assistance of singers, musicians, arrangers, and musicologists, compiled one of the most lasting works in the field, *American Songbag*,

published in 1927. Many years later, in 1951, a sequel was published, called *New American Songbook*.

Sandburg's other works of the late twenties include *Good Morning, America* and *Steichen as Photographer*. In 1930 *Potato Face* was published, *Mary Lincoln Wife and Widow* came out in 1932, and *The People, Yes* followed four years later. During World War II, *Storm Over the Land* and *Home Front Memo* were published while Sandburg was working as a syndicated columnist for the *Times* in Chicago and as narrator of *Cavalcade of America* and other radio programs. His novel *Remembrance Rock* was followed by *Complete Poems*, which was awarded the Pulitzer prize for poetry in 1951. During the early sixties, Carl Sandburg continued his performances and recording of folk songs, and his literary works of this period include *Wind Song*, *Harvest Poems*, and *Honey and Salt*.

On July 22, 1967, Carl August Sandburg suffered a heart attack and died in his sleep at the age of eighty-nine.

# Marc Savoy. *See* The Louisiana Aces.

# Jean and Lee Schilling

*Traditional singers, instrumentalists, producers-directors of the Folk Festival of the Smokies, founders–executive directors of the Folk Life Center of the Smokies and their own record company, Traditional Records, instrument makers, performers, and recording artists*

Dedicated to the preservation of traditional Southern Appalachian Mountain music in its pure form, Jean and Lee Schilling are exponents of old-time music as it was once sung and played throughout the mountains of the southeastern United States.

A descendant of the original Scottish settlers of the Cosby area, Jean Costner Schilling was born and raised in eastern Tennessee. Early in her life, she learned to play the mountain dulcimer and autoharp; and, throughout her adulthood, she has traveled widely, singing and playing the music with which she grew up. As a founder of the Folk Festival of the Smokies, Jean Schilling has endeavored to revive traditional music and crafts, which are part of the proud folkways and folk life of our country's mountain heritage. In an attempt to promote a broader representation of the total way of life of mountain people, Jean Schilling founded the nonprofit, educational Folk Life Center of the Smokies, and she acts as chairman of the board of directors.

Born in eastern Kentucky and raised in West Virginia, Lee Schilling is a descendant of English and German settlers. He graduated with a BS in physics from North Carolina's Davidson College. While employed full-time with the National Aeronautics and Space Administration in Hampton, Virginia, Lee Schilling was engaged in eight years of graduate work in physics and mathematics. During the sixties he abandoned his scientific pursuits and opted for a more fulfilling existence as a craftsman-performer in the Cosby area.

Jean and Lee Schilling were married in May 1969, and, since then, they have worked together to produce and direct the annual Folk Festival of the Smokies and to act as executive directors of the Folk Life Center of the Smokies. They make mountain dulcimers and other handicrafts, and they operate a small merchandising business which handles the work of other local craftsmen and a collection of books and records relating to the life and music of Southern Appalachian peoples. Their own record company, Traditional Records, presents themselves, friends, and selections recorded live at Folk Life Center events and at the Folk Festival of the Smokies.

The Schillings perform at college concerts, workshops, and coffeehouses in various parts of the United States, and their recordings on the Traditional label include *Old Traditions* (JS-5117), by Jean Schilling and *Porches of the Poor* (JLS-617), by Jean and

Lee Schilling; they are both included on *Folk Festival of the Smokies, Vols. 1 and 2* (FFS 528 and FFS 529). Since 1970 Jean and Lee Schilling have served as National Park Service volunteers in the Music Heritage Interpretive Program and have shared their talents in the several weekly presentations of mountain music and heritage.

# Helen Schneyer

*Traditional singer, performer, and recording artist*

A sensitive interpreter of primarily traditional material, Helen Schneyer has been criticized by some for "going too sharp or too flat," and praised by others for her sheer joy of singing. She has been collecting traditional folk music for nearly four decades and has made numerous television, radio, festival, concert, and club appearances. Helen Schneyer was among the founding members of the Folklore Society of Greater Washington and is a former board member of the National Folk Festival Association.

Her only solo recording effort, *Ballads, Broadsides and Hymns* (Folk-Legacy FSI -50), encompasses a broad range of material with accompaniment by such friends as Tony Barrand, Gordon Bok, John Roberts, Ed Trickett, and Jay Ungar, among others. Her album, like her performances, evidences her basic concern with folk melodies, and her musical treatment of a song is largely based on her emotional reaction to combinations of sounds which affect her on a personal level. In her introductory notes to her Folk-Legacy LP, she says: "Any song whose melodic line contains a strong emphasis on a transition from the tonic chord to the fourth almost brings tears to my eyes. I have no idea why that combination of sounds reaches me. It is omnipresent in Scottish music and songs of Scottish extraction; I spent half my time at the Inverness Folk Festival in Scotland last year standing in the rear of the hall and weeping. I guess that means that I like any song that communicates or stirs up some powerful emotion in me. And I suppose *that* means that I experience many feelings that I find hard to express verbally and that the music makes it possible to do so."

Her preference in songs relates to her seriousness, directness, and strength as a vocalist, and the songs in her repertoire represent basic human reactions, from elation to dejection, from fragility to durability. This, in combination with her interest in her subject matter, once caused Jean Redpath to say: "Listening to Helen, I rediscovered what singing should be all about—compassion rather than erudition, spontaneous joy and sorrow rather than affectation.

"The first time I heard Helen sing came as a bit of a shock. I wasn't prepared for her strong contralto voice, and even less prepared for the emotional impact of her songs. The joy is incredibly infectious and one can't help but be caught up in choruses and harmonies and improvisations."

## Dave Schwartz. *See* Bottle Hill.

## Tracy Schwarz. *See* The New Lost City Ramblers; The Strange Creek Singers.

## Earl Scruggs

*Legendary banjoist renowned for the three-finger style, or "Scruggs Picking Style," songwriter, recording artist, and author*

"I was raised on a farm in Cleveland County, North Carolina, where I was born in 1924. My father played the banjo, and the whole family used to play instruments, mainly for the fun of it. One winter, when I was eleven years old, I got my first job picking the banjo for square dances. I got paid three dollars a night, and that was the start of my professional career."

As a boy, Earl Scruggs listened to many local North Carolina finger-style banjoists and to professional country artists who employed the three-finger approach, including the Carolina Tar Heels, Fisher Hendley and His Aristocratic Pigs, DeWitt "Snuffy" Jenkins, Charlie Poole of the North Carolina Ramblers, and Mack Woolbright. Finger-style banjo picking was always popular in this region of the country, and Scruggs was exposed to many nonprofessionals, such as Smith Hammett (probably the first to use three-finger picking) and Rex Brooks, who popularized the technique and performed at festivals and music contests near Scruggs's home outside Flint Hill, North Carolina. His older brother Junie first introduced him to the three-finger style, and Junie's ability as a banjoist influenced the young Earl Scruggs to pursue his own talent as a musician.

In 1939 Scruggs got a job for about eight weeks with one of the best-known groups in the Southeast, the Morris Brothers. At the time, they were broadcasting an early-morning show on WSPA Radio in Spartanburg, South Carolina. Thirty years later, Scruggs was to invite "the boys" to join him in the NET television special, *Earl Scruggs, His Family and Friends*, which included such other notables as Joan Baez, the Byrds, Bob Dylan, and Doc and Merle Watson.

In the mid-forties, Scruggs worked in Knoxville, Tennessee, with entertainer "Lost" John Miller, who, two weeks later, started a Saturday-morning show on WSM in Nashville. After three months, the twenty-year-old banjoist auditioned for Bill Monroe's Blue Grass Boys. By then, the Scruggs style was firmly established, and, impressed with what he heard, Monroe hired Scruggs in December 1945.

A few personnel changes were made in the group: Chubby Wise took the place of Jimmy Shumate on fiddle, and Bill Monroe's brother Birch was replaced by bassist Cedric Rainwater (Howard Watts); and, with Scruggs on banjo, Monroe on mandolin, and Lester Flatt on guitar, one of the most famous and accomplished bluegrass bands was created.

The Earl Scruggs Revue. Earl Scruggs (center) surrounded by members (from left): Randy Scruggs, Gary Scruggs, Jody Maphis, Steve Scruggs.

The term *bluegrass* started with the Blue Grass Boys, and they were responsible for the creation of the modern bluegrass sound. As a member of the band, Scruggs played an important role in popularizing an entire style of music; although he did not originate the three-finger style of playing banjo, its development, perfection, and popularity are attributed to Earl Scruggs, who gave the instrument new prominence.

The Blue Grass Boys toured extensively, and their music began to create an impact on the American music scene. The harmonizing techniques of Flatt and Monroe, and the instrumental sounds, fiddle bursts, guitar styles, and Scruggs's picking, made an indelible impression on traditional music.

After Lester Flatt and Earl Scruggs left Monroe's band in 1948, they soon teamed up with Mac Wiseman and two other former members of the Blue Grass Boys, Jim Shumate and Howard (Cedric Rainwater) Watts. Lester Flatt, Earl Scruggs, and the Foggy Mountain Boys (their name came from the Carter Family's "Foggy Mountain Top," which the quartet used as their theme song) made their first recordings in the summer of 1948 in Knoxville for the Mercury label. They cut four sides, consisting of "God Loves His Children," "I'm Going to Make Heaven My Home," "We'll Meet Again Sweetheart," and "Cabin in Carolina." During the next two and a half years, several classic bluegrass cuts were recorded among the twenty-nine sides made for Mercury, including "Roll in My Sweet Baby's Arms," "Salty Dog Blues," with vocals by Flatt, Wiseman, and Curly Sechler, and, among the instrumentals, the most famous of all, "Foggy Mountain Breakdown."

Although comparisons were made between the Foggy Mountain Boys and the Blue Grass Boys, the image of Bill Monroe began to fade as Flatt and Scruggs eliminated the "high, lonesome" quality associated with their former boss, and added more drive, power, and infectious stage presence to their performances. By 1950 Flatt and Scruggs had established a reputation as a top bluegrass act, and they had their first recording session for Columbia Records on November 21, 1950.

By June 1953, Flatt and Scruggs were sponsored by Martha White Mills, which had radio spots on WSM in Nashville and a half-hour portion on the *Grand Ole Opry*. When Flatt and Scruggs hosted the radio program successfully, they and their band were asked to perform the Tennessee flour company's portion of the *Grand Ole Opry*. During this period, Flatt and Scruggs worked two daily noon radio shows on a station in Crewe, Virginia; a daily show at WRVA in Richmond; and the *Saturday Night Barndance* show in Richmond. They also continued to travel, and made their first appearances on television.

When dobroist Josh Graves was added to the group, less emphasis was placed on a tense and powerful sound. Their music became more relaxed, and the work load of Earl Scruggs's banjo was reduced.

With the advent of the folk music boom, pressure was exerted by Columbia for Flatt and Scruggs to become a folk act. They made the necessary changes in their music which enabled them to survive the commercial demands, but their sound became less dynamic and the banjo work of Earl Scruggs became less inspired.

The group enjoyed its initial national exposure on television in 1960, when they performed on *Folk Sound, U.S.A.* In 1959 Earl Scruggs had appeared at the Newport Folk Festival, and in 1960 he and his Foggy Mountain Boys were among its participants. Among the numerous network television shows on which the group appeared were *The Ernie Ford Show*, *Jimmy Dean Show*, *Tonight Show*, and *The Beverly Hillbillies*. One of their most famous tunes, "The Ballad of Jed Clampett," was used during the midsixties as the theme song for the popular television show *The Beverly Hillbillies*. In 1967 "Foggy Mountain Breakdown," was selected for the movie *Bonnie and Clyde*, and the Scruggs composition made the three-finger-picking banjoist's name a household word. Flatt and Scruggs rerecorded "Foggy Mountain Breakdown" on an album, *The Story of Bonnie and Clyde* (Columbia CS-9649), but this version lacked the vitality of the original 1950 recording. Scruggs's son Randy started playing guitar with Flatt and Scruggs, and this LP marked his recording debut. It was not long before Gary Scruggs was added as a sideman, and the role of Lester Flatt was further jeopardized. In 1969 Flatt and Scruggs parted company and each formed his own new group—Lester Flatt and the Nashville Grass and the Earl Scruggs Revue.

Scruggs explains the formation of the Revue as a change that came about when he felt that he had gone as far as he could go with the music that he had been playing: "My sons were the main influence in changing the direction of my music. My interests were aroused by them playing other types of music. We started combining electric instrumentation with the banjo, and it sounded good. I had jammed with the sax player King Curtis and other people who were playing other types of music, and I was excited by the possibilities. The Revue now plays modern, jazz, blues, folk, rock, and public-domain tunes."

Earl Scruggs's son Randy plays electric and acoustic guitar and slide guitar for the Revue: "He worked with me onstage when he was nine years old, and he started recording when he was thirteen." Together with his brother Gary, who is lead vocalist and electric bass and harmonica player for the group, they recorded two albums for Vanguard, *All the Way Home* (VSD-6538) and *The Scruggs Brothers* (VSD-6579). Scruggs's youngest son, Steve, has become a member of the Revue, and Jody Maphis is the Revue's drummer. Until recently, Josh Graves played dobro for the group, but he has embarked on a career of his own. His first solo album, *Alone at Last* (Columbia KE-33168), demonstrates a talent that is largely responsible for the current popularity of the dobro guitar.

In addition to the numerous albums recorded by Flatt and Scruggs, Earl Scruggs has made many recordings for Columbia Records, including *His Family and Friends* (C-30584) with Joan Baez, Bob Dylan, and others; *Live at Kansas State* (KC-31758); *Dueling Banjos* (C-32268); *I Saw the Light with Some Help from My Friends* (KC-31354); *Rockin' Cross the Country* (KC-32943); *The Earl Scruggs Revue* (KC-32426); *Nashville's Rock* (CS-1007); and, most recently, *Anniversary Special, Volume One* (PC-33416), which includes guest artists Joan Baez, Johnny Cash, Leonard Cohen, Jack Elliott, Dan Fogelberg, Doug Kershaw, Ken Loggins, Roger McGuinn, Jim Messina, Michael Murphey, Tracy Nelson, the New Riders of the Purple Sage, Buffy Sainte-Marie, Loudon Wainwright III, and others.

Scruggs authored the book *Earl Scruggs and the 5-String Banjo*; and he recorded an LP to be used along with the exercise section of the book, *Earl Scruggs: 5-String Instruction Album*, both published by Peer International in 1967. (*See also* Lester Flatt.)

## Gary Scruggs. *See* Earl Scruggs.

## Randy Scruggs. *See* Earl Scruggs.

## Steve Scruggs. *See* Earl Scruggs.

## Sea Island Singers. *See* The Georgia Sea Island Singers.

## John Sebastian

*Contemporary singer, songwriter, guitarist, harmonica player, performer, and recording artist*

A viable entity among the singer-songwriters produced during the 1960s, John Sebastian is a veteran of the New York scene who has managed to retain his appeal as a solo performer and recording artist long after the breakup of his group, the Lovin' Spoonful. For over ten years he has created an impact on contemporary popular music, from his early harmonica accompaniment on albums by Eric Andersen, Judy Collins, and the Mugwumps (Cass Elliot, Denny Doherty, Zal Yanovsky, and James Hendricks) to his founding and composing for the Spoonful and to the launching of his solo career in 1969.

He was born John Benson Sebastian on March 17, 1944, in New York City, the son of a well-known classical harmonica player. His early life was spent in Greenwich Village, where his musical ambitions were molded by an exposure to the many poets and folksingers who were active in New York during this period. He graduated from

Blair Academy in Blairstown, New Jersey, in 1962 and attended New York University from 1962 to 1963. After leaving NYU, he started playing music with a number of people, including the Even Dozen Jug Band and the Mugwumps.

He left New York and traveled down South to study with bluesman Sam "Lightnin'" Hopkins. When he returned home, he put together the Lovin' Spoonful (the name of the group is derived from a Mississippi John Hurt song) with Steve Boone, Joe Butler, and Zal Yanovsky (previously with the Mugwumps). From 1965 to 1969, Sebastian was part of a group that offered a jug band, folk, country, ragtime, ethnic, and gospel repertoire, rivaling the predominant British sound of the late sixties. The group toured widely, performing primarily at colleges and universities across the country, and they recorded a string of hit singles, including "Do You Believe in Magic," "You Didn't Have to Be So Nice," "Daydream" (composed and sung by Sebastian, it was a top hit of early 1966, along with the Mamas and the Papas' "California Dreamin' "), "Did You Ever Have to Make Up Your Mind," "Summer in the City," "Nashville Cats," and "Darlin' Be Home Soon."

John Sebastian's role as lead vocalist, harmonica player, and autoharpist complemented his function as the Spoonful's composer. In 1966 he was the recipient of the highest award points for an individual composer given by Broadcast Music Incorporated (BMI). Toward the end of his career with the Lovin' Spoonful, John Sebastian wrote two film scores, for *You're a Big Boy Now* and *What's Up, Tiger Lily?* After the group's disbandment, he composed some tunes for the Broadway show *Jimmy Shine*, which starred Dustin Hoffman.

As a solo artist, he is well-known for his appearances at the Big Sur, Isle of Wight, and Woodstock folk festivals. His debut solo LP, *John B. Sebastian* (Reprise [S] 6379), was released in 1970; since then, he has recorded four more albums on Reprise. His highly ac-claimed theme song, "Welcome Back," for the television series *Welcome Back, Kotter*, was written by Sebastian in fifteen minutes, and it is the title track of his latest album, *Welcome Back* (Reprise MS 2249).

In recent years, John Sebastian has experimented with a band and performed college concerts, and in 1973 he toured England and Holland. In September John Sebastian appeared in the final concert of the 1975 Schaefer Music Festival at the Wollman Memorial Rink in New York City's Central Park.

During the seventies, John Sebastian composed scores for *Redeye Express*, *I Had a Dream*, *I Don't Want Nobody Else*, and *Lashes LaRue*. (*See also* The Even Dozen Jug Band.)

## Curly Sechler. *See* Earl Scruggs; The Stanley Brothers.

## The II Generation. *See* Eddie Adcock.

## Mike Seeger

*Singer, instrumentalist, solo and group performer, traditional folk music collector, and recording artist*

One of today's most versatile and respected figures in the field of folk music, Mike Seeger has played an instrumental role in the revitalization and performance of Southern traditional music. As a member of the New Lost City Ramblers, he was a representative of traditional music at the first Newport Folk Festival, which was dominated by such groups as the Kingston Trio and the Weavers; and, during the past three decades, Mike Seeger has been an active collector of traditional music, a solo recording artist, and a member of the New Lost City Ramblers and the Strange Creek Singers.

He was born on August 15, 1933, in New York City, to America's foremost folk music family, the Seegers, who moved to the Washington, D.C., area in 1935. His father, Charles Seeger, is a renowned musicologist, and his mother, Ruth Crawford Seeger, was a composer and the author of several folk song books. Folk music was ingrained in Mike Seeger's upbringing, as he remembers his childhood: "I became interested in folk songs about the time of my birth. I was raised on field recordings of Southern rural music and my parents' singing of these songs to me and their friends. We always sang around the house."

He learned to play the autoharp at the age of twelve, but his serious involvement with instruments did not begin until he was about eighteen years old. At this point, he started playing the guitar, banjo, mandolin, fiddle, mouth harp, dobro, and dulcimer. Then it was back to the autoharp; most recently, the jew's harp and pan pipes have been added to his repertoire.

"When I first started playing, I did songs from the usual urban folk music repertoire but heavily based in traditional music. My sister Peggy had started playing guitar about four or five years before me, and we started playing guitar and banjo together and with local square dance bands around Washington."

In 1954 his assignment as a conscientious objector in a Baltimore hospital began an involvement with country music and musicians, including Hazel Dickens and Bob

Mike Seeger

Baker. His interest in bluegrass was aroused, and he played almost exclusively with these musicians until the late fifties. The New Lost City Ramblers were formed in 1958, with Seeger, John Cohen, and Tom Paley; and, during the same year, Mike Seeger was the recipient of first prize in the banjo category at the Galax Old Time Fiddlers' Convention in Virginia.

"About the same time—in the late fifties—I had started recording. Moe Asch [of Folkways Records] had sent me a letter asking me to make some field recordings. I recorded, among others, the Stoneman Family, Libba Cotten's first record, Scruggs-style banjo, fiddlers' convention music, autoharp music, the McGee Brothers and Fiddlin' Arthur Smith, Dock Boggs, Lesley Riddle, and, eventually, bluegrass music and early bluegrass musicians such as the Lilly Brothers and Don Stover.

"Then the Ramblers got started, and I have been playing traditional music for a living since 1960. We performed at colleges and folk festivals, and we did the very first Newport Folk Festival. Tracy [Schwarz] joined the group in 1962. Tom Paley left, and we started going more deeply into country music at that point, and our repertoire changed." Unaccompanied ballads and a modernized bluegrass sound were worked into the group's basic old-time string band format. In the late sixties, Mike Seeger started performing more and more on his own, but he made fifteen or so recordings for Folkways as part of the New Lost City Ramblers.

He had been friendly with Alice Gerrard, Hazel Dickens, and Lamar Grier since the mid-fifties, and they played together from time to time at parties. By the late sixties, they had decided to form a group and record an album: "We got a name, the Strange Creek Singers, after Strange Creek, West Virginia. We worked on and off because each of us was working alone or with other groups. Sometimes Alice and I work as a duet, Tracy and I are with the Ramblers, but I play solo most of the time. I've recorded somewhere between forty and fifty albums, counting collections that I've made for Folkways, five with Peggy, and many with the Ramblers and the Strange Creek Singers. My two most recent albums are on Mercury: *Music from the True Vine* [SRM 1-627] and *The Second Annual Farewell Reunion* [SRM 1-685], with many friends."

Mike Seeger and his family have been living near New Freedom, Pennsylvania, since 1970, when he and Alice Gerrard were married. He became an adviser to the John Edwards Memorial Foundation in 1962; was a trustee of the Newport (Rhode Island) Folk Festival from 1963 to 1971; a director of the Smithsonian Folklife Company from 1970 to 1975; and a member of the board of directors of the National Folk Festival, Washington, D.C., and Southern Folk Cultural Revival Project in Atlanta, Georgia, in 1973. For the past twenty years, Mike Seeger has performed solo, with his wife Alice, his sister Peggy, the New Lost City Ramblers, and the Strange Creek Singers at concerts, festivals, and folk song clubs throughout the United States and in Canada, Europe, Australia, New Zealand, and Japan. His recordings can be found on many labels, including Argo, Folkways, Mercury, Rounder, and Vanguard. (*See also* The New Lost City Ramblers; Peggy Seeger; The Strange Creek Singers.)

# Peggy Seeger

*Singer, instrumentalist, songwriter, performer, and recording artist*

Peggy Seeger, in discussing folk music, wrote: "I should again like to express my debt *en masse* to the people who have put the **folksongs into print; to my parents, Charles** and Ruth Seeger, who instilled in me a real love of folk music and the people who create it; to my brothers, Mike and Pete, who proved to me that city singers really CAN **contribute to folk music; most of all, to** Ewan MacColl, who helped me to crystallize a singing style and, most important, showed me who 'the folk' really are.''

The Seeger name has become synonymous with American folk music, and Charles Seeger's second-eldest child by his second marriage, to Ruth Crawford Seeger, is as well-known for her work in Europe as she is in the United States. In the above statement from *Folk Songs of Peggy Seeger*, published by Oak Publications in 1964, she mentions her indebtedness to others in the folk music field, who, in turn, express the same sentiments in her regard.

Margaret (Peggy) Seeger was born in New York City on June 17, 1935, to piano teacher and composer Ruth Crawford Seeger and ethnomusicologist and professor of music Charles Louis Seeger. During the forties, her parents had begun to transcribe and anthologize American folk music, and the Seeger children were instilled with respect for, and interest in, their country's folk songs. Peggy started piano lessons at the age of seven, and as a teenager played with a mastery of style and technique. When she was ten she picked up the guitar, and she and her father often played guitar duets and sang Spanish songs. Gradually, she learned to play other instruments, including the five-string banjo, autoharp, Appalachian dulcimer, and English concertina.

Peggy Seeger helped her mother with transcriptions, learned music theory, and, when folk artists came to visit the Seegers in their suburban Washington, D.C., home, had the opportunity of meeting musicians who were associated with her older half-brother Pete Seeger or with her parents. It was thus, through listening to other musicians and field recordings of singers and instrumentalists from all over the United States, that she absorbed the folk idiom and developed her singing and playing techniques while growing up in Chevy Chase, Maryland.

Formal music and folk music were an integral part of her education. When she enrolled as a music major at Radcliffe College, she studied harmony, theory, and orchestration and began singing folk songs publicly. In 1955 she went to live in Holland, where she studied Russian at the University of Leiden. Following this, she traveled widely through Russia, Poland, China, and most of the Western European countries. Through her friendship with Alan Lomax, she was brought to England in 1956 to perform in an acting role in a Granada Television production of *Dark of the Moon*, in London. At this point, she became a member of the Ramblers, a singing group which also included Ewan MacColl, the Scottish folksinger, musicologist, dramatist, and songwriter. For a year they worked together on various television and radio programs and began to sing together as a team. In 1957 they embarked (with Charles Parker) upon a series of eight radio-ballads commissioned by the BBC. In the two years before Peggy Seeger and Ewan MacColl were married, she performed throughout the United States in concerts, festivals, and clubs and then traveled to Russia, to participate in the World Youth Festival, to Red China, and finally back to London, where she became a British subject and settled. Since then, she has continued to travel to all parts of the world and has written music (in conjunction with her husband Ewan MacColl) for a number of films and television documentaries.

Peggy Seeger has recorded over three dozen solo LPs, another two dozen with Ewan MacColl, and others with Tom Paley, her sisters Penny and Barbara, and others. Her numerous recordings have been issued by both American and British labels, including Argo, Folkways, Prestige/International, Rounder, and Tradition. She has composed many songs and, as a music editor, has been largely responsible for the publication of several folk song anthologies. Peggy Seeger and Ewan MacColl have produced the music for such television films as *In Prison, Night in the City, The Way We Live, Keeping Their Ends Up,* and *Coventry Kids,* among others. (*See also* Ewan MacColl; Mike Seeger.)

# Pete Seeger

*Singer, instrumentalist, songwriter, performer, recording artist, and author*

In commanding a key position for over a quarter of a century in the social, political, and musical arenas, this American "folk father" has been both a source of inspiration and a marked object of verbal ridicule, criticism, and attack. Sometimes referred to as "America's tuning fork," Pete Seeger has been the touchstone for the climate of his time as well as a model of protest and persistence. "I've never thought of myself as simply an entertainer," he insists, "I think of myself as a storyteller, sometimes as an organizer."

A prime target of McCarthyism, "for seventeen years I couldn't get a job on a network TV show. But maybe it was a lucky thing I was blacklisted—maybe I wouldn't have made any good music if I hadn't been blacklisted." Despite the controversy surrounding his career, his contribution to folk music is indisputable.

His live performances are inevitably highlighted by his magical power to lead in song both audience and other participating performers—heads get thrown back, voices ring out, feet pound the floor, and, always, Pete Seeger is at the center of the musical moment: "If I do my song right, I get people singing with me. I think that's the most important thing I've ever done. I'm not a good singer, I'm not a particularly good banjo player. I'm an old hand at getting a crowd singing, and when the crowd is singing well, then I feel happy. I'm convinced the whole problem of the human race and the machine age is how to get people doing things themselves and not simply being passive spectators." Several decades ago he played an instrumental role in popularizing the five-string banjo, and, over the years, he has placed an important emphasis on using a diversity of folk instruments in performances for peoples around the globe.

Pete Seeger is a shy, gentle, sincere man, modest about his talent as a composer. His philosophy is expressed in his choice of material and in his own original compositions, which include "If I Had a Hammer" (a collaboration with a fellow Almanac Singer and Weaver, Lee Hays), "Where Have All the Flowers Gone?," "The Big Muddy," and "Turn, Turn, Turn" (he composed the music to the passage in Ecclesiastes). The sheer love of music aside, Pete Seeger utilizes the medium as a vehicle for personal expression, and whether he is acting as a proponent of the Progressive party and Henry A. Wallace, the Hudson River Sloop Restoration project and the *Clearwater*, or the right of free speech and the survival of *Sing Out!* and *Broadside*, his treatise on the human condition becomes fused with his actions and his music.

Peter Seeger was born on May 3, 1919, in New York City, to musicologist Charles Louis Seeger and violin teacher Constance de Clyver (Edson) Seeger. "I didn't want to be a musician, I just wanted to have fun," he recalls in looking back on growing up in a musical family. "I'd bang around on musical instruments, I'd make noise, but I wouldn't practice! I played by ear. I didn't want to learn to read and write music." He attended private schools outside of Manhattan, where he "learned to read and write the English language and ended up wanting to be a newspaperman." After studying sociology at Harvard University from 1936 to 1938, "I couldn't get a job as a newspaperman, [and] I ended up singing songs —which I had always done for the fun of it, anyway—and I've been doing it ever since."

In 1939–40 he assisted Alan Lomax on collecting-recording expeditions for the Archive of Folk Song in the Library of Congress, and he appeared on his CBS Radio program. Along with Woody Guthrie, Lee Hays, and Millard Lampell, he organized the Almanac Singers in 1940. "Then World War II came along, and we'd been singing songs against Hitler, and when I went into the army, and Woody Guthrie went into the merchant marine, and so on, the Almanacs broke up. We were only together for about a

year and a half." In his coast-to-coast tours with the Almanacs and Woody Guthrie, he collaborated on composing labor and anti-Fascist songs and sang on overseas Office of War Information (OWI) broadcasts.

In 1945 Pete Seeger became national director of People's Songs, Inc., which "was the forerunner of *Sing Out!* We used the term 'hootenanny,' which Woody and I had found in use out in Seattle when we were singing with the Almanacs, for the fundraising songfests for this new organization. Our slogan was 'Songs of Labor and the American People,' and our aim was to get a singing labor movement. Well, we got kicked out of the labor movement. When the cold war came along, they didn't want radicals like us, and there was no worse name you could call a person than a Communist—and Woody and I and a lot of other people have sung for Communists and radicals and were proud of it. They were the hardest-working people.

"It wasn't generally known, for example, that songs like 'Which Side Are You On?' and 'Solidarity Forever'—all of these songs —would never have been written if it hadn't been for radicals. 'John Brown's Body.' These songs were written not by pop songwriters but by people who wanted to change the world, to get rid of poverty and injustice.

"Well, this kind of thing didn't go down with the establishment in the fifties, and so our hootenannies were attended by a few hundred here and a few hundred there. We were never very big."

Aside from his People's Songs, Inc., activities, Pete Seeger performed in the motion picture *To Hear My Banjo Play* (1946) and appeared in the Los Angeles Repertory Theater production of the folk musical *Dark of the Moon*. He was an ardent supporter of the 1948 Progressive party presidential candidate, Henry A. Wallace. After the election, he formed the Weavers with Ronnie Gilbert, Lee Hays, and Fred Hellerman, in 1949. For the next several years, he toured extensively and recorded for Decca and Vanguard as a member of this in-

fluential folk group, and "in 1950 the Weavers were offered a network, coast-to-coast weekly television show sponsored by Van Camp's Pork and Beans. We signed the contract, but the company hadn't signed it yet. That very week, out came an attack on us in a magazine put out by a professional blacklisting organization called Aware. The contract was torn up, and we never got the job, and for seventeen years I didn't get on network television."

After leaving the Weavers in order to concentrate on his own work, he began recording for Folkways Records in 1953 and traveled throughout this country and abroad: "I used to go around singing in schools and colleges—the one place in America where I was not blacklisted. And then I'd walk into a local TV station and speak to the disc jockey. 'Seeger? Oh yeah, you sang 'Good Night, Irene.' Well, sit down, we'll talk.' I'd be in and out before anybody could complain, and gradually I did more and more of this little TV work. I went up to Canada and worked on TV. I went to England and worked on TV. Australia. Cultural guerrilla tactics."

The height of his legal entanglements with the American government came in 1955, when he held his ground before the House Un-American Activities Committee by pleading the Fifth Amendment. He was indicted on nearly a dozen counts of contempt and was not cleared of the charges until May 18, 1962, when the case was closed in the United States Court of Appeals. Throughout this turbulent period, he gave an "American Folk Music and Its World Origins" concert series at Columbia University's Institute of the Arts and Sciences in 1954–55, was a contributing writer for *Sing Out!* magazine, appeared at the National Folk Festival in St. Louis, assisted in the reorganization (along with Theodore Bikel) of the Newport Folk Festival and was among the original members of its board of directors, helped to found the topical song publication *Broadside*, continued to write new songs, made numerous recordings for Columbia, Folkways, Tradi-

Pete Seeger at the 1965 Newport Folk Festival

tion, and other record companies, and traveled on a global singing tour with his family in 1963–64.

The winter of 1965–66 brought him finally to American television on a regular basis, as host of his own show, *Rainbow Quest*, aired on New York's Channel 47. "Finally, in 1967, I got on the Smothers Brothers' show," which marked his first appearance on network television in nearly two decades. "But the producers cut out the one song that I wanted to sing, 'The Big Muddy.' It didn't mention Vietnam by name, but everybody knew what I was singing about. Who knows? Maybe the song helped do some good. President Johnson decided not to run again a month after I finally got it on the air."

In the mid-sixties, his concern for the pollution of the Hudson River led to the organization of Hudson River Sloop Restoration, Inc., and the building of the *Clearwater*. From 1967 to 1970, Pete Seeger served as chairman of the board of the parent organization, and he became a central figure in the movement for ecological preservation of the United States.

He is the author of *American Favorite Ballads* (1960), *The Bells of Rhymney* (1964), *How to Play the Five-String Banjo* (1965), *The Incompleat Folksinger* (1972), and *Henscratches and Flyspecks* (1973). He is on the editorial advisory board of *Sing Out!* and is a frequent contributor to various other music publications. In 1970 he appeared briefly in the motion picture *Tell Me That You Love Me, Junie Moon*.

He describes himself as basically "a country boy at heart," and with his wife Toshi he cherishes their private life and peaceful home near Beacon, New York: "I'm an old do-it-yourselfer; I went to a school in the country where I learned how to chop trees and do a little slam-bang carpentry—I'm not a good carpenter, but I can slam things together—and my wife had faith in me, Lord knows. She cooked over an open fire for two summers while I threw the walls up and the roof on, and for three years she lugged water from the brook in a pail, till finally I started

earning enough money for us to have running water. Now it's very luxurious, we have a furnace, even. All the comforts of home, including a lawn, which I sometimes cut." (*See also* The Almanac Singers; The Weavers.)

## The Seekers

*Vocal and instrumental group, performers, and recording artists*

The urban folk boom of the mid-twentieth century broadened the possibilities for artistic expression within the context of the folk idiom, which, in turn, fostered its accessibility to the masses. Although popular styles have been scorned by many purists, commercialism was nonetheless an impetus in the creation of an expanded folk music audience. As a consequence, many people have utilized this route of discovery to probe more deeply to find other, more traditional folk forms. The Seekers was an Australian quartet instrumental in bringing to the limelight both traditional folk tunes ("The Water Is Wide," "Sinner Man," and "When the Stars Begin to Fall," among others) and contemporary material written by such prominent composers as Bob Dylan, Malvina Reynolds, and Paul Simon.

Born on January 5, 1940, in Melbourne, Australia, bass player Athol Guy left school at the age of sixteen to work for an accounting firm. During this period, he banded together with two other friends to form a trio, which made several television appearances. During one of his television stints, Athol Guy met Ceylon-born (March 2, 1941) guitarist Keith Potger, and they decided to form another group, called the Escorts. When a throat infection temporarily forced Guy to discontinue singing, the Escorts disbanded. Keith Potger then found employment with the Broadcasting Commission in Sydney, and Athol Guy located a job with an advertising agency.

Coincidentally, another employee of the advertising firm also harbored musical ambitions. Born on July 25, 1942, in Melbourne, Bruce Woodley was a guitarist for Morris Plonk's Moonshine Five, which eventually recruited Athol Guy. The group's widespread popularity stirred renewed interest in Guy's ex-partner Keith Potger, who joined them to tour as a member of Morris Plonk's Moonshine Five. When the number of members dwindled, Athol Guy, Keith Potger, and Bruce Woodley opted for a female vocalist named Judith Durham (born on July 7, 1943), to round out the Seekers' sound.

They played coffeehouses and spots on Melbourne television, and when an audition film of one of their performances was sent to London, the Seekers were asked to appear with singer Dusty Springfield at the London Palladium—only three weeks after their arrival in England. Dusty Springfield's brother Tom composed the Seekers' first hit single, "I'll Never Find Another You," which was released in England late in 1964. The record soared to the top of the British record charts in the early spring of 1965, and Capitol Records issued "I'll Never Find Another You" in the United States, followed by their debut LP, *The New Seekers* (Capitol T 2319).

Before their disbandment in 1968, the Seekers recorded numerous singles, including "Someday, One Day," "Georgy Girl," and "I Wish You Could Be Here," and an additional four albums on the Capitol label.

# The Seldom Scene. *See* Mike Auldridge.

# Joe Selly. *See* Bottle Hill.

# Bryan Sennett. *See* The Serendipity Singers.

# The Serendipity Singers

*Vocal and instrumental group, performers, and recording artists*

With the success of the New Christy Minstrels during the recent folk song revival, the way was paved for another folk choral group, known as the Serendipity Singers. The group's nine members recorded one of the hit records of 1964, "Don't Let the Rain Come Down," and the Serendipity Singers were featured regularly on ABC-TV's *Hootenanny.*

The core of the Serendipities was a collegiate folk trio of University of Colorado students, Mike Brovsky, Brooks Hatch, and Bryan Sennett. To increase the dimension of their sound, three more musicians were added to the group: guitarists Jon Arbenz and John Madden, and bass player Bob Young. Shortly thereafter, the remaining three musicians and singers—Diane Decker, Tommy Tieman, and Lynne Weintraub—joined the Serendipity Singers.

Although their repertoire included traditional folk music, pop songs, topical material, and show tunes, it was their approach and instrumentation that made them classifiable as a folk group. Even the title of their group suggests a freewheeling attitude in the selection of their music, as *serendipity* has been defined as "the faculty of making desirable but unsought-for discoveries by accident."

After performing on college campuses and for Rocky Mountain regional organizations, the Serendipity Singers decided to venture East in an attempt to expand their audience. They auditioned for Fred Weintraub and Bob Bowers at the Bitter End, and, within a matter of minutes, the Serendipity Singers were offered a regular spot on *Hootenanny* and a recording contract with Philips Records. Their album, *The Serendipity Singers* (PHS-600-115), was produced by Weintraub and Bowers and included their hit, "Don't Let the Rain Come Down (Crooked Little Man)."

The commercial success of the Serendipity Singers was immediate but short-lived, and "Don't Let the Rain Come Down" was their only cash box hit. They traveled extensively throughout the United States, performing mostly at colleges, and their tours brought them appearances in Canada and Australia. They were a featured act on *Hootenanny* and the NBC-TV *Today Show*, and were frequently billed at the group's home base, the Bitter End in Greenwich Village.

## Mike Settle. *See* The Cumberland Three; The New Christy Minstrels; John Stewart.

## Bob Shane. *See* The Kingston Trio.

## Shanties

Within the spectrum of folk music are specific categories of work-related songs which are sung by men and women for their own entertainment in their idle hours and for setting a rhythm to enable them to work together in their labors. Shanties, or chanteys, are a by-product of the nineteenth century, when many lives were spent on the open seas.

Every sailor had his own style. An authentic shanty was a work song which was sung unaccompanied, but, in some cases where the work was less complex and required fewer hands, instrumental accompaniment was provided on concertina, whistle, fiddle, or banjo. The tunes were derived from Elizabethan England, British and American folk songs, fiddle tunes, and African chants. The majestic ships and their crews which transported mail, supplies, and passengers are part of a bygone age, but the songs remain to tell their story.

In 1818 the Black Ball Line offered the first packet ship service (they carried packets of mail, among other things) on a regular schedule between Liverpool and New York.

To meet the increased demands of the day, other services, such as the Red Cross Line and Swallowtail Line, were inaugurated. Before long, clipper ships were designed for greater speed and sturdiness, and captains notoriously pushed their crews to cross the Atlantic in less and less time. Shanties such as "Leave Her, Johnny, Leave Her" and "Boston Harbor" (also called "With a Big Bow Wow") express the feelings of the men toward a merciless, hardhanded skipper. Other themes related to whaling, yearning for women, famous ships of that era, sailors, and loved ones left behind.

Forecastle songs, unlike shanties, were sung and played exclusively for pleasure. Variations of old British ballads and American Negro work songs, forecastle songs were usually accompanied by a musical instrument and sung in the early evening—sometimes in the sailors' quarters, or "fo'c'sle."

Different types of shanties were sung for the various tasks that were performed. There were basically three categories: short drag (e.g., "Haul Away, Joe"), halliard (e.g., "Blow, Boys, Blow"), and capstan (e.g., "Santy Anno"). The three categories are all represented in such collections as *Songs & Sounds of the Sea* (National Geographic 705); *Them Liverpool Judies* (Philo 10020), by Craig Morton; *Fo'c'sle Songs and Shanties* (Folkways FA 2429) and *Whaling and Sailing Songs* (Tradition TLP 1005), both recorded by Paul Clayton; *Sea Shanties and Loggers' Songs* (Folkways FA 2019), by Sam Eskin; *The X Seamens Institute* (Folkways FTS 32418), by the Clancy Brothers and Tommy Makem; *Haul on the Bowlin'* (Stinson SLP 80) and *Off to Sea Once More* (Stinson SLP 81), by A. L. Lloyd and Ewan MacColl; *Leviathan!* (Topic 12T174), by A. L. Lloyd; and other collections, featuring various artists, such as *Sailormen and Servingmaids* (Caedmon TC 1162), *Farewell Nancy* (Topic 12T110), *Clearwater* (Sound House PS 1001B/SR0104), *Sea Songs and Shanties* (Topic TPS205), and *The Valiant Sailor* (Topic 12TS232).

**Ernie Sheldon.** *See* The Gateway Singers.

**Dick Shirley.** *See* The Travelers 3.

**George Shuffler.** *See* The Stanley Brothers.

## Paul Siebel

*Contemporary singer-songwriter, guitarist, performer, and recording artist*

Among today's singers and musicians is a poet who combines the directness of Hank Williams and Jimmie Rodgers with a bittersweet lyricism and romanticism. A talented poet-composer, Paul Siebel has maintained a low profile in the music industry, but when he made the transition from singing traditional ballads to writing his own material, everyone began watching him closely.

A native of Buffalo, New York, Paul Siebel is a performer with a genuine country-folk style. An urban environment proved to be unrestrictive in his assimilation of diverse approaches, ideas, and interests, which have yielded a broad range of styles, resulting in his universal appeal. During the sixties, he moved to New York City, where he encountered many folk artists of the Greenwich Village scene, including Bob Dylan, John Hammond, Jr., Tom Paxton, John Sebastian, Pat Sky, Jerry Jeff Walker, and Jesse Colin Young. His initial attempts at performing centered around his interest in traditional folk forms, and he sang old-time ballads with a haunting vocal style which aroused the attention of those around him. However, the most enthusiastic response to Paul Siebel was evoked by his own compositions, which he started writing during this period.

He recorded his debut album for Elektra Records, entitled *Woodsmoke and Oranges*

(EKS-74064), with selections written by Paul Siebel and instrumental accompaniment by David Bromberg, Richard Greene, Gary White, and others. One of his songs, "Louise," became popular among other recording artists, and the entire album was praised by *Rolling Stone* magazine as a milestone in country-rock-pop music. Since then, Paul Siebel has recorded *Jack-Knife Gypsy* (EKS-74081) and has remained a popular performer at concerts and festivals.

## Irwin Silber

*Editor, publisher, author, and producer*

The publication of materials related to folk music has functioned conjointly with live performances and recordings to disseminate the various elements within the idiom. In addition to his significant contributions to People's Songs, Inc., *Sing Out!* magazine, and Oak Publications, Irwin Silber has authored numerous books and articles on folk music and has produced throngs of hootenannies, concerts, and records.

Born on October 17, 1925, in New York City, Silber attended public schools in Manhattan and later enrolled at Brooklyn College. While he was in college, he organized and directed the American Folksay Group, perpetuating his involvement with the group after graduating from Brooklyn College with a BA degree in 1945. Two years later, he began working with others in the field, through the newly formed organization called People's Songs, Inc., to recreate the spirit originally fostered by the Almanac Singers. Along with individuals who had been a part of the Almanac Singers' activities, Ernie Lieberman, Betty Sanders, Irwin Silber, and others joined together to promote progressive causes with music. In contrast to the Almanac Singers, who created an expanded folk consciousness as performers, People's Songs, Inc., was a group primarily concerned with songwriting, then performing. People's Songs was officially incorporated in New York

City on January 31, 1946, and, by the end of the first year, its *People's Songs Bulletin* had expanded from six mimeographed pages to twelve pages with photos. It was during this period that the organization's Executive Secretary Irwin Silber became deeply involved with hootenannies, which were considered its most important enterprises and vehicles for communication. After supporting presidential candidate Henry A. Wallace, the efforts of People's Songs, Inc., were terminated by bankruptcy in 1949.

After the demise of People's Songs, Inc., Alan Lomax, Paul Robeson, Betty Sanders, Pete Seeger, Irwin Silber, and a number of others formed People's Artists, Inc., late in 1949. As Irwin Silber explains: "This organization served as an umbrella organization which obtained bookings for folk and political artists, presented concerts, and published songs. In 1950 People's Artists began the regular publication of *Sing Out!* magazine." After serving in an advisory capacity, Irwin Silber was editor of *Sing Out!* from 1951 until 1967.

Under his editorship, *Sing Out!* was a political and frequently controversial publication, and, says Silber, "during the 1950s, the magazine came under fierce attack. Subpoenaed on three different occasions by various government committees investigating 'subversion,' I was an 'unfriendly witness' who took the position that my politics were not the business of any government agency. In the sixties, when the folk music revival surged, *Sing Out!* grew in size and leadership, but I maintained my generally acerbic critique of the political establishment. In 1964 my 'Open Letter to Bob Dylan,' which criticized the singer's turn away from explicitly political themes, provoked a major controversy among the magazine's readers and within its staff. My regular column, 'Fan the Flames,' frequently drew brickbats from outraged readers."

Silber also continued to produce "more folk concerts and hootenannies than I care to remember, especially during the 1950s, when it was deemed subversive." In the late fifties and early sixties, a close, ten-year association developed between Irwin Silber and Moe Asch, founder and owner of Folkways Records. As editor of *Sing Out!*, Silber had worked with Asch on numerous Folkways recordings. In 1960 they founded Oak Publications, "the first significant publishing company exclusively devoted to books on or about folk and people's music," which, in the next seven years, published some one hundred titles.

In 1967 Oak Publications was sold to Music Sales Limited, London, and Silber resigned as editor of *Sing Out!* in order to devote his full time to political writing and organizing. In 1968 he joined the staff of the weekly *National Guardian*, an "independent radical newsweekly," as a writer and cultural editor. Since 1972 he has served as the *Guardian*'s executive editor.

For the past twenty-five years, Irwin Silber has produced and edited numerous record albums. He has written many articles on folk music, and some of his books include *Lift Every Voice* (People's Artists/Oak Publications), *Reprints from the People's Songs Bulletin* (Oak), *Songs of the Civil War* (Columbia University Press), *Hootenanny Song Book* (Consolidated), *Songs of the Great American West* (Macmillan), *Folksong Festival* (Scholastic), *Great Atlantic and Pacific Songbook* (Embassy), *The Vietnam Songbook*, coedited with Barbara Dane (Guardian), *The Season of the Year* (Oak), *Songs America Voted By* (Stackpole), *Songs of Independence* (Stackpole), and *The Folksinger's Wordbook*, with Fred Silber (Oak).

His work has brought him together with Barbara Dane, "my personal and political comrade—coauthor, coproducer, and copartner in all kinds of schemes relating to people's music," and, together, they operate Paredon Records in Brooklyn, New York. (*See also* Barbara Dane.)

## Shel Silverstein

*Poet, writer, illustrator, cartoonist, composer, performer, singer, guitarist, and recording artist*

Within the field of folk music are many artists who have branched out to explore other media for creative self-expression, and their accomplishments often encompass a broad range of art forms. In his mid-forties, Shel Silverstein is the author of a number of highly acclaimed children's books which he has both written and illustrated; a poet and short-story writer; cartoonist for *Playboy* magazine; performer, guitarist, singer; and composer of many well-known songs recorded by Johnny Cash ("A Boy Named Sue"), the Irish Rovers ("The Unicorn"), Dr. Hook and the Medicine Show ("Sylvia's Mother" and all the songs on their albums), and others.

Born in Chicago in 1932, Shelby (Shel) Silverstein has been compared to James Thurber. Formerly an artist for *Stars and Stripes* magazine, he joined the staff of *Playboy* in the early fifties when the publication first started, and his cartoons were enjoyed by *Playboy*'s readers for nearly two decades. He turned his attention to writing and illustrating children's books and published his first book, *Uncle Shelby's ABZ Book*. It was not long before Silverstein was also engaged in composing music and performing at such esteemed folk clubs as the Bitter End in New York and the Gate of Horn in Chicago.

The lyrics of his songs are generally straightforward, simple, and unforgettable, and a good percentage of his material is in the folk idiom. In his own performances and recordings, he utilizes his unique voice to dramatize his songs, and his style is a blending of energy, joy, a sense of rhythm, whispers, yelps, and groans. His songs are best known through recordings made by other artists. One of his most popular hits was a children's folk song, "The Unicorn," which was a cash box hit single for the Irish Rovers in 1968. "The Unicorn," had been recorded by Silverstein in 1961 and appeared on his LP *Inside Folk Songs* (Atlantic 8072), which also included "Boa Constrictor" and "25 Minutes to Go," recorded and popularized by the Brothers Four. More recently, he has composed popular country songs for such singers as Lynn Anderson, as well as two albums for the rock group Dr. Hook. A tune from his most recent LP, *Freaking at the Freaker's Ball* (Columbia KC 31119), entitled "Don't Give a Dose to the One You Love Most," has been used in anti-VD films and campaigns.

His other books include *Lafcadio, the Lion Who Shot Back, Giraffe and a Half, The Giving Tree, Now Here's My Plan, Uncle Shelby's Zoo*, and *Don't Bump the Glump.*

# Simon and Garfunkel

*Vocal and instrumental duo, performers, and recording artists*

One of the recent contemporary developments in the interest of folk music, particularly among urban dwellers, has been the rise of singers who have combined their talent as songwriters with distinctive personal vocal and instrumental styles. Each highly regarded for his individual achievements, the combination of Paul Simon's lyrics and melodies and Art Garfunkel's pristine soprano vocals created a productive and influential force during the sixties. Simon and Garfunkel succeeded in injecting poetic lyrics and complexly interrelated musical designs into popular music, and Art Garfunkel's blending and interweaving with his partner's vocals made unforgettable their versions of "The Sounds of Silence," "I Am a Rock," "Mrs. Robinson," "Bridge over Troubled Water," "The Boxer," "Cecilia," and other Paul Simon compositions.

Paul Simon was born on November 5, 1942, in Newark, New Jersey, and he met **Art Garfunkel during grade school, when** both families were living in Queens. Garfunkel was born in New York City on October 13, 1942, and his boyhood friendship with Simon resulted in their singing together throughout their school years. Simon earned a BA in English literature at Queens College, while Garfunkel was an education and math student at Columbia University. They per-

Simon and Garfunkel

formed at Gerde's Folk City at the end of their second year of college, and their successful engagement brought them a recording contract with Columbia Records. Their first album, *Wednesday Morning, 3 A.M.* (Columbia CL 2249), was the result of a partnership officially formed that night at Folk City. With album sales slow, the team split up for a while. When one of the cuts, "The Sounds of Silence," began to receive increased airplay, more dramatic instrumental accompaniment was underdubbed and the song was issued as a 45-RPM single. Unaware of this development until "Sounds of Silence" had reached the top-forty charts, Simon then returned from his solo tour abroad and rejoined Garfunkel to meet demands for personal appearances throughout the United States. "I Am a Rock," from their second Columbia LP, *Sounds of Silence* (CL 2469), was a bestselling single of 1966. Simon and Garfunkel toured extensively during the mid-sixties and made several

television appearances on major network programs. In the meantime, their third album, *Parsley, Sage, Rosemary and Thyme* (Columbia CL 2563/CS 9363), was released, and within a year it became a Gold Record.

In 1967 Paul Simon met a new challenge by composing the music for Mike Nichols's film *The Graduate*. One of the songs, "Mrs. Robinson," was a hit single in 1968 and was included on Simon and Garfunkel's next album, *Bookends* (KCS 9529). With the release and sales of the soundtrack album of *The Graduate*, the team of Simon and Garfunkel became known all over the world.

When Garfunkel began to devote more of his time to the pursuit of an acting career, a rift developed in the partnership. Progress in the recording of their next album, *Bridge over Troubled Water* (Columbia KCS 9914), was held up because of Garfunkel's role in the film *Catch-22*, and Simon subsequently decided that it would be in their best interest to split up and to pursue individual careers.

354

Although both Simon and Garfunkel have enjoyed successful solo careers, neither has achieved the level of success that they enjoyed as a team. Paul Simon's first solo LP, *Paul Simon* (KC 30750), was followed by *There Goes Rhymin' Simon* (KC 32280), which was nominated for a Grammy Award as Best Album of 1973. Two songs on the LP, "Kodachrome" and "Loves Me Like a Rock," were released as singles, and both became Gold Records. Simon's most recent album, *Still Crazy after All These Years* (Columbia PC 33540), was released in the fall of 1975.

Garfunkel's initial solo effort, *Angel Clare* (Columbia KC 31474), was released in 1973, produced by Garfunkel and Simon and Garfunkel engineer-producer Roy Halee. Although it had taken over a year to complete, by the spring of 1974 its sales were rapidly approaching the Gold Record mark. In the fall of 1975, *Breakaway* (Columbia PC 33700) was issued with "My Little Town" (which also appears on Simon's 1975 LP) sung as a duet by Simon and Garfunkel. Recording aside, Art Garfunkel has become more established as an actor, with two of his best-known motion picture roles in *Carnal Knowledge* and *Catch-22*.

## Paul Simon. *See* Simon and Garfunkel.

## Sing Out!

*The folk song magazine, published bimonthly*

Twenty-five years ago, the concept of the New York folk song publication *Sing Out!* was formulated by a group of writers and singers who saw folk music as an expression of social discontent and as an extension of the worldwide struggle for equality and justice. The first issue featured the Pete Seeger–Lee Hays composition "If I Had a Hammer" on the cover and, within its pages, Les Rice's "Banks of Marble" and Leadbelly's "It's Almost Done."

### Sing Out!

# SING OUT!

THE FOLK SONG MAGAZINE

VOLUME 21/NUMBER 6          $1.00

Music from Round Peak
Bonnie Raitt   John Davis
Rounder Records
Songs from Women's Workshops
Fiddle & Banjo Teach-In's
Pete Seeger   Michael Cooney
Barbara Dane   Columns
Reviews   Folk Market Place
plus:
THE SING OUT! SOUNDSHEET
WITH MUSIC TO 16 SONGS

A nationally known New York City bimonthly publication

As editor Alan Senauke describes the publication's original premise for selection of material: "*Sing Out!* saw these songs as an alternative to the predigested sounds of pop music, bought and sold by giant record companies and slippery-tongued promoters. Here was a place for grass-roots music—music that people could make for themselves."

Over the past quarter of a century, the world has witnessed many changes and has seen the emergence of a new generation of folksingers. In an attempt to adhere to its original intentions while remaining flexible and responsive to the times, *Sing Out!* has maintained its stature as a viable and meaningful publication which presents the best in both traditional and contemporary folk music. Published six times a year, it includes in each issue twelve to fifteen songs, with words, music, and guitar chords, covering a broad range of material—blues from Chicago's South Side, mountain music, revolutionary songs from Latin America, women's songs, Cajun fiddle music, sea shanties, Celtic ballads, bluegrass, street singers, ragtime guitar, and so on. There are in-depth interviews, articles, and commentaries on all aspects of folk music; columns by Pete Seeger, Michael Cooney, and others; news and reviews; "teach-in's" for a wide variety of folk instruments; a flexible plastic record (to accompany the printed words and music included in the issue) bound into every other issue; black-and-white photographs and sketches; and many other features.

As Woody Guthrie once wrote in a letter to *Sing Out!*: "One little issue of *Sing Out!* is worth more to this humanly race than any thousand tons of other dreamy, dopey junk dished out from the trees and forests along every Broadway in this world."

*Sing Out!* is owned collectively by its staff, its advisers, and some friends. Any money earned is used to improve the magazine and its distribution.

# Patrick Sky

*Singer, songwriter, poet, instrumentalist, Irish Uilleann pipe maker, performer, and recording artist*

This multitalented country boy who came north from Georgia has brought a distinctive individuality and whimsical style to the urban folk scene. His songs cover the gamut of human experience, and his public appearances are a blending of his easygoing pace, his jokes, and a seriousness that contrasts with his humorous side.

Born on October 2, 1940, in Live Oak Gardens, outside Atlanta, Georgia, Patrick (Pat) Sky started playing folk music when he was a youngster, and the interest developed as he was growing up: "As I got older, the folk movement was starting to get under way, and I began to play at little coffeehouses, eventually finding my way to

Florida. I met Buffy [Sainte-Marie] and we were together for about three years, just traveling around and playing clubs, and then I came to the North with her in the early sixties.

"I came to Greenwich Village, and it was just great. There were thousands of places to play, and there was always a lot of music. It was a real scene. I was playing all over for various organizations, and I performed a lot of concerts—*Broadside* concerts—which were really big at that time.

"My recording career actually started with Buffy, who had gotten a record contract, and I was on the record with her. When they heard me play, they wanted me to do a couple of songs for a tape, by myself; and when they listened to them, they liked what they heard, so I recorded *Patrick Sky* [VSD-79179] for Vanguard in 1965. I made another album for Vanguard in 1966 called *A Harvest of Gentle Clang* [VSD-790207], and it wasn't until 1969 that I recorded another record, for MGM Records, *Reality Is Bad Enough* [Verve/Forecast FTS-3052]. After my second album on the MGM label, I made *Songs That Made America Famous* [Adelphi Records AD-R4101] in a small studio called ZBS Media, in upstate New York, in 1971 or 1972.

"Since then, I've been writing a series of articles for *New England Musician's Guide*, and I'm writing a book about my experiences in the music scene. I'm also making Uilleann pipes, which are Irish elbow pipes, but right now I'm only building practice sets. Liam O'Flynn, who played them at the Buffalo Folk Festival in the fall of 1971, got me started on it. I can't make a full set of pipes, which would mean making the drones and the regulators, because I don't have the facilities to make metal keys. Hopefully, I'll be able to make some master keys and have them cast here in Rhode Island sometime in the future.

"I'm not playing professionally anymore—pursuing it as a career. It is mostly a hobby, and I only play certain festivals like the Southeastern Massachusetts University Eisteddfod. I have always liked traditional

Patrick Sky at a *Broadside* hoot, New York City, February 1965

music, and the S.M.U. Eisteddfod is very traditional, with American and British music, country dancing, and storytelling. Since there is nothing that interests me in modern music, I'm going back to the traditional material.

"I was invited to play the Philadelphia Folk Festival for five years in a row, but I don't play it anymore because I think that it's just gotten out of hand. I like the smaller festivals, like Eisteddfod, when only about fifteen hundred to two thousand people show up. Once in a while, I'll play a small club, just for something to do."

Of Creek Indian heritage, Patrick Sky in-troduced the mouth bow to Buffy Sainte-Marie, who uses it occasionally in her performances. During his active years of performing, Pat Sky appeared in solo concerts at New York's Carnegie Hall and Town Hall, the United States Pavilion at the Montreal World's Fair, and the Russian delegation in Washington. He toured colleges throughout the United States, and he was among the artists at the Newport and Philadelphia folk festivals and the Royal Academy Hall Festival in London. In 1966 he composed the musical score for a film on conservation, *Down the Road*, in which he also performed.

# Arthur Smith

*Country singer, musician, songwriter, record and radio producer, and owner of the* Arthur Smith Television Show, Clay Music Company, *and the Arthur Smith Studio*

By the age of twelve, South Carolina–born Arthur Smith had decided that he was going to devote his life to the field of country music. In 1936, when he was in the tenth grade, he recorded for RCA Victor: "The field man, Eli Oberstein, came down through the South with a roll of money in his right pocket big enough to choke a wet dog, and we made records in hotel rooms. In those days, the records were cut in wax, put in a carton to be carried back to New York, and then the 78s were pressed from them."

In 1945 his most successful hit, "Guitar Boogie," was released and became "the first song to cross over from the country field into the pop field." It sold over three million copies and earned Smith a Gold Record. He wrote "Duelin' Banjos" in 1955; when Warner Brothers used the song without his permission in the motion picture *Deliverance*, Smith took them to court with a copyright suit. He had worked out the original composition (which he called "Feudin' Banjos") with five-string banjoist Don Reno and Smith on tenor banjo. Smith was awarded nearly $200,000 by the courts, and in 1973 "Duelin' Banjos" received the Best Country Music Song of the Year Award.

He owns the Arthur Smith Studio in Charlotte, North Carolina, where he produces records and commercials and is the nation's largest producer of syndicated radio shows: "At one time, I built a chain of supermarkets, and, as I got busy, I wouldn't take the time to go to New York or Nashville to record. So I converted a stable on our place into a little studio to keep some records flowing, and it has grown into a very big business! I produce George Hamilton IV, Pat Boone, and Don Reno. And since 1964 we have syndicated the five-minute radio program, *The Johnny Cash Show*, which is broadcast daily on two hundred national radio stations."

Arthur Smith has recorded *Battling Banjos* (Monument Z 32259) and *Arthur & Clay Smith/Smith & Son* (Monument KZ 33429), with his son.

# The Arthur Smith Trio. *See* Fiddlin' Arthur Smith.

# Dan Smith

*Gospel singer, folksinger, harp player, performer, recording artist, minister, and deacon*

Born in 1911 and raised in Perdue Hill, Alabama, gospel singer and folksinger Dan

Arthur Smith

Dan Smith performing at the Friday evening concert at the Eleventh Annual Philadelphia Folk Festival, 1972

Smith taught himself to play the harmonica as a young boy, then abandoned his musical activities until several decades later, when blindness returned him to his boyhood hobby.

When the eight-year-old Dan Smith was caught with his older brother's harmonica, he was scolded by his mother and told to put it down. He started singing a year later, and by the age of ten he had picked up the harmonica again. One of thirteen children, he was raised on a farm and began working at home when he was eleven. When it seemed impossible to earn a living with music, he decided to relinquish his notion of singing and playing on a professional basis. He worked on the railroad while living in Alabama and, when he was twenty-two, left home to work in Georgia. After ten years, he left Georgia and settled in White Plains, New York, in 1943.

In 1960 an industrial accident resulted in the loss of his eyesight. Two years later, when he was at a Spring Valley, New York, camp for the blind, he sang in public by request for the first time in thirty years. Since then, he has sung and played in folk festivals across the country, including Newport and Philadelphia. He has also played with Pete Seeger and the crew of the *Clearwater*, and he has performed at various folk concerts and in church halls. He began writing songs, most of which are spirituals, such as "Keep Goin' On," "Communion in the Lord's House," and many others.

Dan Smith has recorded two albums for

Biograph Records: *God Is Not Dead* (Biograph BLP 12036), primarily gospel with accompaniment by Michael Cooney, Jack Hume, Bessie Jones, and Bill Vanaver; and *Now Is the Time* (Biograph BLP 12053), a folk LP with Nicky Seeger on guitar.

He still lives in White Plains, where he works as a minister and deacon.

## Donald Smith. *See* The Kentucky Pardners.

## Fiddlin' Arthur Smith

*Early country fiddler, banjoist, singer, songwriter, performer, and recording artist*

Fiddlin' Arthur Smith's name is closely tied to country music of the 1930s, when he played with Sam and Kirk McGee on WSM's *Grand Ole Opry*. He achieved national prominence with his own Arthur Smith Trio 1936 recording of "There's More Pretty Girls Than One" and as a sideman for many of the Delmore Brothers' recordings of the late thirties.

In the tradition of handing down an art from one generation to the next within a family, Arthur Smith's father taught his son to play the fiddle at a young age. Working full-time for the railroads, he played with the talented boy in the evenings and on weekends and they sometimes performed together at local gatherings. Arthur Smith followed in his father's footsteps and worked as a railroader, playing the fiddle for his own enjoyment.

In 1930 Arthur Smith joined Sam and Kirk McGee as the Dixieliners. The trio of Tennesseeans was heard on several small local radio stations, and they soon became regulars on WSM's *Grand Old Opry*. With the sponsorship of WSM, Smith could afford to quit his job as a railroad worker, and he toured from 1932 to 1938 with the McGees and with his own group, the Arthur Smith Trio. However, the McGee Brothers and Ar-

thur Smith never made any recordings together, as the brothers recorded either as a team or with Uncle Dave Macon. Smith's recordings on the Bluebird label were made with Alton and Rabon Delmore, and, as the Arthur Smith Trio, they recorded several of Smith's best-known compositions (which have since become country music classics), including "Beautiful Brown Eyes" and "There's More Pretty Girls Than One," which was a hit record for the trio in 1936. After seven years of touring with the Delmore Brothers as the Arthur Smith Trio, and broadcasting on WSM and performing on road shows with Sam and Kirk McGee as the Dixieliners, Arthur Smith left Nashville to work with other small groups during the forties and fifties. He was a relatively obscure country musician until his rediscovery during the folk revival of the mid-fifties and early sixties, when he was asked to perform with the McGees at several major folk festivals, including the 1965 Newport Folk Festival.

The first recording made by Fiddlin' Arthur Smith and Sam and Kirk McGee was the result of efforts by Mike Seeger to tape their traditional country music for the Folkways LP, *The McGee Brothers and Arthur Smith* (FA 2379). Another album was recorded, *Milk 'Em in the Evening Blues* (Folkways FTS 31007), and in 1963 Starday (a small record company which has issued recordings of several old-time performers, such as Ernest Stoneman, Sam and Kirk McGee, Lulu Belle and Scotty, and others) made an album entitled *Fiddlin' Arthur Smith and the Dixie Liners* (SLP 202). (*See also* The Delmore Brothers; The McGee Brothers.)

## Hobart Smith

*Traditional instrumentalist, singer, and recording artist*

Considered by folk purists to be one of America's greatest traditional instrumentalists, Hobart Smith has indirectly influenced an entire generation of young musicians who have learned from others who had the opportunity of listening firsthand to this authentic Saltville, Virginia, folk artist.

Born on May 10, 1897, in Smyth County, Virginia, Hobart Smith was the eldest son among eight children born to King and Louvine Smith. He was musically inclined and by the age of seven had started playing the banjo—influenced by his banjo-picking parents. As a teenager, he learned guitar and then fiddle. His father earned his living as a farmer, an occupation which his son was to adopt, and he taught the young boy a style of banjo playing that Hobart Smith later referred to as the "old-timey rappin' style." Over the years, he developed the skills of single-note picking and double-noting, or "double-thumbing."

Smith helped with the family farming and hauling business, and, twice every week, he played and sang at the community square dance. Throughout his lifetime, Smith was employed as a painter, a butcher, and an entertainer in a minstrel show which traveled to the small local towns of his home state. During the 1920s, he played with his own band, and, before the Depression, he had the chance to play with the legendary Clarence "Tom" Ashley.

After temporarily putting aside his banjo, Smith picked up the fiddle to play at local dances, and, accompanied by his sister, Mrs. Texas Gladden, he performed traditional folk music at festivals in the area. One of the people who listened to them perform was Eleanor Roosevelt, who, in 1936, asked them to come to the White House to play for her husband, President Franklin D. Roosevelt. During the early forties, Alan Lomax recorded Hobart Smith and his sister for the Library of Congress Archive of Folk Song.

Always a local favorite and well-known among collectors, Hobart Smith was highly respected as a banjoist, guitarist, fiddler, and singer of traditional material. The folk song revival of the fifties and early sixties brought Smith more widespread recogni-

tion, and he was invited to perform at such events as the University of Chicago Folk Festival, in February 1964. Prior to his appearance at the festival, he performed at the Old Town School of Folk Music, and he recorded his first solo LP, *Hobart Smith* (Folk-Legacy FSA-17), in October 1963, in the studios of Chicago's WFMT Radio.

After his appearance at the 1964 Newport Folk Festival, Hobart Smith suffered a stroke. He died on January 11, 1965, at his home in Saltville, Virginia.

## Shannon Smith. *See* The Golden Ring.

## The Smoky Mountain Boys. *See* Roy Acuff.

## The Smothers Brothers

*Vocal and instrumental duo, performers, and recording artists*

Among the folksingers of the early sixties was a duo who successfully incorporated its music within the framework of a comedy routine, thereby establishing a new angle from which to explore and introduce folk music. *The Smothers Brothers Comedy Hour* is well remembered for its presentation of such young talent as Donovan, John Hartford, Jennifer, Mason Williams, and others who presented their art to an audience which rivaled in size any of the most popular shows on American television from 1967 to 1969.

Thomas Smothers was born on February 2, 1937, and his younger brother Richard was born on November 20, 1938, in New York City to Thomas B. and Ruth Smothers. The family moved to the Philippines where they lived until the Japanese invasion during World War II. Although the two young boys and their mother returned safely to the United States, their army officer father was captured and later died as a Japanese prisoner.

Tom and Dick Smothers were raised in Redondo Beach, California, and educated in the state's public school system. As they were growing up, the elder brother learned to play the guitar, and Dick Smothers plucked the bass fiddle as they used folk music as a vehicle for 'their comic routines. The Smothers Brothers' popularity during high school encouraged them to continue performing while students at San Jose State College, working initially as a trio with Bobby Blackmore.

After a successful engagement at a San Jose nightclub, a booking was arranged for them at San Francisco's Purple Onion. The response to their act was overwhelming, and their engagement was extended to thirty-six weeks. A recording contract was signed, and they made their debut album while onstage at the Purple Onion. They started receiving offers to do college, nightclub, and concert dates throughout the country, and by 1967 they had produced nine LPs for Mercury Records (five of which are Gold Records).

Their act had been followed with interest by CBS-TV, which offered them a show in 1965. *The Smothers Brothers Show* was geared to emphasize comedy, and although the program was unsuccessful, they were invited to return to CBS as cohosts of the new *Smothers Brothers Comedy Hour*. The show was aired for the first time during the early months of 1967, and its immediate attainment of top ratings precipitated its renewal for the 1967 fall season.

One of their first guests on the *Smothers Brothers Comedy Hour* was Pete Seeger, who had been blacklisted for many years by American television networks. As a result of their invitation, the Smothers Brothers were responsible for Seeger's first post–McCarthy era appearance on a sponsored major network program. This gesture was typical of Tom and Dick Smothers' liberal and innovative thinking, which led ultimately to cancellation of the *Smothers Brothers Comedy Hour* in the spring of 1969, after an incessant battle over censorship of their frank, topical satire.

The Smothers Brothers appeared on an NBC-TV network special and a short-lived *Smothers Brothers Summer Show* on ABC-TV. A lawsuit was filed against CBS, claiming breach of contract, and then the Smothers Brothers went their separate ways. Dick Smothers left show business to engage in a variety of sports activities, particularly race car driving. Tom Smothers starred in the film *Get to Know Your Rabbit*, with John Astin, Katherine Ross, and Orson Welles.

After an eight-week trial, the Smothers Brothers won settlement of their suit against CBS early in 1973. Later in the year, Tom Smothers tested some new routines at the Cellar Door in Washington, D.C. They reunited to perform to nightclub and college audiences. Tom and Dick Smothers signed a "13-week iron-clad contract" with NBC-TV for *The Smothers Brothers Show* in January 1975. The variety show lacked controversy or a strong point of view, and, generally considered bland, this show also vanished.

The Smothers Brothers returned to performing in concerts, nightclubs, and supper clubs, such as Harrahs in Reno, the Hotel Riviera in Las Vegas, the Royal York in Toronto, and the Beverly Hills Club in Newport, Kentucky.

When asked about the prospects for a new Smothers Brothers show, Tom Smothers replied: "We still have at least three good cancellations left in our career."

# John Kilby Snow

*Traditional autoharpist, guitarist, banjoist, songwriter, performer, and recording artist*

When his carpenter father traded an ice cream freezer for his first autoharp, the young Kilby Snow learned to play the old five-bar Zimmerman harp by lying on the floor (which was the only way the small boy could manage the instrument). Now seventy, Kilby Snow ranks among the country's most esteemed autoharpists, and he is known for developing unique picking styles and for using various harplike and slurring techniques.

John Kilby Snow was born in Grayson County, Virginia, on May 28, 1905, and at the age of three he moved with his family to North Carolina. After his early introduction to the autoharp at the age of three or four, one of the state's champion autoharpists, Hubert Ashburn, taught Snow his first song, "Old Molly Hare." When the five-year-old boy won twenty dollars in gold and the state championship at Brown's Warehouse in Winston-Salem, Ashburn made a promise that he would never play the autoharp again. Snow's early success encouraged him to pursue a musical career, and, since then, he has traveled widely while engaged in a variety of jobs.

Kilby Snow is often acclaimed for the special brass fingerpicks and thumbpicks which he developed to enable him to strum both up and down on the strings of the autoharp. He plays a standard twelve-bar autoharp which has been modified, and he picks the melody with his specially equipped index-fingerpick, which allows him to play twice as many notes as the conventional autoharpist. By releasing the bar of the instrument, Snow plays notes that resemble the sound of the harp.

Mike Seeger is largely responsible for Kilby Snow's recording career, and in 1965 Seeger recorded *Mountain Music Played on the Autoharp* (Folkways 2365) with Mike Seeger, Kilby Snow, Ernest Stoneman, and Wade Ward. This was followed by *Kilby Snow: Country Songs and Tunes with Autoharp* (Folkways/Asch AH 3902). Kilby Snow made his first television appearance in 1948 on WHIS (Bluefield, West Virginia) with the Stanley Brothers. Over the years he has performed in such clubs as the Second Fret and Main Point, in Philadelphia, and at the Philadelphia, Mariposa, and other folk festivals.

## Mac Snow. *See* Ernest East and the Pine Ridge Boys.

## The Songswappers. *See* Mary Travers.

## Rosalie Sorrels

*Singer, songwriter, guitarist, performer, and recording artist*

"I have sung all my life. I collected old songs—mostly from Utah and Idaho—as a hobby, and I sang at festivals and I made several albums of traditional songs. I entertained people for a long time before my marriage broke up in 1966, when I started to work professionally."

The turning point in the career of Rosalie Sorrels (née Stringfellow), who is now over forty and lives in the San Francisco area, came in the latter part of the 1960s. Until then, she had sung mostly traditional songs —even though she had already begun to write some of her own material. Her initial commitment as a professional musician (who was trying to support five children) yielded an annual income of $2,800. She made an album in the same year that she and her husband Jim separated; since then, Rosalie Sorrels has made numerous recordings on different labels, including *Traveling Lady* (Sire SI 5902), *Folk Songs of Idaho and Utah* (Folkways 5343), *What Ever Happened to the Girl That Was* (Paramount 6072), *Welcome to Caffe Lena* (Biograph BLP 12046), which includes Rosalie Sorrels singing her original composition "Come On Friend," *If I Could Be the Rain* (Folk-Legacy FSI-31), and *Rosalie Sorrels* (Philo PH 1029), released in the fall of 1975.

"I've never been commercially successful, nor do I expect to be. I guess there are a lot of things in my own personal makeup that prevent me from making a lot of money. I won't do a record unless it's done my way."

She recently edited *What, Woman, and*

Rosalie Sorrels (left) participating in a children's concert, Mariposa '75, with (left to right) Malvina Reynolds, Bruce (U. Utah) Phillips, and Bodie Wagner

*Who, Myself, I Am*, (Wooden Shoe Publishing Cooperative, Sonoma, California, 1974), an anthology of poems, songs, and drawings by women on the subject of womanhood. Her plans for the future include opening a coffeehouse-bar, possibly in Vermont. In the meantime, she is actively playing coffeehouses and festivals, where she is often seen with her good friend Bruce (U. Utah) Phillips.

## The Sour Grapes Band. *See*
Richard Thompson.

## Randy Sparks. *See* The New
Christy Minstrels.

## Andy Spence. *See* Fennig's All-Star
String Band.

## Bill Spence. *See* Fennig's All-Star
String Band.

## Lena Spencer
*Owner-operator of the Caffé Lena, a coffeehouse in Saratoga Springs, New York*

Every field of endeavor has its share of patrons—individuals who remain outside the mainstream of public recognition—whose personal contributions provide priceless nourishment for those whose achievements are more commonly acknowledged. For over fifteen years, Lena Spencer has worked behind the scenes as "hostess" of "the oldest continuously running club in the country," where warmth, congeniality, and good entertainment constitute the Caffé Lena tradition. Once described by writer Andy Smith as the "Grand Lady of the Folk Circuit," Lena Spencer has provided countless opportunities for performers, who, she says, "all come back," and friendship for all.

Lena Spencer was born "in a little town called Milford, in southeastern Massachusetts," and she was the youngest of eight children in her "Victorian-Italian" family. After working as a granite cutter and union organizer, her father opened a restaurant where his youngest child worked while still in high school and "for many years thereafter." When she married Bill Spencer, who was teaching part-time and attending the Boston Museum School of Fine Arts, the idea for opening a coffeehouse was conceived "as a big moneymaking venture to allow us to retire in a year and go to Europe for several years." When Bill Spencer happened to stop over in the college town of Saratoga Springs, New York, on a busy fall weekend, he decided that "this is where we'll have our coffeehouse." On May 21, 1960, the Caffé

Bob Dylan and Suze Rotolo at Caffé Lena, Saratoga Springs, New York, with owner Lena Spencer (right), winter 1961–62

Lena Spencer with Arlo Guthrie at Caffé Lena concert, autumn 1974

Lena opened with Jackie Washington, who was performing around the Boston area, where Bill and Lena Spencer had lived prior to moving to Saratoga. And, Lena Spencer explains: "Most of our contacts were made from people in the Boston folk scene. At that time it was not a matter of auditioning people and bringing them in because I was not as yet that much involved or knew that much about the whole folk music scene, but it just started mushrooming. And most of the people that we came in contact with, either through recommendations from other people or through contacts that we made ourselves, were people who were very much into traditional music. I suppose if we hadn't had some kind of principles or ethics, we may have even gone into presenting a commercial sound, but we liked sticking with the traditional. It was a struggle, but, by the same token, it seemed like we did get some

kind of acceptance by people right from the beginning."

The burdens and financial pressures of operating the coffeehouse created a rift in the Spencers' marriage, and when Bill Spencer left, his wife "chose to stay here. I just kept going and going, despite the rough years of 1962–63, and I got more and more involved in music and in the performers.

"I don't have a formula. I couldn't sit down and write a book on how to run a coffeehouse or to conduct a workshop. All I can say is just 'do it with a whole bunch of love,' not with the attitude that you're in it to make money, but that you're in it to serve."

Don McLean, among many others, continues to return to the Caffé Lena in spite of his enormous commercial and artistic success, and it has become "a tradition for Don to be the New Year's weekend performer." Bob Dylan was one of the early performers at Lena Spencer's coffeehouse—long before anyone knew who he was—along with Jack Elliott, Arlo Guthrie, Jim Kweskin, Tom Paxton, Jean Redpath, Patrick Sky, Dave Van Ronk, and Loudon Wainwright III.

"I feel that the personal touch is the most important thing, not only with the performers but with the audience as well. I would say that in the fifteen years that I have been here, there are probably four or five weekends that I have not been at the Caffé. Three of those because I was too sick to be here, and one when I was invited by Don [McLean] to go to Nashville with him for the Grammy presentations—and another weekend I think I had to go off somewhere. But I'm here every weekend, right there at the top of the stairs, meeting, greeting, and

Lena Spencer with Frank Wakefield (left) and Don McLean at Caffé Lena

Publicity poster used by Lena Spencer for her coffeehouse

seating people, and trying to make them feel that this is not a place where they are going to get ripped off or spend money, but a place where both the performer and the audience are treated with a great amount of respect.

"I have a big house, and a performer doesn't come and spend his spare time in a hotel. A performer comes and stays with me for the weekend and eats with me and that sort of thing. It's all on a very, very personal level. And that's the way it should be."

An organization known as ZBS Media has taped performances at Caffé Lena and distributed the programs to radio stations across the United States. Further recognition of Lena Spencer's vital contribution to folk music came in 1975 when the mayor of Saratoga designated a Lena Spencer Day in her honor.

## Barbara Spillman. *See* Barbara Dane.

## Victoria Spivey

*Blues singer, pianist, songwriter, performer, recording artist, and founder of Spivey Records*

One of the most illustrious blues singers and composers of all time, Victoria Spivey symbolizes the epitome of every female blues performer in the popular music industry today. From her vintage years of 1927 to 1937, to the movies, her own band, Chicago, the Spivey-Adams Comedy Song and Dance Team, semiretirement, and her comeback as a singer, recording artist, and record company executive, Victoria Spivey has maintained the highest caliber of stylings and overall creativity.

She was born in Houston, Texas, where her father and brothers played in a string band. A musically talented child, she was influenced by the legendary blues pianist Robert Calbin. Her early performances included working with the blues-jazz band of Lazy Daddy Fillmore and with the L. C. Tolen band. By the twenties, she was playing

throughout the Galveston–Houston area, often appearing with other blues artists, including Blind Lemon Jefferson. These years saw the development of her sad, moaning stylings, her down-home piano work, and her sparse, raw blues lyrics.

She came into her own from 1926 to 1929, becoming one of Okeh Phonograph's best-selling recording artists of "race" music, or blues, which put her in a class with Louis Armstrong and Lonnie Johnson. She had her first hit record with "Black Snake Blues," and her stylings (adding another meter, doubling up of lyrics, and tacking on four more bars to the regular twelve-bar construction) made her one of the more innovative blues artists of the mid-twenties. Many of the songs which she composed during this period have become blues classics, including "T.B. Blues," "You Done Lost Your Good Thing Now," "Hoodoo Man Blues," "Spider Web Blues," "It's Evil Hearted Me," "Santa Fe Blues," "Arkansas Road Blues," and many, many others. Some of her tunes have been recorded and popularized by such luminaries as Louis Armstrong, Duke Ellington, Leadbelly, B. B. King, Josh White, Sonny Boy Williamson, John Lee Hooker, Sam "Lightnin' " Hopkins, Lonnie Johnson, John Erby, and Porter Grainger, among others.

As the Depression drew closer, she added another laurel to her entertainment career by completing her starring role in King Vidor's all-black, first full-feature talkie, *Hallelujah*. She spent some time in Chicago and was quickly absorbed by a blues scene which boasted such names as Tampa Red, Memphis Minnie, Big Bill Broonzy, and others, and in 1931 she became the band leader of Hunter's Serenaders.

Friendships with Tampa Red and Memphis Minnie led to a historic recording session with the three of them. A year of touring with Hunter's Serenaders took her to various parts of the country, and by 1933 she was heading a traveling show called the Dallas Tan Town Topics, which played throughout Texas and Oklahoma. In the following year, she teamed up with dancer

Billy Adams; they traveled extensively together, receiving favorable reviews with a Louis Armstrong tour, New Grand Terrace reviews, and the Olsen and Johnson *Hellzapoppin'* show.

In 1951, after a death in the family, she terminated her association with Billy Adams and retreated into semiretirement, doing only occasional gigs in the New York area. By the end of 1960, Victoria Spivey had returned to the stage, performing at jazz spots (Jimmy Ryan's & Nick's) and at Gerde's Folk City in January 1961. She recorded for Prestige/Bluesville, and in November she performed at Gerde's in a historic two-week reunion with her good friend Lonnie Johnson. It was not long before she started her own record company—Spivey Records—and she has issued many albums of original productions ever since. Some of the albums on which Victoria Spivey is featured include *Basket of Blues* (LP 1001); *Victoria and Her Blues* (LP 1002); *Three Kings and the Queen* (LP 1004), which includes, in her words, "a blossoming Bob Dylan"; *The Queen and Her Knights* (LP 1006); *The Bluesmen of the Muddy Waters Chicago Blues Band* (LP 1008); *Encore for the Chicago Blues* (LP 1009); *The Bluesmen of the Muddy Waters Chicago Blues Band, Volume Two* (LP 1010); *Spivey's Blues Parade* (LP 1012); *Kings & the Queen* (LP 1014); *Victoria Spivey's Recorded Legacy of the Blues* (LP 2001); *Spivey's Blues Cavalcade* (LP 1015); and *Spivey's Blues Showcase* (LP 1017). In addition, she has recorded for Columbia, Decca, Folkways, GHB, Okeh, Philips, Prestige, RCA Victor, and Vocalion; and she has performed on radio and television, at festivals and club dates.

## Mark Spoelstra

*Singer-songwriter, twelve-string guitarist, performer, and recording artist*

A singer and topical songwriter whose material is primarily related to peace, Mark Spoelstra was among the talented artists who utilized the pages of *Broadside* magazine as an outlet for expression during the 1960s. A onetime companion of Bob Dylan, whose original compositions also appeared on a regular basis in the New York publication, Mark Spoelstra is known in folk music circles as a "peacemaker" who became a participant in Alternative Services in the mid-sixties as a demonstration of his firm antiwar stance.

Mark Spoelstra was born on June 30, 1940, in Kansas City, Missouri, and was raised in California. His initial interest in music stemmed from his attraction to the guitar—not songwriting—and he was a fan of melancholic country & western tunes. Although he wrote songs while living on the West Coast, it was not until he was a part of the folk music scene in New York that he realized the potential interest in original material. At that point, he turned from writing songs for himself to communicating his ideas to others through music—the singer-songwriter phenomenon, largely precipitated by Bob Dylan, which brought many artists into the public eye during that era.

Whether writing about love or peace, his main objective is to relay the message, not himself. His songs are direct, and his gentle voice is typically accompanied by a subdued twelve-string-guitar-playing technique.

After participating in both the New York and Boston music scenes, he returned to California, where he still lives. His strong conviction regarding promotion of peaceful coexistence precluded commercial indulgence, and although he has recorded for Elektra, Folkways, and Verve/Folkways, he has been primarily engaged in social work and community projects. To date, Mark Spoelstra has written over two hundred ballads, children's songs, and songs proclaiming love and peace.

## Spoons

Inexpensive, portable, and relatively durable, spoons are used as a percussion instrument to accompany other band instruments or are played solo for several bars. Two metal spoons of equal size are grasped firmly with one hand and banged together in a variety of finger, thumb, and wrist movements.

One spoon handle is held between the thumb and index finger, while the second spoon handle end is pressed to the base of the thumb muscle and gripped between the index and middle fingers. With the index finger keeping the two spoons about one-quarter inch apart, the round sides (belly-to-belly) of the spoons are brought together with a smooth and easy motion. Different rhythms and beats are employed to produce different effects, and rolls (running the spoons across the fingers of the other hand from top to bottom with the final tap on the thigh of one leg) and trills (thigh-hand-thigh-hand-thigh-hand action in quick succession) may be incorporated with the regular beats of the music.

Spoons are used commonly at festivals and informal gatherings for singing and playing music. The many advantages of this accessible percussion instrument make it popular among children, and spoons may be used for different types of music, including folk, Dixieland, and ragtime.

## Art Stamper. *See* The Stanley Brothers.

## The Stanley Brothers
*Bluegrass vocal and instrumental duo, performers, and recording artists*

Since the mid-1940s, Ralph and Carter Stanley have furnished a link between the disparate components of bluegrass, modern, and old-timey music while simultaneously creating an innovative and personal style based on their mountain heritage. Until Carter Stanley's death on December 1, 1966, the brothers toured through the mountains and the cities of the United States, traveling thousands of miles, to become two of the

most influential contributors to what is now a major movement in music, bluegrass.

The Stanleys were born in the remote Clinch Mountain area of Virginia to logger Fitzhugh Stanley, a widower with six children, and Lucy Smith Stanley, a widow with one child. Carter Stanley was born on August 27, 1925, and his brother Ralph was born on February 25, 1927. Their boyhood was spent on a farm near McClure, Virginia, and most of the music they heard came from around their own home. Their mother often played a clawhammer-style banjo, and a few of the neighbors joined in with another banjo or occasionally a fiddle while everyone sat around to sing old-time mountain ballads. Carter Stanley got his first guitar from a mail-order house, and his brother Ralph started picking on his mother's banjo. Together they worked out duet harmonies, and, while they were in their teens, the Stanley Brothers performed locally.

In 1946 both of the brothers were discharged from military service and they began playing with a band called Roy Sykes and the Blue Ridge Mountain Boys. Soon after, they formed the Stanley Brothers and the Clinch Mountain Boys, with mandolinist Darrell "Pee Wee" Lambert and a fiddle player. They started performing on WNVA in Norton, Virginia, and then began working on WCYB's *Farm and Fun Time*, in Bristol, Tennessee, which featured many early bluegrass acts.

The Stanley Brothers and the Clinch Mountain Boys offered a style of bluegrass that combined an archaic mountain sound and a modernized style that was later to be named after its primary exponent, Bill Monroe. The band played schools and theaters in the Bristol area while they were working the daily radio program on WCYB and, in 1947, recorded "Little Glass of Wine" for the Rich-R-Tone Record Company in Johnson City, Tennessee.

Bluegrass was starting to come into its own as an offshoot of old-time music, and the Stanley Brothers were an important part of its beginnings. Twenty-year-old Ralph

369

Stanley was employing three styles of banjo—old clawhammer, two-finger, and three-finger (as popularized by Earl Scruggs); Carter Stanley was singing lead and playing rhythm guitar; and Darrell "Pee Wee" Lambert was singing tenor and playing Monroe-style mandolin. By the time they went to WPTF in Raleigh, North Carolina, there were five band members. After only two years of performing together, Ralph and Carter Stanley were asked to record for Columbia Records—the same label which carried the work of the most prominent bluegrass artist, Bill Monroe.

The Stanley Brothers' singing was soft, with an unparalleled emotional quality which was subtle but impressive. Carter Stanley composed most of their material, which they sang in two-part harmony or in three-part harmony with Lambert. They are remembered for their moving renditions of such songs as "Drunkard's Hell," "White Dove," "Lonesome River," and others.

When the band broke up in 1951, Carter Stanley went over to Bill Monroe's Blue Grass Boys as guitarist, but within the same year the brothers got back together and resumed performances on WCYB's *Farm and Fun Time*. At this time, they were joined by mandolinists Curly Sechler (of Flatt and Scruggs band fame) and Bobby Osborne. When the Stanleys signed with Mercury Records in 1954, their recording career was given the boost that it needed. When they made their first Mercury recordings, the newly organized Clinch Mountain Boys comprised the Stanleys, Jimmy Williams, Art Stamper, and George Shuffler. This combination of musicians produced the hard-driving bluegrass sound for which the Stanley Brothers are best known today.

As the pressures of touring and recording mounted, alcoholism became an increasingly serious problem with Carter Stanley. His health began to fail, resulting in his death in the winter of 1966. Carter Stanley was the first major personality in the field of bluegrass to pass away, and his death came to symbolize the tragic consequences of the exhausting work, traveling, struggling, and hardships of the bluegrass artist.

After his brother's death, Ralph Stanley continued to perform and act as bandleader of a revised version of the Clinch Mountain Boys. In 1970 Ralph Stanley organized the first annual Carter Stanley Memorial Bluegrass Festival, which has been held every year since then on the old Stanley homeplace in McClure, Virginia. His old-time mountain bluegrass style has become world famous, and his manner of playing banjo has been named the "Ralph Stanley Style" and is one of the most widely imitated by younger bluegrass musicians.

Since the death of Carter Stanley in 1966, the work of Ralph Stanley and the Stanley Brothers has been issued on numerous labels, including County, Jalyn, Jessup, King, King Bluegrass, Melodeon, Nashville, Rebel, and Rimrock.

## John Starling. *See* The Seldom Scene.

## Steeleye Span. *See* Ashley Hutchings.

## Arthur Stern. *See* The Almanac Singers.

## John Stewart

*Contemporary singer-songwriter, guitarist, banjoist, performer, and recording artist*

Singer, performer, and composer of bygone rural Americana and former member of the Kingston Trio, John Stewart is best known for his colorful lyrics, the emotive content, and the dynamic stylization of his original works, such as "Mother Country," "California Bloodlines," and "Survivors." A versatile songwriter, he defies categorization; in addition to material recorded by his first group, called the Cumberland Three, and the Kingston Trio, Stewart also penned cash box hits for his brother Michael's rock group (We Five) and "Daydream Believer" for the Monkees.

Born on September 5, 1939, in San Diego, California, Stewart was raised in Riverside and Pasadena, and he learned to play the ukelele as a boy. In his teens, he was the leader and guitarist for John Stewart and the Furies, which recorded a single for Vita Records, "Rocking Anna," but folk music was a motivating force in his life from about 1958 on: "Burl Ives gave me the first inkling that there was another kind of music that I could play on my guitar besides rock 'n' roll, and then it was the Kingston Trio, and, from there, Pete Seeger and the Weavers.

"After I graduated from high school in Pomona, I worked a club called Cosmo Alley in Los Angeles, with a college buddy named John Montgomery, and we were known as John and Monty. We played there, and then I worked at the Kerosene Club in San Jose with the Smothers Brothers, and it was during this time that I was writing a lot of folk-type songs such as 'Molly Dee' and 'Green Grasses,' which were recorded by the Kingston Trio. I got to know Frank Werber and the guys in the trio, and one day Frank called me and said, 'Roulette Records is looking for a folk group, can you put one together?' So I called John Montgomery and my choir teacher from high school who played bass, Gil Robbins, and we flew to New York. We were the Cumberland Three, and the group was manufactured out of need of a record company wanting a folk group in 1960. Mike Settle joined the group after we met up with him while we were out on the road in Oklahoma, with Shelley Berman. The group recorded three albums for Roulette, but they're all out of print now.

"After a year and a half, Gil Robbins left the group, and then Dave Guard left the Kingston Trio. Nick Reynolds told me to come out to San Francisco to audition for the job, so I went out and auditioned in Bob Shane's basement amidst gun racks and Gold Records. Also auditioning were Chip

Douglas from Hawaii, who later went on to produce about five of the Monkees hits, and I think Travis Edmondson was the other person. In the meantime, Mike Settle was sitting in a hotel in San Francisco, waiting to see whether or not I was going to play an engagement with him—and decided to write songs—and composed 'Sing Halleluja,' which became a folk classic and really started his songwriting career. Trav Edmondson never did show up. I joined the trio, and Mike went on to sing by himself for a while.

"In 1966 I told them I was leaving, and, after ten years, Nick decided it was time to get off the road. So he went up to live on some property in Oregon that he had, and Bob Shane continued and still plays with the New Kingston Trio.

"I had given a year's notice before I left the trio, and during that interim I was looking around to see what I was going to do. For a while, I was going to sing with John Denver. John and I rehearsed two songs, 'Daydream Believer' and 'Leavin' on a Jet Plane.' Everyone sort of yawned and looked pleasant, and later those two numbers went on to be number one in the country. John's writing was going one way and mine was going another, so then I decided to put together a group with Henry Dulce, who was with the Modern Folk Quartet, but we needed a girl singer. We found Buffy Ford about five miles from where I was living, and, when Henry's photography business started picking up, he didn't have time to rehearse, so Buffy and I sang as a duo—John Stewart and Buffy Ford. We did an album for Capitol called *Signals Through the Glass*, but it sold only three thousand to four thousand copies, and we played the Hungry i and a few clubs and college concerts, but mainly we campaigned for Robert Kennedy when he was running for president.

"After that, the songs started to dictate where I was going all along, and it became more and more personal, and that's when I recorded *California Bloodlines* [Capitol ST-203]."

John Stewart recorded one more LP on the Capitol label, *Willard* (ST-540), and two albums for Warner Brothers. In 1973, with his new band, he made his first recording for RCA, *Cannons in the Rain* (LSP-4827), followed by *The Phoenix Concerts* (two- record set, CPL2-0265) in 1974, and *Wingless Angels* (APL1-0816) in 1975. (*See also* The Kingston Trio.)

## Stephen Stills. *See* Crosby, Stills, Nash and Young.

## Bruce Stockwell. *See* Apple Country.

## Lowe Stokes. *See* Gid Tanner and the Skillet Lickers.

## Noel Stookey. *See* Peter, Paul and Mary.

## Win Stracke

*Singer, guitarist, songwriter, composer, performer, recording artist, founder and former president of the Old Town School of Folk Music (Chicago), founder of the Old Town Folklore Center, author, and actor*

A distinguished member of the folk music community who enjoys the honor of being referred to as "Chicago's Minstrel," Win Stracke has made a number of significant contributions to the field, from his organization in 1948 of the performing group known as I Come for to Sing (which included such personalities as Big Bill Broonzy and Studs Terkel), to his founding of the Old Town School of Folk Music in Chicago in 1957 and of the Old Town Folklore Center in 1963. Beyond his achievements in the city where he has lived and sung for all but three years of his life, this influential figure in folk

music is known throughout the rest of the country by his network television and radio programs and by his solo and group recordings with the Golden Ring.

Win Stracke was born on February 20, 1908, in Lorraine, Kansas. His lifelong association with Chicago began when, as the one-year-old son of transferred clergyman Robert Stracke, he moved with his parents to the Windy City. While attending Senn High School, he sang with an *a cappella* choral group—which later led to his participation as soloist in several of the city's churches and as performer of cantorial duties in a number of temples.

He enrolled in Lake Forest College in 1929, and by 1931 he was performing on WLS, followed by appearances on other network and local shows, including *Hymns of All Churches*, *Theater of the Air*, *Alec Templeton Time*, *National Barn Dance*, and *The Meaning of America*. He abandoned his formal education in 1932, but, after a three-year stint in the service during World War II, resumed his studies at the American Conservatory of Music in 1945. In the same year, he began making extensive concert appearances as a folksinger, accompanying himself on guitar. In 1948, a year after he left the American Conservatory of Music, Win Stracke and Studs Terkel put together the initial I Come for to Sing program. In the years that followed, this American folk music panorama presented a number of artists who became established figures in folk music.

During the fifties, Win Stracke made regular appearances on television, costarring on such network programs as *Stud's Place* (1952–55) and *Hawkins Falls* (1953–56), and on his own children's show, called *Animal Playtime* (1954–58). In 1957 he founded the non-profit Old Town School of Folk Music, and he was president from its inception until 1975.

In addition to devoting his time to the courses, workshops, and concerts offered by the Old Town School, he has made a couple of solo recordings, founded the Old Town

Folklore Center in 1963, recorded an album with an ensemble of singer friends informally known as the Golden Ring, coauthored (with Norman Luboff) *Songs of Man*, published by Bonanza Books in 1965, and composed (with Norman Luboff) a musical cantata called "Freedom Country" in 1967.

Win Stracke is currently active in the Midwestern cultural scene and is working on a book about Old Town, Chicago. (*See also* The Golden Ring.)

## The Strange Creek Singers

*Vocal and instrumental group, performers, and recording artists*

The Strange Creek Singers present a wide variety of both traditional and original songs in old-time and bluegrass styles, and, in the words of Mike Seeger, their "uniqueness is the inclusion of Hazel and Alice, original but acoustic country songs, and a strictly individual approach to material that is often quite obscure." With the exception of Lamar Grier, all of the group's members have been making music together in various combinations for over twenty years. The group was formed in the late sixties with Hazel Dickens, Alice Gerrard, Lamar Grier, Tracy Schwarz, and Mike Seeger.

Mike Seeger, who played with Tracy Schwarz in the New Lost City Ramblers, recalls how the Strange Creek Singers came about: "We had all been friends since the mid-fifties, and we played together from time to time at parties and so forth. Then, in the late sixties, it seemed to me that a group could be made with the same five people, so we got ourselves a name and made *Strange Creek Singers* on Arhoolie [4004]. The group is named after Strange Creek, West Virginia. We work on and off as a hobby since all of us have other interests outside the group."

Lamar Grier is best known for his association with Bill Monroe, and he played bluegrass banjo for a number of groups before the Strange Creek Singers.

For five or six years, Tracy Schwarz was

involved primarily with the New Lost City Ramblers. More recently, his attentions have been turned to farming and to working as a solo artist and with his wife Eloise. As a duo, they play old-time American folk and country tunes in a manner reminiscent of the Carter Family and the Monroe and Stanley Brothers styles. They provide accompaniment to their singing on guitar, banjo, or fiddle, and they also sing unaccompanied ballads. Tracy and Eloise Schwarz made *Home Among the Hills* (Folk Variety FV 12007), and Tracy Schwarz also records for Folkways Records.

When she is not performing with her husband Mike Seeger or with the Strange Creek Singers, Alice Gerrard works as a duo with Hazel Dickens. In 1967 Hazel and Alice recorded their first album together, *Won't You Come Sing for Me* (Folkways FTS 31034), and in late 1974 their second LP, entitled *Hazel and Alice* (Rounder 0027), was issued. Along with Nimrod Workman and George Tucker, they recorded *Come All You Coal Miners* (Rounder 4005), which was produced and edited by Guy Carawan from tapes of an Appalachian Music Workshop at the Highlander Center in Tennessee.

The Strange Creek Singers have appeared at most major folk festivals in the United States, and they have toured throughout the United States and Europe.

**Paul Stuphin.** *See* The Galax String Band.

**John Suire.** *See* The Louisiana Aces.

**Dina Suler.** *See* The Pennywhistlers.

**Bill Svanoe.** *See* The Rooftop Singers.

**Dave Swarbrick.** *See* Fairport Convention.

# Sweet Honey in the Rock

*Female vocal group and performers of original and traditional material related to the black American experience*

Formed early in 1974, Sweet Honey in the Rock aims to relate the black American experience through song—spirituals, blues, gospel and work songs, along with original material by group members.

Sweet Honey in the Rock consists of Evelyn Harris, Pat Johnson, Carol Maillard, Bernice Reagon (its musical director), and Louise Robinson, who perform most of the ensemble's repertoire *a capella* or with occasional piano accompaniment. Diana Wharton serves as occasional pianist and composer of accompanied material. Although Sweet Honey in the Rock appears in clubs and festivals in both the United States and Canada, it performs primarily in the Washington, D.C., area, where, says Bernice Reagon, "its audience is predominantly black." The key figure in Sweet Honey in the Rock, Bernice Reagon explains their main objective: "The group is in the process of working out ways to service the community in which they live with its musical needs. To this end, they do weddings, celebrations, funerals, theater, churches, preschool sessions, teacher-training workshops, et cetera. As a result, they have begun to come to the attention of a wider audience, and in the past one and a half years have been seen at the National folk festivals. But this is secondary to what they consider their responsibility as artists." (*See also* Bernice [Johnson] Reagon.)

# The Sweets Mill String Band. *See* Kenny Hall.

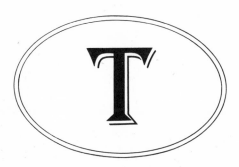

## Holly Tannen

*Traditional and contemporary singer, dulcimer player, pianist, songwriter, contributing writer for* Folkscene *magazine, performer, and recording artist*

Known for her direct confrontation with the strings of the dulcimer, Holly Tannen is considered by many to be one of the most versatile and innovative virtuosos of this particular instrument in the United States. She has earned a well-deserved reputation as a solo artist, but her ability as an accompanist often associates her name with balladeer Frankie Armstrong, with whom she and Susie Rothfield often play.

Born and raised in New York City, Holly Tannen studied anthropology, zoology, and psychology in undergraduate and graduate schools, had some musical training, and played piano. At seventeen she was given her first dulcimer by a boyfriend who had met Jean Ritchie at the Berkeley Folk Festival. From then on, Holly Tannen devoted her time to making dulcimers, teaching herself to play the instrument, and learning tunes by listening to records. After she moved to Berkeley, California, she played and sang most frequently with ballad singer Rita Weill and guitarist Janet Smith. In 1968 she met Will Spires and Dr. Humbead's New Tranquility String Band at the Sky River Rock Festival, and she became so excited about the possibilities of combining the dulcimer with other instruments that she spent the next few months playing with as many old-timey musicians around Berkeley

as possible. As a result, Holly Tannen is capable of playing in a variety of instrumental combinations, and her dulcimer music blends smoothly with almost any stringed instrument.

Holly Tannen was recorded on *Berkeley Farms* (Folkways FA 2436), playing one cut of dulcimer with mandolin and two cuts of dulcimer with a string band. She has been a contributing writer for the California publication *Folkscene* for the past few years, writing the "Dulcimer Corner" and, since her move to England, "Notes from England."

## Gid Tanner. *See* Gid Tanner and the Skillet Lickers.

## Jimmie Tarleton. *See* Gid Tanner and the Skillet Lickers.

## The Tarriers

*Vocal and instrumental group, performers, and recording artists*

The original group, with Alan Arkin, Bob Carey, and Erik Darling, brought the Tarriers into the limelight of the folk music revival with their cash box top single of 1957, "The Banana Boat Song." The Tarriers became progressively more innovative, experimenting and remodeling songs with modern folk and jazz interpretations, and,

The Tarriers, with its original members (left to right): Erik Darling, Alan Arkin, Bob Carey

as the group's members changed, their sound redeveloped with each new influence.

An avid fan of the Weavers' arrangements, Erik Darling organized a quartet with the idea of singing folk songs in harmony. The quartet changed many times, and, after a period of time, finally became a trio consisting of Arkin, Carey, and Darling. Darling had been a performer on Oscar Brand's WNYC program *Folksong Festival*, and had toured the United States with a folk song musical review produced by Mary Hunter of the Theater Guild. He had also played guitar and banjo accompaniment on several albums recorded by Ed McCurdy. Arkin had studied acting at Bennington College, and theater was his primary interest; his particular interest in jazz and modern composition contributed to the group's tendency to shy away from the usual "four-square" harmonic country music sound. The third native New Yorker and member of the group, Bob Carey, received a degree in law, but his interest in music brought him first place on an *Arthur Godfrey Talent Scouts* program in 1953 and in an All-Army Contest for Best Vocalist in Frankfurt, Germany, while he was in the service.

With Darling as tenor and banjoist, Arkin as baritone and guitarist, and Carey as second baritone and guitarist, the Tarriers arranged "Cindy, Oh Cindy" and accompanied Vince Martin in his recording on the Glory Records label. Many months later, the Tarriers recorded "The Banana Boat Song," which was a compilation and partial rewrite of two Jamaican folk songs. The record soared to the top of the trade charts and became a principal stimulus for the consequent popularity of calypso compositions, as Erik Darling explains: "Oddly enough, an earlier version of 'The Banana Boat Song,' which had been called 'Day-O,' had been recorded and released on an album by Harry Belafonte about a year before the Tarriers' recording. But it didn't become popular until after the Tarriers' version, which remained number one on the hit parade for an unusually long time. Then, as time passed, it was the Belafonte version that became better known."

A year or so after the success of "The Banana Boat Song," which had taken the Tarriers to "every imaginable joint in the United States and Canada as well as the Olympia Theater in Paris," as Darling puts it, Alan Arkin left the group to become an actor. At that time, Clarence Cooper became the third member and brought to the group a wealth of unusual black spirituals, which were integrated into the Tarriers' repertoire. The Tarriers never managed to achieve a second national hit, and, when Pete Seeger left the Weavers, Erik Darling was asked to finish recording an album with them. After working in both groups, Darling decided to leave the Tarriers and spent the next four and a half years with the Weavers.

The Tarriers underwent further musical and personnel changes during the sixties, culminating in a last recording made live at the Bitter End coffeehouse in Greenwich Village, *The Tarriers* (Decca DL 4342), with Eric Weissberg, Marshall Brickman (who later co-authored *Sleeper* with Woody Allen), Clarence Cooper, and Bob Carey, the only remaining original member. (*See also* Alan Arkin; Erik Darling.)

## Lynne Taylor. *See* The Rooftop Singers.

## The Tennessee Three. *See* Johnny Cash.

## The Tennessee Two. *See* Johnny Cash.

## Sonny Terry

*Blues singer, harmonica player, performer, and recording artist*

An outstanding harmonica player, Sonny Terry is probably best known for his work with his partner of some thirty years, Brownie McGhee. Over the years, this top blues duo has entertained audiences around the world, and, just recently, Sonny Terry and Brownie McGhee have achieved well-deserved commercial success as recording artists for A&M Records.

Born Saunders Terrell on October 24, 1911, in Greensboro, Georgia, Sonny Terry moved with his father to Piedmont Hills (near Durham), North Carolina, when he was three years old. As the result of a childhood accident, he lost the vision in one eye and, several years later, became totally blind when a piece of metal was thrown in his face. His handicap caused him to channel his energies into music, and he began to play with earnest the instrument which he had played occasionally as a child, the harmonica. Today, one of the unique characteristics of his musical style is his vocal-instrumental interpretation of sounds which he heard as a boy—the cries of hounds chasing a fox, the sound of a speeding train, and so on.

His decision to become a professional musician was influenced by another harp player, DeFord Bailey, whom Sonny Terry met while the Nashville instrumental virtuoso was passing through North Carolina. Terry became partners with Blind Gary Davis, and they traveled from one small town to the next as street performers. When they met up with Blind Boy Fuller, the three blind musicians played for a while as a trio, and after Gary Davis left to pursue preaching, Terry and Fuller continued to work together. Accompanied on guitar and washboard by a local boy named George "Bull City Red" Washington, the group was managed by a Durham politician and department store owner, J. B. Long, who arranged their first recording sessions with Vocalion before World War II. One day, while he was visiting in Burlington, "Bull City Red" met Brownie McGhee, and, before long, Blind Roy Fuller, Sonny Terry, and Brownie McGhee were performing together.

In 1938 Sonny Terry and "Bull City Red" had traveled to New York City to participate in the Spirituals to Swing Concert. After Blind Boy Fuller's death in 1940, the blind harmonica player returned to New York, and, meeting up with Leadbelly, Terry took up residence with him in a Greenwich Village loft. Brownie McGhee also came North and lived for two years with Sonny Terry and Leadbelly. For a brief period during 1941, Sonny Terry, Brownie McGhee, Leadbelly, and Woody Guthrie played as a group called the Headline Singers, and, in the years that followed, Sonny Terry became acquainted with nearly every major entertainer on the folk club circuit.

During the forties, Sonny Terry toured extensively, and in 1949 he made his first

Sonny Terry performing at the Lenox
Music Barn, Connecticut, in July
1961

recordings, for Elektra. The next decade brought offers to record on numerous labels, including Blue Labor, Elektra, Folkways, Stinson, and Riverside, and his work was documented by the Library of Congress. The partnership of Terry and McGhee was reaffirmed at the Leadbelly Memorial Concert on January 28, 1950, and the duo performed consistently at coffeehouses, concerts, and festivals across the United States. They made numerous radio and television appearances, and during the sixties they toured internationally.

Sonny Terry and Brownie McGhee have collaborated on many albums on such record labels as Fantasy, Folkways, Prestige, Savoy, Sharp, and Verve/Folkways. Their names have been added to the roster of A&M recording artists, and some of their early material has been reissued on other labels, including Everest. (*See also* Brownie McGhee.)

**Ambrose Thibodeaux.** *See* Cajun.

**Mrs. Elmerlee ("Mama Lee") Thomas.** *See* The Gateway Singers.

**A. P. Thompson.** *See* The Red Fox Chasers.

**Les Thompson.** *See* The Nitty Gritty Dirt Band.

**Richard Thompson.** *See* Fairport Convention.

**Tommy Thompson.** *See* The Hollow Rock String Band.

**Tommy Tieman.** *See* The Serendipity Singers.

**Ron Tinkler.** *See* The Sweets Mill String Band.

**Arconge Touchet.** *See* The Louisiana Aces.

**Happy and Artie Traum**

*Contemporary singers, songwriters, performers, and recording artists*

Although each of the Traum brothers is a distinctive musician in his own right, both Happy and Artie Traum (born in 1939 and 1943, respectively) have played an important role on the New York folk music scene. For three years Happy Traum was an editor of *Sing Out!* magazine and remains a contributing writer; occasionally, an article or an interview by Artie Traum also appears in the publication. Best known as singers, songwriters, and instrumentalists, Happy and Artie Traum are among the many musicians who are products of the late-fifties Greenwich Village and Pete Seeger influences, as Artie Traum explains: "We were both brought up in the Bronx in a very middle-class neighborhood, and although there was no music in our family's history, there was a propensity toward an acceptance of music and culture, which opened the door for us. As a student at the High School of Music and Art, my brother picked up on music before I did because there was a whole folk movement there, with Eric Weissberg and others. Our involvement was also based on Pete Seeger's influence, and the Weavers and the Tarriers. Happy got drawn into folk music, and I got drawn into it through him."

After listening to Pete Seeger, Happy and

Artie Traum turned to Leadbelly, Woody Guthrie, and other influential folksingers. They spent time in Greenwich Village, attending parties and playing in Washington Square on Sundays. The urban folk revival was at its peak, and the Traums were on hand to hear a multitude of musicians, many of whom have become significant figures on the contemporary music scene.

Guitarist Artie Traum is highly respected for his musicianship, and he recalls his initial involvement with the guitar: "I got interested in the banjo first, and I learned everything I could, and then I moved over to the guitar. I also became involved in jazz guitar as well as folk guitar, and I was constantly going out to see people like Jim Hall, John Coltrane, or whoever was playing, and it held as much interest for me as going to see Pete Seeger, Doc Watson, or the New Lost City Ramblers."

During the late fifties, they played in New York coffeehouses on weekends, and for about two years Happy Traum led Sunday-afternoon sings organized by the Folksingers' Guild. While they were attending college, Happy Traum took guitar lessons with Brownie McGhee, and Artie Traum took lessons with jazz guitarists. Artie Traum played with folk, rock, and jazz groups and taught guitar while living in Greenwich Village and finishing college. He and his brother played together on and off, but each was involved in his own musical sphere of activity. Happy Traum played with the New World Singers and performed at Gerde's and occasionally at the Gaslight. The Beatles influenced the Traums to form a band called the Children of Paradise, with Eric Kaz on electric piano, Marc Silber on bass, Happy and Artie Traum on electric guitars, and a succession of drummers. After Happy Traum left the band in 1967 and moved to Woodstock, New York, the group became known as Bear, with Eric Kaz, Steve Soles, and Artie Traum, and they recorded an album for MGM's Verve/Forecast label.

Since 1967 Artie Traum has been living in Woodstock with his brother, and is actively pursuing a solo career as a singer, guitarist, and songwriter. He has done three film scores: *Greetings*, directed by Brian De Palma; *Parkee Addison*, a TV film by Arthur Barron; and a short animation called *Horses*. Artie Traum also has a production company and works with other artists as a record producer. Happy Traum has written nearly a dozen instruction books, and his Homespun Tapes Music Instruction series for home music study has been very successful in recent years. In his words: "The lessons are unique in that they are the closest thing possible to having a top performing musician teaching you in your own home. Running forty to fifty minutes, each tape is the equivalent (in material covered) of two private lessons," by such names as David Cohen, Stefan Grossman, Bill Keith, Arlen Roth, Mike Seeger, and Happy and Artie Traum.

Happy and Artie Traum recorded two LPs (now out of print) for Capitol Records; more recently, they have made a couple of albums for Rounder: *Mud Acres (Music among Friends)* (Rounder 3001), with Lee Berg, Tony Brown, John Herald, Eric Kaz, Bill Keith, Maria Muldaur, Jim Rooney, and Happy and Artie Traum, and *Hard Times in the Country* (Rounder 3007).

## The Travelers 3

*Vocal and instrumental group, performers, and recording artists*

One of the many folk groups that rose to national prominence during the recent urban folk revival, the original trio of Pete Apo, Charles Oyama, and bass player Dick Shirley turned into a quartet in 1964 when Michael Gene Botta became a member of the Travelers 3.

Both Pete Apo and Charles Oyama had had some musical experience by the time they met as students at the University of Oregon. With Apo's background in songwriting and singing, and Oyama's skill as a twelve-string guitarist, they decided to pursue their musical talents by forming a trio with another college friend, Dick Shirley. After achieving significant local success, Apo left behind his undergraduate studies and Oyama abandoned his work toward a PhD to strive for national acclaim as professional musicians.

During their brief career, the Travelers 3 responded to prevailing musical influences by developing from a basic folk orientation to a folk-rock format. Current trends augmented their popularity, and they were featured on a number of TV shows, including ABC's *Hootenanny.*

Their first album was issued by Elektra in 1962, and their second LP followed within a few months. After the recording of their third album, Michael Gene Botta became the band's drummer and they switched to Capitol Records.

Before the disbandment of the group, they enjoyed widespread favor among college students and club audiences alike, and they are remembered for their appearances at the Troubadour in Los Angles, the Gate of Horn in Chicago, the Exodus in Denver, Harrah's in Reno, and other top nightspots of the folk boom era.

## Mary Travers. *See* Peter, Paul and Mary.

Mary Travers conversing with Pete Seeger at the 1965 Newport Folk Festival

# Merle Travis

*Legendary guitarist renowned for originating the "Travis Picking Style," singer, songwriter, performer, and recording artist*

A legendary guitarist whose name has been tagged to a three-finger-picking style of playing melody and rhythm simultaneously, Merle Travis ranks among the most highly esteemed and most influential musicians in this country. As a songwriter, he has contributed several classic compositions to the folk tradition, including "Sixteen Tons," "Dark as a Dungeon," and "I Am a Pilgrim."

Merle Robert Travis was born on November 29, 1917, in Rosewood, Muhlenberg County, Kentucky. When he was six years old, his father taught him to play the banjo, and, when his brother built a guitar for him shortly thereafter, he adapted his banjo-picking technique to a style of playing guitar. (He was also influenced by other regional musicians who played a "choke" style of guitar.) In 1935 the eighteen-year-old Travis began his career as a professional musician by playing briefly with a group known as the Tennessee Tomcats in Evansville, Indiana. As his reputation spread throughout the Midwest, he was asked to join a better-known country group, the Georgia Wildcats, which had been organized by former Skillet Licker Clayton "Pappy" McMichen. Before long, Travis found himself in Cincinnati, performing on the WLW *Boone Country Jamboree* with the Drifting Pioneers. During his six years with the radio station, he recorded for King Records and formed the Brown's Ferry Four with WLW performers Grandpa Jones and the Delmore Brothers.

After serving in the marines during World War II, Travis settled in California. He signed a recording contract with Capitol and in 1949 recorded his debut album, entitled *Folk Songs of the Hills* (Capitol AD 50), which included his classic "Sixteen Tons" (popularized half a dozen years later by Tennessee Ernie Ford's bestselling pop single recording). During the fifties, Travis continued to write songs and to record, and he was featured on a major West Coast radio barn-dance show, called *The Home Town Party*, and on both local and national TV.

When he moved to Nashville in the mid-sixties, he became one of the stars of the *Grand Ole Opry* while maintaining an international touring schedule. In the early seventies, he settled in Southern California, where he now performs infrequently, due to ill health.

In addition to his numerous recordings on the Capitol label, Travis has been known in recent years for his celebrated appearance on the *Will the Circle Be Unbroken* album spearheaded by Nitty Gritty Dirt Band producer and manager Bill McEuen.

Although Travis plays a hollow-body Gibson Special Super 400, which was specially designed by the guitar virtuoso in 1952, he is generally credited with the design of the first solid-body (flat-top) electric guitar: "It was in '48 ... I was playing dances out in Placentia, California, with Cliffie Stone. That's when I designed the Fender guitar. I got the idea from the steel guitar. I thought, Why can't you get that sustainability of notes out of an electric guitar like you can with a steel? So I built a solid-body guitar, the *first* one, with the keys all on one side like they are on the steel. So you don't have to reach over to tune. It's in the Country Music Hall of Fame in Nashville now."

# Ed Trickett. *See* The Golden Ring.

# Steve Trott. *See* The Highwaymen.

# Michael Tubridy. *See* The Chieftains.

# Gil Turner

*Singer, songwriter, instrumentalist, performer,* *recording artist, collector, founding coeditor of New York's* Broadside *magazine, and actor*

Gil Turner was once described in promotional materials: "Gil 'Jelly Roll' Turner is a raconteur, leather-lunged songster, handmade songmaker and player of anything with string on it, especially 12-string guitar and 5-string banjo. . . . His 100-odd songs include 'Carry It On,' 'If You Ain't Got the Power of Love,' 'Hound Dog.' . . . Can yodel without benefit of microphone . . . did the *first* released recording of many 'early period' Bob Dylan songs including 'Blowin' in the Wind' and 'Don't Think Twice.' His most famous song, 'Carry It On' is also the title and theme of the Joan Baez movie. . . ."

Born Gilbert Strunk on May 6, 1933, in Bridgeport, Connecticut, he early adopted the professional name of Turner, by which he became known both on and off the stage. His German immigrant father was a machinist and singer, who performed regularly in Bridgeport and, on one or two occasions, toured with a group cross-country. His parents' deep religious convictions influenced the teenaged Gil Turner to become a lay preacher at a church in his hometown. His mother sang in the church choir, and through his Baptist upbringing and his love for grand opera, he acquired a strong foundation in music. He majored in political science at the University of Bridgeport and attended the Columbia University School of Social Work. Later on, he wrote papers on the utilization of music in treating autistic children and the therapeutic value of gold and cortisone in treating rheumatoid arthritis—an illness which he endured throughout his lifetime and which caused the crippling of the left side of his body.

When Gil Turner came to New York, he learned to play guitar and banjo from other musicians, including Rev. Gary Davis, but he developed his own innovative style largely through practice. By 1961 he was working as emcee at Gerde's Folk City in Greenwich Village. In 1962, together with Agnes "Sis" Cunningham, Gordon Friesen, and

Pete and Toshi Seeger, Turner founded New York's *Broadside* magazine. He played a decisive role in dictating the course of the topical song publication by bringing to *Broadside* editorial meetings many young singer-songwriters who appeared at Gerde's, including Bob Dylan, Len Chandler, and Phil Ochs. Later in the year, he spearheaded the recording of the first in a series of *Broadside* benefit albums, which included, among others, his own group, the New World Singers. (One of its original members, Bob Cohen, later reorganized the group.)

Gil Turner performed extensively at colleges, schools, camps, organizations, clubs, coffeehouses, concert halls (including seven appearances at New York's Carnegie Hall), and festivals across the United States; made numerous radio and television appearances; completed five successful foreign tours; and recorded for a number of labels, including Atlantic, Broadside, Columbia, and Folkways, in addition to recording material for the Library of Congress. He was a collector of folk songs and tales as well as a prolific songwriter, and many Gil Turner compositions have been recorded by other artists, such as Joan Baez, Len Chandler, Judy Collins, the Freedom Singers, and Carolyn Hester. He was a member of the Student Non-Violent Coordinating Committee (SNCC) and the War Resisters League; and he helped to establish the New York Council of Performing Arts and to coordinate the cultural extension of the Mississippi Freedom Project, known as the Mississippi Caravan of Music, in which twenty-two artists— among them, Len Chandler, Judy Collins, Barbara Dane, Carolyn Hester, Peter La-Farge, Phil Ochs, Cordell Reagon, and Pete Seeger—traveled and performed in more than thirty projects scheduled throughout the summer of 1964 in Mississippi.

In 1966 Gil Turner performed with the National Shakespeare Festival in San Diego, California, and participated in the national tours of *Spoon River* and *In White America*, among other theatrical productions. After moving from Los Angeles to Big Sur, he worked with actor Will Geer on the "Tribute to Woody Guthrie" held on September 12, 1970, at the Hollywood Bowl. In 1971 he was residing in Marin County and working on a Shel Silverstein album, but he was forced to drop his session work when he contracted infectious hepatitis. In the fall of the same year, he moved to San Francisco to live in closer proximity to comprehensive medical facilities.

In the midst of his involvement with the West Coast folk song movement, his recording of an Elektra album, and his preparation for an acting role in a segment of CBS-TV's *The Waltons* and for the portrayal of Lee Hays in a film on Woody Guthrie, his lifelong struggle with the crippling illness ended in death on September 23, 1974, in San Francisco.

**Jay Ungar.** *See* The Putnam String County Band.

## Dave Van Ronk

*Singer, guitarist, songwriter, performer, and recording artist*

One of the many talented performers who was singing his own material and that of others, Dave Van Ronk was a part of the flourishing folk music scene of the 1960s which brought together in Greenwich Village, in New York City, such artists as Eric Andersen, Bob Dylan, Phil Ochs, and Simon and Garfunkel, among others. In this stimulating and productive environment, which many experts feel was the heyday of American folk music, with the revival of old folk tunes and the creation of new material, artists were nourished by one another's art. An integral part of the Village scene, Dave Van Ronk was one of its most colorful personalities, and, with his bawdy, raspy vocal style, he emerged as one of the decade's most distinctive folk performers.

Born in Brooklyn on June 30, 1936, he received his formal education in the city's public school system. His first musical interest was traditional jazz, and, upon completion of his studies at Richmond Hill High School, Van Ronk played with jazz groups in New York City. In 1957 he performed with Odetta, and a new horizon was opened to him with folk music.

His natural inclination was toward blues-related material within the folk music spectrum, and he became an avid fan of Josh White. With an emphasis on blues, Dave Van Ronk started singing folk music in a number of New York clubs and coffeehouses while simultaneously investigating other musical styles such as jug band music. In the late fifties, Van Ronk recorded an album of

Dave Van Ronk performing at the Great Folk Revival held at the Nassau Coliseum, Uniondale, New York, on February 2, 1974

jug band music for Lyrichord, with Sam Charters.

As his reputation spread, Van Ronk started touring more extensively, playing folk festivals and clubs. By 1959 he had signed a recording contract with Folkways, and two albums were issued: *Dave Van Ronk Sings Earthy Ballads and Blues* (Folkways 2383) and *Black Mountain Blues* (Folkway 31020). In 1963 Dave Van Ronk became a recording artist for the Prestige label, and that year he made *Dave Van Ronk, Folksinger* (Prestige FL 14012). The following year, *In the Tradition* (Prestige FL 14001) was released. Both these albums covered a broad range of blues, jazz, and folk material. His performance at the 1964 Newport Folk Festival was predominantly jug-band- and jazz-flavored; and, during the same year, he recorded an album with a jug band that he had just formed, featuring Sam Charters. The Ragtime Jug Stompers' LP was titled after the name of the group, and it

was released in March on Mercury Records: *Dave Van Ronk and the Ragtime Jug Stompers* (Mercury 20864/60864). By August 1964, another solo album by Dave Van Ronk had been issued on the Mercury label.

By the mid-sixties, Dave Van Ronk was well-known as a talented blues guitarist and singer who had brought the relevance of black music to the white middle-class audiences for whom he performed both in the United States and abroad. In 1965 he was a featured performer at the New York Folk Festival at Carnegie Hall. In the spring of 1967 Verve/Folkways issued his next album, entitled *No Dirty Names* (Verve/Folkways 3009), followed by two singles: "Dink's Song"/"Head Inspector" (October 1967) and "Clouds"/"Romping Through the Swamp" (February 1968). In April 1968, MGM Records released an album which included the four sides released as 45-RPM discs on *Dave Van Ronk and the Hudson Dusters* (Verve/Forecast FT/FTS-3041).

Dave Van Ronk is often associated with "Candy Man" (his version of the song brought him attention in his early years as a Greenwich Village folksinger). Some of his better-known original compositions include "Bad Dream Blues," "Bambee," "If You Leave Me," "Pretty Mama," and "Frankie's Blues." His most recent recordings are *Dave Van Ronk* (2-Fantasy 24710) and *Songs for Aging Children* (Cadet 50044).

He was an early intimate of Bob Dylan, and his West Fifteenth Street apartment was periodically Dylan's home. Dave Van Ronk and his wife Terri befriended and supported the talented young "kid" who was then trying to get his foothold in the Village folk scene. The Van Ronks now live on Sheridan Square in Greenwich Village. Now in his late thirties, Dave Van Ronk continues to play clubs and colleges, and teaches guitar. Some of his plans for the future include putting together a string band and playing classic rags.

# Bill Vanaver and Livia Drapkin

*Singers, instrumentalists, dancers, performers, and recording artists*

Following their meeting at a Balkan dance and music festival in New York City in the spring of 1971, sixteen-year folk veteran Bill Vanaver and choreographer-dancer Livia Drapkin joined together to develop a music and dance program which would more fully express their belief in the vitality and communicative attributes of folklore. In an effort to present a wide range of instrumental, vocal, and dance talents, Bill Vanaver and Livia Drapkin organized a company of musicians and dancers known as the "Coming Together Festival of Dance and Music, Inc.," which, in the words of Livia Drapkin, "offers a combination of traditional music and dances as well as our original choreography and music compositions which make use of folk styles and rhythms."

Bill Vanaver was born on September 1, 1943, in Minneapolis, Minnesota. He first became involved in folk music in 1956 while at a Michigan summer camp where he met Pete Seeger and Big Bill Broonzy. Returning home to Philadelphia, he continued to pursue this newfound interest by immersing himself in the early folk song and dance movement—discovering folk music in its traditional forms and styles. He won first prize in a banjo contest at the second annual Philadelphia Folk Festival, and by the time he was a college student, he was performing on radio and television and at various places along the Eastern seaboard. In 1964 he traveled cross-country to study with Bess Lomax Hawes in California and, while there, he had his initial encounter with foreign music and dance. He soon joined an international folk song and dance ensemble called Westwind, and he learned to play various foreign instruments. Upon his return to Philadelphia, he began to frequent a Greek bar and, shortly thereafter, founded and directed Igra (an ensemble similar to Westwind) while simultaneously performing American folk music. In addition to touring throughout the United States and Canada, performing at coffeehouses, colleges, and festivals, and spending two years as accompanist to the Pennywhistlers, Bill Vanaver has recorded for Elektra, Nonesuch, and Swallowtail.

Livia Drapkin was born on April 18, 1951, in New York City. From childhood, dancing has been her *joie de vivre*, and her training prepared her for all forms of the art—ballet, modern, and folk dancing. She earned a BFA in dancing at the New York University School of the Arts. She has worked with various dance companies and dancers, studied Balkan singing with Ethel Raim of the Pennywhistlers, sung with a women's group called Zenska Pesna for several years, taught dance and music to both adults and children, and performed as a solo dancer.

After their initial encounter, Bill Vanaver and Livia Drapkin traveled to Greece, Yugoslavia, and Bulgaria to collect folk dances and music, and when they returned to the United States, she provided vocal accompaniment for his performances and he composed original material for her choreography. Their current concert and workshop presentations as Bill Vanaver and Livia Drapkin, Coming Together Festival of Dance and Music, were conceptualized as a means of incorporating many of the art forms which they both pursue.

In speaking about the Coming Together Festival and their current activities, Livia Drapkin has said: "The original work is not traditional, but rather a unique form. It is challenging and exciting work to combine our knowledge of ethnic form in contemporary material. In fact, one of the workshops we offer is 'The Use of Folklore in Theater.'

"We still give many performances of traditional folk music, here and abroad."

In the spring of 1974, they made a successful three-month tour of England and Scotland, and a European tour is tentatively planned for the fall of 1976. A new album by Bill Vanaver and Livia Drapkin was issued by Philo Records early in 1976; it includes American and Balkan music, as well as compositions for Livia Drapkin's choreography.

**Curley Veroney.** *See* The Louisiana Aces.

**Walter Vinson.** *See* The Mississippi Sheiks.

**The Virginia Boys.** *See* The Addington Family.

**The Virginia Reelers.** *See* Fiddlin' John Carson.

## Loudon Wainwright III

*Contemporary singer-songwriter, guitarist, pianist, performer, and recording artist*

Once described by Jon Landau in *Rolling Stone* (May 8, 1975) as the "last-true-solo-performer-left-alive," Loudon Wainwright III has been criticized for a lack of spontaneity and exuberance in his recordings, with the result that his studio work is the antithesis of his characteristically animated and comic live performances. A highly respected singer-songwriter, who has been compared in ability to Randy Newman, Loudon Wainwright III was performing and recording for a couple of years before receiving widespread recognition in the music industry.

Born on September 5, 1946, Loudon Wainwright III was still in boarding school when the Greenwich Village folk scene was in its prime. When he began his professional career as a performer on the coffeehouse circuit, the Gaslight and other top clubs of the folk boom were on the decline as rock 'n' roll emerged as the major musical force of the late sixties. As a spectator at the early Newport folk festivals, Wainwright was influenced by such prominent folk musicians as Bob Dylan, Jack Elliott, and Richard Fariña, and Jim Kweskin's Jug Band, and his own musical style evolved from an acoustic approach to the art form.

From his early interest in acting Loudon Wainwright III, like so many of his contemporaries, was drawn to folk music during the urban folk movement of the sixties. He ac-quired a guitar—the standard instrument among young folk music enthusiasts—and listened to recordings by major artists in the field. After attending Carnegie Mellon University in Pittsburgh for a year and a half, Wainwright wrote his first song while in Cambridge, Massachusetts, in 1968.

Throughout his songwriting career, his work has displayed a reflective, often sardonic, posture toward life. His performances are characteristically both funny and highly personal. "Dead Skunk," from *Album III* (Columbia KC 31462), considered by many to be his most favorable recording effort, is one of his best known songs. His name is also closely associated with another whimsical country tune, "Swimming Song," an original composition recorded by Wainwright on *Attempted Mustache* (Columbia KC 32710), and included on the McGarrigle Sisters' debut Warner Brothers LP.

After recording two albums for Atlantic, he switched over to the Columbia label. To date, he has recorded three more LPs as a Columbia artist. He plays major clubs and festivals, including Philadelphia, and his television appearances include feature roles on CBS-TV's *M\*A\*S\*H*.

He is now living in New York City with his wife Kate McGarrigle.

## Frank Wakefield

*Mandolinist, autoharpist, guitarist, singer, composer, performer, and recording artist*

Inspired by the mandolin picking of the "Father of Bluegrass Music," Bill Monroe, this talented musician from Emory Gap, Tennessee, has evolved as one of America's most acclaimed and individualistic mandolinists, who is equally at home with bluegrass or classical music. Frank Wakefield has had no formal training on any of the many instruments that he is capable of playing so adeptly, and his musical imaginativeness precludes classification into a particular musical style.

Born thirty-five miles from Knoxville, Tennessee, Frank Wakefield heard many old ballads from his mother and often listened to his father play guitar. He and his thirteen siblings were raised in the railroad junction of Emory Gap, and most members of the Wakefield family could play an instrument: "I was about ten years old when I picked up the harmonica, and, soon afterwards, I played the dobro guitar and then the steel guitar. I gave those up and started playing the banjo, but then I dropped that instrument and ended up with the mandolin. I've stuck with the mandolin ever since."

The first mandolin played by the seventeen-year-old Wakefield was an old "tater bug" or round-belly that was held in his lap. His brother-in-law provided his initial training on the mandolin, but the young Frank Wakefield was also influenced by Jesse McReynolds and Bill Monroe.

In the early fifties, Wakefield went to Dayton, Ohio, to make his professional debut with Red Allen on the *Dayton Barn Dance* radio show. They teamed up with banjoist Noah Crase and called their band the Blue Ridge Mountain Boys, which developed into the Kentuckians. During his years with Red Allen, Frank Wakefield played with many well-known bluegrass musicians, including Billy Baker, Don Reno, Red Spurlock, Eric Weissberg, Chubby Wise, and Bob Yellin.

On September 21, 1963, the Kentuckians came to New York for the first time to perform at Carnegie Hall for the annual *Sing Out!* concert. In 1964 *Red Allen & Frank Wakefield* (Folkways FA 2408) was issued, and, in the same year, Frank Wakefield replaced Ralph Rinzler in the Greenbriar

Boys. When Bob Yellin left for Israel and John Herald headed for California, Frank Wakefield formed the Good Ole Boys, with guitarist Dave Nelson of the New Riders of the Purple Sage. The Good Ole Boys perform when Dave Nelson is not touring with the rock band, and Wakefield and Nelson play "hard grass," country and folk music.

Frank Wakefield has composed over forty mandolin tunes and on several occasions has played mandolin duets with Bill Monroe. Many of his original compositions, written in a variety of keys and tunings, border on classical music, and Wakefield has played classical mandolin with the New York City Ballet Orchestra. He has been recorded on numerous labels, including BMC, Folkways, Rebel, and Starday. In 1972 Rounder Records issued a solo album entitled *Frank Wakefield* (Rounder 0007), which represents an assortment of his work on both mandolin and autoharp. (*See also* The Greenbriar Boys.)

## Cliff Waldron *See* Cliff Waldron and the New Shades of Grass.

## Cliff Waldron and the New Shades of Grass

*Bluegrass band, performers, and recording artists*

Cliff Waldron has been one of the central figures of the recent bluegrass renaissance, and as a major recording artist for Rebel Records he has made nearly a dozen albums for that bluegrass label. Since his appearance on the scene about a decade ago, his recordings (with various combinations of musicians) have influenced the bluegrass world, and many feel that he has contributed to the field by introducing other forms of music, such as pop, country, and traditional, to bluegrass.

During the 1960s, Cliff Waldron teamed

up with banjoist Bill Emerson to form a band called Emerson and Waldron. They recorded several LPs for Rebel: *New Shades of Grass* (Rebel 1485), *Bluegrass Country* (Rebel 1489), and *Bluegrass Session* (Rebel 1493). Dobroist Mike Auldridge joined up with Emerson and Waldron in 1969, and, when Emerson left the band, the New Shades of Grass was organized with Waldron, Auldridge, Ben Eldridge, Bill Poffinberger, Ed Ferris, and Auldridge's brother Dave. This original group comprised strikingly individualistic members, and the early recordings of Cliff Waldron and the New Shades of Grass were both exciting and impressive.

Mike Auldridge and Ben Eldridge left the band about a year later, and they formed their own band, the Seldom Scene. As of the spring of 1975, when *Cliff Waldron and the New Shades of Grass* (Rebel SLP 1539) was recorded, Waldron's personnel included Dave Auldridge, Akira Otsuka, Arthur Penn, Gakusei Ryo, Bill Wheeler, Gracie Williams, and Steve Wilson. Waldron and Dave Auldridge sing duets with close, high harmonies, and Steve Wilson plays the dobro in a manner reminiscent of the Mike Auldridge style.

Some of the other Waldron recordings on Rebel include *Cliff Waldron and the New Shades of Grass* (Rebel 1496), *Traveling Light* (Rebel 1500), *Cliff Waldron: Gospel* (Rebel 1505), *One More Step* (Rebel 1510), *One More Mile* (Rebel 1518), and *Bluegrass Time* (Rebel 1524).

# Jerry Jeff Walker

*Contemporary singer-songwriter, guitarist, performer, and recording artist*

The cohesion of meaningful lyrics and music is a pervasive, contemporary phenomenon precipitated by the poetic works of Bob Dylan, whose songs relate a personal statement and a human experience pregnant with significance for everyone. Influenced by Dylan, many singers and songwriters draw upon a deep well of relevant material, and, in its presentation to an audience, a common spirit permeates the inherent levels of interpretation. Jerry Jeff Walker sings and writes about his life and his friends, and the simplicity of his music and lyrics brings importance to everyday life.

Raised in upstate New York, Jerry Jeff Walker had left the Catskills to go on the road by the age of sixteen. He found his way to New Orleans, where Babe Stovall shed some light on music made by a man's own guitar. Jerry Jeff Walker started playing in the city's bars and streets, passing his hat and making some friends. When he moved on to Texas he met Gary White, and in 1966 the group Circus Maximus was formed with Jerry Jeff Walker on guitar and vocals, Gary White on bass and vocals, Bob Bruno on lead guitar, organ, piano, and vocals, David Scherstrom on drums, and Peter Troutner on guitar, tambourine, and vocals. They appeared with the New York Pro Musica at Carnegie Hall in New York City at the end of 1967, recorded two albums and a single, "Lonely Man"/"Negative Dreamer Girl," and disbanded in 1968 when tensions arose in regard to their musical direction. Jerry Jeff Walker picked up where he had left off with his solo career and recorded an album for Vanguard, *Driftin' Way of Life* (VSD-6521); three LPs on the Atco label; and a single, "Mr. Bojangles"/"Round and Round," released in June 1968. With a yearning for country living, he returned to Texas, bought some land, and built a home.

By the early seventies, he had signed a recording contract with MCA Records, gathered some friends, and made an album called *Jerry Jeff Walker* (MCA-510), which was issued in 1972. In 1973 he and his band spent two weeks in Luckenbach, Texas, about an hour's drive from Austin, and, with producer Michael Brovsky and a mobile recording unit from New Jersey, *Viva Terlingua* (MCA-382) was recorded. His rambling spirit and freewheeling cowboy life are reflected in his music, and his version of Guy Clarke's "Desperadoes Waiting for the Train" has become one of the song's most popular renditions.

Jerry Jeff Walker label on a
beer bottle

Jerry Jeff Walker

Jerry Jeff Walker and his backup band, the Lost Gonzo Band, with Jimmy Baker, Robert Livingston, Donny Dolen, Gary P. Nunn, Kelly Dunn, John Inmon, and Tomás Rameriz, made their most recent album, *Walker's Collectibles* (MCA-450), in 1974. Walker's selection of material demonstrates a diversification of musical form; on his latest album, horns have been added, along with a gospel choir, Dixieland jazz, and a blues sound.

## Charlie Waller. *See* The Country Gentlemen.

## Doc Walsh. *See* The Carolina Tar Heels.

## Drake Walsh. *See* The Carolina Tar Heels.

## Jerry Walter. *See* The Gateway Trio.

## Anne Warner. *See* Frank Warner.

## Frank Warner

*Singer, banjoist, American traditional folk music collector, vice-president of the Country Dance and Song Society of America, performer, recording artist, and author*

Frank Warner and his wife Anne are two of the most devoted and renowned collectors, preservers, and interpreters of American traditional folk music. Their enthusiasm and their pursuit of this genre have brought to the attention of the general public such names as Frank Proffitt, Yankee John Galusha, and Lena Bourne Fish—and a wealth of folk material from the fertile areas of the Southern Appalachians, the North Carolina

Outer Banks, Tidewater Virginia, New England, and upstate New York.

Frank Warner was born on April 5, 1903, in Selma, Alabama. He spent most of his boyhood in North Carolina and enrolled at Duke University in 1921: "While I was in college I was very active in music. I was in the glee club, and some of us were used by our English professor, Dr. Frank C. Brown, to illustrate his lectures on the folk music of North Carolina. I learned then many of the songs he had collected."

After he received his degree from Duke, Warner joined the staff of the YMCA in Greensboro, North Carolina, where he stayed for five years. He then came to New York to join the National Council of the YMCA and eventually became executive director of the YMCAs on Long Island. Throughout his professional career, he maintained, as a hobby, his singing and lecturing on folk music. In 1935 he and Anne Locher were married, and together, during their vacations, they traveled and collected folk material from rural areas all along the Eastern seaboard. In 1937 they met South Carolina folk song collector Maurice Matteson, who had a dulcimer made by Nathan Hicks of Beech Mountain, North Carolina. The Warners wrote to Nathan Hicks and ordered a dulcimer, which he eventually sent them, wrapped in gunny sack and accompanied by a phonetically spelled letter full of archaic words and phrases. The Warners decided they had to pay the Hickses a visit, and Anne Warner describes their first trip to Beech Mountain the next year: "We were so fascinated that we decided to go down, not with the idea of collecting, but just to meet these people. This was before there was electricity in the mountains, and the roads were almost impassable once you got back from the highways, and the Hickses lived way back! When we got there we found Nathan Hicks with a group of kinfolk and neighbors who had come to meet us, and they were all sitting around the front yard. Among them was Frank Proffitt, Nathan's eldest son-in-law." On that first day, Frank

Frank Warner (center) at his home with sons Jeff (left) and Gerret

Proffitt taught the Warners the song "Hang Down Your Head, Tom Dooley," which Frank Warner sang in concerts for the next two decades and recorded on the Elektra label in 1952. The Warners were largely responsible for the recognition given to Frank Proffitt and were instrumental in bringing him North to perform at the first University of Chicago Folk Festival and other festivals and concerts.

In 1939 the Warners traveled to the Adirondacks, where they collected songs from eighty-one-year-old Yankee John Galusha. The following year, they began to collect in New England—especially from Mrs. Lena Bourne Fish of East Jaffrey, New Hampshire. As Anne Warner recalls: "We had a recording machine by this time and small discs. This was long before tape, and because our supply of discs was short, we would record two stanzas of a song—to get the melody—and stop the machine. The fortunate aspect was that I got them all down correctly then and there. From then on, we spent our month's vacation, which we each had each year from our regular jobs, working as hard as we did any other time—usually spending two weeks in the South and two weeks in the North. We have collected, I suppose, more than a thousand songs. And we have collected, too, many, many friends. So many of these people lived close to the roots of America, and they have given us a feeling about the country that I don't think we could have gotten in any other way."

The Warners' two sons, Jeff and Gerret, accompanied their parents on "song-catching trips," performed and recorded with Frank Warner, and now perform and record on their own.

Frank Warner's performances of folk music are authentic, and he often sings in the unaccompanied, traditional manner. His butternut banjo made by Nathan Hicks has 256 signatures (beginning with Carl Sandburg in 1939) of folksingers, folklorists, and others involved in the field of Americana. He has performed throughout the United States and in England for historical societies, club and school programs, and in concerts at colleges and universities. He is a member of the board of the Newport Folk Festival; past president of the New York State Folklore Society; and vice-president of the Country Dance and Song Society of America. For ten years, he was program director of the society's Pinewoods Folk Music Camp.

Frank Warner has performed in such folk festivals as Newport, Berkeley, Chicago, Duke, Cornell, Queens College, and the American Folk Festival in Asheville, North Carolina. He has performed on seven campuses of the University of California and has been a Hoyt Fellow at Yale University. He has appeared many times on radio and television programs and in one Hollywood movie for RKO. His seven albums of collected songs have been recorded on such labels as Disc, Elektra, Heirloom, Minstrel, Prestige, and Vanguard (Anne Warner has written the notes for all the albums), and he is the author of *Folk Songs and Ballads of the Eastern Seaboard: From a Collector's Notebook* (Southern Press, Inc., 1963).

The Warners are currently engaged in preparing their collection for publication at an early date.

# Gerret Warner. *See* Frank Warner.

# Jeff Warner

*Singer, guitarist, concertina player, performer, recording artist, teacher, and director of the Guitar Workshop, Roslyn, Long Island*

As the son of folklorists Anne and Frank Warner, known to most for their fieldwork in North Carolina, where they collected "Tom Dooley" from the singing of Frank Proffitt, Jeff Warner was raised on a steady diet of folk music. Influenced by this background, plus the recent urban folk revival and the Kingston Trio, Jeff Warner became hooked on folk music.

Born on March 9, 1943, in New York City, Jeff Warner was raised on West 12th Street in Greenwich Village, "and, of course, I grew up in the music—Carl Sandburg, Jean Ritchie, and a lot of other singers used to come by." (It is interesting to note that Jeff Warner also went to P.S. 41, along with Harry Chapin and Maria [D'Amato] Muldaur.) When he was thirteen, his father's work with the YMCA took the family to Farmingdale, Long Island, "and I started taking guitar lessons and hated it." With his father's permission, he quit the lessons and joined the glee club, which he stayed with through college. He resumed guitar lessons when he was about sixteen, but his real inspiration to play the instrument came a year later when he heard Happy Traum, and from that point on he "began playing and learning from other people."

After transferring from the University of North Carolina to Duke University (his father's alma mater), Jeff Warner earned his undergraduate degree in English in 1965. Two years later, at the Newport Folk Festival, he was captivated by the concertina playing of Lou Killen: "I vowed to get one, which didn't happen until 1972, but I've been playing the concertina now for about three years and I consider it my favorite instrument.

"As time goes on, I find I am more and more into traditional, unaccompanied singing. I am playing less contemporary material, and even less guitar since guitar is such a relative late comer to the traditional American music scene [about 1918]. I love the 19th century songs and lore of the sea—and I guess I've been labeled as a sea shanty singer during the past few years."

After graduation from college Jeff Warner worked for a few years as an editor for Doubleday & Company, and in 1969 he was asked to join the teaching staff of the Guitar Workshop, which had been founded six years earlier. Since then, he has made music education his primary endeavor "because that's where my forte lies and that's what I care about. I care about preserving not only the old-time songs but the style in which they were sung."

His recording efforts include several children's records and educational projects, and participation on *Clearwater* (Sound House PS 1001B/SR0104), *Songs & Sounds of the Sea* (National Geographic 705), and a few of his father's albums. He is currently the director of the Guitar Workshop and he was recently elected to the Executive Committe of the Country Dance and Song Society of America. For the past three years he has teamed up with another musician, Jeff Davis, to bring music education to elementary pupils, with more than 100 such programs lined up for 1976.

# Washtub Bass

A musical instrument related to the mouth bow, the washtub bass comprises two basic components. An inverted washtub, or metal drum, functions as a resonator, while a perpendicularly secured stick holds taut a string which is extended from the top of the stick to the center of the tub. The string may be secured at the lower end simply by making a hole in the tub, feeding the string through, and tying a large knot; however, more sophisticated instrument makers usually fasten the tub end of the string with a ring bolt. The stick may be any solid, vertically

attached piece of wood, either round or flat (a broom handle or an unfinished length of lumber will do). An upright bass string is most commonly used, with each (E, D, or G string) yielding a distinctive tone. Different degrees of tension on the string produce different notes, and the tautness is controlled by holding the stick away from the tub while plucking the string with the opposite hand. The string can also be fretted (held against the stick while the hand moves up and down on the stick), and the chord can be altered by repositioning the stick while fretting the string. A hose clamp "capo" can be used to tune the washtub bass to other instruments, and if one edge of the tub is slightly propped up on a small object such as a brick, the sound is amplified as a more suitable means of escape is provided. The washtub bass is used commonly in jug band music and for informal accompaniment with other instruments, which may also be homemade.

# Muddy Waters

*Blues singer, guitarist, harmonica player, songwriter, performer, and recording artist*

In the transition from Delta bluesman to Chicago musician playing amplified blues with his own band, Muddy Waters has enthralled devotees of rock, folk, jazz, and country music with his broad range of musical styles. From the grass-roots folk-blues approach of McKinley Morganfield's early career, which bore witness to his impoverished years as a cotton field worker on a Clarksdale, Mississippi, plantation, Muddy Waters's move to Chicago in 1943 changed both the man and his music. His level of musical sophistication and big-city blues sound have appealed to audiences from Chicago's South Side clubs to Newport folk festivals, the Apollo, the Fillmore, the Café Au Go Go, and jazz festivals and workshops in the United States and abroad.

Born on April 4, 1915, in Rolling Fork, Mississippi, young McKinley Morganfield was sent to Clarksdale to live with his grandmother when his mother died three years after he was born. As a child, he learned to play harmonica and guitar, and he worked in the fields where he heard blues sung by local farm workers. He enjoyed singing, and after years of entertaining at parties, he became known throughout the Clarksdale region.

He was discovered by folklorist Alan Lomax, who sought out the cotton field hand to make recordings for the Library of Congress Archive of Folk Song, and in 1940 Alan Lomax and John Work recorded the Delta bluesman singing "I Be's Troubled" and "Country Blues." Within three years, Morganfield made a break with his past—left behind the farm work and the region where he had lived—and headed north to Chicago.

There he supported himself with various jobs, but his main concern was to become a blues performer; and over the years Muddy Waters met others, like Big Bill Broonzy, whose ambitions coincided with his own. By 1946 he had managed to interest a record company that was seeking new artists, Aristocrat Records. After his initial recording of "Gypsy Woman"/"Little Anna Mae," he had two hits with "I Feel Like Going Home" and "I Can't Be Satisfied." Along with Howlin' Wolf and Joe Turner, Muddy Waters was a significant rhythm-and-blues recording artist, and his influence on country music was a contributing factor in the coalescence of racial styles and the emergence of rock 'n' roll as a musical phenomenon of the fifties.

Muddy Waters had organized a band, and their recordings on the Chess label in the early 1950s brought invitations to appear in cities outside of their Chicago home base. As rhythm-and-blues musicians, Muddy Waters and his band performed in various clubs, and, as their popularity became more widespread, they were asked to tour abroad. In 1958 they traveled to England.

John Lee Williamson was one of the pioneers of amplified blues, but Muddy Waters was largely responsible for its popularization around the world. The band made sell-out appearances at folk and jazz festivals during the 1950s and 1960s—"Rollin' Stone," "Got My Mojo Workin'," and "Hoochie Coochie Man" became Muddy Waters standards—and his brand of blues became an influential force in the world of popular music.

He has recorded for varous labels, including Aristocrat, Bounty, Chess, and Pye.

# Doc Watson

*Traditional guitarist, banjoist, vocalist, and recording artist*

"I'm just exactly that feller that early music portrays. I was born in 1923, and I grew up on a little farm in Watauga County in the northwest corner of North Carolina, about three miles from where I live now.

"The music that I grew up with was the sounds of the Carter Family, Gid Tanner and His Skillet Lickers, Clarence Ashley, the Carolina Tar Heels, and the late Jimmie Rodgers. I sang with my family and relatives and friends that lived there locally."

Arthel (Doc) Watson's father made the young boy his first banjo, and two years later, when Watson was thirteen, he got his first guitar. When Watson was fourteen his dad showed him that he could work in spite of his handicap of blindness, and today Watson attributes the success of his musical career to an incident that implanted a sense of personal dignity and courage: "I would not have been worth the salt that went in my bread if my dad hadn't put me at the end of a cross-cut saw to show me that there was not a reason in the world that I couldn't pull my own weight and help to do my part in some of the hard work. He showed me, by doing that, that I wasn't worthless because I was handicapped. I never would have attempted to earn a living as a musician if it hadn't been for my daddy.

"I traveled by myself in the early sixties,

Advertisement announcing an appearance by Doc Watson, and others, at a folk club

playing the coffeehouse circuit, trying to get started, and I barely squeaked by with enough courage and nerve to get out in the world. I needed that little bit of extra courage and the knowledge that my daddy thought I had some capabilities that gave me the edge that I needed."

When Watson was seventeen he played at a fiddlers' convention in Boone, North Carolina. The following year, he joined a group that occasionally played for radio broadcasts. As a teenager, Watson learned finger-style guitar picking from his neighbor Olin Miller, who taught him such songs as "Memphis Blues." He married Rosa Lee Carlton a few years later, and from her father, mountain fiddler Gaither W. Carl-

ton, Watson picked up a wealth of tradition-al tunes such as "Georgie" and "The Old Man Below."

For the next two decades, Watson per-formed mostly country & western music, playing his old favorite traditional songs for his own amusement. His professional career began when Watson was almost thirty years old, and he played in an electric band that performed a combination of musical styles, including country & western, rock, pop, and old square dance tunes.

The turning point in his career came in the early sixties when Watson played with a neighbor of many years, Clarence "Tom" Ashley, whose roots were also in the authen-tic mountain music of the South: "My first professional gig was in 1962 with Clarence Ashley and his friends at the Ash Grove. I went out to California in May and stayed for about three or four weeks."

Doc Watson was recorded with Clarence Ashley on *Old-Time Music at Clarence Ashley's, Volumes I and II* (Folkways 2355 and 2359). These albums became part of a new wave of interest in traditional folk music that brought Doc Watson into the limelight of the sixties' folk movement. Early in the decade, Watson made several appearances with Clarence Ashley, and he played the Ash Grove in Los Angeles and Gerde's Folk City in Greenwich Village, New York. In 1963 Watson performed at the Newport Folk Festival and at Town Hall, New York, with Bill Monroe and his Blue Grass Boys.

In addition to being included as a guest artist on *Old-Time Music at Clarence Ashley's*, Doc Watson made several solo recordings for Folkways. *The Doc Watson Family* (Folkways 31021) and *The Watson Family* (FA 2366) include members of his family, relatives, and neighbors (with his father-in-law Gaither Carlton playing fiddle, his brother Arnold playing banjo, and his son Merle and his wife Rosa Lee joining in on several cuts). Watson recorded an album with Jean Ritchie, entitled *Jean & Doc at Folk City* (Folkways 9026), and *Progressive Bluegrass and Other Instrumentals* (Folkways 2370), with Roger Sprung on banjo.

His son Merle was included on many of Doc Watson's early recordings, and from the beginning, Merle Watson has proved himself to be an accomplished banjoist and second guitarist. Watson's Vanguard LPs testify to the competence and flexibility of the father-and-son team, and, among nearly a dozen albums recorded on the Vanguard label, *Doc Watson & Son* (Vanguard 79170) and *Ballads from Deep Gap* (Vanguard 6576) include some of the best recordings by Doc and Merle Watson.

Over the years, Watson has recorded on several record labels, including United Ar-

tists, Columbia, UA-distributed Poppy, and Verve/Folkways. *Then and Now* (Poppy LA022-F) and *Two Days in November* (Poppy LA210-G) brought Watson two Grammy awards in a row. In 1975 Merle Watson produced *Doc Watson/Memories* (United Artists UA-LA423-H2), which includes songs that reflect Doc Watson's heritage of traditional music—tunes that he learned from his father, his father-in-law Gaither Carlton, the Carter Family, the Delmore Brothers, Jimmie Rodgers, and Clarence Ashley—and an original composition by his son, "Thoughts of Never."

**Jim Watson.** *See* The Hollow Rock String Band.

**Merle Watson.** *See* Doc Watson.

**Howard (Cedric Rainwater) Watts.** *See* The Blue Grass Boys; The Foggy Mountain Boys.

**The Wayfarers Trio.** *See* Mason Williams.

## The Weavers

*Vocal and instrumental group, performers, and recording artists*

In speaking about the Weavers, Carl Sandburg once said: "The Weavers are out of the grass roots of America. I salute them for their great work in authentic renditions of ballads, folk songs, ditties, nice antiques of word and melody. When I hear America singing, the Weavers are there."

Considered by many to have been the single most important folk group in the history of the United States, the Weavers are regarded by others as merely a nexus in the total folk process, as expressed by one of the

The Weavers performing at their Carnegie Hall Reunion Concert, New York City, April 1963. From left: Bernie Krause, Erik Darling, Frank Hamilton, Ronnie Gilbert, Lee Hays, Fred Hellerman, and Pete Seeger

original members, Pete Seeger: "I think the Weavers were an important link in a chain, but no one link is the most important thing—it's the chain as a whole that's important. It's not important to be a long link if you're a strong link. I often think that while the Weavers passed on songs to a lot of other people, there are also totally unknown people from whom we learned the songs who are just as important.

"All four of us [Ronnie Gilbert, Lee Hays, Fred Hellerman, and Pete Seeger] were sitting around a table with a black woman in Brooklyn, and she was singing old hymns. I'd never heard one she sang called 'Twelve Gates to the City,' and I just grabbed a pencil and wrote it down right away. Her name was Marion Hicks. Now, I've since learned that many people know the song—it's not an unknown song—but she was an important link, teaching me that song."

The Weavers bridged the gap between America's rural heritage and the post–World War II urban folk music revival. In the true sense of the term selected by the foursome for their name, the Weavers skillfully intertwined country roots and contemporary city influences. Their voices echoed the message of their predecessor group, the Almanac Singers, and heralded the surging tide of folk-pop groups that followed in their footsteps.

Traditional folk music was extracted from the mountains, plains, and backwoods, and exalted in "a kind of vigorous treatment," says Seeger, "that a lot of folk songs deserve." Similarly, the Weavers brought to the footlights such vital musical statements as Woody Guthrie's "So Long, It's Been Good to Know You" and Leadbelly's "Good Night, Irene," which became the group's first hit record, with sales in excess of two million copies. The quartet celebrated in song all the peoples of the world, and their repertoire included folk songs from many lands.

Few groups have managed to cross over the line of commercialism without forfeiting artistic integrity and qualitative standards. Throughout their career, the Weavers tried to maintain a balance between the purity of traditional material and the polish of professionalism, and they introduced to concert, cabaret, radio, and television audiences sophisticated yet genuine interpretations of the folk song.

The Weavers made their professional debut on the stage of the Village Vanguard in Greenwich Village, New York City, at Christmastime in 1949. Both Lee Hays and Pete Seeger understood the power of group singing as evidenced by the Almanac Singers, and the formation of the Weavers was a direct outgrowth of this perception. In the words of Pete Seeger: "I think the Almanacs did some things as a group that we never could have done by ourselves. Even Woody Guthrie appreciated what the Almanacs could do six years later, in 1947, and said, 'Pete, don't you think we ought to get the Almanacs together again?' He missed the way we could criticize each other and work with each other—have fun. For example, take some songs, like 'When the Saints Go Marching In.' You really need a group of people to sing that properly. So, all of us in the Almanacs appreciated what we could do, but we were kind of unrehearsed on the stage. Woody said that we were the only group that he was in that rehearsed onstage. Later on, Lee Hays, who had also been with the Almanacs, myself, and two others formed another group called the Weavers— we were much better rehearsed, and we even had some written arrangements."

In 1950 their Decca recording of "Good Night, Irene" was No. 1 on the hit parade chart for over three months. At a time when the music industry was dominated by such artists as Perry Como, the Andrews Sisters, Patti Page, and Eddie Fisher, the Weavers demonstrated that folk music was a marketable commodity. With the success of "Good Night, Irene" and "On Top of Old Smoky," the way was paved for the mass marketing of the idiom and the surfacing of other folk groups in the early sixties.

The early days of the Weavers were filled with performances at the Village Vanguard, People's Songs hootenannies, and broadcasts on WNYC. But by 1952 the group was feeling the brunt of McCarthyism, and with blacklisting, invitations to perform began to diminish. This, in combination with personal reasons, led to the disbandment of the group in 1952.

Three years later, their manager-producer, Harold Leventhal, reunited Ronnie Gilbert, Lee Hays, Fred Hellerman, and Pete Seeger for the now-historic Christmas Concert at New York's Carnegie Hall. After a temporary stint of unemployment, the Weavers were reactivated, and, for the next several years, the group enjoyed a period of recording and international touring. Pete Seeger worked as both a solo performer and a member of the Weavers until 1958, when he decided to relinquish his role with the group to pursue his own career. A succession of replacements ensued—Erik Darling, Frank Hamilton, and, finally Bernie Krause —and, after a fifteenth-anniversary Carnegie Hall concert series in 1963, the members of the group went their separate ways.

In recalling their final performances, Pete Seeger smiles and tells the story: "When we had the reunion at Carnegie Hall, we all started singing 'Wimoweh.' Suddenly, everybody began wondering who was going to sing the high part. And we *all* ended up singing it!"

The Weavers came together again for a joint fiftieth birthday party for Pete Seeger and Harold Leventhal, and, says Seeger, "our voices slipped into the old parts just like we'd never been apart."

During the course of their career, the Weavers recorded (in addition to their Decca recordings) several singles and a half a dozen albums on the Vanguard label. In 1960 Harper & Brothers published *The Weavers Song Book*; edited by the members of the group, it was the first book in over ten years (in the early fifties a now-out-of-print booklet was marketed) to offer a representative sampling of the Weavers' repertoire. (*See also* Pete Seeger.)

## Dean Webb. *See* The Dillards.

## George Wein. *See* Newport Folk Festival.

## Lynne Weintraub. *See* The Serendipity Singers.

## Richard Weissman. *See* The Journeymen.

## Hedy West

*Singer, banjoist, guitarist, composer, performer, and recording artist*

A native of northern Georgia's hill country, Hedy West was born to a folksinging family on April 6, 1938. Her father, Don West, was a trade union organizer and a well-known Southern poet, and Hedy West has set some of his verses to music, such as "Anger in the Land," which was recorded on *Hedy West, Volume II* (Vanguard VRS 9126). Although her repertoire includes ballads, broadsides, industrial songs, dance tunes, and original compositions, Hedy West's emphasis is on traditional American folk music.

In the tradition of the West family folk process, she acquired a wealth of traditional material from her paternal grandmother, Lillie Mulkey West, who, in turn, had learned the songs from her parents and grandparents: "I was learning the material before I started, from my parents and from my grandmother, who is from Blairsville in Union County, Georgia. The traditional material was just typical of British-American Southern mountain music. As a folksinger, my father was a big influence but my grandma was the biggest."

At the age of four, Hedy West was taking piano lessons; and she sang and played banjo while she was in high school: "Before leaving the South, I was involved yearly in the festivals. One of them that I used to sing in was the Asheville Annual Folk Festival, and another called the Mountain Youth Jamboree. One year, I got one of the ballad-singing prizes, in 1956."

In 1959 she came to New York City to study music at Mannes College and drama at Columbia University, but was absorbed

Hedy West

by the folk movement almost immediately upon arrival in the North: "During the revival, all those city kids were trying to look like Southerners. I didn't know what they were doing, and they didn't know what I was doing! It started to develop slowly between 1959 and 1961, but people that I knew, knew I sang. My father was an old friend of Pete Seeger, and, when I was nine, my father had sponsored a concert of Pete's in Atlanta—when Pete was still sitting at the side of the stage and playing his banjo, and not standing.

"Pete invited me to participate in several performances. One of them was a *Sing Out!* hoot at Carnegie Hall. And another was an engagement at the Village Gate in 1962, which was my first big date.

"Everything really started happening for me in 1961 when Manny Greenhill heard me sing at Indian Neck Festival and told Manny Solomon at Vanguard Records. I made a record called *New Folks* [Vanguard VRS-9096] with the Greenbriar Boys, Jackie Washington, and David Gude, and everybody that was on the album was contracted to make other albums. I made two more for Vanguard: *Hedy West Accompanying Herself on the 5-String Banjo* [VRS 9124] and *Hedy West, Volume II.* At the same time, I started singing in various places like Caffé Lena and Gerde's while I was making the records.

"I went to Los Angeles and started singing in some places there. I got married and lived there. Then I started going to London. I lived in London for about seven years, and I recorded for Topic [*Pretty Saro and Other Songs from My Family, Hedy West* (12T146), and *Ballads, Hedy West* (12T163)] and one with Fontana-Philips Records [*Serves 'Em Fine, Hedy West* (STL 5432)] in 1967. I lived in Germany for a while, and I recorded an album in 1972 for Folk Variety Records, a German label, and it was called *Getting the Folk Out of the Country* [FV 12008]." She returned to the United States in 1970 to study composition

with David Lewin, and she now lives in Stony Brook, Long Island.

"In the future, I want to continue singing and documenting folk material. I've been working on a project that's going to take me many more years—documenting my specific family. I don't do it from a romantic point of view, but from an exact point of view. I'm afraid that's my personality. The music is collected and transcribed, but I'm trying to fit it into a social context, so I'm interviewing. I spent a month this summer with Grandma, who's eighty-nine and still sings, and I was interviewing her and finding out about her life. She and my father were big influences for getting me started and doing folk music to make a living. But I, like so many other singers, was probably influenced greatly by Pete Seeger, who was a general father figure to a lot of people.

"I think in my performances I've been influenced by people who aren't singers, people who are really good actors. I very much admire good acting. Without an acting technique, a singer can't really sing. I consider the essence of acting also the essence of singing. Without an acting technique, you really can't touch an audience. My music is mixed up with anything that is on the stage, from classical music to pop music."

Other available recordings by Hedy West are *Old Times and Hard Times, Hedy West* (Folk-Legacy FSA-32) and *Love, Hell and Biscuits, Hedy West* (Bear Family Records, West Germany).

# Western Swing

A hybridization of traditional string band, jazz, popular, black, Cajun, and Norteño musical styles, western swing was the Southwestern counterpart of the big cities' Big Band sound of the Swing Era and the Golden Age of country music during the 1920s to 1940s. Also referred to as "hillbilly jazz" or "Oakie jazz," this musical style was brought into national prominence by regional bands such as Bob Wills ("The King of Western Swing") and his Texas Playboys, Milton Brown and his Musical Brownies, Spade Cooley and his Orchestra, and the Light Crust Doughboys.

As the western swing audience expanded, more musicians were generally added to the bands' lineups. From Bob Wills's initial partnership with Herman Arnspiger as the Wills Fiddle Band, Wills became (at the height of his career) a bandleader of nearly two dozen personnel in his Texas Playboys. And as predominant musical infuences— Benny Goodman, the Dorseys, and Duke Ellington, among others—filtered down to the western swing bands, the material in their repertoires also changed.

With newer musical styles competing for attention and less favorable economic conditions during the post–Depression and World War II years, the size of most bands diminished—but the basic stylings remained. Today, the impact of western swing is seen largely in country & western music, which has adopted from this forerunner certain features including employment of the steel and pedal steel guitars, horns, extemporaneous breaks, and imitative solos.

Several commercial record companies have issued albums devoted to western swing (particularly the work of Bob Wills), including Arhoolie, Columbia, Flying Fish, Old Timey, String (Britain), Tishomingo (Pasadena, California), and United Artists. In addition to the increasing number of reissue LPs, the revival of interest in western swing during the past several years has brought forth more printed material in various music publications, as well as a major biographical work by Charles R. Townsend, *San Antonio Rose: The Life and Music of Bob Wills* (University of Illinois Press, 1974).

## Diana Wharton. *See* Sweet Honey in the Rock.

## David "Buck" Wheat. *See* The Whiskeyhill Singers.

## Billy Edd Wheeler

*Singer, songwriter, guitarist, performer, and recording artist*

Outside of his more selective following of country & western and folk music fans, Billy Edd Wheeler is known for his original compositions: "The Reverend Mr. Black," a 1960s hit for the Kingston Trio, and "Jackson," popularized by Johnny Cash and June Carter in 1967.

Born and raised in the coal-mining camps of West Virginia, Billy Edd Wheeler had a restricted exposure to music. Until he was sixteen, he heard mostly hillbilly and church gospel music. He was born on December 9, 1932, in Whitesville, and when he left the mountains to attend Warren Wilson College, Wheeler came upon folk music. After his introduction to the "Jack Tales" of Richard Chase, he sought out their collector; together, Wheeler and Chase journeyed about the mountains in search of folktales and folk songs. Wheeler started listening to records by Burl Ives, Susan Reed, and others, and soon began collecting tapes of ballads as sung by authentic mountain people.

While he was taking courses at Berea College in Kentucky, Wheeler studied under Gladys Jameson, a collector and arranger of folk music. His voice lessons with her were his only formal musical training. In the early fifties, he received his BA degree from Berea College, and, before going into the navy in 1957, he worked as a magazine editor. Wheeler also attended Yale University, and his talents for composing and performing continued to develop as he sang and played guitar at folk concerts and gatherings in the North.

While Billy Edd Wheeler served as an instructor at Berea College from 1959 to 1961, he continued to collect folk material, and produced a substantial body of original works. In 1961 some of his songs were presented in a Lexington, Kentucky, symphony orchestra concert, and during the early sixties, Wheeler had an acting role in a religious pageant, "Stars in His Crown."

Although talented in many areas of the arts, Wheeler was most devoted to songwriting and performing. In 1961 he recorded his first album for Monitor Records, *Billy Edd: USA* (MF 354), with Joan Sommer. He toured throughout the United States, appearing in clubs, concerts, and at fairs, and he was a frequent guest performer at major festivals. He made a second LP on the Monitor label, *Billy Edd and Bluegrass, Too* (MF 367), with two groups in which he played—the Bluegrass Singers and the Berea Three. Billy Edd Wheeler signed a recording contract with Kapp Records, and in 1965 he had a hit with his own song, "The Little Brown Shack Out Back." His albums for Kapp included *Goin' Town and Country* (1479), *Paper Birds* (1533), and *I Ain't the Worryin' Kind* (3567). He has also recorded for United Artists and, most recently, for RCA.

During the early years of his career, Billy Edd Wheeler struggled to find his particular niche in music. His talent for musical diversification makes it impossible to label his artistry as exclusive to any of the forms in which he works. Folk and country & western roots prevail, but his repertoire branches out to include country, rock, pop, and novelty songs.

While his role as a songwriter brought well-deserved recognition and a certain loyal following, some purists criticized Wheeler for his self-expression, and he found himself caught between traditional and contemporary forces. His sophistication made him "unauthentic" to urban audiences, and traditionalists excluded him from singing at some of the grass-roots folk festivals. When his initial solo album was issued in 1961, it was panned by the *Little Sandy Review*, which called him a fake and a composer of poor-quality material.

Gradually, traditionalists began to accept Wheeler, and as he matured as a songwriter, other performers, including Judy Collins, the Kingston Trio, and Johnny Cash and June Carter, selected his songs for recording and thus promoted his status in several musical fields.

# The Whiskeyhill Singers

*Vocal and instrumental group, performers, and recording artists*

The Whiskeyhill Singers was formed by Dave Guard after he left the Kingston Trio in 1961. Guard, who "wanted a quartet like the Weavers," got together world-traveler Cyrus Faryar, who was living in California and was performing as a solo folk musician, Judy Henske, who had migrated from Wisconsin to the West Coast and had been billed with Cyrus Faryar in San Diego, and another Californian, David "Buck" Wheat, who was finishing up an Eastern tour as bass player for the Kingston Trio.

Guard had grown up with Faryar in Honolulu and had heard that he was active as a folk performer on the small club circuit. When Guard presented Faryar with his idea for the new group, Faryar quickly accepted and then told Guard about Henske. Guard flew to Oklahoma City to meet Henske and to listen to one of her performances. As he recalls: "She was great. So I told her that if she did well, she could be famous and have a ranch in Oregon with wild horses on it!" Henske accepted his offer.

Guard's premise in organizing the Whiskeyhill Singers was "to get the smartest people I could find and to try to rack up the most interesting band I could." The formula, however, did not work. The Whiskeyhill Singers were together for only a brief period before the group disbanded. They recorded one album for Capitol, *Dave Guard and the Whiskeyhill Singers* (Capitol T 1728), and they did a soundtrack for the film *How the West Was Won*, which won an Academy Award for Best Musical Score.

## Clarence White. *See* The Byrds.

## Josh White

*Singer, guitarist, songwriter, performer, and recording artist*

Along with Woody Guthrie and Leadbelly (one of the blind black street singers whom he claimed to have led along Southern city streets when he was a young boy), Josh White found in the North a new audience for his music. Once described by Milt Okun as America's nearest approximation of "a national minstrel," White introduced authentic folk songs and the blues to enthusiastic nightclub patrons and, unlike Leadbelly, achieved success in his own lifetime. Beyond his contributions as a significant force in American folk music and as a progenitor of the recent urban folk revival, Josh White used his position of prominence to protest racial inequality, and his name became associated with such songs as "Strange Fruit" and "Jim Crow Train."

Born the son of a preacher on February 11, 1908, in Greenville, North Carolina, Joshua Daniel White spent the early years of his life amid poverty, religion, and share-cropping families in the Carolinas. In lieu of a formal education, he learned about life from musicians who roamed the country roads and small-town alleyways, and, as a young boy, he beat on a tambourine and then passed it around upside down for nickels and dimes. When he was eight years old, he left his hometown of Greenville to travel with a Southern rural singer named Blind Man (John Henry) Arnold, who was the first of a string of blind musicians guided by the eyes of Josh White. During the next decade, he was hired by others, including

Josh White at San Remo Coffeehouse (now defunct) in Schenectady, New York, November 1961

Blind Lemon Jefferson, Blind Joel Taggart, Blind Joe Walker, Willie Johnson, and, reputedly, Leadbelly. He was more than amply paid for his services with the knowledge acquired from these bluesmen, and, with his increasing proficiency as a singer and guitarist, Josh White's name began to spread around the country.

His travels took him to Chicago and then to New York City, where he landed the part of Blind Lemon Jefferson in Roark Bradford's play *John Henry*, starring Paul Robeson. Although the show closed after less than a month, his acquaintanceship with the casting director, Leonard de Paur, led to a cooperative effort in forming a singing group, the Carolinians, with Carrington Lewis, Bayard Rustin, Josh White, and his brother William. With the help of John Hammond, a controversial album recorded for Columbia by the Carolinians in the early summer of 1940 was released, and it was well-received in both the North and the South. Through John Hammond, Josh White met Café Society Downtown club manager Barney Josephson, who arranged the first of White's numerous engagements at the new establishment. Josephson guided him as he perfected his cabaret act, and during these early sessions Josh White laid the groundwork for successful appearances, in the decade that followed, at the Downtown and Uptown branches of Café Society and at the Village Vanguard.

Among the highlights of the forties were his teaming up with Libby Holman for one of the first attempts at billing a black man and a white woman on a cross-country tour, and his association and performances with the Almanac Singers. Josh White won the hearts of the Roosevelts, performing for the First Family in the White House while his brother William worked as a grounds keeper at their Hyde Park residence. Many offers were extended to him to make radio appearances, and during the war he broadcasted for the Office of War Information (OWI).

At the height of his career, Josh White was a victim of the blacklisting of the McCarthy era. He testified on his own behalf before a congressional committee in Washington, D.C., but this purge scarred his career and he became a virtually unknown figure in the fifties. In 1961 he suffered a heart attack, but only half a year later he appeared in concert with his son Josh, Jr., and his daughter Beverly at New York's Town Hall. The sixties brought renewed offers to work clubs and concerts, and he made occasional television appearances. Along with the rejuvenation of his career came three more heart attacks and a serious car accident. Psoriasis of the fingernails often caused his fingers to bleed while he played the steel strings of his guitar, and although the operation to graft artificial fiberglass fingernails to the remains of his own was painful, he did it in order to keep playing.

In "Josh White; a farewell," which appeared in *Sing Out!* (Vol. 19, No. 4; Winter, 1969–70), Don McLean wrote about Josh White: "He was a husky man of medium size, slightly balding with broad shoulders and a handshake like a vise. His hands had to be strong the way he played. The action on his guitar was so high, it was like making chords on an eggcutter. He would mount the stage quickly, trade a few words with his bass player then place his right leg over a straight backed chair, rest the guitar on his right knee, look around for a moment and then from nowhere his hand would snap and curl in a magical motion and over the top of the guitar, his thumb would ride the bass string down the length of the neck. One, two, three times, like the sound of freight cars roaring through a small town station with you standing on the platform so close that the wind almost knocks you down."

Josh White was recorded by the Archive of Folk Song, and, following his first recordings of religious material done in the thirties, (under the name "The Singing Christian") and his "sinful" recordings on the Perfect label (issued "as sung by Pinewood Tom" to avoid offending his mother), he cut discs for numerous commercial record companies, including ABC Paramount, Apollo, Asch, Columbia, Decca, Disc, Livingstone, London, Musicraft, Period, Stinson, Tradition, and Vogue, with reissues on such labels as Ampar, Banner, Blue Note, Brunswick, Elektra, Emarcy, Everest, Harmony, Melotone, Mercury, and Oriole.

## Steve White. *See* The Golden Ring.

## Big Joe Williams

*Country blues singer, guitarist, and recording artist*

In many respects, the life experiences, music, and character of Big Joe Williams are typical of many Mississippi bluesmen, and his blues verses have provided an insight into the man and the image that he portrays.

One of fourteen children born to tenant-farming parents, Big Joe Williams early demonstrated an aversion to the work by which his father made a living. Uninterested in laboring in the fields or sawmill, the young boy was more inclined toward the musical talent that he had inherited from his mother. By the age of four, Williams was experimenting with different sounds as produced by beating on a water bucket, and he discovered how tonal effects related to the pressure of his fingers on the sides of the bucket. Poverty necessitated ingenuity, and Williams constructed his first guitar with materials that were available to him. He used a length of baling wire stapled to a piece of fence wood, with a cotton reel as a bridge; in effect, he created a one-string guitar. As he was growing up, Williams made a series of homemade guitars, and for many years played a "cigar-box" guitar, which was crude but common in his area of the country. Williams started playing at local events, suppers, levee and turpentine camps, and gradually developed his unique

style of playing guitar, for which he is so well-known today.

Indebted to the distinctive rhythm, pronounced swing, and ringing treble notes of the Mississippi blues style, Williams changed from a normal tuning to a "Spanish" tuning, which was popular among blues guitarists. With his guitar tuned to a certain chord, he was able to play innumerable melodies while sustaining a bass rhythm.

For a while, Joe Williams and his friend Peetie Wheatstraw operated a St. Louis club; as a musician, Wheatstraw influenced Williams's guitar style. When his partner died in an automobile accident, Williams acquired his guitar, but he played it infrequently—most often opting for his own well-worn instrument. The club attracted many blues musicians from Missouri and surrounding states, and "Big Joe" Williams, as he came to be called, became an important element on that musical scene until the club closed in the mid-fifties.

Throughout his career, Williams has made a significant number of recordings, with his earliest discs made under the pseudonym King Solomon Hill. His vocal work evolved from a high-pitched, immature style to heavy, dramatic singing. In 1958 he was recorded by Bob Koester, and again, in 1960, by blues collector Chris Strachwitz. After his wife died, Williams settled in Chicago, where he was a featured performer at a coffeehouse called the Fickle Pickle and at Bob Koester's club, the Blind Pig.

During the early sixties, Big Joe Williams toured Europe, and his primitive blues style captivated audiences wherever he performed. When he returned to Chicago, his name attracted a broader range of listeners, and the folk revival quickly absorbed this authentic, folk-blues singer.

Big Joe Williams has been recorded by numerous companies; he appears on such labels as Adelphi, Arhoolie, Blues Classics, Delmark, Folkways, Spivey, Testament, and Yazoo.

# Hank Williams

*Singer-songwriter, guitarist, performer, and recording artist*

In the annals of country music, few aspects are given the special treatment generally reserved for the Hank Williams story—the brilliant career terminated by a tragic death at the age of twenty-nine. At a time when many Americans were tuning in to their rich cultural heritage for the first time, Hank Williams was spinning heads in the direction of country music. Millions were captivated by song after song—"Hey Good Lookin'," "Your Cheatin' Heart," "Cold, Cold Heart," "Jambalaya," "Ramblin' Man," "Lost Highway," "I'm So Lonesome I Could Cry"—many of which have become country standards and have been recorded countless times by artists representing all musical styles.

King Hiram "Hank" Williams was born on September 17, 1923, in Mt. Olive, Alabama. At the age of five, he moved with his tenant-farming family to Georgiana, Alabama, where he earned some extra money for his parents by vending newspapers and peanuts and by shining shoes. As a young boy, he was influenced by the gospel tunes and hymns which he sang in church, and religious material played a significant role in his music throughout his career. When he was about seven years old, he was given a $3.50 guitar by his mother. He acquired basic instrumental instruction from a black street singer by the name of "Teetot," and his later reputation as a country blues vocalist is largely traceable to this influence.

With his song "The WPA Blues," the twelve-year-old Williams took first prize in an amateur contest held at the Empire Theatre in Montgomery, and his already existing desire to become a professional entertainer was further inflamed. He eagerly sought audiences for his singing, and, when he was thirteen, responded to a prevailing contemporary "western" mystique by adopting an image as the "Drifting Cowboy" and by organizing his own band, known as the Drifting Cowboys.

In the following year he was hired to sing on Montgomery's WSFA radio station, and, during the next few years, achieved local recognition for performing—whether in saloons or schoolhouses. He supported his music by working at various odd jobs, and, temporarily discouraged by his slow progress as a musician, abandoned his aspirations and worked in a shipyard during World War II. His mother encouraged him to return to music and helped to get him bookings at several nightspots.

The year 1946 brought Williams his first recording contract—with a small label called Sterling—and acceptance of a number of his original songs by music publishers Acuff-Rose. Impressed with the young singer-songwriter, Fred Rose played an instrumental role in securing a recording contract for him with MGM in 1947. The following August, Williams joined the cast of KWKH's *Louisiana Hayride*. His recognition steadily grew as he produced a series of modest hits; then, in 1949, his version of "Lovesick Blues" became the most highly acclaimed song of that year and one of the best-known numbers of the post–World War II era. His overwhelming success led to a spot on the *Grand Ole Opry*, and until his death three and a half years later, his exceptional rapport with listening audiences was evidenced by his record sales, attendance figures at his live performances, and his financial success. Audiences responded to his direct, genuine approach to country music; when queried about the positive public reaction to this musical form, he once said: "It can be explained in just one word: sincerity. When a hillbilly sings a crazy song, he feels crazy. When he sings 'I Laid My Mother Away,' he sees her a-laying right there in the coffin."

When a heart attack claimed his life on January 1, 1953, he left this world as a financially and popularly successful country music star—but an emotionally distraught and physically ailing human being. In the previous year, he had immediately married Billy Jean Jones after his first marriage had disintegrated, and heavy drinking and irresponsible behavior had led to his dismissal from the *Grand Ole Opry*. His despair and loneliness were reflected in his music (his "I'll Never Get Out of This World Alive" was a bestselling hit of 1952) and in his personal conduct, but despite his public success his personal anguish was inconsolable. He passed away on the back seat of his Cadillac, in Oak Hill, West Virginia, on his way to a New Year's engagement in Canton, Ohio. His funeral in Montgomery, Alabama, was attended by some twenty thousand people who had come to pay their last respects to this country music giant.

Throughout the fifties and sixties, his early recordings were issued by MGM, and his songs were recorded many times over by other artists. In 1961 three bronze plaques, dedicated to three deceased contributors to country music—Jimmie Rodgers, Fred Rose, and Hank Williams—were hung in the Country Music Hall of Fame in Nashville, Tennessee.

His son, Hank Williams, Jr., has followed in his footsteps and is currently enjoying a successful recording and performing career as a country musician.

# Hank Williams, Jr. *See* Hank
Williams.

# Jimmy Williams. *See* The Stanley
Brothers.

# Joe Williams. *See* Fennig's All-Star
String Band.

# Mason Williams

*Contemporary composer, guitarist, singer, performer, recording artist, and author*

At the height of his career in the late sixties,

Mason Williams's list of accomplishments included two Grammy awards for his "Classical Gas," top-selling LPs, an Emmy Award as head writer for the Smothers Brothers' television show, and several successful collections of poetry and humor. His concepts encompass every aspect of the multimedia, and Tom and Dick Smothers were instrumental in providing an audience for his creative genius.

Born in 1938 in Abilene, Texas, Mason Williams studied at Oklahoma City University. He began his career as a traditional folksinger in 1959–60 as a member of a Kingston Trio–like group known as the Wayfarers Trio, which recorded one album for Mercury (Mason Williams also made recordings for the Archive of Folk Song). By 1963 he was on his own as a solo artist, performing and writing material. His early compositions were folk-based, and one of his first satirical songs, "You Done Stompt on My Heart," was recorded by John Denver.

When he was chief writer for the *Smothers Brothers Comedy Hour*, Williams's capabilities were made known to the American public. In addition to devising Pat Paulsen's presidential campaign (for which he was awarded an Emmy) and other material for the Smothers Brothers, he provided ideas for television specials by Glen Campbell, Petula Clark, Roger Miller, Pat Paulsen, and Andy Williams. "Classical Gas" provided the *Smothers Brothers Comedy Hour* with one of its most memorable musical moments, and the song was used as a background for slide collages of art and American history time capsules.

As Mason Williams began to wind down in the wake of television censorship and commercialism, he recorded his last album, which was issued in 1971. His personal appearances became less and less frequent, finally terminating with a symphony concert in Canada early in 1972. He retreated to Oregon, but by 1974 he was musically active once again. With his attention focused on composing, instead of performing, he commenced work on a concert program to integrate bluegrass within a symphony orchestra framework. Returning to his traditional music roots, he formed his own bluegrass band, the Santa Fe Recital.

Mason Williams's work appears in a number of collections on various labels. Some of his earlier recordings for Tradition Records have been reissued on the Everest label, including *Anthology of the Twelve String Guitar* (Tradition/Everest 2071), with Glen Campbell, Bob Gibson, Joe Maphis, James McQuinn, Howard Roberts, Billy Strange, and Mason Williams, and *Anthology of the Banjo* (Tradition/Everest 2077), with Billy Cheatwood, Erik Darling, David Lindley, Joe Maphis, Jim McGuinn, Mike Seeger, and Mason Williams.

To date, four books written by Mason Williams have been published by Doubleday & Company: *Bus, The Mason Williams Reading Matter, Flavors,* and *FCC Rapport.*

## Terry (Benson) Williams. *See* The New Christy Minstrels.

## Bob Wills

*Songwriter, fiddler, bandleader of the Texas Playboys, and recording artist*

Born in Limestone County, Texas, in 1905, this country music pioneer is known as "The King of Western Swing." Bob Wills and his Texas Playboys significantly influenced American music, especially country & western, for over forty years. Related to folk music as a cultural blending of musical styles and backgrounds, western swing is a musical form which originated in the 1920s and enjoyed widespread popularity until the late 1950s.

Wills's career as a fiddler began in 1929, when he joined a medicine show which took him to Fort Worth, where he met and teamed up with Herman Arnspiger as the Wills Fiddle Band. When they were joined by Milton Brown in 1931, they called the group Aladdin's Brown and, later, the Light Crust Doughboys. The trio played fiddle band music, and they created a sound with a strong dance rhythm. The Texas Playboys was formed in 1933 and included Bob Wills, Johnnie Lee, Son Lansford, Don Ivey, Everett Stover, Kermit and June Whalen, Tommy Duncan, and O. W. Mayo, among others. Several personnel changes occurred, with such notable additions as Leon McAuliffe, but by 1935 the Bob Wills Sound was established. The group became the first fiddle and country band to use drums, dual fiddles, steel guitar, and horns—a precedent for today's Nashville Sound.

Although World War II separated the band's members, it was reformed by Bob Wills in the late 1940s. He resumed his rigorous tour schedule, and he and the band made numerous recordings for Columbia, then for MGM, Decca, Liberty, and other companies. Bob Wills finally retired as a bandleader in 1964.

During his lifetime Bob Wills composed "San Antonio Rose," "I Wonder If You Feel the Way I Do," "Silver Lake Blues," "Texas Playboy Rag," "Lone Star Rag," "Texas Two Step," "Wills Breakdown," and "Betty's Waltz," and he starred in twenty-six movies. Old Timey Records has issued some classic recordings on an album called *Western Swing* (Old Timey X-105), which includes Bob Wills, the Light Crust Doughboys, Milton Brown, and others. In 1968 Wills was named to the Country Music Hall of Fame, and on May 30 of the following year, he was honored by the governor and legislature of Texas for his contribution to American music.

He died on May 13, 1975, a year and a half after his final recording sessions with the Texas Playboys and Merle Haggard which resulted in the release of the award-winning album, *For the Last Time* (United Artists LA216-J2).

## George Wilson. *See* Fennig's All-Star String Band.

**Chubby Wise.** *See* The Blue Grass Boys.

# Mac Wiseman

*Bluegrass singer, guitarist, performer, and recording artist*

A distinguished bluegrass singer and guitarist, Mac Wiseman has worked at both the production and the performing ends of the music industry. As an entertainer, he has established a dual reputation, based largely on his earlier association with Flatt and Scruggs and as lead vocalist for Bill Monroe, and on his individual accomplishments.

A native of Virginia's Shenandoah Valley area, Mac Wiseman was raised on bluegrass music. He started playing the guitar seriously when he was in his early teens, and as a high school student he performed with a band called the Hungry Five. After attending the Conservatory of Music in Dayton, Virginia, he worked for several years as a local radio announcer. In 1946 he went to Knoxville, Tennessee, to perform as the featured singer in Molly O'Day's country band. In the following year, he organized his own outfit, known as the Country Boys, which played on the *Farm and Fun Time* show. After leaving their jobs with Bill Monroe, Lester Flatt and Earl Scruggs invited Mac Wiseman to join up with their newly organized Foggy Mountain Boys, along with two other former Blue Grass Boys, Jim Shumate and Howard (Cedric Rainwater) Watts. In the year that he stayed with Flatt and Scruggs, Wiseman recorded four sides of their historic Mercury recordings. From there, he went to Atlanta, and then to the *Grand Ole Opry* with Bill Monroe and his Blue Grass Boys. Before relinquishing his esteemed position as lead vocalist for the "Father of Bluegrass," Mac Wiseman participated in Monroe's final Columbia recording session.

In the early fifties, he reorganized his Country Boys band and, until 1957, toured throughout the United States and in Canada on a road schedule which averaged approximately three hundred one-night stands annually. As a result of the strenuous traveling and performing, the band's personnel changed on many occasions, and included Eddie Adcock and Josh "Buck" Graves (later of the Foggy Mountain Boys and the Earl Scruggs Revue), among others.

During the late fifties and early sixties, Mac Wiseman began performing as a solo act while doing production work (and recordings) for Dot Records. In 1963 his name was added to the Capitol Records roster of recording artists, and his concert appearances took him from college campuses to New York's Carnegie Hall. In 1966 he went to Wheeling, West Virginia, where he ran the WWVA *Jamboree* for four years, operated a talent agency, and owned a mail-order record company. After signing with RCA, he moved to Nashville and has lived there since. In February 1971 he recorded the first of three albums with Lester Flatt, followed by a solo effort entitled *Concert Favorites* (RCA LSP-4845).

He is currently performing with and without Lester Flatt, and he runs the annual bluegrass Mac Wiseman Renfro Valley Festival, Renfro Valley, Kentucky. (*See also* The Blue Grass Boys; The Foggy Mountain Boys.)

# The Womenfolk

*Vocal group, performers, and recording artists*

The recent folk revival generated a proliferation of commercial and pop groups which were characterized by short-term goals and a brief existence. Individuals from all walks of life were brought together for the purpose of utilizing folk music as a business idiom, and as the folk movement waned in the mid-sixties, many groups dissipated and their members pursued prior or new-found occupations.

The Womenfolk, with Jean Amos, Leni Ashmore, Barbara Cooper, Judy Fine, and Joyce James, was a talented group of musi-

**411**

cians from different parts of the country. Most of them came from a musical background, and their singing had an appealing, rich sound. Their repertoire consisted primarily of popular tunes and pop renditions of such folk songs as "The Times They Are A-Changin' " and "The Last Thing on My Mind."

The Womenfolk recorded for RCA Victor; one of their most popular albums was called *Man Oh Man!* (LSP-3527), issued in 1966.

**Bruce Woodley.** *See* The Seekers.

**Norman Woodlieff.** *See* Charlie Poole and the North Carolina Ramblers.

**Gilmer Woodruff.** *See* Ernest East and the Pine Ridge Boys.

**Art Wooten.** *See* The Blue Grass Boys.

**Glenn Yarbrough.** *See* The Lime-liters.

**Peter Yarrow.** *See* Peter, Paul and Mary.

**Bill Yates.** *See* The Country Gentlemen.

**Bob Yellin.** *See* The Greenbriar Boys.

**John York.** *See* The Byrds.

**Paul York.** *See* The Dillards.

**Allie Young.** *See* The Balfa Freres.

**Bob Young.** *See* The Serendipity Singers.

## Israel Young

*Proprietor of the Folklore Center in New York City (1957–73), poetry and music sponsor, and writer*

While operating his Folklore Center, which was once described by Oscar Brand in *The*

*Ballad Mongers* as "a clearinghouse for records, books, and public notices about the folk music world," Israel Young acquired the aura of a Greenwich Village institution, along with his "emporium." His closing of the center and departure for Sweden on April 29, 1973, symbolized the termination of a unique and special period of folk music history.

Israel Goodman Young was born on March 26, 1928, in New York City, and he lived in the Bronx until 1948. After working in his father's Brooklyn bakery and abandoning his premed studies, he opened the Folklore Center at 110 MacDougal Street. Known to most of his friends as "Izzy," he became a pivotal figure of the New York folk scene—whether leading demonstrations for the right to congregate and to make music in Washington Square Park, or presenting Bob Dylan's first concert, in 1961, or providing a "home" where folk musicians and fans could be brought together on an informal basis.

Since the early 1940s, folksingers and folk enthusiasts had gathered in Washington Square Park for Sunday-afternoon hoots. In the early sixties the sessions were banned by the New York City commissioner of parks and the Great Washington Square Park Riot ensued, led by Izzy Young. After several months of battling in the courts and on the streets, the license for the sessions was reinstated.

By this time, Izzy Young had moved the Folklore Center to 321 Sixth Avenue at Third Street, where he was featuring regular weekly folk concerts. In addition to presenting numerous music and poetry events annually, publishing pamphlets and small books, preparing a newsletter, and conducting (with Catherine Grandin) a radio show on WBAI, he was involved in the editorial and financial realignments of *Sing Out!* magazine. His original "Frets and Frails" column first appeared in the New York music publication early in 1959, followed by his "Folklore Revisited," which he still contributes as *Sing Out!*'s European representative (he also continues to serve on its editorial advisory board).

He left the Folklore Center in the hands of Rick Altman, and, since its opening on March 1, 1974, he has been running the Folklore Centrum in Stockholm, Sweden.

# Jesse Colin Young

*Contemporary singer, songwriter, guitarist, performer, and recording artist*

Within the nucleus of the Greenwich Village folk scene of the 1960s were a number of artists who used the folk music genre as a springboard for the pursuit of their art. Initially, Jesse Colin Young was among the talented young performers who began their careers playing in the coffeehouses of New York City; and, like many others, his early accomplishments led to further growth in his music, resulting in his stature as one of today's most popular contemporary musicians.

Born Perry Miller in 1941 and raised in New York City, Jesse Colin Young developed, as a boy, an interest in bluegrass, country blues, and folk songs. By the mid-sixties, he was performing in spots along the Eastern seaboard. In 1964 he met Jerry Corbitt, who was working in the New England area as a performer. Their friendship developed instantaneously, and they started singing together, blending Corbitt's low, ragtime vocals with Young's smooth, melodious voice. They made the changeover from acoustic to electric instrumentation

Jesse Colin Young

and formed a group called the Youngbloods. During their fledgling years, the Youngbloods were based in New York City, but by 1967 the group had moved to the West Coast, and soon embarked on a career as one of California's most popular bands.

Jesse Colin Young acted as the Youngbloods' lead singer and, as the circumstances dictated, played both bass and guitar for the group. Until his recent emergence as a solo pop artist, he was best known for his role as a member of the Youngbloods, to which he contributed his vocal and songwriting abilities. They had their first hit in 1968 with "Get Together," a tune from their first LP, which was used for a commercial promoting racial and religious brotherhood. The Youngbloods have been compared with another popular group of the times, the Lovin' Spoonful. With Jesse Colin Young on bass and vocals, Joe Bauer on drums, Banana on electric piano, guitar, and vocals (he had replaced Jerry Corbitt), the group played a mixed bag of country, blues, jazz, and rock. Produced by Felix Pappalardi, the Youngbloods recorded three albums for RCA and four on their own Raccoon Records label, distributed through Warner Brothers: *The Youngbloods* (RCA LSP 3724), reissued as *Get Together*; *Earth Music* (RCA LSP 3865); *Elephant Mountain* (RCA LSP 4150); *Rock Festival* (Warner/Raccoon WS 1878); *Ride the Wind* (Warner/Raccoon BS 2563); *Good & Dusty* (Warner/Raccoon BS 2566); and *Together* (Warner/Raccoon BS 2588).

After the Youngbloods disbanded in 1972, Jesse Colin Young struck out on his own to record another album. He used some of the musicians who had worked on *Together* as a backup band, and *High on a Ridgetop* (Warner/Raccoon BS 2653) was issued in the spring of 1972. Jesse Colin Young continued to pursue his career as a solo artist, performing club and concert dates across the United States and recording his second album since the breakup of the Youngbloods, *Song for Juli* (Warner 2734), released in the fall of 1973. Since then, he has made several more albums for Warner Brothers: *Light Shine* (Warner 2790); *Songbird* (BS 2845), released in 1975; and, most recently, *On the Road* (BS 2913).

His earliest solo recordings, *Soul of a City Boy* (Capitol T 2070, reissued as ST-11267) and *Youngblood* (Mercury SR61005), are now considered collector's items.

**Neil Young.** *See* Crosby, Stills, Nash and Young.

**The Youngbloods.** *See* Jesse Colin Young.

## Zither

A folk musical instrument consisting of thirty to forty-five strings stretched across a flat soundboard (or sounding box), the zither is held on the player's lap or placed on a flat surface such as a table. Most common in the Tyrol, Bavaria, Norway, and Denmark, the zither provides instrumental accompaniment to folk songs and dances.

A derivative of the ancient Greek *cithara*, the zither has been traced back to Israel and Phoenicia. Prior to the 1700s, the term *zither* was the German designation for the *cithern* (or *cittern*), a stringed instrument resembling the guitar; thereafter, it referred to the Austrian and Bavarian folk-type box zither which was developed from the *scheitholt*, a rectangular-shaped zither of Germany used until the early nineteenth century. By 1830 the zither had found its way to areas beyond its native Alpine region, and its widespread popularity brought about the production of different sizes and types of zithers. During this accelerated phase of its development, the zither acquired the standard forms by which it is known today.

The zither is a flat, rectangular box with a fingerboard on the long side of the instrument nearest the player. In the instrument's center is a soundhole which is cut into the thin, hollow body or soundboard. In addition to the four or five metal melody strings, there are up to thirty-seven gut accompaniment strings. The melody strings are plucked with the right thumb, using a plectrum, while the fingers of the left hand press the strings down on the fretted or fretless fingerboard. The first, second, and third fingers of the right hand are used to stroke the accompaniment strings.

The zither reached its peak in popularity in the United States over a century ago. Since then a select following has been perpetuated by such zitherists as Susan Reed, who brought renewed attention to the instrument during the sixties. One of the best collections of zithers is housed in the Missouri State Capitol, where the Schwarzer and Austrian zithers belonging to the noted Ozark zitherist Adolph Kukler were assembled after his death in February 1963. The State Museum is contained within the Capitol, and it offers a recording of Adolph Kukler playing the zither, which can be heard by the visitor who presses a special button.

## Zydeco. *See* Cajun.

# Illustration Credits
## and Copyright Acknowledgments